LIGHT MOTIVES

LIGHT MOTIVES

German Popular Film in Perspective

Edited by
Randall Halle
and
Margaret McCarthy

WAYNE STATE UNIVERSITY PRESS   DETROIT

Copyright 2003© by Wayne State University Press,
Detroit, Michigan 48201. All rights are reserved.
No part of this book may be reproduced without formal permission.
Manufactured in the United States of America.
07 06 05 04 03   5 4 3 2 1

Library of Congress Cataloging-in-Publication Data

Light motives : German popular film in perspective / edited by Randall
Halle and Margaret McCarthy.
p. cm.—(Contemporary film and television series)
Includes bibliographical references and index.
ISBN 0-8143-3044-4 (cloth) : alk. paper)—ISBN 0-8143-3045-2 (paper)
: alk. paper)
1. Motion pictures—Germany. I. Halle, Randall. II. McCarthy,
Margaret, 1963– III. Series.
PN1993.5.G3L54 2003
791.43′0943—dc21
2002155578

⊗The paper used in this publication meets the minimum requirements
of the American National Standard for Information Sciences—
Permanence of Paper for Printed Library Materials,
ANSI Z39.48-1984.

CONTENTS

INTRODUCTION

Randall Halle and Margaret McCarthy

Despite the rise of cultural studies and its legitimization of popular culture as an object of analysis, Germanists have by and large long neglected a realm that has elsewhere yielded exciting scholarship. Nowhere is this gap more evident than in the field of German film studies.[1] However inadvertently, scholarship here has reflected a very common impulse to divvy up German films, like Germans themselves, into the good and the bad. The "golden era" of Weimar film and the internationally acclaimed New German Cinema of the 1960s and 1970s thus stand apart from embarrassing fascist propaganda, kitschy Heimat films, alpine porn, and the boom of German comedies in the 1990s. More generally, critics have portrayed sweeping landscapes of artistic bounty and commercial wastelands, categories that have yet to be fundamentally challenged. At the same time, scholars of German studies have long been practicing a form of "culture studies" that stands apart from the current developments of cultural studies. Indeed, Germany's turbulent twentieth-century history has brought together scholars from across the disciplines to enliven the field of German culture studies with dynamic debates. Insightful, responsible scholarship vis-à-vis Germany has, in other words, already generated an expanded, bird's-eye view of culture in its many manifestations, with historical and political considerations of paramount importance. Given this wide-angle perspective, it is precisely the field of German studies that can make new, exciting, and serious contributions to our understanding of German film, in particular, and models of film and cultural studies, more generally.

The contributions to this volume pick up these tools of German studies to address certain questions that have arisen alongside a transformation in German film production. The ascension of the German comedy during the early 1990s and the success of German action films like *Run Lola Run* (1998) call for a serious look at the category of popular film across the historical spectrum and the larger cultural, historical, and political meanings suggested by the term "popular." In assessing German culture, Frankfurt School dictates and Goethe House film festivals have long validated high culture, art films over and above popular culture. Those dictates were developed through critical analyses that rejected Hollywood's culture industry productions, as well as the German culture industry of the Weimar era, the Third Reich, and the postwar era. These dictates resulted in rejections of whole eras of film production, blanket alignments of film and fascism, or totalizing rejections of the film form itself.

The origins of such wholesale negativity can be found, in part, in Siegfried Kracauer's influential analysis of Weimar-era film in *From Caligari to Hitler.* In the volume at hand, Christian Rogowski analyzes the far-reaching effects of Kracauer's negative assessment of Weimar film on German popular film production in general. Furthermore, Rogowski returns us to that earlier era to find precisely in its popular and forgotten productions a different narrative than the one written by Kracauer, one filled with subversive visions and potential. While not advocating some naïvely positive approach, throughout this volume the essays undertake similar critical (re)assessments of the possibilities and limits of popular film, with balanced critical analysis.

The reassessment of popular film undertaken by this volume should not be understood as an attack on high culture or avant-garde practice. Of course, where popular and avant-garde cultural productions are understood as each other's negative, a perspective less inflected by traditional generic boundaries becomes difficult. In the area of German film production, such an oppositional understanding, avant-garde versus popular, has often been the basis of critical analysis. A peculiar alignment of German film and art film arose in the 1970s, resulting from a tenuous alliance of the German New Wave filmmakers' interests with those of the state-funded cultural institutions. Nevertheless, the promotion of these films as the height of German culture relied on the presence of German low-brow culture as well. It is often forgotten that the preponderant genre of films produced in Germany in the 1970s were the sex comedies discussed here by Tim Bergfelder. In the social history of German cinema, these films gave form to the film landscape as much as did New German films. Attention to a classic of New German Cinema, Wim Wenders's *Kings of the Road* (1976), or Hans-Jürgen Syberberg's *Sex-Business—Made in Pasing* (1969) discovers direct references to these comedies as defining the landscape. Furthermore, the New

German Cinema set itself up against cultural "lows" from a broader historical period—the general "*Heimatkitsch*" of postwar cultural production, and even further back, to the popular culture of the fascist period. For the state, this high, critical film discussed abroad promoted the success of a West German democratic transformation at home.

The success of this alignment of film production, high art, and state interest has greatly influenced critics and academic analyses both nationally and internationally. Such an alignment lasted through the 1960s and 1970s. In the 1980s the relationship of production, high culture, and state upon which aesthetic analyses had been based underwent a dramatic shift, resulting in general negative critical assessments of German film production. The death of Rainer Werner Fassbinder as a sign of the decline of auteurist film production is cited as one reason for this shift. To this is added the conservative culture war of Helmut Kohl's new government, which transformed the relationship of the state to high culture. Finally, we can add, as is explored in various essays of this volume, processes of transnationalization that transformed the act of film production and the relationship of filmmakers to the German state. Even though the 1980s witnessed great successes in German popular film production, with international hits like *Men* (Dörrie, 1985) *Das Boot* (Petersen, 1981), and *The Never-Ending Story* (Petersen, 1984), 1982 has also been critically identified as the beginning of the decline of German film. However, if all films apart from New German Cinema and some Weimar art films have been written off or pronounced dead, how can one account for the economic viability and viewing pleasure of films from other eras, including the boom of comedies during the 1990s?

Equally important, the critical exploration of popular film raises numerous questions for German film studies. In their obsession with German identity, have cultural critics (like Anglo-American Germanists) privileged films that overtly and "correctly," whether in terms of aesthetics or of politics, situate this identity in relation to Germany's national socialist past? Has such tunnel vision cast the myriad political underpinnings that infuse German popular cinema as being merely reactionary? Does pleasurable, cathartic cinematic viewing, as opposed to a more distanced, Brechtian mode of spectatorship, automatically inhibit critical, if not subversive, ways of seeing? Is Hollywood's influence on German cinema legitimate only when filtered through the lens of a Fassbinder or a Wenders? What is the significance of Germany's substantial influence on Hollywood? How does an analysis of German popular cinema call for new methodologies in understanding all film, German or otherwise? In the face of the Frankfurt School–influenced cultural studies paradigm, can such an examination suggest new directions for debates on popular culture more generally? The essays of this volume explore possible answers to these questions.

The rhetorical nature of these questions, of course, suggests that the traditional periodization of German film, with its discrete categories of worthy or disreputable film genres, is not, nor was it ever, so cut and dry. What this volume does, first and foremost, is offer serious, critical attention to popular films that to this point have remained mostly beyond the pale of critical attention. Moreover, in attempting to answer the questions posed previously, the essays presented here not only challenge the traditional shape of German film history by spotlighting the popular, they also offer their own kind of "Never-Ending Story" of oft-repeated obsessions, overlapping generic forms, omnipresent or subtle nods to Hollywood, and myriad political concerns irreducible to a unified message or aesthetic form. This anthology offers thematic clusters that not only challenge a straightforward, narrative understanding of German film history, but also highlight continuities across diverse historical moments.

In the context of an exploration of popular film, it is also important to question not just the divisions within German film, but the very parameters that distinguish national films as such. The question of how to define national cinemas is hotly debated at the moment, and in effect, some critics have suggested that national cinemas like German or French find their definition in relationship to Hollywood and Hollywood's ability to define cinematic language.[2] In the case of German national film, then, what would make a film German essentially is its difference from Hollywood. Such arguments have been formulated to this point through analyses of art film, identifying in them narrative strategies that directly oppose Hollywood's conventions. Popular film remains unexplored for such potential. Yet in our volume this question is addressed in many of the essays. Christine Haase's essay on that successful German film par excellence, *Run Lola Run* offers a methodology very much in tune with the overall structure of the volume. Recognizing the jumbled mix of Hollywood influences, plus diverse German and American cultural components, that comprise Tom Tykwer's film, she proceeds to analyze this unique fusion of "Hollywood pleasure" and a "*Heimat* identity." Tykwer's playful, pleasurable concoction, with its often surprising, irreverent appropriations, makes it possible to reimagine the field of German cinema as itself not a discrete, closed field of uniquely German components but as an arena in which, to quote Roger Chartier, "common cultural sets are appropriated differently." We hope that what Tykwer's film highlights in pleasurable form is demonstrated throughout the volume by essays that assess not only hybrid elements in popular cinematic production but also the ways in which their appropriation—the pleasures they generate, their political resonances, the obsessions they invoke, an so on—bear witness to the vibrancy of German culture.

Furthermore, Gerd Gemünden's essay stands out as perhaps a corrective or a reminder that Hollywood is also open to influence from "outside." In fact, Gemünden's exploration of the inverse influence of Germany on Hollywood displays an immensely important aspect of the dynamic of popular film production, allowing us to see how permeable Hollywood is. Gemünden focuses on the exile period, a historic moment of great influx of German filmmakers and filmmaking technology to the United States. Many have argued that film noir emerging during the 1930s and 1940s as one of the most American of film movements is a result of this German presence. Gerd's exploration takes us to films like that most American of films, *Casablanca*, and points out how much this film was a product of the work of exiled Europeans, and Germans in particular.[3] Nevertheless it is important in general to recognize that Hollywood's hegemony in part derives from its ability to incorporate the new and dynamic developments of other film traditions. For Canadian and American scholars who come to film studies through routes other than national area studies, or for film scholars whose work focuses solely on Hollywood production, we can appreciate that such questions might be a bit perplexing—although there are, of course, many studies of Canada's relationship to the Hollywood film industry. However, I hope it does not sound like hubris to suggest that this is an area in which German film studies can make an original contribution and say something unique to our American colleagues.

To provide a definition of popular film is a daunting task, enormous in size. Concentrating simply on the history of cinema in Germany, the definition must be long enough to reach from the silent slapstick antics of Carl Valentin's working men to the desperate techno race of Franka Potenta's Lola. It must be high enough to include the tops of Weimar cinema and the flops of postwar restoration. It must be broad enough to include the range of genres: melodrama, comedy, musical, horror, war, and so on. It must be deep enough to hold the populist productions of not just democratic but also national socialist and socialist Germany. Focusing on the content of popular films offers the possibility of only the most general definition. Provisionally, popular film is generally narrative fiction, linear in its development, usually relying on a series of scenes arranged according to genre conventions in order to establish action. Characters are central to this action and generally present themselves as types confronting a central problematic. However, a definition based on such thematic similarities proves ultimately too expansive to be useful. To chart out the dimensions of popular film, we will concentrate not on the content but on the structures of popular film, not on what it "is" but on what it "does." To provide a definition, there follows a series of propositions to be added to the one already listed, along with qualifications and complications. These propositions will cover popular film's mass appeal, entertainment value, political economy, industrial structure, mediating quality, relation to subculture, ability to organize knowledge, role in mediating elite versus popular knowledge, and finally how popular film is affected by the new media and the move into post-industrialism.

Popular film has been frequently defined in opposition to other forms of film practice, especially in opposition to art film. This opposition, a juxtaposition of popular and high culture, draws attention to the mass appeal of popular film. Popular film is generally accessible, relying on unrestrictive knowledge, and therefore it always carries a potential mass appeal. While the potential of mass appeal obtains for popular film, in this opposition art film runs the risk of becoming relegated to the pursuit of a smaller *gebildet,* or educated public. Upon closer inspection, however, the opposition between high cultural and mass film proves difficult to maintain. Certainly, a quick glance at film history reveals the art house successes of Alfred Hitchcock and Douglas Sirk, the Hollywood triumphs of Fritz Lang and Wolfgang Petersen, the genre film fascinations of Rainer Werner Fassbinder and Wim Wenders, or the cross-over hits of Doris Dörrie and Tom Tykwer. The avant-garde and experimental films of Richter, Eggeling, Eisenstein, Dudow, or Riefenstahl oriented themselves toward a mass audience. Indeed, one of the historic goals of at least portions of the avant-garde has been to "popular-ize" high culture, a dynamic explored by Hester Baer in her essay on a Herbert Vesely film. The films of these directors make po-rous distinctions drawn between art and popular film. The basic distinction between film production that appeals widely to a mass audience and one oriented toward a limited public is unsta-ble. All film is inherently a reproducible mass medium, offering the possibility of a mass audience. The spectators themselves cross over. The educated or *gebildet* elite, except in the case of a puritanical few, can also be found among the "hoi polloi" at the multiplex. Art and popular film, therefore, are not in opposition but in a relationship that will be addressed further in the fol-lowing.

In German, one term used in discussions of popular film is *Unterhaltungsfilm*, best translated as entertainment film. Comparing the semantic fields of popular and entertainment film, it becomes clear that diversion, amusement, pleasure, and delight are an integral aspect of popular film's ability to interest an audience. Precisely this aspect of popular film, its entertain-ment value, can distinguish it, although such a gesture does not necessarily mean that other forms of film production are without their pleasures. (Even the most direct attempts to destroy cine-matic pleasure, by directors like Straub/Huillet or Achternbusch, still bring a form of delight to their audience.)

The entertainments of popular film are often denounced as diversionary. They supposedly draw the spectator's attention away from more serious pursuits, offering instead escapist, titil-lating, even morally degrading images. Of course, denunciations of popular film usually mean that the film's audiences are not spending their time pursuing the interests of the denunciator. It is important in this dynamic to recognize the development of "free time" in industrialized countries. Free time did not result in in-creased interest in established institutions. Initial battles over the amusements pursued during leisure hours marked points of larger sociopolitical conflicts between new liberal interests and historic established institutions, such as those of the church, the state, and educational institutions, for example. Popular film emerged precisely along with shorter working hours, and it quickly be-came one of the more lasting and significant pursuits of (the new) leisure time. The battles over the amusements of popular film have thus continually marked sites of social transformation.

These battles have taken two primary forms. First and foremost has been control through restriction or censorship of films. The essays of Janet McCabe, Alison Guenther-Pal, Tim Bergfelder, Stefan Soldovieri, and Randall Halle discuss examples of this type of control. Secondly, but perhaps a more significant form of control, was the realization that the apparatus of film itself could be appropriated for engaged and directed production. For instance, this possibility of appropriation proved significant for the state during World War I, when popular film production was used in the creation of war propaganda. To this end, Lutz Koepnick, Robert Reimer, and Brad Prager, in assessing the films of Wolfgang Petersen and Joseph Vilsmaier, explore how popular film can be used for conservative ends, affirmation of social hierarchy, glorification of state authority, and chauvinistic aims.

On the Left, the particular form of denunciation has historically been on the basis that popular film is politically escapist, the product of a capitalist culture industry that keeps the workers from pursuing their real interests. Certainly, it is possible to recognize that the most diverting of popular films are riddled with contradictions that undermine their easy dismissal as apolitical diversion.[4] The "little shop girl" goes to the movies not to forget her life but to experience better possibilities in "the pursuit of happiness."[5] Marxian critics cannot disregard how she experiences the contradiction between her life and the one on the screen. Perhaps more importantly, critiques of the capitalist culture industry must also at least acknowledge the production of popular films in fascist or socialist systems. Entertainment does not belong to capitalism, although specific forms of entertainment do. If capitalism has specific forms of entertainment, other political-economic systems prove equally capable of appropriating the film apparatus in order to produce specific and unique pleasures. Given the history of dismissal of "escapist film," the exploration of the political aspects and progressive potentials of popular film still proves significant as a basis of analysis. In this volume the work of Antje Ascheid on Nazi cinema and Stefan Soldovieri on GDR film production take up the question of what is specific to the popular films of the particular political-economic systems.

Popular film proves central to film production, regardless of the political-economic systems. To be sure, popular film production in fascist and socialist systems was bound by state-directed censorship and administration. In a planned economy like the GDR's, or in the totally administered society of the Third Reich, the film apparatus was subject to control, just like other branches of industry. Nevertheless, as in capitalist systems, film production had to entice potential spectators with its entertainments. However, capitalism, socialism, and fascism belong as systems to an industrial mode of production, and, as such, share certain structures or apparatuses. The industrial mode of production, like every mode of production, has given rise to its own forms of pleasure and amusement. Film in general belongs to industrial production, and popular film specifically emerged as a form of entertainment for an industrialized era. Indeed, it is possible to offer as further definition that popular film is an industrial system of entertainment for an industrial culture, and through industrialization, the century of cinema brought forward a form of entertainment for everyone. At the dawn of the twentieth century, not just leisure time but surplus wages, the culture industry and the commodification of art, statistical marketing, mass audiences displaced from pre-industrial settings, and new communications technologies coalesced to make popular film possible. This entertainment was available to everybody, proving able to cut across class lines, offering its spectators a commodified form of democracy in its choices. These structures were proper to industrialization, regardless of the political economic system directing the process.

Walter Benjamin understood cinema precisely as a marker of a fundamental transformation of culture in the industrial era. In "The Work of Art in the Age of Mechanical Reproduction," he focused on how, through film, art, formerly unique and distant from the masses, became reproducible and proximate. Benjamin sought a radical politics immanent to cinema's reproduction; the films that end his essay hang between a totalitarian and a communist art for the masses—Leni Riefenstahl versus Slatan Dudow. Yet these films did not reveal practices immanent in popular film; rather, they displayed how popular film reflects larger sociopolitical configurations and conflicts in industrial society. The opposing film practices at the end of Benjamin's essay replicate the conflict that sundered the Weimar Republic—Hitler versus Thälmann. Furthermore, in the audiences to whom these films appealed is a manifestation of the spectators' loyalties to diverging social organizations—National Socialists versus Communists. Even though the film apparatus builds a system of cultural production, its content is not immanent to the apparatus; rather, the apparatus mediates that content. This condition of the apparatus means that popular film is not opposed to libratory practice, nor is it the antipode of politically engaged film. The film apparatus in general, and popular film in particular, simply reproduces all the tensions and contradictions proper to its mode of production—it does not solve them.

Here it is perhaps necessary to underscore that popular film carries only a potential mass appeal, that is to say that popular film should not be understood as synonymous with mass entertainment. Popular film cannot be defined as film that is popular, film that draws in a mass audience. Defining popular films as films that are popular is not tautological, yet it cannot be maintained, as there are plenty of examples of popular films that fail to find a mass audience. Of course, popular film does invite a mass audience, regardless of whether or not the potential spectators perceive the film's enticement. Under current political-economic conditions, with the collapse of state-directed film industries, popular film is produced more than ever in a free market orientation, where popular film production vacillates between two primary market dynamics: the building of increasingly larger audiences and the appeal to specialized audiences. Of course, this type of production is not new but goes back to the earliest days of the film industry. Under these conditions, popular film follows the general dynamic of industrial production in a free market: expansion and further exploitation of the existing markets versus the opening of new markets. The former might be recognized in the development of blockbuster or multigenre films to draw in increasingly larger audiences. The large audience is expanded through the building of interest in star systems, marketing events, product tie-ins, spin-offs, sequels, and so on.

Production for smaller markets, however, is also an important aspect of the popular film industry, and it is reflected in specific genres and subgenres with specialized appeal, such as the *Heimatfilm*, the B-grade sex film, the mountain film, and German underground horror. In their essays in this volume, Alasdair King, Tim Bergfelder, Nancy Nenno, and Randall Halle explore various aspects of this type of production. Production of specialized genres for small audiences is particularly important because in the commodified choices presented by popular film, spectators have proven consistently resilient in countering the homogenizing dynamic of a mass market with their own heterogeneous interests and tastes.

Nevertheless, popular film evidences an ability to organize spectators, producing group cohesion and specific knowledge. This ability is part of the general dynamic of popular culture as it emerged in the twentieth century. We should not underestimate the transformations of consciousness that accompanied production for increasingly larger audiences. Miriam Hansen has argued explicitly that classical cinematic practice presumed a great deal of psychic homogenization in its spectators. While the nineteenth-century theaters and opera houses entrenched a solipsistic and voyeuristic viewing culture—the darkened space filled with mesmerized spectators, absorbed by the spectacle—cinema transformed this viewing practice into a mass event. Gustaf Gründgens the theater actor can appear on only one stage, whereas Ossi Oswalde can appear simultaneously on as many screens as there are exhibition prints of her latest film. In Berlin, Freiburg, and New York, audiences can all thrill to the latest Wolfgang Petersen film. Popular film offers itself as point of communication in the public sphere. Individuals of diverse backgrounds and interests find commonalities through a shared knowledge of popular film. Beyond this general knowledge, each subgenre offers its own conventions and forms of knowledge, for example, women's films or German underground horror. Fan knowledge can even act as basis for subculture, expressing itself not only in information networks but also clothing and behavior. At the same time, these are not, it should be underscored, restrictive forms of knowledge, prerequisite for a viewer's comprehension. Even the sequels and prequels of popular film tend to recap the narrative for new spectators.

Thus, the assumption stated previously that popular film is generally narrative fiction must be qualified. Although in capitalism popular film is dominated by the productions of commercial narrative cinema, popular film is not synonymous with such films. Commercial narrative films, especially the films of Hollywood, do comprise the largest portion of current film production, yet independent and nonnarrative cinema can certainly offer entertainment to their spectators and can go on to find mass audiences. This fact plays an important role outside of Hollywood's film industry and especially in smaller national cinemas. What is popular in the context of one national cinema becomes art house film elsewhere. Popular film production proves flexible and expansive in the development of new genres, and it forces other forms of film production into a relationship that goes beyond competition. Under current conditions, the borders of popular film production expand and sublate the differences with art house and avant-garde film. Films like *Run Lola Run* [*Lola Rennt*] (Tom Tykwer, 1999) or *Buena Vista Social Club* (Wim Wenders, 1999) illustrate this dynamic.

Previously we stated that popular film relied on unrestrictive knowledge. Restrictive knowledge remains as a central point of difference between popular and high cultural film, be it art, avant-garde, or experimental film production. Yet, popular film transforms the significance of high cultural knowledge. In this context, it is important to recall a bit of the history of high and popular cultural knowledge. In the eighteenth and nineteenth centuries, members of the emerging middle class promoted a common high culture as the basis of a universal cross-class human community. A common aesthetic education, described best by Schiller, was to be the anchor of this culture, yet significantly, such high culture was also understood as popular, in the sense that it was and should be available to everyone, although available precisely through *Bildung*, the acquisition of a particular form of restrictive knowledge that would "raise" the common man. Of course, as it developed, the theorists, educators, and producers of this culture were members of the middle class, so that the vision of a common aesthetic education of man promoted by Schiller quickly turned into Hegel's assertion of a common bourgeois society, *bürgerliche Gesellschaft*.

In the nineteenth century a new form of popular culture emerged. Not education but the processes of industrial capital gave rise to it: precisely the commodification of the cultural artifact, the mass reproduction of art and craft, the technological disruption of the uniqueness and discriminations of high culture. In their essays on pre-Weimar and Weimar film, Janet McCabe, Rick McCormick, and Christian Rogowski discuss directly how film served as a means to open up a new mass market that cut across class. They discuss Weimar-era films designed to draw both bourgeois and proletarian into the same exhibition space and to create of them a common viewing public. They return us to the origins of the film market, exploring the parameters of modern popular culture at its point of emergence. In our contemporary era, with its criticisms of the "advanced" marketing techniques, product placement, and ideological influence of film, their essays display how those strategies emerged with the film form itself. Often understood as a leveling or reduction to the lowest common denominator, the modern unfolding of popular culture in the industrial era is of an entirely different order. Popular culture in the era of industrial reproduction was based not on what you knew but on what you consumed. Unrestrictive knowledge of the type found in popular film did not make individuals unfit for the consumption of high culture, rather it represented the type of universal cross-class human community available in the industrial era: mass culture.

As we noted previously, the borders between art and popular film are porous, and filmmakers frequently move from experimental work to unrestrictive popular production. (Unquestionably, even the films intended for a "least common denominator" engage in experimentation with narrative and visual codes, to keep drawing their audience anew.) Attempts to create films with mass appeal and yet retain an aesthetics based in a restrictive knowledge remain more uncommon. During the 1960s in the context of the New Wave, for instance, there were attempts to "elevate" the spectator or create a new audience. However, given such films' position in competition with popular film, the pursuit of the *Bildung* or "knowledge" they afforded never enticed a mass audience. The community offered by restrictive high cultural knowledge lost its inclusive popular quality, and appreciation of these films remained limited to an intellectual elite. Already in his critiques of Weimar films, Kracauer understood art film as on par with popular film. A distinction of art cinema only masked the presence of the shared industrial apparatus of production. For him, high and low were united, in that they shared this means of production that proved such a central tool in the capitalist mode of production. Kracauer recognized little difference in the knowledge conveyed by the two forms of production. In this regard Kracauer derisively wrote: "In their essential details, the "art" film products are no better than the average wares. They are neither less politically biased nor a millimeter closer to reality. They convey nothing of the sphere they presume to capture. They have no content. *Lack of substance is the decisive trait of the totality of established film production*" (319). Ultimately in relationship to popular film, the film industry has fostered a commodification of high cultural knowledge so that in its ability to form community it proves equal to any other form of "fan knowledge." To participate in popular culture, the educated elite actually must go to the multiplex.

Finally and briefly noted, as an industrial entertainment for an industrial culture, the nature of popular film and entertainment in general changes and transforms with the move into postindustrialism. Postindustrialism does not represent the same type of transformation of the mode of production as industrialization once did. Popular film stands in a different relationship today vis-à-vis computer-generated images than it once did vis-à-vis the theater. The new media fundamentally expand x-fold the reproducibility initiated by film. Cable, digital, and computer graphics technologies promise to transform production, distribution, and viewing practices toward personalized heterogeneous forms—a promise of freedom from the homogenization of mass culture. Individualized delivery systems, 1,001 channels, virtual reality, promotion and advertising based on individual or small group-focused rather than mass marketing, and so on promise to free the individual from the mass. Every person will consume according to the refinement of his or her own tastes and interests. Such are the promises of the new popular culture. To be sure, the new media, central to the new economy, have opened up new forms of entertainment, but up until now they have been subordinate to popular film, and the entertainments they offer have not differed dramatically in nature from those offered by the apparatus described here. Perhaps, as the form and influence of the new media expand quantitatively, we can anticipate a fundamental qualitative change in the mode of production, and with it a change vis-à-vis popular film and entertainment in general. However, such a change has not yet taken place.

A complex aspect of these recent developments in the technology of popular culture is explored in this volume through the essays of Brad Prager, Robert Reimer, and Lutz Koepnick, all of which consider the role of historical representation in popular film. Across these essays we discover how the transformation in production technology has also transformed our relationship to reality, to documentary, and fundamentally to the past. All of these essays deal with the form of representation of the Nazi past that has been so significant for Germany and for German film production in particular. Brad Prager sets up this analysis through his discussion of the great success of Wolfgang Petersen's *Das Boot* (1981), placing it clearly in its relationship to the sociopolitical context of its period. Prager describes how the film's techniques for working through the past depended on its position as international blockbuster. However, the filmic precision and historical understanding of this film derived from precomputerized graphics and special effects—unlike Petersen's recent productions. The relationship to history established by *Das Boot* derives from the same period as the forging of the Hitler diaries in the 1980s, parodied in the movie *Schtonk* (1992), and Michael Born's forgeries of more than twenty documentaries for German television—all documents of earlier film technologies.[6] Simultaneously German unification and developments in digital imaging transformed the context of film production and likewise the relationship to the past. In this volume Robert Reimer explores a vision of World War II in Joseph Vilsmaier's *Stalingrad* (1993) that belongs to this new era. Superficially, the film's narrative takes up similar material to that engaged by Petersen, the common soldier confronting a battle situation that the viewer knows is doomed. Pared with Prager's essay, Reimer's discussion displays the intent of the transformations in popular culture. Then Lutz Koepnick explores in Vilsmaier's *Comedian Harmonists* (1997), Vilsmaier's second engagement with the Nazi past, how digital technology now transforms our relationship with the past. Basing his work in current trauma theory, Koepnick critically assesses the vision of historical wholeness and plenitude that spectators can now consume. Recognizing that new critical discussions must follow this new technology, Koepnick's essay establishes their foundation.

Beyond this grouping of essays, similar critical concerns regarding the limits of popular culture inform the work throughout the volume. Haase's essay on *Run Lola Run* examines its use of an MTV aesthetic, animation, grainy super-eight footage, and so on, as a means not so much to master a troubling past but rather to point up the interconnectedness of all things, specifically American and European modes of film production. McCarthy's and Mittman's essays analyze films that mark points of transcultural contact, detailing how such contact is fraught with a dynamic of hegemonic appropriation that adheres to contemporary popular film. McCarthy and Mittman on post-European Union films examine fantasies of geographic boundaries all too easily crossed, whether by the omnipresent cell phones of moneyed, middle-class subjects easily jetting around a unified Europe, or by newly sprung East Germans roaming the European landscape in souped-up Trabis to investigate the promises and pitfalls of German unification.

While the essays appear here ordered according to the chronology of the films discussed, there are many ways we could have arranged them. Readers are invited to approach them in the way that appeals to them. Moving from most to least familiar films might be one form of approach, facilitated by the fact that at this point most of the films discussed here are available on video. The essays can be read in groups of topics and trends that cut across the entire field of popular film production, such as those groupings outlined previously. Other groupings of concerns are also possible.

Beginning with the reevaluation in Christian Rogowski's essay of Kracauer's negative estimation of German popular film, the reader could move on to the essays by Rick McCormick, Hester Baer, John Davidson, and Christine Haase that explore various attempts to infuse popular film with high cultural concerns. These essays take up explicitly the problem of the often antagonistic and constantly shifting negotiations between high and popular culture. A different potential grouping could pick up these considerations but invert them to a certain extent by exploring the relationship of popular film to developments in mass culture like consumerism and tourism. Here the essays of Janet McCabe and Nancy Nenno are particularly important. Popular film offers a wealth of material for explorations of gender and sexuality, especially how popular film production is involved in the production of normative and nonnormative images, but also how film production itself is exposed to regulation. It is certainly the case that popular film has given the censors a great deal of work over the years. In this collection, Alison Guenther-Pal, Tim Bergfelder, Randall Halle, Antje Ascheid, Rick McCormick, and Janet McCabe provide essays that variously discuss socially liberal and conservative depictions of sexuality in popular film. In terms of methodology, the essays of Elizabeth Mittman, Randall Halle, and Margaret McCarthy explore the social psychology of popular film, focusing on ways in which the images, tropes, and narrative structures of popular film reveal their "psychoanalytic" service to their sociocultural setting.

While all of these suggested groupings attend to the political economy of popular film production, through various essays here—Antje Ascheid and Stefan Soldovieri, in particular—readers also can explore the propagandistic deployment of popular film in the service of political interests. These essays look at film production under the administered conditions of the Third Reich and the GDR. Of particular interest in these essays, however, is the difficulties such societies experience as they use propaganda to make a populist appeal. The problem of popular film's relationship to national reconfigurations has a particular resonance in German studies, given the fraught relationship of Germany to nationalism. Of course, popular culture is a global phenomenon and it flows through and across national definitions and state boundaries, making it impossible to understand mass culture as contained by the parameters of the nation-state. Yet we find in the anthology essays that explore specific intersections of popular film and the national imaginary: see, for example, the essays of Gerd Gemünden, Alasdair King, Elizabeth Mittman, Randall Halle, and Margaret McCarthy. All of these films explore forms of national displacement, the experiences of exile, defeat, collapse, and even liberation that resulted from the transformations of 1933, 1945, 1989, and 1992.

What is clear in establishing groupings of essays is that many of them appear in multiple sections, because the topics cut across all popular film production. After reading through this volume it should be quite clear that in the century of cinema, popular film has taken on a function of secularized ritual, achieving something akin to what Geertz would describe as deep play. In popular cinema subjects form and discover their own temperament, and their society's temper as well.

NOTES

1. A notable exception is Thomas Elsaesser and Michael Wedel, eds., *The BFI Companion to German Cinema* (London: BFI Publishing, 1999). Eva Kolinsky and Wilfried van der Will, eds., *The Cambridge Companion to Modern German Culture* (Cambridge: Cambridge University Press, 1998), on the other hand, in effect concentrates solely on high cultural production. In Van der Will's own essay, "The Functions of '*Volkskultur*,' Mass Culture and Alternative Culture," where one might expect a historical overview of popular culture, instead there is a Habermasian review of the problem mass culture poses to high culture.

2. For the article that might be understood as beginning the discussion, see Andrew Higson, "The Concept of National Cinema," *Screen* 10 (1989): 36–46. See also Higson, *Waving the Flag: Constructing a National Cinema in Britain* (Oxford: Oxford University Press, 1995). Stephen Crofts has encouraged the problematization of national cinema, advocating, however, not for its abandonment but rather for an expansion into types of national cinemas. See Stephen Crofts, "Reconceptualising National Cinema/s," *Quarterly Review of Film and Video* 14 (1993): 49–67; Crofts, "Concepts of National Cinema," in *The Oxford Guide to Film Studies*, ed. John Hill and Pamela Church Gibson (Oxford: Oxford University Press, 1998); and Paul Willemen "The National," in *Looks and Frictions*, ed. Paul Willeman (London: BFI, 1994).

3. In German studies the exploration of exile literature (Thomas Mann or Bert Brecht in California, for example) is an active area of exploration. Similar work in film is only beginning, with the discussions of Detlef Sierck/Douglas Sirck or Fritz Lang as the best examples.

4. Richard Dyer has argued in "defense" of the "escapism" of popular film; to dismiss entertainment as simple wish fulfillment or political diversion is to miss out precisely on its utopic thrust. Popular film offers a form of entertainment that acts not as the new opium of the masses, but as that vehicle whereby they are able to experience a moment of unfulfilled promises. Dyer's observations lead us to concentrate, therefore, not so much on the intended diversions of the producers but on the psychological need of the spectator. This defense, which goes against much of the Marxian analysis of

popular film, compels explorations of the social psychology of entertainment. For attempts to negotiate these questions of popular film from a cultural studies approach, see the discussions in Matthew Tinkcom and Amy Villarejo, eds., *Keyframes: Popular Cinema and Cultural Studies* (New York: Routledge, 2001).

5. This effect was, of course, most acutely felt at the class borders, where, as Siegfried Kracauer (1889–1966) observed satirically, "the little shopgirls go to the movies." See the essay with this title in Siegfried Kracauer, *The Mass Ornament: Weimar Essays* (Cambridge, Mass.: Harvard University Press, 1995). On this screen the noble worker marries the billionaire's daughter and the poor girl saves the nation. Kracauer understood film as the imaginary of class society, where even the "stupid and unreal film fantasies are the *daydreams of society,* in which its actual reality comes to the fore and its otherwise repressed wishes take on form" (292). Film becomes the medium not of classless but of mass society, and its fantasies undo the very real restrictions imposed by class structure.

6. The story of Born's forgeries was broken in the weekly *Die Woche.* See Wolfgang Timpe, "Wir sind Opfer. Günther Jauch hat die gefälschten Beiträge des Michael Born gesehen, geprüft und gesendet—schuldig aber sollen andere sein," *Die Woche,* 25 October 1996. For a brief discussion of the case and its relationship to digital forgeries, see Kay Hoffmann, "'I See, If I Believe It'—Documentary and the Digital," in *Cinema Futures: Cain, Abel or Cable? The Screen Arts in the Digital Age,* ed. Thomas Elsaesser and Kay Hoffmann (Amsterdam: Amsterdam University Press, 1998).

WORKS CITED

Adorno, Theodor. *The Culture Industry: Selected Essays on Mass Culture.* London: Routledge, 1991.

Benjamin, Walter. *Illuminations.* Edited and with an introduction by Hannah Arendt, trans. Harry Zohn. New York: Schocken Books, 1986.

Dyer, Richard. *Only Entertainment.* New York: Routledge, 1992.

———. *Stars.* London: BFI, 1979.

Eagelton, Terry. *The Idea of Culture.* Oxford: Blackwell, 2000.

Faulstich, Werner, and Helmut Korte, eds. *Der Star: Geschichte, Rezeption, Bedeutung.* München: Fink, 1997.

Hansen, Miriam. "Early Cinema, Late Cinema: Permutations of the Public Sphere." *Screen* 34, no. 3 (1993): 197–210.

Kracauer, Siegfried. *The Mass Ornament: Weimar Essays.* Thomas Y. Levine, editor. Cambridge, Mass.: Harvard University Press, 1995.

Modelski, Tania, ed. *Studies in Entertainment.* Bloomington: Indiana University Press, 1986.

Patalas, Enno. *Stars: Geschichte der Filmidole.* Frankfurt: Fischer, 1967.

Stacey, Jackie. *Star Gazing: Hollywood Cinema and Female Spectatorship.* London: Routledge, 1994.

Van der Will, Wilfried. "The Functions of 'Volkskultur,' Mass Culture and Alternative Culture." In *The Cambridge Companion to Modern German Culture,* ed. Eva Kolinsky and Wilfried van der Will. Cambridge: Cambridge University Press, 1998.

Williams, Rosalind. *Dream Worlds.* Berkeley: University of California Press, 1982.

CHAPTER 1

From Ernst Lubitsch to Joe May

Challenging Kracauer's Demonology with Weimar Popular Film

Christian Rogowski

For better or for worse, Siegfried Kracauer's classic study, *From Caligari to Hitler* (1947), has set the parameters not only for our perception of the cinema of the Weimar period but for the historiography of German film as a whole. As Theodor W. Adorno has pointed out, Kracauer pursues two distinct yet interrelated objectives by construing the "history of German film after the First World War as the history of the developing ideology of totalitarian power" (Adorno 175 f.). On the one hand, Kracauer suggests a direct linkage between the products of popular culture and the political catastrophe of National Socialism; on the other, he discusses films from the Weimar period as direct manifestations of the "German soul" (Kracauer, *From Caligari to Hitler* 3), with recurring motifs indicating a propensity on the part of Germans to succumb unquestioningly to the power of authority, amounting indeed to a "longing for submission" (Kracauer, *From Caligari to Hitler* 76). This propensity, his claim goes, leads Germans directly from a preoccupation with the demonic powers of filmic hypnotists like the crazed doctor in Robert Wiene's *The Cabinet of Dr. Caligari [Das Cabinet des Dr. Caligari]* (1920) to submission to the real-life dictator, Adolf Hitler. Kracauer thus not only superimposes a teleological narrative onto his account of the history of Weimar cinema; his demonization of Germans as intrinsically inclined to authoritarian rule effectively amounts to a

veritable demonology of German film.[1] Confronted with Kracauer's psychosocial variant of the familiar *Sonderweg* theory, we
are left to conclude that the trajectory of German history is a solitary line that led straight to catastrophe.

Kracauer's dual agenda generates a series of logical incon-
sistencies and methodological conflicts. For one thing, to the extent that Kracauer aims at giving an account of the rise of
National Socialism, and German film's complicity in it, he finds
himself compelled to disregard the complexity of the development of Weimar cinema within the larger context of modern mass
culture. Conceived as a "Psychological Study of the German
Film" (the subtitle of the book), Kracauer's study fails to address
a multitude of historical, sociological, political, economic, and
cultural factors. Even if one were to accept the underlying notion
of cinema as an expression of national psychic dispositions and
collective fantasies, the crucial issue of mediation between
contextual and textual factors remains unexplained. Yet it is
precisely in these mediations—the many "silences and omissions
in Kracauer's account" (Cherchi Usai and Codelli 16)—that a
wide range of alternatives to Kracauer's teleologically linear reasoning reside. It is not surprising, then, that Kracauer's "retrospective teleology" (Elsaesser and Wedel 9) has come under
criticism from a variety of perspectives.[2] To concerns with methodological and ideological narrowness, normativity, essentialism,
and disregard of gender issues, I wish to add a number of further
considerations that all have to do with the embeddedness of
Weimar film in a variety of complex political, sociocultural, and
economic contexts.

Kracauer's book surveys the history of German film from
1895 to the early 1930s by distinguishing four distinct phases,
three of which coincide with the political history of the Weimar
Republic. The first section, "The Archaic Period (1895–1918),"
relegates the many filmic experiments of the *Kaiserreich* era to
the status of "an archaic period insignificant in itself" (Kracauer,
From Caligari to Hitler 15). Section two, "The Postwar Period
(1918–1924)," traces the emergence of Weimar film from the
"Shock of Freedom" (the title of the first subchapter heading; Kracauer, *From Caligari to Hitler* 43) after the military defeat and
the thwarted November Revolution of 1918 to the aftermath of
the hyperinflation of 1923–24 in what is presented as a trajectory
that leads "From Rebellion to Submission" (the final subchapter
heading; Kracauer [1947] 1974, 115). The third section, "The Stabilized Period (1924–1929)," takes a critical look at the precarious

political balances struck in the late 1920s, while section four, significantly entitled, "The Pre-Hitler Period (1930–1933)," suggests that the products of the turbulent final phase of the Weimar Republic could be co-opted by the Nazis only too easily.

My critique of Kracauer here focuses on the first two phases in his chronology, primarily because of the problematic notion of "beginnings" that underpins his project. I wish to test Kracauer's account against popular films produced during the Weimar Republic, paying particular attention to February 1920, the time of the release of Wiene's *The Cabinet of Dr. Caligari*, the film that serves Kracauer as a barometer of German psychic dispositions. In singling out *Caligari* as a starting point, Kracauer construes a quasi-causal logic for the development of German cinema (and for the course of German history in general) that belies the many alternative possibilities that emerged at the same time as, or were present alongside, Wiene's landmark film. By shifting the focus to films that had a more clearly popular appeal (and that, indeed, were more successful at the box office), I wish to challenge some of the key concepts operative in Kracauer's account. In addition to pointing to economic, sociocultural, and political aspects of German popular film, I will discuss Kracauer's problematic notion of a monolithic German national identity, particularly with regard to the role played by Jews in the Weimar film industry. Kracauer's assertions concerning the distinctive characteristics of German cultural products are placed against the backdrop of Weimar films by filmmakers and producers such as Ernst Lubitsch, Fritz Lang, Max Mack, Richard Oswald, and Erich Pommer. I shall then focus on what, in commercial and cultural terms, is perhaps the most remarkable filmic product of early Weimar popular cinema, Joe May's lavish eight-part action-adventure extravaganza, *The Mistress of the World [Die Herrin der Welt]* of 1919–20. As I hope to show, May's film series provides a unique test case for highlighting the ideological and methodological limitations of Kracauer's approach.

I would like to emphasize that the aim of my essay is not to diminish the extraordinary achievement that Kracauer's still influential study represents.[3] Its continuing impact attests to Kracauer's skill in "explaining" the rise of National Socialism through an examination of German film after the first World War. At first glance, Kracauer's reading of the sociopolitical subtext of Weimar cinema appears quite plausible. One thinks of the origins of UFA, the largest German film company, at the height of the

Great War: upon the suggestion of General Field Marshall Luden-
dorff, the main German production companies were merged in
November 1917 with the expressly propagandistic aim of bolstering the German war effort. A nexus of military, political, and economic interests in the German film industry was thus established
that continued after press tycoon Alfred Hugenberg assumed control of UFA in 1927, potentially placing large parts of the industrial conglomerate in the service of propagating right-wing
politics, a situation that made for a virtually seamless transition
when the Nazis assumed direct political control of German film
after 1933 (Kreimeier).

Yet the notion of a distinctly national cinema that underlies Kracauer's investigation is highly problematic. While there is
no denying the importance of political and historical forces specific to Germany in the development of its film culture, it must
be noted that the cinema is, first and foremost, an industrial enterprise subject to economic pressures that transcend national
boundaries. The somber expressionistic style of *Caligari* is perhaps more the product of sober business calculations than an emanation of the tortured "German soul": producer Erich Pommer
initiated the project with the aim of carving out a distinct niche
for German art film in an international market dominated by
American products (Bock and Töteberg 91). *Caligari*'s Teutonic
demonism is thus to a large extent a function of the international
film market of the period, subject to the logic of modern product
differentiation and niche marketing (Elsaesser, *Weimar Cinema
and After* 6).

Quite a number of films before and during the Weimar
period were actually international collaborations, most notably
the German-Danish productions featuring superstar actress
Asta Nielsen and director Urban Gad after 1911.[4] In Kracauer's
periodization, such works appear as insignificant and marginal.
From today's perspective, however, these films necessitate a reassessment of the sociological and artistic potential of early German film. For instance, as Heide Schlüpmann has demonstrated,
much of Wilhelmine cinema, including the highly successful
Nielsen/Gad films, is characterized by a "transgressive femininity" that launches a subtle critique of the patriarchal order (Schlüpmann, *Der unheimliche Blick* 27). In their focus on a female
protagonist and her unprecedented mobility in the public sphere,
such works point to an emancipatory potential of early German
film, a potential, I wish to argue, that runs counter to Kracauer's

notion of German film as a direct (albeit distorted) reflection of a distinctly German authoritarian collective unconscious.

Kracauer does not consider the impact of the international film market in his assessment of German film. Yet, as Thomas Saunders has shown, the development of the German film industry, especially after the First World War, cannot be understood without reference to the presence of the American film industry in the German arena, both as a model to be emulated and as a competitor to be challenged (Saunders). In a climate of understandable international anti-German sentiment following the Great War, it is certainly no coincidence that most German productions actually eschewed clearly identifiable German subjects or settings. For instance, the first German film of artistic significance to be released during the Weimar period, Ernst Lubitsch's *Carmen*, which premiered on December 20, 1918, espouses a Spanish subject, is based on the French novella by Merrimée (and the opera by Bizet), and displays gender conflicts that can hardly be confined to the German collective unconscious. Likewise, Lubitsch's *Passion* (*Madame Dubarry*, 1919), the first work to break the postwar U.S. embargo against German films, in December 1920, whatever its subtextual meaning in the context of the failed November Revolution might be, takes the guise of a historic costume drama set during the French Revolution. Indeed, most of the popular genre films of the early Weimar period significantly avoid Germany as a setting: alongside ersatz-Westerns with titles like *Bull Arizona—The Desert Eagle* (*Bull Arizona— Der Wüstenadler*) (Phil Jutzi & Horst Krahè, 1919), there are the detective serials set in Anglo-American milieus featuring stars like suave hearthrob Harry Liedtke and daredevil Harry Piel, cosmopolitan action-adventure thrillers (such as Fritz Lang's *The Spiders [Die Spinnen]*, 1919–20), period and costume dramas (such as Joe May's *Veritas Vincit*, 1919), and exotic mystery films (such as Robert Reinert's *Opium*, 1919). All these films were clearly made to cater to both a domestic and an international audience in an effort to reestablish the German film industry as a potential rival to Hollywood. Some films, especially exotic extravaganzas such as Lubitsch's *One Arabian Night [Sumurun]* (1920), Fritz Lang's *Destiny [Der müde Tod]* (1921), and Joe May's *The Indian Tomb [Das indische Grabmal]* (1921), with their lavish sets and expensive production values, clearly betray their indebtedness to the popular Italian monumental films of the period and to the blockbuster historical dramas of D. W. Griffith. Early Weimar popular cinema, then, in large part, is the product of transnational genre conventions, feeding on international popular fantasies.

Viewed in this light, the exoticism of much of early Weimar film, including the films mentioned previously, is perhaps more a function of questions of international marketability than an emanation of thinly disguised German imperialistic aspirations, as Kracauer would have it (*From Caligari to Hitler* 57). Motivated by both commercial and artistic concerns, German filmmakers were always eager to absorb new ideas from different countries. The most famous instance of this openness toward the new is perhaps the tremendous impact of the films from the Soviet Union on Weimar cinema after the screening of Eisenstein's *Battleship Potemkin* in Berlin in 1926. The fascination with the "Russenfilme" led to a series of artistic experiments and international collaborations (Bulgakowa). Likewise, alongside the many co-productions with Scandinavian countries, there were joint projects with Italy and Great Britain. Under financial pressure, the German film industry on occasion saw itself compelled to enter into collaborations with its competitors in Hollywood, the most notable example being the famous "Parufamet" deal between Paramount, Ufa, and Metro-Goldwyn-Meyer of December 1925. In this context it is of special interest to note that the stranglehold of American film on the European market even prompted French film producers to set aside their age-old anti-German bias, which understandably had been heightened to fever pitch by the war, in the mid-1920s and seek collaboration with German companies, resulting in a series of Franco-German co-productions (Bock, Jacobsen, and Schöning 169). The joint effort to combat American hegemony on the European market culminated after the advent of sound film in 1930 in an interesting phenomenon, the simultaneous production of parallel versions of German films in additional languages (usually English and French). A famous example of such multiple versions of German films produced in the early 1930s is Erik Charell's romantic operetta, *Der Kongreß tanzt*, the most successful German film of the 1931–32 season (Garncarz 167), pairing Lilian Harvey with French actor Henri Garat instead of Willy Fritsch in both the French (*Le Congress s' amuse*) and the English version *(Congress Dances)*.

Kracauer's operative notion of a German national cinema becomes even more problematic when one considers the extent to which people from a wide variety of countries contributed to the German film industry. Among directors and scriptwriters one finds not only Urban Gad, from Denmark, but also Stellan Rye and Carl Theodor Dreyer; others came from France (Jacques Feyder), Romania (Lupu Pick), Bulgaria (Slatan Dudow), and especially the Soviet Union (Dmitri Buchowertki, Anatol Litvak, Victor Trivas, and Alexander Wolkoff).[5] Many of the filmmakers whose works Kracauer presents as prime illustrations of his theses were not strictly speaking German at all, but hailed from the Habsburg Empire—with its multiethnic tradition distinct from that of Germany—among them Austrian directors and scriptwriters like Fritz Lang, Carl Mayer, Richard Oswald, Wilhelm Thiele, Edgar Ulmer, Berthold Viertel, and Billy Wilder, as well as German-speaking Hungarians such as Béla Balázs and Paul Czinner. These and many other "foreigners" contributed to the creative bustle of Weimar film. Weimar cinema, it becomes clear, was a business, and a highly international one at that.

Kracauer's neglect of commercial considerations and the multinational character of the German film industry is closely linked with his problematic assertion that somehow German film "begins" with Weimar cinema and with *Caligari*. By relegating over two decades of experimentation in the years before 1920 to the status of insignificant "prehistory" (*From Caligari to Hitler* 15), Kracauer downplays the economic, personal, and aesthetic continuities that persist in German cinema during the Wilhelmine and Weimar period. In many ways, the careers of Joe May, Max Mack, Ernst Lubitsch, and others, even master auteur Fritz Lang, are symptomatic of the continuities between pre-Weimar and Weimar cinema. For instance, from 1911 onward, Joe May was influential in the development of the genre of *Serienfilme* (serial films), including the two most important detective serials, featuring "Stuart Webbs" and, later, "Joe Deebs." Together with his wife, actress Mia May, he founded his own film company, May Film, in 1915 and produced, among others, a successful "Mia May Series." Joe May thus emerged as a crucial figure in the regeneration of the German film industry after the First World War, on account of his efforts as producer, director, scriptwriter, and film impresario (Elsaesser, "Filmgeschichte"). It is worth noting that May had been involved in some capacity in over sixty films, some of which were both commercially successful and of artistic significance, before embarking on *The Mistress of the World* together with assistant directors Uwe Jens Krafft and Karl Gerhardt in the summer of 1919 (Bock and Lenssen 151 ff.).

It would appear that Kracauer's dismissal of pre-Weimar film goes hand in hand with a failure to acknowledge the interconnectedness of popular cinema and artistic films that dates back to the Wilhelmine period and continues throughout the Weimar Republic. Alongside May and Lubitsch, a striking example is the work of Max Mack, who today is mainly remembered as the director of what many consider the first true German auteurist "art film," *The Other One [Der Andere]* of 1913, starring Albert Bassermann. Based on a play by Paul Lindau, the film introduces what for Kracauer became a staple of Weimar cinema, the motif of split identity and the encounter with a demonic "other." Like Ernst Lubitsch (who appeared as an actor in several of Mack's films), Mack started out as a theater actor. He appeared in popular film melodramas and comedies before scripting and directing short films, culminating in a prolific series of popular genre movies. These films included slapstick farces, romantic comedies, melodramas, detective films, and exotic adventure dramas, as well as *Serienfilme* featuring a popular Berlin actress, Maria Orska. Like the Lubitsch's films, Mack's extremely varied output was both commercially successful and often artistically sophisticated, attesting not only to the continuities between Wilhelmine and Weimar film but also to the indivisibility of popular and artistic film in early German cinema.[6]

As Anton Kaes has noted, Weimar cinema constitutes a kind of experimental laboratory, where a wide range of filmic genres, such as the detective film, the science fiction film, the intimate family melodrama, and others were developed (Kaes 40). In 1919 alone, the year following the end of the First World War, nearly five hundred feature films were produced in Germany, in a flurry of hectic activity. The collapse of the *Kaiserreich*, the removal of censorship, and the subsequent "Shock of Freedom" (Kracauer, *From Caligari to Hitler* 43) brought about experiments with a wide array of film styles addressing a tremendous variety of different subjects. Among the most remarkable ventures of that period was Richard Oswald's *Different from the Others [Anders als die Andern]* (1919), the first homosexual emancipation film, part of Magnus Hirschfeld's campaign to repeal paragraph 175 of the penal code, which, as Kracauer puts it, somewhat gingerly, "exacted punishment for certain abnormal sex practices" (*From Caligari to Hitler* 45). Kracauer denies that films that openly addressed sexual issues may have had a politically significant dimension beyond the exploitation of the audience's prurient desires. Concerning the removal of censorship after the war, he writes, "the effect was not a transformation of the screen into a political platform, but a sudden increase of films that pretended to be concerned with sexual enlightenment" (*From Caligari to*

Hitler 44). Yet, a case could be made that even the early Weimar sexploitation films signaled an effort to test the limits of the new democracy by calling the Wilhelmine moral code into question and by insisting on the personal liberties the constitution of the new republic was about to promise.

Kracauer relegates such films, alongside most products of early Weimar genre cinema, to secondary status in his emphasis upon the trajectory that he argues emerged with *Caligari*. His treatment of the early films of Ernst Lubitsch is indicative of a disturbing tendency to gloss over difference when it does not fit into his argument. For instance, his complaint that Germans have proven themselves to be "incapable of producing a popular film comedian" (*From Caligari to Hitler* 21) altogether ignores the German comic tradition in early film—modest as it may have been—which included figures such as directors Lubitsch and Mack, and performers like Wilhelm Bendow and Karl Valentin, to name only a few of the most significant ones (see Horak; Brandlmeier). In particular, Kracauer dismisses Lubitsch's early works with a few perfunctory remarks. Yet Lubitsch began as a comic actor in German film before emerging as one of the greatest masters of film comedy, first in Germany, then in the United States. Lubitsch's departure from Germany in the early 1920s, when he was lured to Hollywood, may perhaps be a more important factor in the truncated development of German film comedy than the innate tendency toward brooding introspection that Kracauer ascribes to the Germans (*From Caligari to Hitler* 55).

Ernst Lubitsch, of course, was Jewish. By excluding Lubitsch and the tradition of German Jewish comedy from his account of German film, Kracauer aims at bolstering his notion of a monolithic, somber-minded German national character. Yet the very films that Kracauer enlists in support of his thesis of a demonic German trajectory toward totalitarianism were, in large part, created and produced by Germans and Austrians of Jewish extraction, including, alongside Lubitsch, such figures as directors Fritz Lang (a "half Jew," according to Nazi racial criteria), Max Mack (born Moritz Myrthenzweig), Joe May (born Julius Otto Mandl), Kurt Gerron (born Kurt Gerson), and Max Ophüls (born Max Oppenheimer); scriptwriters like Carl Mayer and Hans Kräly; and producers like Erich Pommer, Jules Greenbaum (born Julius Grünbaum), and Paul Davidson. It should be noted that virtually everyone responsible for *The Cabinet of Dr. Caligari*—Kracauer's crown witness film—had to flee the country after 1933 for "racial" reasons, including producer Erich Pommer, production manager Rudolf Meinert, director Robert Wiene, and scriptwriters Carl Mayer and Hans Janowitz (Belach and Bock 10). Their role and participation in the supposedly Teutonic obsession with subordination to power remains unexplained in Kracauer's oddly essentialist argument. Perhaps the themes of split identities, the double, and the return of the repressed that seem to feature so prominently in German art film of the silent period are not only anchored in the German cultural tradition beginning with Goethe's *Faust* and the German Romantics, but also have something to do with the conflicting allegiances and hyphenated identities of the German and Austrian Jewish filmmakers who created many of them.

The degree to which Lubitsch's early silent comedies, made before the big international successes of period pieces such as *Madame Dubarry* (1919) and *Anna Boleyn* (1920), actually highlight Jewish themes is quite surprising. As an actor in one-reel comedies during the 1910s, Lubitsch developed a distinct comic persona that is recognizable from one film to another and that is clearly identifiable as Jewish. His early films are set in traditionally Jewish milieus, like textile manufacturing and retailing, and feature variations of a rags-to-riches story line: "Lubitsch's antiheros usually arrive in Berlin from provincial places like Ravitch in Poznan. After a series of comic adventures, they conquer the nation's capital and the shop owner's daughter, convincing everyone through their irresistible charm and firm determination" (Hake, *Passions and Deceptions* 26). Overcoming adversity with shrewd wit and resourcefulness, Lubitsch's characters have names like Moritz Abramovsky, Siegmund Lachmann, Moritz Rosenthal, and Moritz Apfelreis, and culminate in the role of Sally Pinkus that Lubitsch played in the first feature film he directed himself, *Shoe Salon Pinkus [Schuhpalast Pinkus]*, in 1916 (Prinzler and Patalas). Lubitsch's comic scenarios, combining business success, social ascent, and sexual wish fulfillment, clearly speak to the economic, social, and erotic aspirations of a general urban mass audience, while also articulating a distinctly Jewish hope for social integration and acceptance.

In dismissing the work of popular directors like Lubitsch and Mack, Kracauer clearly downplays the Jewish contribution to modern German popular culture, a tremendously rich and varied tradition. Mass culture during the Wilhelmine period and the Weimar Republic was to a surprising extent the product of Germans and Austrians of Jewish origin; it is to them that we owe much of the cosmopolitan flair, the ironic wit, and the sensuous glamour of what has come to be known—not, to be sure, without a problematic tinge of nostalgia—as the "Golden Twenties" ("Goldenen zwanziger Jahre," Laqueur). All over German-speaking central Europe, people flocked to the operettas of Victor Holländer, Paul Abraham, and Robert Stolz, and worshiped singers like Fritzi Massary and Richard Tauber. In Berlin, they allowed themselves to be dazzled by the spectacular stage revues of Hermann Haller at the Admiralspalast, Erik Charell at the Großes Schauspielhaus, and Rudolf Nelson at the Theater am Kurfürstendamm. In countless cabarets and theaters, they enjoyed the humorous skits of entertainers like Paul Morgan, Otto Wallburg, and Curt Bois and appreciated the sophisticated ironies of the songs of Friedrich Holländer and Mischa Spoliansky. Numbers from musical films by composers and lyricists like Hans Werner Heymann, Robert Liebmann, and Franz Wachsmann became hit tunes. As Hans Feld has noted, the German film industry attracted many people of Jewish descent, because "there were none of those engrained prejudices against Jewish participation shown in so many other fields of endeavour" (Feld 337). The Weimar-era boom in the German film industry is unthinkable without the influx of Jewish talent, not only in art film but also in popular genre films—if that distinction can indeed be upheld—by lesser known but prolific directors such as Ludwig Berger, E. A. Dupont, Karl Grune, Paul Leni, Richard Oswald (born Richard Ornstein), Willy Prager, Arthur Robison, Reinhold Schünzel, Wilhelm Thiele (born Wilhelm Isersohn), and Willi Wolf.[7] It is estimated that Hitler's rise to power forced some two thousand people active in the German film industry into exile to escape racial persecution (Asper 957). Alongside most of those mentioned previously, they ranged from well-known actors such as Fritz Kortner, Elisabeth Bergner, and Albert Bassermann to a host of technicians, cinematographers, and editors whose names few remember (see Bucher and Gmür; Liebe). This means that many of the people whom Kracauer views as implicated in the German proclivity toward authoritarianism actually ended up as victims of the Nazis—through exile, persecution, and murder.

Kracauer's dismissal of the impact of German Jewish popular culture on German film, in both its auteurist and its populist variant, has much to do, it would appear, with his own conflicted identity as an exiled member of the German Jewish intelligentsia, rejected and persecuted by the very culture with which he so closely identified and to which he and so many other intellectuals of Jewish descent had contributed so immeasurably much. In his

homage written on the occasion of Kracauer's seventy-fifth birthday, longtime friend and colleague Theodor W. Adorno described
Kracauer as "a man with no skin," a person of intense vulnerability and defenselessness (Adorno 161). Viewed in this light, the
essentialist anti-German bias of Kracauer's 1947 book takes on a
special aspect: in demonizing Germans as innately authoritarian
and antidemocratic, Kracauer seems to be wrestling with his own
demons; by distancing himself from the culture with which he
identified, he is, so to speak, exorcizing his own Germanness.
Ironically enough, he does so in that most "German" of man-
ners—by constructing a grand theoretical system.

The overarching causal narrative of *From Caligari to Hitler* stands in marked contrast to the antisystematic, essayistic
quality of Kracauer's work in the 1920s. The key concept of *Zerstreuung, distraction*, first developed in the seminal essay "Cult
of Distraction" ["Kult der Zerstreuung"] of 1926, ascribes to the
products of the entertainment industry a sociologically relevant
function (Kracauer, "Cult of Distraction" 323–28). Early Kracauer, along with other exponents of the left-wing Weimar intelligentsia, like Walter Benjamin, viewed modern mass culture as
potentially emancipatory, initially crediting cultural commodities "with a progressive role in training a different form of perception and attention, socially useful for mastering an increasingly
complex visual environment: a form of perception that Benjamin
called distracted attention, alertness under conditions of disconti-
nuity" (Elsaesser, "Cinema" 80). Recognizing the importance of
pleasure in the newly emerging leisure culture, Kracauer had attributed to the audience an active role in shaping the reception
process of film. To the Kracauer of the 1920s, the "distracted"
mass consumption of cultural commodities replaced the contemplative immersion associated with highbrow (traditional, bourgeois) art. The popularity of a particular film, in this view, is a
reflection of the strength of certain collective hopes and aspirations, a gesture of resistance to the pressures of a depersonalized,
industrialized mass society. Popular culture functions as a recep-
tacle of the subversive potential of collective fantasies that resist
subsumption into the logic of modern capitalism. After the historical catastrophe of National Socialism, the appreciation of popular culture as potentially emancipatory gives way in Kracauer to
a distrust in the gullibility of the masses. Entertainment is now
equated with indoctrination; the popular appeal of cultural products becomes an emblem of a blindness willingly accepted by an
uncritical populace. In his American exile, Kracauer constructs a

narrative based on historical hindsight in which the liberatory function of visual pleasure in the cinema gives way to mindless escapism. Like lemmings, Kracauer's Germans appear to be willingly succumbing to their doom, or accepting Adolf Hitler as a kind of Pied Piper from Braunau.

As understandable as the note of bitterness underlying Kracauer's account may be, it masks the complexity of the film industry during the Weimar period. For instance, rather than recognizing the anarchically subversive element in Lubitsch's popular silent films, Kracauer denounces Lubitsch's historical costume dramas for their "blend of cynicism and melodramatic sentimentality" (*From Caligari to Hitler* 52) and goes on to speculate that "it is highly probable that [Lubitsch's] comedies sprang from the same nihilism as his historical dramas" (*From Caligari to Hitler* 57). It would appear that Kracauer actually never even saw Lubitsch's two masterful comedies of 1919, *The Oyster Princess [Die Austernprinzessin]* and *The Doll [Die Puppe]*, as his strangely tentative remarks on the films indicate. In view of the playful creativity and life-affirming exuberance that both films exhibit, Kracauer's dismissal of them as mere "trifles"—though tempered with the grudging acknowledgment that in Lubitsch's hands "such trifles became truffles" (*From Caligari to Hitler* 57)—is rather odd. Both films provide exquisite visual pleasure through a playful subversion of the economy of erotic and material desires, centered on a liberated female. In fact, *The Doll*, in terms of its filmic techniques and its thematic content, can be read as an interesting countermodel to Wiene's *Caligari*, which it predates by about two months (December 19, 1919, versus February 26, 1920).

In Lubitsch's cheerfully fantastic fairy tale a young man tries to run away from marriage, but then falls in love with a life-size doll who turns out to be a real woman, after all. The comedy thus offers a refreshingly undemonic take on the narratives of male identity in crisis, of which *Caligari* serves Kracauer as the cardinal example. Lubitsch's film shares with Wiene's expressionist masterpiece the painted sets, the frame narrative, and the motif of mastery and subservience. Yet, as Sabine Hake has noted, "In contrast to the former's male universe of horror and insanity, *The Doll*—therein almost *Caligari*'s alter ego—presents a happy childhood paradise. And unlike the claustrophobic set design of *Caligari*, *The Doll* uses painted backdrops to convey a cheerful atmosphere full of play and possibilities" (Hake, *Passions and Deceptions* 94 f.). Lubitsch inherits from Wilhelmine cinema the focus on a strong female lead and experiments with the medium of film by taking recourse to fairy tale motifs. Lubitsch's charming appearance on screen as a master of ceremony at the beginning of *The Doll* contrasts refreshingly with the demonic machinations of Wiene's crazed doctor. Likewise, the somber tale of loss of control, of the dissolution of human agency in murder and madness in Wiene's film is counterbalanced in Lubitsch's other comedic masterpiece, *The Oyster Princess*, by an illness that befalls the characters: at the height of the hilarious confusion surrounding the desire of the spoiled daughter of an American billionaire to marry an impoverished nobleman, everyone is shown cheerfully succumbing to the grip of a "foxtrot epidemic." The social and political turmoil of the early Weimar period in the aftermath of the November 1918 revolution, which forms the backdrop for the anxieties besetting the nightmarish world of *Caligari* and for the spiritual malaise of its male protagonist, here is celebrated as a release of unbridled corporeal pleasure. Gender and class distinctions collapse in an orgy of pure movement in which kinetic and cinematic energy become one. The uncertainties of the beginnings of the Weimar Republic, then, produced not only the brooding introspection of Wiene's film but also the anarchic exuberance of Lubitsch's comedies. Early Weimar cinema, this suggests, rather than charting a predetermined path, presents us with a wide variety of possibilities.

Most of the issues raised in my discussion of Kracauer's historiography of German film can be seen reflected in Joe May's *The Mistress of the World*, the greatest commercial success in the season of 1919–20, far outstripping *Caligari* in popular appeal (which, as Kracauer concedes, "was too high-brow to become popular in Germany" [*From Caligari to Hitler* 77]). May's blockbuster series highlights the continuities between the Wilhelmine and the Weimar period and calls into question the distinction between art and popular film. It combines a focus on gender and class issues with a concern with visual pleasure and a genuinely cosmopolitan and democratic perspective. Taken together with its subtext of Jewish issues, these characteristics endow the film series with a potentially emancipatory political content.

May's initial contribution to Weimar cinema consisted of a German variant of the lavish historical spectacle, modeled primarily on the monumental films produced in Italy at the time. May's first such film, *Veritas Vincit*, released on April 4, 1919, also clearly bears the imprint of the influence of D. W. Griffith's

Intolerance. Like Griffith, May presents a series of historical episodes, here three melodramatic scenarios concerning truth and
fidelity—set in Ancient Rome, in the Renaissance, and in the
present—all featuring Mia May, his actress wife. The spectacular
success of *Veritas Vincit* inspired May to combine the *Serienfilm*
principle with the *Monumentalfilm* (blockbuster) genre to exploit
the popular appeal of both to the fullest. On the basis of a novel
by popular writer Karl Figdor, May conceived a sequence of related yet independent episodes, eight full-length features with a
combined length of over eleven and a half hours. These films once
again acted as vehicles for his wife, whom their many joint films
had established as one of the major movie stars of Wilhelmine
popular cinema.

   Joe May launched *The Mistress of the World* with an unprecedented advertising campaign that was commensurate with
the magnitude of the filmic undertaking. For months, trade journals and the popular press were full of reports about the making
of Germany's most lavish spectacle (Ramm 51). Figdor's novel
was published in book form and serialized in a popular magazine.
Newspapers and trade journals featured multipage spreads with
production stills and descriptions of the upcoming film. *Illustrierte Film Woche* even devoted an entire special issue to a celebration of May's release (no. 47, 1919). The release dates of the
eight episodes of the film were carefully coordinated, starting on
December 5, 1919; a new part of the series was premiered each
subsequent week at the same movie theater, the prestigious
Tauentzien-Palast in Berlin. The considerable advance publicity
generated a tremendous sense of excitement and expectation,
amply reflected, for instance, in Fritz Olimsky's article published
a week before the release of part one:

> The total cost of the film amounts to around six million marks;
> the costumes alone required 200,000 marks; including technical
> personnel, there were some 30,000 people involved in the produc-
> tion of the film; four fifths of all blacks living in Germany were
> hired for several months and housed in shacks in the film produc-
> tion city ("Filmstadt") near Woltersdorf. Nearly 100 temples,
> houses, and huts were set up for the filming, among them the
> immense temple of the legendary land of Ophir, a Chinese vil-
> lage, a neighborhood of Canton, and a negro village. Half the pop-
> ulation of Woltersdorf and Rüdersdorf were pulled into the
> production and flocked there in droves, with an honorarium of 20
> marks a day beckoning. Some parts of the film, with the excep-
> tion of the three main roles, were played exclusively by Chinese,
> others by negroes. (*Berliner Börsen Courier,* November 30, 1919)

The plot of *The Mistress of the World* concerns the adventures of a young Danish woman, Maud Gregaards, played by Mia May. Impoverished after her father's suicide, Maud accepts an invitation to go to China to serve as a governess, where she falls victim to the white slave trade. After many adventures that take her from Asia to Africa and to America, Maud finds the treasure of the Queen of Sheba and returns to Europe. As the richest woman in the world, she establishes the philanthropic "Academy of Humankind" ("Akademie der Menschheit") for the education of young men and helps a young American scientist in the construction of a "peace-making machine." After further complications, Maud finds Baron Murphy, the man who ruined both her own and her father's life, avenges herself on him, and is reunited with their joint son, thought to have died immediately after birth.

This short, and necessarily simplified, plot synopsis of *The Mistress of the World* gives an idea of the tremendous appeal the film had for a contemporary audience: exotic locales, lavish sets, and costumes answer to the scopic desires of the viewer; encounters with enigmatic Chinese "Mädchenhändler" and savage Africans excite the imagination, and incidents such as shootouts, chases, earthquakes, and plane crashes appeal to escapist longings for adventure while inspiring awe of the extraordinary skills of the filmmakers. Taking recourse to trivial myths, May taps into fantasies that in more recent years have been catered to by Tarzan films and Indiana Jones blockbusters. With its many locales and technological gadgets, the film celebrates mobility and modernity in a fashion that anticipates the James Bond films and action thrillers of today. Maud's sidekick, strongman Consul Madsen, is played by popular opera star Michael Bohnen. His exploits invite identification with masculine initiative and resolve; scientist Allan Stanley (Paul Hansen) encourages admiration for American ingenuity and inventiveness. In its unabashed populism, it is worth noting that the film pursues an overtly pacifist agenda, with Maud's "Akademie der Menschheit" clearly mirroring the hopes associated with the founding of the League of Nations after the First World War. Perhaps of greatest importance, however, is the fact that the series is held together by the female lead. Mia May as Maud Gregaards provides the female members of the audience with a source of identification as a role model, while acting as the object of erotic desire for the male audience. In her quest for revenge and social reinstatement, she takes an active role in a domain traditionally reserved for men, finally gaining a degree of autonomy traditionally denied to women (Schlüpmann, "Wahrheit und Lüge").

Kracauer ranks May's film serial alongside other action spectaculars and costume extravaganzas ("*Prunkfilme*") of the early Weimar period as "films of secondary importance," whose main qualities lie in providing the audience with fodder for fantasies that "resembled a prisoner's daydreams," the yearning of the audience to escape "the mutilated and blockaded fatherland" (*From Caligari to Hitler* 56 f.). Kracauer actually misconstrues the identity of the film's female protagonist as German, when the film makes it very clear that May's Maud is Danish. By making his two protagonists, Maud and her companion Consul Madsen, Danish, Joe May clearly aimed at creating characters that would appeal to both a domestic and an international audience. Kracauer's effort to impute expansionist tendencies to products of early Weimar popular culture, even if, like *The Mistress of the World*, they contain a great deal of democratic and emancipatory potential, is thus highly problematic. May's series is clearly aimed not only at a German audience. In the international arena, it presents cosmopolitan fantasies devoid of Teutonic dreams of world hegemony. In the domestic context, it advances a philanthropic democratic agenda that places hope in technological and political progress in the interesting scheme of constructing a "peace-making machine."

The film was greeted with unanimous approval. The consensus was that its production qualities put it on a par with international competition, in particular with that of American movies, which by 1919 had clearly become the standard against which German products wished to compare themselves. With *The Mistress of the World*, experts felt, the German film industry was ready to engage in a "struggle for the World Market" (*Licht Bild Bühne* 46, November 15, 1919, 23). The film's extraordinary critical and public success is a reflection not only of May's skillful publicity efforts but also of the careful layering of filmic qualities, which appeal to its audience on multiple levels. Perhaps the most overt appeal of May's film lies in the escapist fantasies of mobility, wealth, and peace it offers to a population of a nation devastated by war, defeat, social upheaval, hunger, and poverty. In his cursory assessment of a number of such filmic extravaganzas of the period, Kracauer narrows the film's tremendously complex popular appeal down to speculations about the manner in which May's film series supposedly reflects the state of the collective German psyche after the isolation imposed by the war:

"What they called their world mission had been thwarted, and now all exits seemed barred. These space-devouring films reveal how bitterly the average German resented his involuntary seclusion. They functioned as substitutes; they naïvely satisfied his suppressed desire for expansion through pictures that enabled his imagination to reannex the world" (*From Caligari to Hitler* 57).[8] Kracauer largely dismisses May's film series as a German chauvinistic fantasy. Yet in political terms perhaps the most striking element of *The Mistress of the World* is the prominence it affords Jewish themes or themes associated with Judaism. Figdor's story line conflates a variety of popular myths with apocryphal biblical stories: Maud's search for the lost treasure of the Queen of Sheba takes her to China, where it is a rabbi, the last survivor of an ancient Jewish settlement in Canton, who holds the secret of the treasure. In a conversation with the rabbi, Maud's Danish companion, Consul Madsen, reveals himself to be Jewish, establishing a bond of trust that cuts across different nations and cultures. Part five, an episode set in Africa, is centered on Maud's encounter with the people of Ophir, who are revealed to be the descendants of a union of the Jewish King Salomon and the Queen of Sheba. Ophir, that is, is identified as a lost and imperiled Jewish civilization in Africa. At the end of the last episode, after all her travels and travails, Maud is described as "Ahasver," a female version of the archetypal wandering Jew. In combination with the other characteristics noted previously, such aspects speak against a reading of May's film as a Teutonic expansionist fantasy. On the contrary, it would seem that *The Mistress of the World* invites German and international audiences alike to identify with Jews, portrayed here as peace-loving people involved in an arduous quest to set their lives aright.

May's concoction of diverse popular myths, pseudo-scientific speculations, action adventure, and melodrama is far too complex to be subsumed under an easy heading. His forgotten blockbuster *The Mistress of the World* is not brooding and authoritarian; it offers escapist fantasies and visual pleasure to its multiple audiences while propagating, among other things, gender equality (in its resourceful female protagonist), an integrationist agenda (in its positive portrayal of Jews), and an overtly pacifist perspective (in the motif of Maud's philanthropic enterprise). May's action adventure series was a tremendous commercial success. It would appear, *pace* Kracauer, that German audiences voted with their pocketbooks: instead of succumbing to the authoritarian brooding of *Dr. Caligari*, they clearly preferred the emancipatory rule of *The Mistress of the World*.

Weimar popular culture, of which the cinema was a part, can perhaps best be described as an arena in which a wide variety of forces came into conflict, a contested space in which many possibilities were tried out. Far from being the cauldron of demonic chauvinistic aspirations, early Weimar popular cinema— exemplified by the popular successes of Ernst Lubitsch, Max Mack, and Joe May, as well as the work of many others—emerges as an experimental laboratory in democracy. Kracauer's linear teleology fails to acknowledge the coexistence in Weimar cinema of many different discourses, many different collective fantasies. As I hope to have shown, Weimar cinema does not begin with *Caligari;* nor did Weimar film pursue a single trajectory, but many paths that did not necessarily have to lead to Hitler.

NOTES

1. In contradistinction to Lotte H. Eisner's usage in her famous book on German Expressionist film, *The Haunted Screen,* the word "demonic" here is indeed used "in its usual sense of 'diabolical'" (Eisner 8).
2. Heide Schlüpmann takes issue with Kracauer's tendency "to subsume particulars within conceptual constructs" (Schlüpmann 1987, 98). Miriam Hansen notes the contrast between the phenomenological openness to the specificity of filmic experience in the Kracauer of the 1920s and his later "increased commitment to a critique of ideology" (Hansen 62), while Thomas Saunders objects to the "normative" aspect of Kracauer's thought (Saunders 34). Patrice Petro rightly criticizes Kracauer's "circular reasoning," which "makes distinctions without difference by repeatedly conflating narrative with national identity, national identity with subject, and all three terms with male subjectivity and male identity in crisis" (Petro xviii).
3. The book is all the more remarkable if one considers the often difficult conditions under which the project came into being: exiled, isolated in the United States, Kracauer had to rely on memory and on printed sources for much of his analysis of the films he discusses. Lack of access to film prints may account for the occasional vagueness in Kracauer's account and for some of its inconsistencies (Koch 101). Given these limitations, Kracauer's assessment of Weimar film is impressive indeed.
4. Important in this context, Thomas Elsaesser has recently called for a reassessment of early German film in the context of a "New Film History" that is based on an internationally comparative perspective: "Film production and cinema exhibition up to World War I were a highly international business, making nonsense of an idea of national cinema that does not at the same time take note of tendencies in other major film producing countries, such as France, Denmark, Italy and, of course, the United States" (Elsaesser and Wedel 12). The earliest efforts of German film pioneers such as the brothers Skladanowsky and Oskar Messter need to be placed against the predominance of French production and distribution facilities at the turn of

the century. Likewise, the interconnection between Scandinavian, especially Danish, cinema and the German film industry are well known (Behn).

5. Morevover, countless foreign actors and actresses worked in Germany during the first three decades of the twentieth century, especially during the period of silent film, when language posed no discernible barrier. One immediately thinks of Asta Nielsen (Denmark), Nils Chrysander (Sweden), Aud Egede Nissen (Norway), Lyda Salmonova (Czechoslovakia), Lya de Putti (Hungary), Pola Negri (Poland), Vladimir Sokoloff (Russia), and Fern Andra and Louise Brooks (United States).

6. Mack's versatility is displayed by his attempts, on the one hand, to capitalize on the critical success of *Der Andere* with a number of other films based on "highbrow" literary works, such as texts by Felix Salten, Leo Tolstoy, and E. T. A. Hoffmann; on the other, Mack apparently did not shy away from benefitting from the lifted censorship laws after the First World War by supplying an eager market with sexploitation films with enticing titles such as *Freie Liebe* [Free Love] and *Sündiges Blut* [Sinful Blood] (both 1919) (Wedel).

7. Here we might add, alongside Kracauer himself, many of the most brilliant and influential film critics of the Weimar period, such as Rudolf Arnheim, Béla Balázs, Lotte H. Eisner, Hans Feld, Willy Haas, and Alfred Kerr.

8. Significantly, Kracauer bases his reading of the film's alleged expansionist agenda on Figdor's remarks in the program booklet rather than on the film itself (Lenssen 36).

WORKS CITED

Adorno, Theodor W. "The Curious Realist: On Siegfried Kracauer." 1964. Reprint, *New German Critique* 54 (1991): 159–77.

Asper, Helmut G. "Film." In *Handbuch der deutschsprachigen Emigration 1933–1945*, edited by Claus Dieter Krohn, Patrick von zur Mühlen, Gerhard Paul, and Lutz Winckler, 957–70. Darmstadt: Primus, 1998.

Behn, Manfred, ed. *Schwarzer Traum und weiße Sklavin. Deutsch-dänische Filmbeziehungen 1910–1930*. Munich: edition text + kritik, 1994.

Belach, Helga, and Hans-Michael Bock, eds. *"Das Cabinet des Dr. Caligari": Drehbuch von Carl Mayer und Hans Janowitz zu Robert Wienes Film von 1919/20*. Munich: edition text + kritik, 1995.

Bock, Hans-Michael, ed. *CineGraph: Lexikon zum deutschsprachigen Film*. Munich: edition text + kritik, 1984ff.

Bock, Hans-Michael, Wolfgang Jacobsen, and Jörg Schöning, eds. *Hallo? Berlin? Ici Paris! Deutsch-französische Filmbeziehungen 1918–1939*. Munich: edition text + kritik, 1996.

Bock, Hans-Michael, and Claudia Lenssen, eds. *Joe May: Regisseur und Produzent*. Munich: edition text + kritik, 1991.

Bock, Hans-Michael, and Michael Töteberg, eds. *Das Ufa-Buch*. Frankfurt/M.: Zweitausendeins, 1992.

Brandlmeier, Thomas. "Early German Film Comedy, 1895–1917." In *A Second Life: German Cinema's First Decades*, edited by Thomas Elsaesser and Michael Wedel, 103–13. Amsterdam: Amsterdam University Press, 1996.

Bucher, Felix, and Leonhard H. Gmür. *Screen Series: Germany.* London: Zwemmer; New York: Barnes, 1970.

Bulgakowa, Olga, ed. *Die ungewöhnlichen Abenteuer des Dr. Mabuse im Lande der Bolschewiki.* Berlin: Feunde der Deutschen Kinemathek, 1995.

Cherchi Usai, Paolo, and Lorenzo Codelli, eds. *Prima di Caligari: Cinema tedesco, 1895–1920 / Before Caligari: German Cinema, 1895–1920.* Pordenone: Edizioni Biblioteca dell' Imagine, 1990.

Eisner, Lotte H. *The Haunted Screen. Expressionism in the German Cinema and the Influence of Max Reinhardt.* 1952. Reprint, translated from the French by Roger Greaves, Berkeley and Los Angeles: University of California Press, 1969.

Elsaesser, Thomas. "Cinema—The Irresponsible Signifier or 'The Gamble with History': Film Theory and Cinema Theory." *New German Critique* 40 (1987): 65–89.

———. "Early Cinema: From Linear History to Mass Media Archeology." In *Early Cinema: Space, Frame, Narrative,* edited by Thomas Elsaesser, with Adam Barker, 1–8. London: BFI Publishing, 1990.

———. "Filmgeschichte—Firmengeschichte—Familiengeschichte. Der Übergang vom Wilhelminischen zum Weimarer Film." In *Joe May: Regisseur und Produzent,* edited by Hans-Michael Bock and Claudia Lenssen, 11–30. Munich: edition text + kritik, 1991.

———, with Michael Wedel, eds. *A Second Life: German Cinema's First Decades.* Amsterdam: Amsterdam University Press, 1996.

———. *Weimar Cinema and After: Germany's Historical Imaginary.* London, New York: Routledge, 2000.

Feld, Hans. "The Jewish Contribution to the German Film Industry. Notes from the Recollections of a Berlin Film Critic." *Yearbook of the Leo Baeck Institute* 27 (1982): 337–65.

Garncarz, Joseph. "Hollywood in Germany." In *Der deutsche Film. Aspekte seiner Geschichte von den Anfängen bis zur Gegenwart,* edited by Uli Jung and Walter Schatzberg, 167–213. Trier: Wissenschaftlicher Verlag, 1993.

Hake, Sabine. *Passions and Deceptions: The Early Films of Ernst Lubitsch.* Princeton, N.J.: Princeton University Press, 1992.

———. "Siegfried Kracauer." In *The Cinema's Third Machine: Writing on Film in Germany 1907–1933,* 247–70. Lincoln: University of Nebraska Press, 1993.

Hansen, Miriam. "Decentric Perspectives: Kracauer's Early Writings on Film and Mass Culture." *New German Critique* 54 (1991): 47–76.

Horak, Jan-Christopher. "Laughing until It Hurts. German Film Comedy and Karl Valentin." In *Prima di Caligari: Cinema tedesco, 1895–1920 / Before Caligari: German Cinema, 1895–1920,* edited by Paolo Cherchi Usai and Lorenzo Codelli. 202–29. Pordenone: Edizioni Biblioteca dell' Imagine, 1990.

Kaes, Anton. "Film in der Weimarer Republik. Motor der Moderne." In *Geschichte des deutschen Films,* edited by Wolfgang Jacobsen, Anton Kaes, and Hans Helmut Prinzler, 39–100. Stuttgart, Weimar: Metzler, 1993.

Koch, Gertrud. *Kracauer zur Einführung.* Hamburg: Junius, 1996.

Kracauer, Siegfried. "Cult of Distraction." 1926. Reprint, in *The Mass Ornament: Weimar Essays,* translated and edited by Thomas Y. Levin, 323–28. Cambridge, Mass.: Harvard University Press, 1995.

————. *From Caligari to Hitler. A Psychological History of the German Film.* 1947. Reprint, Princeton, N.J.: Princeton University Press, 1974.

Kreimeier, Klaus. *The Ufa Story.* New York: Hill and Wang, 1996.

Laqueur, Walter. "Berlin s'amuse." In *Weimar. A Cultural History, 1918–1933,* 224–53. New York: Putnam, 1974.

Lenssen, Claudia. "Rachedurst und Reisefieber. *Die Herrin der Welt*—ein Genrefilm." In *Joe May: Regisseur und Produzent,* edited by Hans-Michael Bock and Claudia Lenssen, 31–44. Munich: edition text + kritik, 1991.

Liebe, Ulrich. *Verehrt Verfolgt Vergessen. Schauspieler als Naziopfer.* Weinheim, Berlin: Beltz Quadriga, 1992.

Petro, Patrice. "Kracauer's Epistemological Shift." *New German Critique* 54 (1991): 127–38.

————. *Joyless Streets: Women and Melodramatic Representation in Weimar Germany.* Princeton: Princeton University Press, 1989.

Prinzler, Hans Helmut, and Enno Patalas, eds. *Lubitsch.* Munich, Lucerne: Bucher, 1984.

Ramm, Gerald. *Als Woltersdorf noch Hollywood war.* Woltersdorf bei Berlin: Bock & Kübler, 1992.

Saunders, Thomas. *Hollywood in Berlin: American Cinema and Weimar Germany.* Berkeley: University of California Press, 1994.

Schlüpmann, Heide. "Phenomenology of Film: On Siegfried Kracauer's Writings of the 1920s." *New German Critique* 40 (1987): 97–114.

————. *Der unheimliche Blick. Das Drama des frühen deutschen Kinos.* Basel, Frankfurt/M.: Stroemfeld/Roter Stern, 1990.

————. "Wahrheit und Lüge im Zeitalter der technischen Reproduzierbarkeit. Detektiv und Heroine bei Joe May." In *Joe May: Regisseur und Produzent,* edited by Hans-Michael Bock and Claudia Lenssen, 45–60. Munich: edition text + kritik, 1991.

Wedel, Michael, ed. *Max Mack: Showman im Glashaus.* Berlin: Stiftung Kinemathek, 1996. (= *Kinemathek* 88).

FILMOGRAPHY

The Other One [Der Andere] (Max Mack, 1913), Deutsches Institut für Filmkunde, Wiesbaden

Shoe Salon Pinkus [Schuhpalast Pinkus] (Ernst Lubitsch, 1916), Bundesarchiv Filmarchiv, Berlin

Gypsy Blood [Carmen] (Ernst Lubitsch, 1918), Facets Video VHS: S02095

Different from the Others [Anders als die Andern] (Richard Oswald, 1919), Facets Video VHS: S30192

The Oyster Princess [Die Austernprinzessin] (Ernst Lubitsch, 1919), Facets Video VHS: S30211

Bull Arizona—The Desert Eagle [Bull Arizona—Der Wüstenadler] (Phil Jutzi; Horst Krahè, 1919), Stiftung Deutsche Kinemathek, Berlin

Passion [Madame Dubarry] (Ernst Lubitsch, 1919), Facets Video VHS: S02813

Opium (Robert Reinert, 1919), Facets Video VHS: S33057

The Doll [Die Puppe] (Ernst Lubitsch,1919), Facets Video VHS: S49579

Veritas Vincit (Joe May, 1919), Bundesarchiv-Filmarchiv, Berlin

The Mistress of the World [Die Herrin der Welt] (Joe May, 1919–20), Bundesarchiv-Filmarchiv, Berlin

The Spiders [Die Spinnen] (Fritz Lang, 1919–20), Facets Video VHS: S08945,
DVD: DV61788

Anna Boleyn (Ernst Lubitsch, 1920), Facets Video VHS: S35820

The Cabinet of Dr. Caligari [Das Cabinet des Dr. Caligari] (Robert Wiene,
1920), Facets Video VHS: S10765, DVD: DV60034

One Arabian Night [Sumurun] (Ernst Lubitsch, 1920), Facets Video VHS:
S02169

The Indian Tomb [Das indische Grabmal] (Joe May, 1921), Facets Video
VHS: S44378, DVD: DV64556

Destiny [Der müde Tod] (Fritz Lang, 1921), Facets Video VHS: S00327,
DVD: DV63315

Congress Dances [Der Kongreß tanzt] (Erik Charell, 1931), Facets Video
VHS: S02220

CHAPTER 2

Regulating Hidden Pleasures and "Modern" Identities

Imagined Female Spectators, Early German Popular Cinema, and *The Oyster Princess* (1919)

Janet McCabe

"It is . . . an Ossi Oswalda picture—and that is discovered from a number of crude, 'bochesque' details in bad taste," wrote Béla Balázs in his 1923 review of *The Oyster Princess [Die Austernprinzessin]* (Lubitsch, 1919). He felt the plot to be "primitive and meager" and "the funny shots" involving Oswalda "shedding her clothes" to be "downright obscene."(Balázs 16). Balázs was not alone in his disparaging assessment of popular films like *The Oyster Princess* and its frivolous heroine. Cultural watchdogs from the period had firm (if often hysterical) views about the popular cinema that, more often than not, came to be determined by a series of unruly feminine representations about easy pleasures and distracted spectatorship. Theirs was a pejorative discourse marked by a moral skepticism about the suspect, if not outright perilous, diversions offered by popular screen entertainment to the weak-willed mass (Conradt; Hellwig 1911, 1913; Gaupp and Lange; Lange, "Die 'Kunst' des Lichtspieltheaters"; idem, *Nationale Kinoreform*).

The critical devaluation extended into film studies, where until recently the German popular cinema received minimal attention. Academic neglect has been, in part, due to the fact that a vast number of films were lost and the scripts never published. Furthermore, orthodox historiographies have claimed the surviving material to be either minor, in comparison with the critically acclaimed Weimar art cinema (see Eisner; Kracauer 1977), or aesthetically retarded in relation to films produced by Germany's leading foreign competitors, notably America, France, and Scandinavia (Salt 225–36). Despite mass audiences and lucrative financial returns for these generic films, scant attention has been given to understanding the legitimate pleasures associated with the early German popular cinema between 1910 and 1919.

Recent feminist film scholarship has trained our attention on pre-1919 German cinema as a public institution with popular appeal (see Hansen; Schlüpmann, "Kinosucht"; idem, *Unheimlichkeit des Blicks*).[1] Such scholarly efforts seem initially preferable to the orthodox critical condemnations of the popular cinema, if only because they have made it possible to discern some historical norms applicable to the earlier period. Yet, in so doing, this work has proven how elusive and difficult it is to define the German popular cinema. The popular cinema, in comparison with Weimar (classical) cinema, emerges as a countercinema, defined as strange, aberrant, and discontinuous, only to be forgotten as the industry consolidates and gains a greater social reputation. Material, cultural, and historical specificities of the popular cinema thus seem perpetually to be read against the norms governing its celebrated Weimar counterpart. Yet to reclaim the popular as ideologically progressive because it appears so transgressive in relation to classical norms, or to judge it by standards that defined it as somehow inferior, misses the point.

In an attempt to challenge these teleological histories and qualitative judgments, a different schema must be found to make sense of the popular German cinema and its female audience during the second decade of the twentieth century. Rather than view it as a fixed and coherent text, defined by bourgeois criteria, it is my intention to demonstrate how the popular cinema as a *discourse*—its generic products, visual pleasures, and female movie stars who proved a tremendous box office draw—created and described the institutional reality in the process of knowing its imagined female audience. As a discourse, the popular cinema functioned to manage that knowledge and popularize modern identities and representations. It will be thus argued that the institution of popular cinema was organized around a number of discursive processes, with films negotiating various aesthetical and formal, intertextual and extratextual meanings. In this respect, the institution of popular cinema can be seen in relation to be what Michel Foucault understood as "discourse" (Foucault

18–19): a series of statements by which the social world came to be known. To better appreciate the formation of popular cinema as a discourse, a case study will be offered on Ernst Lubitsch's popular feature-length romantic comedy, *The Oyster Princess,* concerning the purchase of an aristocratic husband (Harry Lied-tke) for an American oyster magnate's daughter (Oswalda). By de-scribing how the film sets up its own terms of cultural reference, I aim to provide an alternative model for evaluating how the pop-ular German cinema from 1910 to 1919 defined itself and strengthened its own identity by invoking its imagined female spectator and her sense of being modern.

By 1914, roughly two million Germans were said to be attending the cinema each day. Attempts to police this truly mass cultural phenomenon exposed how unsettling the cinema and its mass audience proved to be for Germany's cultural leaders: "From the bourgeois perspective, the cinema in its early years repre-sented a plebeian counterculture which, without invitation, had established itself beside the mainstream culture" (Kaes 14). In particular, the broadening of the audience to include groups, such as women, previously ignored by public officials caused consider-able consternation among the cultural elite. How the popular cin-ema came to be seen as needing regulation is revealed in the extraordinary series of attempts made to categorize the cinema audience, and in particular women and their cinema-going habits. Firsthand evidence, including educational reports, reformist pam-phlets, state legislation, and journal and newspaper articles, shed considerable light on how the bourgeoisie, often with state ap-proval or support, set about classifying and shaping the unregu-lated "plebeian counterculture." Investigations into why women were so attracted to the cinema demonstrate how the bourgeoisie constructed appropriate representation for cinema's imagined fe-male constituency in the process of getting to know them.[2] At the very least, these audience surveys articulated a tension that was then circulated to speak about the cultural life of the modern city—specifically, related to female sexuality, social control, gen-der relations, public behaviors, and new urban activities.

It is no coincidence that discussions initiated by the intel-ligentsia and cinema reformers (*Kino-reformers*) about the cin-ema as an unregulated site of popular amusement reflect how formless, spontaneous, and ungovernable the moviegoing public must have appeared to them. The need to describe the sheer phys-ical spectacle of the mass, huddled in the darkened auditorium, watching movies, and to explain the appeal of such an experience,

gave rise to decades of intense debate.[3] Therefore, long before
Siegfried Kracauer came to write "The Little Shop Girls Go to the
Movies" in 1927, the equation of lowbrow culture and femininity
had been well rehearsed within the critical discourse (Kracauer,
The Mass Ornament 291–304). Kracauer was to further associate
the most reactionary tendencies of mass-cultural reception with
femininity (and hence the vacuousness of the "silly little hearts"
[*Tippmamsells*]).[4] Although he sought to rethink modes of spectatorship (Petro 139; Hake, "Girls and Crisis" 147–64), Kracauer's
examination of how women on the screen became conflated with
females in the audience was rooted in assumptions so deeply ingrained into the language he used that the implications never entered into the discussion. Consequently, debates about the female
spectator were carried out in a context in which the preeminence
of the bourgeoisie to define the cultural reality of the popular cinema through these reactionary models went unquestioned.

Despite these concerted efforts, bourgeois campaigns had
little impact on the real women who paid regular visits to the
cinema without the slightest concern (or even awareness) that
they were being tracked by conservative forces. In fact, the
"weak-willed" females remained fiercely loyal to popular film
stars such as Asta Nielsen, Henny Porten, and later Oswalda, and
continued to flock en masse to see the condemned "trash" films
(*Schundfilme*), despite official disapproval. Recreation surveys
did little more than count and describe the female audience. Yet,
monitoring the flow and new public habits of the female traffic
within busy cinema auditoriums confronted observers with new
realities, concerns that offer insight into the complex and fast-
changing pace of modern German life. The point is that in each
case the female subject as a textual creation is someone who was
judged, and someone who came to be studied and represented.

Emilie Altenloh's sociologically based doctoral dissertation on cinema audiences in Mannheim is useful in this respect,
especially in its attempt to track the new categories of female
public experience. Framed by her own unquestioned belief in the
bourgeois value system, Altenloh puts forward a case for suggesting that cinema was instrumental in shaping public identities and
privileging respectable patterns of urban behavior for women. Her
audience research made it clear that moviegoing had, by 1910,
become an integrated part of many women's daily routine, especially those living and working in and around the country's newly
expanding industrial centers. For those who were employed in the
modern factories or tertiary sectors, the cinema quickly became

incorporated into new lifestyle habits and expectations. This was a pattern divided between less physically demanding labor and an increased leisure time with disposable income. Of the financially better-off, reasons for movie attendance were divided between those women looking for something to do with their spare time, and those interested in the latest fashions from Paris and elsewhere (Altenloh 91–92). Women from the larger urban centers felt that the cinema provided a welcome refuge from bustling department stores and the hectic city streets. An arduous morning's shopping trip could be rounded off by a relaxing afternoon's entertainment at the movies, often with friends.

Altenloh's findings point out the discrepancies between what the bourgeois community observed and how these women imagined their moviegoing experience. What proves so intriguing is how the women described their public excursions, articulating the conditions of the urban jaunt as highly prescribed around a number of different cultural activities. The respectable woman's city walk was clearly split between two spaces: exterior (difficult and treacherous) and interior (safe and comfortable), in which the cinema was seen as providing sanctuary for unchaperoned females. Implicit in Altenloh's observations is the suggestion that the industry promoted such an identity, through both exciting and regulating female participation, ordering their viewing experience, and offering points of emulation and information, as well as promoting specific patterns of consumer and other social behaviors. Altenloh's statistical data, as a new kind of knowledge about the female spectator, directs our attention toward new formal and institutional strategies used by the film industry to imagine its female constituency differently, and in the process to popularize modern identities for them, as consumers, social beings, and urban travelers.

In the credit sequence of *The Oyster Princess*, the name of the female star, Ossi Oswalda, appears on a title card. This is immediately followed by a head-and-shoulders image, reminiscent of photographic studio portraits, of her dressed in fashionable apparel. Oswalda, framed in a mid-iris-shot, flirtatiously laughs directly into the camera. This vibrant representation of thoroughly modern womanhood appears to confirm conservative anxieties about the feckless, sexually moribund, and economically independent young movie-struck women, an image that Oswalda as the star positively privileges and promotes. Furthermore, the image functions to open up the narrative trajectory, to say something to audiences about the character she will play in the film. It also goes beyond the fictional world, to reveal the star as an industrial category of cinema practice. Competing industrial demands—that is, a blurring of boundaries between character integration and performance virtuosity, between star as spectacle and figure of identification, between fictional pleasures and an industrial commodity, and between conservative resistance and modern identities—become embedded in the construction of the film star as a discourse. Focusing on the Oswalda star image and the multiple pleasures it generated, it is important to challenge bourgeois readings of such an image, and to think instead about how the film industry came to produce these kinds of feminine representation in the first place. It is clear that her image belonged to certain economic imperatives and modes of filmmaking practice associated with the German film business during the 1910's, ones that sought to attract, shape, and retain an imagined female audience.

Born Oswalda Stäglich in Berlin in 1897, Ossi Oswalda was first contracted to PAGU (Projektions AG Union). She began her professional career as a chorus girl in Berlin, debuting in *Lieutenant by Command [Leutnant auf Befehl]* (1916) before appearing briefly as a young flibbertigibbet who flirts outrageously with the eponymous hero in *Shoe Salon Pinkus [Schuhpalast Pinkus]* (Lubitsch, 1916). It was not long before she emerged as one of the most bankable screen comediennes in Germany. Of her comic roles, probably her best-known performances are in *The Doll [Die Puppe]* (Lubitsch, 1919), where she plays a toy-maker's daughter masquerading as an automated doll, and as the spoiled progeny of an American oyster king in pursuit of a suitably aristocratic consort in *The Oyster Princess.*

Oswalda can be seen as a specific example of how the German film industry sought to rationalize its industrial practices around the film star. Oswalda's early film career was, in fact, entirely predicated upon what was known as the "monopoly film" *[Monopolfilm]*. Corinna Müller charts the rise of this unique system for distributing films, and how it both gave a financial boost to production and helped to restructure the exhibition sector. Such an enterprise was based on regulating an exclusive product: an early type of blockbuster that would generate public interest and allow exhibitors to charge higher prices at the box office. It would therefore be fair to say that the star system came into view out of the economic necessity to ensure commercial success and generate public demand for the monopoly film product.

The speed of Oswalda's ascendancy to star status attests
to the efficiency of the monopoly film system in commercially
creating, disseminating, and exploiting her star image as a popular product. Soon labeled as Germany's answer to Mary Pickford
because of her popularity (and suffering a similar fate, forever
typecast as the child-woman), Oswalda's comic persona was perfected over a series of specially written short film comedies, collectively known as *Ossi's Diary [Ossis Tagebuch]* (1917). The
quick and regular release of these comic shorts by PAGU made
sure that she was kept firmly in the public eye. PAGU and later
Union-Film/Ufa carefully nurtured the Oswalda image, and the
film companies found various ways of marketing her as a star,
working hard to build up that profile week after week. Production, distribution, and exhibition strategies were geared to make
sure Ossi Oswalda *looked* popular to the broadest audience possible.

Oswalda's star persona relied heavily on combined elements of sexual libertinage, a sensual joie de vivre, and physical
burlesque. Publicity photographs—postcards, cigarette cards, and
the like—made much of her fresh image. Promoting a daffy, im-
pulsive off-screen image suggested her disruptive on-screen antics
were all part of her natural comic charm, an unscripted and spontaneous extension of a youthful and vivacious personality. The
ostentatious high-spirited pursuit of personal pleasure performed
by Oswalda conveyed a tension between ideas about traditional
genteel feminine behaviors and newer models of femininity, a site
of unease that was to be negotiated in all of her star vehicles.

Generic and narrative conventions of her comic films
function to restrain her playful disorderliness and redirect her disruptive energies, before repositioning her as a companionable
wife within the institution of marriage. *The Oyster Princess*, for
example, flirts with both adultery (or at least sexually adventure-
some behavior) and bigamy, as Ossi enjoys a companionate courtship with one man (Nucki) while married to another (Josef, played
by Julius Falkenstein). Yet, the comedy of errors eventually resolves around mistaken identities and the realization that the
fictional Ossi is technically married to a man named Prince
Nucki. Humor—in this context acted out by Oswalda the performer—allows for several negotiations to take place around points
where traditional social discourses could be seen to be accommodating the new through exposing the mechanisms of screen acting at the moment of its integration into the cinematic
vocabulary. Jokes gave voice to that which in another context

would have been too unsettling, while enjoying public approval because no one was taking what was said too seriously. More significantly, though, by foregrounding the cinematic techniques by which the joke was made, through structuring the female gaze and bringing the artifice of performance to the fore, the film created identities for, and shaped the participation of, an imagined female constituency who were meant to share the joke. Popular film comedy as an industry-regulated discourse creates—but also describes—what is meant to be funny within its own terms of cultural reference.

The star, in the process of performing, emerges as central to the interplay of textual meaning and industrial pleasure. Each performed comic moment is *contained* and *represented* through making visible the rules and mechanisms of the film comedy. This being the case, Oswalda is defined as unruly *only because* the internal logic treats her as someone to be controlled, a problem to be overcome in order to bring about narrative resolution and filmic closure.

How Oswalda's star image and performance were formally and institutionally managed in *The Oyster Princess* offers us insight into how the industry functioned to shape and popularize modern feminine identities. While Josef, posing as Prince Nucki, waits to meet her and her father (Victor Janson) naps, the fictional Ossi takes a bath. Neither conveying narrative information nor progressing the story, the sequence proves curiously long: "For example for suddenly, with no apparent reason [she] . . . step[s] into the bath or get[s] massaged" (Balázs 16). Beyond the patriarchal world, shut away in her private quarters, she gleefully prepares to meet her prospective husband. An army of housemaids, each performing a different service, from cleaning to perfuming her feminine form, attend to their young mistress as she becomes processed along an ever-accelerating beautification conveyor belt. Similar to a time-motion study, and aligned to the new possibilities of portraying speed and movement afforded by the technology of cinema, the ornamentation of Ossi literally suspends narrative flow to allow for a moment of pure spectacle—an exhibition of feminine cleanliness and star glamour. Fashion is represented as a highly technological process, requiring all the latest beauty products. The obvious joy Ossi takes from all the pampering offers the viewer a model of feminine consumerism based on the celebration of the body *made* beautiful. Josef later confirms the results to the audience in a brief moment of intimacy between himself and us. The male verdict, as he looks directly into camera, is expressed through the intertitle and a

knowing smile: Ossi "smells good." Pervasive consumerist fantasies and commodified versions of the feminine self, already identified by the women interviewed by Emilie Altenloh as primary
reasons for attending the movies, are reproduced and promoted
here via Ossi and her ablutions.

Excessive pampering speaks not only of the fashionable
feminine form recently emancipated from corsets, but also about
the construction and deconstruction of the female movie star, and
through this, the female consumer/spectator. Already blurred,
Ossi-the-fictious-American-princess, as an image of urban fash-
ionability and unrestrained American consumerism, collapses
into Ossi-the-German-film-star as template for modern femininity. She is playfully positioned as an instructor on feminine hygiene, cosmetic beauty, and modern cleanliness, simultaneously
flattering and amusing the consumer-cum-spectator. The spectacle of the scene allows Ossi to let the audience in on her private
beauty routines, selling the technology of glamour while conveying the mechanisms of image production. Her direct interaction,
as she catches the audience's eyes, invites spectators to vicari-
ously view various intimate secrets: the sight of a half-naked film
star and the pleasures, sensual or otherwise, involved in beauty
preparation. Direct and personal appeal fosters a high degree of
intimacy between the star and female spectator. Looking, and
being looked at, are crucial here: the star builds fan loyalty with
her natural and spontaneous look directed to the camera. The female spectator is positioned as a consumer of images, of feminine
beauty, of screen glamour, and of movie stardom. There is a stagi-
ness to the whole sequence: heavy drapes mark off intimate
spaces; the edge of the bath denies us the sexual display of her
naked form; and towels, parlor maids, and an oversized dressing
gown allow us only tantalizing glimpses of her bare flesh. Playing
with our desire to see while parodying other disrobing spectacles
as well as the American comedies of Cecil deMille, the scene invites the spectator to make sense of the feminine form as simultaneously constructed and deconstructed. It further encourages an
imagined female spectator to scrutinize her own beauty regimes,
as if the endless task of personal hygiene and self-improvement,
cosmetic or otherwise, was one with which the modern woman
must be constantly engaged.

A moment of presentation for the character gives way to
a moment of performance for the film actress, as she glides, like
the famous movie star she is, through this luxuriant and glamorous interior. A self-conscious nod is thereby made toward the industrial mechanism at work in the star-making process, in the

incessant, week by week, buildup of her profile. It acknowledges other processes, including the selling and marketing of the star-vehicle, the dissemination of news through fan magazines and press releases, and the circulating and collecting of (sometimes autographed) pictures. Playfully exposing how the screen idol is made reveals how identities, star images, and feminine beauty are packaged commodities for sale. Letting audiences in on the hard work that goes into constructing screen beauty offers insight into the very processes with which the imagined female spectators were being invited by the industry to actively engage: the consumption of images, commodities, and identities.

Humor relies heavily on audience identification with the Oswalda star persona, which offers a context to the bathing sequence and its feminine excesses. Reasserting the principles of monopoly film culture that instituted a particular viewing protocol, the star's position within the sequence is industrially motivated, driven by the presold elements associated with the Oswalda brand image. It has industrial implications in terms of soliciting audience identification while retaining their customer loyalty through product differentiation. Precisely by exposing what is funny to the audience through Oswalda's comic antics and burlesque routines, the rules that operate within the cinematic discourse regarding formal vocabulary, textual conventions, and audience expectations, values, and assumptions can be seen functioning.

Issues of audience interaction once more come to the fore, as the female gaze reworks Freud's definition of the tripartite joke structure—male clown, female object, and male audience. The active female gaze is formally positioned as a source of comic excess while simultaneously being narratively sanctioned through social spaces that permit the female joke to take place. Ossi first sees Nucki the day after her marriage to Josef, whom she believes to be the aristocrat Prince Nucki sent by the matrimonial agency. Nucki is brought in drunk to the intemperance society, a charitable organization run by a group of millionaires' daughters. Charity work was known to be a socially respectable activity for bourgeois women in Imperial Germany, as elsewhere. Participation in the female sphere of charitable and religious activism gave middle-class women access to a wider community, where they could exercise considerable autonomy at a time when few opportunities existed for them to participate in the public space beyond hearth and home. Voluntary work effectively offered a training ground for these young bourgeois women. It encouraged feminine virtues of gentility and sexual propriety, and prepared them for marriage and child rearing. However, all is not as it seems at this particular bastion of feminine restraint and decorum.

All the young ladies are assembled together in a panoptican hall, a space designed to keep the offending drunk in view at all times while giving the women visual license to observe docile male bodies. Surveillance and repentance codify such a socially sanctioned gendered space. It is a disciplinary space in which men are answerable to women for their (pleasurable) moral transgressions. However, the high-spirited young women are less interested in a tireless mission to reform wayward alcoholics than in looking for handsome young men among the inebriates brought before them. In a comic reversal of how the cultural guardians sought to police the urban chaos by identifying certain troublesome bodies, the women cynically establish an organization that allows them to track down eligible suitors within the modern world of anonymous crowds under the pretext of moral reform. Ignoring an old dipsomaniac confessing to the errors of his dissolute ways by preferring to gossip instead, these bright young things respond very differently when the suave and elegantly dressed Prince Nucki stumbles into the auditorium. As he falls into a drunken heap, the women immediately jump to their feet in febrile excitement. Fighting is fierce as they clamber to the front for a better look; but then, as the comic premise has already set out, the modern marriage market is a tough place, where only the fittest survive.

Such spectacles of bodily desire over social propriety—the girls refuse to blush—would seem, on the surface at least, to play right into the hands of the reformists and their official assessments about modern young women. However, the spontaneous exhilaration of physical abandon and sexual anarchy is comically sanctioned within a social space defined by female ownership, its rules of exclusive membership and, more importantly, the rules of this particular film comedy. Sequences like this (as well as Ossi's bathing scene) offer a safe haven beyond patriarchal order and male interference. The confidence (rather than progressiveness) of these amusing scenes is an indication of how the comedy discourse sets up its own terms of reference and invites the audience to share in the joke. For example, the text encodes sexually liberated feminine behavior as belonging to the American flapper and her modern sensibilities, thus displacing any possible offense her ostentatious excesses may cause. Yet, the mechanisms of humor make the image funny by converting it into a representation of playful disorder and self-mocking pleasures. The creation of the comical young women to laugh both *at* and *with* allows the comedic discourse to define itself and strengthen its own identity for producing humor by invoking the juxtaposition of two very different types of joking relationship.

How the female spectator is placed in relation to these two alternative joking relationships, through the formal and textual strategies, offers both vicarious and other hidden pleasures. Like his (professional) photograph, displayed on the marriage emporium wall, which invites the spectator/customer to share in the opinion that he is quite a catch, Nucki commands the imaginary visual field. He is positioned as a desired cinematic object rather than an active narrative agent, and as the most appropriate bachelor, despite his inebriated state. Ultimately, though, it is the status of Harry Liedtke as the debonair German film star that defines that suitability. Ossi, panting with sexual excitement at the sight of this man she has never met, is singled out from the other giddy females by an iris shot, which offers a different point of entry for the spectator, as the background momentarily disappears. In the following shot, constructed as belonging to Ossi's lustful point-of-view, Nucki stares straight into camera as his soppy expression gives way to hysterical laughter. Shifting point-of view editing and spatial disruptions thus implicate the audience both within the fiction as spectator-subject and outside it as fans of the stars and collectors and consumers of memorabilia. No sooner has the female spectator witnessed Ossi's sexually charged reaction to Nucki than she is looking at him through Ossi's eyes.

The woman, in her shift from erotic spectacle to erotically lustful spectator, sets in motion a circuit of viewing positions related to desire. These are negotiated between character, spectator, and star, and invite the audience to share in unlicensed visual pleasures. We see here another example of the way in which the film continually repositions its spectator, structurally playing out the terms of the tendentious joke in which, as Freud defined it, repressed desires are given expression through the telling of the joke. The changing status of the gaze, *contained* and *regulated* by the film comedy, means the female spectator is structured to intimately identify with Oswalda on several different levels. On a fictitious level, and in a bold move for a 1919 comedy, the spectator shares a joke with the recently wed Ossi that marriage does not satisfy sensual desires or prohibit the woman from lustfully looking at another man. On a performative level, Oswalda co-opts the spectator to share in the opinion that Liedtke is worthy of their institutional attentions, thus exciting further visits to the cinema, as well as the purchasing of fan memorabilia.

The Oyster Princess has excited little academic interest beyond attempts to understand it as a transitional film in the context of Ernst Lubitsch as auteur, involving a teleological movement between two nations and styles of filmmaking—Germany (counter) and America (classical) cinema (Hake, *Passions and Deceptions*). In an attempt to understand the hidden pleasures and forgotten laughter of the film, it is imperative not to view the comic antics, star performances, and outrageous spectacles as violating classical formal systems and resisting bourgeois cultural norms. It is important, in fact, to judge the popular by different standards and find alternative means by which to talk about it.

It is imperative not to view the German popular cinema between 1910 and 1919 as an archaic relic, to unfavorably compare it with classic masterpieces from the period. Rather, a film like *The Oyster Princess* and its comic star are deeply embedded within the various discursive processes and industrial demands produced at a specific historical moment. By charting reformist campaigns against cinema, and the Altenloh thesis (which was one of the first documents to record how women imagined themselves as modern social beings), it soon becomes apparent how the popular cinema was able to *define* and *represent* its own uniqueness. Regulating its own industrial practices and carefully structuring the formal strategies of the film text, popular cinema sought to appeal directly to its imagined constituency through encouraging considerable audience participation (consumers, spectators, audience members, fans, urban travelers) while inscribing those new institutional identities into the very form of its products.

What makes both the Oswalda star image complex and the film text multilayered are the institutional demands that mapped out a dense network of audience interactions and cinematic experience. The industry was interested in building a heterogeneous yet stable audience for its products, and did so by managing knowledge about, and producing representation for, them. This essay has provided a glimpse, however fleeting, of how the German film industry recognized an imagined female audience and set about producing, circulating, and popularizing a set of modern identities in the process of attracting this audience. The popular star functioned as a multivalent sign—a source of entertainment, a consumer focus, a provider of information, and a reference point for emulation. Each performative and cultural aspect of the Oswalda image was, in turn, assigned meaning and value in relation to how the institution of cinema created its own terms of cultural reference to ensure commercial survival and retain intense customer loyalty.

Finally, how else can the scholar explain the fact that while *The Oyster Princess* proved so popular in its day that further prints had to be struck to keep pace with public demand, by 1926 it had come to be dubbed as merely "an entertainment of unusual character" (*Bioscope*, 1926, 41)? Rather than framing, in terms of historical exclusion and cultural unworthiness, the disappearance of certain stars, the melting down of the nitrate stock after commercial exploitation of the film, and the refusal to publish scripts, it is necessary to rethink the issue. It is important not to view loss as a reclaimed historical object but to consider it as inscribed right in the very form of the popular. Within these terms, *The Oyster Princess* might appear like an isolated aberration, because the popular, as a discourse, organizes certain experiences and identities to speak about specific cultural moments, unsentimentally disregarding the old in favor of the genuinely new. Undeniably, further work needs to be undertaken in understanding the hidden pleasures of seemingly strange spectacles, odd jokes, and almost forgotten movie stars, if scholars are to gain a fuller understanding of how the popular cinema functioned in the cultural life of Germany between 1910 and 1919.

NOTES

1. For example, Miriam Hansen (1983) has considered the function of late-Wilhelmine cinema as a radically new kind of public sphere attracting audiences previously excluded from official cultural address. Another scholar working in this field to draw similar conclusions has been Heide Schlüpmann (1982, 1990, 1992, 1994, 1996). She has in her more recent work on industrial strategies turned to reception conditions and female spectatorship, to argue that the early Germany film industry seized upon an opportunity to construct an alternative, anti-bourgeois public space (Schlüpmann 1990). Casting fresh light on the late-Wilhelmine cinema's bid to improve its cultural reputation and reach an even broader audience, she explores how film production and exhibition (inseparable at this time) promoted a female narrative perspective and appealed to the spectatorial interests of a commercially untapped female constituency (Schlüpmann 1996). Her contribution has, in fact, been to rescue a popular countercinema almost lost from view, eclipsed by Weimar's "golden" years.

2. New research raised concern about how the suggestive effects of

cinema might affect the nation's youth, fueling controversy around female public participation and sexual vice. These studies, including a teachers' commission authorized by the Hamburg senate (Warshadt 128) and selected reformist pamphlets (Hellwig 1911, 1913; Conradt; Lange 1918), provided qualitative data to support a contradictory discourse characterizing young women as inherently vulnerable to seduction and sexually dangerous.

3. Couched beneath attempts to define the female crowds and regulate viewing habits were fears about the immediate pleasures of cinema and the seductive power of the image (see Duenschmann; Mierendorff). Adolf Sellmann (1912, 1914), for example, focused on how dimming the house lights could trigger a dreamlike trance in weak-willed audiences such as women. Konrad Lange (1913, 1918) protested against what he characterized as the fleeting distractions provided by the dissolute representations, simple pulp-fiction-style narratives, and spectacle-attractions of the "trash" films. Through these hypothetical constructs, the mass spectorial experience emerges as a uniquely gendered one, (almost) exclusively written about by male authors and imagined as a "feminine" state.

4. Detailing eight different film narratives and the predictable feminine response, he observed how the female spectator, abandoned to distraction, overidentified with what she saw on screen: "Sensational film hits and life usually correspond to each other because the Little Miss Typists model themselves from the examples they see on the screen." (1995, 292).

WORKS CITED

Altenloh, Emilie. *Zur Soziologie des Kino: Die Kino-Unternshmung und die sozialen Schichten ihrer Desucher.* Jena: Eugen Diederichs, 1914; reprinted in facsimile by Medienladen, Hamberg, 1977.

Balázs, Béla. "Self-Mockery on the Screen," *Hungarofilm Bulletin* 3 (1984): 16.

Cherchi Usai, Paolo, and Lorenzo Cordelli, eds. *Before Caligari: German Cinema, 1895–1920.* Pordenone: Edizioni Biblioteca dell'Immagine, 1990.

Conradt, Walter. *Kirche und Kinematograph.* Berlin: Hermann Walther, 1910.

Duenschmann, H. "Kinematograph und Psychologie der Volksmenge. Eine sozialpolitische Studie," *Konservative Monatsschrift* (1912): 9.

Eisner, Lotte. *The Haunted Screen: Expressionism in the German Film and the Influence of Max Reinhardt.* Translated by Roger Greaves. Berkeley: University of California Press, 1969.

Elsaesser, Thomas, ed. *The Second Life: German Cinema's First Decades.* Amsterdam: University of Amsterdam Press, 1996.

Foucault, Michel. *The Archaeology of Knowledge.* London: Routledge, 1990.

Freud, Sigmund. *Jokes and Their Relation to the Unconscious.* London: Penguin, 1991.

Gaupp, Robert, and Konrad Lange. *Der Kinematograph als Volksunterhaltungsmittel.* Munich: Dürerbund, 1912.

Hake, Sabine, "Girls and Crisis: The Other Side of Diversion," *New German Critique* 40 (winter 1987): 147–64.

———. *Passions and Deceptions: The Early Films of Ernst Lubitsch.* Princeton, N.J.: Princeton University Press, 1992.

Hansen, Miriam. "Early Cinema: Whose Public Space." *New German Critique* 29 (spring-summer 1983): 147–84.

Hellwig, Albert. *Schundfilms, Ihr Wesen, ihre Gefahren und ihre Bekumpfung.* Halle a.s.S: Verlag der Buchhandlung des Waisenhauses, 1911.

———. "Schundfilm und Filmzensur," *Die Grenzboten* 6 (1913): 142.

Kaes, Anton, "The Debate about Cinema: Charting a Controversy, 1909–1929." Translated by David J. Levin. *New German Cinema* 40 (winter 1987): 7–33.

Kracauer, Siegfried. *From Caligari to Hitler: A Psychological History of the German Film.* Princeton, N.J.: Princeton University Press, 1977.

———. *The Mass Ornament: Weimar Essays.* Translated and edited by Thomas Y. Levin. Cambridge, Mass.: Harvard University Press, 1995.

Lange, Konrad. "Die 'Kunst' des Lichtspieltheaters." *Die Grenzboten* 24 (1913).

———. *Nationale Kinoreform.* Mödchen-Gladbach: Volksvereins-Verlag, 1918.

Mierendorff, Carl. "Hatte ich das Kino!" *Die Weißen Blätter* 7:2 (1920): 92. Cited in translation in Sabine Hake, *The Cinema's Third Machine: Writing on Film in Germany 1907–1933* (Lincoln and London: University of Nebraska Press, 1993), 59.

Müller, Corinna. *Frühe deutsche Kinematographie: Formale, wirtschaftliche und kulturelle Entwicklungen, 1907–1912.* Stuttgart/Weimar: Metzler, 1994.

"Oyster Princess, The." *Bioscope,* 10 June 1926, 41.

Petro, Patrice. "Modernity and Mass Culture in Weimar: Contours of a Discourse on Sexuality in Early Theories of Perception and Representation." *New German Critique* 40 (winter 1987): 115–46.

Salt, Barry. "Early German Film: The Stylistic in Comparative Context." In *The Second Life: German Cinema's First Decades,* edited by Thomas Elsaesser, 225–36. Amsterdam: University of Amsterdam Press, 1996.

Schlüpmann, Heide. "Kinosucht." *Frauen und Film* 33 (October 1982): 45–52.

———. *Unheimlichkeit des Blicks: Das Drama des frühen deutschen Kinos.* Frankfurt-am-Main: Stroemfeld/Roter Stern, 1990.

———. "Early German Cinema—Melodrama and Social Drama." In *Popular European Cinema,* edited by Richard Dyer and Ginette Vincendeau, 206–19. London: Routledge, 1992.

———. "Cinematographic Enlightenment versus 'The Public Sphere.' A Year in Wilhelminian Cinema." *Griffithiana* 5 (May 1994): 75–85.

———. "Cinema as Anti-Theatre: Actresses and Female Audiences." In *Silent Film,* edited by Richard Abel, 125–41. New Brunswick, N.J.: Rutgers University Press, 1996.

Sellmann, Adolf. *Der Kinematograph als Volkserzieher?* Langensalza: n.p., 1912.

———. *Kino und Schule.* Mödchen-Gladbach: Volksvereins-Verlag, 1914.

Warshadt, "Aus dem Kampfe um die Kinoreform." *Die Grenzboten. Zeitschrift für Politik, Literatur und Kunst* (1914): 3.

FILMOGRAPHY

The Oyster Princess [Die Austernprinzessin] (Lubitsch, 1919). Distributed by
the British Film Institute in association with the Goethe-Institut
London and the German Embassy, London. http://www.goethe.de/
gr/lon/film/dec10.htm
The Doll [Die Puppe] (Lubitsch, 1919). Distributed by the British Film Institute in association with the Goethe-Institut London and the German
Embassy, London. http://www.goethe.de/gr/lon/film/dec10.htm.

CHAPTER 3

The Carnival of Humiliation

Sex, Spectacle, and Self-Reflexivity in E. A. Dupont's *Variety* (1925)

Richard W. McCormick

The film *Variety* premiered in Berlin in November 1925. Directed by Ewald Andre Dupont and produced by Erich Pommer, the film starred Lya de Putti and Emil Jannings. Both Siegfried Kracauer (*From Caligari to Hitler* 125–27) and Lotte Eisner (278–84), in their canonical books on the German cinema of the 1920s, considered *Variety* (as it was called in its American release) to be a key film in the transition from expressionism in German cinema to the type of realism associated with the *Neue Sachlichkeit*, or New Objectivity. It was definitely a product of the German "art cinema," but it was also a huge box office hit, in Germany as well as in the United States.

    Variety was an "art film" that nonetheless recalled in certain ways the sensational, lurid, and much more "low-brow" early German cinema. Perhaps it is this citation of early German cinema (that is, the cinema before 1918)[1] that helps to make *Variety* such a rich text, one that provides both a mixture of and a reflection upon mass entertainment, innovative cinematic technique, and male insecurities about female autonomy, both sexual and economic. As is true of many famous films made during Germany's Weimar Republic (1918–33)—from Karl Grune's *The Street* (1923) and F. W. Murnau's *The Last Laugh* (1924) to G. W. Pabst's *Pandora's Box* (1929) and Josef von Sternberg's *The Blue Angel* (1930)—this film tells a story of male humiliation. In a plot that resembles the plots of those films, a male protagonist is seduced and then cuckolded by a woman who embodies an interesting mixture of exotic vamp and ambitious working woman.[2] She betrays him with an effeminate, sophisticated, foreign cosmopolitan. The manner in which this familiar story of humiliation and revenge is told, however, indicates a deeper ambivalence about modernity—and about the very mass spectacle that the film itself reproduces.

Variety can readily be related to the emerging New Objectivity of the "stabilized period" of the Weimar Republic (1924–29). Aspects of the film that are arguably "New Objective" include its contradictory move toward both melodrama and documentary, and its embrace—and ambivalent examination—of mass entertainment. The film uses the carnival as a metaphor for the topsy-turvy world of modernity, a metaphor that also can be noted in expressionist films—above all in The Cabinet of Dr. Caligari (Robert Wiene, 1919). However, here it is a very contemporary and very urban entertainment milieu, captured most impressively with virtuoso camera work shot on location in Berlin's famous variety palace, the Wintergarten.

While the film celebrates the modernity of its own camera and editing techniques, it remains very ambivalent about the urban modernity, upward mobility, "Americanism," and destabilization of traditional gender identities it so sensationally depicts.[3] Variety, despite all its citation—and mobilization—of the forms of mass spectacle and entertainment associated with Weimar modernity, remains an "art film." The German "art cinema" of the 1920s is characterized, on the one hand, by a certain aesthetic conservatism that reflects the ambivalence about film and mass culture on the part of intellectuals so well documented in Anton Kaes's Kino-Debatte (Debate about the cinema). On the other hand, the art cinema often manifests a political conservatism typical of large German industries during the 1920s, including the film industry, which was becoming ever more concentrated throughout the decade. By "political conservativism" I mean the generally anti-democratic, class-based hierarchical elitism characteristic of the dominant social groups in the Weimar Republic. Hence the rather cynical (and strategic) contradiction of producing films ambivalent about mass culture and modernity that were themselves stunning spectacles made with all the technical expertise money could buy.

With Variety, one clearly has a film that was the product of Erich Pommer's special division at Ufa, the goal of which was to produce big-budget "art films" of the sort that to this day fill the film-historical canon of the Weimar cinema. At the same time, this was a film that was a box office hit both in Germany and the United States—something for which Pommer and the German industry had long been striving. It thematized popular success in the entertainment world in the way we now expect the "self-reflexive" Weimar art cinema to do. What I would like to examine more closely, however, is precisely the "self-reflexivity" in *Variety*, for this aspect of the film is more problematic than its melodramatic or sensational aspects. It is the self-reflexivity in the film that, far from being politically "progressive," betrays the film's ultimately conservative, elitist, anti-democratic distaste for the mass entertainment it is (cynically) producing.

The 1925 production of *Variety* was the third film adaptation of Felix Holländer's novel, *The Oath of Stefan Huller [Der Eid des Stefan Huller].*[4] The first two film adaptations had been made in 1912 and 1919. That a film about sexual betrayal set in the milieu of acrobats in a variety show was made as early as 1912 is significant, since at that point the cinema in Germany had only recently extricated itself from the lower-class world of variety shows, music halls, and carnivals. In the years after the cinema's invention in 1895, films had primarily been shown in variety halls and in *Wanderkinos,* the "wandering" tent cinemas that appeared at fairs and carnivals; only in 1904 did storefront cinemas begin to compete seriously with these venues. By 1910, German films began to be exhibited in ever grander cinema "palaces," as the German film industry strove for bourgeois respectability, precisely in order to compensate for its quite recent, low-brow origins (Schlüpmann 8–9, 12).

A film presenting a titillating view of the demimonde of carnival and variety performers was still considered marketable in 1925 by Erich Pommer.[5] The German "art cinema" began around 1912 and is often called an *Autorenkino,* or "cinema of authors/auteurs" (Schlüpmann 247; Elsaesser and Wedel 113). By the 1920s, the German art film was only one of many products—and strategies—of a large, commercial film industry. It was certainly nothing at all similar to the concept of a low-budget *Autorenkino* with oppositional ambitions that we associate with the "New German Cinema" of the 1970s.[6] Certainly for *Variety* it is a debatable term, at least if the director Dupont is supposed to be the film's "author"; the producer Pommer and the cinematographer Karl Freund were both arguably much more important for the film. Pommer intended *Variety* to capitalize on the mobile-camera techniques Freund had developed in *The Last Laugh*, the film Pommer had produced a year earlier with F. W. Murnau directing. Pommer wanted to use Freund again to film *Variety*, but for director he chose Dupont over Murnau, apparently because he felt that the latter was unsuited to directing a melodrama so focused on (heterosexual) sex. It was Pommer who persuaded Dupont to film the story in the new dynamic visual style that he wanted to market (Luft, cited in Combs).[7]

Although *The Last Laugh* had been a critical success, and while it had wowed and intimidated Hollywood with its technical virtuosity, it had not been an overwhelming box office hit. Proving Pommer's calculations right, *Variety* did become such a hit, both in Germany and in the United States. Early on, German critics saw it as the film the German film industry had long awaited, one that could compete with American cinema; the German trade journal *Kinematograph* asserted that the film was sure to conquer "even the aloof Americans" ("*Varieté*: Der grosse deutsche Film"). Many American critics agreed, and so did American audiences. Headlines in 1926 about the film's New York reception in another German trade journal, *Lichtbild-Bühne*, tell the story: "Thunderous Success of *Variety* in New York" and "Record Box Office for *Variety*" ("Stürmischer Erfolg von Varieté in New York"; "Rekord-Einnahmen für Varieté").

Variety was for a long time the one great success Ufa managed to achieve in the United States (Esser 165). It had the technical virtuosity of *The Last Laugh* with a story about sexual betrayal so lurid, at least by American standards, that Famous Players Lasky cut it drastically; the version released in the United States in all but New York and a few other large cities was about half an hour shorter.[8] It is this amputated version that is still available today in the United States (and in Great Britain as well—see Combs).[9] Because it is the shorter version with which most North American viewers are familiar, it is worth comparing the two. The longer "German" original is not only sexually more explicit than the "American" version, it also depicts greater social distance between Boss's humble status at the beginning of the film and the success he earns as a star of the Wintergarten later in the film.

Both the original German version and the American version begin in prison. Boss Huller, who has spent ten years in prison for murder, is called to see the prison director. The director has received a petition to grant the prisoner clemency, and therefore he asks that Boss break his long silence and tell his story. In a flashback, Boss does so. In the German version of the film, the flashback depicts Boss Huller as someone who runs a troupe of tawdry female dancers in a Hamburg carnival. His tired and worn-out wife plays piano for the show; Boss appears to be the more energetic and nurturing parent to their infant son. He longs to return to his old career as a trapeze artist, but his wife refuses to allow him to do so. A mysterious, exotic young dancer known as Berta-Marie joins the troupe, and Boss falls in love with her. He runs away with her to a carnival in Berlin, where he resumes his career on the trapeze with Berta-Marie as his partner. Their success leads to an offer from a world-famous trapeze artist, Artinelli, to leave the carnival behind for the more prestigious world of Berlin's internationally famous Wintergarten. They form a trio with Artinelli and are very successful, but now Boss is himself betrayed by the sophisticated and devious Artinelli, who after a somewhat brutal "seduction" of Berta-Marie carries on a sexual liaison with her. When Boss learns that he has been betrayed, he fantasizes about dropping Artinelli during the trapeze act, but instead he kills him later in a knife fight in Artinelli's dressing room. Boss then turns himself in to the police. Here the flashback ends, and the prison director, moved by Boss's story, grants him freedom; the film ends with the gates of the prison opening up to beautiful, sunny skies.

The American version retains the frame of the prison scenes around the main flashback, but in the flashback plot the scenes in Hamburg, including wife and child, are cut. The story begins with Berta-Marie and Boss as trapeze artists at the carnival in Berlin, just as they are about to be discovered by Artinelli. Berta-Marie becomes in this version Boss's wife, not his mistress; Boss has not abandoned his family for her but rather is blameless until he murders Artinelli. Berta-Marie is a faithless wife who succumbs to a clever womanizer, rather than the exotic vamp who seduces Boss away from hearth and home only to betray him for the more wordly and handsome Artinelli.

Eisner credits Dupont for his adroit use of "the last vestiges of Expressionism" in the prison sequences that frame the film (278); Kracauer also notes "traces of expressionism" in the same scenes (*From Caligari to Hitler* 127, 71). The opening high-angle shot shows prisoners in white uniforms moving in a circle against a dark, cavernous background. Emphasis is placed on the number twenty-eight on Boss's back—his face is not shown until the flashback begins; only then does he acquire an identity. This is another convention of expressionist staging, which stressed nameless and faceless masses in ornamental forms, and characters named only by an external designation and a number: "prisoner number 28."

However, both critics see the film as having achieved something other than expressionism.[10] Kracauer writes that *Variety* indulges in the "new realism" that was becoming dominant in 1925 (*From Caligari to Hitler* 125). It is this "realism" that aligns the film with the shift in artistic sensibility of the mid-1920s that came with the waning of expressionism in the German art cinema, an art movement notable for its emphasis on interiority and subjectivity and its anxiety about technology and modernization, and the rise of the so-called New Objectivity (*Neue Sachlichkeit*), with an emphasis on documenting the external surfaces of reality and a more affirmative attitude about technology, the city, and modern mass culture. This transition from obsessive, subjective interiority and distorted, anxious perspectives on modernity to a fetishization of "objectivity," technology, and the "surface" of modern reality is a bit too extreme (or binary) not to be somewhat suspect, and indeed it is belied by certain stylistic and attitudinal continuities—notably an ambivalence about modernity that one finds beneath both expressionist anxieties about and New Objective celebrations of modern mass culture.[11]

Although Kracauer writes about the film's "realism," neither the film's rather generic melodramatic plot nor the dizzying effects of its camera work and editing for the trapeze sequences appear to today's sensibilities to be especially "realistic." Kracauer is right, however: in 1925 *Variety* was famous precisely for its realism. This reputation had much to do with its impressive "documentary" shots of Berlin and Hamburg; for example, the carnival in Hamburg's St. Pauli district, and in Berlin the Friedrichstrasse railway station, certain street scenes, and the interior shots of the Wintergarten (see "*Varieté*: Der grosse deutsche Film"). Shooting on location was still relatively rare in the German art film, which was famous primarily for its carefully constructed studio sets that could be illuminated so precisely and expressively. In this way *Variety* is clearly related to New Objectivity and associated trends of the middle and later 1920s in German film, photography, theater, literature, and painting, in which the attempt to move toward a documentary approach was noted.[12]

However, the film is connected to such trends not merely because of the presence of some documentary footage; what the footage actually depicts is even more significant: carnival scenes, the hectic night life on Berlin's streets, and, above all, famous international variety acts in the Wintergarten—which was not only the venue where the most popular mass entertainment form of the late nineteenth century, the variety show, had its most glamorous home, but also the very hall where the first films by the Skladanowsky brothers had been exhibited in 1895.[13] *Variety* captured a number of variety acts inside (and outside) the Wintergarten, and one of them was the Tiller Girls, the most famous of many troupes of chorus-line dancers who toured Europe during the 1920s and were all the rage, especially in Berlin.[14] Indeed, although the "Tiller Girls" were originally an English troupe (and one that spawned many imitations with the same name), they symbolized Americanism in Germany as much as other phenomena like jazz or Hollywood did.

Americanism—and the ideal of success represented by America—are also crucial to Berta-Marie's "betrayal" of Boss. Artinelli first lures her into his room with a telegraph he has received that contains an offer from America for the trio of acrobats; then he attempts to coerce her sexual compliance with the argument that she owes him her upward mobility—her rise from sleazy carnival performer to the toast of the internationally famous Wintergarten. America represents the pinnacle of achievement in the world of variety shows (or vaudeville, as it was called in the United States). America is also connected—in this film at any rate—to loose sexual morals and other "unhealthy" effects of quick upward mobility and the celebrity offered by modern mass culture. For *Variety*, despite all its citation—and mobilization—of the forms of mass spectacle and entertainment associated with Weimar modernity, remains an "art film," and thus its depiction of modernity, democracy, and class mobility is for the most part negative.

The American critic in Berlin for the U.S. trade journal *Variety* called the style of the German film *Variety* "modernistic" (Trask.). Writing in the *New Republic* in 1926, Evelyn Gerstein went so far as to compare its technique to Leger, Picasso, and Stravinsky. Yet, as Kracauer wrote in "The White Collar Employees" ("Die Angestellten") (1929), the secret of New Objectivity was precisely that behind its modern facade, something very sentimental was often lurking (287). For all *Variety*'s modern technical virtuosity, the film is not merely sentimental but very conservative in its critique of aspects of modernity. It participates in the cynical strategy of dressing its conservative message in the most modern of forms—given its commercial success, one might say that it is one of the most successful examples of the strategy. For the evil that destroys the good-natured family man, Boss, is clearly connected to his desire to be a star of the trapeze again—to be at the center of the spotlight of mass entertainment, the beneficiary of the appetite of the modern masses for spectacle and distraction. His seduction by Berta-Marie is what motivates him to strive again for success in the world of the carnival, and it is Berta-Marie who then pushes Boss to accept Artinelli's offer to move up from the carnival to the classier world of the variety show.

The film's cynical ambivalence creates a distance between narrative and spectacle that is reflexive. Its technical virtuosity is typical of the New Objective fetishization of technology, and its use of a lurid, sensational, melodramatic plot mirrors the move in New Objectivity toward more accessible narratives and an apparent embrace of mass culture.[15] The film's most famous cinematic techniques involve the use of mobile camera from subjective points of view, most impressively in the dizzying shots of the acrobats high above the audience in the Wintergarten, and these techniques tend to foreground themselves through a virtuosity in excess of the needs of the plot. In addition, the film's own constructions of looking are foregrounded, thematized quite explicitly—even melodramatically—in a collage of eyes that is intercut with shots of Boss on the trapeze at his most conflicted moment, as he is indeed being watched by everyone in the huge hall. It can be argued that even the melodramatic narrative itself reflects on the institution of the cinema (although perhaps unintentionally so): the protagonist's precipitous rise from his origins as a "vulgar" carnival performer to a performer in a glamorous hall in which the upper classes ogle him is a trajectory that parallels the rise of cinema itself from despised lower-class entertainment to a more bourgeois one. Yet the comment on cinema is in that case quite negative, for it becomes a part of a topsy-turvy world of glittering mass celebrity that is marked as clearly dangerous and destabilizing.

Also reflexive is the film's thematization of its own specular relations, which, in turn, is closely linked not just to spectacle in the film but also gender. The basic plot of the film is very similar to what Kracauer considers the standard story of the "street film" genre in Weimar cinema: the hero leaves the boring safety of domestic life, lured by a woman of "the streets" into that dangerous but exciting realm, only to meet betrayal at her hands (with help from her criminal accomplices).[16] Yet *Variety* varies this basic plot in some interesting ways: the shift to the carnival milieu turns the domesticity that Boss flees into a shabby, almost lumpen variety—as is his occupation as barker for and manager of a tired and worn-out troupe of exotic dancers. (Predictably, the American version eliminates this initial social degradation, making Boss start as a star of the carnival, about to move even higher, into the world of variety shows.)

Furthermore, while the urban streets of modernity are actually documented here in a more straightforward way than in many "street films,"[17] the chaos of modernity is embodied more compellingly in the milieu of mass entertainment—and not so much in its least glamorous depths, where we first encounter Boss, as in its loftier realms. For what is demonized in the film is clearly the glamorous celebrity and dizzying upward mobility that this subset of modernity offers, whereas the shabby life at the bottom that Boss deserts actually becomes recuperated by the film's narrative frame as the domesticity that in the end "saves" him. The petition for clemency sent to the prison director originates with Boss's wife and son in Hamburg, and it is to this refuge of domesticity that he is allowed to return.[18] When the gates of the prison open before us at the end of the film, revealing a gloriously sun-lit view of wind-blown trees (in what is apparently the film's first exterior shot in daylight that depicts nonurban reality), it is as if Boss's return to his family is "bourgeoisified" with all the glories of nature that middle-class ideology ascribes to the family. The conservative message here seems as much a demonization of upward mobility—that is, of not knowing one's place—as of adultery: both are symptoms and causes of the moral chaos modernity brings through its destabilization of the social and sexual order.

Also, both—unseemly social ambition as well as sexual lust—are connected to the figure of the vamp. Berta-Marie is, certainly in the German version, an archetypal femme fatale, a nameless woman of uncertain identity and mysterious origins. Indeed, in Ufa's program for the film's premiere at the Ufa-Palast am Zoo, 16 November 1925, Lya de Putti's character is not listed as Berta-Marie, but rather as "a foreign girl" ("Ein fremdes Mädchen"). Her real name is never mentioned; the ship's captain who brings the young stowaway to the carnival in Hamburg's harbor district tells Boss that her name is so exotic (so "verrückt," according to the German titles) that the shipmates have named her after their ship, the Berta-Marie.

Thus named for a ship that plies international trade routes, Berta-Marie is no mere woman of the streets, she is truly a foreign element immediately disruptive of the status quo in Boss's life. Her exotic belly dance quickly eclipses the tired troupe of dancers Boss manages, and her solo performance before a leering male audience is so seductive that one man (played by Kurt Gerron) comes onto the stage.[19] Enraged, Boss closes the show, which nearly causes a riot; he then decides to run away with her to Berlin. Berta-Marie is explicitly called a "vampire" in the film's screenplay, for the way she controls Boss with her sexuality.[20] Yet Boss runs away with her not just out of sexual desire, but also out of his longing for stardom: he wants to use her disruptive beauty to ornament his own return to the world of the spectacle on the trapeze. However, he is able to "control" neither Berta-Marie's sexuality nor the ambitious drive to stardom that she motivates and later comes to embody.

Certainly Berta-Marie herself enters Artinelli's room in the first place primarily out of her own ambitions, interested to hear about the offer from America he has received in a telegram. How much she initially desires Artinelli is also unclear, since in the original version of the film his "seduction" of her appears to be a rape (certainly to our sensibilities today). This is an interesting scene, because it gives the viewer a rare insight into Berta-Marie's perspective, something the film otherwise neglects, for her function in the plot is limited almost entirely to the role of catalyst in Boss's story of male crisis. Not only are the origins of this exotic young woman shrouded in mystery, so, too, is her fate at the end of the film. Horrified at Boss's murder of Artinelli, she attempts to stop him as he lumbers down the corridor of the hotel; grabbing his arm, she fails to stop him and falls down the stairs as he continues on, driven to give himself up to the police. We see Berta-Marie for the last time in the background of this shot, collapsed on the stairs; what becomes of her the film never discloses. She is no longer of interest in Boss's narrative.[21]

As is typical of a story of male humiliation, the protagonist is "feminized"—that is, the film frustrates his attempt to achieve the power, control, and autonomy that match the ideal of masculinity in Western patriarchal ideologies. Yet the film seems to be making the point that Boss is susceptible to Berta-Marie because he is *already* "feminized." Boss's nurturant, indeed motherly qualities are visible from the very beginning of the film, notably in his concern for his infant son, whose diaper he changes very cheerfully. Later, sharing a wagon with Berta-Marie

·at the carnival in Berlin, he not only nurtures her but darns the hole in her stocking. While it might be suggested that Boss is here being idealized as a paragon of a new "sensitive" masculinity meant to appeal to women longing for more "companionate" heterosexual relationships,[22] this behavior is highlighted right at the moment of the first covert exchange of glances between Berta-Marie and Artinelli—right at the fateful moment, that is, when the end of Boss's happiness can first be anticipated. The film thus depicts his "sensitive" deviation from more rigid gender roles as a threatening destabilization—a threat to male dominance, a "feminization."

Yet it is not only Boss who is depicted as "feminized." So too is his rival, Artinelli, albeit in a different fashion, for what is depicted in his case is an "effeminate" sophistication. This is made even more explicit through the way he is shown putting on his makeup, filmed from Boss's perspective after he has learned of Artinelli's betrayal of his friendship. Artinelli is depicted negatively here both as "effeminate" and as duplicitous (a combination that one will find in Nazi cinema's anti-French and anti-Semitic caricatures).[23]

The film's destabilization of gender roles is fairly complex. Not only are both male rivals represented as in different ways "feminized," the depiction of women in the film also has some deeper implications.[24] In the German version, the two main female characters obviously represent the two poles of the clichéd madonna/whore dichotomy; nonetheless, both sides of the dichotomy, Boss's shabby wife and the evil Berta-Marie, are discredited to such a great extent that the film's misogyny seems much more powerful—and destabilizing of monogamy—than the somewhat unlikely recuperation of the family at the end of the film would imply. This is perhaps the most subversive aspect of the film's depiction of gender—but this destabilization is clearly demonized throughout the film.

The dynamics of gender in this film are also related to spectacle and specularity in the film and to the film's thematization of its own specular relations. The affair between Artinelli and Berta-Marie is anticipated by a covert exchange of glances between the two; later the audience is continually made aware of their duplicity in manipulating Boss through the film's emphasis on similar exchanges of glances that Boss never notices. Boss himself exhibits the cold, instinctual gaze of murderous jealousy twice in the film—first when the sight of Berta-Marie dancing before the crowd in his tent at the Hamburg carnival incites a riot, and later, after Boss becomes aware that Artinelli and Berta-Marie have betrayed him. Yet Boss's instinctual nature also arguably "feminizes" him: in spite of the power of his gaze in these two scenes, it is not the rational gaze of control so important to the male observer in New Objectivity. Rather Boss's instinctual nature is evidence that he is merely one of the dumb herd, the kind of "creature" ("Kreatur") that Helmut Lethen has written about as the counterpart to the "cold persona" of Weimar culture. This "cold persona," in turn, is the mask of cold impenetrability behind which, according to Lethen, Weimar's male intellectual concealed his own emotions and fears. The "creature," as a member of the urban masses, was precisely what Weimar's "cold persona" feared and despised most. Of course, intellectuals feared and despised the urban masses in no small part because they perceived them as "feminized," as both Klaus Theweleit and Andreas Huyssen have argued.[25] The masses were "feminized" both in the sense of representing a threatening Other as well as representing "downward mobility," that is, the disempowered status into which male intellectuals and artists feared that modern society, with its disregard of their traditional status, was pushing them.

The shifty-eyed, clever Artinelli is in some ways the kind of cynically manipulative "cold persona" behind a mask of smooth sophistication that was the ideal of the mindset Lethen describes. Artinelli, however, is also depicted as "feminized," and in one sense, this happens in a way that is *very* similar to the situation of gullible, instinctual Boss. For all their differences, both men are portrayed in the film as longing to be "on the right side" of the curtain, to be the stars of mass spectacle. Yet, to be the object instead of the subject of the gaze—to be looked at, as opposed to being the one who looks—is to be "feminized," especially in New Objectivity, as Lethen has argued. The male intellectuals and artists Lethen describes attempted to retain mastery amidst the chaos of modernity by wielding a cold, controlling gaze on its excesses and its masses. To be exposed to the gaze of others—especially that of the leering, vulgar, and decadent masses—is clearly to lose power (and thus to become "feminized").[26]

In keeping with the basic conservativism of German art cinema, "Americanist" modernity in this film becomes a world of mass spectacle (and upward mobility) that is clearly marked as negative in the film, a world of faithless tramps, effeminate cosmopolitans, and sensation-hungry spectators. The negative depiction of the leering spectators is nowhere better epitomized than in one striking visual image that consists of a collage of eyes, one that through intercutting appears to be focused on Boss as he sits on the trapeze high above the audience. This occurs at the tense moment in the narrative when Boss hesitates and wipes his brow, afraid that he will kill his rival by not catching him, just as he had earlier envisioned taking revenge upon him. Yet Boss is too honest to kill his rival in this way, and he seems also to want to resist turning his private act of vengeance into a part of the spectacle that the eyes below would greedily devour.

This is a moment of self-reflexivity typical of Weimar art cinema, very ambivalent about mass spectacle and the cinema itself, but also about modernity; again, it is ultimately a very conservative, undemocratic ambivalence. For the Wintergarten variety palace—and in effect the cinema itself—is depicted as a site of degenerate and sexually ambiguous voyeurism in which boundaries between the classes, too, are transgressed. It is this "evil" public sphere that Boss flees by committing his private act of murder offstage, which leads to his being locked away safely in prison. At the end of the film he is returned to the bosom of his family, blessed by a benevolent authority figure, a prison official with white hair and a beard—a character whom Lotte Eisner described aptly as "a cross between Father Christmas and God the Father" (278).

The narrative closure here is the best evidence of the political bent of the film, and while in some films narrative closure seems inadequate to the task of undoing potential subversive elements in the rest of the film, in *Variety* I would assert that there is no significant political difference between the clear demonization of the sensationalized transgressions throughout the film and what the ending posits. Although my emphasis here on reactionary, anti-democratic attitudes in the film would seem to align my reading with Kracauer's overall verdict on Weimar cinema, I would like to stress where I differ with him: Kracauer (at least in his famous postwar book *From Caligari to Hitler*) has more or less the same take on "male retrogression"/ "decadence"/"degeneracy" as the right wing in the Weimar Republic did, namely, that it is bad, one of the serious flaws in Weimar culture.[27] *Variety* sends a very clear—and anti-modern—message about modernity, democracy, and popular culture. Also targeted for attack is the emerging fluidity of gendered and sexual identities that many of us celebrate now (and rightfully so). *Variety* is in tune with elite

opinion in Weimar when it demonizes that fluidity as "degenerate." Yet perhaps the film's fascinated obsession with fluidity is
ultimately of more interest than its strident attempt to make its
disapproval clear.[28]

NOTES

1. Heide Schlüpmann believes that early German cinema, especially
that before 1914, was more subversive in terms of sexual politics than were
later periods of German cinema.

2. As to why stories of male humiliation were so common to the Weimar art film, the most obvious reason in my opinion would involve the fact
that the modernization and democratization that came with the Weimar
Republic were inextricably associated with the humiliation both of the German nation and of its male soldiers in World War I. Defeat on the battlefield
in World War I was combined with the punitive sanctions of the Versailles
Peace Treaty, which led to both political instability and the famous hyperinflation of the early years of the republic that wiped out the savings of the
German middle class. Upper- and middle-class anxieties about class status
in the new republic were aggravated by other threatening innovations, such
as the new public visibility of and roles for working women, Jews, and the
working-class parties, as well as public campaigns for the reform of abortion
laws and laws against homosexuality. See my articles "From *Caligari* to Dietrich" and "Private Anxieties/Public Projections" for an elaboration of these
ideas.

Anton Kaes (for example, in his talk at Hollins College, March
1996) has stressed that much of Weimar cinema can be read as an attempt
to work through the trauma of World War I, and that indeed much of the
depicted trauma in the cinema is an unconscious representation of shell
shock. This suggests a reading of *Variety* that I will not pursue in greater
depth here, yet I want nonetheless to remark that such a reading would
indeed fit the narrative frame of *Variety* uncannily: Boss has spent ten silent
years in prison before he can talk about his traumatic experience; thus, in
1925 (assuming that the "present" in the frame of the story refers to the year
in which the film appeared), Boss has been "imprisoned" in trauma since
1915.

3. The discussion of social mobility in Weimar cinema is indebted to
Thomas Elsaesser, who began discussing this topic in his 1982 essay, "Social
Mobility and the Fantastic." See also his new book, *Weimar Cinema and
After.*

4. Ufa's material for *Variety* in the *Illustrierter Film-Kurier* no. 378
(1925) uses the phrase "Nach Motiven des Felix Holländerschen Romans
Der Eid des Stefan Huller." The motifs on which the film is based are contained in the very beginning of the novel, which focuses not primarily on
the story of the cuckolded circus performer but rather on that of his son,
who grows up haunted by both his father's crime—the murder of his mother's lover—and his father's subsequent suicide. The novel, too, is about upward mobility, but the son's more successful version is solidly bourgeois.

The sexual politics are interesting, because the son grows into a man enlightened enough to forgive his wife's one sexual "transgression."

The 1927 American translation of Holländer's novel, titled *The Sins of the Fathers*, was no doubt occasioned by the film's success in the United States.

5. At just about the same time, production was beginning for Fritz Lang's *Metropolis*, which Pommer also produced. Whereas *Variety* succeeded at the box office in Germany and America, Lang's epic film would result in a monumental financial disaster that bankrupted Ufa and in many ways killed the big-budget art film; it also caused Pommer to leave Ufa and go to Hollywood for his first stint as a producer there. Upon his return to Germany to work for Hugenberg's Ufa in the late 1920s, the second phase of his career as a producer began, in which he would attempt a more American style of film production (Saunders 248–49). This resulted, among other things, in the development of the German musical (or operetta film) in the early sound cinema. On Pommer's career, see Hardt ("Pommer" and *Caligari*) and Jacobsen.

6. On the genesis of the "Autorenfilm" in the 1910s, see Diederichs.

7. Esser gives a great deal of credit for the film's artistic quality to Dupont (165), as does Eisner (278–84), but I think Combs may be correct in his assertion that Dupont seems merely to have been at the right place at the right time to make this film, which is his most famous and most successful.

8. See the 1926 German report from Los Angeles by Reda on the "American" version, as well as the 1926 article, "*Varieté* in 2 Fassungen," which reports that both the "German" and "American" versions were shown in Chicago. Gerstein(of the *New Republic*) and Hall (of the *New York Times*) saw the "German" version in New York; Gerstein comments on rumors that (accurately) predict how the film will be cut for more prudish areas of the United States.

It might be asked why Famous Players Lasky would cut the film this way in 1926, when a film like *The Blue Angel* in 1930 would not have problems with such preemptive censorship. One possible reason for this difference was that by the early 1930s Hollywood was much more willing to take risks, struggling to make money in the Depression with the production of sound films, which was more expensive. This was a time of many "excesses," which in turn led to the much stricter enforcement of self-censorship via the Hays Code beginning in mid-1934 (on "pre-Code" Hollywood, see, for example, LaSalle) . Also significant, as Gertrud Koch reminds us (70), is the fact that *The Blue Angel* wasn't as popular in the United States as it was in Germany, and indeed its Hollywood distributors did not even release it in the United States until after the success of von Sternberg's first American film with *Morocco* (1930), which is what first made Dietrich famous in the States—not *The Blue Angel*.

9. Indeed, there are other versions besides the two I discuss here—the version at the Deutsche Institut für Film in Frankfurt is an Italian version more or less the same as the original, except that it does not use the prison sequences to frame the main flashback. Instead it has them together at the end of the film, thus eliminating the flashback and creating a narrative entirely linear in its chronological progression. This situation reminds us how much artistic "autonomy" counted for in the international marketing of silent films during the 1920s—even for the so-called "art films" of the German film industry. The most famous example is of course Fritz Lang's *Metropolis*; its American distributors authorized massive cuts and re-editing

for the American audience, and its German producers agreed that the new version was more marketable and then released basically the same version in Germany. The original version is completely lost today. Such conditions create a situation for researchers today studying films produced in the 1920s that I imagine is somewhat comparable to what scholars studying medieval manuscripts face.

10. Eisner calls it "Impressionism" (282), stressing the fluidity of the boundary between subjective impressions of the external world and the externalized expressions of internal, subjective reality. Kracauer makes a similar point in contrasting *The Last Laugh*'s use of mobile and subjective camera to depict the doorman's internal reality to *Variety*'s use of the same techniques to "penetrate" external reality (1947, 127). In fact, both films use these techniques ultimately in the service of narrative realism and of enhancing identification with the protagonists—and these techniques (albeit in a more restrained fashion and limited to certain genres) will become part of the repertoire of classical narrative cinema as surely as Freund will end up as a cinematographer in Hollywood.

11. Many film historians, more or less following Eisner, consider all German art cinema of the Weimar Republic to be "expressionist." Obviously this is partly a question of definitions. Nonetheless, of the stylistic techniques often associated with "German expressionism" in the cinema, only the emphasis on excessive or exotic mise-en-scène and the chiaroscuro lighting techniques (the famous expressive use of shadows) actually date from the period in the early 1920s when there was an attempt to adapt expressionism for the cinema. Other techniques, such as the mobile camera, optical printing, and other special montage effects, date from the mid-1920s and are arguably more a part of the "New Objective"/futurist/constructivist celebration of technology than expressionist interiority. Beyond this, however, I would argue that expressionism and New Objectivity, like many other seemingly opposed avant-garde responses to modernity, are more like two sides of the same coin—that is, two versions of the same underlying ambivalence about modernity. On expressionism and New Objectivity as two phases of a much longer series of avant-garde attitude shifts, see Lindner; on recent discussions of New Objectivity, see Lethen, Lindner, Becker and Weiss, and Ward.

12. See, for example, "Der dokumentarische Impuls: Literarische Formen der 'Neuen Sachlichkeit,'" in Kaes 1983, 319–45.

13. The first cinematic productions ever screened in Germany were made by the Skladanowksy brothers and shown in the fall of 1895 in Berlin's Wintergarten, and the films they exhibited depicted—appropriately enough—variety acts. On the Wintergarten's development into a hall that became devoted especially to the increasingly popular variety shows in the late 1880s, see Jelavich 21–22.

14. Their choreographed routines were bemoaned by German intellectuals as the epitome of American mechanization. See Kaes 1983, 242 n. 5; see also Kracauer [1927] 1977, 1931. On the Tiller Girls specifically, see Jelavich 175–86.

15. Melodrama, of course, had long played a role in German film, including the art film; melodrama can be found in expressionist films and "chamber play" films, as Petro's *Joyless Streets* stresses. At one point, however, Petro aligns melodrama with American films, contrasting "American

melodrama" with German expressionism (218). While the melodramatic style of American cinema was influential, melodrama had already had a long history in Germany; it is arguably already to be found within the German "bourgeois tragedy" of the eighteenth century.

16. This is indeed a fair summary of the plot of Karl Grune's *The Street*, the 1923 film Kracauer cites as the prototype of the genre (1947, 125); Petro (160–64) problematizes the genre in her discussion of Bruno Rahn's film *Dirnentragödie* (1927). Miriam Hansen (1991) has commented how Kracauer continually used Grune's film to make larger (and quite different) arguments from the mid-1920s into the period after 1945.

17. Outside of some documentary footage of the city in the impressive montage at the beginning of *The Street,* it is predominantly a studio film.

18. In the American version, Boss's "friends" petition for clemency.

19. According to the film's censorship cards, this is one of the few scenes where the German censors demanded some cuts—during de Putti's belly dance (the intertitle calls it "Der fremde Zauber"). There were only five cuts demanded, four of which were in the Hamburg sequence, all involving Berta-Marie's body—including a close-up of her abdomen in the belly dance scene; the last instance of cut footage occurs at the end of the knife fight, when apparently the dead Artinelli was shown next to a bloody knife.

20. Cited in Ufa's program for the film's premiere at the Ufa-Palast am Zoo, 16 November 1925.

21. In her reading of the film, Jan Wager focuses on the agency and power the film grants Berta-Marie as a femme fatale. While not denying that the film is male-centered, she stresses that this power, in its potential address to female desires, might well have been read differently by female spectators (Wager 36–51). This is a persuasive argument, although I would maintain that the film's narrative as a whole works against this effect.

22. Wager (41–43) suggests such a reading. Her discussion of the two male characters in terms of their desirability to female spectators is very nuanced and complex.

23. I am thinking of anti-French stereotypes in films like *The Old and the Young King* (Hans Steinhoff, 1935) as well as *Fräulein von Barnhelm* (Hans Schweikart, 1940), similar in many ways to the anti-Semitic traits embodied in the title role of *Jew Suess* (Veit Harlan, 1940).

24. I place the term "feminization" in quotes to stress again that the term has no "essential" validity and to underscore my conviction that it is an ideological term within patriarchal belief systems—to mean simply any deviation from some ideal valorization of "masculinity," that is, anything marked as less important, less powerful, less valuable than a certain ideal construction of masculinity. The psychoanalytical term with the same basic meaning would be "castration." The idealized ("uncastrated") concept of masculinity, certainly in Weimar, is almost always misogynistic, but it can also be seen as "männerfeindlich," that is, anti-male, in the sense that patriarchal constructions of masculinity are ultimately inimical to actual male human beings. Ultimately these constructions of "masculinity" and "femininity" are complementary parts of one (oppressive) system.

25. See, for example, the chapter on "Mass Culture as Woman" in Huyssen's *After the Great Divide* (44–62).

26. Many in the audience in the Wintergarten are actually depicted as

wealthy, and thus their desiring gazes (at Berta-Marie, Boss, and Artinelli) are actually less "vulgar" than "decadent," but they are clearly marked as negative by means of a reactionary populism according to which upward mobility is earned by catering to the illicit desires of the decadent.

27. This is, by the way, all the more interesting now that we know, according to Miriam Hansen, that Kracauer was gay ("America, Paris" 173).

28. This disapproval is very clear at the level of the ideology of the film text. One might, however, speculate as to whether the film's popularity in Germany and America might imply a reaction on the part of what Janet Staiger calls "perverse spectators"—a popular reception at odds with the apparently intentional conservatism of the text itself. To pursue such a reading, however, would demand more empirical evidence about the film's reception.

WORKS CITED

Becker, Sabina, and Christoph Weiss, eds. *Neue Sachlichkeit im Roman: Neue Interpretationen zum Roman der Weimarer Republik.* Stuttgart: Metzler, 1995.

Combs, Richard. Rev. of *Variety* (Ufa/Famous Players Lasky film), *Monthly Film Bulletin* 46, no. 546 (1979): 160–61.

Diedrichs, Helmut H. "The Origins of the 'Autorenfilm.'" In *Before Caligari: German Cinema, 1895–1929,* edited by Paolo Cherchi Usai and Lorenzo Codelli, 380–401. Pordedone: Edizioni Biblioteca dell' Immagine, 1990.

Eisner, Lotte. *The Haunted Screen: Expressionism in the German Cinema & the Influence of Max Reinhardt.* Trans. from French by Roger Greaves. (Originally L'Ecran Démonique. 1952; revised 1965.) Berkeley: University of California Press, 1969.

Elsaesser, Thomas. "Social Mobility and the Fantastic." *Wide Angle* 5, no. 2 (1982): 14–25.

———. *Weimar Cinema and After: Germany's Historical Imaginary.* London: Routledge, 2000.

Elsaesser, Thomas, and Michael Wedel, eds. *The BFI Companion to German Cinema.* London: British Film Institute, 1999.

Esser, Michael. "Der Sprung über den großen Teich: Ewald Andre Duponts 'Variete.'" In *Das Ufa-Buch: Kunst und Krisen, Stars und Regisseure, Wirtschaft und Politik,* edited by Hans-Michael Bock and Michael Töteberg, 160–65. Frankfurt/M: Zweitausendeins, 1992.

Gerstein, Evelyn. Review of *Variety* (Ufa/Famous Players Lasky film), *New Republic,* 28 July 1926, 280–81.

Hall, Mordaunt. Review of *Variety* (Ufa/Famous Players Lasky film), *New York Times,* 28 June 1926, 15

Hansen, Miriam. "Decentric Perspectives: Kracauer's Early Writings on Film and Mass Culture." *New German Critique* 54 (fall 1991): 47–76.

———. "America, Paris, the Alps: Kracauer and Benjamin on Cinema and Modernity." In *Amerikanisierung: Traum und Alptraum im Deutschland des 20. Jahrhunderts,* edited by Alf Lüdtke, Inge Marßolek, and Adelheid von Saldern, 161–98. Stuttgart: Franz Steiner, 1996.

Hardt, Ursula. "Erich Pommer: Film Producer for Germany." Ph.D. diss., University of Iowa, 1989.

———. *From Caligari to California*. Providence, R I: Bergahn, 1997.

Holländer, Felix. *Der Eid des Stefan Huller (The Sins of the Fathers)*. 1912. Reprint, translated by Sara J. I. Lawson. New York: Payson & Clarke Ltd., 1927.

Huyssen, Andreas. *After the Great Divide: Modernism, Mass Culture, Post-modernism*. Bloomington: Indiana University Press, 1986.

Illustrierter Film-Kurier 7, no. 378 (1925): Ufa's promotional brochure for *Variety*.

Jacobsen, Wolfgang. *Erich Pommer: Ein Produzent macht Filmgeschichte*. Berlin: Argon, 1989.

Jelavich, Peter. *Berlin Cabaret*. Cambridge, Mass.: Harvard University Press, 1993.

Kaes, Anton, ed. *Kino-Debatte: Texte zum Verhältnis von Literatur und Film 1090–1929*. Tübingen: Max Niemeyer, 1978. English translation of the introduction: "The Debate about German Cinema: Charting a Controversy (1919–1929), trans. David J. Levin. *New German Critique* 40 (1987): 7–33.

———, ed. *Weimarer Republik: Manifeste und Dokumente zur deutschen Literatur 1918–1933*. Stuttgart: Metzler, 1983.

Koch, Gertrud. "Between Two Worlds: von Sternberg's The Blue Angel." In *German Film and Literature: Adaptations and Transformations*, edited by Eric Rentschler, 60–72. New York: Methuen, 1986.

Kracauer, Siegfried. *Die Angestellten*. (1929/30) In *Siegfried Kracauer. Schriften 1*, 205–304. Frankfurt/M: Suhrkamp, 1971.

———. "Girls und Krise." *Frankfurter Zeitung*, 27 May 1931.

———. *From Caligari to Hitler: A Psychological History of the German Film*. Princeton, N.J.: Princeton University Press, 1947.

———. "Das Ornament der Masse." In *Kracauer, Siegfried. Das Ornament der Masse*, 50–63. Frankfurt/M: Suhrkamp, 1977.

LaSalle, Mick. *Complicated Women: Sex and Power in Pre-Code Hollywood*. New York: St. Martin's Press, 2000.

Lethen, Helmut. *Verhaltenslehren der Kälte. Lebensversuche zwischen den Kriegen* Frankfurt: Suhrkamp, 1994. Translated by Don Reneau as *Cool Conduct: The Culture of Distance in Weimar Germany*. (Berkeley: University of California Press, forthcoming).

Lindner, Martin. *Leben in der Krise: Zeitromane der neuen Sachlichkeit und die intellektuelle Mentalität der klassischen Moderne*. Stuttgart: Metzler, 1994.

Luft, Herbert G. *Films in Review*, June–July 1977.

McCormick, Richard W. "From Caligari to Dietrich: Sexual, Social, and Cinematic Discourses in Weimar Film." *SIGNS: Journal of Women in Culture and Society* 18, no. 3 (1993): 640–68.

———. "Private Anxieties/Public Projections: 'New Objectivity,' Male Subjectivity, and Weimar Cinema." In *Women in German Yearbook*, vol. 10, 1–18, ed. By Patricia Herminghouse. Lincoln: Nebraska University Press, 1994.

Petro, Patrice. *Joyless Streets: Women and Melodramatic Representation in Weimar Germany*. Princeton, N.J.: Princeton University Press, 1989.

Reda, Ernst E. "Wie Varieté in Amerika aussieht," *Berliner Zeitung*, 9 July 1926, Mittag (noon edition).

"Rekord-Einnahmen für Varieté." *Lichtbild-Bühne* (Berlin), 21 July 1926.

Saunders, Thomas J. *Hollywood in Berlin: American Cinema and Weimar Germany.* Berkeley: University of California Press, 1994.

Staiger, Janet. *Perverse Spectators: The Practices of Film Reception.* New York: New York University Press, 2000.

"Stürmischer Erfolg von Varieté in New York." *Lichtbild-Bühne* (Berlin), 29 June 1926.

Theweleit, Klaus. *Männerphantasien.* 2 vols. Frankfurt: Roter Stern, 1977, 1978. Translated by Stephen Conway as *Male Fantasies.* Vols 1 and 2. (Minneapolis: University of Minnesota Press, 1987, 1989).

Trask. Review of *Varietee* [sic] (Ufa/Famous Players Lasky film), *Variety*, 20 January 1926, 40.

"Varieté: Der grosse deutsche Film." *Kinematograph* 979 (1925): 21.

"Varieté in 2 Fassungen." Review of *Variety* (Ufa/Famous Players Lasky film), *Film Kurier*, 23 November 1926.

Variety. Ufa's program for the film's premiere. Ufa-Palast am Zoo, 16 November 1925.

Wager, Jan B. *Dangerous Dames: Women and Representation in the Weimar Street Film and Film Noir.* Athens, Ohio: Ohio University Press, 1999.

Ward, Janet. *Weimar Surfaces: Urban Visual Culture in 1920s Germany.* Berkeley: University of California Press, 2001.

FILMOGRAPHY

The Blue Angel [Der blaue Engel]. Josef von Sternberg, Germany 1930. Available in VHS from Facets.

The Cabinet of Dr. Caligari [Das Cabinet des Dr. Caligari]. Robert Wiene, Germany 1919. Available in VHS or DVD from Facets.

Fräulein von Barnhelm [Das Fräulein von Barnhelm]. Hans Schweikart, Germany 1940.

Jew Suess [Jud Süß]. Veit Harlan, Germany 1940. Available in VHS from Facets.

The Last Laugh [Der letzte Mann]. F. W. Murnau, Germany 1924. Available in VHS from German Language Video Service.

Metropolis. Fritz Lang, Germany 1927. Available in VHS from German Language Video Service.

Morocco. Josef von Sternberg, United States 1930. Available in VHS from Facets.

The Old and the Young King [Der alte und der junge König]. Hans Steinhoff, Germany 1935. Available in VHS from German Language Video Service.

Pandora's Box [Die Büchse der Pandora]. G. W. Pabst, Germany 1929. Available in VHS from Facets.

The Street [Die Straße]. Karl Grune, Germany 1923. Available in 16 mm from West Glen or VHS from Facets.

Tragedy of the Prostitute [Dirnentragödie]. Bruno Rahn, Germany 1927.

Variety [Varieté]. E. A. Dupont, Germany 1925. American version (79 mins.) available on VHS from Facets. German version available from the Filmmuseum Berlin.

CHAPTER 4

"Postcards from the Edge"

Education to Tourism in the German Mountain Film

Nancy P. Nenno

"We Germans travel more than perhaps any other people on the face of the earth," declared August Ludwig Schlözer over two centuries ago. "We can count this prevailing taste for travel among our national character traits" (Spoke 13).[1] In light of German travel habits in the twentieth century, Schlözer seems prescient. From the rise of mass tourism at the start of the century through the West German travel wave *(Reisewelle)* of the 1950s to the postunification travel frenzy, in the twenty-first century Germans have emerged as the "European champions of travel" (Schäfer 7). This love of travel has been reflected in German film from its beginnings. In her article in this volume, Elizabeth Mittman plots the tropes of travel in German postwar film culture from the 1950s vacation film *(Ferienfilm)* to the VW- and road films of the 1970s, and finally to the postunification reinterpretations of these topoi in the 1990s. Yet tourism's driving force, what Dean MacCannell calls the "perpetual narrative of adventure" (van den Abbeele 11–12) is also a recurring theme in the earliest German films, from the educational travel shorts *(Kulturfilme)* to exotic adventure serials to the feature-length films set in faraway places.

Popular German cinema not only mimetically reproduces the travel experience but also has produced a self-reflexive meta-discourse about travel and tourism. At the height of the 1950s travel wave, Hans Magnus Enzensberger lamented that "there are few things in our civilization that have been so thoroughly mocked and so diligently criticized as tourism" (120), and devotees of popular German film are familiar with the much maligned figure of the German tourist. Films such as *German spoken [Man spricht deutsch]* (Hanns Christian Müller, 1991) and *Go Trabi Go* (Peter Timm, 1991) revel in the clichéd figure of the German tourist. Far from being a new trend in German cinema, this reflection on tourist practices first appeared in the 1920s within the German genre of the mountain film.[2]

Uttering the word *Bergfilm* among film scholars tends to elicit a chorus of negatives, as the mountain or alpine film *(Alpenfilm)* has fallen from the favored status it enjoyed during the Weimar Republic. Postwar film scholars have rarely diverged from the line of reasoning established by Siegfried Kracauer in his classic film history, *From Caligari to Hitler*.[3] Kracauer's assertion that the mountain film was "rooted in a mentality kindred to the Nazi spirit" (112) may be partly substantiated by the fact that the three most influential directors of the genre—Arnold Fanck, Luis Trenker, and Leni Riefenstahl—remained in Nazi Germany.[4] However, this does not explain the popular appeal the films enjoyed in their heyday, for the mountain film was enthusiastically received by spectators in Germany, Europe, and the New World.[5] The immense popularity of the genre suggests an alternative trajectory for the interpretation of the mountain film, and therewith a legacy for the genre within popular German cinema. This inheritance lies in the genre's simultaneous appeal to and self-conscious reflection on the history and practices of tourism. The typical mountain film stages a conflict between a nineteenth-century trope of alpine tourism and the rise of mass tourism in the early twentieth century, a conflict often presented as a diegetic confrontation between a mountain climber and an urban woman. Poised on tourism's historical fault line, the mountain film registers the tremors caused by the radical shift in tourist practices that accompanied modernity, offering sophisticated analyses and resounding critiques of emerging mass tourism.

Two mountain films of the Weimar Republic explicitly thematize the transformation of the alpine landscape by mass tourism. Both films represent the modern urban tourist as a negative figure, against which the romantic figure of the mountain climber emerges as the superior role model. In his third narrative mountain film, *The Holy Mountain [Der heilige Berg]* (Fanck, 1926), Arnold Fanck represents this shift from nineteenth- to twentieth-century models of tourism and landscape perception.

In the eyes of the urban tourist, the alpine landscape is transformed from inhospitable to accommodating, from turbulent to harmonious; no longer a site of spirituality and pilgrimage, the landscape is transformed by the gaze of mass tourism into a consumer item. Both the narrative storyline and the cinematography of *The Holy Mountain* attack the emerging phenomenon of tourism that values the alpine landscape in terms of its pleasure quotient. *The Holy Mountain* responds to this misrecognition by transforming the mountainscape into a protagonist and reinstating the mountain climber as the appropriate model of tourist perception.

As the mountain film began its slow fade from the screen, Leni Riefenstahl's *The Blue Light [Das blaue Licht]* (Riefenstahl, 1932) overtly thematized the inevitable legacy of mass tourism. The film meditates on tourism's destruction of the natural landscape, ultimately recuperating this loss through cultural tourism, a practice that embraces and enshrines the past. Like *The Holy Mountain*, the film elevates the mountain climber (for the first time a woman) to superior status, although in *The Blue Light* this figure is a lost model, consigned to the past. Riefenstahl's film creates a historical memory for alpine tourism. *The Blue Light* reflects on the practices and impulses underlying the mountain film genre itself as the mountain climber and the mountainscape become twinned objects of cultural tourism.

The mountain film was itself born of the spirit of tourism. The early decades of the twentieth century witnessed a dramatic rise of interest in the alpine regions. Images and stories of mountains appeared in educational short films, magazines, fiction, and popular nonfiction (Rapp 18). In the context of Germany's rapid modernization and urbanization, the "flight into nature" articulated two centuries earlier by Rousseau acquired a distinctly anti-urban flavor. The city appeared as the locus of illness and corruption, the natural mountain landscape as the cure for the cosmopolitan's disease. "A sojourn in nature is ennobling," maintained one critic. "The city's dismal walls are the birthplaces of the most awful crimes, of ultimate depravity" (Cornel 11). The creator and most prolific producer of the mountain film, Arnold Fanck, repeatedly argued that his films responded to escapist impulses in the urban population, and most especially to their "desire for light, sunshine and snow and mountains, that is to say, nature, which he [the film spectator] mostly does without" (Jacobs, "Bergfilm" 30). From his earliest alpine films, Fanck contributed to the transformation of the alpine regions into a popular tourist destination, first in his skiing and sport films and later in the narrative mountain films.

In the context of twentieth-century alpine tourism, Fanck's melodramatic mountain films must be seen as dialogic partners with his comedic ski films *(Ski- und Sportfilme)*. Immediately following the First World War, Fanck created this subgenre of educational film which appealed to touristic sensibilities and urban fashions. His first full-length film was *The Miracle of Skis [Die Wunder des Schneeschuhs]* (Fanck, 1920) which introduced the relatively new sport of skiing. While the sport had initially been rejected by the tight-knit community of alpine sport enthusiasts as a degenerate, bastardized form of alpine athletics, its military usefulness during the First World War led to its widespread acceptance in the postwar period (Rapp 44–45). The success of *Miracle of Skis* and its sequel, *A Ski Chase through Engadin [Eine Fuchsjagd auf Skiern durchs Engadin]* (Fanck, 1922), significantly contributed to the popularity of skiing, also serving as advertisements for Fanck's own Arlberg ski school.

While the mountain film and the ski films both thematize a physical, touristic encounter with the alpine landscape, they radically differ in how they represent the natural landscape. In the ski films, the alpinescape is a backdrop for the sport of skiing, thereby transforming the landscape into what Leslie Stephen disparagingly dubbed "the playground of Europe." These films explicitly play to the rise of sport tourism in the Alps by thematizing the familiar trope of the city-slicker-as-tourist. In *The White Frenzy [Der weiße Rausch]* (Fanck, 1931), Leni Riefenstahl plays "Leni," a woman from Berlin overcome with the desire to learn how to ski. From her initial bumbling attempts to her emergence as a consummate athlete, her comedic performance gently encourages the audience in its pursuit of the sport. In contrast, the mountain films are melodramatic tragedies that invoke tourism's narrative of adventure. The mountain film exhorts the sport tourist to temper his pleasures and historicize his gaze by modeling his perception on the awe-struck, respectful, romantic gaze of the mountain climber.[6] It is no accident that critics and audiences alike praised the splendid imagery of these films, for Fanck dramatically transformed the landscape from a passive setting into an active participant in the story whereby the mountains acquire the status of a dramatis personae. Left-wing film theorist and coauthor of *The Blue Light* Béla Balázs praised this casting of the mountainscape in the role of protagonist. "Is it then possible to represent greatness other than in contrast to the relative insignificance of human daily life?" he asks in "The Case of Dr. Fanck" (1931). Balázs argues that the mountain film counters visual consumption of the landscape because nature's power cannot simply be visualized; rather, "we must experience it in order to feel it, we must suffer it so that we perceive it" (Balázs E11, E12). If recreation and pleasure are the underlying motifs of Fanck's ski films, self-discovery and suffering properly belong to the tragic mountain films. In Fanck's oeuvre, competing models of alpine tourism are coded generically: the comic ski films respond to and thematize the desires of the pleasure-seeking mass tourist of the early twentieth century, while the melodramatic mountain films correspond to the romantic legacy of the nineteenth-century mountain climber. This historical conflict of tourist practices in the Alps informs the main narrative conflict in all of Fanck's mountain films.

At the heart of *The Holy Mountain*, and indeed the originary moment of the entire mountain film genre, is the radical transformation of the alpine landscape brought about by Germany's rapid industrialization and modernization in the late nineteenth century.[7] In 1895, the preeminent sociologist of modernity, Georg Simmel, ruminated on the effect that modern transportation, in particular the railway, was having on the alpine landscape.

> A process which has been in the making for decades in the Swiss transport system has recently been completed. It is something more than an economic analogy to call it the wholesale opening up and enjoyment of nature. Destinations that were previously only accessible by remote walks can now be reached by railways, which are appearing at an ever-increasing rate. Railways have been built where the gradients are too steep for roads to be constructed, as in the Muerren or Wanger Alps. The railway-line up the Eiger appears to have been finalized, and the same number of climbers who have scaled this difficult peak can now be brought up in a single day by rail. The Faustian wish, "I stand before you, nature, a solitary individual" is evermore rarely realized and so increasingly rarely declared. (Simmel 95)

While Simmel admits to feeling some nostalgia for this "Faustian" ideal, he concludes that the consequent democratization and liberation of travel more than compensates for the loss of this earlier model. Where travel had once been considered a birthright, a leisure and educational activity reserved for the middle and upper classes, modern systems of transportation permitted "countless people who previously were barred because of their lack of strength and means . . . to enjoy nature" (95).

Unlike Simmel, who celebrates the democratic spirit and "socialistic leveling" of mass travel, *The Holy Mountain* embraces the elitism implicit in the figure of the "Faustian" tourist who is characterized by his solitary and intimate relationship with the alpinescape. *The Holy Mountain* reaches back into the history of alpine tourism and reinstates the figure of the master climber as the ideal alpine tourist.[8] In this film, the historical figure of the mountain climber, for whom the mountains are neither a consumer item nor a recreational playground, is preserved and elevated. He appears as a Parzifal figure (Mumelter 87), the mountains his proving ground and his grail. In this celebration of mountain climbing, Fanck rejects fashionable Weimar-era alpine tourism as degenerate and superficial, and in so doing he also creates a much loved and often lampooned trope of popular German cinema: the modern tourist.

In *The Holy Mountain*, gender represents the unbridgeable division that separates the romantic tourism of the nineteenth century and consumerist practices of the twentieth, as the former are explicitly masculinized and the latter feminized. The film's prologue establishes this gender dichotomy as it opens on the image of the landscape as metaphor, a screen onto which eternal values and conflicts are projected. Barefoot on the sharp rocks and dressed only in a sheer tunic, Leni Riefenstahl, in her film debut, performs "Diotima's Dance to the Sea." Riefenstahl's performance invokes modern dance's self-conscious thematization of nature and underscores the affinity between her femininity and the ocean. Diotima gestures and sways, her body echoing the water's recurring rhythm, as the film crosscuts between images of the ocean and the dancer. The restlessness of the ocean marks her femininity as inconsistent and restive, associations that persist throughout *The Holy Mountain* to create the narrative conflict of the film's plotline.

The dancer's name, borrowed from Friedrich Hölderlin's *Hyperion*, announces the film's debt to the literary and artistic traditions of romanticism, which swathed the Alps with "a web of poetic associations" (Stephen 268). From its references to Hölderlin and Novalis to its iconographic quotations of Caspar David Friedrich, the genre of the mountain film is rife with self-reflexive references to German literary and visual traditions (Rentschler 32–34; Jacobs, "Visuelle Traditionen" 30). For Anton Kaes, this romanticism, "the subjugation of politics and history in the face of the enormity of nature and the cosmos," constitutes the "German" quality of the mountain film (76). However, romanticism is also the historical origin of modern tourism. Enzensberger has argued that "tourism is nothing other than the attempt to realize the dream that Romanticism projected onto the distant and far away," a dream that was first realized by mountain climbers (125, 126). The mountain climber's search for the uncommon, the elemental, and the pristine is a narrative of adventure that synthesizes the desires of the nineteenth-century romantic artist and the twentieth-century urban tourist, a combination that elevates him to the status of ideal alpine tourist in *The Holy Mountain.*

Diotima's fantasy image of the distant mountains in the prologue firmly establishes the metaphorical masculinity of the romantic gaze and the alpine landscape. A mountainscape is superimposed at the edge of the ocean, and the intertitle reads, "And Diotima dances, delighting in her desire for Him, whom she dreamed on the highest mountain peak." Diotima's dream conjures the image of a man silhouetted against the mountains, whose lack of motion and set, determined stance signify the film's vision of the metaphorical oneness of masculinity and mountain. The male figure and the mountains stand united, rooted and stable in static superiority over the constant motion of the sea. Subsequent shots further underscore the masculinity of this natural world as they frame The Friend (Luis Trenker) and his companion, Vigo (Ernst Petersen) side by side atop the mountain. The intimacy of their comradeship is represented in a series of medium two-shots, while the subsequent narrative disruption caused by Diotima is prefigured by crosscuts between the opposed and gendered landscapes. Later in the film, The Friend's mother sadly predicts that "the mountains and the ocean shall never marry," thereby reiterating the metaphorical meanings attached to the narrative figures of The Friend and Diotima. The prologue effectively establishes a visual and narrative link between opposed landscapes and gendered bodies, transforming their differences into an unresolvable conflict.

The masculinized mountainscape is an enduring trope of the mountain film, and one that Fanck established with his first two films of the genre, *Struggle with the Mountain [Im Kampf mit dem Berg]* (Fanck, 1921) and *Peak of Fate [Berg des Schicksals]* (Fanck, 1924). Although Fanck steadfastly maintained that his mountain films were apolitical, the overt association of the alpine world with masculinity, heroism, and conquest align the

figure of the mountain climber with other, similarly charged figures, such as the explorer and the soldier (Ellis 80; Nenno 315–17).
Loyalty, trust, and self-sacrifice are central tenets of mountain
climbing, and the sport was believed to educate young men to
self-reliance, comradeship, and allegiance to the fatherland
(Stocker 439–40). Fanck repeatedly invokes these traits of the
mountain climber, imbuing his films with a homosocial, military
spirit. The legacy of Germany's humiliation at Versailles is an
ever-present specter on the Fanckian mountainscape; war veterans and national heroes reemerge in the postwar period as athletic
stars who share the screen with champion athletes such as Hannes Schneider and Guzzi Lantschner.[9] Ernst Udet, the decorated
German flyer, appeared in several of Fanck's mountain films, including *The White Hell of Pitz Palu [Die weiße Hölle von Piz
Palü]* (Fanck, 1929), *Storms over Mont Blanc [Stürme über dem
Montblanc]* (Fanck, 1930), and *SOS Iceberg [SOS Eisberg]* (Fanck,
1933). A legacy of military development of aerial reconnaissance
during the First World War, the spectacular cinematography—
panoramas and aerial perspectives—further serves to transform
the mountainscape into a surrogate war-scape. A dominant characteristic of the mountain film, this association of the alpinescape and masculinity is woven into the very fabric of the genre.

The gendered qualities of the two natural landscapes established by the prologue extend to the film's diegesis to define
the tourist practices of the mountain climber and the modern
tourist. Following the prologue, the story finds Diotima living at
the Grand Hotel in a mountain village. The Friend and Vigo fall
in love with her as she performs her interpretive dances of nature,
paeans to the landscape bearing titles such as "Alpine Blossoms."
When Diotima and The Friend meet on the mountainside the
next day, their conversation illustrates the fundamental differences in their natures and their perceptions of the alpinescape.
While Diotima freely rhapsodizes about the alpine world, The
Friend uses his words sparingly. When she suggests that it must
be very beautiful at the heights, he tersely responds, "Beautiful—
hard—and dangerous." To her question about what is sought up
there, he replies, "One's self." When asked what she is seeking on
the mountains, she answers, "Beauty!" The Friend's awareness of
the double nature of the landscape's beauty contrasts sharply
with Diotima's emasculated image of nature. Whereas the alpine
world represents a physical and spiritual encounter for the mountain climber, the modern tourist considers the landscape a consumer good, an item to be desired and visually devoured—a
practice established and encouraged by cinematic practice.

From its beginnings, cinema has always been deeply entwined with the discourse of travel, often cast as an alternative or substitute form. Similar to the nineteenth century's magic lantern show, the travelogues and exotic adventure films of the early twentieth century provided a vicarious experience of travel (Barber 68). Cinema, modernity's step-brother, feeds off the same desires that drive travel and tourism: the wish to escape from daily life and to experience new places, with the photographic image guaranteeing the authenticity and immediacy of the experience. While Fanck appeals to spectators' desire for images of the alpine regions, he does not simply feed the scopophilic desire and "sight sacralization" that MacCannell has argued is the mark of the tourist (MacCannell 44; van den Abbeele 4). His cinematography and editing combat the predisposition of the sightseer (and the filmgoer) toward distanced contemplation and visual consumption. Fanck experiments with the kinetic possibilities of film, dramatically altering conventional spectatorial positionings. In the mountain films, the virtual tourist becomes an active (if virtual) participant in the on-screen action. Fanck's innovative mobilization of cameras, the extreme physical exertions of both actors and crew, and his experimental montage techniques suture the spectator into the action, creating the illusion of participation. The film's audience is transported from the theater to the mountain slopes in such a way that "the intoxications experienced by every sportsman overwhelm the spectator of these images" (Frigo 1)—techniques perfected by Riefenstahl in her monumental sport film, *Olympia* (Riefenstahl, 1938). As the "director of glaciers and avalanches and storms," Fanck rejects the distanced, objective images of "science and postcards" in favor of a physical experience of the alpine landscape (Balázs E12).

The tourist as visual consumer of images is a recurring trope of alpine tourism in the 1920s. In his poem "Vornehme Leute, 1200 Meter hoch," satirist Erich Kästner lampoons those tourists who visually consume the landscape without ever physically experiencing it.

> They sit inside the Grand Hotels
> In raptures over nature
> Their knowledge of the land outside
> derived from picture postcards.
> They sit inside the Grand Hotels
> And talk a lot of sport.

When finally they leave, in furs
They even make it to the door
And once again depart.[10]

In *The Holy Mountain*, Fanck's criticism of the practices of modern tourism is particularly evident in an odd sequence that departs from the narrative story line. This extended, unmotivated hiatus from the plot features Diotima overtly modeling tourist behavior. Seated at the window of her hotel room, Diotima is presented as the visual consumer of an enticingly harmonious view. The composition of the shot, a perfectly balanced frame-within-a-frame, reinforces the harmony of the sight and signals the *mise-en-abyme* of tourist discourse which distances the spectator from the landscape. Resembling the display windows of the department store or "spectacular" on-screen panoramas, the shot illustrates how modern tourist rhetoric and practices aestheticize the natural landscape. Cinema and tourism collaborate to smooth out the wrinkles and soften the edges of the alpine landscape, presenting it as a consumer item. Diotima's encounter with nature in the following sequence might be considered the first overt parody of the tourist in German cinema.

Diotima's walk in the mountains is Fanck's saccharine commentary on the inevitable outcome of a steady diet of postcard images. She emerges from the hotel and throws open her arms as if to embrace all of nature. Donning a modernized dirndl, Diotima thrusts herself into the alpine world, enacting the tourist desire to "share in the real life of the place" (MacCannell 96). In a series of highly artificial parallel edits, Diotima shares the mountain landscape with the alpine peasants, nostalgic, sentimental images of the mountain folk at work and play. She frolics across fields, dances to a shepherd's harmonica, caresses some blossoms, and hugs a lamb. Fanck openly mocks her naiveté—a fact not lost on audiences and reviewers who criticized Riefenstahl's performance (Fanck 164–65). This is a calculated move on Fanck's part; the audience should recognize the trope of the urban tourist but reject this figure in favor of identifying with the romantic tourist represented by The Friend.

Deep respect and intimate familiarity mark the relationship between The Friend and the mountain world in *The Holy Mountain*. True to the pseudoreligious invocation of the film's title, The Friend sanctifies the mountainscape as holy ground, a sacralization represented by the cathedral of ice in which The

Friend fantasizes his marriage to Diotima. The all-encompassing, godlike presence of nature is translated into visual terms; The Friend and Diotima shrink into insignificance as they walk down the aisle of the cathedral, dwarfed by the imposing, glittering walls of ice. This studio creation, which claimed a third of Fanck's budget, concretely represents The Friend's conception of man's relationship to the mountain landscape. Originally titled "*His* Holy Mountain," the film showcases the physical and spiritual connection between the mountain and the mountain climber, a relationship that appears almost symbiotic. The encounter with the landscape reveals the inner essence of the mountain climber's being, and in turn he alone can penetrate the inner secrets of the mountain.

Modern tourism's disruption of this idyllic symbiosis is represented diegetically by the narrative love triangle in *The Holy Mountain*. While The Friend is away, Vigo cajoles Diotima into attending the ski races. When he wins, she permits Vigo to place his head in her lap, unaware that The Friend witnesses the scene. Enraged by her apparent inconsistency, he flees to his mountain sanctuary, despite the storm that rages. Vigo accompanies him and reveals that he was the man that The Friend had seen with Diotima. The two struggle, and Vigo slips from his precarious purchase. Overcome with remorse, The Friend holds Vigo suspended through the night, his undying loyalty to his friend figured as the rope that connects them. With the dawn, his grip loosens and they plunge—together—to their deaths. The film thus resolves the narrative conflict introduced by the urban woman by reinvoking the code of masculinity that properly belongs to the mountain world.

The ideal of the masculine mountain climber clearly reigns over the feminized modern tourist in *The Holy Mountain*. When Diotima receives the news that the two men have ascended the mountain's dangerous north wall, she pleads with her audience for help, but the tuxedoed and pomaded male audience members avoid her gaze. They are effeminate and degenerate when compared to the hearty mountain men who immediately embark on a rescue mission. The deaths of The Friend and Vigo are not meaningless, for they dramatically reiterate The Friend's prophetic remarks about the danger of the mountains and catalyze a shift in the perspective of the modern tourist. The final shots of Diotima illustrate that she has revised her simplistic vision of nature. Finding herself the victim of nature's power rather than the consumer of its beauty, she recants her modernity and dons the veil that visually links her to the rural mountain folk. Within the diegesis, the film has accomplished its task: it has "educated" the modern tourist to the realities of the mountain world.

The Holy Mountain clearly thematizes an anxiety experienced by many mountain climbers that mass tourism to the Alps would threaten their solitude. Henry Hoek, a leading proponent of alpine sports, acknowledged this fear, noting that "we feel wounded by their [the tourists'] presence and behaviour. They disturb our joy and pleasure" (15). Ironically, the mountain film itself contributed to the enthusiasm with which many urbanites greeted alpine sports, and Fanck's films were often criticized by mountain climbers for being inaccurate and misleading, and for luring unprepared neophytes into the mountains. "And afterwards we wonder," cynically remarked one reviewer, "when the number of accidents [in the alpine regions] increases" (Kreimeier E8).

The most famous tourist to answer the siren call of the mountains was Leni Riefenstahl, for whom the mountain film was indeed her introduction to the alpine landscape. In her memoirs, she recalls her first encounter with the mountain film, when, en route to a doctor's appointment, she became entranced by the poster image for Peak of Destiny. The image, which showed "steep walls of rock, . . . [and] the man swinging from one wall to the next," drew her, as if hypnotized, to the cinema.

> The very first images of mountains, clouds, alpine slopes and towering rock, fascinated me. I was experiencing a world that I did not know, for I had never seen such mountains. I knew them only from postcards, on which they looked rigid and lifeless. But here, on the screen, they were alive, mysterious, and more entrancingly beautiful than I had ever dreamed mountains could be. As the film went on I became more and more spellbound. I was so excited that even before it ended I had made up my mind to get to know those mountains. (Riefenstahl 41–42)

Riefenstahl's passionate embrace of the mountain world led her to star in many of Fanck's mountain films in the late 1920s and early 1930s and to write and direct her own mountain film. Like Fanck's Holy Mountain, Riefenstahl's debut film, The Blue Light, also shrouds the mountains in mystery and elevates the sanctity of the mountain climber's intimate relationship to the mountains. Yet while Fanck dismisses the consumerism of modern mass tourism, Riefenstahl seeks to alter the course of these practices by historicizing the modern gaze. In this way, she transforms the consumption inherent in tourism into a thoughtful, respectful gaze.

> Tourism changes the face of the landscape, it extends the culti-
> vated area. By constructing pathways, mountain paths and brid-
> ges, signs and so forth, by putting up plaques and benches at the
> most beautiful sites, by building hotels, inns and shelters, nature
> is robbed of precisely that which the stranger is so often seeking:
> an untouched quality and solitude. . . . Much of a people's singu-
> larity is lost as the result of tourism. (Sputz 291, 293)

If Arnold Fanck's mountain films sought to defend the alpine regions from the ravages of mass tourism, Leni Riefenstahl's *Blue
Light* assumes that the singularity and pristine quality of the
landscape has already been irrevocably compromised. While films
like *The Holy Mountain* intuit the ultimate outcome of mass
tourism, Riefenstahl directs a film that is a panegyric to a landscape already lost. In the narrative structure, the cinematography,
and the editing, Riefenstahl reinscribes the sanctified mountainscape as a past ideal. *The Blue Light* deliberately mobilizes iconographic and literary signifiers of romanticism to swathe the
landscape in mystery and mysticism. From the title's self-reflexive allusion to the "Blue Flower" in Novalis's *Heinrich von Ofter-
dingen* to explicit quotations of the powerful landscapes of
Caspar David Friedrich, Riefenstahl's film transforms the Dolo-
mite landscape into a dreamscape.

　　Tourist practices and the tourist gaze are not only a
theme of the film but also the metadiscourse that structures the
narrative of *The Blue Light*. The first cut of the film, which was
screened in 1932, opens with the arrival of a young couple in a
small, out-of-the-way village in the Sarn Valley.[11] When they in-
quire about the history of Santa Maria, the innkeeper shows them
a book titled "Historia della Junta." With the opening of the book,
the mode of storytelling alters from verbal to visual as flashbacks
take over. The tourists of the frame narrative are replaced by a
Viennese painter named Vigo (Mathias Wieman) who is visiting
the village in the mid-nineteenth century. On nights of the full
moon, the mountain peak above Santa Maria glows with a blue
light—the result of moonlight striking crystals—which acts as a
siren call to the young men of the village. A wild young mountain
girl named Junta (Riefenstahl) is the only one who can safely
climb the mountain, and as a result, the villagers have branded
her a witch, casting her out of village society. Vigo befriends her,
believing that if he can show the villagers a safe route to the
mountain grotto and its crystals he can demystify Monte Cristallo and recuperate Junta. One night he follows her and returns

with a map that allows the villagers to mine the crystals, thereby destroying the grotto. Junta discovers the pillaged cave and, in despair, falls to her death.

Traveling back in time, *The Blue Light* presents the historical changes in the alpine economy and the tragic loss of the landscape that accompany tourism. The film opens with the confrontation between the modern tourist and a landscape already devoured by tourism. The young couple arrives by automobile, dressed in touring attire. As Rentschler has pointed out, the androgynous quality of their clothing marks their modernity, distinguished from the clearly gendered costumes of the villagers (42). Once the car stops, the couple is besieged by the village's children who press them to purchase souvenirs in the form of large crystals and gilt-edged cameos bearing the image of a young woman. As they enter the inn's dark interior, the couple is again confronted with Junta's image, but this appears to be the "original" on which the souvenirs are modeled. The cameo of Junta acquires the significance of a holy icon as it is lit from below as if by a votive candle and placed near a crystal under a glass bell. Thus enshrined and contained, these relics offer themselves to the interpretive powers of the tourist gaze.

The Blue Light illuminates and reflects on the ways in which modern tourism represents "an ideological framing of history, nature and tradition" (MacCannell, quoted in Herbert 1). The village's history is controlled, encapsulated, and displayed for tourist consumption—a strategy that Riefenstahl adopts in the narrative framework that encases Junta's story within a frame story. The film thus exhibits and self-consciously enacts the practice of "heritage tourism," which seeks to restore an original culture for the pleasure and education of tourists. The pedagogical function of this cultural or heritage tourism is represented by the history book, a guidebook that ushers the tourist into the past. Heritage tourism feeds upon the tourist desire for authenticity, which is often found at sites of loss. Much as early alpine tourists were drawn to scenes of mountain-climbing tragedies, Junta's death is transformed by the villagers into the lifeblood that sustains their economy.[12] Simulacra produced by tourist discourse for circulation and consumption, the souvenirs hawked by the children elevate Junta to the patron saint of Santa Maria. However, their status as holy icons does not wash away the grave sin of the village, which paid for its heritage with blood.

Like the nineteenth-century artists and mapmakers

whose images of the Alps were instrumental in creating the alpine tourist industry, the artist in *The Blue Light* is also called to task for his complicity in the destruction of the landscape. Although he intends merely to observe and paint the life he finds in the mountains, his presence and his actions ultimately catalyze the destruction of that landscape. Vigo's decision to provide the villagers with a map to the grotto ultimately destroys the delicate balance of the native culture. The diegetic stand-in for the film spectator and the modern tourist, Vigo's act dramatizes the destruction that the outsider's thoughtlessness can wreak upon the natural landscape.

As Elisabeth Bronfen has argued, the image of the beautiful female corpse is always a double figure (xi), and in *The Blue Light*, Junta's broken body stands in for the landscape that has been metaphorically raped and pillaged by the greedy villagers. Reversing the gender economies of the Fanckian mountain film, *The Blue Light* endows the alpine landscape with a metaphorical femininity, which allows it to appear not as an adversary but as a sacrifice. The landscape-as-victim is represented by Junta; she embodies the beautiful, untouched quality of the mountains as well as the desirability of the crystal grotto. The village boys' attraction to the blue light is simultaneously an attraction to Junta, but, like the blue light, Junta cannot be approached or possessed, although many, including Vigo, attempt to do so.

Ultimately, Junta's dead body conceals the desire that led to her death, namely the villagers' driving wish to control and exploit the economic value of the landscape. The young men who are martyred on Monte Cristallo die because of a fatal flaw in their desires: their wish to conquer and possess the blue light. Unlike the mountain climber, here represented by Junta, who respects and worships at the altar of nature, the young men deviate from and transgress against this ideal relationship with the mountains. An early scene in the film dramatizes the deep division between the villagers and Junta, illustrated by the value each assigns to the mountain's crystals. Soon after Vigo's arrival in Santa Maria, Junta appears in the village to sell a basket of berries. A village boy knocks it from her hand, exposing an enormous crystal that lies on the ground amid the spilled fruit. The crystal attracts the attention of a merchant, who tries to take it from her, without success. In this sequence, it becomes clear that Junta perceives only the intrinsic beauty of the crystal, while the villagers translate the image into the abstract and arbitrary value of money. Despite the nominal admission of guilt in the final pages of the village's history book, Santa Maria ultimately profits from Junta's death. Her life is the price for the grotto's opening and her posthumous sacralization gives the villagers a story to sell. In this way, the film narrativizes the historical despoiling of the landscape and its reconsecration in tourist rhetoric and practices.

The Blue Light invokes the similarity between tourism and film spectatorship, encouraging the film's audience to reflect on the nature and effects of their own viewing practices. By using diegetic stand-ins—the young couple of the frame narrative and Vigo in the main story—Riefenstahl implicates the audience in destruction of the alpine landscape. The editing transforms the spectator into an accomplice of modern tourism, suturing the spectator's gaze to that of the couple in a series of point-of-view shots. As the couple enters the inn, the audience views the image of Junta and the glass-encased crystal at the same moment and from the same position as the diegetic tourists. However, as the innkeeper opens the "Historia," the audience perspective diverges from that of the couple; here the spectator gains direct access to Junta's story through the flashback structure of the film and Vigo's perspective. Within this embedded story the cinematic apparatus permits the audience to identify with both Vigo and Junta. While the point-of-view panorama of Santa Maria that opens the story links the spectator to Vigo, in the climactic sequence in which Junta answers the call of the blue light, eyeline matches and over-the-shoulder shots align the spectator's gaze with that of Junta. This unmediated access to the story is, however, as illusory as the blue light; the fairytale is itself a ghost, the projection of light through the translucent material of film. The projector's light briefly resuscitates a mediated past for the consumption of the film's spectator, completing a circuit of past and present that imitates the historicizing gesture of heritage tourism. The film concludes with a return to the present and to the modern tourists, who appear sobered by the story they have heard. The reflections on tourism in *The Blue Light* contextualize their respectful and thoughtful stance, and their "education to tourism" presents a model for the film's spectator.

In light of the pedagogical message implicit in Riefenstahl's film, it is indeed ironic that she seems unaware of her own imitation of the destructive cycle of tourism in her postwar photographic oeuvre. The narrative of adventure that characterizes tourism is evident in Riefenstahl's travels in Africa and her "discovery" of the Nuba. Riefenstahl's self-styled search for beauty eerily echoes Diotima's desires in *The Holy Mountain*. As a photographer, Riefenstahl links the tourist and the explorer; she discovers new and pristine destinations and peoples, and thereby initiates their destruction. Despite her admonition to tourists in *The Blue Light*, she appears to believe that her photographs merely "capture" the Nuba before the moment of corruption, rather than considering the possibility that her own "sightseeing" helped to bring about the destruction of this culture (Schiff 291).

In a similar fashion, contemporary audiences of the mountain film appear to have missed the "education to tourism" that underlies this genre. Presaging the voices of postwar critics, Weimar-era audiences rejected the mountain film's story lines as formulaic and trite, expressions of "kitsch and struggle" ("Beben-der Berg" [review] 10), while simultaneously glorying in the spectacle of the alpine landscape. However, within the historical context of modern tourism, the "idolatry of glaciers and rocks," which Kracauer diagnosed as "symptomatic of an antirationalism on which the Nazis could capitalize" (112), acquires a different visage. The mountain film reveals itself to be a deeply conservative genre in which the sacralization of the landscape represents a reaction to the explosion of mass tourism in the Alps. Arnold Fanck's *Holy Mountain* accomplishes this by reestablishing the romantic gaze and the nineteenth-century ideal of the mountain climber, while Leni Riefenstahl turns to the rhetoric of heritage tourism in *The Blue Light* in order to historicize and contextualize the landscape for the modern tourist. Not merely reproductions of tourism and travel, the films reflect on the history of tourism and its convergence with cinema. Although predominantly tragic melodramas, the mountain film harbors the seeds of later genres of popular German film, including the nostalgic 1950s vacation films, the adventurous 1970s road films, and the parodic comedies of the 1990s. It is the mountain film's simultaneous appeal to tourist desires and its self-reflexive critique of tourist practices that permits the charting of an alternative—and popular—legacy for the German mountain film.

NOTES

1. Unless otherwise noted, all translations are my own. Early versions of this essay were presented at the Northeast Modern Language Association meeting in 1997 and the South Atlantic Modern Language Association meeting. The essay has benefited immeasurably from the editorial and

substantive comments of Michael Marano, the volume's editors, Randall Halle and Margaret McCarthy, and the anonymous reviewers.

2. Theories of tourism that inform this article are drawn from Enzensberger, MacCannell, van den Abbeele, Feifer, Buzard, and Hennig.

3. After an extended hiatus in which the mountain film all but disappeared, Klaus Kreimeier reestablished discussion of the genre with his seminar "Fanck-Trenker-Riefenstahl" at the Stiftung Deutsche Kinemathek in 1972. In the United States, Susan Sontag reacted to the rehabilitation and recuperation of Leni Riefenstahl by the women's movement in her seminal essay, "Fascinating Fascism." Here she reiterates Kracauer's line of reasoning, arguing that the mountain film read like "an anthology of proto-Nazi sentiments" (76). More recently, Eric Rentschler and Christian Rapp have self-consciously reflected on the postwar reception history of mountain film in their cultural analyses of the genre. See Kracauer 110–12, 155, 258–62, 270; Sontag 75–77; Rapp 11–19; and Rentschler 34–36, 38–40.

4. Of the three directors, Leni Riefenstahl is the most deeply implicated in the Nazi film industry. She made two short documentary films for the party, *Victory of Faith [Sieg des Glaubens]* (1933) and *Day of Freedom— Our Army [Tag der Freiheit: Unsere Wehrmacht]* (1935) before directing *Triumph of the Will [Triumph des Willens]* (1935) and the two-part *Olympiad [Olympia I: Fest der Völker and Olympia II: Fest der Schönheit]* (1938). See also Ray Müller's documentary *The Wonderful, Horrible Life of Leni Riefenstahl [Die Macht der Bilder]* (Müller, 1993). Arnold Fanck made six films during the Third Reich. Despite a somewhat ambiguous relationship to National Socialism (Leimgruber 3), Luis Trenker also completed six films under the Nazis, all of which, Rapp has argued, draw heavily on the generic conventions, if not always the setting, of the alpine film (248).

5. A large number of the German mountain films were exported to the United States, including: *Peak of Fate [Berg des Schicksals]* (Fanck, 1924; U.S. release in 1925), *The Holy Mountain [Der heilige Berg]* (Fanck, 1926; U.S. release in 1927 as *Peaks of Destiny*), *The Struggle for the Matterhorn [Der Kampf ums Matterhorn]* (Mario Bonnard, 1928; U.S. release in 1929), *The White Hell of Pitz Palu [Die weiße Hölle von Piz Palü]* (Fanck, 1929; U.S. release in 1930, also called *Prisoners of the Mountain*), *Grenzfeuer* (Hanns Beck-Gaden, 1929; U.S. release in 1936 under the German title), *Storms over Mont Blanc [Stürme über dem Montblanc]* (Fanck, 1930; U.S. release in 1931, also called "Avalanche"), *The Son of the White Mountains [Der Sohn der weißen Berge]* (Trenker, 1930; U.S. release in 1933), *The White Frenzy [Der weiße Rausch]* (Fanck, 1931, U.S. release in 1938 as "The Ski Chase"), *The Blue Light [Das blaue Licht]* (Riefenstahl, 1932; U.S. release in 1934), *The Rebel [Der Rebell]* (Trenker, 1932; U.S. release in 1933), *The Emperor of California [Der Kaiser von Kalifornien]* (Trenker, 1936; U.S. release in 1937). Following their proven success with American audiences, Hollywood producers sought to stake a claim in this genre. G. W. Pabst returned to Germany from Hollywood in order to oversee the studio shots on *The White Hell of Pitz Palu*, and Fanck's Greenland film, *SOS. Iceberg [SOS Eisberg]* (Fanck, 1933) was financed by German émigré Carl Laemmle at Universal Studios.

6. John Urry has characterized the "romantic gaze" as "Solitary / Sustained Immersion / Gaze involving vision, awe, aura" (22).

7. On the historical development of alpine tourism during the first

decades of the twentieth century, see Rapp 23–70; Hyde; Benesch; Bing, "Alpinismus"; Bing, "Nutzen"; Ogilvie 190–93; Wagner, "Die Alpen"; Matznetter; Wagner, "Das Gletschererlebnis"; and Keitz 52–55, 66.

8. On the history of mountain climbing and the figure of the mountain climber, see Rapp 23–70; Schama 383–525.

9. Luis Trenker's films such as *The Doomed Battalion [Berge in Flammen]* (Trenker, 1931) and *The Rebel [Der Rebell]* (Trenker, 1932) explicitly thematize war. Guiseppe Becce's musical theme, "We Muskateers of the Mountains" ["Wir Muskateere der Berge"], echoes throughout *The Son of the White Mountains [Der Sohn der weißen Berge]* (1930) and *The Doomed Battalion*, contributing to the construction of the mountain world as homosocial space.

10. Quoted in Neubach 38–39, albeit under the wrong title. Neubach calls the poem "Feine Leute, 1200 Meter hoch."

11. The film appeared as three different cuts from the years 1932, 1938, and 1951. See Rentschler 45–46; Hinton 23.

12. Rentschler offers a provocative reading of *The Blue Light* as a vampire film (37–38, 45–46).

WORKS CITED

Abbeele, Georges van den. "Sightseers: The Tourist as Theorist." *Diacritics* 10 (1980): 3–14.

Balázs, Béla. "Der Fall Dr. Fanck." 1931. Reprint, in *Fanck-Trenker-Riefenstahl: Der deutsche Bergfilm und seine Folgen*, by Klaus Kreimeier, E11–14, Berlin: Stiftung Deutsche Kinemathek, 1972.

Barber, X. Theodore. "The Roots of Travel Cinema." *Film History* 5 (1993): 68–84.

Benesch, Erwin. "Die Bergsteigerbewegung in den letzten Jahren." *Der Bergsteiger* 2 (1930): 122–24.

Bing, Walter. "Der Alpinismus und seine Stellung im Sportsystem unserer Zeit." *Der Bergsteiger* 6 (1930): 369–71.

———. "Nutzen oder schaden alpine Filme uns Bergsteigern?" *Der Bergsteiger* 8 (1930): 2–6.

Bronfen, Elisabeth. *Over Her Dead Body: Death, Femininity and the Aesthetic*. New York: Routledge, 1992.

Buzard, James. *The Beaten Track: European Tourism, Literature, and the Ways to Culture, 1800–1918*. Oxford: Clarendon, 1993.

Cornel, F. "Die Reise im Kintopp." *Reichsfilmblatt* 20 (1923): 10–11.

Ellis, Reuben Joseph. "A Geography of Vertical Margins: Twentieth-Century Mountaineering Narratives and the Landscapes of Neo-Imperialism." Ph.D. diss., University of Colorado at Boulder, 1990.

Enzensberger, Hans Magnus. "A Theory of Tourism." 1958. Reprint, translated by Gerd Gemünden and Kenn Johnson, *New German Critique* 68 (1996): 117–35.

Fanck, Arnold. *Er führte Regie mit Gletschern, Stürmen und Lawinen: Ein Filmpionier erzählt*. Munich: Nymphenburger, 1973.

Feifer, Maxine. *Tourism in History: From Imperial Rome to the Present*. New York: Stein and Day, 1985.

Frigo, Conrad. Review of *Der weiße Rausch*, directed by Arnold Fanck. *Reichsfilmblatt*, 12 December 1931, insert 1, p. 1.

Hennig, Christoph. *Reiselust: Touristen, Tourismus und Urlaubskultur*. Frankfurt: Suhrkamp, 1999.

Herbert, David T. "Heritage Places, Leisure and Tourism." In *Heritage, Tourism and Society*, edited by David T. Herbert, 1–20. London: Mansell, 1995.

Hinton, David B. *The Films of Leni Riefenstahl*. 2d ed. Metuchen, N.J.: Scarecrow, 1991.

Hoek, Henry. *Schussfahrt und Schwung: Ein Brevier alpiner Abfahrten*. Hamburg: Gebr. Enoch, 1931.

Hofmeister, Burkhard, and Albrecht Steinecke. *Geographie des Freizeit— und Fremdenverkehrs*. Wege der Forschung 592. Darmstadt: Wissenschaftliche Buchgesellschaft, 1984.

Hyde, Walter Woodburn. "Die Entwicklung der Wertschätzung von Gebirgslandschaften in der Neuzeit." 1917. Reprint, in translation, in *Geographie des Freizeit—und Fremdenverkehrs*, by Burkhard Hofmeister and Albrecht Steinecke, 281–90. Darmstadt: Wissenschaftliche Buchgesellschaft, 1984.

Jacobs, Thomas. "Der Bergfilm als Heimatfilm: Überlegungen zu einem Filmgenre." *Augen-Blick* 5 (1988): 19–30.

———. "Visuelle Traditionen des Bergfilms: Von Fidus zu Friedrich oder Das Ende bürgerlicher Fluchtbewegungen im Faschismus." *Film und Kritik* 1 (1992): 28–38.

Kaes, Anton. "Film in der Weimarer Republik: Motor der Moderne." In *Geschichte des deutschen Films*, edited by Wolfgang Jacobsen, Anton Kaes, and Hans Helmut Prinzler, 38–100. Stuttgart: Metzler, 1993.

Keitz, Christine. "Grundzüge einer Sozialgeschichte des Tourismus in der Zwischenkriegszeit." In *Reisekultur in Deutschland: Von der Weimarer Republik zum 'Dritten Reich,'* edited by Peter J. Brenner, 49–71. Tübingen: Max Niemeyer, 1997.

Kracauer, Siegfried. *From Caligari to Hitler: A Psychological History of German Film*. Princeton, N.J.: Princeton University Press, 1947.

Kreimeier, Klaus. *Fanck-Trenker-Riefenstahl: Der deutsche Bergfilm und seine Folgen*. Berlin: Stiftung Deutsche Kinemathek, 1972.

Leimgruber, Florian, ed. *Luis Trenker: Regisseur und Schriftsteller. Die Personalakte Trenkers im Berlin Document Center*. Bozen: Frasnelli-Keitsch, 1994.

MacCannell, Dean. *The Tourist: A New Theory of the Leisure Class*. New York: Schocken, 1976.

Matznetter, Josef. "Alpinismus und Tourismus." In *Alpinism and Tourism and Other Problems in the Geography of Tourism*, IGU Working Group, Geography of Tourism and Recreation, 3–23. Frankfurter Wirtschafts- und Sozialgeographische Schriften 41. Frankfurt: Institut für Wirtschaft und Sozialgeographie, 1982.

Mumelter, Hubert. "Luis Trenker und der *Heilige Berg*." *Der Film-Spiegel* 7, no. 11 (1926): 86–87.

Nenno, Nancy P. "Projections on Blank Space: Landscape, Nationality and Identity in Thomas Mann's *Der Zauberberg*." *German Quarterly* 69, no. 3 (1996): 305–21.

Neubach, Walther. "Der Alpinismus im Spiegel der Karikatur." *Der Bergsteiger* 1 (1931): 35–39.

Ogilvie, F. W. *The Tourist Movement*. London: P.S. King, 1933.

Rapp, Christian. *Höhenrausch: Der deutsche Bergfilm*. Vienna: Sonderzahl, 1997.

Rentschler, Eric. *The Ministry of Illusion: Nazi Cinema and Its Afterlife*. Cambridge, Mass.: Harvard University Press, 1996.

Review of *Der bebende Berg*, directed by Hanns Beck-Gaden. *Deutsche Filmzeitung* 40 (1931): 10+.

Riefenstahl, Leni. *A Memoir*. New York: St. Martin's, 1992.

Schäfer, Hermann. Preface to *Endlich Urlaub! Die Deutschen reisen*, Exhibition Catalog, 6 June–13 October 1996, by Stiftung Haus der Geschichte der Bundesrepublik Deutschland, 7–8. Cologne: DuMont, 1996.

Schama, Simon. *Landscape and Memory*. New York: Knopf, 1995.

Schiff, Stephen. "Leni's Olympia." *Vanity Fair* September 1992, 252 f.

Simmel, Georg. "The Alpine Journey." 1895. Reprint, translated by Sam Whimster, *Theory, Culture and Society* 8 (1991): 95–98.

Sontag, Susan. "Fascinating Fascism." In *Under the Sign of Saturn*, 73–105. New York: Farrar, 1980.

Spoke, Hasso. "'Zu den Eigentümlichkeiten unserer Zeit gehört das Massenreisen': Die Entstehung des modernen Tourismus." In *Endlich Urlaub! Die Deutschen reisen*, Exhibition Catalog, 6 June–13 October 1996, by Stiftung Haus der Geschichte der Bundesrepublik Deutschland, 13–19. Cologne: DuMont, 1996.

Sputz, Karl. "Wirkungen des Fremdenverkehrs." 1919. Reprint in *Geographie des Freizeit—und Fremdenverkehrs*, by Burkhard Hofmeister and Albrecht Steinecke, 291–99. Darmstadt: Wissenschaftliche Buchgesellschaft, 1984.

Stephen, Leslie. *The Playground of Europe*. London: Longmans, Green, 1871.

Stiftung Haus der Geschichte der Bundesrepublik Deutschland. *Endlich Urlaub! Die Deutschen reisen*. Exhibition Catalog. 6 June–13 October 1996. Cologne: DuMont, 1996.

Stocker, Eduard Paul. "Die Erziehung der Gefühle beim Bergsteigen." *Der Bergsteiger* 9 (1931): 439–40.

Urry, John. "The Tourist Gaze and the 'Environment.'" *Theory, Culture and Society* 9 (1992): 1–26.

Wagner, Monika. "Die Alpen: Faszination unwirtlicher Gegenden." In *Mit dem Auge des Touristen: Zur Geschichte des Reisebildes*, Exhibition Catalog, 22 August–20 September 1981, edited by Kunsthistorisches Institut, 67–86. Tübingen: University of Tübingen Press, 1981.

———. "Das Gletschererlebnis: Visuelle Naturaneignung im frühen Tourismus." In *Natur als Gegenwelt: Beiträge zur Kulturgeschichte der Natur*, edited by Götz Großklaus and Ernst Oldemeyer, 235–63. Karlsruhe: von Loeper, 1983.

FILMOGRAPHY

Leni Riefenstahl's peculiar position in the postwar period means that her films are the most notorious and therefore the most commercially available of the films addressed in this essay. With the exception of *Victory of Faith [Sieg des Glaubens]* (1933), all of her films can be purchased. The revival of Trenker's films at the Telluride Film Festival was the impetus for the re-issue of most of his films. Trenker films available at the Filmmuseum Berlin-Deutsche Kinemathek on film and VHS/PAL include *The Son of the White Mountains [Sohn der weißen Berge]* (1930), *The Rebel [Der Rebell]* (1932), *The Prodigal Son [Der verlorene Sohn]* (1934), *The Emporer of California [Der Kaiser von Kalifornien]* (1936), and *Love Letter from Engadin [Liebesbrief aus dem Engadin]* (1938).

Unlike Riefenstahl and Trenker, there has been no popular revival of Arnold Fanck's films; as a result, very few are publicly available for purchase or rental. Fanck films available at the Filmmuseum Berlin-Deutsche Kinemathek include *SOS Iceberg [SOS Eisberg]* (1933), *Storms over Mont Blanc [Stürme über dem Montblanc]* (1930), and *The Eternal Dream [Der ewige Traum/Der König vom Mont Blanc]* (1934).

Unless otherwise noted, VHS indicates NTSC; PAL format indicates no English subtitles

Leni Riefenstahl, director

The Blue Light [Das blaue Licht] (Riefenstahl, 1932): amazon.com (VHS), amazon.de (VHS/PAL), Facets (VHS), GLVC (VHS with subtitles)
Lowlands [Tiefland] (Riefenstahl, 1954): amazon.de (VHS/PAL), Facets (VHS), GLVC (VHS with subtitles)
Olympia I & II (Riefenstahl, 1938): amazon.com (VHS), amazon.de (VHS, DVD), Facets (VHS)
Triumph of the Will [Triumph des Willens] (Riefenstahl, 1935): amazon.com (VHS, the DVD includes her short film from 1935, *Day of Freedom—Our Army [Tag der Freiheit: Unsere Wehrmacht]*, amazon.de (DVD as of 25 June 2001), GLVC (VHS, subtitled)

Arnold Fanck, director

The Holy Mountain [Der heilige Berg] (Fanck, 1926) [silent]: Facets (VHS), GLVC (VHS—listed as *The Sacred Mountain*)Amazon.com also sells the soundtrack to *The Holy Mountain* together with the soundtrack for *Battleship Potemkin* (Eisenstein, 1925).
SOS Iceberg [SOS Eisberg] (Fanck, 1933): amazon.de (VHS/PAL), GLVC (VHS, no subtitles, rental only)
Storms over Mont Blanc [Stürme über dem Montblanc] (Fanck, 1930): amazon.de (VHS/PAL)
The White Frenzy [Der weiße Rausch] (Fanck, 1931): amazon.de (VHS/PAL) and GLVC (VHS, no subtitles)
The White Hell of Pitz Palu [Die weiße Hölle von Piz Palü] (Fanck, 1929) [silent]: amazon.de (VHS/PAL, DVD) and Facets (VHS)

Luis Trenker, director

The Arsonist [Der Feuerteufel] (Trenker, 1940): GLVC (VHS, no subtitles)
Condottieri (Trenker, 1937): GLVC (VHS, no subtitles)

The Doomed Battalion [Berge in Flammen] (Trenker, 1931): GLVC (VHS, no subtitles)

Duel in the Mountains [Duell in den Bergen] (Trenker, 1950): Facets (VHS, no subtitles), GLVC (VHS, no subtitles, rental only)

The Emperor of California [Der Kaiser von Kalifornien] (Trenker, 1936): GLVC (VHS, no subtitles)

Escape to the Dolomites [Flucht in die Dolomiten] (Trenker, 1955): GLVC (rental only)

Love Letter from Engadin [Liebesbrief aus dem Engadin] (Trenker, 1938): GLVC (VHS, no subtitles, rental only)

Luis Trenker, His Life and Films. A Legend in his Time: GLVC (VHS, no subtitles)

The Mountain Calls [Der Berg ruft] (Trenker, 1937): GLVC (VHS, no subtitles)

The Prodigal Son [Der verlorene Sohn] (Trenker, 1934): amazon.de (VHS PAL), GLVC (rental only)

The Rebel [Der Rebell] (Trenker, 1932): Facets (VHS), GLVC (rental only)

The Son of the White Mountains [Sohn der weißen Berge/Das Geheimnis von Zermatt] (Trenker, 1930): Facets (VHS); GLVC (VHS, no subtitles)

Under the Spell of Monte Miracolo [Im Banne des Monte Miracolo/Der verrufene Berg] (Trenker, 1949): GLVC (VHS, no subtitles)

Other

German Spoken [Man spricht Deutsh] (Hanns Christian Müller, 1988): amazon.de (VHS [Pal format]), Goethe Institut (Montreal)

Go Trabi Go (Peter Timm, 1991): amazon.de (VHS/PAL)

The Wonderful, Horrible Life of Leni Riefenstahl, also called *The Power of the Image: Leni Riefenstahl [Die Macht der Bilder]* (1993): amazon.com (VHS, DVD), amazon.de (VHS/PAL, DVD) and Facets (VHS, DVD), GLVC (VHS, dubbed)

Addresses / URLs / Contact Information

Amazon (US): www.amazon.com

Amazon (Ger): www.amazon.de

German Language Video Center (GLVC)
Indianapolis, IN 46226-5298
Tel.   (317) 547-1257
Fax.   (317) 547-1263
URL: www.germanvideo.com

Facets
Facets Multi-Media, Inc.
1517 W. Fullerton Ave.
Chicago, IL 60614
Tel.   (773) 281-9075
Fax: (773) 929-5437
URL: www.facets.org

Filmmuseum Berlin-Deutsche Kinemathek
(formerly the Stiftung Deutsche Kinemathek)
Potsdamerstraße 2
10785 Berlin
Tel.   (030) 300 903-0/-10/-73/-71
Fax.   (030) 300 903-13
Email: info@kinemathek.de
URL: www.kinemathek.de

Goethe Institut (Montreal)
URL: http://www.goethe.de/uk/mon/

CHAPTER 5

From "Mr. M" to "Mr. Murder"

Peter Lorre and the Actor in Exile

Gerd Gemünden

"The exile is the messenger of misfortune."
Bertolt Brecht

In his poem "The Swamp" ("Der Sumpf") from 1942, Bertolt Brecht describes the slow drowning of a friend, devoured by the morass of a leech-infected swamp. As part of Brecht's "Hollywood Elegies," the poem is one of many in which Brecht vents a thinly disguised indictment of the inhuman practices of the U.S. film industry in Los Angeles:

> Manchen der Freunde sah ich, und den geliebtesten
> Hilflos versinken im Sumpfe, an dem ich
> Täglich vorbeigeh.
>
> Und es geschah nicht an einem
> Einzigen Vormittag. Viele
> Wochen nahm es oft; dies machte es schrecklicher.
> Und das Gedenken an die gemeinsamen
> Langen Gespräche über den Sumpf, der
> So viele schon birgt.
>
> Hilflos nun sah ich ihn zurückgelehnt
> Bedeckt von den Blutegeln.

In dem schimmernden
Sanft bewegten Schlamm. Auf dem versinkenden
Antlitz das gräßliche
Wonnige Lächeln.[1]

Since the only surviving German copy of the poem was found among the papers of the late actor Peter Lorre, it is commonly assumed that it must have been written specifically for Lorre as Brecht's comment on the actor's career in Hollywood, where Lorre had worked since his arrival in 1935. Like Lorre, Brecht himself had come to Los Angeles to find employment in Hollywood, unsuccessfully as it turned out.[2] Brecht had known Lorre since the 1930s, casting him in the role of Galy Gay in his own production of *Mann ist Mann* in 1931. Defending the actor against attacks in the Berlin press, he lauded Lorre's "new art of acting" as exemplary for an actor who not only enacted but also confronted the characters he played.[3] In Hollywood, however, Brecht frequently criticized his friend for what he perceived as a sellout to the studios, even though the poem laments, rather than indicts, the fallibility of the actor in exile.

"The Swamp" not only articulates Brecht's problematic relationship with Lorre but also raises the more fundamental question of what exile has to do with stardom, and, in turn, with the study of German popular cinema in general. Indeed, the career of Peter Lorre, which encompasses performances on Austro-Hungarian and German stages, work within the film industries of Weimar Germany and prewar England, and a thirty-year career in Hollywood, provides a case study that forces us to address the complexity that hides behind the three nouns comprising the title of this anthology. In other words, when talking about Peter Lorre, what does "German," what does "popular," and what does "cinema" actually mean?

To begin with the last term, it must be emphasized that, like so many film actors in Weimar Germany, Lorre was trained on the stage, first in the Viennese theater troupe of Jacob Moreno and then by many renowned directors in Berlin, including Brecht. In his first film role in *M* (1931), Lorre employed a Brechtian notion of *Gestus* in his role as Hans Beckert, showing the character as the intersection of social forces and overdetermined subjectivity. Lorre's acting style, his uncanny physiognomy, and his soft, guttural voice shape the film to such a degree that one may indeed wonder whose imprint shapes the film the most—is *M* not "as much a Peter Lorre film as it is a Fritz Lang film?"[4] While in the United States, Lorre's acting style was forced into complicity with Hollywood's preference for naturalism—a fate alluded to in Brecht's poem—and yet, as I will argue in the following, his American performances continued to entail elements of Brechtian distanciation that allow them to be read as allegories about the exilic circumstances under which they were produced.

Secondly, to what degree was Lorre really a German actor? Born as Ladislav Loewenstein in Rószahegy, Hungary, in 1904, then a part of the Austro-Hungarian empire, Lorre's breakthrough as an actor occurred in the plays and films of Weimar Germany. In *M*, his soft Viennese drawl marked him as an intruder in Berlin, underscoring a sense of otherness and nonbelonging that he would (have to) perform throughout his entire career. In America, where the vast majority of his seventy-nine films were made, his screen persona would remain that of a foreigner, despite the fact that he mastered the grammar and accent of the English language and became a citizen early on. Yet exile also turned him into a stranger in his own country, as his efforts to reemigrate to West Germany after the war failed miserably and he declined Brecht's offer to join him at the Berliner Ensemble in East Berlin.[5] In German popular memory he survives only as the child murderer of *M*, his other eight Weimar films as forgotten as the vast majority of his work abroad. Lorre thus becomes the sad embodiment of Curt Siodmak's observation that "he who has two countries has none."[6]

Finally, Lorre's performances raise interesting questions about the divide of high and low so central to discussions of the popular. Here the modernism of his theatrical career and his performance in *M* needs to be confronted with the rewriting and recycling of his Weimar image in the popular films of the Hollywood studios. In particular, it will be important to analyze the terms of translating Lorre's star persona of *M* into his many incarnations of the uncanny, the perverse, the threatening, and the dangerous that would circumscribe the entirety of his career.

Thus, the exilic dimension of the star persona of Peter Lorre provides a most necessary complement and corrective to the more homogenous notion of national cinema that underpins many essays in this volume. As an actor who has virtually been bypassed in all discussions of German stars, Lorre's case provides an illuminating comparison piece to the study of "very" German stars such as Kristina Söderbaum and Manfred Krug in this volume.

On a more general level, the study of exile cinema forces our attention to the fact that the notion of the national is tied to performativity and cultural mimicry, thereby undermining any definition of national identity based on ontology or authenticity. Furthermore, as an example of the *trans*national dimension in the construction of the star, the case of Lorre offers insight into what one could call an Americanization in reverse—not a tracking of how American culture has shaped the social, political, and aesthetic dimensions of German film during the twentieth century, but rather a study of what Lorre's performances in Hollywood tell us about the function of foreign actors and typecasting in U.S. national cinema. As I argue in the following, the process of transferring popularity and public appeal from one national film culture to another has to be not only understood in terms of positivistic continuities and discontinuities of biography, but also determined by the changing function actors and their roles assume in different historical, geographical, and ideological contexts. My discussion of Lorre's performances will follow a double strategy; I will first map the trajectory from Weimar to Hollywood by discussing the new meanings his performances assumed in prewar and wartime U.S. filmmaking. In a second step, I will read these performances as enactments of displacement that transcend or undermine the circumscription imposed through typecasting, thus rendering visible the strategies of ethnic disavowal and "othering" that informed studio filmmaking in the 1930s and 1940s.

The deterritorialized dimension of Lorre's performances is to a certain degree prefigured in his biography. Although I do not want to read Lorre's life as a chain of events determined by causes and effects, it is important to rehearse some facts in order to see how biography can become part of the intertextual construct that makes up the star. Born to parents who belonged to a German-speaking Jewish minority, Lorre was interested in the theater from early on, acting on various stages in Breslau, Zurich, and Vienna before coming to Berlin in 1929, when Brecht invited him to play the role of Fabian in his production of Marieluise Fleißer's *Pioniere in Ingolstadt*. Performances in *Dantons Tod, Frühlings Erwachen*, and *Die Quadratur des Kreises* followed. Lorre's breakthrough came in 1931. Playing Gala Gay in Brecht's own production of *Mann ist Mann* at night, Lorre would stand in front of the cameras of Fritz Lang during the day in the role of the child murderer Hans Beckert in the director's first sound feature, *M*. The success of the film turned Lorre into an international film star; after *M* he appeared in eight more German films, often in smaller, comical roles. In 1933, Lorre emigrated via the much-traveled route first to Vienna, then to Paris, then on to London, before coming to the United States through a contract with Columbia Pictures.

Known in the United States primarily for his performances as the child murderer in *M* and as the anarchist in Hitchcock's *The Man Who Knew Too Much* (1934), Lorre was typecast from the beginning of his U.S. career as a menacing and enigmatic presence. Following the motto, "Play it again, Peter!," Lorre's Hollywood roles can be read as an extended quotation, rewriting, and mimicking of that of the pedophile and killer Hans Beckert. If the roles he was first offered did not depict him as a pervert or serial killer, he was at the very least always portrayed as a sexual threat or outsider—and invariably as a foreigner (even if it was often not clear from *which* foreign country he hailed). Consider his many roles during the 1930s and 1940s, which include a mad French surgeon *(Mad Love)*; an intellectual Russian criminal *(Crime and Punishment)*; a Mexican-British specialist for murder *(Secret Agent)*; a Hungarian immigrant turned criminal *(The Face Behind the Mask)*; a smart Japanese detective who is a master of disguise (the Mr. Moto series); an unidentifiable, dandylike adventurer, possibly Egyptian *(The Maltese Falcon)*; a Chinese ship captain *(They Met in Bombay)*; a dubious black marketer, possibly Italian or Spanish *(Casablanca)*; several spies or secret agents of Japanese, Russian, and English provenance (*Invisible Agent, Background to Danger,* and *Lancer Spy,* respectively); a German Gestapo officer *(The Cross of Lorraine)*; a French pickpocket *(I Was an Adventuress)*; a patriotic French prisoner *(Passage to Marseilles)*; a Dutch writer *(The Mask of Dimitrios)*; a terrified agent for Franco-Spain *(Confidential Agent)*; a dubious English gambler *(Three Strangers)*; an equally dubious Italo-American nightclub owner *(Black Angel)*; an Italo-American bodyguard and mobster *(The Chase)*; a sly Moroccan police inspector *(Casbah)*; an English book illustrator *(The Verdict)*; and a drunk South African philosopher *(Rope of Sand)*. In very few of his seventy-nine films did he play a character whose nationality was identifiably American, and there was only one film in which he played a German who was *not* a Nazi *(Hotel Berlin)*.

In virtually all of these films, Lorre portrayed someone who would kill or was ready to kill. Yet more often than not his evil was not of will but of madness. A dainty little man with a distinct soft voice and bulging eyes, Lorre's crimes were something uncontrollable—a drive, a perversion, something subconscious—which made him not only the perpetrator but also the victim. Further reducing his responsibility for the crimes was the fact that Lorre was frequently associated with children or with being infantile (yet another important carryover from *M*). Even though Lorre rebelled against this typecasting throughout his career, he never escaped it, even repeating it in the one film he himself directed and co-wrote, *Der Verlorene*, in which he played a serial killer in Nazi Germany. Lorre ended his career, much disillusioned, by co-starring with Vincent Price in Roger Corman horror films and in endless self-parodies on television.

What do these performances tell us about the popularity of German exile actors in Hollywood? On the most obvious level, they indicate that the transition from one national cinema to another was very difficult. Unlike for directors, cameramen, set designers, producers, or even writers, an actor's foreign accent remained an insurmountable obstacle. In a system of production that circumscribed the range of actors in rather narrow terms— sometimes even if they were stars—the accent (and in Lorre's case also the looks) greatly reduced versatility, except when it could be employed to fill the studio's need for exoticism. However, if compared to other famous compatriots, such as Fritz Kortner, Albert Wassermann, Oskar Homolka, or Elizabeth Bergner, who largely failed to continue in the United States their successful German stage careers, Lorre did quite well. Just as Conrad Veidt filled a niche in playing Gestapo officers, secret agents, and spies, and Paul Henreid performed successful variations of the continental lover, so Lorre, too, was able to cultivate a certain persona with his portrayals of the soft-spoken, infantile foreigners of dubious origin whose threat was always associated with hints of sexual perversion or homosexuality. Lorre was able to have top billing only at the beginning of his U.S. career—in *Mad Love* and *Crime and Punishment*, which were specifically intended as Lorre vehicles, and even in the early noir *Stranger on the Third Floor*, where he has significantly less screen-time than the other male protagonist. Surprisingly, the films in which he had a supporting role form a more coherent body of work. Especially the films in which he is paired with Humphrey Bogart and Sidney Greenstreet approximate a mini-genre; they follow a similar set of institutional imperatives, they share certain generic conventions and thematic concerns, and, most importantly, they raise similar audience expectations by virtue of the same cast.

Casting decisions and the creation of a system of stars and supporting characters clearly shape the meaning of genre film beyond narrative and syntax, which traditionally have been considered central in genre theory. This effect can be seen not only within individual Lorre films but also in other films with foreign stars that emphasize horror and the uncanny. Thus the vehicles for Bela Lugosi, a celebrated Max Reinhardt Hamlet whose Dracula roles drove him into drug addiction, and for Boris Karloff, one of the few actors who accepted his synonymy with horror as being natural and useful, provide a contrast and a supplement to the films of Lorre, highlighting their significance through similarity and difference. If one extends this comparison even further, to include other films featuring foreign stars—such as Marlene Dietrich, Carmen Miranda, and Charles Boyer—the significance of the star system for genre films becomes even more apparent. Even though Lorre never achieved the fame of any of these other performers, the way in which he was billed and cast in his films served a very similar function.[7]

However, what interests me in Lorre's roles is not so much how they were shaped by the Hollywood studio system but how these roles in particular were related to his pre-Hollywood career in Germany and in England. In other words, what happened to the popular when transferred from one national cinema to another, no matter how interrelated these were during the 1920s? Discussions about the contributions of Weimar cinema to the Hollywood of the 1930s and 1940s have largely revolved around models of influence, or positivistically have assumed certain continuities by virtue of biographies. Lorre's example certainly complicates this paradigm, asking us to consider exile cinema less in terms of stylistic and thematic continuities and more in terms of the function it played in the host country.[8] The case of Lorre shows that the transformation from Mr. "M" to "Mr. Murder"—as he was known to the American public—was one of successfully mimicking (and later parodying) in order to survive. For American viewers, Lorre's face conjured up the horror of Nosferatu, Caligari, and the Golem, even though he never played these figures. Reenacting the plots of the haunted screen of Weimar, and in fact replaying the past as simulacrum, his first film in Hollywood was *Mad Love* (1934), a remake of *Orlacs Hände* (Robert Wiene, 1924). Directed by cinematographer-turned-director Karl Freund, Lorre interpreted the role formerly played by Conrad Veidt, that of a deranged surgeon who transplants the hands of a murderer onto a pianist.[9] Graham Greene's review of the film sounds the theme of sexual perversion and physical abnormality that would typecast Lorre throughout his career: "Those marbly pupils in the pasty spherical face are like the eye-pieces of a microscope through which you can see laid flat on the slide the entangled mind of a man: love and lust, nobility and perversity, hatred of itself and despair jumping out at you from the jelly."[10]

The transformation of the child murderer Hans Beckert, who elicits as much revulsion as compassion, into the deranged and grotesque Dr. Gogol is indicative of the relocation of the Weimar Republic to "Weimar on the Pacific." Despite obvious borrowings from Weimar silent classics, *Mad Love* lacks the psychological subtlety and moral ambiguity of its predecessor, turning the uncanny into pure horror. Made after the success of Tod Browning's *Dracula* and James Whale's *Frankenstein*, it comes as no surprise that in the public eye Lorre would form, with Bela Lugosi and Boris Karloff, a trio of non-American actors who personified the monstrosity and evil of the Old World. The fact that Lorre was indeed born at the foot of the Carpathian mountains added ample fodder for MGM's publicity department.

More than any other film, it was the success of *M* that determined, and in fact haunted, Lorre's career. The chalk "M" that marked him as murderer in his very first film, as "le maudit" (as the film was called in France), that is, as the notorious, the expulsed, the cursed, the lost, would typecast the actor for his entire career, from Lang, via Hitchcock, von Sternberg, and John Houston to Roger Corman. Even Mr. Moto, Lorre's popular Japanese agent, seems prefigured by the ominous letter.[11] Yet it is of little analytical value to discuss Lorre's Hollywood roles exclusively in terms of (bad) imitations, sequels, and follow-ups, as has so often been done, including by Lorre himself.[12] Such a privileging of Weimar art film over the Hollywood films neglects consideration of the historical circumstances under which each film was produced and the meanings a contemporary audience ascribed to each. Thus, rather than merely tracing stylistic or thematic continuities and differences in Lorre's performances, it is important to historicize deviations and to analyze their respective function in the specific context in which they were made, as a comparative look at two American films that are closely related to *M—Stranger on the Third Floor* (Boris Ingster, 1940) and *All Through the Night* (Vincent Sherman, 1942)—will illustrate.

The close relationship among these three films is most obviously suggested by the similarities of Lorre's roles in these films. However, as we will see, his characters—despite their affinities—assume very different functions in the three films, and

these differences are ultimately more telling than the often com-
mented-on stylistic and thematic continuities. In the early noir,
Stranger on the Third Floor, Lorre plays an escaped lunatic who
stalks the nocturnal streets and threatens to kill anybody who
will disclose his whereabouts. As in *M*, Lorre is cast as a somewhat childish but deadly outsider whose gnomish appearance and
soft voice disguise a deeply troubled psyche. The plot even suggests the film to be a sequel to *M*: the stranger may well be M
who has escaped from the very lunatic asylum in which he was
presumably put after he was apprehended by the police, just before the mobster's kangaroo court could condemn him to death.
(This is, in fact, the scenario that gangster boss Schränker envi-
sions, leading to him to plead for the instant execution of M.)

Like M, the nameless stranger is both hunter and hunted;
both characters pose a threat because of their anonymity, and
both films present the extensive search for the murderer in highly
dramatic terms. Furthermore, both murderers successfully elude
their pursuers for a long time, and when they are finally apprehended it is because their identity has not so much been disclosed
as it has been established. This trajectory is especially visible in
Lang's film, which introduces the child murderer through a shot
of the shadow he casts onto an advertising pillar, where reward
posters demand to know the identity of the murderer. We then
hear his voice, but only much later in the film, in a scene I will
discuss in the following, do we see his face. Even though the police do eventually discover his name, he becomes identifiable
only through the chalk "M" on his shoulder, which literally turns
him into a marked man. In Boris Ingster's film, the stranger remains nameless throughout the film, appearing briefly in the
frame at odd moments but not dominating the screen until the
very end of the film. Even more than M, the stranger has an effect
through his absence. Whereas in *M* the combined forces of the
police and the gangsters are after the murderer, here it is only
Jane, the fiancée of wrongly accused Michael Ward, who searches
for the man with the white scarf whom Ward saw lurking around
the neighborhood. Canvassing the area, she describes him as "a
strange-looking man who has bulgy eyes and thick lips." A mail-
man responds by saying that to him people are just names, and
that sometimes he imagines what these names must look like,
but he "never imagined a man like that." Only when the stranger,
whom she finally encounters in a lunchroom, confesses his
crimes to Jane can she be certain to have found the right man. As
in *M*, this confession of the murderer is indeed the only proof of

his crimes, for in both films the camera never shows us the actual killing of the victims—the only "evidence" lies in a causality suggested through the editing. Since in both *M* and *Stranger on the Third Floor* the confession comes from a mentally deranged or highly disturbed person, each film instills doubt in the viewers about whether or not the accused is actually the real murderer.

In line with this emphasis on uncertainty and ambiguity regarding the identity of the killer and the truthfulness of his confession, both films dwell at length upon the repercussions of the search for the murderer. The hunt for M creates a mass paranoia in Berlin, where everybody begins to suspect everybody, unveiling the brittle sense of security in the modern metropolis as well the moral hypocrisy of many of its inhabitants. Both the law enforcers and the law breakers work with the same mechanical precision and parallel strategies to locate their opponent. The editing of the film fuses them into a coherent body of people, casting one gigantic net through which he cannot escape. If it is the strategy of *M* to expose the ineffectiveness of the law enforcers and the vulnerability of the law breakers (further underscored by the irony that in the end it is a blind man who identifies the hunted by a song he whistles), as well as to critically depict the ensuing processes of mass hysteria, the paranoia in *Stranger on the Third Floor* is confined to Michael Ward, who becomes the suspect for a murder that he claims he did not commit. In the film's stylistically most daring sequence, we are presented with Ward's nightmare of being innocently accused and tried for the murder of his neighbor, Meng. Filmed in a very expressionist style of distorted angles, stark contrasts of light and shadows, and disorienting editing, this sequence cites the formal characteristics of *The Cabinet of Dr. Caligari* as well as its theme of the wrongfully locked-up person, even placing Ward in a cell in which the iron bars' giant shadows encircle him much like a prisoner in Wiene's famous film. It is at this moment of crisis that *Stranger on the Third Floor* alludes to *M* in the most literal sense, while at the same time disrupting the parallel between the two Peter Lorre roles: When Ward wakes from his nightmare, he gets up from his armchair, douses his face with water, and then proceeds to check his features in front of the mirror, much like M in the first scene in which we actually get to see Lorre's face, as he grimaces in front of the mirror. Both scenes forcefully associate the self-examination of one's features with madness and delusion: Whereas in *M* the scene is narrated by a voiceover of a graphologist who proclaims that M's handwriting is symptomatic of "a strain of madness that is hard to prove but can be intensely felt," Ward's self-examination indicates that he begins to doubt the fictitious nature of his nightmare, as he says to himself: "But why don't I hear him [Meng]? I go in there and wake him up!"—only to discover that Meng is indeed dead, and that Ward's nightmare of his prosecution and trial may now come true as well.

What this pivotal scene suggests, then, is that an important parallel exists not only between the two roles played by Lorre, but more importantly between M and Ward. This point is further underscored by linking both men to the sensationalism of the print media. M sends his letter threatening to commit more murders to the Berlin newspapers after the police refuse him any publicity. Ward, a struggling journalist, seems to hit a lucky break when he becomes the main witness in a much-publicized murder case. M and Ward are notably both the generators and victims of this sensationalism; if M's eagerness to claim the headlines produces a much-relished mass hysteria, it also effects the mass mobilization of the police, the gangsters, and the beggars that will lead to his capture. Ward, in his ambition not only to write the headlines but also to be featured in them, provides testimony that almost sends the wrong man—Joe Briggs—to the electric chair, a wrongdoing that is corrected only through his fiancée's discovery of the real murderer. The nightmare of his own prosecution is clearly intended here as a process of purgation and purification that will prevent a future mishandling of his profession.

If Lang's film can be read as a critique of sensationalism (articulated repeatedly in many of his other films) that warns of the dangers of collective violence and mob mentality, Ingster's critique of sensationalism is one that seems to blame only false ambition. Yet the happy end of *Stranger on the Third Floor,* with the killer confessing to his crimes and Ward vindicated at the last moment, contains at least some of the refusal of closure that we find in *M.* While in Lang's film a cut prevents us from hearing the court's decision, thus leaving it to the audience to hand down the verdict on M, the coda in *Stranger on the Third Floor* has Ward and Jane suddenly encounter Joe Briggs, the man who Ward almost sent to the gallows through his testimony. If earlier Jane was wary of Ward's testimony because if proven guilty and executed "he [Briggs] would always be with us," Briggs's sudden appearance as a cab driver who offers them a free ride indicates that, despite his acquittal, he is, and will continue to be, "with them."

This return of the repressed instills in the viewer a profound sense of moral ambiguity regarding the "hero" and his actions rarely found in prewar Hollywood films. The transposition of M, the killer-victim of the Weimar metropolis, into *both* the stranger and Ward is a creative adaptation of Lang's drama of a menace that is both within and outside society—if Lang's film insists, as his initial title indicated, that "the murderers are among us," Ingster's film similarly breaks with Hollywood's facile strategies of othering. Blurring the lines between a lunatic stranger (whose dying confession to the crimes and indictment of mental institutions show humanism and clarity) and a hero whose moral recuperation after a serious lapse of judgment seems all too simple to be believed, *Stranger on the Third Floor* refuses to locate the threat exclusively within the excluded, thus anticipating a cynicism and nihilism that will be fully enunciated in postwar noirs by exile directors.

If the function of the transposition of Lorre's role from *M* to *Stranger on the Third Floor* is to treat the subject of urban living and danger with a hitherto unknown moral and epistemological ambiguity, thereby also questioning the typecasting his previous U.S. performances had cemented, the 1942 film *All Through the Night* recasts *M* in a very different way. Here Lorre plays the pianist Pepi, a sadistic little killer who belongs to a group of fifth columnists threatening to create havoc in New York and elsewhere in the United States. Revisiting the plot from *M*, gangster and racketeer Gloves Donahue (Humphrey Bogart) leads the underworld's feverish chase for a killer—Pepi—who interferes with business. In the process, he discovers the secret dealings of fifth columnists in New York by infiltrating their ranks; saves Leda Hamilton (Kaaren Verne), a singer in the night club where Pepi works, from the claws of the Nazis; and heroically averts the destruction of a U.S. battleship. Cleared of all suspicions of murder, the city celebrates him as hero at the end of the film.

The conventions of the gangster film—the suspenseful search for the killer orchestrated around sequences of chasing and escaping—which *M* and *All Through the Night* share are only the generic vehicles to transport a politically much more relevant point. Both films are cultural productions that intervene in their respective nations' discourse on warfare and mass mobilization. If *M*, as Anton Kaes has argued, presents us with a city in a state of emergency that mobilizes its masses against a serial killer much like an army readies for war, *All Through the Night* portrays the classic conversion story of an apolitical mobster with a penchant for cheesecake into a patriot who risks his life to save his country from a terrorist threat.[13] Produced during the summer and fall of 1941, but not released until January of 1942—that is, after the Japanese attack on Pearl Harbor—*All Through the Night* documents Hollywood's eagerness to do its share in winning the public over for President Roosevelt's politics of U.S. intervention in World War II.

If in *M* Lorre plays the invisible target of a mass rage he himself helped engineer, Pepi, in *All Through the Night*, is a murderer in plain view. Leda Hamilton knows him to be a dangerous killer and warns Donahue of the threat Pepi poses, but the disbelieving Donahue shrugs her off: "Pepi? That squirt!" Underestimating Pepi's danger is symbolic, of course, of overlooking the threat posed by Nazi activity inside the United States, and the main trajectory of the film is to educate Donahue—and the viewers—about the political state of things in contemporary America. Or, in the words of Donahue's friend Barney, it is about the importance of getting "the head out of the sports pages and onto the front page." The film opens with a scene in which we watch Bogart's gangsters play war with toy soldiers and canons in a café while getting into a heated argument about how the British would do best to defeat the Nazis. If this scene suggests warfare as frivolity and make-believe among a bunch of "ignoramuses" (as the mobsters call each other), by the end of the film the necessity for real battle has become more than clear, as Bogart has single-handedly defeated the fifth columnists; what is more, he has been successfully converted into an altruistic patriot who receives a hero's welcome from the city he has protected.

Made thirteen years after the end of World War I and two years before the Nazi takeover, *M* can be read to register both the trauma and shell shock of the lost war, as Kaes claims, and also the impending dictatorship, as Siegfried Kracauer has argued in his famous study *From Caligari to Hitler.* If *M* seems to be critical of processes of surveillance that produce a society ready for war at a moment's notice, *All Through the Night*, by contrast, provides a blueprint for citizen vigilance, courage, and determination in the fight against an enemy much closer to home than commonly assumed. Where *M* leaves us with questions about the killer's accountability and rational responsibility for his crimes, no such ambiguities are allowed when Hollywood fights the Nazis. In line with this clear ideological focus, the figure of Pepi lacks *M*'s tormented psyche, but also the moral ambiguity of the stranger and Michael Ward in *Stranger on the Third Floor.* Even though Pepi, like M, has a penchant for sweets and is heard humming a melody before committing murder, these similarities are a mere homage to Lorre's performance in the Weimar classic, now significantly deprived of its disquieting implications.

In *All Through the Night* emotional engineering of the audience is most clearly achieved through the use of foreign language and accents—always a staple of Hollywood's ways of marking the other. Here the German language is highlighted as the vehicle with which cultural identity and political allegiance are defined, and the film stages the political struggle as a battle of language(s): at stake is the successful defense of American purity against the Germanification of America. Consider the various uses of German we encounter: Leda Hamilton speaks English without any accent, even though there is reason to believe that she is German, because she understands it, and because her father is held in the Dachau concentration camp. The baker Herman Miller speaks with a foreign, though not identifiably German, accent. It is not clear if there exists a German background that first motivated Miller to work for the fifth columnists. Even if he's not German, he seems to understand the language, because when Pepi first greets him, Pepi does so by saying "Hallo, Papa Miller" and is taken aback when Miller responds with an English, "Hello." Miller's wife, Anna, speaks with an even stronger foreign accent, but when alone Miller and his wife converse in English. In contrast to the Millers, Herr Ebbing, the leader of the fifth columnists, and Pepi frequently converse in German. Ebbing speaks with a strong German accent, indicating that he is "the most German of them all," and subsequently the only one willing to risk his life in the attack on a U.S. battleship—when Pepi refuses to help Ebbing with this assignment, Ebbing shoots him. Donahue and Pepi are the only two characters who at least for a certain amount of time can pass as both American and German, and both are bent on exposing an opponent who shares their own linguistic talents for masquerade. When Donahue fakes speaking German at a fifth columnist meeting (in an overt parody of foreigners with accents), Pepi exposes him. If Pepi sees through Donahue's Chaplinesque German, Donahue, too, becomes aware of the uncanny propensities of Pepi's soft accent.

While accents may be the single most important device to steer audience identification, the use of much untranslated German dialogue in the film must have instilled a sense of uneasiness in a contemporary audience. This also resonates with the film's overall ideological message about an unknown threat in our midst. As in most films that involve a fair number of German exiles, there exists a certain irony in *All Through the Night*, owing to the biographies of the actors: Hamilton is played by Kaaren Verne, a German who had come to the United States in 1939 (and who would marry Lorre in 1945); Miller and his wife are played by the Jewish exiles Ludwig Stoessel and Irene Seidner; and Ebbing is played by Conrad Veidt, a fervent anti-Nazi of the first hour.

Such comparisons show how the transformations of various Lorre roles are shaped by different national cinemas at moments of political crisis. Yet, as I indicated earlier, one can also consider Lorre's performances without any such reference to a concrete historical context. Indeed, the particularity of the exile actor Peter Lorre is that in many of his performances he manages to comment on his historical, social, and political predicament despite or beyond the narrative motivation of his characters. While I would not go so far as to call these instances a stepping outside of the role, they do provide a rupture in the complete immersion in the role on which Hollywood studio acting is premised. Employing the notion of gestus of his friend and mentor Bertolt Brecht, Lorre uses bodily posture, accent, and facial expression to exemplify social relationships. While his portrayals of foreigners do follow Hollywood strategies of rendering the other exotic and bizarre, they also show national and cultural identity as a site of multiple competing, often antagonistic impulses and forces, and the complex process of adapting—or not adapting—to another culture. Thus, Lorre's performances are not so much about mimicking as about mimicry— not a simple imitation of a dominant acting style but a blurred copy that always retains the traces of forced assimilation while at the same time mocking the coerciveness of acculturation.

To be sure, such an allegorical reading lies at least partially in the eye of the beholder. The more subtle references to fluid identities and nomadic subjectivity that underlie, for example, Lorre's Joel Cairo in *The Maltese Falcon* or his Zalenkoff in *Background to Danger*—two films that contain virtually identical scenes of Lorre being roughed up by the hero only to be deprived of various passports or identity papers—may have escaped contemporary audiences engrossed in the narrative of the film. Yet there are other moments that foreground self-shaped identities and aspirations to assimilate that are hard to miss. In *Beat the Devil*, Humphrey Bogart (as American Billy Dannreuther) answers Lorre's (O'Hara's) knock on the door with the words:

"What's our wide-eye Irish leprechaun doing outside my door?"
To which Lorre replies: "Why do you always make jokes about
my name? In Chile, the name of O'Hara is a tip-top name. Many
Germans in Chile happen to become called O'Hara." In *My Favorite Brunette*, Lorre plays a knife-throwing killer who fools the
police by pretending to be a gardener. They apologize for the in-
convenience they may have caused him—"Sorry we bothered
you. You're not a bad guy for a foreigner"—to which Lorre replies,
"But I'm going to be a citizen. I'm studying for my examination.
By the way—could you gentlemen tell me who was the eighth
president of the United States?" The police leave without reply,
indicating that the citizens know as little about their country's
history as the aspiring immigrant, but also suggesting that they
and the population in general are largely ignorant about processes
of naturalization.

The film in which Lorre came closest to playing his own
life, and which thus most obviously suggests an allegorical reading, is *The Face Behind the Mask* (Robert Florey, 1943).[14] Here
Lorre is the Hungarian watchmaker Janos Szabo, who immigrates
to New York City. When a hotel fire burns his face and Szabo can
no longer find work because of his disfigurement, he joins a gang
of mobsters, wearing a mask fashioned after his passport photo.
When he leaves the criminals to marry a blind woman, they suspect him of treachery and plant a bomb in his car. The bomb kills
the woman, and this second blow of fate demands a reprisal.
Szabo takes revenge by misdirecting the gang's airplane, landing
it in the desert, where everybody, including Szabo himself, will
die. The tale of the upbeat immigrant who finds out that life is
less forgiving abroad than at home is a familiar one for many first-
and second-generation Americans. The tale of the face that instills fear, and the desire for and impossibility of attaining a new
face, is one that particularly resembles Lorre's fate. Szabo's mask
reduces his expressivity to his eyes and voice—Lorre's trade-
marks—and turns every utterance into a ventriloquism.[15] What is
more, the mask has Lorre's features. When Szabo looks into the
mirror to check his new face—in yet another evocation of the
pivotal scene from *M*—he sees the face of someone else, recalling
the scene from *M* and *Stranger on the Third Floor* where the face
in the mirror does not seem to be his own. The trajectory from
hope to hopelessness, so typical for narratives about coming to
America, is articulated in this film primarily as the futile refuta-
tion of physiognomy. Resigned to his fate, Szabo, the mobster,
pursues a career where looks don't matter, just as Lorre chose to

become an actor because it allowed him to turn a deformation—his small size and bulging eyes—into an advantage.

Lorre's performance of foreigners and of foreignness is closely related to the ambiguity of ethnicity that lies at the very origins of Hollywood itself. Migration and exile are not only processes that led many Europeans to Hollywood but were also constitutive of the American film industry in the first place. We will remember that the studio moguls Carl Laemmle, Samuel Goldwyn, Adolf Zukor, William Fox, Louis B. Mayer, Joseph and Nicholas Schenk, Lewis Selznick, and Jack and Harry Warner were all first- or second-generation Jewish immigrants who strove hard to assimilate to the United States. The "invention of Hollywood," as Neal Gabler has called it, is premised on the repression and disavowal of one's national and cultural origins.[16] This camouflaging is the counterpart to the ostentatious portrayals of otherness that Lorre and other emigrants (many of them Jews themselves) had to play; what this dichotomy suggests is that the notion of a center, that is, that which is not foreign, rests firmly on projections of different kinds of otherness.

Following this kind of reasoning, it is only logical that among the many, many versions of otherness and outsiderness that Lorre had to portray, the one absent form of ethnic stereotyping is that of the Jew. In order not to draw attention to Hollywood's own ethnic origins, the studios' unwritten rule was to downplay Jewish identity, a policy that was kept even as news of the Holocaust increasingly reached the United States. (One of the most striking comments of the 1940s on the disavowal of Jewishness is certainly Ernst Lubitsch's *To Be or Not to Be*.) While some of Lorre's German comic roles, such as the reporter Johnny in *F.P.1 Does Not Answer [F.P.1 antwortet nicht]* (Karl Hartl, 1932) contained stereotypes that contemporary audiences associated specifically with Jews, none of his American roles allowed such allusions. On the contrary, screenplays based on novels or plays that contained references to a Jewish background had to be purged. In *The Constant Nymph* (1943), for example, Lorre played the wealthy Fritz Bercovy, a romantic role that had been stripped of the Jewish background of Jacob Birnbaum, the character of Margaret Kennedy's mildly anti-Semitic novel and play, on which the script was based.[17]

Yet, the many portrayals of outsiders in an industry created by outsiders bent on being insiders suggest that they should be read as allegories of the filmmakers' own repressed ethnicity.

This, at least, is how writer Curt Siodmak, himself a German-Jewish refugee from Hitler, comments on the figure of the wolf-man, which he created: *"The Wolfman* is about fate. I was born as a Jew, in Dresden in 1902. Did I chose this? . . . I didn't have a choice. That's our fate, and *The Wolfman* is about the good and the evil in human beings. He cannot escape his fate. I couldn't escape my fate either. Does that make us monsters?"[18]

It was left to the Nazis to conflate Lorre's performance of the serial killer M with what they perceived as the degenerateness of the entire Jewish race. In *The Eternal Jew* (Fritz Hippler, 1940), the most notorious of the Nazi anti-Semitic films, a clip from Lorre in *M* is commented on as: "The Jew Lorre in the role of a child murderer. Following the saying, 'It's the victim's fault and not the murderer's,' this film tries to twist a normal sense of justice by soliciting compassion for the criminal, thus glossing over the crime and excusing it."[19] For the Nazis, actors like Lorre, Kurt Gerron, Rosa Valetti, or Curt Bois embodied a grotesque deformation of humanity that was considered representative of the Jewish race in general. When these actors appeared on stage or screen, they no longer played a theatrical role but their own lives, allowing, so the Nazis thought, the audience a rare glimpse into the undisguised Jewish soul.

Peter Lorre's Hollywood roles could be described with much of the same vocabulary the Nazis used to deride Jewish artists—"wurzellos," "widernatürlich," "grotesk," "pervers," "pathologisch," (uprooted, unnatural, grotesque, perverse, pathologic)—but they served a different ideological purpose. While these characteristics still had strong negative connotations, they were never associated with things Jewish but instead with foreignness in general—if the Jewish moguls wanted to be American, Lorre's oddity affirmed their assimilation.[20] Lorre's performances point to the profound ambiguity with which Hollywood has typified the roles of foreigners; questioning the film industry's strategies of "othering," these performances offer a forceful critique of Hollywood's disavowal of its own founders' cultural and ethnic origins.

It is interesting to note that Brecht, who taught Lorre much about acting, never read his Hollywood performances allegorically, considering him a victim who remained helpless in the face of the all-devouring Moloch. Yet let us, in closing, take another look at "The Swamp." The last lines about the "ghastly blissful smile" are a reference to the trademark of the many villains Lorre played, read here by Brecht as the actor's last grimace before the swamp will cover him. The meaning of the poem remains ambiguous: Is Brecht implying that Hollywood forces Lorre to smile even as it kills him, thus playing his role unto death? Or are we to understand that Lorre remains blissfully ignorant of the forces that are bringing about his demise? No matter which reading we privilege—whether it is the outsider's perspective who finds everything ghastly, or the insider's perspective who seems content because he is unaware—both of them cast Lorre as the helpless victim devoured by forces much larger than himself. Yet are there no alternatives to Brecht's deeply pessimistic reading of Lorre's ghastly blissful smile? Is it not this very expression that captures best not only the paradox of Lorre's roles but also the fundamental contradiction and incongruity that mark the actor in exile? On one level, the soft-voiced killer's perpetual smirk personifies a seemingly benign peril that harks back to the childishness of the child murderer M while at the same time creatively extending the repertoire of Hollywood character roles. Yet on another level, the ghastly smile also offers an allegorical comment on the proverbial "grin and bear it!" in the drama of coerced assimilation. Brecht knew full well that the paradox of Peter Lorre's life and career was that he had to play the outsider in order to become an insider. We can blame only Brecht's hostility to the culture industry for blinding him to the fact that Lorre's achievement was his talent for making these processes visible, playing the character in the drama while also drawing attention to the drama of his own acculturation.

NOTES

1. The Swamp

   I saw many friends, and among them the friend I loved most
   Helplessly sink into the swamp
   I pass by daily.

   And a drowning was not over
   In a single morning. Often it took
   Weeks; this made it more terrible.
   And the memory of our long talks together
   About the swamp, that already
   Had claimed so many.

   Helpless I watched him, leaning back
   Covered with leeches

In the shimmering
Softly moving slime:
Upon the sinking face
The ghastly
Blissful smile.
(Bertolt Brecht, *Poems 1913–1956*, ed. John Willett and Ralph
Mannheim [New York: Methuen, 1976], 381.)

2. On Brecht's failure in the U.S. film industry, see my essay: "Brecht
in Hollywood: *Hangmen Also Die* and the Anti-Nazi Film." *Drama Review*
164 (1999): 65–76.
3. Bertolt Brecht, "Anmerkungen zum Lustspiel *Mann ist Mann*,"
Gesammelte Werke, vol. 17 (Frankfurt/Main: Suhrkamp, 1967), 980–88.
4. Anton Kaes, *M* (London: BFI, 2000), 26.
5. See Brecht's poem for Lorre, inviting him to join him in Berlin: "To
the Actor P. L. in Exile//Listen, we are calling/you back. Driven out/You
must now return. The country/Out of which you were driven flowed once/
With milk and honey. You are being called back/To a country that has been
destroyed./And we have nothing more/To offer you than the fact that you
are needed.//Poor or rich/Sick or healthy/Forget everything/And come."
6. Curt Siodmak, *Unter Wolfsmenschen: Amerika*, trans. Wolfgang
Schlüter (Bonn: Weidle, 1997), 24.
7. For further discussion of the star system, see, in particular, Andrew
Britton, "Stars and Genre," in *Stardom: Industry of Desire*, ed. Christine
Gledhill (London: Routledge, 1991), 198–206; as well as the more general
discussions in Jackie Stacey, *Star Gazing: Hollywood Cinema and Female
Spectatorship* (London: Routledge, 1994); Richard Dyer, *Stars* (London: BFI,
1986); Thomas Koebner, ed., *Idole des deutschen Films* (Munich: Text &
Kritik, 1997); and Thomas Koebner, ed., *Schauspielkunst im Film* (St. Augustin, Germany: Gardez, 1998).
8. The problematic argument that constructs film noir as a direct de-
scendent of German expressionism can be found most emphatically in Barbara Steinbauer-Grötsch, *Die lange Nacht der Schatten: Film noir und Film
exil* (Berlin: Dieter Bertz, 1997). For a critique of the influence model, see
Thomas Elsaesser, "A German Ancestry to Film Noir?" *Iris* 12 (1996):
129–44; and Thomas Koebner, "Caligaris Wiederkehr in Hollywood? Stummfilm-Expressionismus, 'Filmemigranten' und Filmnoir," in *Innen-Leben:
Ansichten aus dem Exil*, ed. Hermann Haarmann (Berlin: Fannei & Walz,
1995), 107–19.
9. On Karl Freund's career as cameraman, producer, and director, see
Frieda Grafe, "Sehen ist besser als machen: Karl Freund, der Bilderhändler,"
in *Gleißende Schatten: Kamerapioniere der zwanziger Jahre*, ed. Michael
Esser (Berlin: Henschel, 1994), 63–77.
10. Graham Greene, *Graham Greene on Film*, ed. John Russell Taylor
(New York: Simon and Schuster, 1972), 11.
11. Already in Germany, Herbert Ihering warned of miscasting Lorre
after the success of *M*: "Was aber kann Lorre? Welche Rollen formt er durch?
Für welche findet er den richtigen Ton? Es ist falsch, ihn nur für Kranke und
Verbrecher einzusetzen. Eine häufige Beschäftigung mit diesen Rollen geht
auf die Nerven. Es ist erst recht falsch, ihm glatte Strazzis zu geben . . .

Lorres Gebiet sind die ironischen, zweideutigen, liebenswürdig-infamen Zwischenfiguren. Nicht die eindeutig Kranken, nicht die eindeutig Unkomplizierten . . . Lorres Bezirk ist die böse Harmlosigkeit, die infernalische Freundlichkeit, die zynische Sanftmut, die listige Treuherzigkeit, die ironische Spießigkeit. Hier formuliert er darstellerischrichtig, hier kommen 'Können' und 'Sein' zusammen. Hier ist Lorre ersten Ranges" (quoted in: Friedemann Beyer, *Peter Lorre: Seine Filme—sein Leben* [Munich: Heyne, 1988], 62–63).

12. This is the tenor of a recent Lorre biography, *Peter Lorre: Portrait des Schauspielers auf der Flucht*, by Felix Hoffmann and Stephen D. Youngkin (Munich: Belleville, 1998).

13. Anton Kaes, "The Cold Gaze: Notes on Mobilization and Modernity," *New German Critique* 59 (1993): 105–17.

14. Of course, one can also read *M* as a political allegory. In a prophetic twist, the case against Beckert/Lorre is made by none other than Gustaf Gründgens (in the role of mobster boss Schränker), whose career in the Third Reich would thrive through opportunism and cowardice. Lang's film stages their confrontation as that of two murderers—a rationalist for whom murder is a justified means to attain specific goals, and a pedophile for whom it provides temporary relief from oppressive drives. Schränker's self-righteous and rationalized means of persecution, his call for "geordnete Verhältnisse" (law and order), "auslöschen" (extinguish), and "ausrotten" (eliminate) prefigures the Nazi rule that was only two years away. After leaving Germany in 1933, Lorre telegrammed that with Hitler in power, Germany "was too small for two murderers."

15. In a review of Wedekind's *Frühlings Erwachen*, Walter Benjamin commented on Lorre's performance as Moritz Stiefel, which for Benjamin literally and metaphorically presented the disembodied voice of the actor: "Wahrscheinlich sind die Worte des abgefallenen, von seinen Händen aufbewahrten Kopfes noch niemals so—so voll von resigniertem Heimweh nach dem Rumpf—gesprochen worden wie von Peter Lorre." ("Wedekind und Kraus in der Volksbühne," in *Gesammelte Schriften*, vol. 10 [Frankfurt/Main: Suhrkamp, 1980], 551–54.)

16. Neal Gabler, *An Empire of Their Own: How the Jews Invented Hollywood* (New York: Crown, 1988).

17. On the representation of Jews in Hollywood cinema, see Patricia Erens, *The Jew in American Cinema* (Bloomington: Indiana University Press, 1984); and Lester D. Friedman, *Hollywood's Image of the Jew* (New York: Frederick Ungar, 1982).

18. "Im *Wolfman* geht es um Schicksal. Ich bin als Jude geboren, in Dresden, 1902. Habe ich mir das ausgesucht? . . . Ich konnte es mir nicht aussuchen. Das ist unser Schicksal, und im *Wolfman* geht es um das Gute und das Böse im Menschen. Er kann nicht raus aus seinem Schicksal. Ich konnte auch nicht raus aus meinem Schicksal. Sind wir des wegen Monster?" ("'Am Anfang war die Idee': Curt Siodmak im Gespräch mit Manuela Reichart," *Film Geschichte* 11/12 [1998]: 39).

19. "Der Jude Lorre in der Rolle eines Kindermörders. Nach dem Schlagwort 'Nicht der Mörder, sondern der Ermordete ist schuldig' wird versucht, das normale Rechtsempfinden zu verdrehen und durch mitleiderregende Darstellung des Verbrechers das Verbrechen zu beschönigen und zu entschuldigen."

20. It is interesting to note that neither in Nazi Germany nor in Holly-wood was Lorre widely known to be Jewish. Hitler initially considered Lorre one of the most gifted German actors, and invited him back to Berlin after his flight to Austria.

WORKS CITED

Benjamin, Walter. "Wedekind und Kraus in der Volksbühne," in *Gesammelte Schriften,* vol. 10 (Frankfurt/Main: Suhrkamp, 1980), 551–54.

Beyer, Friedemann. *Peter Lorre: Seine Filme—sein Leben.* Munich: Heyne, 1988.

Brecht, Bertolt. *Poems 1913–1956.* Edited by John Willett and Ralph Mannheim. New York: Methuen, 1976.

———. "Anmerkungen zum Lustspiel *Mann ist Mann.*" In *Gesammelte Werke,* vol. 17, 980–88. Frankfurt/Main: Suhrkamp, 1967.

Britton, Andrew. "Stars and Genre." In: *Stardom: Industry of Desire,* edited by Christine Gledhill, 198–206. London: Routledge, 1991.

Dyer, Richard. *Stars.* London: BFI, 1986.

Elsaesser, Thomas. "A German Ancestry to Film Noir?" *Iris* 12 (1996): 129–44.

Erens, Patricia. *The Jew in American Cinema.* Bloomington: Indiana University Press, 1984.

Friedman, Lester D. *Hollywood's Image of the Jew.* New York: Frederick Ungar, 1982.

Gabler, Neal. *An Empire of Their Own: How the Jews Invented Hollywood.* New York: Crown, 1988.

Gemünden, Gerd. "Brecht in Hollywood: *Hangmen Also Die* and the Anti-Nazi Film." *The Drama Review* 164 (1999): 65–76.

Grafe, Frieda. "Sehen ist besser als machen: Karl Freund, der Bilderhändler." In: *Gleißende Schatten: Kamerapioniere der zwanziger Jahre,* edited by Michael Esser, 63–77. Berlin: Henschel, 1994.

Greene, Graham. *Graham Greene on Film.* Edited by John Russell Taylor. New York: Simon and Schuster, 1972.

Hoffmann, Felix, and Stephen D. Youngkin. *Peter Lorre: Portrait des Schauspielers auf der Flucht.* Munich: Belleville, 1998.

Kaes, Anton. *M.* London: BFI, 2000.

———. "The Cold Gaze: Notes on Mobilization and Modernity," *New German Critique* 59 (1993): 105–17.

Koebner, Thomas, "Caligaris Wiederkehr in Hollywood? Stummfilm-Expressionismus, 'Filmemigranten' und Film noir." In *Innen-Leben: Ansichten aus dem Exil,* edited by Hermann Haarmann, 107–19. Berlin: Fannei & Walz, 1995.

———, ed. *Idole des deutschen Films.* Munich: Text & Kritik, 1997.

———, ed. *Schauspielkunst im Film.* St. Augustin, Germany: Gardez, 1998.

Siodmak, Curt. *Unter Wolfsmenschen: Amerika.* Translated by Wolfgang Schlüter. Bonn: Weidle, 1997.

———. "'Am Anfang war die Idee': Curt Siodmak im Gespräch mit Manuela Reichart." *Film Geschichte* 11/12 (1998): 37–40.

Stacey, Jackie. *Star Gazing: Hollywood Cinema and Female Spectatorship.* London: Routledge, 1994.
Steinbauer-Grötsch, Barbara. *Die lange Nacht der Schatten: Film noir und Filmexil.* Berlin: Dieter Bertz, 1997.

FILMOGRAPHY

M. Director Fritz Lang, 1931.
Stranger on the Third Floor. Director Boris Ingster, 1940.
All Through the Night. Director Vincent Sherman, 1942.
The Lost One [Der Verlorene]. Director Peter Lorre, 1951.

CHAPTER 6

The Heroine of Fascist Virtue?

Kristina Söderbaum in Veit Harlan's *The Sacrifice* (1943)

Antje Ascheid

Kristina Söderbaum, the young Swede, who is considered the biggest natural talent in German film these days, certainly isn't educated. Her acting lessons mainly consisted of refining her German pronunciation. . . . [I]t is her untrained skill, her genuineness and the pure nature of her being that is the precious source of her talent. . . . This small, blonde creature with bright eyes and a strong, but finely formed and well-proportioned body comes from the North, where people act restrained. . . . Her art is simple, but not her character. . . . Her severe nature is the foundation for genuine tragedy.

Ufa promotion, 1942

The difficulties in solving problems regarding the nature of the popular within a historically specific political and social context become immediately apparent when we look at the effort to give a name to the approximately 1,100 feature films that were made in Germany in the years between 1933 and 1945. Critics oscillate between the label "Films of the Third Reich" and "Nazi Cinema," revealing the political bent of their analysis through their preference. Thus the notion of the popular as a field of expression that escapes the one-directional trajectory of mass culture by allowing for audience and consumer participation through product selection and street practices seems problematically loaded once we turn to a period of cultural production that effectively consisted of state-controlled populism and propaganda. There can be no doubt that Joseph Goebbels and his Ministry of Propaganda and Public Enlightenment envisioned film in the Third Reich to be nothing other than Nazi Cinema. It is well documented that the Nazis quickly took control of virtually all public and cultural institutions, simultaneously eliminating their political opposition through measures ranging from coercive intimidation to radical persecution. While Goebbels liberally proclaimed that "art is free and art must remain free" when addressing the film community in March 1933, shortly after the Nazi takeover, his definition of what from then on was to be considered "art" revealed his ideological agenda: "[A]rt is only possible if it is rooted in National Socialist soil. . . . We have no intention to tolerate, even in the slightest, that those ideas which will be eradicated in Germany from the roots up somehow, disguised or openly, reemerge in film." (quoted in Albrecht 439) By this Goebbels didn't mean, of course, that there was no room for supposedly apolitical entertainment. On the contrary, he followed the maxim that the best propaganda was one that functioned unconsciously, "which works invisibly so to speak" (quoted in Albrecht 468). Consequently, Nazi entertainment practices that went beyond the political rally or the propaganda newsreel, such as the Ufa pictures at the local cinema, are frequently analyzed as a "bread and circus" aesthetics aimed at streamlining and pacifying the populace by means of the mass media, not least by the National Socialist ideologues themselves. Nevertheless, a closer analysis of many of the manifestations of the popular in National Socialist culture—particularly within commercial cinema, which relied on popular narratives and star discourses—points to significant contradictions even within film texts that were highly ideological.

According to Karsten Witte, German cinema accomplished its most remarkable achievements in its melodramas. Detlef Sierck's films with Zarah Leander, Victor Tourjanski's *Verklungene Melodie [Faded Melody]* (Tourjanski, 1938) and *Illusion [Illusion]* (Tourjanski, 1941), or Helmut Käutner's *Romanze in Moll [Romance in a Minor Key]* (Käutner, 1943) skillfully connected the far-reaching feelings of longing with fatalistic resignation. Here, the superficial extensity of Nazi aesthetics made room for intensity and differentiation, and allowed for modernity and restraint to triumph over exoticism and pathos (Witte 139). Yet, emotion was not the only "star," as Witte put it, in films made by directors who sought to circumvent the kind of political "kitsch" foregrounded in propaganda pictures; pathos and politics were also effectively fused in many of the more infamous Nazi melodramas. "Fascist art," in Susan Sontag's words, "glorifies surrender, it exalts mindlessness, it glamorizes death" (91). Eric Rentschler correspondingly elaborates that "fascist artworks exercise a powerful and persuasive effect: they present seductive intimations of oblivion with visual beauty and operatic glory" (22). Nowhere in film art were these elements more strikingly employed than in the cinematic spectacles created by Veit Harlan: his use of emotion was his stylistic trump card and constituted his unmistakable signature. Moreover, the emotional energy of his narratives almost always centered on Harlan's star wife, Kristina Söderbaum. Ironically, however, Harlan's films with Söderbaum are also particularly suited to illustrate the kind of contradictory double enunciations that emerged within the field of the popular in relation to the female image, pointing to womanhood as an area of unresolved tension within the everyday of National Socialist culture.

Among the actresses who gained prominence in National Socialist culture, Kristina Söderbaum is frequently identified as most singularly representative of the Nazi ideal, as the quintessential Nazi star. Cinzia Romani calls her "the embodiment of the fresh, ingenuous German *Fräulein*—modest and selfless—as well as the strong and healthy Aryan, the fruit of *Kraft durch Freude* (Strength through Joy). The eternal child-wife, she provided an image of the feminine ideal of the Third Reich in a series of films that carried a strong message of propaganda"(84).[1] Richard Grunberger similarly opined that as "a snub-nosed Nordic naiad cocooned in little-girlish femininity she packed cinemas with a series of marrow-withering characterizations which mingled treacle with hymeneal blood" (482). As one of National Socialism's most homogeneous star personae, Kristina Söderbaum starred as the heroine in a number of Nazi Germany's most notorious propaganda films. While other Ufa actresses' success in Nazi cinema was later often mitigated by the ambiguity of their star image, Söderbaum—whose frequent filmic drownings had earned her the nickname "Reich's Water Corpse" *(Reichswasserleiche)*—was later singled out as the prime object of anti-fascist criticism and ridicule. Spectators in the immediate postwar years heckled her off the theater stage or even attacked her by throwing rotten vegetables. When she attempted to attend the 1948 film premiere of *Ehe im Schatten [Marriage in Shadow]* (Maetzig,

1947)—which dealt with the double suicide of the Ufa actor Joachim Gottschalk and his Jewish wife—Söderbaum and Harlan were asked to leave (Zielinski 43). Many of their films were initially banned after the war; *Jud Süß [Jew Suess]* (Harlan, 1940) is still unavailable for commercial viewing in Germany today.

However, Söderbaum also remained remarkably popular with less vocal audiences, who felt a quiet or even defiant nostalgia for Ufa's golden years. In 1953, polls showed Söderbaum to be the second-most popular female star with the German public, despite the commercial failure of her postwar films. The German weekly *Stern* further concluded in 1969, "At one time, Kristina Söderbaum was the blondest of all the Swedish women Germany imported—and the most successful: She was the biggest box-office magnet of German film history. Her films earned more than 200 million Marks, *Die goldene Stadt [The Golden City]* (Harlan, 1942) alone made 43 million" (Ebelseder n.p.).[2] This grandiose assessment of Söderbaum's marketability, however, deserves as much suspicion as does the simplistic reduction of her star persona to a Nazi prototype.[3] That any one actress alone deserves to be considered the most successful is, of course, arguable. Zarah Leander's earnings, for instance, far exceeded Söderbaum's, and star figures whose careers had peaked a decade earlier, such as Lilian Harvey, certainly enjoyed similar success and popularity at that time.[4]

Yet what does separate Kristina Söderbaum from her National Socialist colleagues is that she uniquely condensed what was distinctive in Nazi stars; her star persona as well as many of her screen characters most directly communicated the beliefs of National Socialist ideology. The style and tone of her films, as well as her narrative characterizations and acting style, display an immediate inflection of cultural tenets of Nazi propaganda. Söderbaum's career resonated with National Socialist ideas. Her exclusive association with Harlan, on which he jealously insisted, fixed the couple into a union that is hard to separate. In fact, Harlan is the only film director who was tried (and acquitted) after World War II for creating overtly propagandistic works, in particular for his direction of the anti-Semitic 1940 production *Jew Suess*.[5] "He made me and, in the end, he also destroyed me" (Krause n.p.), she said after his death, forever reenacting the role Harlan had created for her, that of a tragic heroine caught up in a fate that far exceeded her powers. Moreover, as Harlan's creation, the private (postwar) Söderbaum not only mirrored her cinematic representation as the eternal victim of Harlan's National Socialist melodramas, but her micronarrative also articulated a scaled down version of what some have argued to have been National Socialist women's overall position under Nazi rule, constituting a group who equally suffered under the control of a paternalistic despot. At the same time, Söderbaum's character remained forever mired in the controversy surrounding her husband's guilt and responsibility, which appropriately led to questions that addressed her own complicity. The debates raised by feminist historians who argued about women's accountability and victimization in Nazi Germany thus also surfaced in discussions of Kristina Söderbaum.[6]

Conversely, during the Third Reich, Söderbaum, the star, was perceived not as a figure of suffering but as a talented actress who happily united her career with marital and maternal duties, as a performer whose privileged involvement in the artistic family seemed to exempt her from the ideological limitations imposed on women elsewhere. Söderbaum's appearance, argues Stephen Lowry, "conformed to the ideas of beauty and femininity we can also find in the fine arts, the advertising and in the official attestations of the time." She was "blond, young, strong, and more athletic than she was elegant" (61). In addition, her voice and demeanor further emphasized this impression. Her naive mode of self-presentation made her appear childlike, innocent, decent and pure, but also vital and spontaneous (Lowry 61).

In fact, Goebbels at times protested the casting of Söderbaum in roles that seemed to undermine the positive identification of her Aryan image, and insisted on plot corrections for various Harlan melodramas (The Golden City, The Sacrifice) or attempted to replace Söderbaum with a more appropriately brunette actress (The Sacrifice).[7] Unlike Harlan's propaganda films (Jew Suess, Der Grosse König [The Great King,1942], Kolberg [1945]), which were motivated by issues of race and war, the melodramas that centered on Söderbaum as the central protagonist were driven primarily by conflicts produced through their heroines' sexual desires. Furthermore, it was Söderbaum's body, in tandem with its naturalist linkage to the German landscape, whose corporeality marked the visual aesthetics of her films. One of Harlan's most prominent directorial characteristics, as Erich Lüth has proposed, was the director's "exploitation of his own wife's physicality" (quoted in Zielinski 35). Yet, at the same time, the actress's identification with Aryan strength and vitality must be problematized. Several analyses of Söderbaum's character in Jew Süss have linked the role of the female to the role of the Jew, arguing that the film conflates gender and race to some degree to emphasize the unequivocal triumph of German masculinity.[8] Similar arguments can also be made for Söderbaum's role as a half-Czech fallen woman in *The Golden City*. It is as if womanhood, as soon as it came to the foreground and claimed a narrative space that went beyond the simplest of stereotypes, always constituted a problem.

Consequently, the central question we must ask when looking at a star like Kristina Söderbaum is not only whether her star persona and screen representations were capable of expressing the National Socialist ideal of womanhood, but whether her image also stayed contained within this paradigm. Did the Nazis manage to encapsulate their absolute in a star image that solely functioned within the socioeconomic context of Third Reich culture, or did German audiences ask for more than could be accommodated by the framework set up by Nazi ideology—even in the case of Harlan and Söderbaum? In addition, the function of melodrama, a genre that provided National Socialist cinema's most popular films, and its role in articulating social contradictions and conflicts, must be considered in this context.[9] In fact, two of the biggest stars of Third Reich cinema—Zarah Leander and Kristina Söderbaum—were exclusively melodramatic performers. Leander's films began with a worldly "diva" who was then purified, cleaned up, and brought back to a more conventionally moral status quo.[10] Her sexual experience, acknowledged desire, and often her motherhood, constituted the starting point for a narrative development that worked in a direction opposite to that in the films of Söderbaum, who frequently entered her works as a virgin. Söderbaum's melodramas approximated narrative models that pointed toward the "blood and soil" rhetoric of National Socialist ideology through her characters' inherent association with nature and the homeland. Furthermore, while the contradictions that emerged in Leander's pictures pointed to frictions between Hollywood paradigms and Nazi ideals, the problems we encounter in Söderbaum's films derived from inconsistencies that were inherent in National Socialist philosophy and political practice vis-à-vis women's roles: its strange mix of patriarchal conservatism, women's emancipation, and political participation. The tensions that persist in Kristina Söderbaum's narrative characterizations—especially in the films that foregrounded Söderbaum as the main protagonist, rather than those in which she had a supporting role—indicate that in films that thematized womanhood as their main concern, National Socialist models of ideal femininity frequently collapsed to make room for cinematic excess and melodramatic tragedy.[11]

The 1943 film *The Sacrifice* most pointedly illustrates this tendency. In this film, as in earlier Harlan melodramas, Söderbaum's representation of artless, natural womanliness once again functions to describe an ideal femininity that opposes the dominant cinematic model of the glamorous sophisticate, which circulated in both Ufa pictures and Hollywood movies at the time. While many National Socialist divas were modeled after Hollywood stars like Zarah Leander, who was meant to replace Marlene Dietrich in exile, or Lilian Harvey, who had returned from Hollywood to appear in romantic comedies that echoed the American screwball genre, Söderbaum did seem uniquely homely in most of her appearences. Yet in this case, Söderbaum's character also transcends the narrative model with which she is commonly associated. The radical consequence with which her character lives out her "natural" drives toward physical expression—always part of Söderbaum's overall star image as "nature child," but usually contained by the narrative—explodes the narrative framing of the story. Even the heroine's final death is not sufficient to restore the previous status quo convincingly. Instead, the film reveals surprising ideological ruptures and narrative disparities. While *The Sacrifice* engaged particular National Socialist values—especially the myth of naturalness and the notion of glorified death—it explored them in such an overwrought mode that the ideological undercurrents of much of Nazi cinema exploded in its excessive melodrama: on the one hand, the film's overaesthetization made these concerns clearly visible, and on the other, their ideological purpose dissolved in the contradictory nature of the narrative.

Goebbels interjected his objections to the project several times during production. Initially, he protested against the casting of Söderbaum in the role of Aels—a free-spirited young woman who almost destroys the marriage of a haute-bourgeois Hamburg couple—because a seductress of this kind did not correspond to the Nazi ideal of the Nordic type and should better be portrayed by a brunette.[12] Harlan persisted in casting his wife, but Goebbels did successfully change the ending. The original novel by Rudolf Binding culminated in the death of the male protagonist and left the woman alive. Goebbels, however, demanded otherwise. As a result—just like in *The Golden City*—the film finale of *The Sacrifice* deviated from the literary blueprint on which it was based and ended with the death of the heroine. According to Harlan, the minister of propaganda argued "that thousands of soldiers were deserting at the front because they were plagued by the fear that their wives at home were cheating on them. . . . The woman guilty of causing the adultery had to die, not the husband. The marriage must be preserved. This was better not only for the front, but also at home in an educational sense [volkserzieherischen Sinne]" (164). The finished film, moreover, still left Goebbels undecided. Deeply moved by its "erotics of death," as he called it, he privately screened the film frequently, while holding it back from public release, presumably because the film's mood was too dark and hopeless. When *The Sacrifice* finally premiered in December 1944, he had apparently given in to the somber tone of the narrative, knowing well that the war was coming to an end. The public—both in Germany and abroad—liked the film (Beyer 235). Kristina Söderbaum herself would refer to *The Sacrifice* as her best work and her favorite film throughout her life (Krause n.p.).

Like *Die Reise nach Tilsit [The Journey to Tilsit]* (Harlan, 1939) and *Immensee* (Harlan, 1942), *The Sacrifice* essentially centers on a love triangle. However, where *Immensee*'s heroine finds herself caught between two men and two lifestyles (one artistic, the other bound to traditionalist country living), *The Sacrifice* positions the male lead, Albrecht (Carl Raddatz), between two women and their opposite philosophies, Octavia (Irene von Meyersdorff), the overbred ethereal senator's daughter identified with aristocratic "high" culture, and Aels (Kristina Söderbaum), the unconventional but doomed "migrant bird," who even in her association with death embodies pure physicality. The film begins with Albrecht's return to Hamburg after a three-year journey through the world, upholding the German "colonial spirit," as a speaker for Hamburg's Hanseatic League puts it. He has brought souvenirs from his travels to be given to not yet chosen female companions: an Indian statue of Kwannon, the virgin goddess of compassion and mercy, and a red kimono, alluding to the sensuality of the Geisha. The objects will come to stand for the two women in his future: one larger than life, the other firmly of it. "Octavia is heavenly," he will later complain to his friend, to explain his adultery, "Aels is earthly."

Yet, initially Albrecht is attracted to the translucently beautiful Octavia ("How can you give a girl a Roman name these days?" he mocks) with her all-encompassing goodness and empathy, and he soon asks to marry her. Octavia is seen as a creature of luminous light. She is an angel, engulfed, as a contemporary review put it, in a mise-en-scène of visual excess depicting a "snow-white, silky-shimmering palatial salon . . . , the floor covered in an ankle-deep carpet" (Biedrzynski n.p.) The cultural traditions that describe her, however, are also steeped in deep shadows: on Sunday mornings the family gathers in the dark hall of their mansion on the river, the curtains drawn. Octavia plays melancholy tunes, her father, the old senator, recites Nietzsche's morbid poem "The Sinking Sun." In Frieda Grafe's words, "The art of the upper classes is colorless and shy of light. Poems about the premonition of death, Nocturne by Chopin, they give each other orchids from their greenhouses, instead of flowers from their gardens. They favor wearing black and white, and when they allow themselves excess, they wear silver or gold, more shiny than colorful" (quoted in Bock and Tötenberg 455). Albrecht feels suffocated. "Night, night, night, always night and death," he protests, "and outside the sun is shining. . . . Tell me, don't you find this spooky?" Through Albrecht, the film expresses its inherent critique of an "over-educated" bourgeoisie and its perceived lack of physical fitness and joie de vivre, and presents as its counterpoint the daring vitality of bodily expression, a move that resonates with National Socialist attitudes toward class. Insisting that he needs "wind and waves, the burning sun," he storms outside, tolerated by his benevolent fiancée, who will—throughout the plot—selflessly encourage whatever makes him happy. As Albrecht sails out onto the water, his next love, Aels, appears out of the waves like a mermaid holding on to the back of his boat. She is swimming naked, yet is disguised by the water, a virtual spirit of nature. The intrigued Albrecht soon learns that she is Octavia's neighbor, a wealthy Swedish women who restlessly travels the world. "She is like a migrant bird," Octavia explains, "and generally adopts a very unorthodox way of life."

Dora Traudisch consequently juxtaposes the two heroines as personifying binary nineteenth-century types: the trope of the *femme fragile* and image of the mermaid. The first is marked by an anemic beauty free of erotic signifiers, the latter by her engulfing, mysterious, and dangerous sexuality.[13] Yet, despite the film's clear invocation of these literary figures, an unequivocal identification of its female characters with these tropes is made impossible by the continuing narrative. Aels is not at all healthy, but terminally ill, and Octavia's self-sacrificing forbearance will not result in the *femme fragile*'s consumptive demise but give her the strength to win back her husband. As Albrecht runs away from the morose contemplation of night and death in Octavia's drawing room, he embraces a woman who thinks and speaks of nothing else. In his move toward the other lover, he simply turns away from *abstraction* toward *experience*. While Aels initially presents herself as a seductive Lorelei-like figure, the impending narrative doom is directed at her, not Albrecht. It is Aels who is the *femme fragile, pretending* to be the mermaid. It seems that in Harlan's melodramatic universe the only experiences waiting for its occupants are those of loss and dying.

Thus, while an unsuspecting Albrecht begins his daily horse rides with his neighbor and falls in love with her, the spectator is privy to Aels's private conversations with her doctor, in which she defends her attitude of uncalculated risk. Surrounded by a "pack of spotted Great Danes that are meant to express Aels's spiritedness" (Biedrzynski n.p.), she explains that she put her favorite dog to sleep when it became too sick to enjoy life—an analogy that has often been read as the film's implicit approval of euthanasia—insisting that she wants to "live," not "vegetate."

"The erotics of death that bothered Goebbels about the film is undisguised," propounds Grafe, "[i]ts healthy look is only appearance, a sickly red glow caused by fever and excitation. Aels is burning" (quoted in Bock and Tötenberg 455). The Nazi newspaper *Völkischer Beobachter* similarly observed: "The passionate urge to want to die young, to ride on the waves like the elegant bride of the wind, to race along on horseback, that which is unrestrained, feverish, and addicted to life is expressed very effectively through Kristina Söderbaum" (Biedrzynski n.p.). It is precisely Aels's defiant stance and her daring sensuality that attract Albrecht. The couple's continuing excursions into the countryside, which are alluded to in the above quotation, also become increasingly erotic. In one scene Aels, dressed in red, literally aims her (love) bow and hits a bull's-eye. In the following sequence, she is seen riding bareback in a white bathing suit, leading her horse into the ocean to literally ride the waves in a sexually unambiguous manner. She further reveals her underwear while changing clothes and throws herself back onto a haystack, looking up at Albrecht expectantly. Moreover, she also angrily rejects the intervention of Octavia's cousin, arguing for her right to pursue her own unconventional happiness.

Under pressure, it is Albrecht who reluctantly marries his fiancée and leaves town to avoid the collapse of the marriage. His relationship with Octavia, however, is represented as unsuccessful. At an extravagant carnival party, Albrecht's new wife is seen as incapable of enjoying herself. Dressed as a Roman goddess at the masked ball, her attempts to please her husband are merely pretenses of self-enjoyment. While he flirts with two ladies in tuxedos and top hats, a faint allusion to 1920s lesbianism, Octavia is miserable. Gliding down the tongue-slide of a gigantic Harlequin's head, she looks almost violated. When she is elected the queen of carnival and lifted up by the crowd, she escapes in tears rather than delighting in her coronation. Amidst Harlan's spectacular mise-en-scène—meant to suggest a colorful, vibrant world—Octavia longs for the quiet, contemplative atmosphere of her father's river house. Moved by his wife's unhappiness and homesickness, Albrecht decides to return to Hamburg.

However, the "migrant bird" has not moved on. Weakened by love-sickness, Aels is now bound to her bed. Only Albrecht's return lets her regain her strength, and the affair continues. "We are in love, my friend," she tells him, "and it will get bad." Beyond her mysterious disease, love, too, acts like an illness. Furthermore, Aels's unwed motherhood, which is left as unexplained as her exotic malady and remains unexcused by the heroine, serves to portray the character in an equally ambiguous light. As Octavia's acceptance of Albrecht's affair gives way to jealousy, Aels's confusing identity is further investigated. In a striking scene, Octavia and her cousin Matthias follow Aels down the street, because Octavia is intent on discovering Aels's "secret":

> Octavia: Look, how all the men turn to look at her. Nobody looks at *me* on the street, even though everyone tells me that I'm beautiful. You've often told me, Albrecht told me. Why *is* this? She's just like a *magnet!*
> Matthias: You can say *that*, yes! Octavia, be *glad* that no one looks at you on the street. You are a *pure* human being.
> Octavia: No, that isn't it! That, she is too. She is *superior* to me. There's no need in pretending otherwise.

As Traudisch points out, the pair soon detects that Aels has a daughter and thus locates her "superiority" in her "true womanhood"(171). Yet the character's motherhood is simultaneously undercut by the narrative. Aels's nebulous "tropical" fever forces her to live separately from her child in order to avoid the pain of separation she herself suffered when her own mother died young. The hereditary aspects of this curse/disease further complicate her easy identification with the life-affirming stereotype of National Socialist motherhood. Just as for Söderbaum's Anna in *The*

Golden City, the legacy of femininity with its potential for sexual fulfillment comes with an early expiration date; within the fatalist economy of Harlan romances, where there is female pleasure, death cannot be too far. Aels is a good woman, in the National Socialist sense, and simultaneously its opposite.

Likewise, the film's resolution is caught in a number of contradictions. As Aels's illness worsens, a typhoid fever takes hold in Hamburg, threatening Aels's young daughter. Albrecht is sent to rescue the child, but catches the fever himself. Weakened, he apologizes to Octavia for all the suffering he has caused. Moreover, when Octavia learns that Aels is also dying at home, waiting in vain for Albrecht to ride by her house to greet her through the window, Octavia performs her final sacrifice. Fulfilling the deadly love circle, she dresses up as her husband once a day to deliver his silent message of love to her dying rival. Ironically, it is Albrecht's discovery of Octavia's selfless gesture, of her great sacrifice, that finally enables him to separate himself from his desire. In an almost psychedelic superimposition, Aels and Albrecht are both seen in bed, communicating with each other as if in a fever fantasy: he explains that he must return to Octavia, Aels understands and dies. Ironically, then, it is due to Octavia's superiority and altruistic nobility—which, as we have seen, the film associates with aristocratic breeding and high art—that she triumphs in the end, thus resurrecting what the film initially sought to criticize. Its suggested dichotomy between art/death and life/nature is proven false in the end, stripping the film of its ideological consistency to make room for the expression of inescapable doom.

Many critics nonetheless view the film's ending as firmly located within the Nazis' ideological tropes of renunciation and self-sacrifice. "Veit Harlan's *The Sacrifice,*" Rentschler concludes, "culminates in a hypnotic demonstration of sickness unto death as another transgressive heroine takes her place in the procession of female martyrs" (144). In the final scene, the married couple ride along the beach on horseback—Octavia has clearly absorbed some of Aels's characteristics—commemorating the dead woman by throwing roses into the sea; a last gesture, one might be tempted to gibe, for the "Reich's Water Corpse." Cinzia Romani further contends that the filmic ending does not necessarily negate Söderbaum's role: "Once again Söderbaum dies; but despite the unhappy ending, the character she plays is not wholly a negative one. Romanticism and pantheism and the wish to become 'one with the universe' are mingled in a character of a woman who speaks in terms of dreams and other worlds" (87).

Indeed, the film's reliance on romanticism and pantheism is precisely what locks it firmly into a National Socialist framework. As Julian Petley observes, the film is critical of the aristocracy via Albrecht, but uncritical of pantheism, fatalism and romanticized death—all of which are staple components of National Socialist ideology (137). He further argues that the film's "glorification of physicality," even Söderbaum's nudity, firmly connect with the Nazis' simultaneous celebration of the "body beautiful" and its de-eroticization.[14]

Consequently, the question of whether or not Kristina Söderbaum's role in *The Sacrifice* can be read as transgressive is subject to some debate. Petley argues that Aels could "hardly be described as an earthy sensualist, particularly as played by Kristina Söderbaum," suggesting that the actress' star image and performance style worked against the controversial elements contained in the character (135). By contrast, I would like to suggest that the character of Aels condensed the very components that had marked Söderbaum's star construction—naturalness, a large capacity to suffer, physicality, sexuality—in such a way that it was impossible to contain them. It is wrong to argue that the Nazis had stripped their stars—and Söderbaum, in particular—of sexuality, even though the National Socialist discourse itself disapproved of the frivolously "erotic." To a large extent, what Söderbaum melodramas are about *is* sexual desire, as well as its containment. Along these lines, Hartmut Redottée asserts that "a clear-cut definition of a character-type, whom Kristina Söderbaum embodied, is hardly possible. Her description as an innocently naïve blonde, cannot be maintained. Aels in *The Sacrifice* is neither innocent nor naïve." (10)

Moreover, as in earlier Harlan melodramas, the film's embrace of pantheistic fatalism is disconnected from larger nationalist concerns. As is common to female-centered National Socialist narratives, Aels's readiness to live life to the fullest and then die does not serve a purpose; it is uselessly tragic. In fact, both women's sacrifices are intensely private and have nothing to offer to "the people"; neither has the male protagonist, Albrecht, whose preoccupation with leisure and romance overshadows his token introduction as a messenger of German colonialism. In addition, the film's excessive style and pathos—its marked readability as "kitschy" or "corny"—add an element of reflexivity to the film's already confusing ideological messages.[15]

Ultimately, what makes *The Sacrifice* so complicated is that it related to many cultural tropes—some generally linked to

German culture, others specifically connected to National Socialist denominations—albeit in a way that did not fully cohere with
any one of them. While the film wholeheartedly embraces the
notion of sacrificial death, it also maintains an ambiguous attitude toward its "weak" characters—none of whom can be seen as
fulfilling a representative model function—whose obsessive preoccupation with their own identities never leads to their approxi-
mation of a National Socialist "ideal." The characters' self-
absorbed melancholy, their feverish search for self-realization and
self-fulfilment, is not exhausted through an association with Nazi
virtues, but points to German literary traditions and philosophical dispositions that far exceed the proto-fascist. Rather, the
film's elaboration on the tensions between a romanticized death
drive and a rebellious will to live strikingly attempts to interpret
the collective unconscious of a nation nearing its total collapse.
Immediately following the film's premiere, Harlan and Söderbaum relocated to Hamburg to escape the dangers waiting in a
falling capital. Released only five months before Germany's complete capitulation, *The Sacrifice* reached fewer spectators than
earlier Harlan/Söderbaum triumphs. The film does, however,
markedly reflect a national absorption in the very discourses of
death and survival.

    We must conclude, then, that while Veit Harlan's melo-
dramas with Kristina Söderbaum vividly articulated the Nazis'
obsession with nature, sacrifice, and death, they also pointed at
the problems contained within this ideological system. Fritz Göttler explains that:

> . . . [In *The Sacrifice*] appearances are as deceptive as in the pair's
> other films. Söderbaum, who looks like the embodiment of natu-
> ralness and health, is anything but nature impersonated. Like
> Dietrich and Garbo, she is an absolutely artificial creation, the
> perfection of suffering. Synthetic nature, the nature of synthesis:
> with Harlan, melodrama seems to have lost some of its innocence
> by putting itself in the service of propaganda. But melodrama
> wasn't the Nazis' genre. As much as it might have functioned to
> support the state . . . through films which moved Goebbels to
> tears, the closer it moved to the edge of the abyss; and never
> closer than in Harlan's films (n.p.).

In addition, Harlan's films painfully illustrated the problematic
status these ideas assumed, once they were focused on female
protagonists. That is to say, Söderbaum's film characters addressed the very tensions that are inherent in the female-centered

melodrama—namely, the contradiction between the foregrounding of the female figure and the subordinate position of women vis-à-vis men in National Socialist ideology, and by extension, in all patriarchal cultures—which result in her representation as conflicted and torn between different discourses. All of Söderbaum's lead characters oscillate between their desire to fulfill themselves individually and the social pressures embedded in their environment, and thus describe both women's desire to break out and their failure to do so. What was enjoyable about watching Söderbaum, then—especially for female audiences caught in an identical dilemma—were her characters' tireless efforts to fight for their happiness, even if this meant that they might have to die in the process.

Whereas Harlan's propaganda pictures managed to contain the "female problems" that emerged in the narrative by reducing the significance of the female figure to that of a minor character, whose feelings and motives were absorbed into National Socialist stereotypes without deeper investigation, the melodramas fully explored the tragic difficulties of female identity under the Nazis' ideological system. In its recurring odes to death, Nazi cinema revealed German fascism's self-destructive tendencies. Veit Harlan's melodramas show that the trajectory of dying extended far beyond the "glorious" death on the battlefield or the atrocious extermination of "undesirables" in Nazi concentration camps. While National Socialist films celebrated male heroism as active aggression in the service of expansion and domination, women's self-sacrifices were internalized and emotional, leaving them unfulfilled or even suicidal. In the ideological economy of National Socialist philosophy and its cultural fictions, death also called for ordinary German women, all of whom possessed fatal qualities, anchored in their problematic physicality, which could ultimately never be resolved in a positive fashion.

Even in her status as an idealized figure, Söderbaum always remained a victim. The reason for these contradictions might very well be contained within the nature of melodrama itself. Melodramatic forms have often been described as a generic framework, which promotes the articulation of tensions between the individual and the social as the source of insoluble tragedy. In Peter Brooks's words, "[m]an [sic] is seen to be, and must recognize himself to be, playing on the theatre that is the point of juncture, and of clash, of imperatives beyond himself that are nonmediated and irreducible" (13). Thomas Elsaesser further sees

melodrama as containing "elements of interiorization and per-
sonalization of what are primarily ideological conflicts"—
conflicts that consequently reach far and above the capacities of
the individual to understand, let alone solve them (353).

In this respect Kristina Söderbaum's melodramatic roles
may be read as symptomatic, insofar as they expressed the very
conflicts that were also problematic in the Nazis' stance vis-à-vis
women in general. In fact, Söderbaum got much closer to the core
of these tensions than any other star of the period. In the ideological framework of Nazi culture, the positive description of women
as individual figures or characters was extremely difficult because
they could be directed only toward the personal (romance, family), and were therefore only indirectly linked to the concerns of
the nation or the political. That is to say, in the figure of
"woman" there always resided a political tension, albeit not one
between the Nazi ideal of womanhood and its alternatives, but
one that inevitably arose once the focus turned away from the
male and toward the psychologized figure of the female. While
the Nazis advocated a somewhat masochistic stoicism in terms
of their expectation that women bravely endure extraordinary
hardship, the excessive suffering of melodrama exceeded this
framework. In Söderbaum's most popular melodramas the National Socialist meanings transported in the films therefore col-
lided with the expansive energies of their melodramatic excess.
Beyond Söderbaum's image as a National Socialist star, what appealed to German audiences were the tragic components that
were inevitably produced through her womanhood in Harlan's
films. In other words, Söderbaum showed female audiences that
even for women who seemingly corresponded to the Nazi ideal of
femininity, life was a melodrama. In the destructive environment
of Hitler's warfare, Söderbaum thus became the very wartime star
who most passionately addressed the experiences of loss and dep-
rivation that had become an everyday occurrence in ordinary
women's lives—not an idealized super female, but the tragic embodiment of fascist misogyny.

Ironically, postwar accounts turned this description on its
head. While Söderbaum eventually gave up acting to take up star
photography, the news media as well as Söderbaum herself now
embraced the star's prior filmic description as the perpetual victim of male society and applied it to Söderbaum's career as a Nazi
star.[16] If, in National Socialist cinema, she had often been the victim of "degenerate" males (Jews, Czechs, religious zealots, etc.),
now she became the victim of the misogynist figures of Goebbels

and Harlan.[17] The melodramatic description of Söderbaum, the star, thus remained forever mired in the very discourse that had also informed her screen popularity: women's supposed incapacity to take charge of their destiny.

Nazi cinema used its performers to cover a wide range of female representations. Kristina Söderbaum's case points to a number of discourses related to the Nazi concept of "blood and soil," thus linking her star sign to the notion of land and nature as inscribed in the figure of the woman. Her star sign further affirms the prominence of melodrama in Nazi hit films, a generic preference that divulged similar ideological maneuvers but also revealed Nazi cinema's symptomatic inability to address female spectators in an ideologically sound, yet positive and optimistic, manner. The films' tragic narratives and melodramatic excess proved unsuitable to activating the fascist tropes of perpetual renunciation, sacrifice, and death as part of a desirable model for female lives. Instead, National Socialist popular cultural production inadvertently underlined that the position of women in Nazi culture was embedded in negatives.

Furthermore, the invocation of a set number of female stereotypes, which marked the standard narratives of the National Socialist woman's film, carried over seamlessly into the German postwar era. The *Heimatfilme* (homeland pictures) of the 1950s took up the opposing images of womanhood (woman/lady) that had characterized National Socialist heroines: the natural country girl previously embodied by Söderbaum's Aels (which National Socialist ideology attempted to foreground) and the elegant city sophisticate, represented in *The Sacrifice* by Meyersdorff's Octavia.[18] The continuities and legacies that informed female star signs and popular film production of the Nazi period thus also reached beyond German fascism, addressing female viewers, and their concerns and fantasies, in the ongoing economic space of international capitalism. That is to say, the consistent references to cultural tropes that were not ideologically contained within the philosophical framework of National Socialism—even if political measures were taken to appropriate and infuse these referents with National Socialist meanings—indicate the German public's persistent desire to identify with nonfascist traditions, ranging from humanist-idealist to modern expressions. The ambiguity of National Socialist popular culture therefore points to problems that were unresolved in the social sphere of Nazi Germany, suggesting a national adherence to cultural forms that resisted National Socialist philosophy, just as Nazi image makers attempted to appropriate these very proclivities to bolster the functioning of their state.

Yet, attempts to investigate National Socialist culture as productive of "other meanings," as Norbert Grob put it (E4), are often seen as smacking of redemptive revisionism. "Films of the Nazi era," warns Rentschler, "are easy to enlist in campaigns to normalize and neutralize the Nazi legacy" (221). I do not see, however, why a more complicated approach to popular culture under National Socialist rule should necessarily *only* produce apologist interpretations. Instead, it may lead us to revise the Nazis' self-proclaimed assertions about the very functionality of their system, without rescuing "the people" from their potential complicity in Nazi crimes. While it is important to point to the particular weaknesses of systems of totalitarian domination in terms of both their operational practices as well as their ideological foundations, I see no need to hand out medals to "ordinary" Germans for their schizophrenic involvement in antithetical meanings: their engagement in countervailing discourses does not exonerate them from the accusation of failed political responsibility. In looking at the complex interrelations that came into play in Nazi culture—far from clouding the "real" political issues that are at the heart of National Socialist history (racism, imperialism, sexism) by blowing populist or postmodernist smoke—we may, in fact, better understand the dynamics of the fascist totalitarianism that marked the twentieth century.

NOTES

1. Romani refers here to the Nazi recreational program "Strength through Joy," which provided working-class people with state-subsidized vacations such as North Sea cruises or mountain hiking trips. The proclaimed goal was to restore German health through contact with nature, but at the same time the programming of these excursions, which included educational slide shows and the collective singing of patriotic songs, had a highly ideological bent.

2. German newspaper archives and clippings services collect and organize newspaper articles according to date, while page numbers are not noted. All newspaper and magazine citation in this article therefore lack references to pagination.

3. Stephen Lowry argues that *The Golden City* made ten million Reichsmark, at the most (57).

4. Drewniak lists Söderbaum's 1944 salary as sixty thousand Reichsmark per film (Drewniak 162). He further details Leander's and Harvey's contract arrangements, both of which were more lucrative than Söderbaum's.

5. The trial of Veit Harlan began on March 3, 1948. The prosecution accused Harlan of "crimes against humanity," according to allied control law no. 10, which specified that all actions that could be regarded as "having aided the murder, genocide, enslavement, imprisonment, torture, rape and other inhumane acts against the civil population" be included under this rubric. The prosecution argued that Harlan had assisted the Holocaust by directing the anti-Semitic propaganda film *Jud Süß*. Harlan was acquitted twice, both in the initial trial and in the appeal. The controversial rulings were based on the assertion that it was impossible to ascertain Harlan's sole responsibility for the ideological content of the film and that the film could furthermore not be directly causally linked to the mass deportations and murder of Jews. See Zielinski 42–225.

6. See, for example, the debates between Claudia Koonz and Gisela Bock: Gisela Bock, "Ein Historikerinnenstreit?" *Geschichte und Gesellschaft* 18 (1992): 400–404; and Claudia Koonz, *Mothers in the Fatherland: Women, the Family, and Nazi Politics* (New York: St. Martin's Press, 1987), xxxv.

7. See Gabriele Lange, *Das Kino als moralische Anstalt* (Frankfurt/M.: Lange, 1994), 134.

8. See Régine Mihal Friedman, "Männlicher Blick und weibliche Reaktion," *Frauen und Film* 41 (December 1986): 50–64.

9. On the function of melodrama as an articulation of conflict in Hollywood film, see, for instance, Thomas Elsaesser's essay: "Tales of Sound and Fury: Observations on the Family Melodrama."

10. Leander's best known films include *La Habanera [La Habanera]* (Sierck, 1937) and *Zu neuen Ufern [To New Shores]* (Sierck, 1937), both directed by Detlef Sierck, later known in Hollywood as Douglas Sirk, as well as *Heimat [Home]* (Froelich, 1938) and *Die grosse Liebe [The Great Love]* (Hansen, 1942).

11. Patrice Petro's revisionist feminist history of Weimar culture has already explored how Weimar cinema addressed female spectators and represented women's concerns through melodramatic fictions. See Patrice Petro, *Joyless Streets. Women and Melodramatic Representation in Weimar Germany* (Princeton, N.J.: Princeton University Press, 1989). In addition, both Petro and Miriam Hansen have shown that cinema had much to offer to female audiences from its very beginnings. See Miriam Hansen, "Early Silent Cinema: Whose Public Sphere?" *New German Critique* 29 (spring-summer 1983): 147–84; and idem, "Pleasure, Ambivalence, Identification: Valentino and Female Spectatorship," *Cinema Journal* 25, no. 4 (summer 1986): 6–32.

12. Kristina Söderbaum cites this conversation in her memoirs, *Nichts bleibt immer so* (quoted in Lange 134).

13. See Traudisch's inclusive analysis of the film, 150–86.

14. Petley points out that Nazi imagery often featured male and female nudity, best exemplified by the nude athletes in Leni Riefenstahl's *Olympiad*. He further cites the debates about a 1935 farming calendar, which ultraconservatives criticized for the depiction of female nudes, to which the SS responded that reading such images as "erotic" suggested perversion in the spectator, not the image (136). I would like to caution, however, that Nazi statements concerning matters of eroticism were often merely rhetorical; many cultural phenomena in the National Socialist media can be understood only if we see them as attempts to package eroticism in such an

ambiguous way that it could pass the censors without losing its enticing effect.

15. Swiss newspapers, for instance, which published uncensored reviews, found *The Sacrifice* "unrealistic," "overly sentimental," "superficial," and "anesthetizing." Swedish reviews also often adopted an ironic tone when discussing the film (Drewniak 677). This contemporary response suggests that the film was read as excessive in terms of story and style, pointing to the possibility of similar readings by German spectators.

16. Söderbaum's memoirs, *Nichts bleibt immer so,* were instrumental in creating this impression. In Régine Mihal Friedman's interview with the actress, "Mein Tag mit Kristina," she also points to her role as an innocent caught in a bad marriage and a political system she didn't understand.

17. Söderbaum firmly stood by her husband in the postwar years. She testified on his behalf in the Harlan trial and further rejected all offers to return to Sweden without him to resume her film career. Only after Harlan's death did Söderbaum begin to publicly voice her criticism of him and describe the often oppressive relationship she experienced as his wife.

18. Homeland pictures typically contrasted both figures without eliminating either and resolved the narrative problematic by physically separating the oppositional protagonists allocating each their own space (city/country). The immensely popular *Sissy*-trilogy starring Romy Schneider further united both paradigms. Sissy, the Bavarian mountain child who becomes the celebrated empress of Austria—enshrined in the luxury of the imperial court and simultaneously imprisoned by it—is, in fact, emblematic for the preoccupations of postwar kitsch and excess.

WORKS CITED

Albrecht, Gerd. *Nationalsozialistische Filmpolitik; eine soziologische Untersuchung über die Spielfilme des Dritten Reichs.* Stuttgart: F. Enke, 1969.

Althen, Michael. "Totentanz," *Süddeutsche Zeitung* (Munich), 29 June 1995.

Beyer, Friedemann. *Die UFA-Stars im Dritten Reich. Frauen für Deutschland.* Munich: Heyne, 1991.

Biedrzynski, Richard "Liebe, Leid und Luxus," *Völkischer Beobachter* (Berlin), 31 December 1944.

Bock, Gisela, "Ein Historikerinnenstreit?" *Geschichte und Gesellschaft* 18, 1992.

Bock, Hans-Michael, and Michael Tötenberg, eds. *Das Ufa-Buch. Kunst und Krisen, Stars und Regisseure, Wirtschaft und Politik.* Frankfurt am Main: Zweitausendeins, 1992.

Brooks, Peter. *The Melodramatic Imagination.* New Haven, Conn.: Yale University Press, 1976.

Drewniak, Boguslaw. *Der deutsche Film, 1938–1945. Ein Gesamtüberblick.* Düsseldorf: Droste, 1987.

Ebelseder, Sepp. "Eine Witwe knipst sich durchs Leben." *Stern,* no. 44, 23 October 1969.

Elsaesser, Thomas. "Tales of Sound and Fury: Observations on the Family

Melodrama." in *Film Genre Reader,* edited by Barry Keith Grant, 350–80. Austin: University of Texas Press, 1995.

Friedman, Régine Mihal, "Männlicher Blick und weibliche Reaktion," *Frauen und Film,* no. 41, December 1986.

———. "Mein Tag mit Kristina," *Frauen und Film,* no. 44/45, October 1988.

Göttler, Fritz. "Die Frau des Verfemten. Kristina Söderbaum wird 80," *Süddeutsche Zeitung,* 6 September 1992.

Grob, Norbert. "Veit Harlan." *CineGraph,* installment 15. Munich: edition text + kritik, 1989, E4.

Grunberger, Richard. *A Social History of the Third Reich.* Harmondsworth, UK: Penguin, 1974.

Hansen, Miriam, "Early Silent Cinema: Whose Public Sphere?" *New German Critique,* no. 29, Spring-Summer 1983.

———. "Pleasure, Ambivalence, Identification: Valentino and Female Spectatorship." *Cinema Journal* 25, no. 4, Summer 1986.

Harlan, Veit. *Im Schatten meiner Filme,* Gütersloh, Germany: Sigbert Mohn Verlag, 1966.

Kienzl, Florian. "Kristina Söderbaum, das Naturtalent." In *Text- und Bildinformationen zu dem Ufa Film "Die goldene Stadt,"* n.p. Berlin: Ufa Informationen, n.d.

Koebner, Thomas, ed. *Idole des deutschen Films.* Munich: edition text + kritik, 1997.

Koonz, Claudia. *Mothers in the Fatherland: Women, the Family, and Nazi Politics.* New York: St. Martin's Press, 1987.

Krause, Siegfried. "Ihr liebster Film ist 'Opfergang.'" *Rheinische Post,* 2 September 1977.

Lange, Gabriele. *Das Kino als moralische Anstalt.* Frankfurt/M., Germany: Lange, 1994.

Lowry, Stephen. *Pathos und Politik: Ideologie in Spielfilmen des Nationalsozialismus,* Tübingen: Niemeyer, 1991.

Petley, Julian. *Capital and Culture: German Cinema 1933–1945.* London: bfi, 1979.

Petro, Patrice. *Joyless Streets: Women and Melodramatic Representation in Weimar Germany.* Princeton: Princeton University Press, 1989.

Redottée, Hartmut. "Versuch über Harlan." In *Die Ufa—das deutsche Bilderimperium,* Ufa-Magazin, no. 20, 9–13. Berlin: Stiftung Deutsche Kinemathek, 1992.

Rentschler, Eric. *The Ministry of Illusion,* Cambridge, Mass.: Harvard University Press, 1996.

Romani, Cinzia. *Tainted Goddesses: Female Film Stars of the Third Reich,* New York: Sarpedon, 1992.

Sontag, Susan. "Fascinating Fascism," *New York Review of Books,* 6 February 1975.

Traudisch, Dora. *Mutterschaft mit Zuckerguss? Frauenfeindliche Propaganda im NS-Spielfilm.* Pfaffenweiler, Germany: Centaurus, 1993.

Witte, Karsten. "Film im Nationalsozialismus." In *Geschichte des deutschen Films,* edited by Wolfgang Jacobson, Anton Kaes, and Hans Helmut, 119–70. Stuttgart/Weimar: Verlag J.B. Metzler, 1993.

Zielinski, Siegfried. *Veit Harlan. Analysen und Materialien zur Auseinandersetzung mit einem Film-Regisseur des deutschen Faschismus.* Frankfurt/M.: R.G. Fischer, 1981.

FILMOGRAPHY

Ehe im Schatten [Marriage in Shadow] (Kurt Maetzig, 1948).
Die Goldene Stadt [The Golden City] (Kurt Maetzig, 1942). Video: Facet
    Video.
Der grosse König [The Great King] (Veit Harlan, 1942). Video: German Lan-
    guage Video Center.
Illusion (Victor Tourjansky, 1941).
Jud Süß [Jew Suess] (Veit Harlan, 1940). Video: with subtitles, International
    Historic Films Inc.
Kolberg (Veit Harlan, 1945). Video: with subtitles, Facets Video.
Opfergang [The Sacrifice] (Veit Harlan, 1943). Video: German Language
    Video Center.
Die Reise nach Tilsit [The Journey to Tilsit] (Veit Harlan, 1939).
Romanze in Moll [Romance in a Minor Key] (Helmut Käutner, 1943). Video:
    with subtitles, Facets Video.
Verklungenen Melodie [Faded Melody] (Victor Tourjansky, 1938). Video:
    German Language Video Center.

CHAPTER 7

Placing *Green Is the Heath* (1951)

Spatial Politics and Emergent West German Identity

Alasdair King

Although it seems immediately obvious that the *Heimatfilm* is a genre which numbers among its concerns the ideological meaning of territory, critics have tended not to seek to establish a more exact topography of the genre, nor to explore the reasons behind its success with German audiences. In their entry in the recently published and extensive *BFI Companion to German Cinema*, contributors Joseph Garncarz and Thomas Elsaesser remind readers that the *Heimatfilm* is one of a number of popular film genres unique to Germany (133). Like other successful domestic genres such as the *Problemfilm* or the *Arbeiterfilm*, the *Heimatfilm* has proved popular at different moments in Germany's development, and hence, despite its lowly standing among many critics, is central to the history of German national cinema. Although *Heimatfilme* were produced during the Weimar Republic and under the Third Reich, the genre achieved its most notable popular successes in the 1950s. Summarizing the conventions of the genre, and inadvertently hinting at the reason behind its low critical status, Garncarz and Elsaesser emphasize its indebtedness to the representation of traditional values: "Love triumphs over social and economic barriers, and the story is usually set in an idyllic German countryside, highlighting maypoles and other folkloric traditions" (Garncarz and Elsaesser 133). This summary usefully indicates some of the superficial thematic features shared by many *Heimatfilme,* though plotlines and settings can be surprisingly diverse. Social issues, rarely entirely absent despite the romanticized settings and plots, find positive resolution at the end of the films, often through the triumphal restoration of traditional village (rather than urban or modern) values. However, the rural locations chosen, and the characters placed filmically within their borders, are represented in a highly stylized manner. *Heimatfilme* rarely seek to represent authentic rural communities but rather utilize authentic and recognizable locations to construct imagined, and highly idealized, communities where contemporary tensions can ultimately be negotiated and defused. In this way, the *Heimatfilm* can be seen as a popular genre that addresses, albeit tangentially and mostly conservatively, social contradictions and ambiguities. Elsaesser has argued convincingly that this genre, despite its often reactionary plot resolutions,

> . . . is nonetheless one of the most accurate and sensitive barometers of shifts in public opinion across a wide spectrum of social and moral issues. . . . The *Heimatfilm* has always been the vehicle of crisis, an expression of conflicts that extend beyond the boundaries of its setting and the limited perspectives of its characters. While selling comforting ideological solutions it nonetheless gave the emotional dilemmas a fair airing. Its perennial usefulness—for filmmakers as well as audiences—would be then that it articulates, albeit in cliches and stereotypical formulas, the crises of authority and legitimation so crucial to German history and Germany as a nation. (Elsaesser II/5)

It is, however, important to add to this reading of the genre an analysis of its use of space in addressing German history, for so often in Germany's political development its crises have been conflicts over borders, territory, and identity. Indeed, the word *Heimat,* which is almost untranslatable but relates most closely to homeland or native region, has been employed in political discourse to win popular support for acts of territorial expansion on many occasions in recent German history.[1] To understand the popularity of the *Heimatfilm* in German history it is necessary to include in any assessment of its aesthetics its use of landscape and hence its spatial politics.

In recent years film scholars have begun to recognize the importance of the category of space to their understanding of the narrative strategies of European cinema. Drawing in particular on the work of André Gardies, but also on theorists as diverse as

Mikhaïl Bakhtin, Walter Benjamin, and Henri Lefebvre, they have attempted to establish frameworks for formal analyses of the utilization of place and location in specific films.[2] Gardies has proved particularly useful, both for his efforts to establish that space in literary and cinematic narrative is as important as characterization and also for his attempted redefinition of space with regards to narration. Rather than adhering to the conventional understanding of place as merely the environment in which objects take their place, he argues for the recognition that place in any narrative is a textual manifestation of a latent social ordering of space.[3] The place of the narrative therefore becomes a site offering significant representations of the inclusion and exclusion of characters from any given society's public and private domains.

Not surprisingly, much of the scholarly work on space in European cinema has concentrated on the mappings of city spaces by canonical directors such as Antonioni, Pasolini, and Wenders, mappings that self-consciously explore the social and political dimensions of urban space. The streets, squares, parks, and suburbs of Rome, Paris, and Berlin, above all, become the preferred locations in European cinema for the representation of hierarchies of inclusion, and also, of course, as Konstantarakos notes, of "spatial challenges to class, gender and ethnic exclusion, which occur often by representing forbidden movements across frontiers" (6). City spaces, and the (im)possibility of movement across and between them, form one of the enduring themes of European art cinema.[4]

However, the representation of space in European filmmaking is significant not only in its art cinema. Much less common has been critical work that explores the landscapes and locations that characterize popular genres such as the German *Heimatfilm*. Like popular American genres such as the western or the film noir, the *Heimatfilm*'s generic conventions foreground the representation of key recognizable and iconic spaces just as prominently as they do identifiable characterization or specific narrative dynamics. The representation of space and location in the *Heimatfilm* is central to an understanding of the narrative conventions of the genre, and, significantly, to its great popularity at specific moments in Germany's troubled political history. The use of landscape and location exceeds the mere provision of the narrative setting within which events unfold. Instead, space is organized symbolically in the *Heimatfilm* to offer German audiences access to a site where contemporary social and ideological problems, often concerning territory and identity, achieve a positive resolution.

Although the *Heimatfilm* often appears to be set in a timeless, unchanging landscape, a location somehow outside any historical matrix, its specific organization of space, as well as its appeal to tradition, can be historicized and is in fact meaningful only when considered within a political history of German space and place. It is easy to overlook that the *Heimatfilm* achieved its greatest popularity at the beginning of the 1950s, at a historical moment when political debates concerning territorial borders, mass migration, and new constructions of German national identity were particularly prevalent. As Mary Fulbrook has argued, in the immediate aftermath of the defeat of National Socialism in 1945, the geopolitical identity of postwar Germany was not only defined by changes to its external borders and the loss of territory to Poland and the Soviet Union. The physical landscape of the four zones of occupation, and subsequently after 1949 of the two German states, was subject to complex transformations in attempts to remove or re-present reminders of Germany's recent past:

> Germans continued to inhabit the same soil, but the landscapes became different. Streets and squares were renamed, buildings were put to different purposes, some places were transformed and re-presented, others allowed to tumble into ruin. There was an almost infinite variety of ways in which the landscapes of the past became all but unrecognizable, except to the eyes of those trained to perceive and imagine. (Fulbrook 27)

In addition, as Fulbrook points out, for millions of Germans in this period the landscapes were actually different in another way: around twelve million people resettled in different parts of Germany between 1945 and 1960. The census of 13 March 1950 in the newly founded Federal Republic of Germany recorded almost eight million ethnic Germans from the former eastern parts of the Reich and from East Central Europe who had emigrated between 1945 and 1949.[5] Approximately 16 percent of the Federal Republic's total population, then, were refugees, many of them considered expellees, or *Heimatvertriebene,* in the new state, having been subject to expulsion, forced migration, and ethnic cleansing from Germany's lost territories in the East. Despite the fact that much of this huge influx could be considered domestic migration, albeit often over great distances, there still remained the challenge of integrating ethnic German migrants into the very different German communities in the western states. Linked to this attempt to achieve a new sense of belonging, or *Heimat*, in the western states came the task of forging a new *West* German identity appropriate to the borders of the new Federal Republic.

The conditions under which integration was achieved were desperate: in addition to the personal trauma and loss that accompanied forced migration, it should be remembered that in the aftermath of defeat Germany lay in ruins, lacking adequate food or shelter to support its rapidly growing population. Mass homelessness, ill health, and starvation were prevalent, provoking numerous initial conflicts over scarce resources between native communities and refugees in western Germany.[6] Despite this unpromising environment, assimilation was relatively swift and successful, not least, according to Fulbrook, because "the concept of the ethnic German *Volk* readily encompassed those who often spoke in very different dialects and practised very different customs" (90). These displaced and fragmented heterogeneous communities were, over the course of the 1950s, largely integrated into the economically successful society of West Germany, not least because of the pressure exerted by the right-of-center *Bund der Heimatvertriebenen und Entrechteten* (BHE; Association of Refugees and Those Deprived of Rights), which ensured that economic restitution to refugees remained on the political agenda.[7]

It was exactly at this historical moment, when questions of place, belonging, and identity were so significant to the establishment of a new political consensus in the Federal Republic, that the *Heimatfilm* achieved its spectacular successes. What the *Heimatfilm*, particularly the most popular of all films in this decade, Hans Deppe's *Green Is the Heath [Grün ist die Heide]* (1951), appears to offer its German audiences is a stylized reworking of the issues surrounding displacement and locale. This reworking culminates in the *Heimatfilm*'s presentation of a harmonious imagined community, composed of displaced and native ethnic Germans, visibly at home in an iconic (West) German landscape, which all acknowledge as their genuine *Heimat*.

Green Is the Heath, directed by Hans Deppe in 1951, was actually a remake of the successful film of the same name that appeared in 1932. After Hans Deppe's surprise hit, *Black Forest Girl [Schwarzwaldmädel]*, in 1950, the production team decided to rework the 1932 version of *Green Is the Heath*, confident that the combination of stars, director, music, and attractive location shooting, which had proved so winning in *Black Forest Girl*, would find success a second time. At this point, *Heimatfilme* were not viewed in a positive light in any quarter, by critics, audiences, or the domestic film industry, which was experiencing a crisis over film quality and poor audience figures.[8] As Marc Silberman notes, *Black Forest Girl* was not only the biggest German box office success between 1945 and the release of the even more popular *Green Is the Heath* in late 1951, it was awarded the German equivalent of the Oscar, the Bambi, in 1951 (117). The unexpected success of *Black Forest Girl* offered the moribund domestic film industry a useful blueprint for winning back German audiences at a moment when German cinemas were dominated by foreign, particularly Hollywood, films.[9] In its increasing commitment to the *Heimatfilm* in the 1950s, the German film industry, far from manipulating its audiences into watching escapist fare, was actually responding to public demand.[10] The increasingly formulaic nature of much 1950s cinema reflects the attempts by the domestic industry to exploit, rather than to create, audience interest in *Heimatfilme*, and to cash in on the astonishing success of films like *Black Forest Girl* and *Green Is the Heath*.

Several important elements link *Black Forest Girl* with *Green Is the Heath*. Both were produced by the Berlin-based Berolina Company and utilized Deppe as director of a Bobby E. Lüthge screenplay. Both draw on popular folk music, particularly so in *Green Is the Heath*'s explicit references to Hermann Löns's songs, and both exploit color film stock, thereby distancing themselves technically, as well as in terms of theme, from the monochrome series of *Trümmerfilme* (Rubble films) that characterized the immediate postwar period. The innovative use of color photography in Deppe's films draws instead on German experiments in color film stock which came to fruition in early 1940s productions like Veit Harlan's melodrama *The Golden City [Die goldene Stadt]*, a notable box office success in 1942.[11] Both Deppe films, of course, cast Sonia Ziemann and Rudolph Prack in the leading romantic roles, with Hans Richter and Ernst Waldow supporting. The "Zieprack" combination became, despite an age difference of more than twenty years between the couple, a celebrated element of 1950s *Heimatfilme*.

Despite many shared ingredients, there are also interesting differences between Deppe's two great popular successes. Silberman argues convincingly that *Black Forest Girl* operates largely as a comedy of errors, utilizing visual motifs of disguise and blindness: "The confusion between real and fake, which surfaces in every relation, signals a more fundamental uncertainty that underlies existence in this narrative world. The uneasiness these characters experience is that of a society in rapid transition and demanding adaptability in order to survive" (121). The character played by Ziemann, Bärbele, stands at the center of the film's narrative, a down-to-earth and practical secretary who wins an American sports car in the lottery. She is fully able to negotiate successfully the space of the modern city (in this film, Baden Baden) and yet comfortable with her real identity as the Black Forest girl of the film's title. Her ability to be at ease, at home, in both environments makes her not duplicitous but, within the dynamics of the film, the guarantor of authenticity in a film dominated by disguise.[12] Rather than providing evidence of Bärbele's schizophrenic attitude to very different German spaces, the film demonstrates, as Silberman argues, how pervious the opposition between city and countryside can be, and this is echoed in several positive references to city life by other characters. In *Black Forest Girl*, then, the rural space of the *Heimat* is not foregrounded as a utopian counterpoint to the ills of modernity in general or contemporary city life in particular. In this, *Black Forest Girl* stands outside the strict separation of urban and rural worlds which features strongly in subsequent 1950s *Heimatfilme* and which has a long tradition in German cinema.[13] The film suggests instead that the authentic and adaptable Bärbele can herself help to construct a harmonious, happy community, a true *Heimat*, wherever she finds herself, whether it be in the village or in the city.

The position at the center of the narrative occupied by Ziemann *and* the location in *Black Forest Girl* is filled very differently in *Green Is the Heath*. As the title suggests, the subject of the latter film is the locale rather than any one character. The film, noticeably darker in mood than *Black Forest Girl*, is clearly positioned within debates about the geography of the new Germany and about spatial politics: the film unfolds around questions of law, of order, of appropriate behavior within new boundaries. In *Green Is the Heath* ethical considerations are foregrounded as much as the tropes of romance. Identities are more stable than in *Black Forest Girl*, and the plot hinges not on a comedy of errors, where no crime is really committed, but on poaching and, ultimately, on a murder. Whereas *Black Forest Girl* offered audiences two counterposed realms, the materialistic (and partly fake) urban milieu of Baden Baden and the (fictional) Black Forest village of St.Christoph, every sequence in *Green Is the*

Heath is set within the *Heimat,* here a village (unnamed in the film, but shot in Bleckede) on the northern Lüneburger Heide. Although characters make reference to other locales throughout the film, visually there is no counterpoint to the world of the heath (even the visiting circus is contained diegetically within the borders of the rural *Heimat*). As in *Black Forest Girl,* there are only limited attempts to document authentically the rural location in *Green Is the Heath.* Instead, the location shooting is used to frame a *performance* of German identity, an identity anchored in an attachment to selected customs and traditions of the village-as-*Heimat.* This performance is seen most clearly at the *Schützenfest* (shooting match), where the village community is shown to be surprisingly heterogeneous, composed of refugees and newcomers from several different German regions. Despite the differences in traditional regional dress, banners, and songs between the different groups, they are united in their ability both to remember lovingly their old *Heimat* and to respect and commit fully to their new habitat. The performance of a form of German identity based on commitment to one's native region is carried through the theatricality of the parade of regional costumes as well as being articulated, albeit rather self-consciously, in speeches of thanks to the local dignitaries.

This performance draws not only on the location shooting for its claims to authenticity but also on the actual villagers from Bleckede and surrounding areas. One of the leading regional newspapers carried an article at the time about the film, which was just beginning to be shot, repeating Berolina's call for villagers to attend wearing Sunday best and to play themselves. In fact, they were asked to recreate the annual shooting competition and accompanying village fair, which had actually taken place shortly before filming began:

> Although Bleckede celebrated its authentic, traditional shooting match only a few weeks ago, outside on the shooting grounds a number of stalls have been constructed again, together with carousels, beer tents and a travelling circus appropriate to a local country fair, and both young and old are enthused again. Smiling, the bearded old marksmen of the village are being made up and powdered. Film posters at the scene have urged local tailors to work overtime for several days. The extras are natural and authentic. (Textor 36)

The article reveals in passing, and surely by accident, much about the film's highly selective attitude toward local authenticity.

While so many details of everyday life in the local community are laboriously recreated for this fictional account, the film averts its gaze from direct representation of the broader realities of the Lüneburger Heide in the early 1950s. The journalist notes that in traveling north from Hanover to Bleckede, the Lüneburger Heide, far from being a natural refuge from political and historical tensions, is in reality of extreme strategic importance:

> "Caution! Tank damage!"—"No entry for tanks" and similar signs show just as clearly as the long columns of British vehicles, upon which soldiers with tired and dust-smeared faces are sitting, that we are travelling across the largest area for allied military manoeuvres in North West Germany. However, as we come into the small heath village of Bleckede other bright red posters can be seen: "Berolina is shooting *Grün ist die Heide* on the shooting grounds in Bleckede. Come wearing Sunday best if you want to appear in the film." (Textor 36)

In his casual remarks on the signs that attempt to claim the heath as, alternately, an area for allied military maneuvers and for the creation of a fictional, authentically German space, Textor's article touches on the tensions and contradictions that lie at the heart of *Green Is the Heath*. The film attempts to claim the heath as an appropriate site for the construction of a new German identity, an identity anchored in a commitment to an authentic local identity. It is this identity that is able to provide resolution to present social tensions without the need to delve deeply into Germany's recent past. Incredibly, at the moment that the completed film was meeting with such popular acclaim, a nearby part of the Lüneburger Heide with a very different set of resonances was also the focal point for considerable political debate. An attempt, instigated under the British forces of occupation in 1945, to ensure that this part of the heath would be retained as the site of a national memorial to the victims of National Socialism, was finally successful. On 30 November 1952, the former concentration camp of Bergen-Belsen was officially opened by the president of the Federal Republic, Theodor Heuss.[14]

Green Is the Heath's thematization of the legacy of National Socialism shows only Germans as victims. The original 1932 version was updated whereby the impoverished landowner, Lüder Lüdersen, became a refugee from an estate east of the Elbe. A new character, Nora, was added, a friend of Lüdersen's daughter, Helga, an orphan who was similarly an expellee from her eastern *Heimat*. Beyond this, the plot touches only obliquely on the

German past: the war figures as a natural catastrophe. It has no author but unsettling repercussions (Fehrenbach 153). After fleeing from the lost eastern territories, Lüdersen and his daughter Helga are fortunate to have found a refuge at the moated castle on the Lüneburger Heide that is owned by wealthy relations. Although Helga seems to have adapted to her new surroundings and is ready to start a new life, her father's full integration is in jeopardy because of his obsessive need to hunt on the heath, an activity forbidden under local law. A new forester is eager to prove his worth by catching the elusive poacher and manages to follow him back to the castle, where he meets Helga, who suspects her father but covers up for him. Lüdersen subsequently confesses his secret to Helga and promises to stop hunting. However, when a gendarme is found shot on the heath, the local district judge increases attempts to apprehend the poacher, who is suspected of murdering the gendarme, too. The arrival of a traveling circus brings with it Nora, a long-lost friend of Helga, another refugee, who is performing with the circus in order to travel with it to America in search of a new life. Romance is in the air, as Forester Rainer falls for Helga and the district judge is taken with Nora. As Lüdersen cannot control his impulse to hunt, Helga decides that they must leave the heath for the city before he can cause further damage. Rainer is torn between love for Helga and his duty to catch the poacher. At the shooting match, Helga and Lüdersen bid farewell to the area. Lüdersen disappears into the woods one last time and sees someone killing a deer. When he confronts the man, he is shot and wounded, at which point the perpetrator, who was poaching for food for the circus animals, is arrested by the gendarmes and confesses to the earlier murder. Helga and Rainer are reunited after Lüdersen's good deed, and they are able to remain part of the community on the heath. Nora also stays— she breaks her leg falling from her horse and is unable to leave with the circus—to the delight of the district judge. This basic account of the key plot developments leaves out one important feature of the film, the songs and comical escapades of three vagabonds who live rough on the heath.

Given the prominence of displaced persons in the film, the central tension of *Green Is the Heath* can be characterized in the form of a question, namely: how should we behave in the territory we must now occupy? This is, though, a deceptively complex question, because, on closer examination, it seems to beget many other questions, concerning, for example, identity (who are we in this context?), morality (what are the new rules governing behavior post-1945? what counts as transgression?), geography (what exactly comprises the territory of the new republic?), and international politics (why *must* we live here?). *Green Is the Heath* can be read, at first glance, as a romance in which all the obstacles in the way of Helga and Rainer, played by Sonia Ziemann and Rudolf Prack, must be overcome, and similarly in the form of the resolution of the conflicting ambitions of the district judge and Nora. Yet, interwoven with the narrative of romance one continually finds questions of law and order. The real concern of the film is to establish a legal code for the space of the film, the stylized space of the heath. This explains why the film has so many false endings, when Helga and Rainer are together and Lüdersen has confessed and promised not to poach again. However, all the while a poacher and murderer is still at large, the rule of law has not been firmly anchored in the heath, preventing the satisfactory resolution of the romance. In this respect, *Green Is the Heath* operates in a similar way to the conventions of the western or film noir, which are motivated by the need to establish law and order on an unruly or uncertain terrain. At the very beginning of the film the three vagabonds, excluded from the communal table for the village luminaries and yet key members of a wider community on the heath, reject suggestions that they adopt an unfamiliar routine by saying, albeit comically, "Ordnung muß sein" (order rules). Similarly, a character who does not feature too prominently in motivating plot development and yet is on screen for substantial periods and at key moments is the district judge, the man charged with the just maintenance of law and order.

In addressing these issues of law, territory, and identity, it is important to reexamine that most problematic German term, *Heimat*, a word that has never been far from German debates about national identity, place, and belonging. Although the concept of *Heimat* had often served to justify xenophobia, not least in the propaganda of National Socialism, as Celia Applegate has argued at length, it is such an ambiguous, flexible concept that it has also been employed in political discourse to argue against excessive nationalism. Applegate identifies how it served also as a key concept in the immediate postwar period in attempts to salvage an acceptable idea of a modest democratic German identity based on local, integrated, communities, in contrast to the excesses committed in the name of the German *Volk* under National Socialism. She notes that the concept of *Heimat* was "pulled out of the rubble of the Nazi period as a victim, not a perpetrator" (229), and that *Heimat* "came to embody the political and social community that could be salvaged from the Nazi ruins" (242).

In *Green Is the Heath, Heimat* is both a physical space—the beautiful Lüneburger Heide, a landscape of nature at its most idyllic—and a cultural concept that is connected with the reconstruction of German identity. Earlier *Heimatfilme* had offered a natural idyll as counterpoint to the corrupt modernity of the city. Although the undesirability of city life is broached at the shooting match, the binary opposition of countryside/city is not a dominant theme. For a film that, one might assume, is firmly rooted in the countryside, in a natural world, *Heimat* as space of nature features less than one might expect. True, the heath is a space where Rainer and Helga in part conduct their courtship, it is obviously the terrain in which Lüdersen poaches and in which other crimes are committed, and it is the space inhabited by the loveable rascals, the three musicians. Yet this is in no way a film anchored in an authentic portrayal of a natural way of life. The dominant characters are either refugees, who have little to do with that specific landscape, or they are bourgeois patricians, who are administrators of a just and healthy society, not farmers or people who actually work *with* the land. The two foresters whose strategic function is to administer the health of the natural world can hardly be counted as embodying an altogether successful relationship with the countryside. Neither the outgoing *Förster* nor Rainer, his newly appointed replacement, are able initially to establish law and order in the *Heimat*. Forester Rainer's seriousness and devotion to the order of the heath is presented visually through his frequent appearances in carefully maintained uniform and in dialogue through his sense of natural hierarchies as he is deferential to the outgoing forester and mistrustful toward the vagabonds. His pursuit of the poacher is dogged and motivated as much by a genuine empathy with the natural world as out of a desire to make a name for himself and thus to embark on a notable local career. However, the rigidity of his worldview shows him to be incapable of truly understanding the dynamics of life on the heath and therefore of establishing an appropriate sense of order there. He claims presumptuously that he has full knowledge of the heath despite having spent only three weeks in his new job, he assumes with little evidence that the three vagabonds must be guilty of poaching because they live rough, and he is adamant about the importance of duty over possibly conflicting compassionate impulses. Consequently, he is, at least in the beginning, as disturbing to the order of the heath as Lüdersen or the poacher. As in *Black Forest Girl*, the ability to adapt to changing circumstances is a prerequisite if a character is to be able to function successfully in uncertain times.

Prack's well-intentioned but occasionally officious *Förster* can be compared to Rudolf Lenz's portrayal of the title role in *The Forester from Silberwald [Der Förster vom Silberwald]*, which appeared in 1954. Although an Austrian production, this *Heimatfilm* can be usefully considered in this context on account of its phenomenal and completely unexpected success with West German audiences, attracting twenty-two million visitors in the three years it was exhibited in the Federal Republic.[15] Lenz's Forester Gerold, a newcomer who, like Lüder Lüdersen, has been forced to relinquish an estate as German borders were altered after the war, finds his world order threatened at the outset of the film by the more materialistic members of the village community in which he has settled, who are chopping down the trees for commercial reasons. Although motivated by strong ecological concerns for the health of the forest and for the wildlife that inhabits it, Forester Gerold is unable to impose his sense of order on his community without the intervention of a local councillor. Lenz's character may well wear the uniform of local authority and be permitted to bear arms, but he is as impotent in resolving the conflicts of interest in the forest as he is in dealing with a rival for his beloved Liesel. After discovering that his rival, Max, an abstract artist from Vienna and occasional poacher, has shot a deer, he refuses to charge him, as he believes that Liesel provided the weapon. Assuming that his position is now untenable, Gerold resigns and leaves. Although selfless here, and acting out of compassion toward Liesel rather than the strictest dictates of duty, Lenz's forester is again unable to resolve the misunderstandings that have caused his departure. It is Liesel who acts to find out the truth and to pursue Gerold, persuading him to return. Despite his attachment to the idyllic space of the forest, the forester is unable, acting alone, to guarantee the survival of its traditions, to impose law and order on the threats to its stability. The dilemmas in *The Forester from Silberwald* are solved with recourse to an older man's authority and to the perseverance and perception of the leading female character.

Although lacking much of Gerold's deep understanding of the natural world around him, Prack's forester is more eager to intervene to guarantee the order of the heath in *Green Is the Heath*. However, like Gerold, Forester Rainer is unable to achieve alone the restitution of the law within this world and has to rely ultimately on a combination of elements. The policing introduced by the district judge, an older civil servant, makes the heath a scene of surveillance, Helga's repeated confrontations with her father help him to recognize his transgressions and to find ways of coming to terms with the new rules on hunting, and finally Lüdersen's moral deed, his individual sacrifice when he confronts the real criminal, ensures the arrest of the murderer. Yet, in the course of the narrative Rainer learns to understand, and hence love more deeply, his new *Heimat,* and this is why he, like Helga, becomes such a positive force within the space of the heath. The ability to love and respect the heath as *Heimat* is the precursor to full acceptance by the community within the ethical code of the film.

The love of *Heimat* so central to *Green Is the Heath* must be understood in connection with attempts to salvage a positive form of national identity after the horrors of National Socialism and the ravages of military defeat and territorial division. *Heimat* is a crucial concept, in two ways. First, it offers a sense of German identity tied to a number of discrete regional areas—highly appropriate given the new boundaries. Second, it acts as a moral imperative. Full German (or rather *West* German) identity is available to all who inhabit its new spaces, regardless of their place of origin, as long as they are prepared to love the *Heimat* appropriately—that is, as long as they adapt to the new laws concerning appropriate behavior. This explains why there are so many characters who claim the Lüneburger Heide as their *Heimat* when their accents, names, or role in the narrative mean that they cannot have been brought up there. It also explains why so much of the plot hinges on Lüdersen's schizophrenic attitude toward the heath.[16] He can love it as *Heimat*—in fact, he calls it his second *Heimat* at the shooting match—and yet he is not fully integrated because he cannot reconcile himself to its codes of behavior. In contrast, Rainer, who at the beginning makes many naive assumptions about his new *Heimat,* learns quickly, adapts, becomes fully integrated, and is rewarded with the girl. However, Lüdersen's turmoil is presented sympathetically, especially when set against the situation of the real criminal, Ristek. Lüdersen, after all, shows that he can love and adapt to his new home, whereas Ristek, the animal trainer at the circus, belongs to a rootless institution. He literally has no *Heimat,* and so it is hardly a surprise that he is capable of killing men and animals for cold-hearted gain. Interestingly, this is a case where, in contrast to the famous rubble films, the film strives to announce that "The Murderers are NOT Among Us." Love of *Heimat*, of the new boundaries of the Federal Republic, excludes the capacity to commit (and, by extension, to have committed) murderous crimes.

Significantly, Nora, who for most of the film is adamant that America is fertile soil for a better future, explicitly rejects as sentimental the idea of the Federal Republic as new, redemptive *Heimat*.[17] The district judge's attempts to persuade her by wooing her with Hermann Löns songs, which he refers to by name, are unsuccessful with such an independent, resilient, postwar survivor.[18] At this point, with the inclusion of an element of self-referentiality, the film acknowledges its own project: it lets the audience know that its sentimentality is part of a scheme to win it over to a commitment to the *Heimat*. The popularity of *Grün ist die Heide* and of subsequent *Heimatfilme* suggest that, like Nora, many spectators responded positively to the stylized representations of community life on the heath. The heath as *Heimat* actually points to a future, possibly utopian, resolution of the social tensions of the Federal Republic. In this society, refugees can be integrated without resentment, there is space for everyone, the heath is a world of plenty, and the community cheerfully supports those who are short of food or who live in poverty. The familial structures devastated by the war are stabilized by the strength, compassion, and adaptability of women like Helga and Nora, able to compensate for the aging, ineffectual, or guilty male figures who surround them.

In his article on Hollywood musicals, "Entertainment and Utopia," Richard Dyer argues that such films are organized around the representation of idealized communities and utilize many non-narrative elements, such as music, dance, color, and spectacle. For Dyer, the Hollywood musical can be understood as offering a utopian sensibility—"what utopia would feel like rather than how it would be organised" (222–23). This utopian sensibility acts to propose solutions to real needs and lacks, like, for example, scarcity or the lack of community, and attempts to resolve social contradictions. If we take into account the popularity of *Heimatfilme* in general, and *Grün ist die Heide* in particular, with audiences in the early 1950s, despite the massive competition from Hollywood imports, then Dyer's argument can be appropriated and utilized for understanding the attractions of this German genre. As Heide Fehrenbach has pointed out, "the *Heimatfilm* could and did address German audiences as potential consumers, but Hollywood never addressed German audiences as

Germans, with reference to their national past, present, or future" (163).

I would like to end by suggesting that *Green Is the Heath* be usefully considered as a utopian fantasy, a cinematic space that projects the problems of the German present into an imaginary, harmonious future. In fact, it anticipates in its sense of abundance and in its inclusive community certain aspects of the Federal Republic later in the decade as it profited from rapid economic growth. This is not to argue that all *Heimatfilme* in the 1950s function in exactly the same way. Indeed, in *The Forester from Silberwald* there is already perceptible an inclination to interrupt the narrative not with folk songs but with numerous semidocumentary scenes of the mountainous landscape and of various forms of wildlife. Although these episodes are occasionally motivated in the narrative by the need for the watchful *Förster* to observe developments in the forest, more often they are presented as enjoyable spectacles, either for visitors like Liesel or Max, or simply directly to the audience. The *Heimat* as spectacle that is notable in *The Forester from Silberwald* points to an emerging trend in *Heimatfilme* in the mid-to-late 1950s, namely the packaging and commodification of the *Heimat* for potential visitors and tourists, rather than to the resolution of the social questions that inform the earlier *Green Is the Heath*. While the landscapes of *Green Is the Heath* are not yet offered to the audience as a potential tourist destination, they are constructed as utopian spaces. They find little place for Germany's recent past, but they do frame a performance of German identity that is firmly anchored in the social and political reality of the early Federal Republic, providing a utopian resolution to specifically German problems.

NOTES

A version of this paper was presented to the DAAD Filmseminar: *Deutsches Kino & Co.—Geschichte, Gegenwart, Didaktik,* Cumberland Lodge, Windsor Great Park, United Kingdom, 24–26 June 1998.

1. See, for example, Elsaesser's discussion of the concept of *Heimat* in "The Heimat-Film," II/1.
2. See, in particular, Konstantarakos 1.
3. "L'Espace n'est plus seulement ce décor sur le devant duquel s'enlève l'action, il est un des acteurs évoluant sur la scène narrative. Il est aussi et surtout l'un des facteurs primordiaux de toute stratégie de récit" (Gardies 2).

4. See also Möbius and Vogt 9.

5. See Münz and Ulrich 69.

6. See Fulbrook 90–91.

7. See ibid. 92. Fulbrook argues that by the late 1950s the views and votes of the BHE had been largely absorbed by Chancellor Adenauer's ruling conservative party, the Christlich-Demokratische Union (Christian Democratic Party).

8. See Fehrenbach 148–49.

9. See Silberman 114–15 and Fehrenbach 148–49.

10. See Fehrenbach 150–52.

11. See King 110–11.

12. See also Silberman 121.

13. See ibid. 123.

14. For an account of the establishment of such sites of memory in the Federal Republic, see Fulbrook 36–45.

15. See Bliersbach 47.

16. Silberman also notes how, in comparison with earlier films, a schizophrenic attitude to *Heimat* is discernible in certain films. This is characterized by "nostalgia for the security of home and fear of the phantoms in that home" (117).

17. Again, the film touches on a contemporary social issue: at the end of the 1940s there was a noticeable desire among some Germans to emigrate. As Rainer Münz and Ralf Ulrich note, "The motivation for some was better career opportunities; for others, it was the desire to escape the atmosphere of political restoration in postwar Germany. Still others married soldiers and staff of the allied forces and later joined them when they returned to their countries of origin, especially the United States" (76).

18. The Löns songs were a key element of the film's success, and were also available as a record in the series, "Heimat, schöne Heimat," Polydor 21219 EPH.

WORKS CITED

Anderson, Benedict. *Imagined Communities. Reflections on the Origin and Spread of Nationalism.* Rev. ed. New York: Verso, 1991.

Applegate, Celia. *A Nation of Provincials. The German Idea of Heimat.* Berkeley: University of California Press, 1990.

Bade, Klaus J., and Myron Weiner, eds. *Migration Past, Migration Future. Germany and the United States.* Providence, R I: Berghahn, 1997.

Barthel, Manfred. *Als Opas Kino jung war—Der deutsche Nachkriegsfilm.* Frankfurt am Main: Ullstein, 1991.

Bessen, Ursula. *Trümmer und Träume. Nachkriegszeit und fünfziger Jahre auf Zelluloid.* Bochum: Studienverlag Dr. N. Brockmeyer, 1989.

Bhabha, Homi K., ed. *Nation and Narration.* New York: Routledge, 1990.

Bliersbach, Gerhard. *So grün war die Heide. Der deutsche Nachkriegsfilm in neuer Sicht.* Weinheim: Beltz, 1985.

Bullivant, Keith, and C. Jane Rice, "Reconstruction and Integration: The Culture of West German Stabilisation 1945–68." In *German Cultural Studies. An Introduction,* edited by Rob Burns, 209–55. Oxford: Oxford University Press, 1995.

Carter, Erica. *How German Is She? Postwar German Reconstruction and the Consuming Woman.* Ann Arbor: University of Michigan Press, 1997.

Ceserani, David, and Mary Fulbrook, eds. *Citizenship, Nationality and Migration in Europe.* New York: Routledge, 1996.

Dyer, Richard. "Entertainment and Utopia." In Bill Nichols (ed.), *Movies and Methods,* vol. 2, edited by Bill Nichols, 220–32. Berkeley: University of California Press, 1985.

Elsaesser, Thomas. "The Heimat-Film." In "Deutscher Heimatfilm," II/1–II/14, a pamphlet prepared by the Goethe-Institut, London, in 1988.

Elsaesser, Thomas, with Michael Wedel, eds. *The BFI Companion to German Cinema.* London: British Film Institute, 1999.

Fehrenbach, Heide. *Cinema in Democratizing Germany. Reconstructing National Identity after Hitler.* Chapel Hill: University of North Carolina Press, 1995.

Fulbrook, Mary. *German National Identity after the Holocaust.* Cambridge, U.K.: Polity, 1999.

Gardies, André. *L'espace au cinéma.* Paris: Méridiens Klincksieck, 1993.

Garncarz, Joseph, and Thomas Elsaesser. "Heimat Films and Mountain Films." In *The BFI Companion to German Cinema,* edited by Thomas Elsaesser and Michael Wedel, 133–34. London: British Film Institute, 1999.

King, Alasdair. "Landscape, Ideology and National Identity in the German Cinema: A Case Study of *Die goldene Stadt* (1942)." In *Deutschland im Spiegel seiner Filme,* edited by Martin Brady and Helen Hughes, 96–117. London: CILT, 2000.

Koebner, Thomas, ed. *Idole des deutschen Films. Eine Galerie von Schlüsselfiguren.* Munich: Edition Text und Kritik, 1997.

Konstantarakos, Myrto, ed. *Spaces in European Cinema.* Exeter and Portland, U.K.: Intelleck, 2000.

Massey, Doreen. *Space, Place and Gender.* Cambridge, U.K.: Polity, 1994.

Möbius, Hanno, and Guntram Vogt, eds. *Drehort Stadt. Das Thema "Großstadt" im deutschen Film.* Marburg: Hitzeroth, 1990.

Morley, David, and Kevin Robins, eds. *Spaces of Identity. Global Media, Electronic Landscapes and Cultural Boundaries.* New York: Routledge, 1995.

Münz, Rainer, and Ralf Ulrich. "Changing Patterns of Immigration to Germany, 1945–95. Ethnic Origins, Demographic Structure, Future Prospects." In *Migration Past, Migration Future. Germany and the United States,* edited by Klaus J. Bade and Myron Weiner, 65–119. Providence, R.I.: Berghahn, 1997.

Schuck, Peter H., and Rainer Münz, eds. *Paths to Inclusion. The Integration of Migrants in the United States and Germany.* New York: Berghahn, 1998.

Silberman, Marc. *German Cinema. Texts in Context.* Detroit: Wayne State University Press, 1995.

Textor, Jan Jörg, "Wer mitgefilmt werden will . . ." *Hannoversche Presse,* 22 September 1951, p. 36.

CHAPTER 8

Sexual Reorientations

Homosexuality versus the Postwar German Man in Veit Harlan's *Different from You and Me (§175)* (1957)

Alison Guenther-Pal

In October 1957, Veit Harlan's *Different from You and Me (§175)* [*Anders als du und ich (§175)*] premiered in West German cinemas across the nation and was marketed by its distributors as a film worthy of earnest discussion.[1] Advertisements heralded it as a movie that "everyone wants to see," about which "everyone is talking" (quoted in Noack 359).[2] Promotional materials described the film as tackling "a burning issue of our times," promising audiences a frank treatment of the "ethical" and "legal" problems of §175 of West Germany's penal code, the statutory prohibition against same-sex relations (*Anders als du und ich* 12). However, moviegoers expecting a cinematic discussion of the statute would have been sorely disappointed. Nowhere in the film is the law itself mentioned, nor is any overt reference as to whether or not homosexuality should be decriminalized, despite Hans Giese's enlistment as "scientific advisor."[3] While this marketing tactic suggested a more tolerant and progressive view of homosexuality, the film's hardly subtle homophobia is revealed through its sensationalistic representation of homosexuals as being in need of family intervention to "rescue" and "cure" them of their transgression onto the *Irrweg,* or "wrong path" (*Anders als du und ich* 12).

Ultimately, *Different* is primarily preoccupied with the patriarchal family and its importance in West German reconstruction efforts. Homosexuality is merely utilized as a means to stage the public anxieties surrounding gender and the status of the family that were intimately tied to the postwar reconstruction of a national identity that was neither emasculated[4] nor corrupted by the pathological authoritarianism of fascism. The attempts to come to terms with the war (albeit often quite indirectly) and reconstruct this new conception of national identity occured not only in the realm of politics and public policy but entered the wider popular sphere through the vehicle of cinema.[5] Throughout the 1950s, film production, ticket sales, and the number of movie theaters rose steadily (see Prinzler 182–225, passim). By 1957, going to the movies was the most popular leisure activity among West Germans; during the ten-year period from 1946 to 1956, box office ticket sales skyrocketed from an estimated 300 million to 817 million, which represented nearly sixteen annual theater visits per capita (Noelle and Neumann 387; Prinzler 165, 208; Höfig 449).

Judging by the frequent controversies and public debates among politicians, religious leaders, and intellectuals, the cinema was seen as decisive in the ideological reconstruction of the social realm.[6] Both celebrated and reviled by conservatives and liberals alike, film became a preoccupation of the postwar era ostensibly because it could be used to represent and consolidate specific aspects of German culture and national identity.[7] Of course, popular film in the 1950s was primarily produced for domestic consumption, and thus was particularly adaptable as a means of representing specifically German issues. However, the cinematic treatment of such issues has typically been criticized for being aesthetically unsophisticated, escapist, and lacking social or intellectual merit. Although such criticisms are not without justification, especially given the generally oblique way that West Germany went about coming to terms with the recent past *(Vergangenheitsbewältigung)*, popular film functioned to represent the nation's collective concerns, in particular those surrounding the professed crises of gender, sexuality, and the family.

Linked to efforts to redefine a national sense of culture and social identity that had been devastated by the war and National Socialism, the rehabilitation of masculinity and redomestication of femininity dominated not just the much maligned yet immensely popular *Heimatfilm*, but other genres that purported to address more socially relevant concerns, such as the *Trümmerfilm* (rubble film) and the *Problemfilm* (social problem film). While overt references to the Holocaust were nearly absent from the popular films of the period, the problems represented on-screen were "real" to the extent that they responded to the socio-economic and moral instability produced by the war and its aftermath. From the *Arztfilm* (doctors' film) and the elaborately staged costume dramas to the rubble and social problem films, and in features as diverse as *The Sinner [Die Sünderin]* (Forst, 1951), *Green Is the Heath [Grün ist die Heide]* (Deppe, 1951), and *Roses for the State Prosecutor [Rosen für den Staatsanwalt]* (Staudte, 1959), millions of viewers witnessed the redefinition and reconstitution of a putatively postfascist, democratic German culture, played out in part on thousands of movie screens nationwide.

This essay endeavors to reveal the complex relationship between the popular film *Different from You and Me (§175)* and its broader social context, ultimately locating those areas of public and private life that were being actively contested in 1950s West Germany. The articulation of these contests converges here on the overdetermined site of homosexuality. The figure of the male homosexual functions as an organizational locus for the production of a specifically non-German category of otherness against which the "new German man" is constituted.[8] Because sexuality and gender, national identity, and the status of the patriarchal family occupied center stage throughout the socially turbulent period of the "economic miracle" *(Wirtschaftswunder)*, *Different*'s thematization of these issues can serve as a particularly instructive example of the ways in which popular culture is implicated with other institutional centers of power (for example, the law, the family, politics) in an effort to manage the ideological concerns preoccupying a particular moment in time.

Early historiographies and contemporary public conceptions of the founding years of the Federal Republic have tended to represent May 1945 (the *Stunde Null,* "zero hour") as a historical point of rupture from fascism, and have neglected the dynamic tension between past and present. Since the 1980s, however, a vast amount of scholarship has been produced to reconceptualize the history of the nation's early years. In this particular example, the social anxieties addressed in *Different* via the figure of the homosexual male necessarily rely on earlier constructions of homosexuality. By revealing these traces of Nazi doctrine in *Different,* I demonstrate how, alongside the obvious breaks, disturbingly visible continuity also existed between the Third Reich and the Adenauer era.

Applying the notion of the zero hour to the cinema is particularly erroneous, given the overwhelming continuity between the personnel of the Nazi film industry and those who continued making movies after the war. Most notable, of course, is Veit Harlan, arguably the Third Reich's star filmmaker, who directed *Jew Suess [Jud Süß]* (1940), perhaps the most frequently cited cinematic example of unapologetic anti-Semitism and fascism.[9] Harlan's early postwar film career was quite successful, though not without controversy.[10] Ultimately, his popularity waned, and after several box office flops he was approached by Arca Films, a small Berlin production company, to direct *Different*, a film that was supposed to be his comeback (Noack 354–55). *Different* was one of some forty films made by Arca, which had the reputation of producing provocative and titillating cinematic fare *(Kolportage)*. *Different* was no exception.

Different is an example of the social problem film, a popular genre that was supposed to represent the marriage of entertainment and social analysis. It enabled specific contemporary social issues to be explicitly addressed, although its conventional narrative and cinematic style, as well as its mandate to appeal to the tastes of a broad public, limited its potential for in-depth social critique. In its treatment of controversial subjects such as prostitution, teen gangs, and "mulatto" children, the social problem film of the 1950s tended to be exploitative, sensationalistic, and unsophisticated, although there were noteworthy successes, for example, *The Hooligans [Die Halbstarken]* (Tressler, 1956) and *The Girl Rosemarie [Das Mädchen Rosemarie]* (Thiele, 1958). For the most part, however, the social problem film avoided promoting radical social change or even moderate reform; and while it did bring attention to contemporary social concerns, it ultimately tended to present viewers with a vision of society that solidly affirmed the status quo.

The promoters of *Different* were surely banking on turning the controversy its subject matter would no doubt provoke into box office profit. While movie posters promised its viewers a topic worthy of thoughtful conversation ("We present for discussion"), the film's representation of homosexuality is lurid and sensationalistic. This is perhaps best exemplified in the over-the-top depiction of the wrestling game "Catch as catch can," in which muscular adolescent boys clad in tight metallic lamé bikini briefs roll around on the floor, limbs entwined. The shock value of this scene is heightened by the use of an extreme oblique camera angle and shrill electronic music.

The film's title, *Different from You and Me (§175)*, alludes to the Weimar film *Different from the Others [Anders als* die Andern] (Oswald, 1919), which marks one of the very first depictions of homosexuality in the cinema. The cause of riots and protests, Different from the Others was banned a year after its release, presumably due to its positive treatment of homosexuality.[11] In terms of its narrative, Different from You and Me (§175) is by no means a remake of Different from the Others, sharing only its general theme of homosexuality. Yet the slight title change is significant, for it demonstrates a notable change in point of reference. In the Weimar film, the homosexual is opposed to an unspecified other—that is, heterosexuals are positioned as "the others," while the homosexual is the reference point from which the film proceeds. The 1950s film, on the other hand, contrasts the homosexual as fundamentally different from "you and me"—the new reference point—suggesting his deviance from the norm, heterosexuality.[12]

Different from You and Me (§175) opens in a German courtroom in which Christa Teichmann (Paula Wessely, the star of numerous films during the Third Reich) is on trial for violating §§180 and 181 of the federal penal code. Frau Teichmann has been charged with aggravated pandering (schwere Kuppelei): providing the opportunity for unmarried individuals to engage in illicit sexual relations. Specifically, she is accused of deliberately leaving her seventeen-year-old son, Klaus (Christian Wolff), home alone with their attractive young housekeeper, Gerda Böttcher (Ingrid Stenn). The narrative, except for the final courtroom scene, proceeds by means of a flashback that chronologically details the events leading to the trial. Klaus, it is disclosed early on, is not like "normal" men his age: he has no interest in girls and rejects the stuffy bourgeois values of his father by pursuing modern art, poetry, and eerie electronic music. By leaving Klaus and Gerda home unsupervised, Frau Teichmann hopes that her son will be encouraged to experience what she believes is natural between a man and woman and be cured of his abnormal attachment to his best friend, Manfred Glatz (Günther Theil).

The characters are introduced in succession under the premise of reporting to the court as witnesses, but the cinematic techniques employed in this opening sequence reveal their symbolic position in the film and postwar society in general. Introduced first is the antiques dealer, Dr. Boris Winkler (Friedrich Joloff), a man approximately in his fifties who leads Klaus into a shadowy underworld of homosexual decadence. The camera cuts from a head-on long shot of the witnesses to a medium shot of

Boris filmed from the left side of the cinematic space. The camera's oblique position serves both to depict him as socially marginalized as well as to establish him as deviant from the norm. Boris's demeanor and dress in the courtroom, including his dark, modish sunglasses, mark him as a rather ominous, perhaps foreign presence. The judge orders him to remove his sunglasses, deemed inappropriate for the austere setting of the courtroom, thus further designating Boris as an outsider, an individual who either does not understand or chooses not to respect the rules that maintain the democratic social order of the new Germany.

Manfred is depicted similarly as he begins to return to his seat and is ordered by the judge to stay where he is. On his way to the front of the courtroom, he and Boris touch, briefly alerting the viewer to a more intimate relationship. Manfred's bad posture, sickly complexion, and slight build signify illness and vulnerability, which each point to a physiognomic construction of homosexuality; that is, homosexuality as a contagion that enters the body because of moral weakness and lack of individual character. Herr Teichmann's later characterizations of Manfred as an "unbaked biscuit" and as "proven to be predisposed to homosexuality" as well as the fact that he is indeed sick enough to require an extended period of bed rest at one point in the film, again point to this conflation of homosexuality with physical and spiritual illness.

The fatherless Manfred is a sensitive, budding young writer of experimental prose whom Boris has taken under his wing. Manfred's relationship with Klaus is portrayed as one in which he has little power, either physically (Klaus rescues him and fights on his behalf against the class bullies) or emotionally (he is obsessively jealous of any erotic attention—hetero- or homosexual—Klaus receives). As Manfred's widowed mother, Frau Glatz (Hilde Körber), stands before the judges, her posture and the seemingly desperate manner in which she clutches her purse, indicate maternal weakness and a suffocating attachment to her son. Her status as a widow suggests that part of Manfred's sexual disorientation originates from his father's absence. Evidently, his relationship with Boris is an attempt to replace his father as the paternal role model from which heterosexuality and gender identity are supposed to develop. Manfred's homosexuality has clearly been produced by identification with the wrong kind of man.

Gerda appears next as the picture of controlled femininity in an attractive suit and white gloves, her blond hair in a bun, wearing a deferent expression. Unlike Boris and Manfred, Gerda is well aware of how a respectable individual should fulfill his or her prescribed gender role. Gerda's comfort with her feminine role in the domestic sphere is depicted throughout the film.

Klaus's father and the family autocrat, Werner Teichmann (Paul Dahlke), is dressed traditionally in a suit, has neatly groomed hair and a tidy mustache, and has removed his hat at some point before the proceedings, manifesting his awareness of the social rules governing the courtroom. His demonstration of respect for and knowledge of the legal system foreshadows his unsuccessful invocation of the law to save his son. However, he represents the unproblematic acceptance of convention and tradition, a position that is critiqued throughout the film by subtly aligning him with National Socialism.

Next the viewer is introduced to the boyishly handsome Klaus Teichmann, the focus of his parents' grave concern. Contrary to his portrayal in most of the film, his courtroom behavior demonstrates his successful alignment with heterosexual patriarchy and his commitment to his role in revitalizing the German nation and culture. He places himself physically between Gerda and his father, symbolizing this transformation as well as his position as his father's successor, the postwar German man. Unlike Boris, who is associated with sexual and cultural depravity, and unlike Herr Teichmann, whose tastes are stuffy, old-fashioned, even fascist, Klaus represents the healthy articulation of masculinity as well as the reconsolidation of German bourgeois culture. This new concept of national identity is thus produced both through an explicit and self-conscious distancing from the Third Reich and also through the rejection of the sexual deviant, whose construction relies, as I will demonstrate, upon the ideological remnants of National Socialism.

Finally, the camera's attention is placed on Frau Teichmann, who personifies the middle-aged maternal ideal of woman. Her fear and emotional anguish as she sobs and puts her head in her hands contrasts with her husband's stoicism. As she begins to relate Klaus's story to the judge, she speaks reluctantly but eloquently. Her face dissolves into a long shot of her son leaving school at the end of the day, and with this the flashback representing the greater part of the film's narrative begins as Klaus first encounters Boris.

Boris has befriended the sickly Manfred, with whom Klaus has an intimate relationship, the specifics of which are never overtly revealed, though it clearly transgresses heterosexuality. Both Herr and Frau Teichmann recognize that there is something not quite "normal" about their son, but take different approaches to helping him. Initially, Herr Teichmann believes that Klaus's supposed sexual confusion can be resolved within the family, through disciplinary measures, such as locking him in his room. When this approach proves ineffective, he turns to the public sphere and presses charges against Boris for homosexual seduction of youth, which indirectly leads to Frau Teichmann's arrest.

Frau Teichmann's attempts to cure her son, however, never move into the public realm, except to enlist the advice of supposed child-rearing experts: a psychologist and the family doctor. The psychologist, Dr. Schmidt, whose appearance and demeanor invoke images of Freud, recommends that she remove the usual parental restrictions intended to prevent romantic attachments between adolescent girls and boys; the family doctor confirms this advice, declaring that only the true love of a woman can save Klaus from permanent psychological damage. Having the attractive young housekeeper suitable for converting Klaus to heterosexuality already in residence, Frau Teichmann encourages Gerda to pursue her romantic feelings for Klaus. Frau Teichmann's return to the family realm indicates her acceptance of the conservative gendered discourse limiting women to the domestic sphere, which, if transgressed, may only be so briefly and for the purposes of reinstating familial harmony.

Left alone together one night, Klaus paints Gerda's portrait and is overcome with lust when her robe opens to expose her naked breast. Klaus's conversion to heterosexuality is made official on the Teichmann lawn, when Gerda submits to his persistent and now insatiable desire. During the remainder of their time alone together, they "play house," portraying the picture of matrimonial domestic bliss: they go on romantic picnics, she cheerfully prepares dinner for her "husband," and his sexual desire for his "wife" cannot be sated. Klaus's aesthetic sensibilities undergo a transformation as well. Instead of painting her in his usual abstract modernist style, Klaus's portrait of Gerda is now realist. Thus, the conflation of the avant-garde with deviant sexuality, a relationship that was established in the depiction of Boris, Manfred, and previously Klaus, is mirrored in the analogous conflation of representational art with heterosexuality.

When Boris learns of Klaus's unsupervised festival of passion with Gerda, he files charges against Frau Teichmann, accusing her of pandering. A police investigation ensues, and the camera returns to the courtroom as Frau Teichmann is found guilty. Despite having just been convicted of a crime, she emerges as the film's heroine. Her maternal intervention, though illegal, is justified by having brought about Klaus's eleventh-hour conversion to heterosexuality. Consequently, the sexual normalcy of the family is (re)established, a duty to which Frau Teichmann is morally obligated even when it involves personal sacrifice, superceding any juridical particulars.

Although Klaus's "cure" and transformation from sexual deviant to healthy, red-blooded heterosexual certainly reveal a manifestly conservative politics of sexuality, *Different* in fact presents the viewer with a more ambiguous position. There is evidence that the film both denounces homosexuality and advocates tolerance (albeit limited) for it. Despite the lack of overt references to §175, a close reading of the film reveals subtle allusions to state-sanctioned homophobia and suggests ways in which *Different* reflects and participates in the discursive production of gender and national identity through its construction of homosexuality.

It is not insignificant that the film's narrative is framed in the context of a trial, for the legal system itself was an important focus of restoring democracy, which included (ostensibly, at least) cleansing it of any traces of Nazi ideology and bringing previously existing laws into agreement with the Federal Republic's 1949 constitution (*Grundgesetz* or Basic Law). In the early 1950s, two men convicted under §175 appealed their case by challenging the law's constitutionality as well as arguing that because it had been revised in 1935, it was a product of National Socialist racial teaching *(Rassenlehre)*. The Federal Constitutional Court rejected each argument of their case in its 1957 decision, more than seven years after the initial criminal charges had been made and approximately a year after one of the appellants had died. Hans Giese was one of many experts called upon to testify in the appeal, and ironically, his testimony was ultimately used to support the state's case to retain the criminalization of male homosexual conduct and the continued exclusion of lesbians from the statute.[13] The intense scrutiny to which the legal code and judicial system were submitted is evidently reflected in *Different*.

Perhaps the most direct reference to the criminalization of homosexuality occurs early in the film, when Klaus visits Manfred late one night. Manfred scolds Klaus for being so loud as to wake up his mother. Klaus responds that Manfred is treating him as if he were a criminal, to which Manfred replies: "There are simply loud and quiet crimes. Even a glance can be enough."

Explained from within the narrative, the comment refers to Manfred's suspicion that Klaus has been unfaithful to him. However, the reference can also be read to refer to the Nazi enforcement of the antisodomy law, in which physical contact need not have occurred to qualify as illegal conduct (Schönke 392). The notion that homosexuals are criminals is a sentiment most frequently voiced by Herr Teichmann. When he discovers, after locking his son in his room, that Klaus has escaped through the window, he thunders: "Criminals climb through windows!" He then recounts the news story of a recent murder by a young man and reports that "Such criminals after all come from these circles!" conflating criminal behavior as serious as murder with homosexuality.

However, it remains unclear whether the film should be read as contesting or promoting the stereotype that homosexuality leads to criminal behavior, since such sentiments originate from the undeniably unsympathetic Herr Teichmann. He represents the stereotype of the authoritarian Third Reich male and is depicted in the by now predictable fashion that implicated men of his generation in the consequences of National Socialism.[14] His interpersonal skills leave much to be desired: he runs his household like an army base, constantly barking out orders and raising his voice even in casual conversation. Although homophobia is far from absent in *Different,* the only overt homophobe is the tyrannical and anachronistic Herr Teichmann. Here homophobia is linked with fascism and hints at an attempt to expose the Nazi tendencies inherent in §175. Herr Teichmann's repeated association with fascism complicates the film's treatment of homosexuality: by implicitly linking his blatant homophobia to the Third Reich, the film represents his prejudices as archaic, indeed as originating from an ideology being actively contested, though the film arguably falls short of endorsing the political reform of §175.

The statutory endorsement of homophobia is explicitly portrayed from Boris's perspective, although his difficulties are given less than sympathetic treatment. For example, during the police investigation prompted by Herr Teichmann's accusation against Boris for homosexual misconduct with minors, Boris is blackmailed by one of his underage protégés, which implies that the charges against him are not altogether false. Upon finding Boris's name familiar, the investigator recalls that he questioned Boris in a recent homicide in which the murderer came from "homosexual circles." Boris's behavior is constantly monitored—he is a suspect in every crime, because his identity as a homosexual is criminal.

Such episodes underscore the incessant scrutiny to which Boris is submitted simply because he is openly homosexual. The effect of these scenes, however, does not evoke sympathy for his unjust persecution. Rather, the implication is that the accusations are true, only the evidence to prove them is lacking. Also, Boris's designation as a *Triebmensch*, "creature of instinct," sexualizes his identity, suggesting that his actions are solely motivated by his perverse desire. Each of these examples, and there are many more, marks Boris as psychologically deviant, morally depraved, and pathologically driven by his excessive sexual urges and thus reveals a second position of *Different* toward homosexuality—condemnation. How does one account for the film's different treatments of homosexuality? The answer lies in the narrative context within which these sentiments are expressed. A sympathetic treatment of homosexuality as a temporary transgression is associated with Klaus; deviance is depicted in the treatment of Boris. Klaus, in fact, as we learn by the end of the film, is not homosexual at all.

In his exemplary article on West German postwar conceptions of gender and homosexuality, Robert G. Moeller contends that homosexuality was not necessarily regarded as an immutable trait under Nazi ideology; there was a difference between "seducer" and "seduced," "weak" and "strong" homosexual tendencies ("The Homosexual Man," 258–59). Heide Fehrenbach rightly argues that Klaus belongs in the category of the "seduced" male, possessing "weak" homosexual tendencies, and concludes that "his sexual inclinations are attributable to social influences and therefore subject to modification" (196). This distinction between social and biological homosexuals is also made by the family physician: he differentiates between "crisis and destiny." Klaus's transgression is merely a developmental crisis of adolescence, and Frau Teichmann's efforts to "cure" her son are successful because he is not predetermined to be homosexual. In contrast, men destined to be homosexual (for example, Boris) are portrayed as sexual predators, pederasts even, who possess the power to transform an adolescent crisis into lifelong sexual deviance.

This connection to Nazi ideology has important consequences for postwar social attitudes concerning gender relations. Moeller reports that according to Nazi doctrine homosexuals were considered agents of the "death of the *Volk*," because their sexual practices did not propagate the "Aryan race" ("The Homosexual Man," 256). This attitude was shared by politicians and others attempting to restore social, economic, and political stability to the Federal Republic, in particular through their promulgation of a social ideology that homed in on the family and gender relations. A distinctive demographic fact of the 1950s, and of postwar periods in general, is the existence of the so-called surplus of women *(Frauenüberschuß)*. Nearly 4 million men died in combat, and at the end of the war there were 7.3 million more women than men (Frevert 257–58, 264); by 1950, even with the return of those men in prison camps, the gender imbalance still existed—in the age group of twenty-five to thirty-nine, for every 1,000 men there were 1,400 women (Moeller, "Reconstructing," 111; Castell 121). Due to this gender skew, the number of "intact" families had dramatically decreased, and this had far-reaching social implications.

Women, as a result of having had to survive without male support, in some cases for more than a decade, had gained substantial emancipation from their traditional gender roles. As their husbands returned from the war or prison camps, often physically and psychologically wounded, they were faced with wives whose sphere of authority had expanded dramatically. According to Helmut Schelsky, a prominent family sociologist and member of an advisory committee to the Ministry of Family Affairs under Adenauer, this was an "emancipation out of necessity," and furthermore a "dubious gain in so far as the rights won for women turn out to be largely a burden," particularly given the tremendous importance of the maternal role in child rearing ("Die Gleichberechtigung," 130; "Die gegenwärtigen Problemlagen," 293–94). Experts cautioned that the "dismantling" of the social differentiation between men and women upon which all cultures were ostensibly constructed would "disrupt the roots of our civilization" (Schelsky, "Die gegenwärtigen Problemlagen," 293–94; Schelsky, *Wandlungen,* 344). A woman's primary social function was not in the public sphere but in the family, providing the most favorable domestic environment necessary to nurture her children.

Correspondingly, remasculation became of critical social importance to the restoration of German male identity. The postwar period has been psychologically characterized as a "crisis of masculinity" (Fehrenbach 95), in which the retraditionalization of the patriarchal family and gender roles was central in reconstructing the German nation ravaged by the war and National Socialism.[15] Fehrenbach asserts that public rhetoric "advocated a specific brand of German masculinity that linked gender roles and sexuality in a complex way with nationality and national pride" (98). Consequently, the task of normalizing the new family and, concomitantly, gender roles, moved to the forefront of political discourse and social policy. The stability of the Federal Republic was understood to be dependent on the presence of traditional family units. Single men and women were encouraged to marry so that they might contribute to the restoration of the nation by producing progeny to support the infant postwar economy and offset fears of a declining national birthrate. Thus, Konrad Adenauer's 1952 inaugural speech called for the "strengthening of the family and thereby the strengthening of the desire for children" (quoted in Stümke 139–40). Pronatalism and the idealization of heterosexuality were tied to concerns of economic recovery and growth as relying on an increasing population of citizens who would contribute to the nation.[16]

In *Different*, Frau Teichmann's willingness to sacrifice herself for her son's benefit is exemplary of the conservative social ideology of motherhood that characterized the Adenauer era. The psychologist whom the Teichmann's consult claims that the real problem is the pathological generation gap between father and son, though instead of suggesting that the father attempt to bridge this gap, he advises that in such cases a mother can be of greater benefit. Klaus's alienation from his family is thus explained as resulting from his father's authoritarian intractability, but the responsibility of bringing the family back together rests squarely on his mother's shoulders. However, her love alone is not sufficient; she must sacrifice herself to prove her total devotion to the family. Her renunciation of any moral, as opposed to legal, guilt only further demonstrates her undying commitment to her son and her obligation to provide the nation with the new German man, capable of heading the patriarchal family, though without the authoritarian pathology of the father. Should the viewer still doubt whether Frau Teichmann's actions were justified, the close-up of Klaus and Gerda holding hands at the end of the trial dispels any such reservations.

Moreover, homosexuality was understood to be a contributory factor in the disequilibrium of gender relations. Schelsky, whose testimony (along with Giese's) was used to uphold the constitutionality of §175, also argued that homosexuality was a consequence of the interaction of specific "social constellations," including "the difficulty of the male role," which developed in part due to "female social emancipation," but also the increased functionalization of modern society, which caused men to lose their "personal authority in the family" (*Soziologie*, 83–84). To counter the "flood of sexual perversions" brought about by political, social, and economic destabilization (*Soziologie,* 82), Schelsky and others maintained that the reinstatement of patriarchal authority into the family was central to reestablishing the nation's stability, normalizing sexual behavior, and promoting democracy.

Examined within this rhetoric, homosexuality was viewed as blatant repudiation of one's familial and political responsibility as a citizen of West Germany. In the same way that homosexuals were considered the enemy of the state under National Socialism, homosexual men could be accused of renouncing democracy, or, perhaps more incriminatingly, supporting communism by relinquishing their obligation to reinstate the patriarchal family as the cornerstone of society (Moeller, "The Homosexual Man," 279–80). Klaus's conversion to heterosexuality represents his acceptance of the socially prescribed role of the new West German man. While Herr Teichmann's generation symbolizes the past and is held responsible for the atrocities of the war and its social and economic consequences, Klaus embodies the new ideal—the anti-authoritarian, yet patriarchal man. On the one extreme, this reconstructed masculine ideal is produced against the allegorical figure of the father; yet, this anti-authoritarian "softness" must also be clearly defined as potent and masculine. Not simply through the rejection of the fascist father, hegemonic postwar masculinity is constituted through the cipher of the homosexual man as weak, unpatriotic, and decadent. Furthermore, the homosexual also acts as an abject site of containment for all that is non-German, against which a healthy expression (that is, neither Weimar decadence nor Nazism) of a uniquely German culture is developed. Ultimately, then, he acts as a point of confluence for multiple cultural anxieties related not only to gender and sexuality but to national identity as well. Homosexuality thereby becomes a necessary and constitutive element in the construction of postwar national identity as a multiple embodiment of otherness that includes such categories as the avant-garde, communism, Jewishness, and the foreign. This strategy, while superficially representing the explicit effort to distinguish the Federal Republic from the Third Reich, in fact creates a bridge between the two states through its reversion to the Nazi strategy of conflating homosexuality with other "undesirable" groups. As Moeller remarks, "In the easily decoded categories of Nazi ideology, it was possible to associate pressures for homosexual rights in Weimar with Jews and communists, and Nazi rhetoric emphasized the 'indissoluble joining of Marxism, pederasty, and systematic Jewish contamination'" ("The Homosexual Man," 256).

In *Different*, it is Boris who personifies this allegorical use of the homosexual. His commitment to postwar reconstruction is challenged not only because of his homosexuality but also because he is frequently associated with non-German culture. His aesthetic preference for avant-garde *musique concrète*, "oriental" décor, and classical Greek statuary suggest a renunciation of his patriotic duty to revive a uniquely German national culture. His sustained contact with adolescent boys—the nation's future, desperately in need of healthy role models—underscores his portrayal as a menace to German democracy. Boris's attempted flight to Rome serves to further emphasize his homelessness and disavowal of his role as a citizen of the new nation.

Boris's Slavic-sounding name evokes another cold war conflation: that of homosexuality and communism. With the banning of the Communist Party (KPD) in 1956, anticommunism was seen as way to guard against the godless masses of the East, especially those other Germans in the German Democratic Republic (GDR), and to ensure socioeconomic prosperity through proliferation of the values of capitalism and democracy, even patriarchy.[17] The conflation of communism with homosexuality raised the stakes of the threat. Richard Gatzweiler, a judicial authority in Cologne who argued against the abolition of §175, wrote that homosexuals were an "enormous danger to the young German democracy," and that one must consider that "the East Zone virtually continues to tolerate homosexuality, thus one recognizes the magnitude of the danger, when the Bolshevists bend the inverts in the Federal Republic to their will" (quoted in Stümke 144). Thus, the political meaning of homosexuality no longer remains in the domain of sexuality or even gender, but becomes an overdetermined category signifying, among other things, a threat to the success of the democratic state.

Furthermore, as Fehrenbach indicates, though she makes a distinct effort not to overemphasize her point, Boris may be Jewish (200). In his scathing review of *Different*, which differed little in tone from the film's general critical reception, the film critic identified as E. P. (most likely Enno Patalas) also remarks on Boris's Jewishness: "The suspicion actually arises here as to whether this aesthete and sexual pervert, this intellectual cosmopolitan 'Dr. Winkler' might perhaps also be a Jew: with this the characterization of the Nazi enemy of the *Volk* would be complete."(191). Analogous to the cold war strategy, during the Third Reich Jews were conflated with homosexuals and communists. The persistent association of Boris with modern art suggests the corresponding association between Jews and degenerate art *(entartete Kunst)* under the Hitler regime.[18] Likewise, Klaus's characteristic style of abstract painting becomes realist just at the moment when his switch in erotic attachment from the sickly Manfred to the socially responsible Gerda is completed. This transformation from sexual deviant to healthy heterosexual, moreover, parallels an analogous transformation from a morally depraved, anti-German avant-garde aesthetic, associated in general with Weimar decadence, to a purely exaltive expression of German beauty and bourgeois normalcy, though supposedly without the Nazi pathology. This serves to further stigmatize Boris and ennoble Klaus.

Finally, the representation of the perceived threat of homosexuality is also achieved through specifically cinematic means in *Different;* that is, through the mise-en-scène, music, and camera angles used to portray Boris and his surroundings. Boris's home has been aptly described as a "den of Uranism" (Fehrenbach 196), and indeed, its decor could easily be characterized as decadent: life-size statues of young men, modern art, and large, ornate candelabras dripping with candle wax adorn his home. His preference for wearing pajamas in the middle of the day is suggestive of retrogression and marks him as an un(re)productive member of society. The living room appears to be lit only by candlelight, creating chiaroscuro effects that obscure the actors' faces, particularly Boris's; in fact, the Winkler residence seems to be totally devoid of windows and is never shown from the outside, emphasizing his separation from the rest of the world. The cinematic techniques employed to represent Boris serve to physically mark him as immutably deviant: extreme-oblique angles are used to film him, and the camera often lingers on him for uncomfortably long periods of time, accentuating his menacing and penetrating gaze. Shrill and disquieting electronic music accompanies many of the scenes depicting Boris, further marking him as degenerate and strange. This technique is most successful when it is cross-cut with the Chopin piece that is associated with Gerda and later with the portrayal of Klaus and Gerda's idyllic romance. The explicitly cinematic means of representing Boris's milieu, positioned against a normative version of sexuality and culture, again demonstrates the latter's dependence on the abject homosexual subculture for its constitutive identity. This putatively postfascist expression of masculinity, located in Klaus's character, is produced precisely through its complementary rejection of all that is symbolically consolidated in the socially pathological figure of the homosexual. Sexuality is redeployed in the service of national identity, and in part through the representational shorthand of the cinema, the ideological conflicts surrounding the patriarchal family, democratization, and culture are staged.

Without overlooking Harlan's cinematic legacy during the Third Reich, it is still possible to expose the ideological ties to Germany's National Socialist past that were replicated, albeit more subtly, in the broader social and cultural discourses of the postwar period, and especially in the construction of homosexuality. On the other hand, the movement to retraditionalize the family represents an attempt to break from the past and embrace a new German man, one who stands for patriarchal values but rejects the authoritarianism of his father's generation. The homosexual man is incapable of embodying this role, not only because of his supposed sexual deviance but also because he has repudiated his obligations to participate in the instrumentalization of the West German family. The homosexual acts as a specific site onto which the anxieties of West German reconstruction efforts are projected, against which national identity is produced.

Given its virtually unprecedented popularity in the 1950s, the mainstream cinema appears to be an especially representative source through which to uncover the social anxieties that circulated in postwar Germany. Particularly because of the extensive degree to which the film industry was regulated in the 1950s, the cinema should be viewed as being positioned within regulatory networks of power and functions to produce, reproduce, and reify the historically specific discourses surrounding given clusters of social identity. My interrogation of the representational and narrative strategies in *Different* reveals the underlying ideological concerns and regulatory mechanisms within their sociohistorically specific context to demonstrate the multiple ways in which homosexuality functions discursively. The figure of the homosexual ultimately comes to stand not simply for sexual deviance, but all that is threatening to the new, "democratic" Germany.

NOTES

1. *Different from You and Me (§175)* was initially released in Austria under the title *Das dritte Geschlecht [The Third Sex]*. Due to substantial

changes required by the FSK *(Freiwillige Selbstkontrolle der Filmwirt-schaft)*, the West German censorship board, the film premiered in the Federal Republic as *Anders als du und ich (§175)*. Although the English release retained the original title, *The Third Sex*, I refer to the film here as *Different from You and Me (§175)*, the literal translation of the title, to capture the inflection it had in Germany more precisely.

2. All translations in this essay are my own, unless otherwise noted.

3. Giese was one of the pioneers of research on homosexuality and campaigned for the reform of §175; the Institute for Sexual Research, of which Giese was then director, is prominently listed in the opening credits of *Different*. Giese (and Harlan) protested against the massive cuts demanded by the FSK. The revisions required and the ensuing protest by the Catholic and Protestant churches were fueled by what was perceived to be a "pro-homosexual bias" associated with Giese's participation in the project (Fehrenbach 201; see also Theis 62–72 and "Ist Harlan wirklich der große Uebeltäter?") In a letter to the *Frankfurter Allgemeine Zeitung*, Giese criticized the unchecked authority afforded the unidentified FSK, whom he accused of having created the sensationalistic tenor of the film primarily through censorship and editing: "If one very impartially and soberly observes how even a scientifically interesting topic, for example, the maturing youth of these times, is prepared, tackled, and depicted in the world of film and finally presented to the public, then one recognizes with horror the overwhelming power of anonymous people, who serve up, censor, edit and somehow finally put works of art back together again" (Giese, 10). Giese's letter demonstrates the enormous influence of the FSK, but also points to the potent relationship between the institutional regulation of sexuality and popular culture during the 1950s. In particular, it demonstrates the degree to which the popular realm is frequently targeted through other centers of power as representing a potentially dangerous origin or reproducer of social ideology.

4. This was a common Nazi indictment of the Weimar era.

5. For an intelligent and meticulously researched treatment of the role of the cinema in the construction of national identity, see Fehrenbach. This essay is intellectually indebted in particular to Fehrenbach's analyses of the postwar crises of gender, the family, and national identity, and their relationship to popular cinema.

6. For sophisticated treatments of two such controversies see Fehrenbach 92–117 on *The Sinner* and McCormick on *Roses for the State Prosecutor*.

7. In this regard, Heide Fehrenbach writes, "Culture was feared as a corrupter of national morals at the same time that it was embraced as a means—in a new bipolar world—to promote a particular vision of a distinctly German identity. In the postwar period, as in the Third Reich, the cinema again became a crucial focus for constructing social ideology in Germany" (117).

8. My investigation presupposes that historically specific categories, such as sexuality or national identity, do not exist in isolation, but rather intersect to constitute each other in particular representational clusters. Scholars of gay and lesbian history have argued that sexuality can serve as a powerful "surrogate medium," "an especially dense transfer point," or a "vehicle," upon which social anxieties are displaced, particularly during

times of great social and economic upheaval (Moeller, "The Homosexual Man," 253–54; Weeks 74; Foucault 103; Rubin 267). Thus, any discursive examination of (homo)sexuality must necessarily include an examination of other historically produced categories.

9. Harlan's activities during the Third Reich were the target of several legal proceedings after the war, though he was ultimately categorized as a fellow traveler *(Mitläufer)* by the denazification court. Harlan first appeared before the denazification court and was acquitted, for he was found not to have been a formal member of any Nazi organization. In 1949, he was charged with crimes against humanity for his participation in the production of *Jew Suess*. Again, he was acquitted, though the acquittal was nullified by the court of the British occupation zone. Harlan was eventually retried again in 1950 and was acquitted for the third and final time. His defense in each case consisted largely of claiming that he was simply following the orders of Joseph Goebbels, minister of propaganda under Hitler; he alleged, in fact, that his life would have been endangered had he not done so. During one of his trials, Harlan brazenly claimed to have secretly been a fighter in the resistance. For a discussion of these trials see Muhlen 245–47; Schwab-Felisch; and Zielinski 42–66. For his own account, see Harlan's autobiography, especially 213–38.

10. Harlan's first two postwar films, *Immortal Beloved [Unsterbliche Geliebte]* (1950) and *Hanna Amon* (1951), were tremendous commercial successes: in fact, despite threats to boycott Harlan's films, *Immortal Beloved* was the third most successful film of the year, surpassed only by the family film *Two Times Lotty [Das doppelte Lottchen]* (von Baky, 1950) and the nostalgic *Heimatfilm, Black Forest Girl [Schwarzwaldmädel]* (Deppe, 1950) (Noack 318). With the release of *Immortal Beloved,* Erich Lüth, a film critic and head of the Hamburg press club, called for a boycott of all of Harlan's films. The producers and distributors of the film sued Lüth, arguing that because Harlan had been cleared of all charges against him, Lüth was impinging on his constitutional right to freedom of expression and free trade. The court initially sided with Harlan despite public support and demonstrations supporting Lüth's cause, but this decision was ultimately overturned by the Supreme Court in 1958. See Muhlen 247; Schwab-Felisch; and Zielinski 66–82. Harlan briefly mentions the controversy in his autobiography (238–39).

11. Richard Dyer remarks that "the plot of the film makes it absolutely clear that the 'problem' is social attitudes towards homosexuality and the codification of those attitudes in §175" ("Less and More," 14).

12. Dyer makes a similar point when he states that *Different from the Others* indicates "the otherness of the straight world," while *Different from You and Me (§175)* "firmly locates the film in the irremediably normal world of 'you and me,' who could never be other" *(Now You See It,* 271).

13. The defendants, Günter R. and Oskar K., charged that the law was unconstitutional because it discriminated against (homosexual) men—lesbians could not be prosecuted under the law. They argued that this violated the Basic Law guaranteeing equal rights for men and women. Giese's testimony focused on the differences between male and female sexuality. He argued that because male sexuality is less tied to the "generative-vegetative" aspects of reproduction (that is, men do not become pregnant, give birth, or lactate), they are more likely to fall prey to the destructive satisfaction of their greater sexual desire. This biological difference between male

and female sexuality had consequences for the male homosexual, since because of his increased sexual appetite, he was more likely to engage in "perversion," which Giese defined as sexual contact outside of a monogamous, long-term relationship between two consenting adults. Giese thus demonstrated that men and women were essentially, that is, naturally, different from one another and therefore the state was able to justify their unequal treatment under §175. The court rejected the appellants' argument that §175 was tainted with Nazi ideology and ruled that prohibiting homosexual conduct was indeed compatible with the principles of democracy. See in particular, Moeller's incisive analysis of the case ("The Homosexual Man"). See also Stümke and Finkler 358–65 and 460–77. The actual opinion of the court is published in Mitglieder des Bundesverfassungsgerichts. For a summary of Giese's testimony see 402–5 of the court's opinion. It is worth noting that during the 1950s alone nearly twenty-seven thousand men were convicted of homosexual relations; the number of arrests was, of course, significantly greater (Dose 131). The statute was finally stricken from the penal code in 1994.

14. This is a familiar trope in postwar films. See, for example, the portrayal of the father in *Roses for the State Prosecutor*, though his connection to National Socialism is more overtly represented as part of the narrative (McCormick 289).

15. Of course, gender crises necessarily implicate constructions both of masculinity and femininity, in that challenges to one come about as a result of a shift in the other, or rather the blurring of the two. Specifically, the crisis as it is constituted for men is that masculinity is threatened by a potentially emancipatory expansion of women's autonomy during the war and early postwar years. The femininity crisis, or perhaps more appropriately, the feminist crisis, represents an "imbalance" that appears to demand a "corrective" measure in order to preserve an idealized construction of masculinity that had been significantly challenged as men returned from the war to a social economy that had existed for years without them. Consequently, traditional female roles had to be reestablished, or rather, the sphere in which women had previously been allowed to operate was radically restricted.

16. The role of the family in postwar West Germany has been the focus of a tremendous amount of research. For a contemporary perspective, see especially Schelsky, *Wandlungen;* for an excellent historical treatment, see Moeller, *Protecting Motherhood.*

17. On the constitutive relationship between West German conceptions of democracy and anticommunist rhetoric, especially that directed at the GDR, see Weitz.

18. This apparent reversion to Nazi tactics was not lost on contemporary critics who reviewed the film; Harlan's cinematic body of work certainly invites such readings. See especially the review by Paul Schallück and "A Study in Perversion."

WORKS CITED

Anders als du und ich (§175). Promotional Material. Constantin-Film Distributor, 1957.

Castell, Adelheid zu. "Die demographischen Konsequenzen des Ersten und Zweiten Weltkriegs für das Deutsche Reich, die Deutsche Demokratische Republik und die Bundesrepublik Deutschland." In *Zweiter Weltkrieg und sozialer Wandel: Achsenmächte und besetzte Länder,* edited by Waclaw Długoborski, 117–37. Göttingen: Vandenhoeck & Ruprecht, 1981.

Dose, Ralf. "Der §175 in der Bundesrepublik Deutschland (1949 bis heute)." In *Die Geschichte des §175: Strafrecht gegen Homosexuelle,* edited by Freunde eines Schwulen Museums in Berlin, 122–43. Berlin: Verlag rosa Winkel, 1990.

Dyer, Richard. "Less and More than Women and Men: Lesbian and Gay Cinema in Weimar Germany." *New German Critique* 51 (1990): 5–60.

———. *Now You See It: Studies on Lesbian and Gay Film.* London: Routledge, 1990.

Fehrenbach, Heide. *Cinema in Democratizing Germany: Reconstructing National Identity after Hitler.* Chapel Hill: University of North Carolina Press, 1995.

Foucault, Michel. *The History of Sexuality: An Introduction.* Translated by Robert Hurley. Vol. 1. New York: Vintage Books, 1990.

Frevert, Ute. *Women in German History: From Bourgeois Emancipation to Sexual Liberation.* Translated by Stuart McKinnon-Evans. New York: Berg, 1988.

Giese, Hans. "Anders als du und ich." Letter. *Frankfurter Allgemeine Zeitung,* 9 November 1957, sec. Briefe an die Herausgeber, 10.

Harlan, Veit. *Im Schatten meiner Filme.* Gütersloh: Sigbert Mohn, 1966.

Höfig, Willi. *Der deutsche Heimatfilm: 1947–1960.* Stuttgart: Ferdinand Enke, 1973.

"Ist Harlan wirklich der große Uebeltäter?" *Der Weg* 8, no. 3 (1958): 83–87.

McCormick, Richard W. "Memory and Commerce, Gender and Restoration: Wolfgang Staudte's *Roses for the State Prosecutor* (1959) and West German Film in the 1950s." In *The Miracle Years: A Cultural History of West Germany, 1949–1968,* edited by Hanna Schissler, 281–300. Princeton, N.J.: Princeton University Press, 2001.

Mitglieder des Bundesverfassungsgerichts. "Urteil vom 10. Mai 1957 (1 BvR 550/52)." In *Entscheidungen des Bundesverfassungsgerichts.* Vol. 6, 387–443. Tübingen: J. C. B. Mohr, 1957.

Moeller, Robert G. "The Homosexual Man Is a 'Man,' the Homosexual Woman is a 'Woman': Sex, Society, and the Law in Postwar West Germany." In *West Germany under Construction: Politics, Society, and Culture in the Adenauer Era,* edited by Robert G. Moeller, 251–84. Ann Arbor: University of Michigan Press, 1997.

———. *Protecting Motherhood: Women and the Family in the Politics of Postwar West Germany.* Berkeley: University of California Press, 1993.

———. "Reconstructing the Family in Reconstruction Germany: Women and Social Policy in the Federal Republic, 1949–1955." In *West Germany under Construction: Politics, Society, and Culture in the Adenauer Era,* edited by Robert G. Moeller, 109–33. Ann Arbor: University of Michigan Press, 1997.

Muhlen, Norbert. "The Return of Goebbels' Film-makers: The Dilemma Posed by Werner Krauss and Veit Harlan." *Commentary* 11, no. 3 (1951): 245–50.

Noack, Frank. *Veit Harlan: "Des Teufels Regisseur."* Munich: Belleville, 2000.

Noelle, Elisabeth, and Erich Peter Neumann. *Jahrbuch der öffentlichen Meinung: 1958–1964.* Allensbach am Bodensee: Verlag für Demoskopie, 1965.

P., E. (Enno Patalas?) "Anders als du und ich (§175)." *Filmkritik* 12 (1957): 191.

Prinzler, Hans Helmut. *Chronik des deutschen Films: 1895–1994.* Stuttgart: J. B. Metzler, 1995.

Rubin, Gayle S. "Thinking Sex: Notes for a Radical Theory of the Politics of Sexuality." In *Pleasure and Danger: Exploring Female Sexuality,* edited by Carole S. Vance, 267–319. Boston: Routledge, 1984.

Schallück, Paul. "Anders als du und ich." *Filmforum* 7, no. 1 (1958): 5.

Schelsky, Helmut. "Die gegenwärtigen Problemlagen der Familiensoziologie." In *Soziologische Forschung in unserer Zeit,* edited by Karl Gustav Specht, 282–96. Cologne: Westdeutscher Verlag, 1951.

———. "Die Gleichberechtigung der Frau und die Gesellschaftsordnung." *Sozialer Fortschritt* 1, no. 6 (1952): 129–32.

———. *Soziologie der Sexualität: Über die Beziehungen zwischen Geschlecht, Moral und Gesellschaft.* Hamburg: Rowohlt, 1955.

———. *Wandlungen der deutschen Familie in der Gegenwart: Darstellung und Deutung einer empirisch-soziologischen Tatbestandsaufnahme.* 2d ed. Stuttgart: Ferdinand Enke, 1954.

Schönke, Adolf. *Strafgesetzbuch für das Deutsche Reich.* 2d ed. Munich: C. H. Beck, 1944.

Schwab-Felisch, Hans. "Die Affäre Harlan." *Der Monat* 3, no. 28 (1951): 414–22.

"A Study in Perversion: Herr Harlan back in business." *The Guardian,* 29 November 1957.

Stümke, Hans-Georg. *Homosexuelle in Deutschland: Eine politische Geschichte.* Munich: C. H. Beck, 1989.

Stümke, Hans-Georg, and Rudi Finkler. *Rosa Winkel, Rosa Listen: Homosexuelle und "Gesundes Volksempfinden" von Auschwitz bis heute.* Reinbek bei Hamburg: Rowohlt, 1981.

Theis, Wolfgang. "'Anders als du und ich (§175).'" In *Vergessene Zukunft* (Forgotten future), edited by Christian Phillip Müller, 56–75. Munich: Kunstverein München, 1992.

Weeks, Jeffrey. *Sexuality and Its Discontents: Meanings, Myths and Modern Sexualities.* Boston: Routledge, 1985.

Weitz, Eric D. "The Ever-Present Other: Communism in the Making of West Germany." In *The Miracle Years: A Cultural History of West Germany, 1949–1968,* edited by Hanna Schissler, 219–32. Princeton, N.J.: Princeton University Press, 2001.

Zielinski, Siegfried. *Veit Harlan: Analysen und Materialien zur Auseinandersetzung mit einem Film-Regisseur des deutschen Faschismus.* Frankfurt am Main: Rita G. Fischer, 1981.

FILMOGRAPHY

Black Forest Girl [Schwarzwaldmädel] (Hans Deppe, 1950): not available on video

Different from the Others [Anders als die Andern] (Richard Oswald, 1919): (complete film is no longer available): www.facets.org

Different from You and Me (§175) [Anders als du und ich (§175), aka Das dritte Geschlecht] (Veit Harlan, 1957): www.alpineimporters.com or www.germanvideo.com

The Girl Rosemarie [Das Mädchen Rosemarie] (Rolf Thiele, 1958): www .amazon.de

Green Is the Heath [Grün ist die Heide] (Hans Deppe, 1951): www .alpineimporters.com

Hanna Amon (Veit Harlan, 1951): not available on video

The Hooligans [Die Halbstarken] (Georg Tressler, 1956): www.amazon.de

Immortal Beloved [Unsterbliche Geliebte] (Veit Harlan, 1950): not available on video

Jew Suess [Jud Süß] (Veit Harlan, 1940): www.facets.org

Roses for the State Prosecutor [Rosen für den Staatsanwalt] (Wolfgang Staudte, 1959): www.amazon.de

The Sinner [Die Sünderin] (Willi Forst, 1951): www.amazon.de

Two Times Lotty [Das Doppelte Lottchen] (Josef von Baky, 1950): www .amazon.de

FILM SOURCES

Alpine Importers
833 W. Torrance Blvd.
Torrance, CA 90502
Phone: (310) 327-6985
www.alpineimporters.com

Facets Multi-Media, Inc.
1517 W. Fullerton Ave.
Chicago, IL 60614
Phone: (800) 331-6197 or (773) 281-9075
Fax: (773) 929-5337
www.facets.org

German Language Video Center
Division of Heidelberg Haus
7625 Pendleton Pike
Indianapolis, Indiana 46226-5298
Phone: (317) 547-1257
Fax: (317) 547-1263
www.germanvideo.com

CHAPTER 9

Negotiating the Popular and the Avant Garde

The Failure of Herbert Vesely's
The Bread of Those Early Years (1962)

Hester Baer

Occupying a liminal space between the cinema of the 1950s and the later productions of the New German Cinema, Herbert Vesely's 1962 film *The Bread of Those Early Years [Das Brot der frühen Jahre]* united conventional narrative elements with new, experimental aesthetic strategies. The film sought to appeal to popular audiences with a narrative about contemporary issues that incorporated generic aspects of the detective story and the love story, while encoding this narrative within formal structures emblematic of the emergent new wave. Despite its attempt to mediate between popular and avant-garde filmmaking strategies, however, the film was, by all accounts, a resounding failure.

The Bread of Those Early Years, the first new wave film to be released after the "Oberhausen Manifesto," failed to appeal to either popular audiences or critics invested in a rejuvenation of the German film landscape. The film's lack of success in either regard caused the co-signers of the Oberhausen Manifesto to rethink their strategy for future film productions.[1] Had the film been successful in its attempt to mediate between the popular film culture of the 1950s and the theoretical possibility of a new, experimental cinema in the 1960s, German film history might have turned out differently. The film thus casts doubt on the notion of the "rebirth" of the German cinema after Oberhausen, and provides insight into the failure of postwar German filmmakers

to create a cinema that could be aesthetically innovative and politically relevant while still appealing to domestic audiences.[2]

   While *The Bread of Those Early Years* is, in hindsight, not
wholly successful in its filmic project, neither does it fail completely in its attempt to mediate between two polarized ideas of
what the cinema can or should be. *The Bread of Those Early Years*
is situated, historically and aesthetically, between the popular yet
provincial West German cinema of the 1950s and the emergent
postwar European avant-garde cinema. The discourse of failure
that surrounded the film can be explained as a confused reaction
to the film's attempt to reconcile disparate film forms (neorealist
elements and a highly fragmented, "abstract" narrative style) and
to mediate between high and low culture. In its attempt to synthesize these dichotomies, the film ends up articulating a highly
ambivalent gender politics, at the levels of form and content. It is
my contention that the reason for its failure with audiences and
critics in 1962 lies in the fact that it reflects an instability and
confusion of categories, in particular an instability of gender roles
and an instability of definitions of the avant garde or the modern
in cinema. This instability touched a nerve in the public sphere
at a time when these categories were not only in flux but were
vexing and confusing to audiences and critics alike.

   In this chapter, I argue that the public discourse surrounding the film is based on a complex set of repressions and elisions
of what is truly at stake in the critical and popular rejection of
The Bread of Those Early Years: anxiety over the sense in which
(narrative) authority is gendered as female in the film, an anxiety
that is of course emblematic of larger social and political anxieties in postwar West Germany at a moment when the "economic
miracle" began to tip into the upheaval and transformations in
society that reached their pinnacle around 1968. I further suggest
that an analysis of this particular film and the anxieties surrounding it sheds light on larger issues in German film history, in particular on the vexed relationship of the New German Cinema to
its more popular precursors.

   The Bread of Those Early Years premiered at the Cannes
film festival on 18 May 1962. Much fanfare surrounded the premiere of the film, which had been publicized for months as the
first production of the recently proclaimed New German Cinema.
Responses at Cannes were muted, and when the film opened in
Cologne the next week, it was panned. "A Dream Has Ended,"
mourned the *Abendzeitung* in Munich, and other reviewers
agreed.[3] While *The Bread of Those Early Years* was shown widely

in West German cinemas and went on to win several Federal Film Prizes, it clearly failed to live up to popular or critical expectations. Critics were receptive to the film's experimental visual style and fragmented narrative, but reviewers in both mainstream newspapers and film journals agreed about the film's primary faults. Not only did its attempt to espouse a new wave, avant-garde style appear synthetic, but the film was too "cold," and failed to capture emotion or to create any possibilities for identification. Incessant comparisons to recent French new wave films, in particular Alain Resnais's *Last Year at Marienbad,* not only fueled embarrassment over the continuing provinciality of German cinema and resentment over the reaction to the film at Cannes, but also highlighted the "inadequacy" of the film's borrowed formal qualities in dealing with its uniquely German content.[4] As one reviewer said of Vesely, "Instead of bread, he gives us papier-maché petit-fours" (Kaul n.p.).[5]

The massive popular and critical backlash against Vesely's film was not entirely surprising, given the immense expectations whipped up by the media and by the publicity campaign engineered for the film by the vocal young film critic Joe Hembus, who stressed the film's popular appeal as much as its experimental, "artistic" aspects.[6] Expectations for the film were already high in January 1962, when *Filmkritik* published an article about the production of *The Bread of Those Early Years* that concluded: "We will know in March [the projected release date of the film], then, if the German film, despite all skepticism, is in fact in the position to make a contribution to world cinematography after all" (Thiel 16). Then, in February, as shooting of the film wrapped, the Oberhausen Manifesto was proclaimed. Director Herbert Vesely was among those who signed the call for a New German Cinema, as were the film's producer, Hansjürgen Pohland, the cameraman, Wolf Wirth, and the principal actor, Christian Doermer.

While their film adaptation of Heinrich Böll's novella had gone into production long before the manifesto was written, the film was nonetheless quickly cast as the vanguard in the attack against "Papas Kino."[7] As the publicity campaign emphasized, the film was made for a measly DM 400,000 at a time when most films cost five times that amount. The cast and crew were industry outsiders, none of whom was over the age of thirty-five, save for Böll, who adapted the dialogue from his novella. Extensive newspaper coverage during production provided an "insider's look" at the glamorous young rebels of the cast and crew on the set of the film, which was shot on location in West Berlin. Given the drama and excitement surrounding the production itself, and the buzz that it would be a radical departure from the typical cinematic fare of the day, it was almost a foregone conclusion that the film could not fulfill these expectations.

Nonetheless, the fact that the film generated high expectations does not account for the venom of the criticism to which it was subjected, nor for the actual content of the critiques leveled against it. By 1962, film critics routinely decried the sentimentality and melodramatic affect of popular German cinema; it is thus all the more ironic that one of their chief qualms with *The Bread of Those Early Years* was its emotional detachment and "coldness." Agreeing that the film was an optical tour de force, critics in publications as diverse as the leftist journal *Filmkritik*, the film evaluation organ of the Protestant Churches *Evangelischer Film-Beobachter*, and the teen fan magazine *Bravo* suggested that the film's failure to address spectators clearly, and the absence of possibilities for spectator identification, left audiences with no access to the social and historical critique of West Germany during the economic miracle that the film meant to articulate.[8] A reviewer for the *Beratungsdienst Jugend und Film* put it this way: "The epic form of theater, the new attempt in literature to substitute the 'stream of consciousness' for plot: these certainly constitute a new task for film. But it cannot be carried out in such a cold and bloodless manner. For in this film, the feelings of the spectator are hardly addressed" (2).

The popular women's magazine *Film und Frau*, on the other hand, published one of the few positive reviews of the film, focusing on the strong female characters and the love story the film narrates as points of identification for (female) viewers of the film ("Das Brot der frühen Jahre" 106–8). Indeed, an informal poll by one reviewer of responses to *The Bread of Those Early Years* found that the only spectators who had positive things to say about the film were women. The snide tone of the article utilizes the fact that only women liked the film as evidence of how awful it was. Nonetheless, the article offers one of the few attempts to gauge the actual responses of average spectators to the film, and it is interesting that gender becomes a category of analysis as a result.[9] The fact that the film was received positively by these female viewers and by a popular women's magazine (and almost nowhere else) suggests that gender is imbricated with definitions of the popular and avant garde that shaped the public discourse surrounding the film, as well as in the conceptions of spectator address and identification at play in the critiques of the film.

There is much in the film's narrative and structure that substantiates this idea. While most reviewers assumed that the film was "about" Walter Fendrich's subjective transformation, the *Film und Frau* review focused primarily on the subjective transformations of the female characters and on their role in Walter's self-realization, thus highlighting an important aspect of the film that remained repressed in much of the public discourse surrounding *The Bread of Those Early Years*. As the *Film und Frau* review suggests, the film did, in fact, provide possibilities for spectator identification, but with its female characters rather than its male characters.

Like Böll's novella, the film version of *The Bread of Those Early Years* tells the story of Walter Fendrich (Christian Doermer), a washing-machine repairman who is successful at his job, engaged to his boss's daughter, and well on his way to bourgeois bliss in the "Wirtschaftswunder" of West Germany. This all changes one day in March, when he falls in love with Hedwig (Karen Blanguernon), a girl from his hometown whom he picks up at the train station when she moves to the city. Through the intensity of emotion he experiences in his immediate love for Hedwig, Walter is able to realize his alienation and reject the life he has been living. He renounces that life, failing to report to work and breaking off his engagement to his fiancée Ulla (Vera Tschechowa). Throughout the day, he remembers the time when he was plagued by a constant hunger for bread, which Ulla and her family never gave him; the desire symbolized by this bread is what propelled Walter into the alienated life he now leads, but, of course, the desire itself has only been sublimated as a result. Through Hedwig, the narrative suggests, Walter finds access to his desire once again. With several exceptions, *The Bread of Those Early Years* remains true to the narrative of Böll's novella. The film transposes the action of the story from Cologne (the implied setting of Böll's narrative) to divided Berlin.[10] With the exception of one flashback sequence that projects images of Fendrich's childhood and features a voice-over by his father, the narrative is compressed into one day in the life of Fendrich, the day when Hedwig comes to town and he ditches his job and his fiancée for her.

The viewer of the film comprehends this narrative fully, however, only by piecing together its fragments bit by bit. *The Bread of Those Early Years* is set up almost as a detective story, in which various characters, and by extension the film's viewers, are engaged in a quest for knowledge about the motivations for Walter's strange behavior on this day. The film is characterized by a fragmentary, repetitive narrative style and a strong disjuncture between sound and image tracks. Only slowly do we as viewers begin to discover who Walter is, what it is that he has done, and why it is of consequence. Bit by bit, we hear different versions of Walter's story in a montage of sound and image that at times resembles a documentary.

Vesely himself explained his project in terms of an attempt to document contemporary reality by repeating certain narrative events from different perspectives, a device that he saw as creating an intensified mode of realism absent from German filmmaking in the 1950s (Baer n.p.). Vesely's 1960 treatment for the film explains his conception of temporality and perspective in the attempt to portray visually a transformation of consciousness: "The past and the present permeate each other. The gaze is synchronous and everywhere. No plot with flashbacks, but rather synchronous occurrences: reflections, possibilities, realities. This interlacing of levels creates an expanding consciousness, the consciousness of Walter Fendrich, 23, electrical mechanic and specialist in washing machines, on this Monday, the 14th of March" (Hembus, "Suche," n.p.). What is striking about *The Bread of Those Early Years* is that those characters who observe Walter and comment on his behavior—those who structure our knowledge about him—are almost exclusively women: Ulla, Hedwig, Walter's landlady, Frau Flink and the women who work in her laundromat, as well as the woman from Kurbelstraße who has a washing machine that Walter repairs. If, as Vesely's treatment suggests, "the gaze is everywhere," Walter is very much the object of that gaze, while the subject of the gaze is most often a woman.[11] In both form and content, the film grants an unusual amount of narrative authority to its female characters. In as much as they control the gaze and structure our knowledge within the context of the film's narrative, the female characters are also the characters with whom spectators are encouraged to identify. If, as feminist film theorists have long argued, dominant Hollywood cinema placed female spectators in a double bind (they must either masochistically identify with the objectified female character or "masquerade" as other in an attempt to identify with the male character), then *The Bread of Those Early Years* wholly inverts this model.[12] Female spectators likely found plenty of opportunities for identification, in particular with

Walter's ditched fiancée Ulla, but male spectators clearly lacked such opportunities.

Like other films of the European new wave, *The Bread of Those Early Years* invokes the model of the Hollywood film noir in its mood and structure. Yet, while the narrative of the classic film noir is constructed around a quest (by the male protagonist, and by extension the male spectator) for knowledge about the mysterious and dangerous femme fatale, in Vesely's film, again, the tables are turned. Here it is the women who are engaged in a quest for knowledge about Walter, who takes on the structural role of the "femme fatale" in the film. Mary Ann Doane has described the femme fatale in the following way:

> The femme fatale is the figure of a certain discursive unease, a potential epistemological trauma. For her most striking characteristic, perhaps, is the fact that she never really is what she seems to be. She harbors a threat which is not entirely legible, predictable, or manageable. In thus transforming the threat of the woman into a secret, something which must be aggressively revealed, unmasked, discovered, the figure is fully compatible with the epistemological drive of narrative, the hermeneutic structuration of the classical text. Sexuality becomes the site of questions about what can and cannot be known. (1)

This description is strikingly accurate as an explanation of the role of Walter Fendrich in the film. Like the femme fatale, Walter turns out to be not at all as he had seemed, and he thus constitutes a threat not only to Ulla, whom he rejects, but also to Hedwig, whom he loves all too dangerously. In this instance, Walter is the secret that must be aggressively uncovered by the female characters of *The Bread of Those Early Years*; as such, he becomes the epistemological drive of the narrative. As Doane maintains, sexuality—and sexual difference—are at the center of this narrative questioning of what can and cannot be known; but again, it is the women in the film who are vested with subjectivity and narrative authority, while Walter Fendrich is the object of their quest for knowledge. By extension, as the viewers of the film participate in this quest for knowledge that propels the film's narrative, they are encouraged to identify with the film's female characters.

This inversion of gender roles is accomplished most strikingly, not only through the realignment of the gaze but also through the use of disjunctive voice-over. As Kaja Silverman has

argued, there are no instances within mainstream cinema of disembodied female voices, because the disembodied voice is a signifier of phallic, abstract power, of epistemological authority in the
production of discourse. The woman, lacking phallic power, is
obsessively specularized in mainstream films: if she is heard she
must be seen, though she may be seen without being heard. While
even disembodied male voice-over is unusual in fiction film,
when it does occur, "the dis-embodied voice-over can be seen as
'exemplary' for male subjectivity, attesting to an achieved invisibility, omniscience and discursive power" (Silverman 134). Invisibility is thus a representative trait for male subjectivity—most
fully realized in the disembodied voice-over—while specularity,
or visibility, is exemplary for female subjectivity as it is represented in dominant discourse. *The Bread of Those Early Years*
inverts this model to a large extent: Walter Fendrich is highly
visible, even specularized by the female gaze, and disembodied
female voices vested with narrative authority comment upon and
interpret his actions.

Because of the taboo against disembodied female voices
within mainstream cinema, feminist cinema has often focused
on the female voice as a site of aesthetic experimentation through
which to reinvest female subjectivity with agency. As Silverman
suggests, a great deal is at stake in this disassociation: "the freeing-
up of the female voice from its obsessive and indeed exclusive
reference to the female body, a reference which turns woman—in
representation and in fact—back upon herself, in a negative and
finally self-consuming narcissism" (137). Feminist filmmakers
have worked with a number of strategies to "challenge the imperative of synchronization"; these include aligning the female voice
with the male body (and thus challenging the reification of sexual
difference), and presenting several female bodies to which voices,
sounds, and stories could be attributed (thus frustrating cinematic codes by denaturalizing the voice-body alignment). *The
Bread of Those Early Years* employs both of these strategies, in
particular the latter.[13] Ulla's voice is often matched to the landlady's image, and vice versa. Though Hedwig's voice is almost always aligned with her body, she and Ulla have such similar faces
and voices that at times (when they are shot from a distance or
behind glass) they seem almost indistinguishable.[14] The fact that
the film was shot without sound, and only "synchronized" later
in a sound studio, contributes further to the nonalignment of
voices with bodies and thus to the denaturalization of this semic

link. In what follows, I examine the consequences of this disjuncture of the female voice from the female body, and the concomitant specularization of the male body, as one way of explaining the negative response to the film: lacking clear-cut possibilities for identification with male characters—and, in fact, being encouraged by textual structures to identify with female characters—clearly proved confusing and frustrating to male critics and spectators alike.

The opening sequence of *The Bread of Those Early Years* structures the spectatorial relation to the subsequent disjuncture of sound and image by establishing an epistemological correspondence of images with narration despite their lack of an organic or naturalized connection. During the credit sequence, a train approaches Berlin's Gleisdreieck train station, which itself functions as a metaphor for the love triangle between Walter, Ulla, and Hedwig, and for the tripartite structure of the narrative.[15] As the train arrives at the station, two female voices are heard in dialogue:

> "And then he went to the train station . . . at least that's what he says."
> "Which station was that?"
> "I don't know."

The camera cuts from the train to the Gleisdreieck station sign, and a (male) voice announces the arrival of the train from the station's loudspeaker. An extreme close-up of a lighted cigarette segues into a pan up to the loudspeaker, a pan that creates spatial confusion because it is subsequently clear that the cigarette smoker is not in the station. The camera zooms in on the loudspeaker in a shot that establishes the epistemological authority of the disembodied voice, which now directs passengers to board the train. The image now shifts to a shot of hands dialing a pay phone in the station, then cuts to a mouth smoking the same cigarette we have seen before. Women's voices discuss the disappearance of Walter Fendrich, attempting to reconstruct his actions over the course of the day. The symmetry of the loudspeaker and the telephone, both transmitters of disembodied voices, grants credence to the narrative authority of the (female) voices that will construct our knowledge about Walter over the course of the film. Finally, we see a woman behind the glass of the phone booth (the glass functions as an obstacle to organic sound-image correspondence), followed by a full-face shot of the woman smoking the cigarette. While it is clear that the women we see are the

women whose voices make up the soundtrack—the voices of the
women, that is, are definitively linked to their bodies here—it is
unclear which voice belongs to whom, or even who these women
who speculate on Walter's actions are. Nonetheless, in contrast
to the classic film noir narrative, it is not the women about whom
our curiosity is aroused but Walter Fendrich, the absent object of
their speculations. The epistemological correspondence of narration and image that has been established throughout this sequence structures the spectatorial relation to the ensuing
narrative, which is enunciated in an increasingly disjunctive fashion, albeit one that utilizes a set of generic conventions in an
attempt to offset the narrative fragmentation to some extent.

As in a detective story or film noir, we are drawn into the
action by a set of mysterious occurrences about which we are
given little information. Indeed, the impression of a detective narrative is confirmed shortly after the sequence just described when
the screen fades to black and a snappy jazz soundtrack accompanies images of Walter Fendrich in full face and profile that recall
mug shots. A male voice tells us he is "Fendrich. Walter Fendrich.
Twenty-four years of age, refugee from the East." Walter is thus
constituted again as the object of the gaze, of inquiry, of the filmic
narrative.

The narrative is subsequently divided into three overlapping and partially repeating sections, loosely constructed around
three parallel subjective sequences that record the perspectives of
the three protagonists: Walter Fendrich, his fiancée Ulla Wick-
weber, and his new beloved, Hedwig Muller. In these sequences,
in which images are accompanied by voice-over narration, each
protagonist projects a possible future life that is ultimately nullified by the events of this particular day: Walter imagines a regi-
mented, bourgeois married life with Ulla; Ulla imagines herself
as the accommodating and flexible but proper wife for Walter,
who would himself be stable and provide for her, even if he might
have occasional affairs; and Hedwig imagines a detailed future in
a marriage to a man she has just met on the street. These circumscribed, "subjunctive" projections of a stable future stand in stark
contrast to the fragmentary and uncertain events of the preceding
and succeeding narrative, when the lives of all three characters
are turned upside down almost despite themselves.

This present-day narrative, which parallels the three subjunctive, subjective sequences, is also tripartite in structure,
though now marked by the "objective" perspectives of those who

speculate on Walter's actions. The *Evangelischer Film-Beobachter* described this narrative in the following way:

> The spectator who is prepared to think it through can ascertain three clusters of experience: At the beginning stands Ulla's search for her fiance, who roams the streets with a troubled face, and therein lies the story's search for its "hero." The comparison of the two women and Fendrich's decision between them constitutes the middle portion of the film. The new pair in the old environment is the end piece of the work. (Review 257)

This description of events is fairly accurate, though it is a stretch to suggest that Walter actually makes a choice between Ulla and Hedwig. Unlike Böll's novella, which suggests that Walter Fendrich, after meeting and falling in love with Hedwig, is able to break out of the oppressive conditions of a bourgeois lifestyle for which he has never been suited, the film does not attribute such explicit agency to Walter. Instead, the film's narrative structure takes the events of the day as assumptions about reality, deconstructs them through visual and aural fragmentation and repetition, and reconstructs the events as a richer tapestry of reality through the perspectives of the various women who observe Walter. Reconstructed through the perspectives of these female characters (including Ulla and Hedwig), Walter's actions lack definitive meaning: they are invested with a multiplicity of meanings, all of which are subjectively determined by female perspectives. Although the film's ending, in which the camera circles around Walter and Hedwig embracing in the street, leaves little doubt that the two are united, the closure is arbitrary in both form and content. Not only does the episodic nature of the film make clear that this is just one moment in time (and things could change again in the next moment), but according to the film's narrative logic, Walter or Hedwig easily could have ended up with someone else instead.

Walter's lack of agency is confirmed on a formal level by his lack of narrative or epistemological authority in the film. The first time he is allowed to speak at all in the film comes in the subjective sequence in which he imagines his future married life with Ulla. This sequence is sandwiched, and thus circumscribed, by Ulla's commentary on the events. As if this weren't enough to destabilize his authority, Walter says at the end of his subjective sequence, "I know nothing of this future, which will never be present. I don't see myself or hear myself, I don't smile or talk, shake hands, go to movies or to visit people, open doors, nothing, nothing, I know nothing." Though the sequence is marked as subjective because of Walter's voice-over—it is the first time we hear his voice—it ends with a statement that functions to disavow even this subjectivity through the symbolic castration represented by his admission of blindness and deafness to the sounds and images of a future that spectators of the film can hear narrated and watch as they occur.

Reviewers of *The Bread of Those Early Years* were particularly disturbed by Walter Fendrich's lack of agency and impotence in the face of the events that befall him. Unlike the Fendrich of Böll's novella, the Fendrich of the film is granted only limited agency in the events that take place, and limited authority in the narrative interpretation of these events. As such, the film does not inscribe possibilities for spectator identification with him. This was clearly disturbing to critics who hoped for a New German Cinema featuring strong male characters who would provide a contrast to the male characters of 1950s cinema, who were perceived as passive and compromised subjects.[16] The angry young men who confronted the problematic filmic legacy of the 1950s with their Oberhausen Manifesto were themselves so self-prepossessing that they were expected to present mimetic versions of themselves on screen: young, potent subjects brimming with agency. Instead, many of the early (pre-1968) productions of the New German Cinema, like *The Bread of Those Early Years*, depicted young men who seemed to mirror their filmic fathers in their passivity, crisis, and subjective oblivion.[17]

Most accounts of the cinema of the 1950s—film criticism contemporaneous to the 1950s as well as film history written since—tend to portray it as an aesthetically and politically problematic monolith thematizing the continual crisis of male subjectivity after fascism. Influenced by Siegfried Kracauer's account of the passive men of Weimar cinema[18]—best epitomized by characters with their bowed and defeated heads in their wives' sheltering laps—critics and historians have placed 1950s films in a continuum with the problematic films of the Weimar and Nazi periods. During the 1950s, critics such as Joe Hembus and the collective that published the journal *Filmkritik* called for a new mode of filmmaking that would break with this problematic continuum that they labeled "Papas Kino" (Papa's Cinema). The Oberhausen Manifesto was drafted as a response to this call, and has subsequently been seen as the moment of radical break from the cinematic past.[19]

The idea of "Papas Kino," so integral to the discourse surrounding *The Bread of Those Early Years,* itself effects an interesting assertion and displacement of male authority. Taken literally, "Papas Kino" refers to the cinema produced by the generation of the fathers; indeed, there were few young film directors or producers during the 1950s, and many of the most popular directors and producers of that period had been active in the Nazi film industry.[20] Declaring "Papas Kino" dead was thus an Oedipal gesture on the part of a younger generation of men, who in so doing sought to assert their own (male) subjectivity. At the same time, however, the derogatory label "Papas Kino" refers to certain formal and functional qualities embodied by 1950s German films. In a sidebar entitled "Papa's Cinema—A Definition" in their March 1962 issue, *Filmkritik* defined these qualities by reprinting an ad from the studio Ufa-Film-Hansa (the caption gleefully notes that the studio went broke several weeks after the appearance of the ad):

Was wir unter Film verstehen:

Format und Farbe: verschwenderisch
Inbegriff unbegrenzter Unterhaltung
Lösung aus den eigenen vier Wänden
Mehrerlebnis weil Massenerlebnis

What Film means to us:

Format and color: extravagant
Ideal of boundless entertainment
Liberation from one's own four walls
More experience through mass experience

This definition of "Papas Kino" calls to mind the formula of the Hollywood studios, but it is important to note that these traits (boundless entertainment that induces a loss of subjectivity and feelings of oneness with the diegetic space of the film, liberation from the domestic sphere into the "mass experience" of the cinema) are "feminized" traits that are linked to the "mass cultural" realm of modernity.[21] These traits are also closely associated with the female viewer's experience of film, at least since Siegfried

Kracauer's description of "the little shop girls" at the movies.[22] Indeed, postwar German film audiences were comprised of many more women than men, and the film studios, clearly cognizant of this fact, made a concerted attempt in the 1950s to address female viewers in their genre and star choices and in product tie-ins.[23] Indeed, it was not uncommon in the films of the 1950s to find textually inscribed possibilities for spectator identification primarily with female characters rather than male characters. If this was a cinema produced *by* the fathers, it was also a cinema produced *for* the mothers. In a sense, then, in declaring the old cinema dead, what the rebels of Oberhausen wanted to kill off was just as much a "Mamas Kino."

Barton Byg has suggested a gendered reading of the development of new wave cinema in Europe that links the issues I have been discussing to the emergent cold war. Byg argues that a number of films set in Berlin in the late 1940s very clearly represented male subjectivity and masculinity in crisis in the wake of World War II; in so doing, they actually helped to demonstrate the need for the emergent cold war and its culture. According to Byg, the cold war recuperated masculinity both by reasserting a nonproblematic military prowess differentiated from Nazism and by promoting a rejuvenation of cinema:

> Regarding the latter [the rejuvenation of cinema], a cultural recuperation of masculinity emerged through film noir and the subsequent renewal of the institution of the cinema, propelled by male-oriented critical appreciations of noir and Italian Neo-Realism, and resulting eventually in the "new waves" of European cinema. In one sense, all these cinematic movements can be seen as narrative ways of restoring the vitality of a masculinity left vulnerable in the wake of the war and the abdication or disgrace of the "fathers." In another, as "modernist" movements within the popular context of the cinema, they are examples of the masculine impulse in art to resist the threats posed by the feminine aspects of modernity/modernism (177–78).

Byg's analysis implies that the task of new wave films was indeed, as I have argued, to effect a double displacement of the problematic masculinity represented by the idea of "Papas Kino" as well as of the feminized aspects of mass modernity I am referring to here as "Mamas Kino." After fascism, the medium of film itself had become suspect as a result of its exploitation at the hands of Goebbels's "Dream Factory." The propagandistic but pleasurable film spectacle of the Nazi years was associated with the feminized "other" of mass culture, and could be overcome only by new cinematic movements.

While in the United States film noir emerged as a strategy for confronting emasculated men and aggressive women in the aftermath of the war, in Germany male subjectivity had become so marginal that it could not stand at the authoritative center of any filmic narrative. As Barton Byg points out, "In the German films, the women cannot be shown as either physically weak or aggressive; instead their threat resides in the fact that the male characters are the weak ones" (181). This default attribution to female characters of the traits lacking in their male counterparts continued to structure the representation of gender roles in German films even after the emergence of the new wave. In contrast to the new wave films of other national cinemas, early German new wave films rarely portrayed strong, modern women or addressed the disruption of traditional, binary gender roles in ways that moved beyond default inversion.[24]

Similarly, in the attempt to dispense with the Nazi past and its problematic cultural heritage, new wave German filmmakers (again in contrast to their counterparts in other countries) ultimately found that the most successful strategy was to reinstate the absolute alterity of the popular versus the avant garde, or of mass culture versus autonomous art.[25] This is arguably what the New German Cinema ultimately did, sacrificing the possibility of truly transforming West German cinematic culture and reaching wider audiences, and instead setting itself up in opposition to "Papas Kino" and "Mamas Kino," articulated together as the residually fascistic realm of mass culture. Yet this strategy emerged only slowly.

In the early 1960s, cinematic culture was at a turning point in many respects. In the 1950s, the cinema still provided one of the primary (public) spaces in which West Germans were able to express emotion openly. The melodramatic and sentimental films of the era offered thinly veiled representations of problems that faced many people (in particular women) at the time; as such, they presented a space in which to contemplate public and private histories, and to do so with emotion at a time when affect was slowly being drained from the public and private spheres, especially within the realm of visual culture.[26] By the late 1960s, the cinema was beginning to lose this role in society, as the student movement made history a subject of public confrontation, and the countercultures provided new forums for the public and private expression of emotion. The Oberhausen Manifesto hinted at this transformation in the role of cinema by emphasizing its contested nature already in 1962.

Within this complex constellation of gendered expectations surrounding the emergence of a triumphant new German film, *The Bread of Those Early Years* was introduced as the first great hope of the German new wave. In short, the film was charged with the tasks of displacing problematic masculinity and asserting a renewed masculine modernity that would shut out the threatening, feminized aspects of mass modernity. The film failed miserably at both these tasks, seeming almost to embody the very issues with which it was supposed to dispatch. It narrativized problematic male subjectivity in a highly self-conscious fashion, turning the tables of classical cinematic convention to vest female characters with abstract authority while specularizing the male subject. In so doing, it provided identificatory possibilities only with its female characters, as had so many German films in the 1950s. At the same time, it self-consciously attempted to straddle the great divide, to merge the popular and the avant garde. In so doing, the film ended up displacing familiar formal qualities and inverting gender norms in ways that proved confusing to critics and spectators.

Like the rubble films of the immediate postwar years, *The Bread of Those Early Years* uses the real settings of Berlin as a backdrop, but this time the city is no longer in ruins. Instead, it is both the prosperity of the miracle years and the cold war threat of the wall that are at stake. Like the city itself, Walter Fendrich is a divided subject who is pulled between the prosperity represented by Ulla and the desire represented by Hedwig, the woman who arrives from the East. Here as well, *The Bread of Those Early Years* constitutes a departure from the particularly German tendency (since the Weimar street films) to equate the city with "Woman" in the cinema.[27] Indeed, it is Walter who is equated with the city, while Hedwig is seduced by the streets of Berlin. Toward the end of the film she escapes the constricted space of Walter's car and (like a Weimar film hero) loses herself in the night city. It is here that she meets the man whom she considers marrying in the subjective sequence where she imagines her future. Walter, afraid of losing Hedwig to the seductions of the city, rushes madly through the streets in pursuit of her. At the end of the film, the two are united, not in the secure domestic space that would ensure a happy ending, but under a street light out in the public space of the city.

To its credit, the film does not rely on the overdetermined symbolism of divided Berlin, nor does it invoke facile allusions to the cold war politics of which Berlin was emblematic. Nonetheless, its subtle equation of the symbolically castrated Walter Fendrich with the symbolically castrated city of Berlin is revealing. If the ruined Berlin of the rubble films symbolized Nazism, which was embodied in these films, according to Barton Byg, by the femme fatale, here Berlin symbolizes the cold war, which is in turn embodied by the "feminized" Fendrich, who is placed in the role of femme fatale in the film.

It is precisely this subtle invocation of cold war politics and divided Berlin, in conjunction with the inversions and displacements the film effects in regard to male subjectivity, that helps to explain the seemingly paradoxical accusation against the film that it was too cold and failed to provide adequate structures of spectator identification. There is an inherent repression evident in the reviews of the film, which almost never mention the representation of Berlin, except in passing.[28] Reviewers of the film had contradictory expectations: they hoped for an exemplary new wave film that would avoid sentimentality and expunge the "feminized" aspects of mass modernity from its formal canon, yet they continued to need the cinema as a forum for working through emotion, as a site of mourning—in this case, mourning over the division of Berlin. Reviewers approached *The Bread of Those Early Years* as a work of autonomous art, but criticized it for not providing the structures of identification they expected from mass culture. This double bind continued to plague the New German Cinema through the 1970s and 1980s, as directors increasingly developed formal strategies based on distantiation and alienation effects to mourn and work through the Nazi past that failed to address the emotions of spectators.[29]

Yet, again, what is particularly interesting about *The Bread of Those Early Years* is that this critique was articulated primarily by male spectators and reviewers. Female viewers apparently liked the film, in large part due to the clear identificatory possibilities it offered them. The magazine *Film und Frau*, which tended to approach films from the perspective of the female spectator, gave it a positive review. A standard feature of *Film und Frau* was the pictorial retelling of a given film plot illustrated with stills from the film. The pictorial retelling of *The Bread of*

Those Early Years focuses as much on Ulla's subjective transformation as it does on the emergent love story between Hedwig and Walter. A close-up of Ulla is accompanied by the caption: "Ulla waits in front of the house in which [Walter] lives. She waits an entire night, and a transformation occurs in her as well. She sees how superficial her relationship with Walter was" (106). The accompanying article focuses on the ways in which Hedwig and Ulla shape Walter. Perhaps the film also appealed to female spectators because it worked with the generic conventions of "Mamas Kino" to challenge them in interesting ways. While 1950s films presented highly encoded narratives of unstable gender roles and traits that appealed to female viewers struggling to redefine their own place as women within both the family and the public sphere, *The Bread of Those Early Years* foregrounded this instability of gender in both its narrative and its self-conscious form.

Yet, despite all the formal inversions it effects, the film does not really break with modes of representing gender that were typical for German cinema in general. In contrast to the female protagonists of other new wave cinemas—strong and unique modern women who often challenged traditional gender roles— the female characters in *The Bread of Those Early Years* are almost indistinguishable from each other, functioning more than anything as signifiers for male lack. In granting narrative authority to these female characters and in specularizing Walter Fendrich, the film inverts traditional gender dichotomies but does not attempt to unmask them.

Finally, the failure of *The Bread of Those Early Years* cannot be attributed exclusively either to the inherent faults of the film itself or to a failure of reception. On the surface, *The Bread of Those Early Years* accomplishes what the new wave films of other national cinemas accomplish: it is self-reflexive about its construction; it makes a statement about the contested nature of reality as constructed through the cinematic process; it provokes both pleasure and discomfort in looking; in short, it puts into question both the process of filmmaking and the process of film spectatorship. In terms of content, too, the film addresses issues pertinent to the European new wave at large: it critiques consumer capitalism; questions traditional values (such as the work ethic); problematizes love, marriage, and desire; and evidences discomfort with the liberal status quo of the cold war West. Within the cinematic context of postwar West Germany, the film also does manage to meld certain aspects of popular cinema with new experimental filmmaking strategies. What the film ultimately lacks in comparison to its new wave counterparts, however, is the dynamic energy that characterizes the successful fusion of the avant garde with the popular, the novelty and vitality that exemplify popular modernity. *The Bread of Those Early Years* is marked by a feeling of exhaustion that manifests itself in the repetition of visual images, sound bites, and entire sequences. This cinematic fatigue is mirrored, and was perhaps in part provoked, by the endless repetition of public discourse surrounding the film, in the endless debates and commentaries that it inspired both before and after its release.

The conception of postwar Western Germany as the site of an exhausted scopic regime has become commonplace. After the iconological ecstasy of fascism, the wealth of visual pleasure, and the abundance of ideologically overburdened images of all kinds, visual culture in the postwar years, it is argued, was completely bankrupt. This explanation is generally used to vilify or dismissively excuse the provincial and frivolous West German cinema of the 1950s. Yet, that cinema, in all its provincialism and frivolity, was a dynamic, popular, and successful cinema, fueled by the national need for escapist entertainment tailored to the highly specific life experiences and visual frameworks of reconstruction-era West Germans. As the West German nation attained economic, political, and social stability toward the end of the 1950s, this cinema went into decline, in part because it was no longer needed to fulfill this purpose.[30]

Rather than returning to innovate on the earlier model of popular modernity represented by the German films of the Weimar era, *The Bread of Those Early Years* attempted to fuse aspects of this declining 1950s West German cinema with recent avant-garde filmmaking strategies appropriated from the French new wave. The popular modernity of Weimar films was still considered suspect by many German filmmakers and critics in the early 1960s, in part due to the valence given to the idea first proposed by Kracauer that these films encoded a kind of residual fascism, and in part out of ignorance: the Weimar films were not easily available, and many young filmmakers had not seen them. While the French new wave filmmakers were busy utilizing the technical developments of the past thirty years to innovate on the accomplishments of the first wave of cinematic modernity, which they were actively addressing in their work, filmmakers such as Vesely could not bridge the gap created by fascism and exile so easily. What remains compelling about *The Bread of Those Early*

Years is that Vesely and his team tried. Precisely in foregrounding the instability of their project, the difficulty of reinstating an unproblematic, rejuvenated masculine modernity in the visual landscape of postwar West Germany, the film addresses both the promise and the curse of popular modernity as deployed in the German context.

NOTES

1. Films associated with the New German Cinema that were released after the failure of *The Bread of Those Early Years* could be much more easily aligned into the "experimental camp" or the "popular camp." Examples of the former include Danielle Huillet and Jean-Marie Straub's two Böll adaptations, *Machorka-Muff* (1962) and *Nicht versöhnt* [*Unreconciled*, 1965], and Vesely's own next attempt, *nicht mehr fliehen* [*Flee No More*, 1965]. These films had no pretension of addressing a popular audience and were aggressively fragmentary and experimental. It was not until 1966 that New German films began to emerge that managed to combine a new form with a more straightforward and accessible narrative style that would prove popular among critics, if not with vast audiences. The two German submissions to Cannes in 1966, Ulrich Schamoni's *Es* [*It*] and Volker Schlöndorff's *Der junge Törleß* [*Young Törleß*], are exemplary of this group, as is Alexander Kluge's 1966 *Abschied von gestern* [*Yesterday Girl*]. Nonetheless, all films associated with the New German Cinema were increasingly marginalized as "difficult," experimental, and unpopular—in short, as other than the popular cinema produced by the German studios and, of course, by Hollywood.

2. Many critics have sought to problematize the "break" between the popular German cinema of the 1950s and the new cinema that emerged in the 1960s and 1970s through the adoption of various descriptive terms to characterize different stages of the latter. Thomas Elsaesser's distinction between the Young German Film and the New German Cinema, with the "Autorenfilm" as a concept that mediates the two, has perhaps become the most accepted usage. See Elsaesser, *New German Cinema: A History* (New Brunswick, N.J.: Rutgers University Press, 1989), 2. I have chosen not to use this distinction in writing about a period during which it was as yet unclear how the various and sometimes competing notions of what the new cinema should or could be would evolve into specific styles, genres or platforms. Instead, I refer to the "new wave" as a general designator for the various new films that sought to distinguish themselves from the popular cinema of the 1950s, and to the New German Cinema as the more programmatic agenda according to or against which these films developed.

3. See *Die Abendzeitung* (Munich), 19–20 May 1962. Other pithy headlines indicating the dominant response to the film included the following: "Der deutsche Film wurde noch nicht gerettet" (*Der Tagesspiegel*, [Berlin] 3 June 1962); "Das Brötchen der frühen Jahre—Herbert Veselys Experiment rettet das deutsche Kino kaum" (*Der Weser Kurier*, [Bremen] 16 June 1962); "Ist Vater doch der Beste?" (*Bravo*, 24 July 1962).

4. Critics quickly developed an ironic nickname for *The Bread of*

Those Early Years: "Letztes Jahr atemlos in Mariendorf" (Last Year Breath-less in Mariendorf), which punned on Godard's *Breathless* and the Resnais film, while expressing through the substitution of "dorf" (village) for "bad" (spa) the provinciality of the German film in comparison with its cosmopoli-tan French counterparts.

5. This and all other translations from the German are my own, un-less otherwise specified.

6. Hembus was the author of a widely read pamphlet from 1961 ironi-cally titled "The German Film Couldn't Be Better," and a contributor to the journal *Filmkritik*. See Joe Hembus, *Der deutsche Film kann gar nicht bes-ser sein. Ein Pamphlet von gestern. Eine Abrechnung von heute* (Munich: Rogner & Bernhard, 1981). Hembus's press book for the film is a brilliant attempt to convince potential exhibitors and audiences of the modernity of the film's style and to educate them about its meaning. He explains the plot in straightforward detail, and then goes on to explicate the formal style: "Independently of its relationship to its literary precursor, however, the film follows the legitimate principle of art: decomposition of reality towards the composition of a world which matches the vision of the artists, or, to oper-ate in filmic terms: a new montage of the elements of reality." See the *Pres-seheft: Das Brot der frühen Jahre*, in File 8023 on *Das Brot der frühen Jahre*, Schriftgutarchiv der Stiftung Deutsche Kinemathek, Berlin.

7. Reporting in *Filmkritik* on the events at the Oberhausen festival, Enno Patalas articulated the incredible expectations drummed up by the manifesto: "A chance like this—the public bankrupting of all principles ac-cording to which films are produced and directed in this country—a chance like this will not return again so quickly. It will depend on the decisions of the next months as to whether a fourth decade of dominance by Philistines follows the three previous ones, or whether a new beginning can finally be risked." Enno Patalas, "Die Chance: Neubeginn im deutschen Film?" *Film-kritik* 4 (1962): 150.

8. See Review of *The Bread of Those Early Years, Filmkritik* 6 (1962): 262–64; Review of *The Bread of Those Early Years, Evangelischer Film-Beobachter* 14 (9 June 1962): 257; and Heinz Martin, "Ist Vater doch der Beste?" *Bravo*, 24 July 1962, n.p.

9. The reviewer wrote, "In contrast, a few female voices: 'Wonderful photography,' 'Deeply impressed by the images and words(!)'—Apparently men have worse nerves." See Ponkie, "Wie finden Sie Bubis Kino?" *Die Ab-endzeitung* (Munich), n.d.; from the file on *Das Brot der frühen Jahre* in the Clippings Archive, Bibliothek der Deutschen Film- und Fernsehakademie Berlin.

10. The building of the Berlin Wall on 13 August 1961, had logistical consequences for Vesely's plans for the film and led both to narrative incon-sistencies and to more fraught political meanings in the filmic narrative. The film was shot wholly on location in West Berlin streets, trains, and cafes, and in the occasional apartment of friends of the film team. In the film, Fendrich is a refugee from the East who has emigrated to West Berlin years earlier. When Hedwig arrives from his hometown, it thus must be assumed that she is arriving from East Germany—the fact that she simply arrives at the Gleisdreieck station with no fanfare does not square with this assumption. On the other hand, the many shots in the film of empty S-Bahn trains rattling over elevated tracks constitute a subtle but omnipresent re-minder of the situation in West Berlin during a time when the boycott of

the S-Bahn was still in effect. Similarly, Hedwig and Walter board a tram in the Tauentzienstraße labeled "Endstation Bernauer Straße," a tram leading directly to the new wall, to a street where people had jumped from buildings to land in the West and avoid separation from their families. Very few reviews of the film make mention of this backdrop, which, though not foregrounded, does lend direct contemporary political implications to an otherwise more subtly critical narrative. I will return to these issues later in this essay.

11. My use of the term "the gaze" in this essay refers to the system of looks encoded by the cinematic apparatus through the alignment of camera shots with the perspectives of individual characters within the filmic narrative. "The gaze" functions also to inscribe a textual address to an implied or ideal spectator, which may (or may not) align the gaze of real viewers in the audience with the gaze of characters within the film—and by extension with the camera itself—through mechanisms of identification and conventions of viewing. Because it helps to structure and provides perspective for what is and is not seen on screen, "the gaze" is a primary tool through which knowledge, authority, identity, and subjectivity are constructed and attributed within the filmic text, as well as for the implied spectator and, potentially, the real viewer of the film. For a productive reconsideration of the gaze (in particular as it was articulated in 1970s apparatus theory) and of larger issues surrounding the theorization of spectatorship, see Judith Mayne, *Cinema and Spectatorship* (New York: Routledge, 1993).

12. See, among others, Laura Mulvey, "Visual Pleasure and Narrative Cinema," *Visual and Other Pleasures* (Bloomington: Indiana University Press, 1989), 14–26; and Mary Ann Doane, "Film and the Masquerade: Theorizing the Female Spectator," in *Femmes Fatales: Feminism, Film Theory, Psychoanalysis* (New York: Routledge, 1991), 17–32.

13. With this in mind, I do not believe that *The Bread of Those Early Years* can be read as an example of explicitly feminist cinema. On the contrary, the film grants agency and authority to its female characters more by default than by way of political intention. Through a feminist reading of the film, I seek to uncover the ways in which it displays the fractured nature and instability of gender (both masculinity and femininity). Without delving into questions of authorship that are beyond the scope of this chapter, I am wary of aligning Vesely's film with the project of feminist filmmakers who explicitly seek to dismantle gender constructs and dichotomies as they are encoded in traditional forms of (cinematic) representation.

14. Reviewers commented uncomprehendingly on the astounding similarity between the two actresses. See, for example, Walter Kaul's review in the *Kurier.*

15. "Gleisdreieck" literally means "triangle of tracks," a place where three sets of tracks converge and diverge again. The action of the film returns to this symbolic train station again and again.

16. See Heide Fehrenbach, *Cinema in Democratizing Germany: Reconstructing National Identity after Hitler* (Chapel Hill: University of North Carolina Press, 1995), especially chapter 3, "*Die Sünderin* or Who Killed the German Man?: Early Postwar Cinema and the Betrayal of the Fatherland," 92–117.

17. This can be said, for example, of the male characters in the next big New German Cinema productions to gain widespread attention: Ulrich

Schamoni's *It* and Schlöndorff's *Young Törleß*. Both films offer (very different) explorations of male subjectivity, but the male subjects evince impotence and lack of agency in both cases.

18. See Kracauer, *From Caligari to Hitler: A Psychological History of the German Film* (Princeton, N.J.: Princeton University Press, 1947).

19. *Filmkritik* imported the phrase "Papas Kino" from the French journal *Arts* which ran a review of *Last Year at Marienbad* with the title "Le cinéma de papa est mort," a phrase that quickly became a kind of motto for the French new wave. The first mention of the phrase in *Filmkritik* comes in the title of a "Letter from Paris" about the French new wave written by Hans Dieter Roos. See Hans Dieter Roos, "Papas Kino ist tot," *Filmkritik* 1 (1962): 7–11. *Filmkritik* immediately adopted the phrase as a catchword for its longstanding call for a New German Cinema. Although it responded to *Filmkritik*'s call for a break with "Papas Kino," the Oberhausen Manifesto itself does not use the term "Papas Kino." Rather, it declares: "The old film is dead. We believe in the new one." For the purposes of this chapter, however, I retain the term "Papas Kino," even in relationship to the declaration of the Oberhauseners, because the term is consistently used in the public discourse surrounding both the manifesto and *The Bread of Those Early Years*. The Oberhausen Manifesto is reprinted in German in *Augenzeugen. 100 Texte neuer deutscher Filmemacher*, ed. Hans Helmut Prinzler and Eric Rentschler (Frankfurt am Main: Verlag der Autoren, 1988), and in English in *West German Filmmakers on Film*, ed. Eric Rentschler (New York: Holmes and Meier, 1988).

20. There were almost no women involved in directing or producing films during the decade.

21. See Andreas Huyssen, "Mass Culture as Woman: Modernism's Other," in *After the Great Divide: Modernism, Mass Culture, Postmodernism* (Bloomington: Indiana University Press, 1986), 44–62.

22. See Siegfried Kracauer, "Die kleinen Ladenmädchen gehen ins Kino," in *Das Ornament der Masse: Essays* (Frankfurt am Main: Suhrkamp, 1963), 50–63. In English as "The Little Shop Girls Go to the Movies," in *The Mass Ornament: Weimar Essays*, trans. and ed. by Thomas Levin (Cambridge, Mass.: Harvard University Press, 1995), 291–306.

23. While no concrete statistics of ticket sales exist that would allow an inference about the gender breakdown of the moviegoing public, it seems clear that the majority of tickets were sold to women. In 1945, German women outnumbered men by at least 7.3 million; this so-called *Frauenüberschuß* (surplus of women) lasted well into the 1950s. In addition, as a number of critics have pointed out, the cinema was a space where women—especially young and single women—could go unaccompanied, and as such, film viewing was an essential leisure time activity and an important part of everyday life for many women at the time. See Angela Delille and Andrea Grohn, *Blick zurück aufs Glück. Frauenleben und Familienpolitik in den 50er Jahren* (Berlin: Elefanten-Press, 1985), 90; see also Erica Carter, *How German Is She? Postwar West German Reconstruction and the Consuming Woman* (Ann Arbor: University of Michigan Press, 1997), 175.

24. Temby Caprio complicates this point in her "Women's Film Culture in the Sixties: Stars and Anti-Stars from *Papas Kino* to the German New Wave," *Women in German Yearbook* 15 (2000): 201–26. As she suggests, for

crossover audiences who saw the films of both "Papas Kino" and the New Wave, the transition from watching star actresses to watching the women featured in the new wave films (many of whom were not trained as actresses) would certainly have been an experience that disrupted traditional images of women on screen and traditional notions of authenticity in regard to film. Caprio mentions, for example, the career of Sabine Sinjen, who starred in both *Heimatfilme* and the new wave film *It*, where she played a woman who has an abortion. Most paradigmatically, she discusses the character Anita G. in *Yesterday Girl*, who was played by Alexandra Kluge, a physician by training and the sister of director Kluge. Anita G. was the most iconic character of new wave film, and certainly represented a departure from female characters of the past. Nonetheless, as Caprio writes, Anita G. "functions like a 'seismograph' (Kluge) of postwar German society, ricocheting between paternalistic lovers and various other authority figures on her seemingly aimless journey through the legal, cultural, and educational institutions of the Federal Republic" (Caprio 212). While Anita G., as many critics have argued, was a character with whom audiences could identify in multiple and complex ways, precisely this "seismograph" quality ultimately denies her a real subjectivity in the film. It could almost be argued, following Barton Byg, that Anita G. represents a departure from earlier depictions of women in German film primarily in the sense that, with *Yesterday Girl*, woman is once again able to structurally assume the role of the weak or passive character at the hands of paternalistic male authority figures. However Caprio's reading, again, productively complicates any easy conclusions regarding the transformations of women's roles in new wave cinema, focussing as it does on the continuities and disruptions in star culture and the responses of (female) spectators to images of women on screen.

25. See Lutz Koepnick, *The Dark Mirror: German Cinema Between Hitler and Hollywood* (Berkeley and Los Angeles: University of California Press, in press).

26. The rise and eventual hegemony of abstract art during the 1950s is emblematic of the taboo on expression and affect during this "leaden time." Abstraction was equated with a forward-looking, scientific rationalism, and was charged with the task of cleansing visual art of residually fascistic traits such as expression. The rise of abstraction was concomitant with the repression in the 1950s of any discussion or representation of the Nazi past, in the public or the private sphere.

27. On the German street film, see, for example, Siegfried Kracauer, *From Caligari to Hitler*, and Patrice Petro, *Joyless Streets: Women and Melodramatic Representation in Weimar Germany* (Princeton: Princeton University Press, 1989).

28. It was an Austrian reviewer who noted this fact: "Vesely elucidates the dividedness of German consciousness after August 13, 1961: the film is set in Berlin. Only the people don't seem to notice this. They don't see that an empty S-Bahn train goes by again and again (it's being boycotted still, and the public is supposed to take note of this)." Review of *The Bread of Those Early Years*, *Profil* 7 (1962), n.p.

29. This was, of course, the lesson brought home most explicitly by the success of the television miniseries "Holocaust" in 1979. See Andreas Huyssen, "The Politics of Identification: 'Holocaust' and West German Drama" in *After the Great Divide*, 94–114. See also the articles on the subject collected in Anson Rabinbach and Jack Zipes, eds., *Germans and Jews*

Since the Holocaust: The Changing Situation in West Germany (New York: Holmes and Meier, 1986).

30. Of course, many other factors played a role in the decline of German cinema at this juncture in time, not the least of which was the rise of television.

WORKS CITED

Baer, Volker. "Heinrich Böll als Drehbuchautor." *Der Tagesspiegel* (Berlin), 24 December 1961, n.p.

"Das Brot der frühen Jahre. Ein Film nach Heinrich Böll." *Film und Frau* 6 (1962): 106–8.

Byg, Barton. "Nazism as Femme Fatale: Recuperations of Cinematic Masculinity in Postwar Berlin." In *Gender and Germanness: Cultural Productions of Nation*, edited by Patricia Herminghouse and Magda Mueller, 176–88. Providence, R.I.: Berghahn Books, 1997.

Caprio, Temby. "Women's Film Culture in the Sixties: Stars and Anti-Stars from *Papas Kino* to the German New Wave." *Women in German Yearbook* 15 (2000): 201–26.

Carter, Erica. *How German Is She? Postwar West German Reconstruction and the Consuming Woman.* Ann Arbor: University of Michigan Press, 1997.

Delille, Angela and Andrea Grohn. *Blick zurück aufs Glück. Frauenleben und Familienpolitik in den 50er Jahren.* Berlin: Elefanten-Press, 1985.

Doane, Mary Ann. *Femmes Fatales: Feminism, Film Theory, Psychoanalysis.* New York: Routledge, 1991.

Elsaesser, Thomas. *New German Cinema: A History.* New Brunswick, N.J.: Rutgers University Press, 1989.

Fehrenbach, Heide. *Cinema in Democratizing Germany: Reconstructing National Identity after Hitler.* Chapel Hill: University of North Carolina Press, 1995.

Hembus, Joe. *Der deutsche Film kann gar nicht besser sein. Ein Pamphlet von gestern. Eine Abrechnung von heute.* Munich: Rogner & Bernhard, 1981.

———. *Presseheft: Das Brot der frühen Jahre.* File 8023: Das Brot der frühen Jahre. Schriftgutarchiv der Stiftung Deutsche Kinemathek, Berlin.

———. "Suche nach der verlorenen Zeit. Junger deutscher Spielfilm auf neuen Wegen." *Spandauer Volksblatt*, n.d., n.p.

Huyssen, Andreas. *After the Great Divide: Modernism, Mass Culture, Postmodernism.* Bloomington: Indiana University Press, 1986.

Kaul, Walter. Review of *The Bread of Those Early Years. Kurier* 10 July 1962, n.p.

Koepnick, Lutz. *The Dark Mirror: German Cinema Between Hitler and Hollywood.* Berkeley and Los Angeles: University of California Press, in press.

Kracauer, Siegfried. *From Caligari to Hitler: A Psychological History of the German Film.* Princeton: Princeton University Press, 1947.

———. "Die kleinen Ladenmädchen gehen ins Kino." In *Das Ornament der Masse: Essays.* Frankfurt am Main: Suhrkamp, 1963.

—————— "The Little Shop Girls Go to the Movies." In *The Mass Ornament: Weimar Essays*. Translated and edited by Thomas Levin. Cambridge: Harvard University Press, 1995.

Martin, Heinz. "Ist Vater doch der Beste?" *Bravo*, 24 July 1962, n.p.

Mayne, Judith. *Cinema and Spectatorship*. New York: Routledge, 1993.

Mulvey, Laura. *Visual and Other Pleasures*. Bloomington: Indiana University Press, 1989.

"Papas Kino—Eine Definition." *Filmkritik* 3 (1962): 98.

Patalas, Enno. "Die Chance: Neubeginn im deutschen Film?" *Filmkritik* 4 (1962): 150.

Petro, Patrice. *Joyless Streets: Women and Melodramatic Representations in Weimar Germany*. Princeton: Princeton University Press, 1989.

Ponkie. "Wie finden Sie Bubis Kino?" *Die Abendzeitung* (Munich), n.d., n.p.

Prinzler, Hans Helmut and Eric Rentschler, eds. *Augenzeugen. 100 Texte neuer deutscher Filmemacher*. Frankfurt am Main: Verlag der Autoren, 1988.

Rabinbach, Anson and Jack Zipes, eds. *Germans and Jews Since the Holocaust: The Changing Situation in West Germany*. New York: Holmes and Meier, 1986.

Rentschler, Eric, ed. *West German Filmmakers on Film*. New York: Holmes and Meier, 1988.

Review of *The Bread of Those Early Years*. *Die Abendzeitung* (Munich), 19–20 May 1962, n.p.

Review of *The Bread of Those Early Years*. *Beratungsdienst Jugend und Film* 5 (1962): 2.

Review of *The Bread of Those Early Years*. *Evangelischer Film-Beobachter* 14 (9 June 1962): 257.

Review of *The Bread of Those Early Years*. *Filmkritik* 6 (1962): 262–64.

Review of *The Bread of Those Early Years*. *Profil* 7 (1962): n.p.

Silverman, Kaja. "Dis-Embodying the Female Voice." In *Re-Vision: Essays in Feminist Film Criticism*, edited by Mary Ann Doane, Patricia Mellencamp, and Linda Williams, 131–49. Los Angeles: American Film Institute, 1984.

Thiel, Reinhold E. "Mutmaßungen über Walter." *Filmkritik* 1 (1962): 16–18.

FILMOGRAPHY

The Bread of Those Early Years [Das Brot der frühen Jahre] (Herbert Vesely, 1962)

Breathless [À bout de souffle] (Jean-Luc Godard, 1960)

Flee No More [nicht mehr fliehen] (Herbert Vesely, 1965)

It [Es] (Ulrich Schamoni, 1966)

Last Year at Marienbad [L'année dernière à Marienbad] (Alain Resnais, 1961)

Machorka-Muff (Danielle Huillet and Jean-Marie Straub, 1962)

Unreconciled [Nicht Versöhnt] (Danielle Huillet and Jean-Marie Straub, 1965)

Yesterday Girl [Abschied von gestern] (Alexander Kluge, 1966)

Young Törleß [Der junge Törleß] (Volker Schlöndorff, 1966)

CHAPTER 10

Exotic Thrills and Bedroom Manuals

West German B-Film Production in the 1960s

Tim Bergfelder

The 1960s occupy a curious place in historical accounts of German cinema, bracketed by the landmarks of the Oberhausen Manifesto in 1962 (signed by a new generation of filmmakers opposed to the popular German cinema of the 1950s) and the feature film debuts of, among others, Rainer Werner Fassbinder and Werner Herzog at the end of the decade which heralded the emergence of the New German Cinema. What happened in between these two landmarks, however, is often less clearly understood. Fifteen years after the end of World War Two, and after one and a half decades of reasonable recovery, the early 1960s witnessed a serious economic crisis in the German film industry, which manifested itself in a decline in national production, a sharp fall in audience figures, and the demise of many established German film companies. Yet, despite the Oberhauseners' triumphant rallying cry of "Daddy's cinema is dead," the declared corpse of the commercial German film establishment remained obscenely lively and stubbornly productive for most of the 1960s. In terms of box office success, the main protagonists of the decade were not Oberhausen signatories such as Alexander Kluge, but the resolutely populist distributors Constantin and Gloria, and production companies such as Horst Wendlandt's Rialto and Artur Brauner's CCC.

   If this survival of the commercial film in the 1960s beyond Oberhausen is acknowledged in histories of German cinema, it is often perceived as nothing more than a negligible continuation of what is referred to as the provincial "cottage industry" of the 1950s, with its popular genres such as the *Heimatfilm*, musicals, or Hapsburg romances (Corrigan 2). Even a cursory comparison, however, reveals a number of significant differences in production patterns and generic formulae from the 1950s to the 1960s: a move from largely indigenous to increasingly pan-European co-production deals coupled with an increasing fragmentation of German production and distribution outlets; a demographic shift from a traditionally female and family core audience to younger, male, and international markets; and a move from female-centered genres such as melodrama and Heimatfilms to Westerns, adventure genres, horror, crime and spy thrillers, and sex films, often conceived as a series format (Bergfelder 139–52). These changes are borne out by the two most popular and financially successful franchises of the West German film industry in the 1960s, Rialto's Karl May Westerns (eleven films between 1962 and 1968) and the Edgar Wallace crime film series (thirty-three films between 1959 and 1972).

If the genres and production patterns of the 1960s constitute a significant departure from the 1950s, they still can be placed within the context of long-standing popular German traditions. Thus the Karl May films not only draw on a widely read German novelist of the late nineteenth century, they are also part of a cinematic canon, German-made Westerns, that can be traced back to the 1910s (Göktürk 174–200). Equally, the German fascination with the British crime author Wallace dates back to the 1920s, while the detective crime serial more generally had been a staple of popular German film production since the early 1910s (Knops 132–42). What both the Karl May and Edgar Wallace case studies attest to is the extensive intertextuality of popular German film genres from the early days well into the 1970s, and their close dependence on and relationship with other media and leisure activities, such as popular or pulp literary fiction, tabloid journalism, and later television and tourism.

If the films produced by Rialto and CCC can be seen as the populist mainstream of the German film industry in the 1960s, similar developments occurred at the lower strata of production. The producers I am dealing with in the following pages operated from the fringes of the industry. They specialized in low-budget and disreputable genres (such as horror and sex films), and they often gained notoriety among the traditional German film establishment. The turn of the decade witnessed not only a generational shift from the commercial industry to the auteurs of the

New German Cinema. A similar change of guard occurred within the commercial sector itself. By the end of the 1960s, few of the traditional German producers and distributors remained in business, superseded by producers and exhibitors of what in other national contexts has been termed exploitation cinema. This chapter, then, traces the ascendancy of the B-film sector in the 1960s, and the production strategies, generic formulae, and social contexts that made this shift possible.

Among West German B-film producers, Wolf C. Hartwig is possibly the best known and most reviled. Attacked equally by the film establishment and by the emerging protagonists of the New German Cinema, his Munich-based company, Rapid, was labelled a "filth factory," occupying "the basement of German film production" ("Protest gegen Schmutzfabrik," n.p.). Hartwig's regular clashes and disputes with the FSK, the German film industry's self-regulating censorship board, were widely reported in the national press. In conservative newspapers of the late 1950s Hartwig was seen as a corrupter of moral values who could furthermore tarnish German respectability abroad.

What enraged conservative critics in particular was that Hartwig made no effort at all to disguise what they perceived as the exploitative nature and motivations of his productions. On the contrary, notoriety and scandal were skilfully employed by Hartwig in publicizing his films (Kuntze-Just n.p.). In a press interview Hartwig was disarmingly frank about his ambitions and limitations: "I am a sober businessman. You won't hear me using phrases such as artistic endeavour and humanistic problem film. I have researched the market situation, tested the audience demands, while always remaining realistic about the possibilities of my company" ("Film-Sex nicht mehr gefragt?" n.p.). On a less moralistic note than the conservative press, Joe Hembus, one of the earliest critics to champion the New German Cinema, wrote about Hartwig in the early 1960s: "It is not that terrible that there is someone like Mr Hartwig. It is terrible that we don't have a Resnais, a Kubrick or a Bolognini. You can't blame Mr Hartwig for that" (Hembus 10). It must have been galling for conservative and progressive critics alike not only that by the end of the 1960s Hartwig's special brand of disreputable B-film had moved from the "basement" to the center of German film production, but that he was one of very few German producers who made a highly successful and profitable transition into the 1970s.

A look at Hartwig's output and the gradual movement toward soft porn in the 1960s is instructive in understanding the changing production strategies, generic formulae, and audience expectations of the decade. At a time when the German mainstream was dominated by feel-good musicals and Heimatfilms intent on forgetting the Nazi past, Hartwig's first production, *Until Five Past Twelve [Bis fünf nach zwölf]* (Grindel, 1953), offered the public a lurid exposé, compiled mainly from newsreel footage, about the private lives of Adolf Hitler and Eva Braun. Between 1957 and 1960 Hartwig's company, Rapid, established its position as Germany's foremost producer of *Sittenfilme*, or vice films. The term had first been coined in the aftermath of World War One for a number of sensationalist melodramas dealing with issues such as prostitution, venereal diseases, and homosexuality. The most prominent exponent of the early Weimar *Sittenfilm* was the director Richard Oswald and his *"sozialhygienische Filmwerke,"* or socio-hygienic film productions (Belach and Jacobsen).

Hartwig revived this tradition, albeit within a very different social context. Generically speaking, his films were difficult to define, the only common denominator being a gratuitous amount of female nudity, often amply provided by the "German Jayne Mansfield," Hartwig's discovery Barbara Valentin, who in the 1970s would resurface as a character actress in the films of, among others, Rainer Werner Fassbinder. Valentin's image in the late 1950s and 1960s was that of a buxom, peroxide-blonde, and dangerous vamp from the wrong side of town. In Hartwig's films she was often required to engage in wrestling matches or violent catfights with other women, and her low-class status was further underlined by her broad southern dialect.

Valentin's screen persona stood in sharp contrast to the demure, desexualized, and middle-class ideal of womanhood German mainstream films projected at the time. Indeed, she remains to this day one of very few genuine sex icons postwar German cinema has produced. In the late 1950s and early 1960s, the Karl May Westerns and Edgar Wallace films were basically male-centered affairs, while more typical female stars of the time were prim bourgeois actresses such as Ruth Leuwerik, tearful tragediennes such as Maria Schell, teenage waifs such as Christine Kaufmann and Conny Froboess, or tomboy comedians such as Lieselotte Pulver. Only Nadja Tiller and Elke Sommer occasionally approximated the impact of Valentin's sexualized persona, though the former's bad girl roles were far too refined, while the latter lacked Valentin's menacing dimension. In its uncomfortably raw vulgarity, Valentin's screen image in Hartwig's productions, on the other hand, articulated and elicited class and gender anxieties to a degree that amounted to public scandal in the twilight years of the Adenauer era.

Hartwig's films in the late 1950s and early 1960s can be subsumed under the definition of exploitation cinema, as suggested by Pam Cook: "schematic, minimal narratives, comic book stereotypes, 'bad' acting, and brief film cycles which disappear as soon as their audience appeal is exhausted" (367). *The Nude and Satan [Die Nackte und der Satan]* (Trivas, 1959) and *A Dead Man in the Spider's Web [Ein Toter hing im Netz]* (Böttger, 1959) are horror films. The latter of these, about a group of shipwrecked go-go dancers in various stages of undress, hunky sailors, mutant giant spiders, and a werewolf prowling the jungle of a radioactively contaminated desert island, has been reappropriated as a cult favorite by young urban cinema audiences since the 1980s. *Final Destination: Red Lantern [Endstation Rote Laterne]* (Jugert, 1959) belongs in the white slavery genre, another longstanding tradition in German cinema that had its heyday in the 1910s with the productions of the Danish company Nordisk (Behn). *Satan's Love Temptation [Der Satan lockt mit Liebe]* (Jugert, 1959) is a torrid gangster melodrama, replete with noirish *femmes fatales*, and *Amazon Island [Insel der Amazonen]* (Meyer, 1960) is an exotic adventure story, again set on a desert island inhabited by scantily clad women.

As this list indicates, Hartwig liberally plundered not only the repertoire of earlier German genres but also elements from Hollywood B-serials and drive-in movies, and other European genre traditions. What made, and still makes, these generic hybrids so refreshing is less their unashamed cannibalization of established genres than the sheer ingenuity employed in creating these incongruous concoctions. Pam Cook has argued that a "contradiction is generated by the exploitation film's schematic form and its appeal to audiences who are assumed to care little about style" (368). As Cook has shown for the American context (and for Roger Corman's productions in particular), this paradoxically gave exploitation filmmakers a sometimes greater scope for stylistic experimentation than that allowed to their mainstream generic counterparts. Many of Hartwig's films bear out this argument.

Until 1962, Hartwig produced without the financial backing of a major distributor, which required cost-cutting measures in terms of production values, such as sets and costumes, and tight shooting schedules. Like other European producers at the time, Hartwig frequently used the tax loophole of registering his productions in Liechtenstein, which officially functioned as a co-production partner. All of the fifteen Rapid films produced be-tween 1957 and 1962 were based on original (though clearly deriv-ative) scripts, to avoid expensive copyright acquisitions. Hartwig's production teams consisted mostly of inexperienced newcomers, the industry's second or third league, and tax exiles from Hollywood (for example, the actor Alex D'Arcy, who had played opposite Marilyn Monroe in *How To Marry A Millionaire* [Negulesco, 1954]) and Britain (such as the Rank starlet Belinda Lee). Yet his teams also included veterans from Weimar days who had slipped through the net of the postwar industry (for example, the director of *Die Nackte und der Satan*, Victor Trivas), and oc-casionally technicians of international caliber, such as the cine-matographer Georg Krause, who in 1957 had shot Stanley Kubrick's *Paths of Glory*. In this respect, Rapid (like Roger Cor-man's film factory) provided a fertile training ground for younger commercial filmmakers, many of whom would later move into television.

In 1962, Rapid changed its corporate strategy in a number of ways. First, Hartwig distanced himself from the *Sittenfilm* and publicly announced a new cinematic cycle: "As a genuine coun-terpart and competition to the small television screen I envisage the widescreen adventure film in color, where suspense and exot-icism are effectively combined, and where the beauty of foreign countries can be realistically captured in images" ("Film-Sex nicht mehr gefragt" n.p.). This, of course, meant location shoot-ing in these countries, and consequently cooperation and co-pro-duction agreements, about which Hartwig was confident: "These days I can produce more cheaply in Spain, Bangkok, Rangoon, Hong Kong or Manila than in Germany where the costs have gone through the roof. In various trips around the world I have acquired detailed knowledge about the technical aspects and personnel is-sues of film production in these countries" ("Film-Sex nicht mehr gefragt" n.p.).

In the following years, Hartwig gained the reputation of an expert in coordinating the production of relatively low-cost adventure films and later spy thrillers in the Far East, particularly in Hong Kong and Thailand. His know-how and established con-tacts overseas frequently attracted French and Italian co-produc-tion partners, but they also gained Hartwig access to, and the support of, the major German distributor Constantin. A relatively minor company in the 1950s, Constantin had achieved a domi-nant position among German suppliers in the early 1960s, not least by targeting a younger and male market with new genres, a decidedly international and devolved approach toward production, and aggressive marketing and brash advertising campaigns (Garncarz and Elsaesser 93). Hartwig's films fit this strategy perfectly.

From 1962 to 1968, Rapid almost exclusively concentrated on the exotic adventure genre, providing Constantin with a steady stream of inexpensive, yet highly marketable products both for the domestic market and for European export. Hartwig's films were frequently based on the multiauthored pulp novel series "Rolf Torring," centering on the adventures of a private agent in Asia. Torring conveniently provided Hartwig with a homegrown version of James Bond. By this time, the Bond series had become one of the most successful imports in the German market, and imitation series mushroomed in many European countries. Hartwig had nearly unlimited supply of Torring material, and he could safely rely on its indigenous box office appeal: an estimated one thousand novels had been published in Germany since the 1930s. In foreign markets, Rapid's Torring films were formulaic and recognizable enough to pass as standard Bond imitations.

Hartwig was not the only B-film producer operating on this international scale during this period. Like Rapid, Theo Maria Werner's Munich-based company Parnass established connections in Southeast Asia, and arranged a production deal with Constantin's major distribution rival, Gloria (run by Ilse Kubaschewski, West Germany's only female film tycoon and the godmother of the 1950s Heimatfilm boom). Following Hartwig's example, Werner discovered another German cousin of James Bond in *Kommissar X*, a pulp novel series about a secret agent which had spawned about five hundred novels. The series resulted in seven films between 1965 and 1971.

Clearly modeled on the James Bond cycle and its cold war ideology, the films' narratives centered on foreign villains threatening world peace with, among other weapons, mass hypnosis, deadly bacteria, laser rays, and LSD, and they focused on fast-paced action and pyrotechnic special effects. The *Kommissar X* films were German-Italian co-productions, with Hungarian, Yugoslav, Turkish, Canadian, and Austrian co-financiers, locations in India, Pakistan, Ceylon, Thailand, and Lebanon, and were often supported by the tourist boards in these countries. Germany, France, and Italy provided the main distribution areas for the series, whereas the series had next to no impact in Britain and the United States (Austen 43).

Competition for the *Kommissar X* series in the cinemas came from yet another German pulp novel hero, the FBI agent Jerry Cotton, aptly described by one literary critic as a "well-behaved James Bond" (Kunkel 559). Since 1956 the adventures of the incorruptible and brave G-man Cotton against New York mobsters had been published in weekly installments, written (like the *Kommissar X* and *Rolf Torring* novels) by mostly non-professional and anonymous authors. A team of editors at the down-market publishing house Bastei ensured that the series' formula and ethical values were upheld: "sadism," "realistic descriptions of murder and sexual activities," "psychological causes of crime," and "corrupt authority figures" were strictly forbidden (Kunkel 566–67). By the early 1960s, the readership of the Jerry Cotton novels was estimated in Germany at 2.8 million (Kunkel 569).

When the series was brought to the screen in 1965 by the small company Allianz (with the financial backing of Constantin), the Bastei publishing house retained significant control over its franchise, and the right to veto script and casting choices. Eight Jerry Cotton films were made between 1965 and 1969, starring the Hollywood actor George Nader. Despite French and Italian investment, the series firmly catered to the German market, and appears to have made little impact elsewhere. Unlike Hartwig's and Werner's pulp series, which tried to emulate the James Bond films, the Jerry Cotton series oriented itself on American television formats such as *The Untouchables* and *FBI*, which were highly popular with German television audiences at the time.

One reason for the temporary success of the exotic spy and adventure films produced by Hartwig and Werner may have had to do with their generic adaptability. Chameleon-like and composed of various generic influences, they could fit a number of current European subgenres in circulation. German press reviews, for example, alternately referred to them as crime films, exotic spectacles, horror films, spy thrillers, adventure films, and even as science fiction. The strategy of casting actors from other established genre cycles (such as James Bond films, Edgar Wallace adaptations, and Hammer Horrors) fostered a mutual referentiality between different genres and a blurring of generic as well as national distinctions. While the Kommissar X, Jerry Cotton, and Torring films may not have been able to compete with the James

Bond series in terms of production values, they could easily be adapted in terms of narratives or casting, and marketed according to changing audience preferences in different countries. By 1966, however, the various spy and exotic adventure cycles showed early signs of exhaustion, and the trade press became increasingly concerned about the variety of films being offered ("Kommissar X soll Jerry Cotton nicht ins Gehege kommen" 4).

In the late 1960s, West German B-film producers changed course and moved into the highly profitable production of sex films. Costume sex romps such as the French-Italian-German co-productions *Lady Hamilton* (Christian-Jacque, 1968) and *The Tower of Forbidden Love [Der Turm der verbotenen Liebe]* (Antel, 1968) indicated a shift in Rapid's generic output, and a return to its origins in the vice film, but now in a sexually more explicit format. Hartwig's East Asian adventure series, which had already begun to display a greater interest in the Asian sex industries than in action, ebbed out with *The Young Tigers of Hong Kong [Die jungen Tiger von Hong Kong]* (Hofbauer, 1969). Werner's company, Parnass, went bust in 1968, though two further *Kommissar X* sequels were made by other producers.

One significant trigger for this change in direction was the unexpected European box office success of the sex-education semidocumentary *Helga* (Bender, 1967). The film, which told the story of a young woman from the first stages of pregnancy to a graphically shown birth, had been commissioned by the government-funded *Bundeszentrale für gesundheitliche Aufklärung* (Federal Centre For Health Education), and was originally intended to be shown in educational contexts. Instead, it went straight into general release and became the biggest indigenous box office success of the year, surrounded by widespread public debate and inevitable protests by church leaders and right-wing lobbying groups such as the *Aktion Saubere Leinwand* (Action for a Clean Screen).

Apart from breaking box office records in Germany, *Helga* (which spawned two sequels) also proved an export hit in several European countries, particularly in Italy, leading the trade paper *Film-Echo/Filmwoche* to proclaim rather grandly that "Germany has begun to educate Italy about sex" ("Deutschland klärt Italien auf!" 8). Georg Seesslen speculates that the Italian success of *Helga* was possibly helped by the Nordic name and appearance of the film's main protagonist, played by the actress Ruth Gassmann (Seesslen, *Der pornographische Film* 175). In the following years, German-made sex films recorded the highest box office figures among films imported into Italy, which explains why Italian companies increasingly invested in co-productions of these films. Owing to Italian censorship regulations, however, Italian and German release versions often differed significantly in their sexual explicitness.

Following the success of *Helga,* Hartwig bought the rights of the best-selling book *Schoolgirls Report [Schulmädchen-Report],* first serialized in the tabloid press, by Günter Hunold, which documented, through interviews, the changing sexual attitudes, fantasies, and experiences of fourteen-to-eighteen-year-old girls. The filmic version of this exposé, directed by Ernst Hofbauer and released in 1970, was basically a compilation of soft porn sketches (largely focusing on teacher-pupil and teenage relationships), linked by a framing story in which a "reporter" conducted surveys of public opinion and "authentic" interviews on the streets of Munich. The film's interminable parade of cheerful nymphets was a far cry from the aggressive sexuality Valentin had provided in Hartwig's earlier films. Indeed, the cast consisted mostly of physically uninhibited but otherwise rather wooden amateur performers who had to be dubbed by professionals during postproduction. Cinematography and editing comprised a patchwork of static shots, wobbly camera movements, disorientating zooms, and perfunctory cutting, all of this supposedly indicating a documentary feel.

The sketched, unfinished-looking images and awkward performances were accompanied by a psychedelic musical soundtrack. At the time of the film's release, what emerged out of this audiovisual concoction was a tabloid portrait of what may have been intended to look and sound like swinging Munich, but which set up instead a deep chasm between a supposedly hip and sexually transgressive (though still firmly middle-class) teenage scene and a puzzled moral majority (something the score's eerie and feverish melodies emphasize). Re-released on CD in the 1990s, however, the soundtrack seems to have caught the mood of a new generation's appreciation for the weirder realms of 1960s easy listening, now rebranded under the term "lounge-core." In Germany, the composer Gert Wilden has seen his career revitalized in recent years, touring urban nightclubs with his synthesizer, and attracting audiences largely composed of listeners who had not been born when Wilden's soundtracks were first heard[1].

Requiring next to no production values, *Schulmädchen-Report* was completed in less than three weeks. The film eventually had a box office turnover of 8.5 million DM, leaving Hartwig with a profit of at least 6 million DM. During the next ten years, Rapid produced in total thirteen School-Report sequels (which were also exported and seen by an estimated one hundred million cinemagoers worldwide), as well as *Holiday Report [Urlaubsreport]* (Hofbauer, 1971) and *Nurse Report [Krankenschwestern-Report]* (Boos, 1972). Other producers followed suit, with reports on, among others, housewives, pool attendants, postmen, apprentices, flight attendants, and ski instructors, clearly relishing the potential for sexual innuendo, and confirming all the salacious rumors these professions invited.

Following the prototype of *Helga* and the report films, sex-education cycles mushroomed, combining scenes of scientific information with feature film narratives or episodic sketches. After the report series, the most prominent protagonist of this subgenre was the journalist Oswalt Kolle. Like Hunold, Kolle had originally published his ideas about sexual reform (strongly influenced by the Kinsey reports in the United States) in Germany's tabloid press, acquiring a reputation as the country's foremost sex guru. In this function he introduced, narrated, and occasionally directed a series of eight films between 1968 and 1972, where, again, "exemplary" narratives were commented on by academic experts (in later years these were frequently played by actors).

After the first three films, *The Miracle of Love [Das Wunder der Liebe]* (Gottlieb, 1968), *Sexual Partnership [Sexuelle Partnerschaft]* (Neve, 1968)*[Deine Frau—das unbekannte Wesen]*, and *Your Wife—The Unknown Being* (Neve, 1968), Kolle mostly abandoned any pretense of serious eduction. Subsequent films dealt with nudist families and child sexuality (*Your Child—The Unknown Being [Dein Kind—das unbekannte Wesen]*, Lenz, 1970) and group sex (*Love As A Party Game [Liebe als Gesellschaftsspiel]*, Lenz, 1972). The seventh entry, *What, By the Way, Is Pornography? [Was ist eigentlich Pornographie?]* (Kolle, 1971), included a number of (albeit heavily censored) Danish hard-core extracts, interspersed by Kolle's plea to banish censorship.

The second major subgenre was the sex comedy, initiated in the late 1960s by a series of bawdy historical farces, and, like the education films, spawned their own distinctive cycles. Prototypical was the Constantin release *Susan, the Innkeeper from the Lahn River [Susanne, die Wirtin von der Lahn]* (Antel, 1968), a comedy set during the Napoleonic Wars in provincial Germany. The film, based on a fictitious character from German folklore and oral storytelling traditions, charted the sexual trajectory of its eponymous heroine through brothels and courtly boudoirs.

Susanne, die Wirtin von der Lahn, an Austrian-German-Italian-Hungarian co-production, became the fourth top-grossing film in Germany during the 1967–68 season, and the film sold well into Italy, France, and Britain, where it was released under the title *The Sweet Sins of Sexy Susan*. Between 1968 and 1973 five further Sexy Susan films were made, all of them directed by the Austrian director Franz Antel under the pseudonym Francois Legrand and distributed by Constantin. Unlike other sex-film cycles, the series gave a much more professional impression in terms of editing and cinematography. It regularly featured an international cast of established actors (which included Jeffrey Hunter, Edwige Fenech, and Margaret Lee), and it took care and imagination in details of decor, costumes, and narrative construction. Even Joe Hembus grudgingly conceded that the films "at least occasionally gave the illusion of some charm and flair" (Hembus and Fischer 204–5).

Unlike the sex reports, with their contradictory messages about social acceptability and cautious sexual experimentation, the Sexy Susan films relished their frivolity and their status as erotic fantasies. The films' escapist settings and historical distance allowed them in many cases to be less repressed, or at any rate more relaxed, in their attitude toward sex. As portrayed by the Hungarian actress Terry Torday, Sexy Susan comes across as an early nineteenth-century rebel for sexual libertinage whose exploits sometimes bear a striking (and very likely not coincidental) resemblance to the happenings organized by German (and other Western) students at the time. Thus in one instance Sexy Susan leads a protest march of naked women through the streets to demand political changes, although the demand itself—the abolition of entertainment taxes—would, of course, hardly have agitated the generation of '68. Compared with the empty sociological ciphers the anonymous schoolgirls represented in the report films, however, Sexy Susan and her female co-conspirators managed to convey a more affirmative, if still stereotypical, version of femininity.

Although comedy has often been regarded as one of the most culturally specific, and least exportable, of European popular genres, this cannot be said of the costume sex comedies of the late 1960s, which performed remarkably well across Europe. Like the contemporary British *Carry-On* films (and later the British TV farces of Benny Hill), the Sexy Susan series combined social and gender stereotypes, puerile innuendo, and cultural pastiche with a fairly universal sense of visual slapstick and the carnivalesque. Geoff Brown, commenting on the British release of the last entry in the series, *The Innkeeper's Feisty Daughters [Frau Wirtins tolle Töchterlein]* (Antel, 1973, British title: *Knickers Ahoy!*), gave a pretty accurate, if rather terse, summary of the vaguely Rabelaisian humor of the series:

> Admirers of Franz Antel's costume romps *The Sweet Sins of Sexy Susan* and *Sexy Susan Rides Again* will have no difficulty in recognising the Susanna of *Knickers Ahoy!*, for it is the same actress and the same lady, with her name slightly changed by the sprightly American dubbing. Within five minutes of the film's opening, however, she lies dead, victim of her own "highly developed sense of humour," as someone generously terms it (she laughs too much at her maid and an undertaker making love in a cupboard); but she returns at odd intervals to relive her past adventures in flashback form. We also see her five attractive daughters in action, frightening a rotund monk with displays of bottoms and breasts. . . . But it's unlikely that audiences will follow Susanna's example and die of laughter, unless their sense of humour is developed enough to relish a naked girl riding around on a goat or a man's trouser button flying off under stress. . . . (Brown 81)

Hartwig's and Antel's success indicates a change in the profile, backgrounds, and business strategies of West German producers during this period. Traditional producers such as Horst Wendlandt or Artur Brauner either reluctantly (and then rather coyly) followed the sex-film boom in order to compete or kept out of the market completely. Many established figures of the industry's "old guard" disappeared from the scene altogether.

Typical of a new breed of producer were figures such as Erwin C. Dietrich and Alois Brummer. Dietrich, originally an exhibitor with various cinema outlets in Switzerland, added sadomasochism and fetishism to the ingredients of the sex-film, most successfully in *The Colonel's Wife and her Nieces [Die Nichten der Frau Oberst]* (Thomas, 1968), allegedly based on a Guy de Maupassant novel, which became the top German-Italian coproduction at the Italian box office in 1971 (Phelix and Thissen 194). In Germany, the film's tag line was "Banned as a book for decades. But even Maupassant did not go that far" ("Die Nichten der Frau Oberst" 13).

The career of Alois Brummer exemplifies perhaps most drastically how weak the traditional production and distribution sector had become by the end of the 1960s. Brummer, formerly the owner of a provincial Bavarian haulage firm and several small rural cinemas, specialized in the production of low-budget, simpleminded, and technically amateurish soft-porn farces with titles such as *Count Porno and His Nymphomaniac Daughters [Graf Porno und seine liebesdurstigen Töchter]* (Hendel, 1969), which proved surprisingly successful (Seesslen 1998, n.p.). Ignoring the previously held monopoly of the major distributors, Brummer released the films on his own. With production budgets of less than 350,000 DM, the films brought Brummer profits of about 2 million DM each. Between 1968 and 1983 Brummer (who died in 1984) independently wrote, directed, produced, and distributed about twenty-five films. His crude blend of soft porn and conventions borrowed from traditional Bavarian stage comedies and rural folklore was widely imitated by other producers, leading to a seemingly endless series of titles such as *From the Lederhose With Love [Liebesgrüsse aus der Lederhose]* (Marischka, 1973) and *Yodelling in Knickers [Gejodelt wird im Unterhöschen]* (Hofbauer, 1974).

Watching these films today, the German sex-film boom of the late 1960s, and particularly its scope, is difficult to comprehend. As their original cultural and social context has disappeared, the films seem historically more remote than the exotic adventure genres that preceded them (perhaps partly because very similar formulae to the latter genre are still being provided by the continuing James Bond series, and, of course, Hollywood's action blockbusters). The Oswalt Kolle and other sex education films may provide unintentional hilarity among younger generations of cinemagoers, while some of the Sexy Susan films may be appreciated for their comedy and production values. Brummer's films are plainly bizarre and grotesque, though a cult film aficionado may be attracted by what could be seen as a very Teutonic equivalent of Russ Meyer. The Schoolgirls' reports and their numerous clones, on the other hand, seem to operate according to a specific code and horizon of expectations that is likely to confound most contemporary viewers, and they even seem to refuse the kind of camp appropriation or postmodern irony the Kolle or Brummer films may facilitate.

The report films of the late 1960s and early 1970s appear incoherent, elliptical, and muted, marked by strangely emotionless characters, and, even in a narrowly sexual sense, unconvincing performances. Overall, they frustrate rather than confirm visual pleasure and narrative expectations in a manner that, perversely, is closer to avant-garde cinema than to the conventions of popular genres. Moreover, although their perfunctory narrative structure resembles the standard of pornographic genres, they neither achieve the gloss nor the directed gaze of what could have been the cinematic equivalent of glamour photographs in men's magazines, nor are the sex scenes explicit enough to pass off as real pornography. They lack, of course, what the porn trade refers to as "meat" (that is, penetration) or "money" (ejaculation) shots. Linda Williams has argued that "hard core tries *not* to play peek-a-boo with either its male or its female bodies. It obsessively seeks knowledge, through a voyeuristic record of confessional, involuntary paroxysm, of the 'thing' itself" (49). An obsessive quest for knowledge is certainly at the heart of the report films, and even more so in the education cycles. Yet, at the same time, the quest for what Williams refers to as the "thing itself" becomes deflated, interrupted, and frustrated in the films' visual and narrative trajectories. This strategy of displacement, of course, questions for whom these films were originally made and what kind of function or use value they provided at the time.

Thomas Elsaesser has claimed that the sex films catered to a "pornography clientele, largely recruited from Germany's two million immigrant workers" (1989, 23). His argument that "the mainly male *Gastarbeiter* from Southern, Catholic countries" represented a "volatile and furtive but none the less numerically quite sizeable clientele" (1989, 67) sounds suggestive, and corresponds to the success of these films in countries such as Italy and Spain. However, given that the sex films were regularly awarded prizes for reaching more than three million cinemagoers per film in the domestic market alone, Elsaesser's target audience appears too narrowly defined. Moreover, as far more explicit foreign sex films (particularly from Denmark, where pornography had been legalized in 1968) became available on the German market, albeit in a different distribution and exhibition context, one has to wonder why a pornography clientele would have bothered with the comparatively tame reports or sex farces at all.

Box office figures suggest that, rather than catering exclusively to ethnic minority or fringe audiences, sex films attracted viewers from across the social spectrum, across the urban-rural divide, and across all ages. What is significant, however, is that the films themselves address an implied middle-class audience, the bedrock and proclaimed core of West German society. The report films in particular emphasize the ordinariness of their characters, centering on middle-class (and in the case of the male performers, mostly middle-aged) protagonists in average surroundings. Even the sex scenes, where one would normally expect elements of fantasy, or exaggeration, are firmly rooted in relatively plausible, everyday, and overall rather subdued situations. Unlike in similar genres from other countries, there seems to be no attempt to cast particularly attractive performers—in fact, the permed, portly, and mustachioed male actors so beloved of German sex film producers became internationally renowned as an arbiter in bad taste. Where sexual routine threatens to become either narratively or visually excessive, the reports frequently diffuse this with elements of comedy and farce, or provide "scientific" and sobering instructions of properly executed sexual positions. Comedy is also the mode by which the costume sex films contain possible transgression.

Georg Seeßlen has suggested that the German sex film boom, and the reports in particular, "legitimated a new liberalism. However, they also demonized what went too far. Principally the genre was about constructing a new social consensus which was less prudish but which still required its abnormal other" (1990, 180–81). In other words, the genre can be seen to have provided a relatively safe outlet for sexual curiosity, which was fuelled by a more general shift in behavior. In the late 1960s and early 1970s West German society witnessed a number of conflicting developments in sexual openness: the expansion and increased visibility of sex shop chains under the crusading aegis of the formidable sex entrepreneur Beate Uhse (a graduate of the Nazi Youth movement and a passionate aviatrix); the publication of ever more risqué tabloid papers; and the growing influence of American popular culture on German teenagers which manifested itself not least in a yearning for greater sexual independence. At the more alternative end of the spectrum were the various Reichian, Marcusean, or anarchist splinter communes of the student movement, staging their protest in public exhibitions of sexual nonconformism, which the West German tabloid press was only too eager to publicize with a mixture of shocked indignation and leering voyeurism. What rendered the sexual stunts of the 68ers, by today's standards rather tame and overall fairly isolated, particularly threatening was the conflation of sexual liberation and political revolution. Furthermore, as Dagmar Herzog has argued, sexual liberation in West Germany had a nationally specific vantage point and distinctive aims: "Much of what the 68ers were actually rebelling against were their own experiences in the postfascist 1950s and the interpretations of Nazism's sexual legacies proffered by parents and political and religious leaders in that decade" (396).

Thus, although part of the same momentum toward greater visibility in sexual matters, the sex film wave and the actions of the 68ers had clearly divergent agendas. For the latter, sexual liberation was one of a number of means (pursued with deadly seriousness) to destroy the complacency they perceived to be characteristic of West Germany's insistence on social, sexual, and gender relations that they belived had their origins in, and had helped to sustain, Nazism. The reports, on the other hand, initiated a sensible interest in sex and promoted the responsible consumption of soft porn as an act of maturity, enlightened citizenship, and matrimonial duty, thus preserving the status quo of these social and domestic institutions, and to some extent affirming West Germany's democratic legitimacy. If one can speak of an ideological project at work in these films, it is to circumvent and suppress the dangerous link between sex, politics, and history that the 68ers addressed, while taking on board some of their more superficial attractions.

What the sex films offered their mainstream audiences were visual induction manuals for sexual efficiency, pleasure enhancement, and, perhaps most importantly, new consumerist identities and lifestyles. One contemporary review tellingly compared the sex films' mise-en-scène to the presentational style of a mail-order catalogue ("Helga und die Männer" n.p.), underlining the fact that these films were firmly placed within a consumerist agenda. If there is one recurring mantra in the sex films, and one that is prevalent throughout public discourse in West Germany in the 1970s, it is the belief (a curious melange of Freud, Marcuse, and capitalist work ethic) that sexual freedom leads to mental and physical health, which, in turn, leads to greater social and economic efficiency, thus providing a blanket solution to all political ills. Thus, watching a sex film could be legitimated as an expression of worldly libertarianism or, for younger audiences, as an initiation ritual into sexual maturity (and, by implication, patriarchal hierarchies).

The Kolle and report films were explicitly advertised to function, at least in part, as counselling services to sexually dysfunctional couples, and it is reasonable to assume that they were used in that way by a considerable number of cinemagoers. At the same time, the sex films clearly set the rules and boundaries for sexual permissiveness. West Germany's sexually as well as politically transgressive hippie communes, not to mention any major deviation from the heterosexual norm (except for decorative lesbian scenes), are either conspicuously absent in the reports or depicted as comic or exotic aberrations. Rosa von Praunheim's celebrated gay agit-prop film *Not the Homosexual Is Perverse, but the Situation in Which He Lives [Nicht der Homosexuelle ist pervers, sondern die Situation, in der er lebt]* (1970), released at the height of the sex film boom, can be seen as a countercultural attack on this kind of (non)representation, couched in a parodic subversion of the report films' narrative and didactic strategies, and their attendant ideology of exclusion.

One reason for the success of the report films particularly may be precisely that, unlike real pornography, they promised more than they delivered. If the German sex films, veering between repression and libertarianism, appear in hindsight confused about their aims and intentions, this could be read as an apt reflection of an equally uncertain audience, trying to negotiate deeply ingrained moral and social conventions with an increasing pressure from the media and psychologists, among other authorities, to conform to new models of sexual and consumerist behavior. Ironically, although the 68ers had originally set out to use sex as a weapon against a culture of commodification, they finally contributed to the consolidation of precisely the same commodification process, something, as Dagmar Herzog has documented, the West German feminist movement by the mid-1970s acutely recognized and bitterly condemned (418–25).

The sex film boom not only initiated changes in production and consumption patterns, it also coincided with, and accelerated, significant changes in the German exhibition sector. Throughout the 1960s, the number of first-run, inner-city cinemas had dramatically declined. While the Karl May, Edgar Wallace, and adventure films targeted a younger market, family audiences increasingly stayed at home in front of the television set. Film producers were only too aware that color, wide-screen formats, exotic locations, and greater sexual explicitness remained the only attractions with which film production in the 1960s could compete with the still relatively studio-bound, black-and-white, and family-oriented formats of television. In terms of exhibition, however, what was left were smaller provincial and suburban outlets, among them the notoriously seedy *Bahnhofskinos* (cinemas in the proximity of rail stations and red-light districts), which had either always specialized in the exploitation end of the market, or which now began to veer ever more closely toward this market segment. The cheaply available reports and Kolle films, with their transparent masquerade as serious research, provided the perfect genre for such venues, while also giving a relatively wide spectrum of audiences a designated space and a filmic format that was just about respectable enough to satisfy their sexual curiosity.

The remainder of the big urban exhibitors accelerated this process even further in the early 1970s. Large venues were subdivided into shoe-box cinemas, at least one of which was continually screening a report or a sex comedy, thus further normalizing the genre as mainstream entertainment. Unlike with previous genres, individual sex films had inordinately long runs in these cinemas, in some cases lasting more than a year. This, in turn, was detrimental to the major distributors, who had been the dominant force in the German film industry since the 1950s. Gloria and Constantin, the only German companies that had managed to maintain profits throughout the 1960s, gave up by the mid-1970s.

What is often overlooked, however, is that the production of sex films continued long after the New German Cinema had consolidated itself as the officially approved version of national cinema, and they remained its abject and embarrassing other. Brummer and report films were made throughout the 1970s, although no longer possessing their initial mass appeal, and increasingly displaced between the artistic aspirations of the New German Cinema, proliferating hard-core porn venues, and the by now dominant box office presence of Hollywood. Sex film producers responded with attempts to update their formula with variants such as "Ibiza reports" (copying the combination of sex and glossy tourist promotion popularized by international hits such as *Emmanuelle* [Jaeckin, 1973]) and, in the wake of a late-1970s boom in zombie and cannibal films, horror-sex hybrids. Not all B-film veterans became stuck in the genre. Drawing on the profits he had made with his reports in the 1960s and 1970s, Wolf Hartwig produced two international, big-budgeted World War II epics in 1976 and 1978, Sam Peckinpah's *Cross of Iron,* and its sequel, *Breakthrough/Sergeant Steiner* (McLaglen). Erwin C. Dietrich, on the other hand, has concentrated his efforts since the late 1970s on his distribution outlet, Ascot-Elite, achieving respectability and box office success with foreign acquisitions as diverse as *The Wild Geese* (McLaglen, 1978) and, more recently, *Four Weddings and a Funeral* (Newell, 1994).

As their sexual content gradually became more explicit

and lurid, the sex films of the late 1970s and early 1980s now genuinely targeted a niche clientele. The final convergence of the sex film with the hard-core industry was complete in a wholesale retreat from cinema exhibition to video distribution in the mid-1980s. The cinematic back catalogue of the previous decades was sold off at cut-down prices to newly emerging cable-TV channels, where the report films experienced a ghostly renaissance in late-night slots from the late 1980s to the mid-1990s. Whether this revival was simply a matter of cheap availability, or whether there was genuine audience demand for these films (perhaps among viewers in the former GDR) is difficult to ascertain. Nonetheless, if it could be argued that "Daddy's Cinema" was in the mid-1980s finally laid to rest as a viable mode of theatrical exhibition, it occurred at the same time as the New German Cinema began to lose its direction. In an ironic twist to the long-standing battle between the New and the Old German film, and between art and commerce, the patricidal sons and daughters capitulated alongside their dissolute fathers.

This Oedipal conflict embedded in German cinema, as Thomas Elsaesser has pointed out, continues to the present day (2000, 3–16). The populist "Grandchildren's Cinema" that emerged in the 1990s has mostly rejected the aspirations of the New German Cinema. Instead, it has rediscovered the gender farces of the early 1930s and 1950s, which it remakes and repackages as *Beziehungskomödien,* or relationship comedies. The 1990s has also seen the phoenixlike reappearance of the brand name Constantin (as Neue Constantin), under the aegis of the transatlantic producer Bernd Eichinger. For the Ascot-Elite Group, Erwin Dietrich's son Ralph has produced *Condom of Terror [Kondom des Grauens]* (Walz, 1997), a gay crime and horror comedy set and shot in New York.[2] What this turn of events proves is that the popular genres of German cinema, and their institutions, had far too many resurrections and transformations in the past to be pronounced safely dead.

NOTES

1. Wilden's case is not unique in this respect. Other 1960s German film composers also have become unlikely pop icons for a new generation. These include Peter Thomas and Sigi Schwab, whose score for the German-Spanish horror film *Vampyros Lesbos* (Franco, 1968) was used for the soundtrack of *Jackie Brown* (Tarantino, 1995).

2. The film was based on the gay underground comic book by Ralf

König, who already provided the source for the biggest German box office hit of the 1990s, *Maybe, Maybe Not,* a.k.a. *The Most Desired Man [Der bewegte Mann]* (Wortmann, 1996).

WORKS CITED

Austen, David. "Kiss Kiss Kill Kill." *Films and Filming* 15, no. 3 (1968): 43.

Behn, Manfred, ed. *Schwarzer Traum und weisse Sklavin. Deutsch-dänische Filmbeziehungen 1910–1930.* Munich: Edition Text und Kritik, 1994.

Belach, Helga, and Wolfgang Jacobsen, eds. *Richard Oswald. Regisseur und Produzent,* Munich: Edition Text und Kritik, 1991.

Bergfelder, Tim. "The Nation Vanishes: European Co-Productions and Popular Genre Formulae in the 1950s and 1960s." In *Cinema and Nation,* edited by Mette Hjort and Scott McKenzie, 139–52. London and New York: Routledge, 2000.

Brown, Geoff. "Knickers Ahoy!" *Monthly Film Bulletin* 42 (1975): 81.

Cook, Pam. "The Art of Exploitation, or How to Get into the Movies." *Monthly Film Bulletin* 52 (1985): 367–68.

Corrigan, Timothy. *New German Film. The Displaced Image.* Bloomington and Indianapolis: Indiana University Press, 1994.

"Deutschland klärt Italien auf!" *Film-Echo/Filmwoche,* 1 June 1968, 8.

"Die Nichten der Frau Oberst." *Film-Echo/Filmwoche,* 2 August 1968, 13.

Elsaesser, Thomas. *New German Cinema. A History.* London: BFI/Macmillan, 1989.

———. "German Cinema in the 1990s." In *The BFI Companion to German Cinema,* edited by Thomas Elsaesser and Michael Wedel, 3–16. London: BFI, 2000.

"Film-Sex nicht mehr gefragt?" *Filmgeflüster,* 13 November 1962. n.p.

Garncarz, Joseph, and Thomas Elsaesser. "Constantin." In *Encyclopedia of European Cinema,* edited by Ginette Vincendeau, 93. London: Cassell/BFI 1995.

Göktürk, Deniz. *Künstler, Cowboys, Ingenieure.Kultur-und mediengeschichtliche Studien zu deutschen Amerikatexten 1912–1920.* Munich: Wilhelm Fink, 1998.

"Helga und die Männer—Die sexualle Revolution." *Film-Dienst* April 1969, n.p.

Hembus, Joe. *Der deutsche Film kann gar nicht besser sein. Ein Pamphlet von gestern. Eine Abrechnung von heute.* Munich: Rogner und Bernhard, 1981.

Hembus, Joe, and Robert Fischer. *Der neue deutsche Film 1960–1980,* Munich: Goldmann, 1981.

Herzog, Dagmar. "Pleasure, Sex, and Politics Belong Together: Post-Holocaust Memory and the Sexual Revolution in West Germany." *Critical Inquiry* 24, no.2, (1998): 393–444.

Knops, Tilo. "Cinema from the Writing Desk: Detective Film in Imperial Germany." In *A Second Life. German Cinema's First Decades,* edited by Thomas Elsaesser and Michael Wedel, 132–41. Amsterdam: Amsterdam University Press, 1996.

"Kommissar X soll Jerry Cotton nicht ins Gehege kommen. Die Angebote der Verleiher müssten unterschiedlicher sein." *Film-Echo/Filmwoche*, 2 March 1966, 4.

Kunkel, Klaus. "Ein artiger James Bond. Jerry Cotton und der Bastei Verlag." In *Der Kriminalroman, Band 2*, edited by Jochen Vogt, 559–78. Munich: Wilhlem Fink, 1971.

Kuntze-Just, H. "Die Wahrheit über Wolfgang Hartwig." *Echo der Zeit*, 23 August 1959, n.p.

Phelix, Leo, and Rolf Thissen. *Pioniere und Prominente des deutschen Sexfilms*, Munich: Goldmann, 1983.

"Protest gegen Schmutzfabrik." *Berliner Morgenpost*, 30 August 1959, n.p.

Seesslen, Georg. *Der pornographische Film*, Frankfurt and Berlin: Ullstein, 1990.

———. "Alois Brummer." In *Cinegraph. Lexikon des deutschsprachigen Films*, edited by Hans-Michael Bock, n.p. Munich: Edition Text und Kritik, 1998.

Williams, Linda. *Hard Core. Power, Pleasure, and the Frenzy of the Visible*. London: Pandora Press, 1991.

FILMOGRAPHY

Amazon Island (*Insel der Amazonen*, 1960, Meyer)

Breakthrough/Sergeant Steiner (*Steiner—Das eiserne Kreuz 2. Teil*, 1978, McLaglen)—available on video and DVD in German and English versions.

The Colonel's Wife and Her Nieces (*Die Nichten der Frau Oberst*, 1968, Thomas)

Condom of Terror (*Kondom des Grauens*, 1997, Walz)

Count Porno and His Nymphomaniac Daughters (*Graf Porno und seine liebesdurstigen Töchter*, 1968, Hendel)

Cross of Iron (*Steiner—Das eiserne Kreuz*, 1976, Peckinpah)—available on video and DVD in German and English versions.

A Dead Man in the Spider's Web (*Ein Toter hing im Netz*, 1959, Böttger)— available on DVD in dubbed version as *Horrors of Spider Island*.

Emmanuelle (1973, Jaeckin)

Final Destination Red Lantern (*Endstation Rote Laterne*, 1959, Jugert)

Four Weddings and a Funeral (1994, Newell)

From the Lederhose with Love (*Liebesgrüsse aus der Lederhose*, 1973, Marischka)

Helga (1967, Bender)

Holiday Report (*Urlaubsreport*, 1971, Hofbauer)

How to Marry a Millionaire (1953, Negulesco)

The Innkeeper's Feisty Daughters/Knickers Ahoy! (*Frau Wirtins tolle Töchterlein*, 1973, Antel)—available on video as *Devils in the Convent*.

Kiss, Kiss, Kill, Kill (*Kommissar X—Jagd auf Unbekannt*, 1965, Kramer)

Lady Hamilton (1968, Christian-Jacque)

Love as a Party Game (*Liebe als Gesellschaftsspiel*, 1972, Lenz)

The Miracle of Love (*Das Wunder der Liebe*, 1968, Gottlieb)

Not the Homosexual Is Perverse, but the Situation in Which He Lives (*Nicht der Homosexuelle ist pervers, sondern die Situation, in der er lebt*, 1970, von Praunheim)

The Nude and Satan (Die Nackte und der Satan, 1959, Trivas)
Nurse Report (Krankenschwestern-Report, 1972, Boos)
Paths of Glory (1957, Kubrick)
Satan's Love Temptation (Der Satan lockt mit Liebe, 1959, Jugert)
Schoolgirls Report (Schulmädchen-Report: Was Eltern nicht für möglich halten, 1970, Hofbauer)
Sexual Partnership (Sexuelle Partnerschaft, 1968, Neve)
Susan, the Innkeeper from the Lahn River/The Sweet Sins of Sexy Susan (Susanne, die Wirtin von der Lahn, 1968, Antel)
The Tower of Forbidden Love (Der Turm der verbotenen Liebe, 1968, Antel)
Tread Softly (Jerry Cotten: Schüsse aus dem Geigenkasten, 1965, Umgelter)
Until Five Past Twelve (Bis Fünf nach Zwölf, 1953, Grindel)
What, by the Way, Is Pornography? (Was ist eigentlich Pornographie?, 1971, Kolle)
The Wild Geese (1978, McLaglen)
Yodelling in Knickers (Gejodelt wird im Unterhöschen, 1974, Hofbauer)
The Young Tigers of Hong Kong (Die jungen Tiger von Hong Kong, 1969, Hofbauer)
Your Child—The Unknown Being (Dein Kind, das unbekannte Wesen, 1970, Lenz)
Your Wife—The Unknown Being (Deine Frau, das unbekannte Wesen, 1968, Neve)

CHAPTER 11

The Politics of the Popular

Trace of the Stones (1966/89) and the Discourse on Stardom in the GDR Cinema

Stefan Soldovieri

Considerations of the East German cinema have concentrated primarily on its ideological function, on its role in the legitimation of—and intermittent resistance to—official narratives on the history and identity of the GDR state. The reasons for this focus are apparent enough. Film production in the GDR was a highly administered affair that could prompt the participation of an astounding assortment of state and party agencies. Mandated to promote a socialist film culture, the centralized studio, known as DEFA (Deutsche Film-Aktiengesellschaft), was obliged to engage the political agenda of the ruling Socialist Unity Party (SED) throughout its history.

Despite the ideological pressures to which they were subject, however, filmmakers and culture administrators alike nonetheless recognized the importance of attending to the entertainment needs of GDR audiences. A comprehensive early 1960s initiative to improve the DEFA's feature-film production, for instance, included a call for the production of more and better films in a range of popular genres. One of the measures designed to promote more entertaining films was a plan to increase the studio's material interest in the production process with the help of a system of bonuses based in part on success at the box office. The impetus behind this specific effort to bolster DEFA's popular film output can be located in an industry crisis in the early 1960s, in which increasing pressure on the domestic film industry from television—particularly the Western films and programming that could be received in the GDR via West German stations—converged with a period of tentative liberalization in the GDR's exceedingly bureaucratic society.

These media-related and political factors provide the context for the discourse during the first half of the 1960s on the merits of promoting stars to increase the popularity of DEFA's films. They also form the backdrop to the eventual suppression of the major DEFA feature scheduled for release in 1965–66. The film was director Frank Beyer's *Trace of the Stones [Spur der Steine]* (1966/89); its star, the ruggedly charismatic Manfred Krug, who was one of the most visible personalities on the East German entertainment scene.[1] Conceived by its makers as *Gegenwartsfilm*—a feature set in the GDR present addressing social, political, and cultural issues—*Trace of the Stones* was not a genre film in the sense of a light entertainment. On the other hand, the film's production history and promotion were strongly influenced by DEFA's designs to capitalize on the drawing power of Manfred Krug, the previous star of comedies and adventure films and a public figure known for his nonconformity and outspokenness. Manfred Krug's subversive performance in *Trace of the Stones* was not the only factor that came into play in the film's suppression in the wake of the infamous Eleventh Plenary of the Socialist Unity Party in December 1965, an ideological housecleaning that led to the withdrawal of nearly an entire year's film production and other far-reaching reprisals. Nonetheless, the circumstances surrounding the actor's collision with the party's suppression of liberal trends in GDR society highlight the challenge that the star phenomenon posed to the system of film regulation and the contradictions inherent in DEFA's popular and genre-film production.

The star is a highly composite textual phenomenon, consisting not only of the image on the screen, but the texts produced by film agents and studios and those disseminated in various other media. In recognition of this complex structure, the star has been aptly described as "an intertextual construct, produced across a range of media and cultural practices that is capable of intervening in the working of particular films" (Gledhill xiv). This notion that the star image can impinge on the film text suggests the point at which the star phenomenon and political interests intersect, for the possibility that an actor's persona can imbue dialogue and gesture with shades of meaning external to the diegesis complicates the censor's work in trying to contain a film's possible interpretations.

Theories of stardom have been concerned primarily with film industries in liberal capitalist societies, but important aspects of the economy of stardom, that is, the dynamics of desire, identification, and ideology involved in the social production (and inescapably social control) of meaning, also bear on the context of state-administered film industries. To judge from most accounts of DEFA, however, the East German cinema failed to generate stars at all. Popular actors, perhaps, but surely not stars. The lack of attention to the issue of stardom is symptomatic of a more general unwillingness to approach the GDR film industry—and the industries of the former socialist countries of Eastern Europe—in the terms commonly applied to other cinemas. Treatments of DEFA continue to neglect issues such as genre film and stardom in favor of a view of the GDR cinema as a window on East German society or an unmediated extension of state power. Even where film scholarship has entertained the issue of stars in the context of the GDR, there has been a tendency to revert to the vocabulary of GDR film policy itself, namely, to the rhetoric of the *Leitbild* or positive model and mechanistic concepts of audience identification.

Most commonly associated with Hollywood, the phenomenon of stardom, with its connotations of excess, elitism, and individualism, would, in fact, seem to be largely antithetical to centralized film industries and the strictures of officially authorized production plans. What better symbol of the Western cinema's capitalist pedigree than the glossy image of the star? Yet while the GDR film industry did not generate a full-blown "star system" in anything like the Hollywood sense of an extensive apparatus for grooming and promoting actors, DEFA did give rise to its share of film personalities, who were by no means exclusively identified with the upstanding anti-fascists and worker-heroes whom they were regularly called upon to portray in the studio's more earnest subjects. DEFA actors played roles in films whose production was shaped by a range of ideological concerns, but this says nothing about how GDR moviegoers appropriated DEFA's images and film paraphernalia for their own purposes—particularly given the widespread knowledge of censorship in the GDR cinema and other spheres of public communication.

In many ways the GDR cinema sought to adapt the forms (while transforming the contents) of Western film industries. DEFA dabbled in detective films, musicals, and ice revues, and even repoled the Western in the form of "Indian films," which were distributed with success throughout Eastern Europe. Although the last of these films, which took the side of native North American peoples against the white colonizers, appeared in 1983, their hero, actor Gojko Mitic, remains popular today, with a stint in the FRG soap opera *Forbidden Love (Verbotene Liebe)*, several recent film roles, and fan web sites to his credit. DEFA actors were featured on star postcards and in collectible programs. There were fan contests, most-popular-actor polls, and a film magazine with a fair share of international coverage, industry gossip, and pin-up-type photos. DEFA performers were even enlisted in advertising campaigns, putting in plugs for everything from GDR fashion to sparkling wines made in Eastern Europe.

Although film regulators in the GDR were well positioned to influence the entirety of the filmmaking process from scriptwriting through postproduction, controlling the meanings that audiences could construct in conjunction with the star was a largely futile endeavor. The reason for this lies in the aforementioned discursive complexity of the star phenomenon: Stars are not merely images on the screen sprung upon naive spectators, but intertextual spaces for the projection of political, sexual, and social fantasies. Thus, casting an actor like Manfred Krug, who by 1965 had earned a reputation for resistance to the party line, could raise expectations about the film roles in which he was scheduled to perform. Whether singing opposite a Bulgarian starlet in Vladimir Jantschev's comedy adventure *The Ancient Coin [Die antike Münze]* (1965) or in the guise of an antifascist hero of the Spanish Civil War in Frank Beyer's *Five Cartridges [Fünf Patronenhülsen]* (1960), the Krug persona remained present in the imaginations of GDR spectators as something larger than any one role, charging films with latent ironies and double meanings.

During the first half of the 1960s, the film industry in the GDR was compelled to confront the growing significance of television and a decline in movie attendance. This development led various publications to consider the question of how to make films, particularly DEFA films, more attractive to the public. "Empty Cinemas?" was the cover story of the *Neue Berliner Illustrierte* (NBI) in mid-1964, which addressed with unusual candor topics such as the effectiveness of film advertising, the causes of DEFA's chronic underproduction of genre films, and the possible role of stars in the East German cinema ("Kinos leer?" 8–13).

Culture administrators were understandably interested in improving DEFA's image, and even tentatively accepted the need to promote popular actors. Yet, despite the recognition that the film industry needed a boost, officials continued to frown on stardom as a Western evil. DEFA's distributor, VEB Progress Film-Vertrieb, faced the dilemma of creating attractive film advertising without appearing to revert to the practices of Western film industries. Especially rigorous ideological standards were applied to the promotion of GDR features as compared to Western or even Eastern European imports. The publication in 1962 of a book of actor's photos and short bios reflects this state of affairs. Although the book's "popular" format seemed to embrace the idea of stars in the GDR, its preface, penned by none other than the deputy minister of culture, indicates how the makers of cultural policy hoped to frame the discourse on stardom. He wrote, "Although the title of this book is 'Film Stars' this is by no means a call for 'star' arrogance . . . which we unfortunately so often find in the case of the 'top performers' in the Western film industry" (*Unsere Filmsterne* 5). Additionally, the book's title, *Unsere Filmsterne* in the original German, refrained from using the ideologically objectionable English word "star," which was otherwise in common use as loan word. The title's "our" also signaled the calculated distinction between serious GDR film personalities and their shallow capitalist counterparts. Accustomed to navigating officious preambles, GDR film fans no doubt proceeded directly to the photos and commentaries, where they could find background information on the lives of prominent GDR actors and DEFA productions and far more moderate ideological tones. Star discourse in East Germany was extremely heterogeneous and contradictory, with anti-Western diatribes coexisting uneasily with the publicity put out by DEFA for its own films and imports and the light-handed coverage supplied by *Film Spiegel, NBI,* and other publications. On the whole, anti-star polemics subsided somewhat after the discourse on stardom peaked in the 1960s, a shift linked to the production goals that DEFA eventually set for itself during the course of the 1970s. While DEFA never completely abandoned its genre-film efforts, meeting the public's demand for popular entertainments was increasingly left to foreign productions, which were acquired by special delegations sent abroad to screen and purchase films.

When *Trace of the Stones* went into production in 1965, Manfred Krug, who had been cast in the lead role, was already an established media personality. A genuine crossover performer, Krug was well known as a jazz interpreter and had toured and recorded a number of popular titles with the ingeniously named

"Jazz-Optimists" and other groups. Krug had by this time also played leading parts in several television and DEFA films, among the latter Ralf Kirsten's *On the Sunny Side [Auf der Sonnenseite]* (1962), the actor's breakthrough role, which also featured music by Krug and the "Jazz-Optimists." The title track for this film topped the charts on GDR radio.

As a prominent performer with a large youth following, Krug's activities on and off the screen and stage did not go unnoticed by state officials, who were eager to take advantage of the actor's celebrity to further cultural policy objectives. At the same time, they also recognized that an actor like Krug, whose popularity was of a piece with his reputation for indifference to the party line, could become a serious political liability. Although it was possible to discipline disobedient personalities through orchestrated media campaigns and publication or performance bans, familiar practices used against troublesome public figures, restrictive measures generally only served to stir up resentment among GDR citizens. Krug would later get a dose of such medicine following his support in 1976 of dissident poet Wolf Biermann, shortly after which the actor left the GDR for West Germany.

The subversive edge to Krug's persona drew from different sources. For one, there was his association with jazz, a form of music rejected by culture functionaries as another example of Western decadence and "pessimism." The name of Krug's sometime group, the *Jazz-Optimisten,* suggests a conscious effort to deflect such trumped up charges of cultural negativity. Krug's rebel image was also the product of a number of early film performances in which he had been repeatedly cast as a young, leather-jacketed tough on the margins of society, a kind of GDR "rebel without a cause" or *Halbstarke,* as the jargon of the time had it. Studio-encouraged legend building surrounding Krug's pre-DEFA career as a steelworker also sought to foster the image of an actor in touch with the concerns of the common people.

In June 1965, shortly after shooting for *Trace of the Stones* began, two Central Committee departments conferred to check up on the results of a running probe concerning the prominent and problematical actor. The exchange between the Security Department *(Abteilung Sicherheitsfragen)* and Culture Department *(Abteilung Kultur)* had to do with the perception that Krug's public statements on the GDR's armed forces were not sufficiently supportive. Behind the Security Department's concern about Krug's position on the army was the state's continuing effort to increase the acceptance of mandatory military service, which had been instated in early 1962. At the same time that Krug's sentiments regarding the army were being scrutinized by the Central Committee, the party's youth magazine was using Joachim Kunert's *The Adventures of Werner Holt [Die Abenteuer des Werner Holt]* (1965), a DEFA feature about a young German soldier who comes to realize the immorality of the war, as the occasion for airing official positions on Western militarism, the GDR's legitimacy as an antifascist state, and the historical significance of military service in the GDR ("Wie stehen wir zu Werner Holt?" 3).

Citing the actor's growing fame, the security official investigating Krug urged the Culture Department to step up its efforts to rein him in. Recognizing the potential for public embarrassment, the well-informed bureaucrat noted that Krug was under consideration for the leading role in a historical documentary on the German communist Richard Sorge (Letter, 26 April 1965). From the perspective of the party, an actor who could not be relied upon to support the proper standpoint on the defense of the GDR offscreen was clearly a rather poor candidate to play such a prominent political figure on it.

In response to the Security Department inquiry into progress in the Krug case, culture officials urged the studio to arrange a meeting with the actor to discuss his public statements on the military (Letter, 3 May 1965). DEFA later reported back to the Central Committee that the requested discussion had taken place and that Krug had no intentions of creating any problems in the event of his assignment to reserve duty. Defending his important asset, the studio head offered that Krug's seeming uncooperativeness merely reflected his concern that his physical condition was below par and that he might be harassed due to his fame.

According to the studio, in the interest of dispelling any rumors that he was a refusenik, Krug was prepared to go on tour for army units and to appear in uniform at all events, televised or otherwise, in which he was required to participate. The studio head also promised that his star performer would behave himself at conscription interviews and in related situations. Emphasizing that DEFA had big plans for Krug in 1966, the studio head requested that any engagements be cleared with him beforehand. In his report, the studio head also suggested a way of handling Krug that would be more effective in terms of public relations and less disruptive of DEFA's production plan than his enlistment. He wrote, "My recommendation in this whole matter is to appoint

Manfred Krug—if he is in fact to be drafted—to the Erich Weinert Ensemble. This [having Krug join the army orchestra] would generate more public interest than assigning him to six weeks of training duty somewhere" (Letter, 31 May 1965).

Apparently satisfied with these assurances from the studio, and no doubt aware of the limits to the kind of influence that could be effectively and inconspicuously exerted on Krug, culture officials reported back to the Security Department that the appropriate steps were being taken and that Krug appeared to be willing to help deflate damaging rumors surrounding his person. Taking the cue from the studio head, the suggestion was made to find a way of working with the difficult actor to promote a favorable image of military duty among GDR youths (Letter, 3 June 1965).

The dilemma of containing Krug became alarmingly clear following the Eleventh Plenary and his public support of Wolf Biermann, who had been attacked by party officials for his purportedly seditious sentiments. Krug had previously sung one of Biermann's ballads at a 1964 concert in Berlin. Following the Eleventh Plenary, the Central Committee sought to subsequently squelch the recording of the event, entitled "Jazz und Lyrik," which had been released in early December 1965 ("Aktennotiz"). Scrambling to find a way of coping with Biermann, the Central Committee's Agitation Department *(Abteilung Agitation)* pondered a commissioned study of GDR radio and newspapers, including *Neues Deutschland, Junge Welt, Berliner Zeitung, NBI,* and *Wochenpost,* which sought to assess the widespread public opinion that the state was overreacting in its denunciation of the dissenting singer-poet ("Information"). In this context the authors of the media analysis also reported on Krug's endorsement of Biermann in a GDR radio program, which had, in turn, prompted a harshly worded article in *Junge Welt* condemning Krug for contributing to problems among GDR youths. Krug had responded in letter form, demanding that his reply be published unabridged, a condition that the spin-conscious newspaper editors rejected. According to the Agitation Department report, the tone of the article had prompted an alarming number of letters objecting to the publication's treatment of Krug.

In terms of production values and expectations, *Trace of the Stones* was the most important project in DEFA's production plan for 1965–66. Based on the acclaimed novel by Erik Neutsch, which had first appeared in serial form in *Junge Welt,* the high-budget, 70mm release was originally scheduled to open in dual celebration of the twentieth anniversary of the party and DEFA.

Although *Trace of the Stones* was ultimately produced as a standard-length feature film, initial plans were for nothing less ambitious than a two-part, 4,500–4,800-meter epic. Befitting a feature film of this importance, the main character, Hannes Balla, was to be cast with a performer of the appropriate stature, namely Manfred Krug. To direct the film, the studio enlisted the services of an eager Frank Beyer, the respected director of the well-received *Five Cartridges* and *Carbide and Sorrel [Karbid und Sauerampfer]* (1963), the latter a lighthearted film relating the adventures experienced by a worker in search of the supplies needed at his war-ravaged factory.

Trace of the Stones is set in the GDR around 1960 at the problem-ridden construction site for a huge industrial complex. The chaotic working conditions at the site are characterized by incompetent functionaries, poor planning, material shortages, and a general lack of discipline. Under these circumstances, Hannes Balla, the roughly charismatic, rebellious, but hard-working head of a carpenter's brigade, has taken the situation into his own hands. Dependent on Balla's competence, his authority among the other workers, and his indispensable role in meeting production deadlines, administrators at the project must grudgingly tolerate the raucous brigadier's outlaw justice and his open disregard for socialist or any other authority.

Events are set into motion by the arrival at the site of the new party secretary, Werner Horrath, and the engineer, Katrin Klee. The young newcomer sent by the party, a reform-minded technocrat, quickly recognizes that improving the state of affairs at the construction site means winning over Balla. He also knows that this can be accomplished only by appealing to Balla's pride in his work. The slight, intellectual functionary and the physically intimidating Balla become first allies and then rivals when they both fall in love with Klee. Klee subsequently becomes pregnant by the married party official, which leads to a tribunal regarding his private and official conduct. In the end, the demoted secretary joins Balla's brigade as an ordinary worker, and Balla appears to accept the value of working collectively for a better future. The film concludes on an equivocal note with Klee's nocturnal departure from the site; a concluding voice-over relates her thoughts: "I would like to begin all over again."

The promotion of *Trace of the Stones* reflected the studio's high hopes for the film as a way of combining an endorsement of liberalization trends in GDR society with the entertainment appeal of a high-budget film with a star actor. In the publicity for the film, of course, the emphasis was on the latter. In this regard, the character of the press notices and promotional material that appeared in GDR media differed markedly from those for the rest of the films of its production year, several of which appealed to the same progressive policies as *Trace of the Stones*. Lacking the exposure that had been lavished on *Trace of the Stones*, however, these films could be less conspicuously withdrawn after the Eleventh Plenary. Despite the importance of the film's treatment of issues like party discipline, socialist development, and the integration of nonconformist elements into society, the film's publicity was organized largely around the drawing power of actor Manfred Krug.

The buildup for the premiere of *Trace of the Stones* commenced in summer 1965 and culminated with a two-story billboard mounted in East Berlin's center, which depicted a swaggering Krug in the role of Balla. Advertising such as this had far more in common with the publicity surrounding recent Krug genre-film vehicles than *Trace of the Stones*'s serious subject matter would seem to warrant. One preview went so far as to insinuate a kind of sequel to *After Me, Scoundrels! [Mir nach, Canaillen]* (Ralf Kirsten, 1964), a successful Rococo-era action-comedy, in which Krug had played a swashbuckling peasant-turned-rebel ("Der Krug geht zu Wasser" 4–7). For this high-budget costume film the actor even had had a hand in shaping his role, as co-author of the screenplay, which was shot in wide-format "Totalvision" (DEFA's answer to Cinemascope), ORWO-color, and the best sound system at the studio's disposal. The elaborate premiere took place out of doors along a regatta stretch between Berlin and the environs of Grünau. For the occasion Krug appeared on horseback in front of the open-air screen in what the actor later recalled as "a[n] extremely American entrance for the GDR" (Krug 16). A mounted, pistol-wielding Krug leaped from the flashy, color film program put out for the film's promotion by *Progress*. Inside, fans were given a preview of an uncharacteristically blond-haired Krug sailing out of a castle window and wooing female lead Monika Woytowicz. Typical of Krug publicity, the caption applied to a still of Krug and a corsetted Woytowicz played on the blurred lines of biography and screen persona indicative of star discourse, divulging that the actress was also Krug's partner off-camera *(Mir nach Canaillen)*.

This type of slippage had been exploited to even greater effect in the publicity for the aforementioned picture *On the Sunny Side*. "A DEFA comedy in which LAUGHTER, LOVE, and

JAZZ are writ large," "A DEFA comedy with cool champagne and hot music"—these were just a few of the enticements to be found in Progress's packet of promotional material for local theaters (*Auf der Sonnenseite*). The story of a steelworker's acting ambitions, *On the Sunny Side* is something of an anomaly among DEFA's films. Although Krug would star in other films conceived as vehicles for him, *On the Sunny Side* was billed as a film based in part on the life of actor Krug, who had been a steelworker and, according to fable, had been expelled from acting school, just like the film's hero. Even the star-skeptical *Junge Welt* participated in this kind of star promotion, printing an interview on *Trace of the Stones* in which Frank Beyer remarked on the actor's credentials in the world of work. "Several brigade members," Beyer was quoted as saying about the actors in Balla's troupe, "are no strangers . . . to hard manual labor. It's well known that Manfred Krug, for example, worked at a forge for years . . . " (Beyer 4).

The 30 June 1965 issue of *Filmspiegel* took a similar focus on Krug in reporting on the filming of *Trace of the Stones*, trumpeting from its cover, "Krug Takes to the Water!" ("Der Krug geht zu Wasser"). The reference was to a notorious scene from the film's literary source in which a skinny-dipping Balla and crew throw the local guardian of law and order into a reflecting pond in front of the town courthouse. This same episode was also the subject of an *NBI* feature issue later in the year, which dedicated its cover to Krug and warned its readers with tongue in cheek: "The Balla brigadiers! In *Trace of the Stones*—readers, there's no cause for alarm—even if they are coming to the theater with Manfred Krug at the fore!" ("Ballas gehen baden" 20). The feature contained a two-page spread with photos of a pearl-earringed Krug in full gear, with the broad-rimmed hat and traditional costume of the carpenter's trade—an outfit that made him look like a cowboy straight off of a Hollywood set. "That's Hannes Balla," read the caption, "You're right, he looks like Manfred Krug. Whether or not you imaged the carpenter from Erik Neutsch's best-selling novel quite like this—soon you'll have the chance to meet DEFA's Balla yourselves" ("Ballas gehen baden" 21).

What is telling about the coverage of the pond scene is the way in which it adroitly played on the subversiveness associated with the Krug persona without openly condoning the irreverent treatment of state authority at the hands of the Balla brigade. By suggesting a discrepancy between the character in the novel, who becomes a party member and an exemplary worker, and the

Krug persona, the text solicited the magazine's readership to consider how the anarchic actor would go about portraying this worker-hero. The captions supplied to the pond scene stills went on to sarcastically boast that the photos were so "exclusive" that they wouldn't even be appearing in the completed film. This initially disconcerting news about the stills is diffused by the punning explanation that, as opposed to the magazine's color photos, the film was being shot in black and white. Given the text's provocative undertone, sophisticated GDR readers no doubt perceived behind this tease an allusion to the censor in the notion of somehow "absent" images. At the very least, the treatment of the scene ensured that future moviegoers would be alert to see how far Krug and DEFA could go in representing the challenge to state authority embodied by the dousing of a GDR policeman.

Later, this press coverage would also make it considerably more difficult for film administrators to argue for the scene's omission. Following the political crackdown of December 1965, culture officials reacted with outrage at the handling of the pond scene by the *NBI*'s editors for precisely this reason. At a party meeting on the grounds of the DEFA studio, the story was used as ammunition against the filmmakers, who were accused of harboring a political agenda directed against the GDR state ("Diskussionsbeitrag des Gen. Frank Beyer").

As the magazine publicity surrounding the pond scene demonstrates, *Trace of the Stones* offered scenarios that were perfectly suited for the unfolding of the subversive Krug persona. Not surprisingly, the majority of the changes demanded of the DEFA Studio during the production of *Trace of the Stones* targeted scenes featuring Krug. Yet, despite numerous alterations, officials remained dissatisfied with the effort to dampen the actor's impact through cuts and reworking dialogue.

The introduction of the Balla brigade in the film's second sequence contains some of the film's most visually striking images, and these play an important role in establishing the disruptive presence of the Balla figure. Exploiting the film's wide-screen format, the sequence begins with a shot of the brigade striding toward the camera seven abreast in the distinctive regalia of traditional German carpenters, with broad-rimmed hats and black leather vests gesturing to the imagery of the Hollywood western. Sporting cocked beers instead of revolvers, the brigadiers force their way through a crowd heading in the other direction to an official gathering. "A rally in this heat," mocks Balla, as he leads his boisterous troupe to a tavern out of sight of the proceedings.

Balla's dramatically choreographed entrance in this scene as the leader of a proletarian posse situated the character in the context of previous Krug roles, suggesting to the film's audience that they were in for a rather different workplace epic.

Even in his less conflicted literary incarnation, the rowdy Balla figure, who rebuffs party ceremony in the previous scene, would have been a prime role for Krug. In the novel Balla develops from an egotistic rebel, willing to resort to outlaw justice to finish a job, into a responsible member of the working collective, a transformation that is symbolically tied to the triumphant completion of the industrial complex. A measure of the text's investment in the closure of Balla's biography is provided by the novel's final paragraph, in which the formerly restless Balla lays claim to the GDR as his socialist "Heimat," or homeland" (Neutsch 844).

As rendered by Krug, the film character retained rougher edges than his literary complement, and the tribunal involving the new party secretary, which the scriptwriters had transformed into a narrative frame for reorganizing the lengthy novel, had relieved him of much of the burden of having to sustain the film's positive ideological message. With some of the political weight shifted away from the Balla character toward the young functionary at the center of the party hearing, spectators were free to privilege the construction site cowboy's rebelliousness and down-to-earth humor over and against any gains in maturity and political orientation during the course of the story. Although in the film Balla also comes to recognize the virtues of cooperation, the final scenes leave a number of issues open. In the film, the link between his maturation and the triumphant completion of the construction project has been broken. The narrative no longer peaks with Balla's affirmation of a sense of place in a socialist homeland, but troughs with the ambivalence of Klee's departure.

Even before *Trace of the Stones* went into production, the script had been the subject of heated negotiations between the DEFA studio and officials in the Film Bureau and the Central Committee. Objections to a treatment of the script by culture officials were raised in late 1964 in an expertise submitted to the studio head in which the scriptwriters were charged with polarizing a number of conflicts between party representatives and construction site administrators, on the one hand, and those confronted with the everyday problems of the workplace, on the other. This was apparent, said the Central Committee, in a sequence in which Balla proposes a strike to protest delays in the supply of building materials to his brigade. The reference to a "strike" was seen as an unconscionable provocation, suggesting quasi-capitalistic working conditions in GDR society. The culture functionaries were also convinced that the Balla figure had lost much of its force as a model for personal and political development in socialist society (Letter, 16 October 1964).

Like the studio readers who had assessed the novel for filming, however, Central Committee functionaries did not fully anticipate at this stage the extent to which the Krug persona would radicalize the Balla character. At key junctures in the film—and in numerous, seemingly innocuous shots—Krug's gestures and delivery infused the Balla character with multiple levels of significance and irony. Particularly in the tense post-Plenary atmosphere, a situation in which film and studio administrators approached films and scripts with a heightened sense of the symbolic or allegorical meanings that could be attributed to dialogues, narratives, and images, critics of *Trace of the Stones* recognized that script revisions and postproduction editing, including the reshooting of several scenes, had not sufficiently diffused Krug's anarchic energy.

With the momentum behind reform policies coming to a grinding halt in late 1965, the initial cut of *Trace of the Stones* found few sympathizers among culture officials, who found themselves scrambling to adjust to the new political course. In order to save the production, director Frank Beyer was compelled to submit to the Ministry of Culture a list of alterations designed to dampen the film's more provocative scenes—half of which featured Balla. The suggested changes included the abbreviation of a scene in which Balla provokes a brawl at the festivities for the GDR's anniversary; major rearrangements to justify Balla's actions in the aforementioned "strike" sequence; and dialogue changes in a scene in which Balla and a senior brigade member ruminate on the two Germanys ("Betr. Film 434").

Even in the version that briefly made it into GDR cinemas, this latter scene was another instance in which the Krug persona encouraged spectators to seek heterodox levels of meaning. Set in a deserted workers' barracks at Christmas, the scene depicts an exchange between Balla and an older carpenter, who have been left behind amid a clutter of empty vodka bottles. The dialogue on the topic of Germany is initiated in a seemingly accidental way. Fumbling with the television in his drunken state, Balla stumbles onto a West German station that is airing the same sentimental holiday songs to be found on the GDR program. Disgusted, Balla switches off the set. Suddenly reflective, he turns to his partner and acknowledges his respect for the young party secretary and his idealistic efforts to improve conditions at the project. This, in turn, inspires his companion to consider how his own generation's ideals were destroyed under Nazism. "Destroyed?" interrupts Balla,

> You sawed Germany in half—in a big lump and a little lump.
> The difference is: Over there . . . crap.
> Over here [gesturing to empty bottles and apparently losing his train of thought] . . . we just had a pile of bottles on the table.
> Didn't I just get a bottle of vodka from everybody [for Christmas]?

Like a number of other situations in the film, this scene, too, operates on two levels. While the (in effect illegal) reception of the West German channel is presented as inadvertent and parallels between the GDR and the FRG do not become more explicit than the suggestion of a common affinity for sappy holiday music, the staging of this scene has connotations that exceed what could be explicitly portrayed in a DEFA film. Namely, that GDR citizens regularly watched television from the West and that both East and West Germany could be seen as deformations of the cold war. Krug's humorous performance and the fact that the characters are intoxicated at once enable and neutralize the threat to the distinct and antifascist identity of the GDR.

Despite the changes promised by director Beyer, not all of which were actually carried out, culture functionaries remained discontented with *Trace of the Stones*, and the Balla figure in particular, whose rebelliousness was perceived as threatening to socialist morals. In acknowledgment of the influence of Krug's persona in enhancing the attractiveness of Balla in the film, officials warned that moviegoers with uncertain political loyalties would uncritically identify with the character's disregard for authority. "There is no need," as one official remarked, "to emphasize the extent to which Manfred Krug's powerful performance encourages this effect" ("Kritische Überlegungen").

Manfred Krug's rebellious aura was, of course, by no means solely responsible for *Trace of the Stones*'s ultimate withdrawal in summer 1966. Paradoxically, it was in part the publicity surrounding the star actor that had contributed to the pressures on film administrators to arrange a displayable version of the film that could withstand the ideological scrutiny of the Eleventh Plenary. Long after the termination of most of the films that had gone into production at the same time as *Trace of the Stones*, the film was still at the center of negotiations between DEFA and culture officials, who were hoping to salvage the anxiously awaited feature. DEFA even succeeded in securing the controversial film's release, although it was short-lived: *Trace of the Stones* was removed from circulation after only a week, under the pretense of public outrage over the portrayal of contemporary GDR society.

In contrast to director Frank Beyer, who was fired from the studio along with the studio head, Manfred Krug suffered no appreciable setback as a result of the scandal of the ban. He continued to entertain GDR audiences—and ruffle the feathers of culture bureaucrats—until his relocation to the West in response to Wolf Biermann's forced expatriation. Characteristic of the relationship between the star and the state, GDR officials grudgingly agreed to allow Krug to leave the country rather than suffer additional bad publicity at the hands of one of the GDR's most popular performers.

NOTES

1. Among the suppressed films of 1965–66, *Trace of the Stones* has received most of its scholarly attention since its re-release following the demise of the GDR. For comprehensive descriptions of the film's complicated production history, see Feinstein, Schenk, and Soldovieri. Reid provides a reading that compares film, novel, and play; Lohmann's highly theoretical account touches on the concerns of the present study in its attention to the film's various registers.

WORKS CITED

"Aktennotiz zur Herausgabe der Schallplatte *Jazz und Lyrik*." 21 January 1966. BArch DY30 IV A2/906/10.
Auf der Sonnenseite. Progressdienst für Presse und Werbung. January 1962.
"Ballas gehen baden." *Neue Berliner Illustrierte* 45 (1965): 20–21.
"Betr. Film 434—*Spur der Steine*." 29 March 1966. BArch DR 117 A/1188.
Beyer, Frank. "Dem Balla bei Filmaufnahmen in Coswig auf der Spur." *Junge Welt*, 28–29 August 1965, 4.
"Diskussionsbeitrag des Gen. Frank Beyer." 23 December 1965. BArch DY30 IV A2/906/123.
Feinstein, Joshua. "The Triumph of the Ordinary: Depictions of Daily Life in the East German Cinema, 1956–66." Ph.D. diss., Stanford University, 1995.
Gledhill, Christine. Introduction to *Stardom: The Industry of Desire*, edited

by Christine Gledhill, xiii–xx. London and New York: Routledge, 1991.

"Information über Argumente und Diskussionen zum 11. Plenum." 6 January 1966. BArch DY 30 IV A2/9.02/107/1.

"Kinos leer?" *Neue Berliner Illustrierte* 22 (1964): 8–13.

"Kritische Überlegungen zur dramaturgischen Konzeption der Egel-Beyerischen Filmversion des Neutsch-Romans *Spur der Steine*." 8 July 1966. BArch DR 117 A/1188.

"Der Krug geht zu Wasser." *Filmspiegel*, 30 June 1965, 4–7.

Krug, Manfred. "Ich bin immer, wie ich bin . . . Ein Gespräch mit Manfred Krug." In *Manfred Krug. Die großen Kinofilme*, edited by Ralf Schenk, 9–21. Berlin: Parthas Verlag, 1997.

Letter. 16 October 1964. BArch DR 117 A/0129b.

Letter. 26 April 1965. BArch DY30 IV A2/906/10.

Letter. 3 May 1965. BArch DR 117 A/240.

Letter. 31 May 1965. BArch DR 117 A/240.

Letter. 3 June 1965. BArch DY30 IV A2/906/10.

Lohmann, Hans. "'Kellerfilme' damals und heute." *Beiträge zur Film- und Fernsehwissenschaft* 40 (1991): 30–49.

Mir nach Canaillen. Progress Film-Programm 56 1964.

Neutsch, Erik. *Spur der Steine*. Halle/Saale: Mitteldeutscher Verlag, 1964.

Reid. J. H. "Erik Neutsch's *Spur der Steine*: The Book, the Play, the Film." In *Geist und Macht: Writers and the State in the GDR*, edited by Axel Goodbody and Dennis Tate, 58–67. Amsterdam: Rodopi, 1992.

Schenk, Ralf, ed. *Regie Frank Beyer*. Berlin: Henschel Verlag, 1995.

Soldovieri, Stefan. "Negotiating Censorship: GDR Film at the Juncture of 1965–66." Ph.D. diss, University of Wisconsin-Madison, 1998.

Unsere Filmsterne. Berlin: Verlag Junge Welt, 1962.

"Wie stehen wir zu Werner Holt?" *Junge Welt*, 20–21 February 1965, 2–3.

FILMOGRAPHY

Trace of the Stones [Spur der Steine] (Frank Beyer, 1966/89)
The Ancient Coin [Die antike Münze] (Vladimir Jantschev, 1965)
Five Cartridges [Fünf Patronenhülsen] (Frank Beyer, 1960)
On the Sunny Side [Auf der Sonnenseite] (Ralf Kirsten, 1962)
The Adventures of Werner Holt [Die Abenteuer des Werner Holt] (Joachim Kunert, 1965)
Carbide and Sorrel [Karbid und Sauerampfer] (Frank Beyer, 1963)
After Me, Scoundrels! [Mir nach, Canaillen] (Ralf Kirsten, 1964)

CHAPTER 12

Beleaguered under the Sea

Wolfgang Petersen's *Das Boot* (1981) as a German Hollywood Film

Brad Prager

The chief difficulty in contextualizing recent popular films lies not in asserting that many such films are made in global contexts, but rather in isolating from the manifold those historically specific discourses out of which particular popular films emerge. The case of a film such as *Das Boot* (Petersen, 1981) is unique in that the film's popularity bespoke the coincidence of a number of overlapping film-historical and cultural-historical moments. *Das Boot* was simultaneously an extension of New German Cinema projects and a Hollywood-inspired film that arguably marked the end of those projects. Additionally, it was distinctive as a German representation of World War Two defined by the ideological spirit of the 1980s, in which it was produced. Petersen's film, with its specific agenda of absolving the German soldier—through the figures of the submarine's captain and his overwrought crew—navigated, so to speak, the working-through of the past in a way that guaranteed its American *and* German popularity. The interpretation of that success must then be understood in light of *Das Boot*'s cross-cultural position at the point at which popular German film, and particularly those films that took Hollywood form as their model, met Germany's own discourse about its military past.

Before considering *Das Boot* in particular, it is worthwhile to reflect on a related watershed German-American event in May 1985, when President Reagan visited Germany's Bitburg

Cemetery at Kolmeshöhe—a cemetery in which Nazi soldiers, in-cluding forty-eight SS-officers, were buried. In his speech that day, Reagan explained his motivation for making the trip, for which he had been strongly criticized. Although he acknowl-edged that "the crimes of the SS must rank among the most hei-nous in human history," he added that others who were buried there "were simply soldiers in the German army." He then con-tinued: "How many were fanatical followers of a dictator and willfully carried out his cruel orders? And how many were con-scripts, forced into service during the death throes of the Nazi war machine?" ("Remarks of President Reagan at Bitburg Air Base" 259). Reagan's rhetorical question, by virtue of its unan-swerability, voices an ambivalent historical relation to that par-ticular group of dead veterans; an ambivalence with which German historians have long been grappling.

If one is to claim, as did Reagan, that German soldiers during the Second World War were coerced into fighting, either through force or through an extremely effective propaganda ma-chine—a position not wholly without merit—difficulties and contradictions abound. One problem produced by a disavowal of the German soldiers' responsibility for Nazi atrocities is that it produces a nonidentity of soldiers with themselves: How can it be the case that all German soldiers were victims of the ideologi-cally driven war in which they fought? When Reagan defended his visit to Bitburg in the face of objections not only from Ameri-can Jews but from the U.S. House of Representatives—who in a 390 to 26 vote encouraged him to reconsider the inclusion of Bit-burg Cemetery in his trip—he simultaneously pardoned himself and the German soldiers, asserting: "I think that there's nothing wrong with visiting that cemetery where those young men are victims of Nazism also, even though they were fighting in the German uniform, drafted into service to carry out the hateful wishes of the Nazis." He then added a statement that provoked very strong responses on both continents: "They were victims, just as surely as the victims in the concentration camps" ("Re-marks of President Reagan to Regional Editors" 240).

Reagan's trip served political and economic as well as ex-plicitly ideological ends. The real goals of the public display in which Reagan and Chancellor Kohl engaged, whereby they si-multaneously came to terms with World War Two, have been treated in various essays. Jürgen Habermas, in particular, argues that this historic visit and the handshake over the graves of the

SS-soldiers "was a symbolic reaffirmation of the loyalty of the [current German-American] alliance more than a response to the interests of the German populace" (44). These highly political motivations were made explicit in Reagan's own remarks at the time. During the same speech in which he forgave the soldiers, Reagan first referred to the importance of NATO, and then added a personal reflection with a certitude that raised skeptical eyebrows among not only German historians: "believe me, [the Germans] live in constant penance, all those who have come along in later years, for what their predecessors did, and for which they're very ashamed" ("Remarks of President Reagan to Regional Editors" 240).

The gesture by which soldiers are universally exonerated for participation in a war that was morally questionable is something that popular U.S. films frequently do for their national military history. Considering that Reagan's speeches were made in the mid-1980s, one could argue that the actor cum president got the idea from Hollywood itself. The depiction of the soldier as the victim of war is exclusive neither to German World War Two representations nor to German culture. This German tendency in fact shares a cultural-ideological disposition with the same longstanding American tradition. In contrast with representations of American World War Two soldiers, who are, in the tradition of Hollywood—through *Saving Private Ryan* (Spielberg, 1998) and the *Das Boot*-derivative *U-571* (Mostow, 2000)—uniformly heroic, Hollywood films have busily constructed the Vietnam veteran as a casualty of war. American cinema in the pre-Bitburg decade attempted to work through its ambivalent relation to the U.S. presence in Vietnam in films such as *The Deer Hunter* (Cimino, 1978) and *Apocalypse Now* (Coppola, 1979). This structure was repeated continuously throughout the 1980s, in films such as *First Blood* (Kotcheff, 1982), *Platoon* (Stone, 1986), and *Casualties of War* (de Palma, 1989) to name but a few. In these Hollywood films, soldiers are—unwillingly and typically at too young an age—shipped off to Vietnam with no guidance other than the indifferent orders handed down from "high command." Within the films, the military administration generally lacks the organizational skills to support its soldiers, who find themselves abandoned in a foreign country. The chief distinction in these discourses becomes one between the soldiers (in the position of beleaguered laborers) and the high command that exploits them (equated with management). American filmmaking on the subject, as is consistent with Hollywood projects in general, tended to have an affirmative ideological function: It told the viewers, by way of their identification with the soldier-as-victim, that they, too, were the victims of the horrors associated with that particular military intervention, rather than implicated in the military-industrial complex that produced it.

What is unusual and particularly transcultural in the case of Petersen's *Das Boot* is that it functioned analogously to those American popular films, yet it was made in Germany. American audiences were infrequently exposed to the disavowal of soldiers' responsibility in the case of foreign troops, and still less often in the case of fighting Germans. Though there were notable exceptions, from *A Time to Love and a Time to Die* (Sirk, 1958) to *Cross of Iron* (Peckinpah, 1977), German soldiers tended to be stereotyped in American films as sadists. They were traditionally the articulators of explicitly evil ideological intentions, including anti-Semitism, rabid nationalism, and simple greed. German popular literature of the postwar period, however, consistently took a more redemptive tone, a literary trend examined by Hans Wagener, who summarizes: "With the form 'Hitler = Betrayer; Soldier = Betrayed Idealist,' who in a heroic act of self-delusion fights for his comrades, the Third Reich is cleverly disavowed and the infantryman is justified as a heroic, tenacious hero" (244).

If one agrees with film historian Timothy Corrigan that *Das Boot* is a co-optation of German cinema by Hollywood (204, n.3), then the film is consistent with the assessment of soldierly responsibility made during the Reagan administration. It is, in other words, a film that came to prominence in the same historical moment in which forgiveness for military activity was acceptable or even *au courant*. The soldiers in *Das Boot* appear simply as grunts in the trenches, who could have been any soldiers, Axis or Allied, and who don't bear any responsibility for that war's atrocities. When the film's characters demonstrate any signs of rabid nationalism, those gestures are tied more to the success and failure of the German soccer team than to their military projects. If *Das Boot* is, on the contrary, taken to be part of the historical tradition of New German Cinema, one might note that the film doesn't represent the first time that that movement tackled the project of working through the Nazi past. Fascism is the subject of Volker Schlöndorff's well-known adaptation of Günter Grass's *The Tin Drum* (1979), for example. Despite the fact that fascism may not be the only thematic concern at work in that film, insofar as it sustains a distinct oedipal narrative as well, *The Tin Drum* relentlessly depicts the ideological apparatus of the Third

Reich, holding the psychosexual development of its protagonist in tension with economic and social developments.[1]

Although some maintain that the end of New German Cinema did not occur until after the cold war (see Davidson 68), many of the filmmakers associated with the movement felt, after *Das Boot,* that it was finally all right to make it in Hollywood—a sentiment that was to be the death knell of a wholly independent German cinema tradition (Rentschler "How American Is It?" 279–80). Eric Rentschler points out that the end of New German Cinema is usually understood to have come around 1982, in conjunction with the death of Fassbinder and the entry into office of Interior Minister Friedrich Zimmermann, who declared war on the *Autorenfilm* in the name of "entertainment." ("Film der achtziger Jahre" 286–88). *Das Boot,* from this perspective, rests squarely on the cusp of a cinema-historical shift, from overwhelming enthusiasm for the *Autorenfilm* to a revolution against it in the name of popular culture. Through the 1970s New German Cinema had been committed to low-budget, unspectacular, and insistently anti-Hollywood film. The producers of *Das Boot,* however, from the outset wanted their film to be a spectacle and a crowd-pleaser in the Hollywood style, a decision that rendered their moneymaking intentions distinct from New German Cinema's agenda of developing a national style untainted by Hollywood. Initially, according to Petersen, in the mid-1970s Bavaria Studios bought the rights to adapt *Das Boot* and thought, "We need American money, American brilliance, an American director, an American superstar and American know-how." (Thomas 22). They considered a number of possible combinations of actors and directors, including Don Siegel and Robert Redford, but after the successes of two German-made World War Two films—*The Marriage of Maria Braun* (Fassbinder, 1979) and *The Tin Drum*—Bavaria Studios finally summoned up the courage to go ahead and make the film under the supervision of a German. In the tradition of spectacular Hollywood films, *Das Boot* was viewed primarily as a technical achievement, and in this way distinct from Fassbinder's and Schlöndorff's films of the same period.

Petersen, in particular, had long wished to ingratiate himself with America. After *Das Boot* he went on to direct a number of blockbusters, including *In the Line of Fire* (1993) and *Air Force One* (1997)—both films that, not incidentally, feature an idealized representation of the U.S. president. It may be the case that with *Air Force One* he finally achieved the acceptance in America he had always wanted. Petersen explains that before he had made that film, he had had a constant and recurring nightmare. He elaborated: "I'm sitting in a huge plane, hunting through narrow streets—American streets. I have to maneuver the aircraft through one curve after another. I'm scared, I panic, and I finally wake up, bathed in sweat." Finally, however, he reported having been cured of the anxiety, adding that, "Since the filming of *Air Force One* I haven't had this horrible dream again. Maybe you can film yourself to health" (Petersen and Greiwe 35). In the terms of the dream, Petersen had finally overcome his anxiety associated with controlling his own destiny in America.[2]

It is not only Petersen, however, who wanted to "film himself to health" *(sich gesundfilmen)*. As I have argued, cinematic representations of the Vietnam War were the means by which the American public had rid itself of its feelings of guilt. If one identifies with the soldier-victims of *The Deer Hunter,* for example, then one need not feel culpability for the policies of the government that supported and staged that war. In a similar tradition, if one identifies with the soldier who was a victim of the Nazis, one need not confront the question of whether the collective identifications that produced the war continue to exist. From this perspective, Theodor Adorno concludes, "We will not have come to terms with the past until the causes of what happened then are no longer active. Only because these causes live on does the spell of the past remain, to this very day, unbroken" (129). In this regard *Das Boot* can be understood as a persistent symptom of the collective denial of the past. America, in particular, produces affirmative war films to deal with these anxieties, films that choose cathartic self-help over cultural psychoanalysis, a juxtaposition that one finds in the work of Peter Homans, who argues that not choosing to work through the past is equivalent to continuing to choose fascism (see esp. 338).

Das Boot is based on Lothar Buchheim's 1973 novel and is an aggregate of his experiences on board German submarines. Both the text and the film explicitly fight against any identification of the soldiers with Nazi ideology. In a separate memoir entitled *U-Boat War,* Buchheim writes:

> when I read the sentence by my *[New York Times]* reviewer . . . that of the 40,000 men who had gone forth as volunteers in German submarines to wage total war against innocent civilians, the 30,000 dead had fully deserved their dreadful fate at sea, I was incensed by the cold-bloodedness of the verdict. However horrific the idea that these young men, lured into action by every form of

propaganda, came very close to bringing down an empire, it is not the individual sent to his doom that merits such merciless condemnation. (*U-Boat War* 9)

It is curious that he believed his reviewer was bitter toward Nazi soldiers because they almost brought down an empire. By contrast, it was more likely that they were accused of attempting to establish one. Mostly, however, Buchheim's defensive remarks bespeak the truth that sometimes individuals can be identified with ideologies. If the line that divides the individual (and the soldier in particular) from the ideologies for which he or she fights were always clear, then misidentification would never occur. In other words, Bucheim's response seems to tacitly acknowledge the possibility that some soldiers *were*, in fact, Nazis.

Petersen, who shared writing credit for the screenplay, had intentions similar to Buchheim's; he, too, wanted both German and American audiences to feel sympathy for the sailor-soldiers in the film. For Petersen, however, the film's American popularity was paramount. In an interview, he described the first time that he showed his film to an American audience. He explained: "There were around 1,500 people in the theater. At the beginning of the film, the explanation appeared that of the 40,000 German submarine sailors, 30,000 never returned. At that moment everyone loudly applauded, which sent a chill down our spines. I thought: This is going to be a catastrophe! If they were applauding the death of 30,000, we knew we were in trouble." Petersen recounted with pride, however, that his film managed to change their minds. He added: "It was uncanny: In the next 150 minutes the film turned the audience completely around. I'll never forget it. At the end, I was greeted on stage by thunderous applause and I discussed the film with the viewers. Without exaggeration, *Das Boot* made a triumphal march through America" (Petersen and Greiwe 174). Some may find his remark that the film made a "triumphal march through America" unsettling insofar as it is understood as a film explicitly about salvaging the memory of the German soldier while failing to mention at any moment either nationalism or anti-Semitism.

Petersen was interested in discussing neither the ideological conditions that led to the war nor those that persisted after it. He was interested primarily in representing the experience of war without referring to its circumstances. In answer to the question of the political project of his own film, Petersen explained, "I was reproached that we Germans were still far from ready to depict the submariners on the U-boats as normal people like you and me. We were always aware that we were the war criminals, we were the guilty ones! But that's not what *Das Boot* is about. The film simply tries to point out what war really means" (Petersen and Greiwe 167). He was concerned, in other words, not with thinking through the causes of the war, but rather with the improbable and difficult project of representing war in itself; his intent was simply to show "what war really means." This particular desire on Petersen's part, to represent the horror of war but not the horror of Nazi ideology, explains much of what makes this film's particular space of representation interesting. It is no coincidence that the film he chose to make takes place on a submarine, and that the dark depths to which the submarine plunges effectively erase the signs and marks of historical context, signs and marks of fascism and anti-Semitism that would have been more pronounced had the film taken place on the surface.

What makes the film most formally interesting is indeed the narrow space of the boat itself, similar to that of the plane on which Petersen's *Air Force One* took place. In this respect it is unlike contemporary popular films that emphasize the breadth of nuclear submarines, such as the Hollywood-produced *Crimson Tide* (Scott, 1995), in which Denzel Washington can be seen taking a jog along the decks of that film's high-tech war machine. Close quarters are not simply symptomatic of an attempt at historical accuracy; they are also a means of underscoring the camaraderie between the men necessary for the logic of the film—the men are ultimately more loyal to one another than to the high command who betrays them.

Das Boot has five principal stages: Its prologue takes place in a bordello, in which the young men who are to ship out the following day indulge in a final bacchanal. After some drills, boredom, and frustration, the crew then engages in a difficult and psychologically demanding sea hunt and firefight with British destroyers and attempts to head home. They are given orders instead to stay at sea and maneuver through the Allied-controlled Strait of Gibraltar, which they take to be an impossible task. The U-Boat, before heading for the Strait, connects with a supply ship in a Spanish port and then continues on to certain death in the Mediterranean. After being attacked at the Strait, the decks are flooded and the ship sinks. The crew resourcefully and heroically bails out the ship, repairs the engine, and surfaces again. In the film's ostensibly anti-war epilogue, they return to a small and dispassionate heroes' welcome, but as the submarine pulls into the port, Allied bombers attack from above, blowing the harbor to bits. Every character in the film lies bleeding or dead on the pier, with the exception of the author-narrator, who is left behind to assess the damage.

As in the case of many German war novels written during the 1950s, the novel of *Das Boot* was "literature of and by a generation that was still strongly under the influence of the Third Reich and World War Two. It was literature of a time in which moral self-evaluation was the first logical step of those who returned home from the war and who had survived the bombings" (Wagener 261). Immediately on the first page of Buchheim's work, he explains that it is not a mere work of fiction. The author claims to have experienced everything that he described. The events are real, he asserts, but the characters are fictive. *Das Boot* can be treated as yet another representation in which the German soldier, instead of standing in for absolute evil, is the victim of evil as well. As Alexander and Margarete Mitscherlich assert in *The Inability to Mourn,* this type of equivocation is standard among postwar tropes that inhibit the process of working through or reprocessing World War Two from the German side. In their influential book, they argue that Germans had identified with Hitler as a national father figure and attached libidinal energy to him. With the agenda of mandating the expansion of psychoanalysis and its institutions in Germany, the Mitscherlichs maintained that in order for healing after the Second World War to begin, the Germans would have to work through the devastation of their libidinal investments in the Führer as well as those of their group identifications with the *Volksgemeinschaft.* German culture, in short, was in need of psychoanalysis so that it could properly come to terms with the loss of those attachments. Freud, in his essay "Mourning and Melancholia," which serves as the basis for much of the Mitscherlichs' book, opened the door to this type of social-psychological description of the mourning process when he claimed that mourning is not only the reaction to the loss of a loved one, but also may be a reaction "to the loss of some abstraction which has taken the place of one, such as the fatherland, liberty, an ideal and so on" ("Mourning and Melancholia" 164). The loss of Hitler (and National Socialism), in the Mitscherlichs' hypothesis, takes the form of a loss of a part of the self for the mourner who refuses to acknowledge the difference between him- or herself and the abstractions and ideals the lost father figure embodied. The failed mourner (the postwar German) then inflicted the damage that was intended for the lost object upon his or her own ego, and became, drawing on Freud's schema, a melancholic.

In summarizing their conclusions about the effects of this process on individual postwar German psyches, the Mitscherlichs conclude:

> To the conscious mind the past then appears as follows: We made many sacrifices, suffered the war, and were discriminated against for a long time afterward; yet we were innocent since everything that is now held against us we did under evil orders. This strengthens the feeling of being oneself the victim of evil forces; first the evil Jews, then the evil Nazis, and finally the evil Russians. In each instance the evil is externalized. It is sought for on the outside, and it strikes one from the outside. (46)

Their argument maintains that postwar Germans universally had become melancholic because of a failure to properly mourn. Rather than acknowledging the loss of that about which they had felt so strongly, the identifications of many Germans shifted from Hitler to the victims. The Mitscherlichs discuss case studies in which, for example, a former Hitler Youth, who eventually became a soldier, suffered from repeated anxiety attacks that came as a consequence of disavowing how much more he had shared the collective beliefs of the Nazis than he had been willing to admit. They also discuss a nervous man who was made melancholic by the "dreadful deeds committed by other Germans," but, as was determined in the course of analysis, was really feeling a sense of guilt about his own ambivalence toward the atrocities committed during the war (42).

Though the Mitscherlichs wrote their influential text in 1967 and it bears traces of the psychoanalytic discourse pervasive at the moment in which it was produced, it provides compelling insights into the motivations that belie Petersen's film as an attempt to facilitate a popular "coming to terms" with the war through exonerating ordinary German soldiers. Regardless of whether one agrees with the Mitscherlichs, one might be inclined to consider *Das Boot* in the context of this question of reprocessing the past *(Aufarbeitung der Vergangenheit)* or, as Eric Santner articulates it, as a possible attempt to set aside the difficult questions about World War Two in favor of "abolishing of any moral or psychological willingness to feel the painful affects that form the inner lining of the mourning process" (739). *Das Boot* participates in exactly the process that they describe: The soldiers in the film are identified not as the aggressors, but as having been the victims of external forces. In sum, the interiority of ordinary Germans is juxtaposed with the demands of bad Nazi rhetoric, located external to the self. In this way, the film can be seen as an affirmative account of the war that externalizes the evil in the form of the Nazi high command.

Long before "Mourning and Melancholia," Freud had written on the way in which the unconscious deals with loss. He underscored that ambivalence was a fundamental feature of dreams that present an alternation between death and life. He described one analytical problem associated with mourning in particular in *Interpretation of Dreams*. Freud reflects that often there is a

> particularly strongly marked emotional ambivalence which dominates the dreamer's relation to the dead person. It very commonly happens that in dreams of [dead people] the dead person is treated to begin with as though he were alive, that he then suddenly turns out to be dead and that in a subsequent part of the dream he is alive once more. This has a confusing effect. It eventually occurred to me that this alternation between death and life is intended to represent indifference on the part of the dreamer. . . . This indifference is, of course, not real, but merely desired; it is intended to help the dreamer to repudiate his very intense and often contradictory emotional attitudes and it thus becomes a dream-representation of his *ambivalence*. (*Interpretation of Dreams* 466)

Noteworthy in this account, particularly in relation to *Das Boot*, is the way the mourner's dream reevaluates and replays not only the life of the lost object, but the death as well.

In the case of *Das Boot*, the past is given meaning and rendered comprehensible for its broad audience through the depiction of the death of the submarine captain. In a way reminiscent of Walt Whitman's "O Captain! My Captain!" (1865–66), the psychic life of the ship's captain is the support for that of his crew. He is the father figure on whom the survival of the crew depends and the man whose death stands in for the fate of the fighting nation. The emphasis of this argument is therefore not so much on the image of the boat itself, but rather on the representation of what one might describe as the captain's heroic interiority. It must be understood that *Das Boot* is, above all, an affirmative film, and one in which the viewers are asked to identify with and mourn for a father-protagonist, who for reasons of the film's political agenda has a cynical distance from the demands of German ideology.

The character who represents Buchheim, the novel's author, is Lieutenant Werner, played by the German pop star Herbert Grönemeyer. As a war correspondent, he has been assigned to a German submarine manned by an extremely young crew but commanded by a very experienced captain (Jürgen Prochnow) referred to simply as "Herr Kaleun," which is an abbreviation for Captain-Lieutenant *(Kapitänleutnant)*. Throughout the novel, and at various points in the film, his character is referred to as "the Old Man" *(Der Alte)*. The psychic life of the protagonist, when confined by the limited space of the ship, opens a discourse similar to that surrounding the world of chess as depicted in Petersen's earlier *Black and White Like Day and Night [Schwarz und Weiß wie Tage und Nächte]* (1978), a film he made shortly before *Das Boot*. In that film, Bruno Ganz plays a fictive German chess master whose character and eccentricities are clearly based on the American chess grandmaster Bobby Fisher. Ganz becomes obsessive, and the same questions that one asks during *Das Boot* arise: is the opponent externalized or is the opponent really the self? Herr Kaleun is the chess genius of *Das Boot*, whose acquaintance with the barrier between internal and external, made manifest in his ability to differentiate genuine conflict from paranoia, defines his psychological health.

Those characters against whom Herr Kaleun is defined are not the Allied troops, who hardly appear, but other Germans. With the few exceptions of the brothel at the beginning, the supply ship in the middle, and the harbor at the end, one almost never explores the world beyond the walls of the vessel. This means as well that the "enemy," in this case the British fleet, is reduced to a pure abstraction. The captain's interiority is, therefore, developed by means of contrasts with the other Germans he encounters. There are a number of identities in the film that define who Herr Kaleun is, through his implicit differentiation from them. These figures include the young men who constitute his crew; his ardent and ideological first lieutenant, who has come all the way from Mexico to join the fight; the seasoned veteran sailor Thomsen; the Nazis on the supply ship near Vigo; and Johann, the engineer, who is referred to as "the ghost in the machine."

In both the novel and the film, an explicit distinction is made between Herr Kaleun as the experienced sailor and the young soldiers. That he is "the Old Man" reminds the viewer of the difference between the captain—the voice of experience—and the young men who are shipped out one after another to die at the hands of the superior British fleet. In a dialogue in the novel that Petersen partially reproduces in the film, Herr Kaleun reflects on the kind of crew with whom he has set out to sea. He contemplates aloud in the presence of Lieutenant Werner:

> After getting back to port, when they've shaved and then come on watch, I ask myself how on earth I could have put to sea with this kindergarten. They're just kids, nurslings who belong at their mothers' breasts. . . . I've often thought: please, God, only photos of returning boats for the newsreels and the papers; with bearded crews. No departure pictures, if only out of consideration for the enemy's feelings. (Bucheim, *The Boat* 86)

That Herr Kaleun's discourse is so radically gendered (that they should have beards rather than looking as though they are nursing at their mothers' breasts), is no surprise, as the film is in many respects about turning the boy soldiers into responsible men, primarily in the image of the captain, who appears as the submarine's father figure.

Petersen's film differentiates in its opening between two types of German fighting men: the "high command" and the ordinary soldier. An expository intertitle provides the historical context for the film's events. On a dark screen the introductory text explains that the film begins in the port of La Rochelle in occupied France in 1941. The German army, it continues, had suffered "enormous setbacks." The high command had ordered more boats with younger and younger crews into battle. It subsequently informs us that of the forty thousand German sailors who took part in the Second World War, thirty thousand never returned. Already, in the film's first moments, Petersen underscores the difference between Nazis on the basis of those who gave the orders and those who died following those orders.

In the film's first extended sequence, in the brothel in occupied France the night before the submarine is to depart, one comes to understand the captain defined against the many virtually adolescent males who will constitute his crew. The captain is represented as a man among boys insofar as he knows not to go wild in the brothel—his hallmark is his reserved behavior. He acknowledges the existence of his libido but asserts his masculinity through his control over it. His self-control renders his character consistent with one trope of masculinity identified by Klaus

Theweleit in *Male Fantasies*. Where libidinal urges are defined through metaphors of streaming and flooding, as argued by Theweleit, masculinity becomes about controlling these urges—one's ability, in other words, to dam the flood. Theweleit elaborates that because the water metaphors, which play a large role in *Das Boot*, historically share metonymic relations with women's bodies, this trope of masculinity routes male desire through women. It is for this reason, in his argument, that women are less often rendered as subjects capable of the alternatives of restraining themselves, or of letting loose. Men, by contrast, are defined through their ability or inability to master their libidinal "currents." Theweleit goes on to argue that "in all European literature (and literature influenced by it), desire, if it flows at all, flows in a certain sense *through women*. In some way or other, it always flows in relation to the image of woman" (272).

In the film's first scene, Herr Kaleun observes the young sailors in the bordello. In the parallel scene in the novel, he explains: "I stare at this assemblage of young heroes as though I were seeing them for the first time. Hairline mouths with sharp grooves on either side. Rasping voices. Swollen with their own superiority and crazy for medals. Not a thought in their heads but 'The Führer's eyes are upon you—our flag is dearer than life'" (Bucheim, *The Boat* 9). In the film, the sailors throw themselves into the orgy, destroying the brothel. The hand-held camera work underscores the chaos as the men, among other activities, fire pistols at the sex organs of the paintings of female nudes that line the walls, and spray soda water at the crotch of the French singer who had been entertaining them. The captain opts not to participate. In this way, the captain can be understood as the experienced ego with the capacity for self-reflectivity, in contrast with those of the fighting men, who act in direct conformity with ideological injunctions. The captain's ego, however, because of his capacity for discernment, is implicitly ambivalent. He knows that he is both the subject and the object of history; both the self and the self-observing self. This acknowledgment of an inability to play a role in his own fate produces an ambivalence about his actions. He knows enough, in other words, to know when he may not be doing the right thing. The sailor-soldiers are represented, by contrast, as egoless objects that are acted upon—pawns whom the Nazis put to horrible use. During the course of *Das Boot*, however, the crew ultimately adopts the captain's disposition. They reproduce his ability to understand that he is simultaneously free (possessing the capacity to use reason) and unfree (a victim of the sloppy military planning of the Nazi high command). The ambivalent relationship Germans are said to have to their own past is reflected in the meditative personality of the captain, which the crew comes to emulate.

Herr Kaleun's cynical distance separates him from the political positions of the party ideologues. In an early scene, when the men are getting to know one another, they listen to a Party radio broadcast. Herr Kaleun refers to the politicians in Berlin as braggarts *(Maulhelden)* and rejects the abuses heaped on Churchill. Kaleun recognizes the fact that although Churchill may be a "drunken cripple," that doesn't prevent him from giving the Nazis a "sound beating." Kaleun distinguishes the ideological injunctions to believe from the real facts, adding soberly in response to his first lieutenant's party-line optimism: "Churchill is far from being on his knees" *(auf den Knien ist [Churchill] noch lange nicht)*.

The first lieutenant (Hubertus Bengsch) is, by contrast with the captain, the paradigmatic fighting man. He is the character who is ultimately most closely associated with party ideology, having come of his own free will all the way from Mexico to fight for Germany. That he has come from so far surprises the other officers, who apparently would not have made the same decision, a decision upon which the lieutenant boasts that he did not even pause to reflect. He explains proudly, "for me as a German it was self-evident" *(für mich als Deutsche war das aber selbstverständlich)*. The viewer first encounters him when he arrives at the brothel after having driven past the drunken sailors outside. The sailors urinate on all the arriving cars, creating "a pissing honor guard" *(ein pissendes Spalier)*. The officer recounts to the captain that he, too, had been urinated upon as he pulled up, but can't get the words out, and the Old Man has to finish the sentence for him. The lieutenant is the opposite end of the spectrum from the reveling men. He finds the sailors' unrestrained micturation shocking because he stands for absolute control; they are too much id, he is too much superego. Both extremes, however, reduce to two sides of the same phenomenon—an inability to navigate libidinal waters.

Additionally, the lieutenant sees his personal hygiene as consistent with party mentality, citing respect for the Führer as the reason he keeps so clean. He, too, winds up infected with crabs *(Sackratten)*, like the rest of the crew, and his ideological emphasis on cleanliness yields to the same conditions to which the rest of the men are subjected. His refusal to engage in the pervasive discourse about flatulence and sitting in one another's smells is finally given up as posturing and artifice. His conversion indicates that the entire crew, in the end, is in the same boat.

A horrific vision of the captain's future is presented in the figure of Thomsen (Otto Sander). Older than the captain, his boat has been out numerous times. His presence underscores the difference between those who have experienced the horrors of war and those who know only its surface—a before and after representation. In the novel, Thomsen (who is there named Trumann) gives a longer version of the same speech he gives in the film. The experienced sailor gets up on a table and drunkenly proclaims:

> Our magnificent, esteemed, abstinent, and unwed Führer, who in his glorious ascension from painter's apprentice to the greatest battle-leader of all time . . . is something wrong? . . . The great naval expert, the unexcelled ocean strategist, to whom it has occurred in his infinite wisdom . . . The great naval leader who showed that English bedwetter, that cigar smoking syphilitic . . . ha, what else has he dreamed up? Let's see . . . has shown that asshole of a Churchill just who knows which end is up! (Bucheim, *The Boat* 15–16)

On the one hand, he is the voice of experience, having been long at sea. He knows the difference between the surface of Nazi appearance and the depth of Nazi reality, and has, therefore, a cynical relationship to politics of all kinds. On the other hand, like the inexperienced men and unlike the captain, he is unable to hold his fluids. In Petersen's film, he ultimately winds up vomiting and unconscious on the floor of the bordello bathroom, muttering in English, "I am in no condition to fuck."

Petersen reflected on the distinction between appearance and reality that he tried to achieve in his film. Too young to remember the war himself (he was born in 1941), he writes that his mother spoke of the glamour that was pervasive during the Nazi era:

> My mother told me about it—about all the glamour that dominated throughout the first Hitler years, about all the propaganda tales and the movies that insisted on the "new" German mentality, and about how she was seduced by the Nazis. As I was filming *Das Boot,* that was important for me to recognize. Irritatingly, I haven't been able to silence the critics who were fascinated with this period, with the submarine weapons, the uniforms of the heroes and the sailors. The film shows that they were idolized, almost like pop-stars, and the way the submarine sailors were bid

farewell to as they set out to sea before thousands of spectators, with that music that carried the crowd along with it. That was a grandiose and heroic spectacle—for a twenty-year-old it was naturally very seductive. The film contains all that. Moreover, it shows the ideas that were clouding the boys' heads, and the sad truth. (Petersen and Greiwe 166–67)

The first scene, in which the crew sets out to war with the sensation that they are heroes and pop stars, is meant to contrast with the glum and subdued return that precedes the final massacre.

Consistent with the idea of representing a decontextualized "reality of war," the sailors in *Das Boot* are meant to be neither Nazis nor even German sailors, but soldiers in a universal sense, identified with other soldiers in the world. When the crew is depressed, Herr Kaleun plays an old record on the ship's public address system. The song he chooses is the British World War I drinking song: "It's a long way to Tipperary." One of the crewmen exclaims "now we're the Royal Navy" *(jetzt sind wir die Tommies)* and both the crew and officers gleefully sing along. At this moment, they cross-identify as the enemy. The highest point of the cross-identification comes when they destroy a British tanker. Their submarine surfaces once they are sure that the remaining survivors have been rescued. They watch the conflagration and fire a shot to sink the empty ship for good. After the shot hits the apparently abandoned vessel, it becomes clear that there were still men on board. The Germans are shocked that the British sailors hadn't been picked up yet, and they watch their enemies, bodies on fire, leaping from the hull of the burning craft. In that moment, the soldiers view themselves as having been turned into killers, not by their captain, who gave the order, but by the British high command that, like their own, has failed and disappointed its men. Herr Kaleun asks despondently, "Why didn't anyone come to rescue them?" *(warum hat die keine vom Schiff geholt?)*. They recognize themselves in the drowning men, but feel compelled to retreat as the soldiers in the water plead to be saved. They identify with the other soldiers, but find themselves forced to behave cruelly.

The captain demonstrates allegiance neither to the nation nor to any of its *Maulhelden,* but to his men only. He and his officers stop on board a supply ship in Vigo shortly after they receive orders to continue on to the Mediterranean. Herr Kaleun and his men are greeted as heroes as they come on board the ship, although at first the neatly pressed first lieutenant is mistaken for the ship's captain by the Nazi supply officers. They welcome the submarine's party "with a triple 'Sieg heil'" (mit einem drei-fachen 'Sieg heil!') that Herr Kaleun refuses to return. The supply officers embarrass themselves studying every movement of the sailors, ascribing authenticity to the smallest of gestures. They anxiously await war stories from the crew, but Herr Kaleun refuses to indulge them.

Finally, the machinist Johann provides yet another contrast with the captain. As "the ghost in the machine," he is directly identified with the machinery of the ship itself. This very identification, however, means that he, as the boat, yields to the pressure of the flood outside. In one of the first drills, as the submarine creaks and groans, Johann and the men begin to sweat and lose their bearings. The captain keeps a level head, as he does later during the firefight. The boat begins to sink, and the captain inspirationally and quietly adds, "Keep calm, men, keep calm." As the bolts burst, Johann comes undone. Herr Kaleun fears that Johann's inability to keep his psychic floodwaters dammed will be contagious, and he reaches for his revolver, prepared to sacrifice the broken and fearful engineer.

In the film's last protracted segment, in the Strait of Gibraltar, the submarine is hit and sinks. As the crew repairs the boat, one hardly sees the face of Herr Kaleun. We are seeing what has finally become the rational and heroic crew, inspired by the captain, through his subjective perspective. The viewers no longer observe the captain himself, but they see through his eyes. It is clear that the men finally have adopted his rationality *tout court*; even Johann redeems himself. Everyone works together to keep the boat from being flooded, and as Theweleit's work makes clear, their ability to manifest control over their anxieties takes the form of holding back the explosive floodwaters. As Lieutenant Werner thinks the end is near, he confirms Theweleit's claim that male fantasies, especially in this context, are predicated on the controlled flow of the libido through women's bodies. Werner lyrically and fearfully longs for the return of the comfort of fantasy over this moment of uncontrolled reality, declaiming a portion of Rudolf Binding's poem "Schlacht—Das Maß":

To head into the inexorable
where no mother will care for us,
no woman crosses our path,
where only reality reigns with cruelty and grandeur . . .
   well this is reality.

Even in the moments when the crew most fear for their own lives, they never blame or resent their captain, only the invisible high command. They take care to point out to one another that trying to "ram through" the Strait of Gibraltar wasn't the captain's idea. Even the attack of the Allied forces at the end confirms that they were safer on board in the hands of Herr Kaleun. After the bombardment, virtually all the characters we have come to know lie dead on the pier. Herr Kaleun stares enraptured at his boat, sinking in the harbor. In that instant, identified with his ship, he finally loses his grip on the post to which he had been holding fast. Through replaying the death of the film's heroic character, Petersen reevaluates Herr Kaleun's military service in a positive light. The uncertain terms that had plagued his memorialization dissolve. For the viewer, identification with the captain's own ambivalence about his war activities replaces an ambivalent relation to the past, the acknowledgment of which would be the primary constituent part of its working through.

Das Boot indeed resembles American popular films whose success it emulated. Petersen, together with Bavaria Film Studios, not only set out to prove he could make a film in the American style but began in that moment to cultivate the popular approbation he finally acquired. *Das Boot* now appears thoroughly consonant with the hit films to which it gave birth, such as *The Hunt for Red October* (McTiernan, 1990), *Crimson Tide*, and *U-571*, formally indistinguishable from those bigger-budgeted Hollywood productions. The film's popular success, however, is not simply a consequence of technical precision and mastery in a Hollywood style, but also about the particularities of its historical context. It stands at the end of the era of auteur cinema in Europe, and it participated in introducing a new period in which the demand for popular entertainment films supplanted the thoughtful response to purely affirmative postwar German films. Additionally, *Das Boot* resonates with its transatlantic counterparts, in that, like so many American Vietnam films, it was part of the process of exonerating the soldiers, and, by extension, the public themselves. In both respects, the blockbuster German film *Das Boot* makes manifest the desire to dispense with the difficult project of cultural psychoanalysis and the critical demand that subtends works of art.

NOTES

This essay refers to the 210-minute director's cut of Wolfgang Petersen's *Das Boot*, first released in the United States in 1997. The original theatrical release opened in Germany and the United States in 1981. Also, please note that all translations from German texts are my own, except where a translation is mentioned in the list of Works Cited.

1. The link between *Das Boot* and *The Tin Drum* is explored by Thomas Elsaesser. He argues that

For national cinemas struggling to get into the international market, history (and Nazism in the case of Germany) has become a system of referents to some extent substituting for generic formulas and codes. In films like Schlöndorff's *The Tin Drum*, Petersen's *The Boat* or Fassbinder's *Lili Marleen*, Fascism and its visual paraphernalia function simultaneously within several (generic, psychological, authorial, economic) discourses, so that the filmic status of Fascism, as signifier and referent becomes quite problematic. This disjunction between sign and referent allows questions of history to become questions of representation in a very precise sense. It allows any number of metaphorical discourses (about outsiders and minorities, about honor and loyalty, family and oedipal rivalry, about show-business and warfare) to be supported by the same set of signs. (*New German Cinema* 303)

In a later essay, however, Elsaesser modified his position, arguing that *Das Boot* was a German "Hollywood" film, and deemed it inconsistent with other New German Cinematic projects such as those of Fassbinder ("*Lili Marleen*" 255). Elsaesser's comments are among the very few scholarly references to *Das Boot*. Apart from these remarks, and note taken of the film's success by Eric Rentschler and Timothy Corrigan, the lack of close readings of this enormously successful film underscores the need for protracted discussions of popular film.

2. Rentschler associates Petersen's hopes with those of other internationally ambitious German filmmakers at that moment, such as Doris Dörrie. He writes: "After a disappointing experience with America (the Columbia Pictures production *Me and Him* [1987]) Doris Dörrie returned to Germany. At the same time, others hunted for the American dream of participation in international markets. . . . Wolfgang Petersen cooperated with Bavaria Films and [Bernd] Eichinger's 'Neuer Constantin' on the sixty million mark project *The Never-Ending Story* (1984) based on Michael Ende's best-seller. With its special effects, the ambitious undertaking was supposed to be a blockbuster German neo-film that would directly compete with *Star Wars* and *Close Encounters of the Third Kind*. Ende referred to the resulting film as a 'gigantic melodrama made of kitsch, felt and plastic'" ("Film der achtziger Jahre" 296).

WORKS CITED

Adorno, Theodor. "What Does Coming to Terms with the Past Mean?" Translated by Timothy Bahti and Geoffrey Hartman. In *Bitburg in Moral and Political Perspective*, edited by Geoffrey Hartman, 114–29. Bloomington: Indiana University Press, 1986.

Binding, Rudolf G. "Schlacht—Das Maß." In *Dichtungen*. Bielefeld and Leipzig: Velhagen and Klasing, 1941.

Buchheim, Lothar-Günter. *The Boat*. Translated by Denver and Helen Lindley. New York: Alfred A. Knopf, 1975. (Translation of *Das Boot* [Munich: Piper, 1973].)

———. *U-Boat War*. Translated by Gudie Lawaetz. New York: Knopf, 1978.

Corrigan, Timothy. *New German Film: The Displaced Image*. Bloomington: Indiana University Press, 1983.

Davidson, John E. "Hegemony and Cinematic Strategy." In *Perspectives on German Cinema*, edited by Terri Ginsberg and Kristen Moana Thompson, 48–71. New York: G. K. Hall, 1996.

Elsaesser, Thomas. *New German Cinema: A History*. New Brunswick, N.J.: Rutgers University Press, 1989.

———. "*Lili Marleen*: Fascism and the Film Industry." In *Perspectives on German Cinema*, edited by Terri Ginsberg and Kristen Moana Thompson, 253–76. New York: G. K. Hall, 1996.

Freud, Sigmund. *Interpretation of Dreams*. New York: Avon, 1965.

———. "Mourning and Melancholia." In *General Psychological Theory*, 164–79. New York: Collier, 1963.

Habermas, Jürgen. "Defusing the Past: A Politico-Cultural Tract." In *Bitburg in Moral and Political Perspective*, edited by Geoffrey Hartman, 43–51. Bloomington: Indiana University Press, 1986.

Homans, Peter. *The Ability to Mourn: Disillusionment and the Social Origins of Psychoanalysis*. Chicago: University of Chicago Press, 1989.

Mitscherlich, Alexander, and Margarete Mitscherlich. *The Inability to Mourn: Principles of Collective Behavior*. Translated by Beverley R. Placzek. New York: Grove, 1975. (Translation of *Die Unfähigkeit zu Trauern: Grundlagen kollektiven Verhaltens*. [Munich: Piper, 1967].)

Petersen, Wolfgang, with Ulrich Greiwe. *Ich liebe die großen Geschichten: vom "Tatort" bis nach Hollywood*. Köln: Kiepenheuer und Witsch, 1997.

"Remarks of President Reagan at Bergen Belsen." In *Bitburg in Moral and Political Perspective*, edited by Geoffrey Hartman, 253–56. Bloomington: Indiana University Press, 1986.

"Remarks of President Reagan to Regional Editors." In *Bitburg in Moral and Political Perspective*, edited by Geoffrey Hartman, 239–40. Bloomington: Indiana University Press, 1986.

Rentschler, Eric. "Film der achtziger Jahre." In *Geschichte des Deutschen Films*, edited by Wolfgang Jacobsen, Anton Kaes, and Hans Helmut Prinzler, 285–322. Stuttgart: Metzler, 1993.

———. "How American Is It?" In *Perspectives on German Cinema*, edited by Terri Ginsberg and Kristen Moana Thompson, 277–94. New York: G. K. Hall, 1996.

Santner, Eric. "Alexander and Margarete Mitscherlich's *Die Unfähigkeit zu trauern* Is Published." In *Yale Companion to Jewish Writing and Thought in German Culture*, edited by Sander Gilman and Jack Zipes, 736–41. New Haven, Conn.: Yale University Press, 1997.

Theweleit, Klaus. *Male Fantasies*. Translated by Stephen Conway. Minneapolis: University of Minnesota Press, 1987.

Thomas, Kevin. "The Men Who Launched the Movie." *Los Angeles Times*, 2 May 1982, Cal 22.
Wagener, Hans. "Soldaten zwischen Gehorsam und Gewissen. Kriegsromane und Tagebücher." In *Gegenwartsliteratur und Drittes Reich: Deutsche Autoren in der Auseinandersetzung mit der Vergangenheit*, edited by Hans Wagener, 241–64. Stuttgart: Philip Reclam, 1977.
Young, Robert S. "A Sailor Views *Das Boot*." *Los Angeles Times*, 2 May 1982, Cal 22, 24.

FILMOGRAPHY

Air Force One. Dir. Wolfgang Petersen. Columbia Pictures, 1997.
Apocalypse Now. Dir. Francis Ford Coppola. Zoetrope, 1979.
Black and White Like Day and Night [Schwarz und Weiß wie Tage und Nächte]. Dir. Wolfgang Petersen. Westdeutscher Rundfunk, 1978.
Das Boot. Dir. Wolfgang Petersen. Bavaria Film 1981, 1997.
Casualties of War. Dir. Brian de Palma. Columbia, 1989.
Crimson Tide. Dir. Tony Scott. Simpson/Bruckheimer, 1995.
Cross of Iron. Dir. Sam Peckinpah. EMI, 1977.
The Deer Hunter. Dir. Michael Cimino. MCA/Universal, 1978.
First Blood. Dir. Ted Kotcheff. Carolco, 1982.
The Hunt for Red October. Dir. John McTiernan. Paramount, 1990.
In the Line of Fire. Dir. Wolfgang Petersen. Columbia Pictures, 1993.
Lili Marleen. Dir. Rainer Werner Fassbinder. Bayerischer Rundfunk, 1981.
The Marriage of Maria Braun [Die Ehe der Maria Braun]. Dir. Rainer Werner Fassbinder. Filmverlag der Autoren, 1979.
Me and Him [Ich und Er]. Dir. Doris Dörrie. Neuer Constantin and Columbia, 1987.
The Never-Ending Story [Die unendliche Geschichte]. Dir. Wolfgang Petersen. Neuer Constantin and Warner Brothers, 1984.
Platoon. Dir. Oliver Stone. Hemdale, 1986.
Saving Private Ryan. Dir. Steven Spielberg. DreamWorks SKG and Amblin Entertainment, 1998.
A Time to Love and a Time to Die. Dir. Douglas Sirk. Universal International, 1958.
The Tin Drum [Die Blechtrommel]. Dir. Volker Schlöndorff. Bioskop, 1979.
U-571. Dir. Jonathan Mostow. MCA/ Universal, 2000.

Das Boot: The Director's Cut is distributed by Columbia Tristar Video and is widely available on both video and DVD.

CHAPTER 13

Crime and the Cynical Solution

Black Comedy, Critique, and the Spirit of Self-Concern in Recent German Film

John E. Davidson

The problems of studying the "popular" are notoriously vexing. Tzvetan Todorov (1977) claims that the popular in literature is an arena where there is no tension between genre and artwork. The individual popular work succeeds because it exemplifies the genre rather than reshaping it, as a piece of high literature would. He is then able to argue that a logical rather than historical movement identifies a popular genre such as detective fiction. The curiosity that centers the "whodunit" gives way to the suspense of the "thriller," which finally generates a synthesis in the "suspense novel." What determines this movement is the elevation of one type's points of concern to "pure form" (52). Thus, the whodunit's all-important original crime becomes merely a formal excuse for the action of the thriller, which adds milieu and violence to the mix; then milieu, emptied of significance, becomes the starting point for the suspense novel. Though Todorov's Hegelian attempt to revitalize genre through a typology of detective fiction fails to take into account the complicated history of detective fiction and the historical specificities of (for example) the hard-boiled tradition, his analysis contains insights that will be useful for the following study of socially critical crime comedies. We will trace a similar pattern in post-World War II cinema, one moving from an attitude of satirical criticism to self-critique and finally a self-affirmation. The final two phases have entered the realm of black comedy.

Gerd Henninger has delineated a black humor tradition in post-World War II West German literature using "absurdity" and "death" as the twin markers of this form. His scheme is problematic in part because it sees certain post-World War II authors as conduits of a displaced public trauma in the wake of the war, conduits that enable a cathartic effect with their work. Nevertheless, his idea that black humor is a force in contemporary German-language literature certainly seems sound, and absurdity and death will be useful markers to take note of in our analyses. Yet in this chapter we are not interested in generic definitions in the narrow sense, nor will we participate in the bickering about whose national tradition can lay a longer claim to the genre.[1] The rubric "black humor" corresponds here to a kind of attitude that has reappeared often in cultural history, bearing the marks of both the critique and the cynicism that Peter Sloterdijk discusses in his *Critique of Cynical Reason.* As Andreas Huyssen points out in the introduction to the English translation, Sloterdijk gives this eternally returning sentiment some historical specificity by always thinking in reference to the late 1960s and 1970s, even though he places the weight of his examples squarely in the Weimar Republic. The reason for this parallel would be the willingness of the postrevolutionary intellectuals (say, post-1923 on the one hand and post-1968 on the other) to return to a distanced, cynical participation in a system despite their full knowledge of its corrupt nature. In what follows I explore the role black humor has in mediating the relationship between a real and grounded critique that Sloterdijk, borrowing from the Greeks, terms "kynicism" and the enlightened false consciousness coming out of the post-World War II era that he calls "cynicism," that is, between self-critique and an attitude of self-concern once best exemplified by Friedrich Nietzsche in *Ecce Homo.* This attitude resurges noticeably in postwall cinema, and I want to put this resurgence into historical context by considering different moments of humor in post–World War II German film. I will not be arguing that this development follows a unique historical progression, for both the logic of forms and the historical circumstances play a role here;[2] nonetheless, in the half century between 1949 and 1999 we do see a telling parallel between the socioeconomic zeitgeist and the formal address to the audience that anchors the satirical criticism, self-critique, and then self-concern in these comedies.

As has been true in most areas of *Germanistik* concerned with the twentieth century, work on German film has been a very serious affair. The reasons for this are obvious and important, but the effect of such seriousness has been self-limitation. For example, the Adenauer era was long written off as having no cinematic significance because it did not examine the past, yet it produced many real classics of German film, some of which indeed engaged in serious political criticism. Among others, *Roses for the State Prosecutor [Rosen für den Staatsanwalt]* (Wolfgang Staudte, 1959) looks through a glass darkly at the hidden crimes of Germans past and present, provoking a laughter that is not (or not only) cathartic but scathing. There is no mistaking its razor-sharp attacks on West German society that are packaged in a more enjoyable, yet no less frightening form than heavy-handed works like John Brahm's *The Golden Pestilence [Die goldene Pest]* (1954) or Staudte's *The Beacon [Leuchtfeuer]* (1954). *Roses* tells the story of Rudi Kleinschmidt, who wanders across the Federal Republic as a street hawker without a steady home or identity. He hitches a ride one day that happens to take him through a city in which he has an old flame. While there he runs up against the locally prominent state's attorney, who has managed to hide his past participation in the Nazi judicial system in order to continue his careerist rise in the new Germany. Our wanderer knows firsthand about that participation, because this very man had condemned him to death in the late phases of the war for stealing two bars of chocolate. This earnest situation allows a dark comedy to arise, and the prosecutor twists and turns to try to protect his position as we watch with both glee and astonishment at the normality of these circumstances. After trying to rob Rudi of his livelihood in order to drive him out of town, the prosecutor himself must flee, flinging his judicial robes on the courthouse steps as he disappears.

If, as Henninger comments, absurdity and death are the two main poles around which black humor functions, then *Roses* might well qualify, for the absurdity of the death penalty handed down at the beginning of the film is insisted upon unmistakably. Yet, I would not use the label, for both absurdity and death are eventually chased out of the film and the problem is made individual rather than systemic. The criticism in this film remains satirical precisely because the crimes are seen not as being terminally absurd and structural, but as being individually grounded, contingent, and manageable. Furthermore, Staudte's film clearly aims at further participation in the system. While criticizing the potential of continuities within the judicial system, and poking gentle fun at the weakness of the solid citizens of the Federal

Republic, the major subtext of the film is the domestication of Rudi. This implies not simply settling down but participating in the new economy of savings, investments, and returns, and becoming an entrepreneur like his friend Vera. The final resolution of the love story shows Rudi getting out of the truck that was to take him on the road again to embrace the woman who has worked her way up from waitress to be the owner, and modernizer, of the little bar that has been the center of the story. Rudi's impulse has been to live hand to mouth, to spend his day's earnings the following evening, and to avoid anything that looks like the normal rooted life; now he is settling, saving, and spending. Thus the clear moral stance against the prosecutor is coupled with the insistence on the daily participation in the world that brought him forth. This sense of a continuing participation in the society that is being criticized corresponds precisely to the liberal attitude of the socialized market economy. As in most of Papas Kino, the morally superior position of those who want to expose crimes is never formally in doubt in Staudte's comedy. Screenwriter Wolfgang Kohlhaase remarks succinctly on the popular nature of this kind of comedy, which requires that the audience and author be largely of one mind about the object of comedy's barbs (Schenk 167).[3]

Contrary to the common wisdom that assumes the New German Cinema merely preaches to the converted, the easy moral security afforded the viewer in Papas Kino is called into question by the new cineastes. Its critical examination of this continued participation in liberal models arrives at a level of critique through black humor by insisting on the terminal absurdity of the revolt within the system. Much more than in the work from the economic miracle, these filmmakers turn their gaze upon themselves, that is, on the intellectual Left and its desire for revolution mediated through culture, which is inherently conservative. At the very least, they want to examine as best they can the self-indulgence embedded in certain moments of their own resistance. While many critics have spoken of the reflexive nature of the New German Cinema and pointed out that this was never a unified movement, much less the expression of a common political or aesthetic sensibility, few have considered the way this self-depreciating humor balances its critical attitude. My initial contention will be that some of these important films aim a critique at the social totality without turning that project into a self-assuring one or the vehicles of that critique into (heroic) figures of identification within the representations themselves.

"This region has torn me apart, and I'm staying until all of you notice it!" insists the artistic main character about his Bavarian homeland in Herbert Achternbusch's *Bavaria, Adieu* (*Servus Bayern*, 1974). Achternbusch has long been one of the most bitterly humorous artists in German film, consistently deadpanning his way through all of the major issues of his day, local, national, and international.[4] In this film, the small-mindedness of the local population causes a writer to develop a block, after which he wanders about his village as if he were the ghost of a conscience that his neighbors do not have. It seems quite an indictment of the cruelty that can go hand in hand with the pettiness of parochialism, at a time when many were seeking to radicalize the cinema with a "new regionalism" (Geisler 29), and the artist's final departure for foreign shores might be seen as an embrace of the international. Yet that move is blatant self-parody, since the writer goes into complete isolation in Greenland to experience warmth after the frigidity of his Bavarian homeland. Furthermore, neither the lead character (played by Achternbusch himself) nor his project is presented in a particularly sympathetic light. The extreme self-centeredness of his concerns leaves the viewer no easy point of identification, no place to feel assured of being in the right. The crimes of his fellow Bavarians are not just in this man's head, but they are also there, and his obsession with himself seems just as false as the world that is abhorrent to him.

We can make a preliminary distinction between satire, of the type found in *Roses*, and black humor, of the type found in *Bavaria, Adieu*. Satire has a self-righteous audience, black comedy a self-critical one. I am calling black comedy the humorous variation showing the world to be powerful and yet insubstantial, which happens when the popular runs up against itself in a manner that structures self-critique. It confronts us with the question of our own participation in that world and, thus, urges us into a comical yet uncomfortable position. As we will see when we begin our analysis of postwall films, black humor can also remove its own self-critical impulse if it pushes beyond this recognition of the problems to an attitude of profound distance. That such a distance is neither desired nor facilitated in the black humor of the New German Cinema can be established by further scrutiny of *Bavaria, Adieu*, in which long takes resemble a tableau vivant centered on a single still life, a mug shot balancing out the Bavarian "crime" of tearing him apart with the profile of the man arrested in his pursuit of art and change.

The writer's obsession drives him to want his moral superiority to be visible in his self-presentation, so we are treated to many shots of his stoic visage in medium close-up. Yet the camera at times places the viewer in a position of enforced coincidence with this figure, most disturbingly at the moment that his moral superiority clearly breaks down. As the writer's wife, who runs the local pub, berates him for his jealousy, mistreatment, and inability to see to her needs, she is filmed from precisely his point of view in a take of exceptionally long duration. For nearly three minutes she talks to "us," moving about the bar cleaning up but occasionally stopping to address the camera directly; the camera remains absolutely still during this take. Abruptly, the film cuts to an extreme close-up of the writer's eyeball ("ours" as well, given the previous point of view), which occupies the screen for only a second or two, when another cut returns us to the former position of watching and listening to the wife for another full minute. The address to the audience, and the uncomfortable conflation of the viewers with this egocentric figure, changes our relationship with the artist entirely. He has shifted from being a comic imp disturbing the balance of this sleepy village to being an extension of the self-obsessed viewer, whose comfortable position of distanced criticism is shattered, forced into a position of self-critique. Thus, when the viewer is asked throughout the film to examine the artist's desire to be noticed in these medium shots of very long duration that have no apparent connection to the plot (such shots recur often in Achternbusch's work), what becomes visible is an image of a figure lost to reflection, which also becomes a critical self-reflection on the viewer. He maintains his self-obsessed pose right to the end, an absurd death at the hands of a fake polar bear.

Similar to Achternbusch, Alexander Kluge consistently explores a social order in need of critique over and against a self-centered rebel, also often relying on long takes of characters. In Kluge's films these tend to be uncomfortable close-ups that bring the viewer into the characters' immediate proximity, made more disturbing because he does not distinguish between establishment figures and his protagonists, between the professor and Anita G. in *Yesterday Girl [Abschied von Gestern]* (1966), for example. The undertaking so often critically associated with Kluge—namely, developing a dry pedagogy to politicize cinema culture—is called into doubt through a recognition of his techniques of humor. In *Artists under the Big Top, Perplexed [Artisten unter der Zirkuskuppel, ratlos]* (1968), Leni Peickert sets up her modern circus of alternative history, an enterprise that falters, among other things, on its needing financing by corporate and governmental sponsors. They have developed acts that fall far outside popular notions of entertainment, among others a particularly brilliant rendition of the execution of Mexico's Emperor Maximillian acted out with toys. The film itself shifts between blatant and obscure entertainment episodes as well, often revolving around coming to terms with German history. In one sequence we see circus elephants in their tents while hearing their innermost thoughts in voice-over: they are obsessed, of course, with never forgetting. It would be a mistake, however, to see this (only) as a trite bit of overt symbolism referring to the need to examine the German past, for it both insists on and lampoons that need simultaneously. The scene in which Leni tries to spirit these animals away so that they will not be repossessed by her financial bankers makes this point again by using the film language of silent comedy to show the farcical nature of the undertaking. As we consider the resistance involved in the wry images of stealing the elephants of history, perhaps we must ask ourselves the ultimately Brechtian question about culture—what is the crime of robbing a circus compared with that of founding a circus?

If montage is the key to developing a new relationship between the viewer and history, as is often noted about Kluge's work, then there are intimate camera positions and long interludes without cuts that ask the viewer to confront the confounding nature of that project within the given historical conjuncture. Picturesque shots from a stationary camera of the characters at rest, such as those of the contemplative Leni, sitting hands-on-chin on the edge of the ring in her absurd circus costume, show that the attitude of morally informed rebellion is a contradictory task in this cultural context, one that is quietly, absurdly, funny. We have much the same sense when faced with images of Anita G. looking down in the courtroom after sparring with the judge in *Yesterday Girl* or of Gabi Teichert sitting with her shovel, tired from her naïve attempt to unearth the "real" German history in the omnibus film *Germany in Autumn [Deutschland im Herbst]* (1977), later expanded in *The Patriot [Die Patriotin]* (1979).

Ironically, nowhere is the effective deployment of Kluge's self-critical humor more evident than in *Germany in Autumn*. This goes well beyond Gabi trying to shovel in the frozen fields of German history. For example, interlaced between the docudrama-style segments of a young woman's brush with a terrorist on the run and the documentary footage of Max Frisch speaking to the SPD (Social Democratic Party), we see Gabi Teichert furiously taking notes, a fictional send-up cut right into the reality of the liberal project. Along with the archeology of the historical moment, the central figures in Kluge's black comedies always show the near impossibility of using spectacular media to evoke a new relationship between the audience and history under the capitalist mode of production. At the end of *Artists under the Big Top, Perplexed*, Leni Peickert begins to move into the world of television, and is soon to come in contact with Korti, the brains of the media system in Germany. The final verdict on the project of revolutionizing culture, a project in which the audience of the film is assumed to be fully invested, remains in doubt. Does this impending meeting with Korti indicate that the Leni Peickerts of the world will have changed the system or have been co-opted? The joke seems to be ambiguously on us, as the lecture on the complexity of culture's history, which begins in a TV studio as the film ends, is about the plot of Verdi's *Troubadour* and delivered by a pedant of the oldest school: the intercut shots of a smirking Leni do nothing to dispel our discomfort at this image of the revolutionized media, however humorous.[5]

To this point I have argued that in particular the black comedies of the New German Cinema use formal techniques to question exactly the audience that might think itself to be securely in line with leftist political criticism, confronting "us" through the filmic representation of the attitude of the main figures. These formal devices invite us to pursue the critical path back to the undertaking of the filmmakers, and ultimately to anyone enjoying the position of the opposition, as continuing participants in this world. In doing so these works hope to laugh their way around the kind of repressive tolerance that enabled the critical voices in the humor of Adenauer cinema. We should remember that this earlier period of liberal economic expansion also was dominated by the policy of containment, which was the cornerstone of the Western (U.S.) strategy in the cold war. As a situation of permanently structured binary opposition made concrete with the building of the Berlin Wall in 1961, the cold war served as a vital structuring principle for much of the culture produced in both East and West Germany at the time. The black humor in the New German Cinema violates the moralizing imperatives inherent in that structure, which admits only those "for us" and those "against us."[6] The struggle for containment at the level of film form is precisely where the historical resonance of those structuring principles can be found. In these black comedies that structure fails to hold, even while they carve out a position of self-consciously uncomfortable participation within it.

In the postwall euphoria the fate of this kind of critique, which refused to choose sides while remaining within the liberal camp, can be briefly illustrated through a comparison of two films by Niklaus Schilling: *The Willi Busch Report [Der Willi Busch Report]* (1980) and its postwall update, *German Fever [Deutschfieber]* (1992). We find the view that a symbiotic relationship exists between the state and media/corporate interests, on the one hand, and their opponents, on the other, again at the heart of *The Willi Busch Report*. Schilling's Willi Busch owns and operates a small newspaper in Friedheim, a little town situated in immediate proximity to the East German border. The paper is being squeezed out of existence by corporate competition and by being at the end of the line in the middle of nowhere since the inner-German border was erected. In order to boost circulation, Busch begins to commit and report petty crimes, a strategy that eventually snowballs into a full-blown investigation of espionage and sabotage, with reports that the stability in the region is threatened. Though Busch seems initially to have an enlightened view of the town's situation, his stability is questionable as well. A chronic drinker, yet a charismatic character whose one-seater Messerschmidt car is hailed far and wide, Busch soon cannot distinguish between his own intrigues and those of others. Schilling's film takes a savage look at the paranoia of the cold war mentality, the propensity of the (unscrupulous) press to perpetuate the crimes it reports for profit, and the complicity of liberals in the cold war, despite all sympathies with the East. The viewer is brought to share and then to question Busch's cynical vision of the world in sequences that intercut medium shots of him typing with point of view shots through his binoculars at the "activities" around him, from which he concocts the day's yellow journalism. The self-critical darkness of this comedy arises as death and absurdity take root around him in such a way that neither Busch nor the viewer can be completely sure where the border is, mental or political.

It seems no coincidence that the main character here is named after the nineteenth-century cartoonist who is one of Germany's most popular purveyors of dark humor. With his motto of "what is popular *[beliebt]* is also allowed," the historical Wilhelm Busch made comics that cut across the various borders erected to maintain order and discipline in the social structures of the German Empire. Regimes of class, gender, government, and knowledge take quite a beating in his work, as do the naughty boys who are often the vehicles for showing up those boundaries. The choice seems an apt one for Schilling's impish character of the early 1980s; more recently the figure seems somewhat lost and out of place. The dissolution of the division between East and West is no longer a phantom of the protagonist's mind, but rather built into the fabric of the *German Fever*. The aged and now reclusive Willi Busch emerges to wander through crowds coming across the opened border, occasionally enjoying a bit of celebrity, and rediscovering a daughter he has never known. It is indeed the end of history as Willi Busch has known it, a history that had been physically and temporally bounded by the policy of containment. There is no crime to report in the euphoria of spontaneous reunification: the borders have all broken down and the people fill to capacity the canal that had separated them. It comes as no surprise that for this New German cineaste, working in cooperation with the nearly defunct East German DEFA, film history can only repeat itself as farce here, not as black comedy.

In postwall cinema, critical perspectives do not seem to have opened themselves up to this humorous style of presentation. Coming to terms with the German past, where it continues to exist at all, has become largely a matter of dealing with the East German past, which remains by and large a matter of utmost seriousness, allegory, or farce.[7] The same could be said of the issues of reunification, depicted as "crimes" that are treated either as dark or as comedy, but rarely as both at once (Misselwitz; Schlingensief; and Buck). Where one does find black humor in postwall cinema, it replaces the historically specific perspective on crime that we found in the Adenauer and New German Cinemas with a generic one—the formula becomes the context, and our relation to the genre becomes the issue. As Todorov pointed out in his discussion of detective literature, the key elements of concern become merely an excuse for generic form, causing a different type of form to emerge.

Matthias Glasner's *Sexy Sadie* (1996) and Volker Einrauch's *The Mother of the Killer [Die Mutter des Killers]*(1997) clearly have particular generic traditions in mind. Each has the schematic structure and images of a newly established genre (based on fresh Hollywood faces such as Quentin Tarantino) to draw on and does so with hilarious impunity.[8] The former works in the vein of criminal-redemption movies, involving a journey that brings the convict from beyond the pale to the glow of forgiveness. The latter works similarly, but instead of the road-to-renewal movie it evokes the double-cross crime comedy in a lower-class milieu. These pregiven forms make them more readily (although not immediately) accessible to a broader audience. The participation of stars with a high degree of visibility (Corinna Harfouch, Jürgen Vogel, Peter Lohmeyer, Richie Müller, Thomas Heinze, and others) and increased advertising budgets certainly play a significant role in their appeal as well. Yet we must also take note here of their strategies of spectator address, which invite the viewer to become aligned with the narrative perspective in a celebration of a radical individuality that seems unique and self-sufficient. Both these films empower the audience at all levels to feel that they are "in the know" and thus to laugh at the victims of the structures represented, while maintaining the impression that these structures are necessarily inalterable. The mechanism delivering these multiple levels of spectator address is a kind of reflexivity, but the reflexivity in this new popular presentation is limited to generic structures rather than formal or even topical components, and becomes the basis of an affirmative self-citation rather than self-critique. While showing the problems of self-citation as a critical project, I also contend that by making this move to genre, postwall black comedy, in some ways despite itself, recasts containment yet again and thus bears traces of the historical conjuncture that can and should be read critically.

Sexy Sadie takes place in Berlin and tells the story of the last days of an arch criminal named Edgar. Learning in the opening scene that he has but a few days to live due to a brain dysfunction, he breaks out of prison, taking his doctor with him as hostage, chauffeur, and later, companion. The news that "Edgar's out" spreads like wildfire, often disseminated by a hand emerging from behind the camera, and reaches a number of seemingly ordinary citizens, who all have reason to exact revenge upon this man. Edgar refers to himself as "the most unscrupulous guy of all," and, despite his seemingly moderate behavior in reference to Lucy, his doctor, we learn that he has indeed been without a conscience. Each encounter with figures from his past paints anew the picture of Edgar as the ultimate villain, running the gamut of generic evil deeds: he broke a woman's heart and ruined her career; he killed his foster family; he blinded a coworker with a cutting torch; he killed a little girl's father and then made her love him as if he were her real father; and he cut out a man's tongue. The attempts of these figures to get back at Edgar lead him on a killing spree that he did not intend, for he has broken out only to have a few nice days before he dies and, perhaps, to seek some kind of closure.

In addition to being the most unscrupulous murderer in Berlin, Edgar is also a vessel of the particularly German variation of bourgeois normality *(Spießigkeit)*. Two repeated motifs bring this to the fore: Edgar's quotations of wisdom from his father, and his regular habits. In one incident he goes to a club to hear a chanteuse, who eventually pulls a gun on him, insisting that he accompany her one more time on the piano before dying. At the moment when the woman has again been won over to him through the passion in her own singing, Edgar stops his accompaniment and, after a brief embrace, kills her. Asked why he does it, since the woman would not have shot him at that point, he responds that his "Daddy" told him, "when things are serious, you can't put your trust in a woman's love." Asked why he even went there that night, he says, "I always go there on Sundays." Like a contemporary update of Brecht's MacHeath, Edgar's mania for regularity nearly does him in at this point. In fact, the regularity rooted in this bourgeois solidity finally does do him in. When the medicine that keeps his seizures in check runs out, he plans to take his own life in a quiet spot on Berlin's famous Peacock Island, but the doctor reveals that he does not necessarily need to die. It turns out that she has been slowly poisoning him by means of the prescription she began giving him while still in prison. Lucy did this in order to rid herself of her obsession with Edgar, but then felt guilty about it and developed the injections to counteract his pain. If he simply stops taking the pills, he should recover completely. This makes little impression on Edgar, who gets ready to carry out his plan to shoot himself, saying for the third time: "My Daddy always told me that once you decide something, you should stick to it."[9]

Sexy Sadie teases us with two potential historical frames of reference that should be introduced before going further. First, we learn early in the film that Edgar was incarcerated in 1989 and has "missed the [early] 1990s." Given the somewhat schizoid nature of his character as the most unscrupulous and the most mundane one, we might want to see him as the embodiment of a violent German normality that was temporarily suspended during the initial period of euphoria surrounding unification. This normality could be seen as East German or, following up on the view that Edgar is a contemporary MacHeath, as the individual-ized violence inherent in the controlled liberalism of cold war West Germany. His reemergence in the mid-1990s would be sig-nificant in such a reading, since the film questions the unique-ness of Edgar's character even as it builds on the cult of his personality: everyone in the postwall age seems to be infected with Edgar's fabled self-interest and violence, indicating the dis-persal of his values in reunited, neoliberal Germany. The second historical reference to which the film gestures is the possibility that Lucy stands in for all those obsessed with the utmost horrors of the past. Lucy becomes fascinated with the most unscrupulous one, the one with the ability to perpetuate the most heinous crimes against humanity, and thus she could be an allegorical figure for fascination with (perpetrators of) the Holocaust. This reading would mean that the film assumes such a fascination to be dishonest about its investment in coming to terms with the past and, hence, dangerously prone to falling into barbarism itself.

Both the immediate political and the more distant histor-ical frames of reference here suggest ways to make a reading of this film richer. They also offer up multifaceted moments for au-dience members with particular (intellectual) interests to latch onto. Yet, just as *Sexy Sadie* never really directly addresses the postwall situation, it also never directly addresses the historical specific of the crimes of National Socialism, since that would ex-ceed the limits of generic representation. These elements are sim-ply tossed in as spices in the mix; what is (always) at stake in this film is *only* the world of representation itself. I do not say this merely to dismiss *Sexy Sadie* as a work in which the world is all text, where pastiche is the only mode of procedure. Understand-ing Glasner's generic play opens a reading in which the film offers a darkly comic exposé on the relation of the cultural medium to violence, a reading supported, for example, by the discussion of the new possibilities of cable television, of which Edgar has no conception.

Significant in this regard is that Lucy serves as the overt surrogate for the viewer within the film, making all would-be as-sassins stop to explain *why* they want to kill Edgar. Thus, she provides the mechanism that satisfies the viewers' morbid curios-ity about his deeds. Indeed, even as she rids Germany of its most unscrupulous character, Lucy takes on his lack of scruples—assuming, of course, she ever had any. Lucy is every bit as schiz-oid as her captor, since she has saved the brain, and occasionally takes on the character of, her dead sister, Sadie. As Edgar is the bourgeois element of the criminal world, so is Lucy the criminal element of the bourgeois world and, more importantly, of the film-going audience. Seeing that he plans to kill himself anyway, she asks if she can do it. "Could you live with yourself, if you do that?" he asks. "I don't think I could live with myself if I don't do it," is her reply. The idea of denying herself this opportunity would be a greater crime than killing this man. The camera rests briefly in medium close-up on her after she dispatches him, showing only a face of satisfied curiosity, and, as she then walks off, the film ends.

Certainly, absurdity and death are the mainstays of this black humor. Yet, in *Sexy Sadie* this absurdity remains within the realm of generic necessity, and the pleasure it generates arises from a secure and unquestioned love of completing the form in the face of its obvious ridiculousness. Though Lucy is our surrogate in the film, the criticism is all at the level of character: we are not aligned with her formally to any degree that becomes uncomfortable, and so she both keeps us in and out of the film. The play with generic violence here remains, well, generic, pro forma, and the stance over and against the main figures takes account of nothing besides what is presented in the film. Glasner does not make the step that marked the examples from the New German Cinema, the step to self-critique directed outside the world of the representation, for his positioning of the audience invites it to be distanced from and "in control of" the narrative perspective at all times. If we look for evidence of the critique embedded in the film's formal properties other than those of the narrative, we find that long takes of the protagonists from medium distance occur here, much as they did in *Servus Bayern*; however, in *Sexy Sadie* their use always stays confined within the formal systems of the film, both narrative and stylistic. While we do not necessarily know the thoughts that are occupying the protagonists at the points at which these sequences arise, there is never any doubt that they are contained within the representation. First Edgar sits in a chair in the hotel room, glancing at what establishing shots and an earlier shot-reverse-shot sequence have shown to be the bedroom where Lucy is sleeping. Placing that room in the background of this shot (and "pointing" to it with Edgar's glances), Glasner invites the viewer to fill in his contemplation as part of the narrative: whether to kill or leave her, or where to go next. Since his next move is to wake her decisively and take her to the nightclub, our surmise seems retrospectively justified by his decision, and thus we are more eager to participate in a later sequence, in which the roles are reversed.

Again, a shot-reverse-shot progression locks us firmly within the narrative, with Lucy sitting in a similar position in a similar hotel room, looking in the direction of Edgar, sleeping but unseen. She is also thinking about what to do with him, and decides: after retrieving Edgar's pills from the bedroom, she leaves him—albeit temporarily. Although these are moments of decision that have moral implications, they are moments over which we have a sovereign distance because they are fully contained in a world in which morality plays no role. A kind of identification is called for by these shots, but nothing asks us to consider our alignment with these figures; on the contrary, we are asked to advance the narrative at these moments, furthering our sense of control over and distance from it, which lessens any self-critical potential in the duration and construction of these images. Finally, there is the brief sequence just after Lucy has shot her victim. Nothing in these shots causes us to look beyond the frame of the representation, unless perhaps it is the proximity of the final sequence to "The End" on the screen. Yet, if we are asked to reflect retrospectively on our desire as viewers to participate in this (fascination with) violence, the request comes from a self-affirming narrative stance that claims to be above the petty moralizing attitude of such questioning, and that is the attitude we've been invited to share all along. With the crimes of the most unscrupulous as a backdrop and as an endpoint, *Sexy Sadie* never relents in its pursuit of pulp crime fiction's absurdity, managing, in true Nietzschean style, both to reject and to adopt the great imperative of self-concern.

Volker Einrauch's *The Mother of the Killer* begins with the final words of a similar kind of pulp story, words being typed on an old machine: "Even the lowest dog can piss on the proudest dead man." The author is Theo Bono, who mails off the short story (entitled, of course, "The Mother of the Killer") and then proceeds to fake his own death in order to commit the perfect murder with his lover. In a bit of dumb luck, the story wins "The Golden Canon" after his "death," the big prize in a crime-fiction contest sponsored by a local car dealership. Despite being able to write with such apparent aplomb about murder, Theo is incapable of shooting the old man whose young wife and insurance money are the apples of his eye. This inability causes his plan to fail and will eventually get him killed, having only briefly tasted his fame.

As the reader will surmise, *The Mother of the Killer* is about losers all the way around, all of whom are "lowest dogs," even though some are more sympathetic than others. Eddie is the most likeable figure here, the central character we follow through the seediest residential and most stifling industrial sections of Hamburg in his pursuit of alcohol, Theo, and Theo's "widow," Olga. He spends his time trying to avoid the wrath of his own wife's boyfriend, Bomber, to patch up relations with his mother, and to keep things together at his job at a funeral home. These are not easy tasks. Bomber, the brute out to avenge the fright that his girlfriend experienced when Eddie pulled an unloaded gun on her, waits outside his front door. His mother says that he is a curse to all those around him, and proves as much by using her homemade rhubarb schnapps to heal the mark of that curse spreading on Olga's neck. (That "wart" looks like a passion mark, which is an embarrassing bit of stained skin on the day after your husband dies.) She also sings the praises of her other boy, who spends his time marching around their yard with a shovel shouldered, wearing a Confederate Army cap and burying small dead things. The mother's comments stoke a sibling rivalry that neither Eddie nor the viewer can really understand, but certainly they provide us the generic motifs of absurdity and death necessary. Eddie returns to work (after several drinks in transit), where his boss, who is in on Theo's plot, then tries to trick him into using his embalming expertise to make another corpse pass for Theo. Despite all this adversity, Eddie remains the figure endowed somehow with a spark of human decency in this milieu. His irresponsibility (drinking and driving, for example) seems almost understandable, given the dialogue with his mother or with his unpleasant wife. ("Where are you going?" he asks in the film's first exchange. "To fuck. Whadda you think?" she retorts.) Our sense of sympathy for Eddie is the only thing that seems to lighten the dark contours of this self-described "proletarian comedy" (*Prol-Komödie*).

Nothing enters into this world to indicate that another one might exist: no images of Hamburg as an affluent city, no characters who come from other classes, no sense that class relations might exist at all. Nothing, that is, except the dream behind Theo's plan to get the money and run, a dream illustrated in deep focus fleetingly by the cover of the travel magazine his girlfriend examines. Yet even these are the dreams of losers. This does not mean that there is no resolution to the narrative. The old florist, the target of the plot, returns safely to his shop with his young wife, and Eddie eventually convinces Olga that Theo is still alive and cheating on her, and, thus, is able to convince her of the honesty of his feelings for her. The film ends with a grand reconciliation between Olga, Eddie, his mother, and his brother, so we certainly can speak about a resolution, even, perhaps, a happy ending. Yet nothing about the film displaces the necessary connection between these figures and this milieu, nothing asks us to feel in any sense near to the space offered us through the narrative presentation. Here there are no shots of Eddie in contemplation, for we are steadily in motion, and all the close-ups only further the plot and character development. Our laughter at this film arises from recognizing the generic necessity of these figures within this representation: necessity is the mother of invention, and these characters are necessary for inventing *The Mother of the Killer.*

One element returns twice in this film, however, that not only does not seem to fit, it is an encroachment on the rigorous exclusion of worlds different than Eddie's. When Sylvester, something of a literary ambulance chaser, arrives to tell Olga that her dead husband's short story has won the prize and will be published, his character itself does not seem out of place. Yet on his baseball cap we read the incongruous slogan, roughly, "It's all Nietzsche, isn't it?" ("Alles Nietzsche oder was?"), which the camera keeps centered in the frame for almost the entire sequence of their conversation. No other comment is made on the hat at this point, but it returns in a later discussion between Sylvester and Olga, now drunk from her medicine. Accosted by an angry Eddie wanting to know just who he and this Nietzsche are, Sylvester begins his reply by stating that Nietzsche was a German philosopher, born in 1844. Yet he never mentions his date of death as he goes on to banter back and forth with Olga about the way some authors are born only after they die. Of course, this provides a parody of Theo, whose "death" precedes his birth as an author of pulp fiction, but it is also a clear, if unconscious on Sylvester's part, reference to the Nietzschean maxim: "some are born posthumously" ("einige werden posthum geboren"; Nietzsche 74). So, one might say that *The Mother of the Killer* is a bit of pulp fiction in which Nietzsche is resurrected. "Alles Nietzsche oder was?" opens a window through which we enlist in this film, affirming ourselves as provisional intellectuals in league with the attitude of the film, assuming ourselves to be "in the know," which assumes that others (such as the hapless Sylvester)

are not. The binary world of those with us and against us constantly shifts and reforms itself, yet always with self-certainty
and -affirmation. This is the mechanism at work in an aesthetics
of popular quotation, where quotation serves no other purpose
than offering the possibility of being in the know, referring back
to other works of familiar representation.

The black humor of the New German Cinema held up a
world to critical scrutiny, and with our laughter we oppose it;
however, our opposition is egocentric, like that of the rebels
shown in self-centered self-absorption, and that, too, is held up to
our own, uncomfortable, ridicule. In *Sexy Sadie* and *The Mother
of the Killer*, we are neither of this world nor with the figure
within the representation who thinks he differs from it: the right
attitude is the one of the narrative perspective that we construct,
a constantly shifting attitude of implied aesthetic objectivity.
This Nietzschean moment of identification does not require a
sacrifice of ones self; on the contrary, one is offered the opportunity for self-assertion, self-affirmation, given as many chances as
possible to reject the lowly dogs cynically, those not in the know.
Postwall black humor's cynically reasoned rejections and parodic
pleasures, which mark much of the play with genre and form as
well as much of the camp aesthetic in contemporary cultural
products, take part in this Nietzschean identification. Of course,
there can be no doubt that a great deal has been won for identity
politics through such strategies, and that is as it should be. Yet
there is a danger that the surety of these strategies is anchored in
a deadly "cultural self-evidence" in the literal sense of the term
("kulturelle Selbstverständlichkeit," Engler 262), because it is ultimately only self-concerned.

Self-evidence, constantly giving testimony for the self, is
one answer to a culture of uncertainty masquerading as self-
assurance, and it has a corollary in "necessity": if things are self-
evident, then there seem to be no other choices, and we should
embrace what must be. It is here that I think we find both the
problems and the possibilities for socially motivated criticism in
contemporary black humor. On the one hand, the move to genre
cinema, supposedly responding to the opportunities of the market
and corresponding to "what the people want," furthers the pervasive logic first made famous as a motto of Margaret Thatcher's
neoliberalism—"there are no alternatives." So, we have infinite
possibilities within the world of representation and can take aim
at it from many different angles, yet there is no other choice
about what popular culture and, by extension, our society is

about. Thus we have returned to an attitude prefigured by Nietz-sche: *amor fait* (embrace necessity; Nietzsche 72). Of course, there is one significant difference between his age and ours. In Nietzsche's day, economic liberalism was being furthered, yet was radically divorced from the progressive liberal politics that had accompanied it in the early part of the nineteenth century; today, economic neoliberalism is being heralded *as* progressive and necessary politics by the German state and others pushing the "American model" of fiscal reform. Self-promotion is now the accepted imperative of the day, and the only real crime, so the implicit argument of much contemporary culture goes, is placing limitations on oneself.

I contend that the black humor in the New German Cin-ema should be understood as a critique of liberalism from within, while that in postwall film must be seen in the context of the triumphant march of neoliberalism.[10] This is the form we see re-turning to prominence in the postwall era, which calls forth shift-ing, self-affirmative stances rather than a self-righteous one or self-critical ones. Having said this, I feel that Glasner and Ein-rauch's films also show the potential within the containment of genre to actualize a critique informed by a non-Nietzschean tradi-tion. Black humor in this vein shows up one of the most basic absurdities of our society, namely that of epidemic overproduc-tion, which is just as much a facet of the service and information economies as it was when Marx and Engels diagnosed it as a mainstay of the capitalist mode of production in its industrial phases (Marx and Engels 86). The overproduction of entertain-ment commodities fetishizing death comes into absurd focus here, in a manner that might indicate its structural relationship to cultural production and lived experience. *Sexy Sadie* and *The Mother of the Killer* both take generic material and push it to the point that it shows traces of the deadly and absurd structures that determine it. By remaining focused exclusively within the popu-lar form, they allow the tongue-in-cheek question to arise: "This is inevitable, there are no alternatives: don't we love that it is not us?" And "we" are the surplus value that is contained in our response of laughter.

NOTES

1. The term "black humor" can be traced to André Breton (1950). When it resurfaced as a subject of critical inquiry in the 1960s and 1970s, many scholars concentrated on the U.S. context, seeing in figures like Joseph

Heller, Thomas Pynchon, and Terry Southern the critical consciousness of America at its most edgy. German thinkers were quick to point out the bias in that scholarship, which focused myopically not only on the United States but on the immediately contemporary as well.

2. In addition to Sloterdijk, see Jameson for a theoretical discussion of historically specific repetition in the context of his analysis of recurring debates about cultural realism.

3. Of course, this idea is not specific to Kohlhaase, but it seems especially appropriate since he is speaking in self-critique about the popular failure of *Sunday Drivers [Sonntagsfahrer]* (Klein, 1961), the GDR comedy containing one of DEFA's first and least well received treatments of the building of the Berlin Wall.

4. For an excellent discussion of Achternbusch's use of a "primitive aesthetic" to explore problems of German national culture in the international, post-World War II world, see Gemünden 89–129.

5. Though editorial considerations make it impossible to do so in this space, fully pursuing black humor as an exploration of the tensions between media and revolution would require an extended analysis of Fassbinder's *The Third Generation [Die dritte Generation]* (1979), perhaps his most bitingly political film. Fassbinder leaves no doubt about the effect of the ambiguities that inhabit that relation, and already in the promotional blurbs the director is quoted as saying, "I don't throw bombs, I make films." The film goes on to trace the activities of a terrorist group that is planning its big coup, but which is also thoroughly bourgeois and interwoven in the world of the media it is seeking to overthrow. Given the immediate tendency for voices from across the public sphere and even outside of Germany to misunderstand the radicals as a return of the repression of Nazi violence or, even more daftly, as "Hitler's Childern" (Becker), Fassbinder's film stunningly rejects such easy labeling. It does so even while exercising a chilling critique of the ethos of rebellion that ultimately is grounded in personal gain and tied to the apparatus of state media.

6. As I have argued elsewhere, we need to keep in mind the exclusion of another "third"—the third world—from this structure as a mode of mutual complicity in the forces with (West) and against (East) us (Davidson 1999).

7. For powerful representative examples, see, respectively, Schönemann; Kipping; and Föth.

8. An important aspect of genre is its recognizable, potentially transnational character, particularly given the dominance of Hollywood in many foreign markets. "Genre films are produced after general identification and consecration of a genre substratification, during the limited period when shared textual material and structures lead audiences to interpret films not as separate entities but according to generic expectations and against generic norms" (Altman 53).

9. This brings us to the final twist of the Edgar-as-the-most-heinous spiral. At this last reference to "Daddy," Lucy exclaims in exasperation that he must mean his stepfather, since he didn't even know his real father. Edgar replies: "No, I mean my real father. He used to talk all the time, well, at least while he still had his tongue." In retrospect the viewer realizes the oedipal moment in an earlier, brilliantly over-the top scene that dispatched the tongueless man.

10. U.S. discussions of black humor often link it explicitly to liberalism (see, e.g., Davis). This observation has been used both to bolster and to criticize the style of the writers lumped under this rubric. Perhaps the most famous and virulent attack came from Burton Feldman, who labeled such writers "affluent terrorists," since their material was not nearly dark or comic enough for their time. "Black humor," he writes, "does not differ in its rejection of affluence, but only in rejecting it affluently" (159).

WORKS CITED

Altman, Rick. *Film/Genre*. London: BFI, 1999.

Becker, Jillian. *Hitler's Children : The Story of the Baader-Meinhof Terrorist Gang*. Philadelphia: Lippincott, 1977.

Brecht, Bertolt. *The Three Penny Opera*. Translated by Ralph Mannheim and John Willet. New York: Arcade, 1984.

Breton, André. *Anthologie de l'humour noir*. Paris,: Éditions du Sagittaire, 1950.

Busch, Wilhelm. *Sämtliche Werke in zwei Bänden*. Bielefeld: Bertelsmann, 1982.

Davidson, John E. *Deterritorializing the New German Cinema*. Minneapolis: University of Minnesota Press, 1999.

Davis, Douglas M. *The World of Black Humor : An Introductory Anthology of Selections and Criticism*. 1st ed. New York: E. P. Dutton, 1967.

Elsaesser, Thomas. *Der Neue Deutsche Film*. Munich: Heyne, 1994.

Engler, Wolfgang. "Anhang: Die höhere Aufklärung." In *Die ungewollte Moderne. Ost-West Passagen*, 247–81. Frankfurt: Suhrkamp, 1995.

Feldman, Burton. "Anatomy of Black Humor," *Dissent* 15 (March-April 1968): 158–60.

Geisler, Michael E. "'Heimat' and the German Left: The Anamnesis of a Trauma." *New German Critique*. Special Issue on "Heimat." 36 (fall 1985): 25–66.

Gemünden, Gerd. *Framed Visions: Popular Culture, Americanization, and the Contemporary German and Austrian Imagination*. Ann Arbor: University of Michigan Press, 1999.

Henninger, Gerd. "Zur Genealogie des schwarzen Humors," *Neue Deutsche Hefte* 13, no. 2 (1966): 18–34.

Hussyen, Andreas. "The Return of Diogenes as Postmodern Intellectual." Foreword to *Critique of Cynical Reason*, by Peter Sloterdijk. Minneapolis: University of Minnesota Press, 1987.

Jameson, Fredric. "Culture and Finance Capital." *Critical Inquiry* 24, no. 1 (1997): 246–65.

Marx, Karl, and Friedrich Engels. *The Communist Manifesto*. New York: Penguin, 1979.

Nietzsche, Friedrich. *Ecce Homo. Wie man wird, was man ist*. Frankfurt: Insel Verlag, 1977.

Schenk, Ralf, ed. *Das zweite Leben der Filmstadt Babelsberg*. Berlin: Henschel, 1994.

Sloterdijk, Peter. *Kritik der zynischen Vernunft*. Frankfurt am Main: Suhrkamp, 1983.

Todorov, Tzvetan. "The Typology of Detective Fiction". In *The Poetics of*

Prose, translated by Richard Howard, 42–52. Ithaca, N.Y.: Cornell University Press, 1977.

FILMOGRAPHY

Achternbusch, Herbert. *Bavaria, Adieu [Servus Bayern]* (Herbert Achternbusch Produktion, 1974), Atlas/Zweitausendeins.

Brahm, John. *Die goldene Pest* (Occident, 1954), Bakiros International.

Brustellin, Alf, Hans Peter Cloos, Rainer Werner Fassbinder, Alexander Kluge, Maximiliane Mainka, Edgar Reitz, Katja Rupé, Bernhard Senkel, and Völker Schlöndorff. *Germany in Autumn [Deutschland im Herbst]* (Hallelujah/Kairos, 1977), New Line Cinema.

Buck, Detlev. *Wir können auch anders. . . .* WDR, 1993.

Einrauch, Volker. *The Mother of the Killer [Die Mutter des Killers]* (Josephine Film/Glückauf, 1997), MFA.

Fassbinder, Rainer Werner. *The Third Generation [Die dritte Generation]* (Tango Film, 1979), Polygram Video.

Föth, Jürgen. *Letztes aus der DaDaEr* (Gruppe DaDaEr, 1990).

Glasner, Matthais. *Sexy Sadie* (Glasner/Vogel, 1996), Filmgalerie 451 Video.

Kipping, Herwig. *The Land beyond the Rainbow [Das Land hinter dem Regenbogen]* (Gruppe DaDaEr, 1992).

Klein, Gerhardt, K. G. Egel, and W. Kohlhaase. *Sonntagsfahrer.* DEFA, 1962.

Kluge, Alexander. *Yesterday Girl [Abschied von Gestern]* (Kairos, 1966), West Glen Film, 16mm.

———, *Artists under the Big Top, Perplexed [Artisten unter der Zirkuskuppel, ratlos]* (Kairos, 1968), West Glen Film, 16mm.

Misselwitz, Helga. *Engelchen* (Wilkening, 1997), Arsenal.

Schilling, Niklaus. *The Willi Busch Report [Der Willi Busch Report]* (Visual, 1979), West Glen, 16mm.

———, *German Fever [Deutschfieber]* (Visual/DEFA, 1992).

Schlingensief, Christoph. *The German Chainsaw Massacre [Die deutsche Kettensägermassaker]* (DEM/Rhewes/Hymen II, 1990), Video Search of Miami.

Schönemann, Sybille. *Verriegelte Zeit* (WDR, 1990), Zeitgeist Films.

Staudte, Wolfgang. *The Beacon [Leuchtfeuer]* (DEFA/Pandora, 1954).

———, *Roses for the State Prosecutor [Rosen für den Staatsanwalt]* (Kurt Ulrich, 1959), Kinowelt Home Entertainment.

CHAPTER 14

Unification Horror

Queer Desire and Uncanny Visions

Randall Halle

If this were a film, right now trailers would be flashing on the screen, teasing us with spectacles of blood, gore, splatter, mayhem, screams, and lurid exposed flesh. Such scenes attend to any retrospective of the horror genre, including this one. We might begin to shift in our seats and giggle in nervous anticipation of the emotional roller coaster ahead, with all its terror, horrific shocks, gut-wrenching twists, and bone-chilling surprises. We might wrinkle our noses in disgust at the spectacle but the horror genre occupies a consistent and central position in popular film production. Such base images and visceral emotions both repel and draw in spectators. Indeed, the horror genre has a particular appeal, especially at certain historic junctures, like at the onset of the Weimar Republic in Germany and in the midst of the Great Depression in the United States. More generally, the genre attracts spectators in the midst of a state of psychological upheaval, like puberty—as Hollywood discovered in the 1950s.

If this were a film, right now images of eerie somnambulists, abject vampires, uncanny *Doppelgängers*, and terrifying serial killers would flash by, as a review of the long history of German cinema's engagement with the haunted screen. There is a certain urgency to have another look at horror film in Germany, given that contemporary studies of German film have largely disregarded the horror genre. The neglect is understandable, given that the Third Reich ended production of horror films, and after World War II, unlike in the United States, German horror films never gained a mass audience. What reemerged after the war bore little resemblance to the classics of Weimar Art cinema. As post-war film production went into crisis in the 1960s, horror film production targeted ever increasingly specialized interest with increasingly lower budgets. Finally, horror film disappeared from mainstream production and moved into underground and subcultural milieus, spending decades so far on the fringes of the culture industry that they fell off the cultural map.[1] However, as this chapter will review, in the underground the horror genre has occupied a significant position, and it played an overlooked social psychological function at the point of the *Wende*, the unification of the two Germanies. Furthermore, a new wave of horror production since the end of the 1990s might indicate that the genre has now returned to dominant culture.

If this were a film, here our trailers would shift and names would flash on the screen, like Christoph Schlingensief, Jörg Buttgereit, Andreas Schnaas, or Olaf Ittenbach. These young German filmmakers have produced important contributions to the horror genre, and I want to pay particular attention to their contributions at the point of unification. They generally do not appear in critical works on German cinema, in part because of their underground production and in part because of the lowbrow status of the genre. In this chapter, I hope to contribute to the scholarship of German horror film; however, I will first move through general reflections on genre, horror, and the history of the horror genre in German film production. I will then narrow the focus to explore German Underground Horror of the 1990s and its social psychological function. Finally, I will concentrate my analysis even further on the example of Jörg Buttgereit's *Nekromantik 2: The Return of the Loving Dead [Nekromantik 2:die Rückkehr der liebenden Toten]* (1991). If this were a movie, here the trailers would end.

Genre studies are a central aspect of the analysis of popular films and popular culture, given that films produced as genre occupy the center of popular film production. In analyses of the Hollywood studio system, genre studies have recognized the film industry and its profit motive as the source of generic consistency. The labor of a culture industry, its audience marketing strategies and an army of scriptwriters, regiment genres, produce scripts with interchangeable generic elements, and "give the people what they want."[2] Classic studies of popular culture undertaken variously by Adorno, Laszerfeld, Merton, Williams, Hess, Wright, and so on identified this as a normative, ideologically conformist, narcotizing dysfunctionality. However, it seems revealing of something more than sheer market-induced dysfunctionality that spectators happily return time and again to see the stranger ride into the sunset, Godzilla sink to the bottom of the ocean, the Forester of the *Heimatfilm* get the prettiest girl in town, "Bond, James Bond" order a Martini, and so on. Furthermore, in genre distinctions we recognize how popular films become sites of address to particular audiences. Popular film, although often described as mass entertainment, is not synonymous with mass film. The various genres have their specific fans, with specific interests and expectations, so that those spectators who are pleased to see the girl get her boy in the end are revolted if she then cuts off his head—whereas fans of the horror genre might expect the latter. Individual spectators happily return time and again to genres that address their interests, creating subcultural cohesion and fan expertise.

The production of popular films outside of Hollywood takes place in film and culture industries that do not have comparable resources. German horror films prove particularly revealing of what these conditions of production entail because they have been produced within an industrial market-oriented system, yet precisely one that never achieved the level of output or stability of Hollywood. Nevertheless, from the earliest days of film production, German cinema produced horror films, with some of the greatest and internationally best known films from Germany making defining contributions to the genre. Already before World War I *The Student of Prague [Der Student von Prag]* (Rye, 1913) amazed its audiences with state-of-the-art special effects, and after the war *The Cabinet of Dr. Caligari* (Wiene, 1920), reopened the market in the United States on the draw provided by its distinctive semantic qualities.[3] German production for the horror genre differed, and continues to differ from the prevailing Hollywood model. Comparing films like *Caligari* and *Nosferatu* (Murnau, 1922) to the Hollywood *Frankenstein* and *Dracula* films, it is clear that the German film industry produced films that in their generic qualities could be understood as related only in very broad terms of narrative development and horrific disruption, whereas Hollywood produced films that relied on a precise replication of the successful elements of a previous film. Furthermore, in these films Germany marked the point of emergence of new generic elements, which are picked up and emulated elsewhere, especially in Hollywood, yet in the case of the horror genre it is not easy to identify any reverse influence, even though it is standard to understand the relationship of German cinema as minor to a hegemonic Hollywood dominant cinema. Early German contributions reveal the international processes at work in film production, in which a transfer of ideas and expertise took place, and continues to take place, toward the more advanced and lucrative culture industry, Hollywood. This type of production also establishes a particular relationship to genre fans in other national markets, who consume internationally but nevertheless find themselves addressed specifically in national genre productions.

In the history of German film production, horror films represent significant contributions during World War I and the chaotic beginning of the Weimar Republic.[4] However, as mentioned previously, their production all but ended during the Third Reich because the totally administered film production of the Third Reich viewed horror films as disruptive of the goals of National Socialism. For those who had not already emigrated to Hollywood, the Third Reich forced many of the best filmmakers active in horror films into exile.[5] Moreover, horror production by the German film industry did not return in any significant form until the late 1960s. A cursory review of movie databases reveals that in the fifty-six years from 1933 to 1989, we can find thirty-four contributions to the horror genre in German and forty-five further co-productions with primarily Spanish or Italian companies. The majority of these films appeared in the midst of the German film industry's crisis of the late 1960s, and they flourished in the 1970s with very low budgets and production values. These films, shot mostly in black and white, had to compete in the same market with the brilliantly colored films produced by Hammer studios in England or with Hollywood productions like *Psycho* (Hitchcock, 1960), *Rosemary's Baby* (Polanski, 1968), and *The Exorcist* (Friedkin, 1973), but given their budgets, even small audiences could produce a profit. During this time Herzog's opulent remake of *Nosferatu* (1979) appeared as a notable exception.

In general, much of European film production of the period relied on an erotic quality to help in the competition with Hollywood, and likewise horror films incorporated titillating scenes but adopted the innovative tactic of substituting a horrific turn in the narrative for explicit sex.[6] The fun of pursuing the semantic and syntactic structure of an exploitation film like *La Isla de la muerte* (Franco,1969), a.k.a. *die Jungfrau und die Peitsche*, a.k.a. *De Sade*, a.k.a. *Eugenie, the Story of Her Journey into Perversion* belongs to a different study.[7] I am interested in these films for making explicit a mixture of sex and horror, but also as foil to the new subgenre of German horror films that emerged around the time of German unification.

In the late 1980s a sudden production of horror film emerged again with the debuts of Jörg Buttgereit, Andreas Schnaas, and Olaf Ittenbach, filmmakers who have become significant names in German Underground Horror.[8] Then, starting in 1989, there was a sudden jump in horror film production so that in the next three years at least twelve full-length feature films were produced in Germany.[9] Compared to the output of Hollywood, it seems exaggerated to talk about a horror wave, however for German film production there was a clear quantitative and qualitative shift at this time. The wave of sexploitation horror had ended almost a decade earlier and the horror genre had all but disappeared out of German film production. The sudden increase to about four films per year marks a significant and sudden jump in horror film production. Further, we should keep in mind that at this time the average year's production for Germany was between sixty and seventy films, and that in 1990 there was even a dip down to forty-eight, so that these films represent 5–6 percent of the total production. We can also note that horror film production subsequently has continued in both above and underground productions, so that at least seventeen further films have been made in the years from 1993 to 2000.[10] Against this background, these films begin to appear sociologically interesting.

If we look more closely at the films of what begins to appear as a horror wave, we note that they share certain sociohistorical contextual characteristics. Like the generation of filmmakers of the New Wave, their fairly young directors were mainly autodidacts, shooting their films on super 8 and video when they could not get better materials. The film schools at the time did not welcome them in. Like the leftist cineaste subculture that built an audience for the New Wave, these directors were supported by an attendant subcultural milieu. The filmmakers emerged out of centers primarily in Berlin, Hamburg, and Munich, where an audience already existed. The audience that consumed the images consisted of specialists with a broad international knowledge of the genre, that is, horror fans. In these cities international horror and fantasy books, comics, and videos were distributed by a few fan shops, and interest in the genre was supported by fan zines of which the German zine *Splatting Image* continues as perhaps the best known. Films were screened in bars, art spaces, and late-night theaters, or in conjunction with the Fantasy Filmfest that had begun in the summer of 1986.[11]

If we can detect a prehistory to these films, it derives from an international tradition of slasher, trash, splatter, or Euro-gore films, nevertheless a new direction for German filmmakers. All of these films appeared as solely German productions on a very low budget with very crude production values. Yet in Christoph Schlingensief's films we also find actors who count as some of the most significant of New German Cinema: Margit Castensen, Volker Spengler, and Irm Hermann, as well as international bad boy Udo Kier. In general, the narrative plotting of the films proceeds at a rapid pace, with cinematic mayhem displacing narrative development. They rely on irony and parody, along with gallons of fake blood. In the press some of the films and filmmakers have gained a certain notoriety, capitalizing on new shock journalistic techniques that turned the directors themselves into sites of public dread and anxiety.

To this point little academic attention has been paid to the filmmakers and their films, with one notable exception. The most broadly known of these films is Schlingensief's bitingly satirical slasher/gore film *The German Chainsaw Massacre [Das deutsche Kettensägen Massaker]* (1990). The film appeared at the point of unification as a shockingly negative and bitter satire in a media landscape filled with positivity and not the least bit of triumphalism. At the heart of *German Chainsaw,* like the storyline of *Texas Chainsaw* (Hooper, 1974), on which it is based, is an economically impoverished butcher family. They recognize "cheap meat" in the East Germans passing over the old border into the West and begin turning them into sausage. The film received excessive commentary and a great deal of negative publicity in the popular press, ultimately drawing academic attention to Schlingensief. In academic assessments he is placed as a next generation filmmaker in the tradition of New German Cinema, thereby rhetorically his films are elevated nervously to the level of high aesthetic form.[12] However, as with the rest of this group of filmmakers, his work challenges the very categories used to appraise it. The films of Schlingensief, Buttgereit, Ittenbach, and Schnaas fall quickly out of any high aesthetic category, unless those categories can account for the "making [of] art out of sleaze," as Jörg Buttgereit might describe it (Kerekes 61).

Emerging out of a subcultural milieu but not as a unified movement, the quantitative change in German Underground Horror production begins in the late 1980s and takes off particularly around the point of German unification, the *Wende.* Not simply a quantitative transformation, there is also a qualitative change in horror film production at this time. Attempts to describe commonalities run up against the dynamic described previously, in that, typical of the history of horror production in Germany, there is a great deal of diversity with respect to the generic elements of the actual film narratives. The lack of industry relations and the subcultural nature of the audience result in a greater degree of directorial (auteurist) specificity and experimentation.[13] Nevertheless, they do share a certain aesthetic rooted in the particular pleasures the horror genre offers its spectators, an aesthetic based in not simply the motifs but also the thrills they presumably offer to their viewers.

The particular nature of the horrific disruption provides an immediate form of commonality among these films. The horror genre relies consistently on a monstrosity that appears to undo the stability of everyday life, and in the horror narratives of the early 1990s this transgression takes the form of a disruption of once stable borders, boundaries, and limits. Institutions that once offered stability prove ineffective or are themselves sites of terror. Schlingensief relies in particular on portrayals of the disruption of political borders at the time of unification. The border in *German Chainsaw* is the site of the psychotic butcher family.[14] Likewise, a sleepy town on the Polish border in *Terror 2000* (Schlingensief, 1992) is the site of violent attacks against foreigners.[15] *Burning Moon* (Ittenbach, 1992) carries the suggestive extension to its title "this film transgresses all borders," and in it, the institutions of the family and church certainly do fall apart. An older brother left to baby-sit his little sister shoots up on heroine and spends the night telling his sister as a form of bedtime story horrific tales of extreme violence committed by, among others, devil-worshipping priests. Similarly, in *Babylon* (Huettner, 1992) the maternity ward, the modern institution of life and innocence, becomes a site of sexual violence and deadly carnage. Further, the more fantastical of these films combine a loss of institutional control with a violation of the most fundamental border, that between life and death. In *Zombie 90, or Extreme Pestilence* (Schnaas, 1991),because of a military industrial accident, the dead rise to feast on the living. In *The Deathking, or Club Extinction* (Buttgereit, 1990), the reverse takes place as the films depict societies beset with unexplained suicide plagues. The necrophilia of *Nekromantik 2* (Buttgereit, 1991) portrays a different violation of the border between the body and the corpse. For the spectator of German Underground Horror, the absence of happy endings extends this disruption beyond the final frames of the films.

Another consistent aspect of these films derives from the type of emotional relationship established with their spectators. The films of German Underground Horror adequately portray their characters' experiences of horror; nevertheless, the buckets of fake blood, butcher shop entrails, pasta for skin, and other kitchen cupboard special effects that fill the frames of these films seem to aim only at eliciting an experience of revulsion from their spectators. The very speed with which a Schlingensief film progresses, or the extended scenes of violence that belong to the splatter films of Schnaas, Ittenbach, Panneck, and Hollmann, undermine suspense, mystery, or terror possibilities typical of horror films. The pacing and the excess of carnage here push the films to a different level, where they border on a parody of their own genre, and instead of the periodic screams and starts of more conventional or mainstream horror productions, the spectator responds with a constant stream of nervous, repulsed laughter.[16]

A further fairly common dynamic in these films is a nexus of violence and pornography to establish an affective state. In general, the elements of a horror film—rapid heartbeat, perspiration, quick, shallow breathing, and so on—seek to be a direct cognitive cause of a physical state of excitation.[17] The violent sexual excesses portrayed here exceed a shock effect or a desire to provoke moral outrage. For example, Schnaas and Ittenbach rely on extensive genital mutilation scenes perpetrated by degraded subhuman characters. Likewise, Huettner's *Babylon* portrays a series of women raped and impregnated by a demonic character who then are torn apart from inside by the developing fetus. Buttgereit directly portrays necrophilia, among other forms of shocking sexuality. One of his signature scenes from the end of *Nekromantik* and repeated as a flashback at the opening of *Nekromantik II* is a suicide scene in which the character Rob disembowels himself as a form of masturbation. The scene ends with an ejaculation first of semen then of blood. These ghastly sexual acts appear as a primary vehicle for the experience of revulsion.

Beyond revulsion, scenes of degradation, murder, defilement, perverse sexuality, and cannibalism push the films into the *abject* as site of the horror of the films; indeed *Cinema of Abjection* could serve as a description to capture further the common aesthetic. The abject is commonly understood as that which is defiled and/or defiling, and abjection as an act of self-degradation. Psychoanalytic discussions, taking the work of Julia Kristeva as impetus, understand abjection as a type of expulsion, and the abject as an expelled other, an object, the exclusion of which is necessary to constitute a subject. This expulsion and the expelled other produce horror in these films. For example, we recognize the abject clearly in a scene in *Babylon* in which a fetus that threatened to destroy its mother is aborted but afterward crawls out of the operating room. Abject is that which is excluded physically *and* psychically from a body to make it clean, to keep it intact. Usually removed from sight in everyday life, such excluded bodies abound in German Underground Horror: Buttgereit's corpses, the various zombies, the foreigners of *Terror 2000*, and so on. The expulsion or exclusion of abjection actually establishes the physical and psychical topography of a body, putting things in their "proper place." Zombies belong in the ground. Psychotic cannibal serial killers belong in prison. When they appear above ground and in the forests outside your house, these abject characters become sites of horror. In regard to "proper place," Schlingensief's narratives represent what one could describe as battling abjections; his films seem manically to question who will be expelled—the former East Germans or the butcher family, the foreigner or the Germans.

A central problem of abjection for body and psyche, however, is that the borders of every living body are only provisional, always under threat of disruption, constantly in need of reassertion. The body-ego, established by abjection, must constantly assert its contours through expulsion. Abjection becomes a constant "self-defense," yet in this constancy the subject is always close to its abject, leaving the subject horrified but also ultimately compelled by it. The horrifying figures of this cinema of the abject give in to this compulsion and revel in otherwise abject objects or acts of abjection. The butcher family, for instance, lives amidst the cadavers and offal of its victims. Kristeva describes victims of the abject who are overcome by this compulsion. As if reflecting on Rob's suicide, she writes suggestively, "One thus understands why so many victims of the abject are its fascinated victims—if not its submissive and willing ones" (9).

In the Cinema of Abjection, this dynamic of the submissive and willing "victim" should be noted among the spectators. Abjection here goes beyond the representations of the screen such that the viewing space constituted by the films becomes itself a space inflected by the abject. Cadavers and gore are certainly not the same as images of cadavers and gore, so that in comparison to the abjection of those who spend real time in a morgue or cemetery, time spent in the cinema could be considered only as constituting a contained form of secondary abjection. Nevertheless, such abjection is important for the constitution of the subculture of horror fans. The Cinema of Abjection belongs to its fans, to a subculture that excludes or repels the random viewer. The secondary abjection of these films repels some viewers and attracts others. The Cinema of Abjection on the one hand repels a mainstream audience, and on the other hand, without speculating on the experiences of the willing spectators, we can say any subcultural status of the horror fan comes about as a result of his or her proximity to "gross" images—taboo and repellent to most. Here we move from abject representations to the audience's real lived experiences of abjection.

If it is clear that the viewing of a horror film has the potential to affect its spectators emotionally, physically, and psychically, we might ask why such an effect attracts viewers? In this particular case, why are viewers attracted to the abjection of German Underground Horror? Subcultural cohesion is clearly important, but beyond general belonging, does the subculture offer its viewers any other pleasures? Isabel Pinedo describes how the spectator of fantastic scenes approaches them as a bounded experience of dread, suspending disbelief, knowing that this is a contained moment, and she identifies this function as "recreational terror." Such a description proves insightful as another aspect of what horror films offer their spectators, but not as an explanation of why viewers seek out this experience in the first place. In Freud's discussion of the uncanny, *das Unheimliche,* from which Pinedo developed the idea of recreational terror, Freud described as uncanny precisely those moments when the familiar becomes defamiliarized and frightening (220). Further, in his analysis of this experience, Freud suggested that the better oriented a person is in his or her environment, the less likely the uncanny appears, which is to suggest that during periods of disorientation the experience of the uncanny, this sense of defamiliarization, appears more frequently (221). Freud withheld any speculations on the cause of production of the uncanny, but in terms of reception, then, the suggestion is that the genre world somehow acts as a reflection of the real one, offering a rehearsal of the anxieties induced by defamiliarization.

Production for the horror genre (re)emerges during periods of social turmoil. Horror film produces a particular and popular form of mass space that both emerges out of a historically chaotic period and further offers its audience a pointed experience to address that chaos. Generally speaking, the visions of monstrosity, the uncanny, the abject in horror films create for individual spectators a nexus of social context and mass psychology.[18] Specifically speaking, the German Underground Horror films do not only mark a new figuration of cultural anxiety, they mark general points of transition in culture, cultural labor as such.[19] Taking Schlingensief's direct reflection on the process of unification in *German Chainsaw* and *Terror 2000* as an indication, it borders on understatement to observe that this period establishes the ground of these generic representations. The year 1989 represents, of course, the beginning of a process that has proven profoundly disorienting for many, and it is clear that the loss of borders that occurred was experienced as much geo-politically as psychologically. Thus Unification Horror can serve as another possible designation for the German Underground Horror films produced during the wave from 1989 to 1992. The aesthetic commonalities described previously become a rehearsal of the anxieties induced by the defamiliarization of the *Wende*.

Of course, the experiences of unification provided a ground not just for the horror genre. More conventional and realistic genres, such as documentary and melodrama, also emerged during this period, directly portraying the transformations of unification.[20] Yet, none of these films offers the type of emotional experience afforded by Unification Horror. Any tears shed over the melodrama *The Promise [Das Versprechen]* (von Trotta, 1994) could result only from a very specific identification with the narrative. Unification Horror performs dramatically different cultural labor than the "realistic" films, not a document of the social but rather a provocation of the psychological context.

Nekromantik 2: The Return of the Loving Dead proved to have a particular uncanny ability to provoke its spectators; in 1991 the authorities banned the film and its distribution. The film was censored and tried according to § 131 of the criminal code, which regulates the presentation of violence, precisely on the grounds that it glorified violence. Amidst the ever increasing explosions and murders of popular films from Hollywood, censorship marks the success of the techniques of abjection and the film as a specific site of cultural anxiety. The court case lasted until 1994, when it was decided in favor of Buttgereit and the film was again made available for screening.

In the defense of *Nekromantik 2*, Knut Hickethier argued that the film was not about necrophilia but a "metaphorical interpretation of the decline of East Germany and the effects of the Berlin Wall coming down" (Kerekes 122). Certainly the film's narrative does not represent the historical events or any of the political debates of the moment; however, the film opens with the loss of the border between East and West Germany. The original *Nek-romantik* had a surreal space as setting, most of the scenes filmed in an unlocalized apartment, with exterior scenes either shot in a studio interior with a black backdrop or out in nondescript nature. Thus, it stands out that after a short black-and-white reprise of the final scenes of the original *Nekromantik*—the autoerotic suicide of Rob—the sequel opens with a color shot of a burnt-out Trabi and a pan over crumbling building facades. Such scenes clearly mark the locale as East Berlin at the time of unification. The unlocalized action of the original is interpolated into the space of the East. In a city so clearly visually and socially divided as Berlin was at the time, the subsequent exterior shots of the film define locations as either East or West. Monika, the main character and necrophile of the film, has an apartment in the East that serves as the central location of action. West locales appear to present an opposition to this apartment and to Monika herself, as when Mark, the second lead, meets a former girlfriend to discuss his relationship with Monika.

It is important, however, to modify Hickethier's defense. Asserting that the film was a metaphor suggests that the film is not really about what it depicts. Yet, certainly this film is about necrophilia, and it is important to modify the "defense" to insist that representations of necrophilia not as metaphor but in themselves provide a significant means to address the process of unification. In his contributions to German Underground Horror Buttgereit has developed sophisticated techniques that take control of our imagination and undermine our ability to differentiate between the real and the fantastic. Like his contemporaries, with his tale of necrophile love, he narrativized the loss of border, combining the border that once separated East from West and that between life and death. At the same time, Buttgereit concentrated not just on representing the disruption of border but on filmicly accomplishing various types of border crossings, disorientations, and defamiliarizations in the spectator. Like German Underground Horror in general and Unification Horror in particular, the film accomplishes this effect by representing abject acts and by drawing its spectators into an experience of abjection.

The film appears to be a horror film, yet it could easily belong to the romance genre of the very traditional type as well: girl meets boy, girl loses boy, girl gets boy back. The twist, of course, is that the boy here is a corpse. After the opening scenes that serve to localize the film in the East, we move to a new sequence consisting of claustrophobically extreme close shots. A woman, Monika, prowls about in a cemetery. The frame, typical of horror films, remains tight, dissecting her body, preventing any overview. This lack of visual plenitude forecloses the possibility of any sense of spectatorial control. The camera clearly calls the shots, according to a logic that is exterior to our own. We start to piece together the bits of information offered by these shots. This proves difficult because Monika is dressed as if for a date, not for the heavy digging she undertakes. It becomes clear only when we recognize that she is exhuming the "body" of Rob, the main character of the previous film, and that it is, in fact, a "date."

This scene ends with the introduction of a parallel narrative line when we cut to Mark on his way to work. He misses the streetcar on the recognizable corner of Dimitroff Street and Lenin Allee. The action then cuts back to Monika bringing the body home, cleaning it, and eventually engaging in her first sexual encounter with Rob. The scene imbues the corpse with a certain subjectivity by focusing on its open eyes, and thereby intensifies the fascination of the abject. The head of the body rocks gently in pace with Monika, and the firm borders between living and dead become confused. There is then a quick cut to an extreme out-of-focus shot that confuses the viewer, as do the sounds of a couple, a woman and a man, having sex. This cut gives the momentary appearance that Rob has come back to life and that the film is a fantastical film. Instead, as the camera pulls into focus we find ourselves following the second narrative line. We are at Mark's place of work, a dubbing studio for sex films, one of the postwall centers of economic "success." Mark dubs the sounds of male participants in sex films.

Buttgereit's films do not proceed at the same pace as those of his colleagues, but rather with a slowness that concentrates on establishing atmosphere and mood. Nevertheless, Buttgereit's films exhibit a profound ability to disturb, precisely, then, through idiosyncratic techniques. This scene at the dubbing studio establishes two of these techniques. First, his films play with different media and genre, presenting here "real" pornography and "real" exploitation, whereby the necrophile sex scenes appear all the more distinctive and enter into an imaginary space. This confusion continues in the scenes of Monika and the cadaver to which we cut back, which are wrenched out of the realm of fantastical film, juxtaposed to "real" pornography, and then aligned with art film practice through the shots now being accompanied by classical romantic extradiegetic music and filmed in slow motion with various types of filters. Second, there is here a technique of narrative offset and overlay, which is employed to appeal to the emotional affective state of the audience. The cut here causes a break in the narrative that is not immediately comprehended by the spectator. The action is offset to a later moment of comprehension. The sex scene with Monika is then overlaid with the sounds of sex from the following sequence, and as a result of the confusion there is the momentary sense that Rob is alive and then quickly the opposite realization, disorientation.

As the narrative unfolds further, a chance meeting at an art cinema brings Monika and Mark into contact. Mark is quickly smitten with the attractive Monika, and it seems that she is with him. So much so that Monika cuts up Rob's body and discards it, all except for the head and penis. She takes up with Mark, presumably having "gone straight." They engage in the activities of new lovers. They spend a day at the amusement park. She shows him pictures of her relatives—in their coffins. Increasingly the film displays scenes to indicate that all is not "normal." Spectator anxiety increases as Mark begins to ignore the signs that there is something "queer" about his girlfriend, including when he finds Rob's penis Saran-wrapped and in the back of the refrigerator.[21]

The technique of offset and overlay is used to great effect in a pivotal scene that opens at Monika's apartment. A group of unnamed women has gathered there, described in the credits as simply members of a "Necro gang." Their unexplained presence reinforces the film's refusal of psychological investigation and suggests that Monika is not alone but part of a larger network. They have gathered for a little familiar fun: to drink coffee, eat cake, and watch a video. The video, however, is a documentary first of seals playing and then of their dissection. On the coffee table amidst the food is Rob's severed head, looking as fake as ever. The opening of this scene is usually met with laughter from the audience. Then the film begins to cut back and forth between the group watching TV and the documentary they are watching. There is a slow pan across the women, as they smoke, drink coffee, and pass each other sandwiches and chocolates. When the dissection gets underway, the scene takes over the frame. As unmediated images, clearly documentary, clearly referencing a real event, confront the spectator, it becomes increasingly difficult to limit our revulsion with the dissection to the particular shots. We continue to cut back to the women eating. Soon the spectator cannot emotionally differentiate the revulsion of the dissection from the scenes of women eating. Even though we are firmly sutured into their point of view, the women's lack of disgust sets them outside our comprehension. Mark, who shows up on a surprise visit, provides a point of identification for the spectator; as he watches the film he experiences a state of revulsion and leaves.

Throughout the spectators are forced into a flux of identification based on varying attractions and repulsions of desire encoded in the film. *Nekromantik 2* is particularly successful at relying on the abject to accomplish this flux, taking up scenes that reference typical romantic activities and twisting them: a chanteuse sings a melancholic song in French while images of a decaying skull circulate in the background; lovers take Polaroids of each other, except one is a corpse dressed up and posed in *heimlich*, familiar positions. In the end we have to reanalyze any identification with or form of sympathy we have given Monika. After the initial sequence, the film appears to suture us in to Monika's perspective. Subjective shots, point of view, even flash shots depicting Monika's uncanny desires lead us to believe we have access to her interior life. For example, a romantic ride on a Ferris wheel, filled with shots of Mark and Monika responding to each other lovingly, is suddenly broken by the quick insertion of shots of Rob, presumably suggesting Monika's internal struggle against her queer desires. In the end, however, when Monika, whom we have come to believe has been struggling against her necrophile tendencies, actually behaves in such a way as to prove the contrary (I don't want to give away the ending), we realize that her configuration of desire had never changed. Even though she cut him up, she has in effect never broken up with Rob.

The ending of the film forces the spectator to reanalyze his or her reading of the entire film. This forced reanalysis is perhaps the most significant effect of the film as Unification Horror. The horror of the film lies for us in the way that we are sutured into a subject position that we cannot possibly comprehend. The film does not imbue Monika with any explanation. Her desire does not carry any signs of madness; to the contrary, she appears as rational and articulate throughout. Her desire simply is. Like an outside force that sweeps up the audience against its will, we are sutured into the film, yet we remain outside of the desire it depicts. It does not present itself to our comprehension; we must simply experience it.

As if commenting on Monika's attraction to the corpse of Rob, Kristeva notes, "the erotization of abjection, and perhaps any abjection to the extent that it is already eroticized, is an attempt at stopping the hemorrhage [of subjectivity]" (Kristeva 55). As discussed previously, subjectivity is embattled and in flux, the physical and psychic borders of the subject always rupturing, hemorrhaging, always in need of reassertion. In necrophilia we go to the absolute limits of the subject. The dead body, that abject object of peaceful decay, utterly desireless, confronts all living bodies with their absolute opposite. In necrophilic desire, the subject that desires the dead body, that cold absence of all desire, becomes thereby positioned as pure desire. Monika's necrophilia establishes her as a fully contained coherent self.

Is it significant that at the point of unification precisely such a contained self appears to horrify? This was the point of emergence of the longed-for coherent German political body, a whole country, no longer defined by dismemberment or East-West opposition. Instead of producing such coherency however, the loss of the border reshuffled the possibilities of subjective unity and disunity. The subject position of the East German citizen became impossible; moreover, in fairly unexpected ways the new sociopolitical condition hemorrhaged the West German subjects, who kept their citizenship but lost their state as well. The Berlin Republic appeared as designation of a Federal Republic new to all its citizens. Is it possible, then, that *Nekromantik 2* and Unification Horror in general marked an attempt to stop the hemorrhage of subjectivity experienced at the point of unification?

The representations of the film contain a clue as to how this might be possible in a Cinema of Abjection. In the diegesis of the film, we find a representation of contact with the abject that serves as metaphor for the audience's own experience. Monika becomes fascinated with the abject and in her necrophilia abjects herself. Yet her first encounter with the corpse ends abruptly with Monika running to the bathroom to vomit. This could be understood as a sign of her own struggle against her fascination with the abject, a revulsion of her own abject state. Yet the expulsion of vomiting itself is a process of abjection whereby we experience the propriety of the internal and external. The act of expulsion makes felt a coherent body. The process of abjection reaffirms Monika's borders, leaves her self-contained, an absolute, monadic subject. The abjection of the spectator of the film is similar. It is not the "gross out" that is desired, but the experience that ensues, the reassertion of subjective borders and coherency. In Unification Horror there are no happy endings that restore normalcy, only better-equipped subjects. Horror films, then, appear here as a cheap therapy, available at every screening, a ninety-minute stop-gap to make bearable the lack of cohesion of the social body outside the film fantasy.

If I suggest that Unification Horror was better equipped to engage the social psychology of the *Wende* than contributions to other genres, with such an observation I do not mean also to suggest that they were successful, and certainly not "massively" successful in their attempt. These films belong to the category of "popular" film, yet not as films that appealed to a "mass audience." As I noted in the opening, this specific address to fans is part of genre film and of national production in particular, although, interestingly, the international quality of horror fans means that German Underground Horror has acquired a cache outside of Germany. Years after their initial release, Buttgereit's *Nekromantik* films 1 and 2 continue to be screened, they have been transferred to DVD, and their international distribution on video and DVD has expanded. The moment of unification is over, but the ongoing incohesion of life affords these films a resonance beyond their point of emergence.

NOTES

1. In a reference work like the recent British Film Institute's *Companion to German Cinema*, which specifically attempts to orient itself "towards popular traditions (the entertainment cinema, the despised, supposedly mediocre, genres, and the stars and directors of popular cinema often unknown outside of their own countries)," the horror genre does not appear. See Thomas Elsaesser, and Michael Wedel, eds., *The BFI Companion to German Cinema* (London: BFI Publishing, 1999), viii.

2. We catch a glimpse of what it means to produce popular genre films in an advanced industrial system when we consider how it is possible that different Hollywood studios could produce in the same years films with almost identical semantic and syntactic elements: for example, two alien invasion films, *Mars Attacks* and *Independence Day* (1996); two volcano films, *Volcano* and *Dante's Peak* (1997); two asteroid films, *Armageddon* and *Deep Impact* (1998); two terrorists on a plane films, *Con Air* and *Air Force One* (1997); two terrorists in either a rain or firestorm films, *Hard Rain* and *Firestorm* (1998); three virtual reality "are we real or is this cyberspace" films, *Matrix*, *ExistenZ*, and *The Thirteenth Floor* (1999), and so on. The semantic and syntactic elements these film share do not appear interesting in themselves, rather they become markers of something else, a marketing process behind them. In effect, we can identify these films as consciously produced as genre for a market by studios in heated competition for a lucrative summer audience. See, in particular, Rick Altmann, *Film/Genre* (London: BFI Publishing, 1999) or Barry Keith Grant, *Film Genre Reader II* (Austin: University of Texas Press, 1995).

3. There are many discussions of these films, but under the aspect of expressionist film or Weimar Art Cinema. Here the critical work of Siegfried Kracauer and Lotte Eisner set the example. See Christian Rogowski's discussion of Kracauer in this volume. For discussions that explore these films as

horror films, see Paul Coates, *The Gorgon's Gaze* (Cambridge: Cambridge University Press, 1991) or Siegbert Prawer, *Caligari's Children* (New York: Da Capo Press, 1989). For a work on the horror genre that includes German sources in its broader cultural and historical considerations, see Noël Carol, *The Philosophy of Horror* (New York: Routledge, 1990).

4. In addition to those films already mentioned, a quick survey includes: *Alraune* (Illes, 1918), *The Hunchback and the Dancer [Der Bucklige und die Tänzerin]* (Murnau, 1920), *Cagliostro* (Schünzel, 1921), *Genuine* (Wiene, 1920), *The Golem [Der Golem, wie er in die Welt kam]* (Wegener, 1920), *The Hound of Baskerville [Der Hund von Baskerville]* (Zehn, 1920), *The Head of Janus [Der Januskopf]* (Murnau, 1920), *Figures of the Night [Nachtgestalten]* (Oswald, 1919), *The Hands of Orlac [Orlacs Hände]* (Wiene, 1924), *The Plague in Florence [Die Pest in Florenz]* (Lang, 1919), *The Student of Prag [Der Student von Prag]* (Galeen, 1926), *Dance of Death [Totentanz]* (Rippert, 1919), *Eerie Tales [Unheimliche Geschichten]* (Oswald, 1919), *Madness [Wahnsinn]* (Veidt, 1919), and *Waxworks [Das Wachsfigurenkabinett]* (Birinsky, 1924). Notable for films from the end of the Weimar Republic are *The Secret of the Blue Room [Das Geheimnis des blauen Zimmers]* (Engel, 1932), *Five Sinister Stories [Unheimliche Geschichten]* (Oswald, 1932), and *The Vampire [Vampyr: Der Traum des Allan Grey]* (Dreyer, 1932).

5. At the outset of the Great Depression the classic horror films of Universal Studios arose, drawing much of their sets, lighting, casting, and themes directly from German Expressionist films. There are numerous examples of émigré and exile filmmakers with direct backgrounds in the horror and thriller genres who worked on the Universal films. Gerd Gemünden discusses the career of Peter Lorre elsewhere in this volume. Karl Freund was cameraman for films like *The Golem* and *Metropolis*, then went to Hollywood, where he worked on films like *Dracula* (Browning, 1931) and directed *The Mummy* (1933). Conrad Veidt, the somnambulist in *Caligari* and star of numerous horror films, wound up playing a different type of horror figure in exile—that of the Hollywood screen Nazis.

6. Tim Bergfelder's analysis in this volume alludes to the production of sexploitation horror and also provides a great deal of information regarding the specific history out of which it emerged. During the late 1960s and through the 1970s the borders between pornography, exploitation film, and art film proved rather fluid both in terms of themes and material resources, to the point where Erwin Dietrich produced for the German sex industry in this period and his son, Ralph Dietrich, now acts as producer for a contemporary high-budget dark comedy/horror film like *Killer Condom* (Walz, 1996).

7. The actual variations of the titles are more elaborate, marking its international releases and certain attempts to draw audiences. These include *La Isla de la muerte* (1969, Spain), *Die Wildkatze* (West Germany), *Decameron francese* (Italy), and *Les Inassouvies* (France). England generated a series of titles, varying in suggestion and innuendo: *Eugenie,* or *Eugenie, the Story of Her Journey into Perversion,* or *Philosophy in the Boudoir,* or *De Sade 70.* The film returned to West Germany in 1972 under the title *Die Jungfrau und die Peitsche.*

8. Jörg Buttgereit, *Nekromantik* (1987); Andreas Schnaas *Violent Shit* (1987); Olaf Ittenbach, *Black Past* (1989).

9. Given the underground nature of the films I am discussing here, and the presence of direct-to-video productions, it is possible that there are more. It is certain, however, that in the quantitative analysis that follows there are at least twelve films that appear representing further a qualitative change. Films in the period from 1989 to 1992 include *Black Past* (Ittenbach, 1989), *Der Todesking* (Buttgereit, 1989), *German Chainsaw Massacre [Das Deutsche Kettensägen Massaker]* (Schlingensief, 1990), *My Lovely Monster* (Bergmann, 1990), *Nekromantik 2: The Return of the Loving Dead [Nekromantik 2: die Rückkehr der liebenden Toten]* (Buttgereit, 1991), *Zombie '90: Extreme Pestilence* (Schnaas, 1991), *The Burning Moon [Burning Moon: Dieser Film überschreitet alle Grenzen]* (Ittenbach, 1992), *Violent Shit II* (Schnaas, 1992), *Urban Scumbags vs. Countryside Zombies* (Panneck and Hollmann, 1992), *Babylon [Babylon—Im Bett mit dem Teufel]* (Huettner, 1992), and *Terror 2000 [Terror 2000: Intensivstation Deutschland]* (Schlingensief, 1992). Even though the director is French, I include *Club Extinction [Docteur M.]* (1990) by Claude Chabrol because it was filmed as a German production and its setting is Germany. The films by Ralf Huettner, Michael Bergmann, Sebastian Panneck, and Patrick Hollmann are further debut films.

10. It becomes problematic to exactly trace out production at this point. There is much direct-to-video work that remains isolated and travels in underground circles outside of major distribution mechanisms. Furthermore, direct production for television increased as well. If we exclude these forms for an arbitrary definition of "pure film" then we are still left with the question of syntax. As John Davidson discusses in this volume, there are a number of "Black Comedies" that could be assessed as horror films. However, if we apply "strict" generic definitions then films produced in the subsequent period to the present include *Schramm* (Buttgereit, 1993), *Amoklauf* (Boll, 1994), *The Fallen Angel [Premutos: Der gefallene Engel]* (Ittenbach, 1997), *Over My Dead Body [Nur über meine Leiche]* (Matsutani, 1995), *The Deathmaker [Der Totmacher]* (Karmakar, 1995), *Kiss My Blood* (Jazay, 1998), *Night Time [Sieben Monde]* (Fratzscher, 1998), *Anthropophagous 2000* (Schnaas, 1999), *Holgi* (Knarr, 1999), *The Thirteenth Floor* (Rusnak, 1999), *The Valley of Shadows [Das Tal der Schatten]* (Gutmann, 1999), *Anatomy [Anatomie]* (Ruzowitzky, 2000).

11. The "Fantasy Filmfest" tours Berlin, Frankfurt, Stuttgart, Munich, Cologne, and Hamburg, in the summer. It began in Hamburg in 1986 on a small budget in the Alabama-Kino, where Rainer Stefan screened a number of films from the 1950s and 1960s that he had collected. He continues to work on the festival, which now lasts three days and includes a full international program with numerous world premiers. For program and dates look under *www.fantasyfilmfest.com*

12. Almost universally, the term *"enfant terrible* of German film" appears in discussions of Schlingensief, a characterization that might reveal something about his affect but little about his work. Schlingensief's activities incorporate a broad variety of cultural production, punk performance art, theater staging, filmwork on varied topics, and television programming. Indeed, Schlingensief's activities do resemble those of Fassbinder in many ways, including his assembling of a company of actors around himself, many of them veterans of work with Fassbinder. Critical attention, however, has focused on his two films concerned with the unification of Germany. See,

for instance, the discussion in Thomas Elsaesser and Michael Wedel, eds, *The BFI Companion to German Cinema* (London: BFI, 1999), 212–13.

13. We do not witness in this form of production the same sort of generic repetition that marked the new German comedies of the 1990s, where, amidst the revitalization efforts of the film industry, suddenly at least ten films in three years, all varying the same relational comedic theme, could appear. For a detailed discussion of this problem of genre see my own Randall Halle, " 'Happy Ends' to Crises of Heterosexual Desire: Toward a Social Psychology of Recent German Comedies," *Camera Obscura* 44 (2000): 1–39.

14. The transgression of border is highlighted early on in *German Chainsaw* when Clara arrives at the old German-German border. This is a lengthy, slow-paced episode that appears oddly out of place with the tempo and visual style of the rest of the film. It portrays how a group of East German border guards who cling to their anachronistic function inspect Clara and her Trabi. They harass her, trying to assert a lost authority, yet at the same time they also seem to augur future terror. In the end Clara ignores them, defies their authority, and simply runs the gate. The black backdrop setting and blue and red high-contrast lighting as well as the characters' behavior imbue this episode with a surreal quality, highlighting border crossing itself as a central problematic of the film.

15. A conspiratorial neo-Nazi organization is the cause, and the representatives of the government sent in to restore order prove ineffective. If the premise of this narrative seems to be realistic, given the well over three thousand attacks by neo-Nazis reported annually in Germany, it is important to note that the film was done in 1991, at a time when the attacks were just beginning. The film, which began as horror satire, portrayed an unfolding central problematic of unification and it has ceased to be a horror film per se and has become a realistic prediction—horrifying in its own right.

16. To be sure, the laughter is also not the laughter elicited by the contemporaneous gore comedies like *Frankenhooker* (Frank Henenlotter, 1990). In those films the narrative relies on satirical and ironic citations and transpositions of classic horror tropes, for example, the story of the Frankenstein monster and his bride condensed into the character of dead fiancée regenerated as a super powerful sex worker. The works under examination here remain within the slasher genre, but accelerate the effects and the gore to a chaotic mayhem, as if the energy of the long chase scene that ends *Texas Chain Saw Massacre* (Tobe Hooper, 1974) were extended to infuse the entire film.

17. As a result of this effect a number of critics have placed the horror genre in the proximity of pornography, given that pornography also draws its spectators into a similar state, though by different means. This point has been explored primarily by feminist film criticism. As much as pornography has resulted in productive debates for feminist scholars, so, too, has horror film criticism, for similar reasons. For varying approaches, see the excellent collections by Barry Keith Grant, ed. *(Dread of Difference: Gender and the Horror Film* [Austin: University of Texas Press, 1996]); Carol Clover *(Men, Women, and Chain Saws: Gender in the Modern Horror Film* [London: BFI, 1993]); and Barbara Creed *(The Monstrous-Feminine: Film, Feminism, Psychoanalysis* [London and New York: Routledge, 1993]). It is interesting to

note that the lifting of censorship laws at the advent of the Weimar Republic meant that *Caligari* emerged amidst a flood of pornographic and sensational-ist films. Certainly, a lack of censorship, the basic freedom to produce hor-rific images, is a fundamental prerequisite for the genre. For a discussion of the lifting of censorship at the time, see Malte Hagener, ed., *Geschlecht in Fesseln: Sexualität zwischen Aufklärung und Ausbeutung im Weimarer Kino, 1918–1933* (Munich: CineGraph Edition Text und Kritik, 2000).

18. It is important to note that if we withdraw from Siegfried Kra-cauer's problematic assertion of a submissive collective German spirit, he identified a function of film in establishing a relationship between the socio-historical conditions (here the new freedoms of the Weimar Republic) and the affective psychological state of an audience. Such a connection between sociohistorical ground and generic qualities is the basis of the term "social psychology" in this chapter.

19. Rick Altman wrote eloquently of the cultural labor performed by genre: "Each generic crossroads is a worksite, a place where cultural labour is performed. Though not all spectators can be expected to recognize or accept the invitation extended by any particular generic crossroads, those who do participate implicitly activate at each crossroads both cultural and generic standards. Within the real world, cultural values of course reign supreme. In the genre world, however, generic values systematically domi-nate—as long as we consider crossroads experiences individually" (152).

20. By realistic I simply mean a form of narrative that does not turn to the supernatural, fantastical, or uncanny. Films in roughly the same period depicting the process of unification include, among others, *The Wall [Die Mauer]* (Böttcher, 1991), *Ostkreuz* (Klier, 1991), *All Lies [Alles Lüge]* (Schier, 1992), *Rising to the Bait [Der Brocken]* (Glowna, 1992), *Hello, Comrade [Grüß Gott, Genosse]* (Stelzer, 1993), *No More Mr. Nice Guy [Wir können auch anders]* (Buck, 1993), *The Blue One [Der Blaue]* (Wawrzyn, 1994), and *The Promise [Das Versprechen]* (Von Trotta, 1994). The sequel to Wender's *Wings of Desire* (1987), *Far Away, so Close* (1991) relies on the fantastical. It picks up the angel theme of his earlier film to explore the transformed conditions of Berlin after the wall; however, it also combines realistic repre-sentations with the fantastical, including significant historical figures, like Mikhail Gorbachev playing himself.

21. It should be clear that the use of the term "queer" here is not syn-onymous with gay or lesbian. Originally "queer" emerged in part as a term that could build larger coalitions among sexual minorities: lesbian, gay bi-sexual, transgendered, and so on. However, in Queer theory, "queer" has moved away from a strict relationship to identity politics and acts as a gen-eral designation of actions that present an antipode to heteronormativity. Here I am exploring abject desires like necrophilia as queer. If "gay" readers resist designating necrophilia as queer, that only reveals normative limits in their applications of the term "queer."

WORKS CITED

Altmann, Rick. *Film/Genre*. London: BFI Publishing, 1999.

Benshoff, Harry. *Monsters in the Closet: Homosexuality and the Horror Film*. Manchester: Manchester University Press, 1997.

Bronfen, Elisabeth. *Over Her Dead Body: Death, Femininity and the Aesthetic.* New York: Routledge, 1992.

Carol, Noël. *The Philosophy of Horror.* New York: Routledge, 1990.

Clover, Carol. *Men, Women, and Chain Saws: Gender in the Modern Horror Film.* London: BFI, 1993.

Coates, Paul. *The Gorgon's Gaze.* Cambridge: Cambridge University Press, 1991.

———. *Film at the Intersection of High and Mass Culture.* Cambridge: Cambridge University Press, 1994.

Creed, Barbara. *The Monstrous-Feminine: Film, Feminism, Psychoanalysis.* London and New York: Routledge, 1993.

Eisner, Lotte H. *The Haunted Screen: Expressionism in the German Cinema and the Influence Of Max Reinhardt.* London: Secker and Warburg, 1973.

Elsaesser, Thomas and Michael Wedel, eds., *The BFI Companion to German Cinema.* London: BFI Publishing, 1999.

Freud, Sigmund. "The Uncanny." In *The Standard Edition of the Complete Psychological Works of Sigmund Freud,* vol 18. London: Hogarth P, 1966.

Grant, Barry Keith. *Film Genre Reader II.* Austin: University of Texas Press, 1995.

———. ed. *Dread of Difference: Gender and the Horror Film.* Austin: University of Texas Press, 1996.

Halle, Randall. "'Happy Ends' to Crises of Heterosexual Desire: Toward a Social Psychology of Recent German Comedies," *Camera Obscura* 44 (2000): 1–39.

Hagener, Malte, ed. *Geschlecht in Fesseln: Sexualität zwischen Aufklärung und Ausbeutung im Weimarer Kino, 1918–1933.* Munich: Cine-Graph Edition Text und Kritik, 2000.

Hermann, Max. "Eine Begegnung mit Jörg Buttgereit." *Artechock Filmmagazin* 22 (1997). <http://www.artechock.de/film/magazin/magaz 722.htm>.

Kerekes, David. *Sex, Murder, Art: The Films of Jörg Buttgereit.* Manchester: Head Press, 1998.

King, Stephen. *Danse Macabre.* New York: Berkeley Books, 1982.

Kracauer, Siegfried. *From Caligari to Hitler: A Psychological History of the German Film.* Princeton, N.J.: Princeton University Press, 1974.

Kristeva, Julia. *Powers of Horror: An Essay on Abjection.* New York: Columbia, 1982.

Pinedo, Isabel Cristina. *Recreational Terror: Women and the Pleasures of Horror Film Viewing.* Albany: State University of New York Press, 1997.

Prawer, Siegbert. *Caligari's Children.* New York: Da Capo Press, 1989

Rohlf, Oliver. "Schreddern & Fleddern: Horror-König wider Willen: Das 3001 zeigt eine Retrospektive mit Werken des Splatter-Filmers Jörg Buttgereit." *taz* (Hamburg), 8 July 1998, 23.

FILMOGRAPHY

Bergmann, Michael. *My Lovely Monster* (1990).

Boll, Uwe. *Amoklauf* (1994).

Buttegreit, Jörg. *Nekromantik* (1987).
———. *Der Todesking*, (1989).
———. *Nekromantik 2: The Return of the Loving Dead [Nekromantik 2: die Rückkehr der liebenden Toten]* (1991).
———. *Schramm* (1993).
Chabrol, Claude. *Club Extinction [Docteur M.]* (1990).
Franco, Jesus. *Eugenie, the Story of Her Journey into Perversion [La Isla de la muerte]* (1969).
Fratzscher, XXX. *Night Time [Sieben Monde]* (1998).
Gutmann, XXX. *The Valley of Shadows [Das Tal der Schatten]* (1999).
Huettner, Ralf. *Babylon [Babylon—Im Bett mit dem Teufel]* (1992).
Ittenbach, Olaf. *Black Past* (1989).
———. *The Burning Moon [Burning Moon: Dieser Film überschreitet alle Grenzen]* (1992).
———. *The Fallen Angel [Premutos: Der gefallene Engel]* (1997).
Jazay, David. *Kiss My Blood* (1998).
Karmakar, Romuald. *The Deathmaker [Der Totmacher]* (1995).
Knarr, Günter. *Holgi* (1999).
Matsutani, Rainer. *Over My Dead Body [Nur über meine Leiche]* (1995).
Murnau, F. W. *Nosferatu* (1922).
Panneck, Sebastian, and Patrick Hollmann. *Urban Scumbags vs. Countryside Zombies* (1992).
Rusnak, Josef. *The 13th Floor* (1999).
Ruzowitzky, Stefan. *Anatomy [Anatomie]* (2000).
Rye, Stellan. *The Student of Prague [Der Student von Prag]* (1913).
Schlingensief, Christoph. *The German Chainsaw Massacre [Das deutsche Kettensägen Massaker]* (1990).
———. *Terror 2000 [Terror 2000: Intensivstation Deutschland]* (1992).
Schnaas, Andreas. *Violent Shit* (1987).
———. *Zombie '90: Extreme Pestilence* (1991).
———. *Violent Shit II* (1992).
———. *Anthropophagous 2000* (1999).
von Trotta, Magarethe. *The Promise [Das Versprechen]* (1994).
Wiene, Robert. *The Cabinet of Dr. Caligari* (1920).

In general these films are difficult to find and travel in underground circles often as pirated copies on video. In the United States, Facets Video, *www.facets.org*, is, of course, a good source, as is German Language Video Center, *www.germanvideo.com*. Kim's Video, *www.kimsvideo.com*, has proven very helpful. These sources carry some videos by Buttgereit, Ittenbach, and Schlingensief, as well as many of the classic horror films mentioned here. In Germany, *www.splatting-image.de* and Splatter.de are good websites for information and addresses for the latest on German Underground Horror. Schlingensief's films can be purchased on video from absolut MEDIEN GmbH, Boxhagenerstr 18, 10245 Berlin, *info@absolutMEDIEN.de*. Ittenbach's films are available through Videodrom, Fürbringrerstr. 17, 10961 Berlin.

CHAPTER 15

Picture-Perfect War

An Analysis of Joseph Vilsmaier's
Stalingrad (1993)

Robert C. Reimer

"We have seen it before," writes film critic Stanley Kaufmann, referring to Joseph Vilsmaier's war epic *Stalingrad*, released in 1993, on the fiftieth anniversary of that (in)famous battle. "The data are different, naturally," continues Kaufmann, "but we know from past war films that friendships will be ended by bullet, that some hothead will fire at the wrong time, that one or two men will simply crack under pressure, and in a German film, there will be some soldiers who despise Hitler" (32). Yet have we seen this war film before? Does *Stalingrad* follow the formula of the generic war film so closely, changing the data to suit the peculiarities of the battle, but recycling ideas and images from other films to satisfy audience expectations? The answer is ambiguous because the film's stance toward war is ambivalent. On the one hand, *Stalingrad* is a conventional war film. Its scenes of fighting, camaraderie, bravery, and sacrifice valorize the spirit of war, speaking to its necessity as a human endeavor. The movie shows the tendency of many war films, especially those from Hollywood about the Second World War, to valorize the necessity of fighting. Yet here, as in many of the Hollywood war films, the images of heroism also provide antiwar rhetoric, as the deeds of glory that the images represent occur within a context of death and destruction. On the other hand, *Stalingrad* is also an antiwar film. As with other antiwar films, the images of carnage, destruction, death, and cynicism condemn war's existence by their very presence in the film. The director wants to disturb viewers and move them to promise "never again." Vilsmaier's movie thus avoids most scenes of heroism, emphasizing antiwar rhetoric that questions the value and need of this battle and exposes the waste in terms of human suffering.

We have indeed seen the conventional war film that is found in *Stalingrad* before. Examples of the genre range from epics starring John Wayne, such as *The Fighting Seabees* (Edward Ludwig, 1944) or *Flying Leathernecks* (Nicholas Ray, 1951) to the recent Steven Spielberg film, *Saving Private Ryan* (1998). As representative of "the dominant tendency of war films which is to glorify victory and heroize the individual" (Hayward 390), these films about the Second World War give value to the actions of those who fight the Axis powers. Of course, the point of view is reversed in *Stalingrad*, but the tendency to valorize at least some of the virtues of war is present. We have also seen the antiwar film that is found in *Stalingrad* before. Even though war films "only rarely . . . look at the horrors of war" (Hayward 396), Vilsmaier's movie presents these horrors clearly enough to be reminiscent of Lewis Milestone's *All Quiet on the Western Front* (1930) or even Oliver Stone's *Platoon* (1986). Like Milestone and Stone, Vilsmaier examines the misguided patriotism and questionable government policies that put young men in harm's way. To be sure, this is the wrong war, as most of the antiwar subgenre focus on wars other than the Second World War. Yet even the Second World War spawned films such as *Catch 22* (Mike Nichols, 1970) and *Slaughterhouse-Five* (George Roy Hill, 1972), whose antiwar rhetoric questions the military mind, especially as it pertains to lines of command, objectives, and motives.[1] Film historian Susan Hayward offers a definition of the war film whose iconography satisfies both the conventional war movie and the antiwar film. "Combat is either on a grand scale (military maneuvers, tanks and so on) or on a small, even individual one (as with fighter pilots). Quite frequently there is a target to be obtained (a hill, a bridge). There is an ensemble within the corps of servicemen with whom we identify . . . and who display different types of courage. Comradeship is paramount. The enemy is absent except as an impersonal other (and therefore bad)" (Hayward 407). The war formula described here could apply equally to conventional as well as antiwar films.

It is hardly surprising that Vilsmaier's *Stalingrad* gives critics a sense of déjà vu, for Vilsmaier adopts familiar war film iconography for the film. Yet he also adapts the images and ideas generally found in a film about the Second World War, as well he must. As a German director telling of a battle from the German perspective, he is not merely telling a war story but the story of German defeat. Moreover, most of the world, including Germans, professes satisfaction and relief that the Allies defeated the Axis powers. Hence, the film may use conventional formulae but must find ways to counter a positive reading of the exploits of fighting. In this way, *Stalingrad* resembles films about wars that were unpopular, fought for questionable motives, or ended in defeat. Yet, even as an antiwar film, its iconography nonetheless occasionally suggests valorization of war and not just its condemnation. Vilsmaier's ambivalence places viewers in a double bind, for when viewing iconography familiar from other war films, viewers are predisposed to identify with characters similarly to the way they identify with characters in these other films, which generally means validating their actions. Yet the characters are clearly supporting a corrupt cause. The director faces his problem of making a war film from a German perspective by subverting conventional iconography with a decidedly antimilitary code of ethics and subverting antiwar imagery with aesthetic composition. That is, he tries to turn the conventional war movie and the typical *antiwar* film into an anti *war-film*. In the remainder of the chapter I compare *Stalingrad* to its models, looking at structure, imagery, and characterization to show that the mixed messages of the film create tension that pulls viewers in multiple directions. Sometimes the film asks us to see war as natural. Sometimes it asks us to see it as the construct of a few powerful men. At times *Stalingrad* wants us to experience the virtues of fighting, comradeship, bravery, and sacrifice, and at other times to condemn those aspects of war. Finally, the film wants us to understand the meaning of the battle for today, and yet it wants us to recognize that this battle took place a long time ago. The result of the conflicting messages can be nostalgia, confusion, or dismay at what the film says about Germany today and its war legacy.

In its three guises as conventional war film, *antiwar* film, and anti *war-film*, *Stalingrad* is quintessential Vilsmaier.[2] In his review of the movie, Urs Jenny, film critic of *Der Spiegel*, refers to the director as a "complete emotionalist" ("handfester Pathetiker") (127), and, indeed, the film asks for our emotional participation, thanks in large part to an almost ever-present musical score by Norbert Schneider. A Neapolitan-like melody captures our attention from the beginning, reminding us of sunny beaches and young love. This gives way to a shrill whistle as a troop train enters a long dark tunnel in Italy and reemerges in the Soviet Union. The music track then returns to the film's main motif, a slow, mournful march rhythm that plays during the opening credits and reappears whenever the men are moving closer to their inevitable fate. Trailers, reviews, and publicity for the film remind potential audiences of the depressing numbers, should they not already know them from history books. Interspersed among brief images of love and battle the trailers announce:

> 450,000 men marched into one city.
> Only 10,000 returned.
> This is the story of four of them.
> In the winter of 1942, it was too cold for tears.

The trailer features Vilsmaier's signature emotionalism, using scenes from the film that suggest a love story as well as a war film.

The film asks for contemplation as well as tears, however. With an eye for the visually striking, sometimes shocking, Vilsmaier seduces viewers into thinking about his alarming images by making them aesthetically beautiful. In so doing, he often renders the images harmless. He composes his film such that almost any frame reveals a well-balanced composition whose lighting, colors, and placement of characters and objects appeal to the eye. As a consequence, when bodies are blown apart, blood spurts from a head wound, or men freeze to death in the snow, viewers are apt to see composition before they see the composition's content. We thus think about what we see before we experience it, reacting in shock only afterward at the horror. That is, Vilsmaier uses the aesthetic composition of the image to force contemplation of the horror the image depicts, but with only partial success. A battle scene halfway through the film illustrates this well: During a particularly destructive battle, two members of the German squadron with whom the film has asked viewers to identify stare out from their foxhole (toward the camera) in a close-up that suggests horror and disbelief. An edit then reveals what the men see, a comrade who has been cut in half, his lower body lying on the ground with feet away from the camera. The upper body is upright in the snow. The man is not yet dead but rather screams in agony as his head bows to the side, signifying his death. A thin line of blood runs between the two halves of the body, connecting them in the otherwise white landscape. Whatever revulsion and ultimate antiwar sentiment the scene may produce in viewers is delayed by its painterly composition, which forces the eye to scan the "painting" rather than focus immediately on the horror of the moment.[3] Eventually the horror of the moment overpowers the beautiful form, but its effect as antiwar statement is diminished. The next scene subverts the film's antiwar rhetoric and reverts to a conventional war film formula, according to which the slain man's comrades exact quick if irrational revenge on the enemy. Moreover, as the dead man's comrades succeed in their attack on tanks and Soviet soldiers in stopping the enemy advance, they also give viewers a small victory within the impending ultimate defeat, the only reminder of which is the film's signature leitmotif, a slow processional series of notes suggesting the German military's march to inevitable disaster.

Stalingrad indeed recycles the war iconography of conventional and antiwar films. In order to examine how the film embeds the unconventional within the conventional, I want to introduce a more specific template of influence, namely war films told from the German perspective. When film critic Stanley Kaufmann suggests that we have seen the way Stalingrad represents "some soldiers who despise Hitler," (32) he is surely referencing the films of German directors whose works emphasize the separation between Nazi leaders and the men fighting the battles. Beginning with Paul May's 08/15 trilogy in 1954 and continuing through Frank Wisbar's Officer Factory [Fabrik der Offiziere] (1960), a number of films appeared in West Germany whose narratives revolve around the German enlisted man during the Second World War. The majority of these films helped viewers to cope with Germany's past by focusing attention on the exploits of the common soldier or sailor in both comic and tragic situations and away from the ideology of the Third Reich. The more conventional of these war films emphasize valor, comradeship, and sacrifice fighting the Allied enemy, but they also show a second enemy, the National Socialist leadership, which the men combat with cunning, humor, and sometimes subversive activity. The less conventional of these films focus on the brutality of war, like Bernhard Wicki's The Bridge [Die Brücke] (1959), for example, or foreground Nazi Germany as aggressor and the Soviet Union as victim of the war, as in the films from East Germany.[4]

Stalingrad is most often compared to Wolfgang Petersen's The Boat [Das Boot] (1981) and Lewis Milestone's All Quiet on the Western Front (1930), two films considered by most critics to be antiwar. Comparing Stalingrad to The Boat, critics reveal ambivalence to films told from the perspective of the Germans, accepting the films as representation of "war as Hell," but rejecting the portrayal of the men who are fighting. For example, Pat Dowell comments in *Air Force Times* that like the film *The Boat*, *Stalingrad*, "succeeds as an indictment of war by keeping its focus largely below politics. It concentrates on the life of the German grunt in one of the most desperate situations soldiers have faced." He adds, however, that Vilsmaier's film, "glosses over some big moral questions in the process" (42). Mark Jenkins, film reviewer for the *Washington City Paper*, is seemingly neutral on the effect of the film's perspective, writing that the film "makes the customary effort to clear the central characters from any implications of Nazism; as in *Das Boot*, they're just soldiers doing their job" (38). Louis Menaashe, reviewing the film in *Cineaste*, remarks that the perspective gives him greater understanding for the common soldiers' suffering: "As with the riveting *Das Boot* . . . , while I find myself not exactly rooting for the Germans—I know they were stunningly defeated, anyway, and got what they and their war aims deserved—I can't refrain from feeling some sympathy for some of them in their miserable end" (50).

The comparison between *Stalingrad* and *The Boat* should not be overstressed, however. To be sure, both films are told from the German perspective and both start with a celebration of victory that ends when the men are suddenly called back to duty. Petersen's film, though, is more overtly exculpatory than Vilsmaier's, and at the same time also stresses the virtues of military discipline more. In *The Boat* battle fatigue may indeed precipitate a cynical attitude toward the German High Command on the part of the enlisted men, the officers, and their captain, which dominates the movie, but the submarine crew never wavers in its allegiance to military virtues. Petersen gives substance to the cynicism in a scene in which the men of the submarine confront the officers during a brief leave in Gibraltar. Yet besides emphasizing the mistrust of the crew vis-à-vis their superiors in ways reminiscent of Germany's war films in the 1950s, the scene gives no indication that the men doubt the righteousness of the war, and makes clear that the men will perform their duty. Indeed, after this confrontation, the story follows the formula of the conventional war film. The submarine escapes through the strait with the ensuing bombardment from Allied ships in a scene that is portrayed with traditional suspense and close calls. Moreover, the mission succeeds, regardless of how foolhardy and meaningless it seems. Indeed, it is not until after the boat arrives safely at its destination that the film acknowledges that the Germans lost the war. It is as if Petersen belatedly realizes the sub fought not only for the losing side in the war but for the side that history agrees should have lost. The attack on the harbor, which sinks the submarine and kills most of the crew, solves the dilemma.

Stalingrad, in contrast to The Boat, introduces the gulf between officers and enlisted men from the start and opens the divide ever wider as the film progresses, creating cynicism that saps the men's resolve to fight and eventually leads to their decision to desert. Vilsmaier restructures the elements of the typical war film, locating suspense and drama not in battle scenes, or not only in battle scenes, but rather primarily in confrontations between officers and their men. That is, he develops the divisions between the leadership and the enlisted men into outright hostilities. In so doing he focuses conflict outside the battles and relocates tension from the battlefield to personal confrontations between the men and their superiors. In the defining scene of the film, the four principles, representing the usual suspects in a war film—a hardened veteran, a raw recruit, a cynic, and a naïve lieutenant—are commanded to execute a band of old men and children. After vigorous protest, they comply, but their action so demoralizes them that they desert. Emotionally drained from their complicity in the death of civilians, the men separate themselves as good soldiers from the evil captain. By emphasizing the men's moral dilemma, the scene saves the characters from total condemnation. They do not blindly follow orders; they do so for reasons of self-preservation, a valid although not an ennobling action. Moreover, once they recognize how dehumanized they have become, they regain their humanity by deserting.

Comparisons with All Quiet on the Western Front seem at first inappropriate. Milestone's film, after all, is about the First World War, not the Second, and it was directed in Hollywood by a Ukrainian of Jewish descent, not by a German. Yet the film is based on a German novel, and even if about another war, Stalingrad references several scenes from Milestone's film, which suggests a comparison is in order. Moreover, the two films are related in tone. Milestone, as does Vilsmaier, focuses on war as death, as negation of value, rather than as a showcase for displaying the virtues of war, as in conventional films, or merely as a battlefield on which men die, as in the typical antiwar film. In perhaps the best remembered scene of All Quiet on the Western Front, a young German soldier must wait for rescue in a foxhole as an enemy soldier lies next to him dying. As the day drags on, it is clear to the soldier and to us how life slowly drains from the body, a fate that awaits all young men in war. In another scene, friends are with their injured comrade in a field hospital. The film has to this point emphasized the comrade's pride in his expensive boots, now worthless to him as his leg has been amputated. It would seem that even simple pleasures cannot survive war's destructive power.

Stalingrad achieves its own level of pathos with images and situations that could be borrowed from Milestone's film. Twice Vilsmaier includes scenes of a Russian soldier dying in the presence of the Germans. The point of war, as the men know, is to kill the enemy. Yet, just as in Milestone's film, giving the enemy a face emphasizes not only the common link between soldiers but their common fate as well. Stalingrad, too, has a scene in a field hospital in which the friends must beg to get care for their dying comrade. Absent, however, is the pathos surrounding the amputee's boots. Vilsmaier refers to Milestone's film instead in a scene on the battlefield, where one recruit steals the boots off a dead comrade, who "won't be needing them anymore." The change in venue also allows Vilsmaier to stress the lack of adequate clothing associated with the Russian campaign. The films most resemble each other in the portrayal of the death of their films' main character(s) in the last scenes of the movies. As All Quiet on the Western Front nears its end, there is a deception of a satisfactory outcome for the character in whom the audience has expended the most emotional energy. Yet as he reaches out for a butterfly, a symbol of ethereal beauty as well as of the soul, the young man is killed. The negation of life and beauty could hardly contain more pathos. Vilsmaier ends with a similar appeal to the emotions in a visual comment that freezes the frame as two of the men we have invested time in freeze to death and become a frozen sculpture to the futility and stupidity of war.

As much similarity as Stalingrad has with All Quiet on the Western Front and The Boat, however, its true antecedent and model is Frank Wisbar's Dogs, Do You Want to Live Forever? [Hunde, wollt ihr ewig leben?] (1958).[5] Surprisingly, most critics and reviewers have overlooked the similarities between the two films, although the question of their relationship is begged not only because of their common theme (Battle of Stalingrad) but also because of their common approach to the material. Moreover, Vilsmaier's changes in the material suggest he may be responding to the lack of political awareness of Wisbar's film, which at its release was described as "routine amateur stuff" (Bandmann 216).

Released in 1958, *Dogs, Do You Want to Live Forever?*
reflects the second wave of interest in films about the past.[6] Following the model set forth by Paul May's film trilogy *08/15* and
fictionalized accounts of the Stalingrad battle, *Dogs, Do You
Want to Live Forever?* approaches Germany's military history
cognizant of viewers' emotions, allegiances, and feelings. Like its
predecessors, it presents itself as an apologia, justifying the actions of Germany's military in fighting for the Third Reich. Accordingly, enlisted men, the chaplain, and young officers through
the rank of lieutenant are victims of an uncaring, incompetent,
cynical, and callous leadership. Wisbar follows Fritz Wöss's
novel, on which the film is based, up to the actual capitulation
and therefore excludes any direct description of imprisonment
and death at the hands of the Soviets other than what is implied
in the statistics. The film captures the spirit of the novel, which
Jens Ebert describes as "a song of praise to the will-power and
maturity of the fighting man" (271). In addition, it reflects the
question of responsibility found in the novel, which, according to
Gerd Steckel, "speaks again and again of guilt and innocence"
(310). Michael Kumpfmüller, in an exhaustive study of the literature on Stalingrad, similarly describes both novel and film as
therapeutic works, quoting an early review of the film: "Every
German man who comes out of the theater feels he has been ex-
cused"(226). Indeed, responsibility shifts around in the film until
it comes to rest exclusively on Hitler.

The outline for *Dogs, Do You Want to Live Forever?* could
come from any number of war films: a young officer, sent to the
front to command his first squadron, works to earn the respect
of his men, harnesses their otherwise unmilitary energies into a
fighting unit, loses some of them, and in the process gains insight
into his strengths and weaknesses and learns how to be a leader
of men. Wismar changes the formula only to conform to the German point of view from which the story is told and to underscore
the disastrous outcome of the battle. A new lieutenant (Wisse) is
sent to the eastern front to fight in Stalingrad. On the way he
helps a woman of Russian and German parentage, a character
who is then dropped from the story only to reappear again shortly
before the final defeat. Arriving at the front, the Lieutenant bonds
with his men but makes an immediate enemy of a major, who
reappears at crucial scenes in the film as a stand-in for the corrupt, cynical, and ultimately cowardly nature of the leadership.
Wisse goes from enthusiastic to realistic to dejected as the campaign drags on, until finally, as one of the few survivors of the

battle, he surrenders to the Soviets. *Stalingrad* tells the same story, changing names and using 1990s production values, rougher language, more graphic violence, a more cynical representation of religion, somewhat less moralizing by the characters, and greater emphasis of Nazi evil. A young lieutenant (Witzland) goes to the front, meets a woman of Russian/German parentage, a character who disappears until just before the end of the film. He bonds with his men, makes an enemy of one officer who reappears at crucial moments in the story, and goes from enthusiastic to realistic to cynical. Vilsmaier also increases the pessimism of the story, in that the lieutenant deserts and dies. Though similar in their narratives and in their treatment of the legend of guilt that surrounds the Battle of Stalingrad, a number of differences exist that shift the focus from exculpating the guilt of the individuals to contemplating the tragedy of the battle.

As is to be expected, their differing approach to the material is clearest in the elements where the two films are dissimilar. In keeping with Wöss's novel, Wisbar encloses *Dogs, Do You Want to Live Forever?* in a narrative frame that serves multiple purposes. First, the opening and closing scenes place the story in a historical framework that adds distance to an event about which Germans at the time of the film's release still had emotional memories and with which they had been trying to come to terms even before the war had ended.[7] Second, the final eight-minute sequence of scenes reinforces the myths that the film has been creating: namely that this was Hitler's war and that members of the military were his personal victims. Hitler provides the penultimate speech of the film, responding to the news that the Sixth Army has been destroyed: "Don't get so emotional. It's only an army. Put together a new one." Third, the opening scene of victoriously parading Nazi troops contrasts with the closing shots of the defeated soldiers on their way to the camps from which most never returned, echoing other war films of the period that offered viewers a warning about repeating the mistakes of the past. The last words of the film are those of the chaplain and a soldier's response: "Perhaps we will learn from all of this." "And perhaps not." Whether the warning pertains to allowing oneself to be seduced by Nazism or to committing mistakes in fighting the war, remains open. The chaplain's words would suggest a more general warning. Yet in the first part of this closing, Paulus refers to "enormous errors that were committed by all," implying a more limited understanding of responsibility.[8]

Vilsmaier's *Stalingrad* commemorated the fiftieth anniversary of the Battle of Stalingrad. Historical remoteness thus creates its own distance, and Vilsmaier accordingly eschews the narration and overt warnings that Wisbar employed to provide safe haven from the painful memories of the past. Indeed, Vilsmaier seems to realize that the distance afforded by fifty years may be too great for viewers to traverse and goes out of his way to make the horror real enough so that they aren't able "to forget what war really is"(Jaenecke 71).

Realism and a more linear style of telling the story, then, are the biggest differences between *Dogs, Do You Want to Live Forever?* and *Stalingrad*. Vilsmaier's film begins in sunny Italy. Music, camera, and location shooting work together to bring viewers into the film. The carefree attitude of the men who will become the story's principle characters interests us from the beginning, since we know this is a film about total destruction and wonder which, if any, of the men will live. The beginning also introduces the division between the good (enlisted) men and their overbearing officers, giving viewers two conflicts about which to worry, the war on the front and the war behind the lines. Equally as important, though, for reception of the film, is that the beginning moves viewers toward identifying with the unheroic heroes of the story and thus provides from the beginning a barrier against an uncritical acceptance of the values of war.

The two films come together and differ most clearly in the way they divide the military into soldiers and their leaders. As mentioned, Lieutenant Wisse in *Dogs, Do You Want to Live Forever?* has an enemy in the person of a major who appears at critical times in the story. Yet he is never more than an annoyance to Wisse, and matters hardly at all to the viewers, since his cowardice marks him as other and less than the men. In addition, through their own obvious heroism, the men render him as no danger to the company. This is borne out when Wisse kills the major as he runs toward the enemy with a flag of surrender. The structure of the scene allows viewers to reject the major's cowardice and as corollary recognize bravery in the face of uncertain even if meaningless death as a virtue. In contrast, Lieutenant Witzland and three of the men under him in *Stalingrad* must deal with a more updated, cinematic enemy, a captain whose portrayal reflects the stereotyped Nazi officer familiar from Hollywood films. His appearance whenever the lieutenant and his men display some semblance of humanity, whenever they come to some notion of the criminality of the Nazi regime, is clearly a danger to the men, since he could have them court-martialed and shot if he wanted to. They kill him not because he is trying to desert but because he is trying to prevent them from doing so, his killing providing for viewers a momentary rejection of the values of war. Since Hitler appears only once in *Stalingrad,* as a disembodied voice on the radio, the captain functions to extend the criminality of Nazi action beyond the Berlin leadership. Clearly his death also exonerates the men for their act, since they do the right thing, not only by deserting but also by rejecting Nazism. I will return to this ambiguity and ambivalence in my conclusion.

The commonalties between *Dogs, Do You Want to Live Forever?* and *Stalingrad* extend to characters as well as individual scenes. For example, Vilsmaier leaves undeveloped a subplot that involves a relationship or nonrelationship between Lieutenant Witzland and a Russian woman whose mother was German. It may be that the directors felt their films needed a female presence as a balance to the war. Indeed, the Russian woman in *Dogs, Do You Want to Live Forever?* offers solace to Wisse when he is trapped behind enemy lines. She also provides Wisse a humanitarian pedigree, as his last act before going to the front is trying to get her a visa to stay behind the line of battle. The inclusion of a woman serves a different purpose in *Stalingrad.* Beyond giving a role in the film to his wife, Dana Varovna, who appears in almost all of his films,[9] Vilsmaier includes this minor character to redeem the lieutenant for his earlier support of the war but also to offer a more general condemnation of Germany. As the campaign nears its end, the Russian woman, who had earlier tricked the lieutenant and pushed him into an underground canal, thereby almost drowning him, reappears in a bunker as the sex-prisoner of the commanding officers. Although Witzland's men want to rape her, he protects her, thus revealing the distance he has come from enthusiastic supporter to weary dissident. The scene precludes smugness as the woman not only refuses to thank her rescuer but instead taunts him and finally announces that she will never forgive herself for once having loved the German language. The scene is reminiscent of Konrad Wolf's *I Was 19 [Ich war 19]* (1967), an East German film, in which a teacher asks how he should explain to his students how the German language can contain both the word Goethe and the word Auschwitz.

Most importantly, though, the Russian woman allows viewers to recognize Witzland as victim. In an artfully composed shot in which the two characters sit on opposite sides of the bed, their backs to each other, as if they were a mirror reflection, Vils-maier equates their common experience of guilt, pain, and absolution.

> Woman: "I'm a German's whore."
> Lieutenant: "Nonsense. You were forced."
> Woman: "I should have killed myself."
> Lieutenant: "I thought the same."

Their position in relation to each other and the significance of the dialog to both their situations transfers the violation of the woman at the hands of her captors to Witzland, who has been violated, indeed emasculated, by his superiors, his demoralization making him incapable of fighting.

Although *Dogs, Do You Want to Live Forever?* and *Stalingrad* are careful to locate negative traits in the leadership and positive ones in the men, both films also allow for bonding with at least one of the commanding officers. In *Dogs, Do You Want to Live Forever?* one of the commanding officers as well as the chaplain treats the men well, indicating that not all leadership was corrupt. In *Stalingrad,* the purpose of the good commander's role is ambiguous. On the one hand, he treats the men no more harshly than one would expect of a no-nonsense officer. On the other hand, Vilsmaier gives his commander the persona of John Wayne, from both his Second World War and Western movies. In addition, he outfits him with a mechanical hand that has a mind of its own, reminiscent of the mechanical hand of Dr. Strangelove, from Stanley Kubrick's 1964 film of that name. Thus, when the captain is not seen raising his hand and motioning forward, exhorting his men "follow me," he is hitting his prosthesis, attempting to get it to function properly. The captain furnishes the only comic relief of the film,[10] at the same time that he focuses attention on the role of charisma in war, albeit without development. At one point the men accede to a suicide mission as long as the captain will be in command, and at another he is present when their ranks are reinstated after a punishment.

Stalingrad references two additional scenes from *Dogs, Do You Want to Live Forever?* with an attempt to deflate the received history. In the first, the film alludes to a scene from the army field hospital, also found, as mentioned above, in *All Quiet on the Western Front.* Wisbar had borrowed the homage to Milestone's film, or Remarque's novel, to indicate a change in the attitude of the men toward the war.[11] During a radio speech by

Göring, the chaplain enters the hospital and turns the radio off, signaling that the death and suffering on the floor surrounding the radio exposes the lies of the regime. Vilsmaier then references that scene to drive home not only the suffering caused by war and its sheer inhumanity but the callous attitude of those in command. The four principles have come to the hospital in futile search for a doctor to treat a comrade. Vilsmaier uses actual amputees in the scene to give his film the realism necessary to reflect the horrors of war (Jaenecke 71). When the four men are punished for wanting to help their friend, the criminality of the leaders and the innocence of the men in their ordeal are once again highlighted. In the second of the scenes, Vilsmaier places a legend found in films about the First and the Second World Wars into question, namely the momentary truce when troops listen to music (sometimes Christmas carols) and gather their dead. In *Dogs, Do You Want to Live Forever?* the cease-fire is agreed to easily by the Germans when the Russians request it. During the operation, one of the soldiers plays a piano conveniently available in the rubble of a building, and both sides collect their dead and wounded without incident, restarting hostilities at the exact appointed half hour. Vilsmaier places the legend into question first by characterizing the Germans as reluctant to engage in the cease-fire out of mistrust of the Russians. Indeed, the lieutenant has difficulty in locating volunteers for the mission. Second, he emphasizes the mistrust by having one of the division fire on the Russians during the operation. The scene is important because it is one of only a few instances in the film when the Russians are shown as the co-victims of this war, a point of fact that Wisbar, and other films told from the German side, completely ignore.[12] That Vilsmaier intends to introduce the Russian as victim here is suggested by the length of screen time devoted to their suffering. Although the scene of truce comprises only a few minutes of the overall movie, it focuses almost exclusively on the Russian wounded.

Judging from critics' reviews, the contradictory images of *Stalingrad* make them uneasy. The film asks them to identify with men who fought for a government whose role as aggressor in the Second World War it never makes clear. Kaufmann's comments, quoted previously, disparage the film's use of formula, to be sure, but also its use of a German cliché of apologia ("and in a German film, there will be some soldiers who despise Hitler") (32). Barbara Schulgasser, film critic for the *San Francisco Examiner*, commenting on the film's German point of view, finds that

Stalingrad exonerates the German soldier more than she is willing to accept: "You can argue that as an anti-war document *Stalingrad* has merit, but it still is a defense of German behavior . . . the movie just seems to let the Germans off the hook a little more than this viewer is willing to tolerate" (C6). Hal Hinson writes similarly, "Vilsmaier is arguing that no one is responsible, no oaths hold, no morality applies. . . . Still, no matter how it is presented, Vilsmaier asks that we join him in a game of pass-the-buck" (www.washingtonpost.com). Finally, some critics refer to the similarities with Hollywood films about the Vietnam War, *Platoon* in particular. Film critic J. Hoberman, for example, refers to the film as an "arctic Vietnam" movie (47).

Comparisons to *Platoon* and other Vietnam films may seem innocuous at first. We must keep in mind, though, that Hollywood's films of the war in Southeast Asia are often seen as redeeming the Vietnam veteran and as failing to show a connection between the men fighting the war and the government responsible for the war.[13] Thus, just as films that portray the glory of battle often have an antiwar subtext, films that show the horrors of war can contain a subtext that excuses the soldiers fighting the war. As discussed earlier, and as suggested by critic Mark Jenkins in his review, *Stalingrad* reveals exactly such a disconnect. "The script (by Johannes Heide, Jürgen Buscher, and the director) makes the customary effort to clear the central characters from any implications of Nazism; as in *The Boat*, they're just soldiers doing their job, and guardedly skeptical of the ideology that's sent them to Russia" (Jenkins 38). In this case, then, the comparison takes on added meaning, suggesting a similar process of redemption is at work. Perhaps such worries are well placed. One of the many Internet reviews of *Stalingrad* reveals how strong a subtext of rehabilitation of the fighting man's image might be: "The Nazis may have been 'Jew-hating power-mad sickos,' but *Stalingrad* shows us they were also human-beings—something we rarely see in films" (Steinbacher).

Stalingrad remained in the top ten at the box office in Germany for over five weeks, during which time a million Germans saw the film. Although not a success in theaters in the United States—it played mainly in the larger metropolises or at film societies—the number of guest comments on Internet sites that sell the video indicate the film has been successful in America in its video afterlife. If one considers the popularity of the film in Germany and the uncritical and unreflective "guest comments" found on database film sites, it is easy to become concerned about the film's subtext of victimology.[14] Whether we choose to see *Stalingrad* as a conventional war film, as some critics and viewers do, however, or as an antiwar film, as others do, the subtext of the film that soldiers are not responsible for their acts remains.

Despite its serious tone and its antiwar message, ultimately *Stalingrad* fails to rise above its predecessors in the 1950s. That should not be surprising since the movie fits into the body of Vilsmaier's other works, works in which either gentle nostalgia or lyrical aesthetics detract from or prevent a critical reception of the subject matter. Joseph Vilsmaier's films are commercial in a way that films of the New German Cinema are not. The signers of the Oberhausen Manifesto may have declared 1950s cinema dead, banishing sentimentality, likable characters—or at least ones with whom viewers can identify—and an unproblematic world from the screen, but Vilsmaier was not listening. He makes films like they used to in Germany. Echoing the tone, style, and politics of 1950s cinema, the director offers viewers a world they recognize and a worldview with which they feel comfortable, even as he presents images of a far from perfect past. His films, which include *Autumn Milk [Herbstmilch]* (1988), *We're Cleaning Up [Rama dama]* (1990), *Charlie and Louise [Das doppelte Löttchen]* (1993), *Stalingrad* (1993), *Brother of Sleep [Schlafes Bruder]* (1995), and *The Harmonists [Comedian Harmonists]* (1997), transport viewers to simpler, if sometimes harsher and more primitive, times.

Viewers easily shed tears at Vilsmaier's movies,[15] but they just as easily leave the movie house feeling that the world is as it should be. In *Autumn Milk*, Vilsmaier's directorial debut, the director conjures up a fairy tale existence for the film's heroine, who must endure a series of folkloric hardships, including suffering at the hands of a mean-spirited mother-in-law during the period of the Third Reich. Filming in atmospheric colors, Vilsmaier eschews confronting history in favor of nostalgic remembrances. The high point in the movie comes as Anna Wimschneider, on whose memoirs the film is based, confronts a district leader, demanding he grant her request for a prisoner of war to work her farm and at the same time distancing herself from "his thousand year Reich." Unlike other films set on the home front made only a decade earlier in which women who have been left at home are still alone when the war ends, *Autumn Milk* has a happy ending. Anna's husband returns home just as she is about to be turned out of the home by her mother-in-law. Banishing his mother from the house, as one would banish an evil sorceress, the husband takes his wife out in the yard to dance, and the film ends, suggesting normalcy has returned and the reign of Nazi terror is over.[16]

Autumn Milk is what Germans call a Heimatfilm (a nostalgic film about one's home region or country). It was one of the favorite genres of German filmmakers in the 1950s, referring to states of mind but also to actual places, suggesting nation while being specific to region. The Heimatfilm of the 1950s presented a safe haven, a place to which to escape. Moreover, it was a way to disavow the cultural rupture of 1933–45. The Heimatfilm was also anathema to the signers of the Oberhausen Manifesto, calling forth their dismissive attitude of films of the 1950s. For the years of New German Cinema (1962–83) the anti-Heimatfilm became the preferred format for this genre. For example, Volker Schlöndorff parodied the historical idyll found in the Heimat ideal in his The Sudden Wealth of the Poor People of Kombach [Der plötzliche Reichtum der armen Leute von Kombach] (1971). Peter Fleischmann parodied the genre's rural idyll in Hunting Scenes from Lower Bavaria [Jagdszenen aus Niederbayern] (1969).

Unlike his Oberhausen predecessors, Vilsmaier prefers to recycle 1950s images without Schlöndorff's or Fleischmann's irony. His second film, We're Cleaning Up (1990), for example, tells the story of a young couple separated by the Second World War. When the husband fails to return after the war, the woman eventually begins a new relationship, and as her life is being rebuilt, her husband returns, her new lover leaves, and the film ends. Whatever problems the film's story suggests are lost in nostalgia for late 1940s Munich, as thousands of women helped rebuild the city. Yet Vilsmaier avoids the political aspects of postwar Germany in favor of a generic love story. Again a comparison with films of New German Cinema with a similar theme helps illuminate the nostalgic quality of Vilsmaier's work. The heroine of Rainer Werner Fassbinder's The Marriage of Maria Braun [Die Ehe der Maria Braun] (1979) represents a generation of women who, in rebuilding Germany, lose their soul in the process and ironically their power as well, once the men return. Likewise, the heroine of Helma Sanders-Brahms's Germany, Pale Mother [Deutschland, bleiche Mutter] (1980) grows in her role as independent woman and has difficulties reconciling her loss of autonomy once her husband returns after the war. In contrast, the heroine of *We're Cleaning Up* represents a generation of women who rebuild their lives as they clean up Germany, fitting back into their traditional roles as the men return.

Stalingrad shares with Vilsmaier's other films the director's propensity for striking imagery. From beginning to end, the film is dominated by "beautiful pictures," scenes that are artfully composed but depict horrific content. The director uses light and heat to show a progression from sunny Italy, where all is bathed in sunlight, to the frozen tundra, where in spite of the time of day, no visible sun is present. In between, as the men trek from Mediterranean to tundra, they become part of a series of seemingly endless tableaux of characters marching, riding, fighting, standing, and lying down, lit by fires coming from barrels used for heat. When the barrels are absent, light comes from exploding shells and mines or burning houses. In spite of the fire, though, there seems to be no heat, only light. The first of the tableaux occurs soon after the arrival in Russia, as soldiers, fatigued and injured, sit and lean in toward the center of the composition, their faces illuminated by a flame from a barrel in the lower right hand of the scene. Even though the mise-en-scene is constantly moving, each successive frame reveals a similarly studied shot. It is as if the stasis of the battle in the "kettle" has caused stasis in the film's movement, and nonmovement has caused loss of heat. In the penultimate scene when the deserting men find a bunker, the only heat again comes from the fire in a barrel in the middle of the room, its light illuminating each successive shot. Vilsmaier, though, has reserved his most striking tableau for last, a painterly scene that depicts the surviving two deserters transfigured into a monument to the Battle of Stalingrad. As the two surviving men settle down in the snow, their bodies form a sculptural triangle in a sea of blinding white light. As the men slowly die, snow begins to cover them. The shot is held for over a minute before the credits roll and then remains on the screen for the duration of the credits. Long absent is any resemblance to a conventional war film. Also absent, though, is any allusion to the horrors of the *antiwar* film. In place of the conventional war film and the *antiwar* film, Vilsmaier has crafted an anti *war-film*. It speaks not about the virtues of war or the sacrifice of dying, nor does it speak of the horror of death. Instead it turns war and dying into an object for aesthetic contemplation.

NOTES

1. In addition to these obvious favorites of the 1960s culture of protest, other films about the Second World War at least in part subvert their

own war rhetoric with antiwar tendencies. For a detailed analysis of the sociology of the war film, in particular of the antiwar rhetoric and texts within supposedly conventional war films, see Gaile McGregor, "Cultural Studies and Social Change: The War Film as Men's Magic, and Other Fictions about Fictions," *Canadian Journal of Sociology/Cahiers canadiens de sociologie* 18, no. 3 (1993): 271–302.

2. Although Vilsmaier broke with his usual practice of serving as his own cinematographer on this film, his camera eye is evident throughout.

3. Terrance Malick's *The Thin Red Line* (1998) approaches America's Pacific campaign in a similar aesthetic, contemplative fashion. Malick, however, stresses the philosophy of dying much more directly than does Vilsmaier.

4. Films from the German Democratic Republic generally treat the German military harshly and focus their treatment on reeducation of the common soldier and creating a myth of an unbroken line from the soldiers who were converted to the Soviet cause and the East German government. Konrad Wolf's *I Was 19 [Ich war 19]* (1967) and *Mama, I'm Alive [Mama, ich lebe]* (1976) are indicative of such films.

5. Wisbar (Also known as Franz Wysbar) directed several films about the Second World War, including *Sharks and Small Fish [Haie und Kleine Fische]* (1957), *Night Fell on Gothenhafen [Nacht fiel über Gothenhafen]* (1959), and *Officer Factory [Fabrik der Offiziere]* (1960).

6. If we see the second wave as comprising war films beginning with Paul May's *08/15* trilogy in 1954, then the first wave began with Wolfgang Staudte's *The Murderers Are among Us [Die Mörder sind unter uns]* (1946), the first in a series of rubble films released in the first years after the war.

7. Michael Kumpfmüller assays the literature on the Stalingrad story from Hermann Göring's *Appell an die Wehrmacht* (30 January 1943) to Alexander Kluge's *Schlachtbeschreibung* (1964–78).

8. Warnings from other films of the time are less ambiguous. For example, Kurt Hoffman ends *Aren't We Wonderful [Wir Wunderkinder]* (1958) with an inscription on a memorial, "We warn the living." The camera closes in on the word "living," whose German equivalent, "*Lebende*," gives us the word "End" to close the film but also the outcome if we don't heed the warning. Paul May is equally blunt. *08/15* (1954/55) ends with a screen text: "And so ends the darkest chapter in German history. Let's be on our guard that we never again have a dictatorship of the 08/15 mentality." Quoted in Robert C. Reimer and Carol J. Reimer, *Nazi-Retro Film: How German Narrative Cinema Remembers the Past* (New York: Twayne Publishers, 1992), 182–88.

9. Vilsmaier takes this desire to showcase his wife in his films to the ultimate level in *We're Cleaning Up [Rama dama]* (1990), where he included the actual birth of their child. See Joseph Vilsmaier, *Rama dama: Eine Dokumentation über den Film* (Berlin: Ullstein, 1991), 58–61.

10. I am assuming that a scene in which a Russian soldier who has been shot and continues to stumble forward as if a refugee from *Night of the Living Dead* (George A. Romero, 1968) was unintentionally funny.

11. The similarity in tone between the films *Dogs, Do You Want to Live Forever? [Hunde, wollt ihr ewig leben?]* (1958) and *All Quiet on the Western Front* (1930) can be traced to the similarity in tone between Wöss's novel *Hunde, wollt ihr ewig leben?* (1958) and Erich Maria Remarque's novel *Im Westen nichts Neues* (1928).

12. Wolfgang Petersen in *The Boat [Das Boot]* (1981) portrays the British as real victims of an attack by focusing on the helplessness of the German submarine crew in helping the burning, drowning sailors of the ship their boat has just torpedoed. Konrad Wolf in *Mama, I'm Alive [Mama, ich lebe]* (1976) portrays Nazi Germany's enemy as victim by telling the story from a non-German perspective.

13. Michael Selig writes about the film *Jacknife* that "it reiterates the proposition the U.S. GI was a victim" (174). See "From Play to Film: *Strange Snow, Jacknife,* and Masculine Identity in the Hollywood War Film," *Literature/Film Quarterly* 20, no. 3 (1992): 173–80.

14. The comments from general viewers are admittedly often uncritical, but they offer an overview of the film's reception by the public and support the critics' assumptions of how the film reflects public reception.

15. One of the trailers for *Stalingrad* announces that "it's too cold for tears" in an allusion to the battle on the frozen tundra and the death of the heroes in the snow. Yet tears flowed as easily at the end of this film, as at the end of *Autumn Milk [Herbstmilch]* (1988) and *We're Cleaning Up [Rama dama]* (1990).

16. For a more detailed analysis of the film, see Reimer and Reimer, *Nazi-Retro Film,* 182–88.

WORKS CITED

Bandmann, Christa, and Joe Hembus. *Klassiker des deutschen Tonfilms 1930–1960.* Munich: Goldmann, 1980.

Dowell, Pat. "The Other Side of Stalingrad." *Air Force Times* 56, no. 38 (1996): 42.

Ebert, Jens. "Wie authentisch ist das eigene Erlebnis? Heinrich Gerlach: *Die verratene Armee* (1955) und Fritz Wöss: *Hunde wollt ihr ewig Leben* (1958)." In *Von Böll bis Buchheim: Deutsche Kriegsprosa nach 1945,* edited by Hans Wagener, 265–78. Amsterdam and Atlanta, Ga.: Rodopi, 1997.

Hayward, Susan. *Key Concepts in Cinema Studies.* London and New York: Routledge, 1996.

Hinson, Hal. "'Stalingrad': Germany's Boys in Brown." Review of *Stalingrad.* 29 March 1996, http://www.washingtonpost.com/wp-s...gterm/videos/stalingrad.htm.

Hoberman, J. Review of *Stalingrad. Village Voice,* 30 May 1995, 47.

Jaenecke, Heinrich. "*Stalingrad:* Rekunstruktion eines deutschen Traumas." *Stern* 48 (1992): 62–84.

Jenkins, Mark. Review of *Stalingrad. Washington City Paper,* 29 March 1996, 38.

Jenny, Urs. "Fiese Fratze." *Spiegel* 47, no. 1 (1993): 126–27.

Kaufmann, Stanley. "A Battle." *New Republic* 212, no. 23 (5 June 1995): 32–34.

Kumpfmüller, Michael. *Die Schlacht von Stalingrad: Metamorphosen eines deutschen Mythos.* Munich: Wilhelm Fink Verlag, 1995.

McGregor, Gaile. "Cultural Studies and Social Change: The War Film as Men's Magic, and Other Fictions about Fictions." *Canadian Journal of Sociology* 18, no. 3 (1993): 271–302.

Menashe, Louis. "*Stalingrad.*" *Cineaste* 23, no. 2 (1997): 50–51.
Reimer, Robert C., and Carol J. Reimer. *Nazi-Retro Film: How German Narrative Cinema Remembers the Past.* New York: Twayne Publishers, 1992.
Schulgasser, Barbara. "Germans Get Off Too Easy." *San Francisco Examiner,* 27 October 1995, C6; http://www.sfgate.com...rchive/1995/10/27/WEEKEND10076.dtl.
Steckel, Gerd. "'Mißverhältnisse in der Buchhaltung.' Alexander Kluge: *Schlachtbeschreibung* (1964)." In *Von Böll bis Buchheim: Deutsche Kriegsprosa nach 1945,* edited by Hans Wagener, 309–23. Amsterdam and Atlanta: Rodopi, 1997.
Steinbacher, Bradley. Review of *Stalingrad.* http://www.film.com/filmreview/1993/9469/24/default-review.htm.
Selig, Michael. "From Play to Film: *Strange Snow, Jacknife,* and Masculine Identity in the Hollywood War Film." *Literature/Film Quarterly* 20, no. 3 (1992): 173–80.
Vilsmaier, Joseph. *Rama dama: Eine Dokumentation über den Film.* Berlin: Ullstein, 1991.
Wagener, Hans, ed. *Von Böll bis Buchheim: Deutsche Kriegsprosa nach 1945.* Amsterdam and Atlanta: Rodopi, 1997.

FILMOGRAPHY

08/15—Part Two. [08/15—Zweiter Teil]. Dir. Paul May. Divina, 1955.
All Quiet on the Western Front. Dir. Lewis Milestone. Universal Pictures, 1930. (VHS [PAL]; VHS [NTSC]; and DVD [Region 1]).
Aren't We Wonderful [Wir Wunderkinder]. Dir. Kurt Hoffmann. Filmaufbau, 1958.
Autumn Milk [Herbstmilch]. Dir. Joseph Vilsmaier. Senator Film, 1988. (VHS [PAL]).
Boat, The [Das Boot]. Dir. Wolfgang Petersen. Bavaria Film, 1981; Triumph Releasing Corporation (U.S.), 1982. (VHS [PAL] and DVD [Region 2]; VHS [NTSC] and DVD [Region 1]).
Bridge, The [Die Brücke]. Dir. Bernhard Wicki. Deutsche Film Hansa, 1959; Allied Artists (U.S.), 1961. (VHS [PAL] and DVD [Region 2]; VHS [NTSC]).
Brother of Sleep [Schlafes Bruder]. Dir. Joseph Vilsmaier. Senator Film, 1995; Sony Pictures Classics (U.S.), 1996. (VHS [PAL] and DVD [Region 2]; VHS [NTSC]).
Catch 22 Dir. Mike Nichols. Paramount Pictures, 1970. (VHS [PAL]; VHS [NTSC] and DVD [Region 1]).
Charlie and Louise [Das doppelte Lottchen]. Dir. Joseph Vilsmaier. Senator Film, 1993. (VHS [PAL]; VHS [NTSC]).
Dr. Strangelove. Dir. Stanley Kubrick. Columbia Pictures, 1964. (VHS [PAL] and DVD [Region 2]; VHS [NTSC] and DVD [Region 1]).
Dogs, Do You Want to Live Forever? [Hunde, wollt ihr ewig leben?] Dir. Frank Wisbar. Deutsche Film Hansa, 1958. (VHS [PAL]; VHS [NTSC]).
Fighting Seabees, The. Dir. Edward Ludwig. Republic Pictures Corporation, 1944. (VHS [PAL]; VHS [NTSC] and DVD [Region 1]).

Flying Leathernecks. Dir. Nicholas Ray. RKO Pictures, 1951. (VHS [PAL]).
Germany, Pale Mother. [Deutschland, bleiche Mutter]. Dir. Helma Sanders-Brahms. Basis-Film-Verleih, 1980; New Yorker Films (U.S.), 1984. (VHS [NTSC]).
Harmonists, The [Comedian Harmonists]. Dir. Joseph Vilsmaier. Senator Film, 1997; Miramax (U.S.), 1999. (VHS [PAL] and DVD [Region 2]; VHS [NTSC]).
Hunting Scenes from Lower Bavaria [Jagdszenen aus Niederbayern]. Dir. Peter Fleischmann. Rob Houwer Productions, 1969.
I Was 19 [Ich war 19]. Dir. Konrad Wolf. DEFA, 1967. (VHS [PAL]; VHS [NTSC]).
Mama, I'm Alive [Mama, ich lebe]. Dir. Konrad Wolf. DEFA, 1976.
Marriage of Maria Braun, The [Die Ehe der Maria Braun]. Dir. Rainer Werner Fassbinder. Filmverlag der Autoren, 1979; New Yorker Films (U.S.), 1979. (VHS [NTSC]).
Murderers Are among Us, The [Die Mörder sind unter uns]. Dir. Wolfgang Staudte. DEFA, 1946; Artkino Pictures (U.S.), 1948. (VHS [PAL]; VHS [NTSC]).
Night Fell on Gothenhafen [Nacht fiel über Gothenhafen]. Dir. Frank Wisbar. DFH, 1959. (VHS [PAL]).
Officer Factory [Fabrik der Offiziere]. Dir. Frank Wisbar. Deutsche Film Hansa, 1960. (VHS [PAL]).
Platoon. Dir. Oliver Stone. Orion Pictures Corporation, 1986. (VHS [PAL] and DVD [Region 2]; VHS [NTSC] and DVD [Region 1]).
Saving Private Ryan. Dir. Steven Spielberg. Dream Works, 1998. (VHS [PAL] and DVD [Region 2]; VHS [NTSC] and DVD [Region 1]).
Sharks and Small Fish. [Haie und kleine Fische]. Dir. Frank Wisbar. Zeyn-Severin, 1957.
Slaughterhouse-Five. Dir. George Roy Hill. Universal Pictures, 1972. (VHS [NTSC] and DVD [Region 1]).
Stalingrad. Dir. Joseph Vilsmaier. Perithon Film, 1993; Strand Releasing (U.S.), 1995. (VHS [PAL] and DVD [Region 2]; VHS [NTSC] and DVD [Region 1]).
Sudden Wealth of the Poor People of Kombach, The [Der plötzliche Reichtum der armen Leute von Kombach]. Dir. Volker Schlöndorff. German TV, 1971; New Yorker Films, 1974.
Thin Red Line, The. Dir. Terrence Malick. Twentieth Century Fox Films, 1998. (VHS [PAL] and DVD [Region 2]; VHS [NTSC] and DVD [Region 1]).
We're Cleaning Up [Rama dama]. Dir. Joseph Vilsmaier. Senator Film, 1990.

CHAPTER 16

Fantasizing Integration and Escape in the Post-Unification Road Movie

Elizabeth Mittman

At the beginning of Peter Timm's *Go Trabi Go* (1991), the Struuz family from Bitterfeld is preparing to depart for their first vacation to the West. When their neighbors, who are all outside washing their new VWs, ask where they are headed, the father, Udo, beamingly replies: "Naples," at which one of the men laughs, mocking the idea that their old Trabant will get them any further than Leipzig. In the opening scene of Detlev Buck's *No More Mr. Nice Guy [Wir können auch anders]* (1993), Kipp exits the gates of the home for the mentally retarded in which he has been living, looking something like an overgrown boy in his outmoded confirmation suit. He smartly crosses an open field to speak with a land surveyor at work there, and proclaims: "I'm going away now." When the surveyor replies, with a patronizing smile, "Why don't you stay where you belong," Kipp persists: "I'm a free man. I can go wherever I want."[1]

Against all admonitions, these travelers, each liberated from states of relative confinement, set out undeterred. Their journeys—one from East to West and the other from West to East—follow paths as distant from one another as the styles of the films themselves. There is, however, much that unites these films from the early 1990s: both offer complex commentaries on the promise and the impossibility of unification, and do so by describing simultaneous and apparently contrary desires for the integration of East and West, as well as escape from the German cultural context altogether. Before exploring the unification fantasies at work in these films, I will first situate them within the context of contemporary German film culture and popular culture in general, for, as popular comedies, they belong to a relatively unexamined category within German film studies.[2]

The recent boom in German film comedies—in particular, apolitical "relationship" comedies—has received wide attention from movie critics, film scholars, and filmmakers. This move toward more audience-pleasing films is linked to large-scale changes in German cinematic production, whose origins are all traced back to the early 1980s: some cite political and structural problems creating an increasingly unfriendly climate for independent filmmaking;[3] others describe the palpable shift in filmic styles as the result of both audience fatigue toward *auteur*-oriented films and the decline of leadership in the New German Cinema that was foreshadowed with the death of Fassbinder in 1982.[4] In the epilogue to his valuable study on the New German Cinema, John Davidson echoes the concern of many critics when he wonders whether the recent wave of popular films made and marketed in Germany is a sign of the disappearance of an oppositional cinematic public sphere that emerged in the Federal Republic in the wake of German fascism and the subsequent American occupation (155–64).

If these changes did not begin in 1990, they have come to be associated with the decade of unification. It is here, between the cinematic and sociopolitical realms, that a curious silence emerges, for the dominant political experience of the decade remains strangely unhooked from the debate around the ascendancy of comedy. While a considerable number of comedies about German unification have appeared since 1990, little mention is made of them in the critical literature.[5] It seems as though the terms of discussion of current German cinema, on the one hand, and the trauma of unification, on the other, are so separate that there is no available discursive space for those films that have emerged on the seam between the two phenomena. Reading against this tendency, I would argue that film comedy, from slapstick to satire, offers fertile ground for nuanced depictions of the state of the German polity after 1989. In a May 1999 interview with *Der Spiegel*, Werner Herzog shrugged off the lack of a German presence at Cannes, saying that Germany has produced nothing of late that would be of international interest: "What is finding success with the German audience above all is comedies, which are only understandable within their own culture" (196). While Herzog's remarks derisively set the cosmopolitan setting of Cannes against an implied new German provincialism, I would take his observation and turn it in another direction: if comedy functions precisely by foregrounding cultural specificity, does it not offer a legitimate forum for the expression of political and social tensions? Could comedy perhaps even be particularly well positioned, albeit within the parameters of generic conventions (for example, conflict resolution and heterosexual coupling), as a vehicle to address explosive topics that are generally associated with "issue" or "problem" films?

Building on developments in cultural studies, a significant body of recent critical work has begun taking comedy seriously, focusing on the complicated relationship of comedy and politics.[6] In her study of 1980s and 1990s Hollywood comedies, Nicole Matthews asserts that such products of the cultural mainstream "pose the intriguing question of whether popular cultural forms might be pleasurable and playful or ideologically coercive, or indeed both" (4). Put differently, are any and all critical spaces that might be opened up inside the frame of popular comedy— whether by way of parody, irony, satire, or other comedic means—simply foreclosed by its participation in the larger entertainment industry, à la Horkheimer and Adorno? Do visual pleasure and viewer identification necessarily "tame" and thereby depoliticize audience response? Or is it possible that some potentially subversive trace remains when the lights go up and the credits roll?

Both of the films at hand were produced in the early 1990s, a time that witnessed the often painful processes of unification, not only of political structures but also of mass media and hence of its consumers, and East and West Germans were offered a common pool of images on television and movie screens. I will argue that, for their East-West German audiences, these two comedies of unification reveal ideological contradictions at least as much as they conceal them, and place their viewers into positions alternately of identification and of alienation. Both films explore the implications of crossing borders within and beyond Germany: *Go Trabi Go* describes the adventures of an East German family whose summer vacation takes them through West Germany and, literally following in Goethe's footsteps, to Italy. *No More Mr. Nice Guy* follows the travels of two West German brothers who set out for a village on the Baltic Sea in search of their inheritance and end up in the heart of Russia. Despite their production in mainstream Western studios, neither of these films mindlessly reproduces the invisibility of the East. Rather, both films represent unification as an experience fraught with considerable difficulties, and, within their popular context, significantly problematize visual representation and the mapping of boundaries and terrains, concepts central to the negotiation of cultural identities.

A comparison of *Go Trabi Go* and *No More Mr. Nice Guy* reveals that, beyond their comedic foundations, the two films' fantasies of unification and escape share a number of common themes and motifs identified with the genre of the road movie: the journey, conflicts (and sometimes danger) arising from interactions with strangers, the deepening of bonds among the travelers as they negotiate "foreign" territory, and above all the iconography of the automobile.[7] Frequently described as prototypically or essentially "American," the road movie has exercised particular fascination and undergone countless permutations abroad.[8] In this case, the generic grounding of *Go Trabi Go* and *No More Mr. Nice Guy* in the road movie provides a rich field of references for the portrayal of unification. As East and West Germans travel into the other half of Germany—each effectively moving from home into a foreign country—they perform an act of rejection, or of leaving something behind.

In contrast to the classical American road movie, however, departure is portrayed in these films less as conscious rebellion than as the involuntary result of the ubiquitous displacements of unification, which are capable of turning the most innocuous of journeys into an existential road trip. Thus, in *Go Trabi Go*, the Struuz family flees from the industrial decay of Bitterfeld and the claustrophobic space of their neighborhood. In *No More Mr. Nice Guy*, one could argue that the rejection occurs yet more obliquely in the construction of the unwitting characters themselves: Buck's brothers—illiterate outcasts—already represent a rejection of the West and its symbolic dominance. Ironically, the Struuz family of Bitterfeld and the brothers Kipp and Most share an outsider status with respect to capitalism: having previously been denied direct access to the socioeconomic order—locked away, whether in a socialist country or a mental institution—they are presented as precapitalists journeying into a new capitalistic world of experience. The degree to which they succeed lies at the heart of the two films.

Both films also draw upon the road trip as an enactment of freedom. In the representation of their characters' emergence from situations of confinement, a core difference between the two films as road movies surfaces. As we shall see in the discussion to follow, the asymmetry of East-West relations inscribes both films and their relationship to the thematics of freedom: *Go Trabi Go* readily feeds viewer expectations in its description of a "typical" East German family leaving the (nasty) confines of the East for the (idealized) freedom of the West, while *No More Mr. Nice Guy* contrives a plot that works against the grain of precisely those ideological expectations, integrating the brothers into the East. Does this mean, then, that Timm's film is destined to act out the ideological interests of Western capitalism, and that Buck's is guaranteed a more subversive stance? Although the two films reveal significant intellectual and cinematic differences that may lead many to valorize the latter film over the former as more politically critical and aesthetically complex, I would argue that such a view reduces both films to simplistic categories that obscure their underlying affinities.

Here it is perhaps useful to turn to Robin Wood's work on genres. Wood proposes that "the development of the genres is rooted in the sort of ideological contradictions" issuing from the conglomeration of values and assumptions embodied in classical Hollywood cinema, that genres rarely stand alone, but rather are best looked at "in terms of ideological oppositions, forming a complex interlocking pattern," and that they in fact "represent different strategies for dealing with the same ideological tensions" (61–62). In this view, genres are not merely vessels for the transmission of dominant cultural values, but can also be activated as a tool for the renegotiation of those values. In order to represent the peculiar tensions obtaining to the encounter of East and West, *Go Trabi Go* and *No More Mr. Nice Guy* create their own hybrid genres, combining the basic structure of the road movie with motifs and iconographies of additional genres from diverse historical and cultural contexts. Rooted in a parallel thematic of unification, and charting the problematic encounter with the other by means of automobile journey, these two films project different solutions for their differently situated travelers, and reach their literal and figural destinations by recourse to different traditions in popular film genres: *Go Trabi Go* evokes the nostalgic 1950s vacation film, with its apparently touristic vision and air of breezy innocence, while *No More Mr. Nice Guy* works in a more parodic mode, relying heavily on citations from rather darker genres that imagine forces of good and evil at work, such as the Western and the detective film. In both cases, I will argue, these comedies work with and through the genres to reveal complicated realities. This chapter will further endeavor to show that the fantasies that fuel both films contain powerful utopian impulses beyond "mere" entertainment.

The desire to escape defines both image and sound in the opening sequence of *Go Trabi Go*. A huge coal-processing plant fills the screen, while a lone steam engine chugs across the desolate scene in the foreground. As the camera pans slowly right, the image is revealed to be framed by the window of the room where Jacqueline, the Struuz's teenage daughter, is fixing her hair in front of a mirror. The walls are plastered with images of pop idols; stuffed animals line the bed. In the background, a rhythmic beat, which seems to originate with the steam engine, gradually grows in volume and erupts into the energetic title song, and Jacqueline changes clothes and packs her duffel bag as if in time with the extradiegetic music. As the song and opening credits end, Jacqueline comes out of the front door of the house and immediately battles soot in her eye. Dreary and polluted surroundings thus frame the exuberance of the title song and the girl: Jacqueline's overt dissatisfaction with home and her identification with pop culture situate her as a potential rebel and prime candidate for a road movie.

It immediately becomes clear, however, that a competing force is acting as a potential damper on her desires: the family vacation. The Struuz family's trip from their home in Bitterfeld—emblem of industrial nightmare and the GDR's undesirability—to beautiful southern Italy pays homage to the travel fever *(Reisewut)* that seized East Germans in the early 1990s. The question is: what does the film do with that desire? I will argue that this film creates its own hybrid genre, building both on the road movie and on the more sedate vacation film *(Ferienfilm)*, in order to sort out the particular challenges for East Germans traveling to the West after 1989.[9] A kind of foreign variant on the *Heimatfilm*, the vacation film emerged as a genre in 1950s West Germany and Austria, in part as a celebration of the newfound affluence and consumer culture that emerged with economic recovery after the war. In these films, a family generally travels to sunny southern Europe by car, the experience of the exotic contained by the touristic romp through beautiful landscapes. Georg Seeßlen has suggested that the vacation film is in part about the integration of the new Federal Republic into a larger European whole (159). Embedded within the motifs of travel and superficial engagement with the "natives," the core narrative involves the family unit itself. The father's authority (and, implicitly, his virility), weakened by the war and his diminished position in the domestic sphere afterward, is restored in the course of their travels, and the parents' marriage is revitalized. Conflicts between parents and teenage children—who, "under the influence of American youth culture, [have become] a bit sassy" (Seeßlen 140)—are ultimately resolved as well.

Go Trabi Go revives many of these typical motifs. Yet what does the specific insertion of an *East* German family as central protagonists into this 1950s genre mean? Observing a renewed popularity in the 1990s of 1950s German film culture, Tassilo Schneider has speculated that there is "a manifest desire on the part of Germany's popular culture audiences in the 1990s to make sense of the present by taking recourse to the meanings of the past" (313). I see the transposition of generic conventions of the vacation film here not as a nostalgic gesture but as a complicated comment on the contemporary context of German unification. Though the Easterners' travels mimic those of the 1950s, they do so with a marked, even embarrassing, belatedness that forces the viewer to register a historical jolt in the asynchronicity of East and West. Ultimately, Go Trabi Go is not primarily a film about cementing paternal authority in the family but rather about self-preservation in the face of unification, or, to put it somewhat differently, integration into a new representational order. The good-natured Struuz family—traveling in their overloaded Trabant, speaking Saxon dialect—face particular trials on their trip, for unlike the motoring family of the 1950s, they are not affluent tourists, and, especially in the first part of the film, they are repeatedly made aware of their lack as they attempt to enter and navigate capitalist culture.

Indeed, in many ways the most treacherous terrain they encounter on their journey is the other half of Germany, where they are immediately confronted with their status as lesser citizens—even as foreigners—at their first stop at the home of Rita's relatives in Regensburg. The family is pure parody: Uncle Bernd is greedy, materialistic, and decidedly chauvinistic; Aunt Gerda plays the overly manicured, subservient wife; and son Alfons, the fleshy, spoiled boy with his own computer. As Bernd watches the Struuz family pull up in front of their house, he says: "I knew it, one day the Saxons would stand at our door, with all their junk. Looks like a caravan of Turks. Alfons—clear the table." At this, father and son anxiously hide the enormous chocolate cake they

have been eating, while Gerda pulls out two dusty Christmas or-
naments—valuable handcarved treasures sent as gifts from the
GDR, but clearly unappreciated here. Bernd's obsession with the
monetary value of objects extends to people as well. It is no coincidence that the Struuz family is forced to sleep in the backyard
RV, in which Bernd has already housed others for profit: first
Turks, then ethnic Germans from the former Soviet Union *(Aus-
siedler)*, and finally former East Germans *(Übersiedler)*. The Struuzes are only the last in a string of second-class foreigners, who,
because they are family, unfortunately cannot be charged for the
privilege.

What marks the travelers most readily is, of course, their
automobile, which, from one breakdown to the next, calls attention to itself.[10] While this most central element of the film's iconography identifies the East German as a potential object of
derision, it also functions as strong object of fetishistic identification for some East Germans (and as a central icon in the phenomenon of nostalgia for the East *[Ostalgie]*). The vacation film
motif of the car, then, offers a strongly overdetermined focus for
Udo's extreme anxiety at entering capitalist culture. On numerous occasions, the film shows us that Udo is utterly cathected
to the anthropomorphized vehicle, "Schorsch": whenever the car
suffers a mishap, he appears physically ill himself, and he routinely cares for his car before tending to his own needs.

The vacation film enacts a crisis of paternal authority
whose cause is only implicit; in *Go Trabi Go*, the *pater familias*
is explicitly traumatized by his visible lack, and as Schorsch is
cast down and reviled, Udo is compelled to work through his
second-class status by way of identification: whatever happens to
Schorsch happens to him. Udo's anxiety about his own desirability and virility is thematized repeatedly. As they leave Bitterfeld,
Rita realizes with a start that she has forgotten her birth control
pills, then says consolingly, "Don't worry, keep driving, Papa, you
don't need them anyway with your stress." Later, when they are
being given a lift by a truck driver who tells Trabi jokes, the connection between man and car is made explicit. The driver asks:
"What is the difference between a Trabi and a condom?" Rita fills
in the punchline: "There isn't one—they both block traffic [inter-
course]." At first, Udo and Rita join in the trucker's guffaw, but
they become somber as they exchange a meaningful gaze, and
Udo looks away with a pained expression. The film underscores
the earnestness of this problem when, in an ensuing series of

shots and countershots, close-ups of Udo's troubled visage alter-
nate with the view from his seat: panoramic vistas of the Austrian
alps reduced to a scrap of mountain framed by a dusty windshield.
Subjective shots like this, which have no place in the vacation
film, reveal a disturbed relationship between Udo and the terrain
of his vacation.

The other key element of Udo's anxiety—his daughter's
budding sexuality and independence—is never far from sight. For
the duration of this scene we see Jacqueline, asleep in a berth
behind the front seats, her backside to the camera. The silent
presence of her rear end in the middle of the screen, encased in
provocatively torn jeans, punctuates the boorish driver's endless
stream of Trabi jokes and highlights the dynamic that turns the
East into the butt of all jokes. Throughout the film, Jacqueline
constitutes the unambiguous focus of the camera, and *Go Trabi
Go* revels in the dominant tradition of filmic language, with its
implicitly male spectator and female spectacle. The constant thematization of the male gaze and the fetishization of the daughter
bring to mind the often cited "feminization" of the East in representations of unification. When faced with an exorbitant car re-
pair bill, the Struuz family stages a fund-raising "Trabi peep
show," inspired by Jacqueline's offhand comment that she could
go turn a trick or two to raise money. The equation of the feminized body with the Trabant and, by metonymic extension, with
the GDR per se, is complete.

While the film indulges the West's acquisitionist gaze, on
one level, the act of looking (and being looked at) is exaggerated
in ways that call attention to itself and thereby create potential
for a thematization of problems of representation. Jacqueline's
playful self-awareness can be read both affirmatively and critically in the context of the encounter with the other that is so
central to the genre(s) the film invokes.[11] While Jacqueline is
ogled by the West Germans, she saucily engages in acts of posing
everywhere they go: for the neighbors, for *Wessis* on the Auto-
bahn, and for the film's spectators. On the surface, her aggressive
sexuality offers sheer visual pleasure in the most traditional
sense. At the same time, however, she insists upon a vision of
female sexuality that possesses the power of agency, refusing the
status of passive object for the camera or anyone or anything else.
This is most clearly demonstrated in a department store scene
in Munich, where a "playboy"—wearing a leather jacket, comb
protruding from the back pocket of his jeans—tucks a bill into
the hole in her jeans as if she were an exotic dancer. She wheels

around furiously and shoves the money back into his pocket, saying: "No hair on your balls yet, and already a comb in your pocket, eh?"

From the outset, then, Jacqueline's awareness of her status as commodity serves as her best weapon in the battle for her own agency—and just incidentally undermines the implicit masculinity of the West. In marked contrast to Udo, whose auto-anxiety prevents him from joining in the fun throughout the trip, Jacqueline grabs the bull of unification by the horns and rides it for all it's worth. Ironically, for all of her flirtations, she never actually engages in sexual behavior; nor does she, for all of her awareness of how capitalism functions (in marked contrast to her parents), display any real interest in becoming a consumer. Rather, the dream of flight from the everyday that is intoned in the opening scene of the film carries her through the whole journey, coalescing in a pivotal sequence around an Italian campground at Lake Garda. At the high point of her flirtations, she heads off to a dance by the lake with two young Italian men and her mother. Her energies take a sudden turn when she breaks away from them to dance with abandon alone along the pier, remarkably enough, to a rap song that decries arrogance, bigotry, and greed.[12]

As she stops posing for anyone and dances for herself under the night sky, the underlying idealism of *Go Trabi Go* comes fully to the fore, and Jacqueline's desire becomes an emblem of the utopian hope of the first months after the Wall came down. In an odd scene that unfolds the following day after a row with her parents, she sets out barefoot, guitar slung over her shoulder, along a dusty road to the next town, where she sits on a stone wall and sings a soulful song about the "Gates of Eden." While she doesn't remain a lone figure for long—soon she is back in the family fold and they are on their way on to Rome—the break is striking enough, and the aura of the road movie surfaces: Jacqueline's embeddedness within the music of popular culture— her singing, dancing, and guitar playing—point toward a narrative of rebellious youth in search of independence and a place of one's own. While her parents are happy to set out on a vacation that will, by definition, deposit them back where they began, Jacqueline gives expression to that desire for escape, freedom, and unalienated experience that the other genre promises. As they enter Rome, her father hands her the camera, telling her excitedly to take a picture, to which she replies, a bit bewildered: "of what?"

In contrast to the camera-clicking of tourists, for Jacqueline, experience takes precedence over a gaze- and consumption-oriented travel; in this sense, she belongs in a different movie.

However, she is needed in the more domestic vacation film as the agent for renewal in her own parents' marriage, albeit through the rather troubling, contradictory means of creating a(nother) sexual spectacle. As the sole family member who understands and can manipulate the representational economy of the West, the adolescent daughter, steeped in practices of self-representation for the benefit and attraction of others, can effect the integration fantasy of the (vacation) film. It is Jacqueline who drags her mother into the swimsuit section of the Munich department store; it is she who takes her mother to the dance under the stars in Italy, where Rita actually replaces her as object of desire for the Italian men. Significantly, after returning from that dance, Rita rekindles her romance with Udo. Finally, it is Jacqueline who takes her mother shopping at the Spanish Steps in Rome, with the result that, on the level of visual consumption, Rita is desirable for Udo once more.

In the end, Rita literally resembles Schorsch, who has undergone parallel makeovers both in Munich and in Rome: her colorful new dress creates a perfect graphic match with the car, which has acquired several new body parts after an exciting night out with Udo and a gaggle of Italian women, who shower much attention on both Udo and his beloved Trabi. With this playful affirmation of difference, sexual balance is restored between husband and wife, and while Schorsch still has an important role in the family, Udo no longer needs to identify with him. Rather, the car can reassume its function as a vehicle that supports the emotional attachments of the family members (at the movie's close, Udo confesses to Jacqueline that she was conceived in Schorsch—as was the baby that Rita now carries, symbol of a night of passion at the campground).

With this twist, the movie closes on a simultaneously conservative and emancipatory note. The conventions of comedy demand the reaffirmation of heterosexual coupling, and *Go Trabi Go* is no exception. If there is a difference here, it is in the fantasy of simultaneously celebrating and overcoming difference *within representation*. The camera that Udo so proudly acquires just before they depart for their trip—but which is never used until they reach Rome—hints at this; the theft of the camera as they drive into Rome unleashes the climactic sequence in the film. With the retrieval of the camera by the women, anxiety about representation is reined in; that is, the gaze is recuperated for the East by the East. The Struuz family is integrated into the representational culture of the West, but not—and this is a critical part of the utopian dynamic of the film—in West Germany. While they survive their experiences there, they begin to enjoy themselves only in the other space of Italy. Thus, the fantasy of integration is at once a fantasy of escape: the trajectory pointed to by Jacqueline's rebelliousness, and by the idealism of the soundtrack, posits a utopian "other" place. While they do ultimately reach their stated destination—Naples—they do not drive into the city, but rather, keep on going. As we watch the Trabant winding its way across the Italian countryside in a final aerial shot, the earnest closing song—"White doves have crossed the borders"—describes a journey beyond all boundaries.

The sheer sensual pleasures of the vacation are bundled together with an optimism that marks it as belonging to a specific historical moment early in the process of unification. Elements of the vacation film and the road movie are combined in order to grasp that moment in its contradictory enthusiasms, and to fantasize a place where it is possible to escape the East-West binary. The Struuz family's rejection of the place of West Germany does not, however, imply a rejection of all things German. In fact, the trip offers up a variation on an old German theme: Udo is a German teacher, and the family's travel guide is Goethe's *Italian Journey*. Having left the *Wessis* in the dust, the East Germans become implicit heirs to the unified German traditions of culture and *Bildung*; they are offered up, in a sense, as the better—indeed, the more genuine—Germans.[13]

If *Go Trabi Go* asserts that East Germans can successfully navigate the landscapes of the West, and moreover successfully navigate its representational grid, Detlev Buck's *No More Mr. Nice Guy* poses the question in reverse. What happens when West Germans go east? Like *Go Trabi Go*, this film acts out an alternative fantasy of integration; in this case the less likely integration of West into East. Here Kipp and Most, two hapless and illiterate West German brothers, set out to find and claim the property they have inherited from their grandmother near the Baltic Sea. The change in direction is accompanied by a shift in generic orientation. In contrast to *Go Trabi Go*, the markers of the road movie dominate throughout *No More Mr. Nice Guy*, with its motifs of wandering social outcasts, the appearance of mysterious (and sometimes dangerous) strangers, and mishaps that threaten their

progress. Rather than incorporating the narrative structure of another genre wholesale, here other genres are interwoven in the
narrative of wanderings in an associative and fragmented manner.
The resulting pastiche implies an overarching lack of coherence
to the entire experience of the road trip, and transforms the generic markers—most notably from the Western and the detective
film, but also from sci-fi and the Soviet agricultural epic—into a
means of commentary on what is happening to and around the
brothers.

    This layer of filmic commentary is crucial for the con-
struction of meaning in a film whose central characters are so
lacking in consciousness. Detlev Buck has claimed that he made
Kipp and Most illiterate out of necessity: "You can only make a
road movie in Germany with illiterates. Anyone else will be able
to read the signs and reach their destination in six hours" (quoted
in Arnold 40). Given the larger context of German unification, I
find Buck's explanation disingenuous and problematic, for it
elides the political dynamics underlying the selection of such
outsiders as protagonists. By casting the travelers as mentally
handicapped brothers who drive a dilapidated old truck, the film
introduces its viewers to the East through the eyes not merely of
atypical Westerners, but indeed of blank slates who carry no real
cultural baggage. It is this lack of a sense of belonging—of inheritance in the broadest sense—that casts them as potential road
movie heroes, rather than any particular desire for adventure, rebellion, or freedom. Indeed, in marked contrast to the typical road
movie, these brothers seem utterly unaware of the genre they are
inhabiting.[14] In this sense *No More Mr. Nice Guy* refashions the
road movie in order to produce a parody of the dominant story of
unification—namely, that of the overbearing Westerner coming
to "reclaim" the East. The subversion of that colonizing narrative
fuels the film's twin fantasies of integration and escape.

    In an attempt to impress two East German women mid-
way through the film, Kipp, playing the wealthy capitalist, proposes joint boat excursions "to Scandinavia—Sweden, Norway,
Denmark . . . Romania . . . Denmark, whatever you like." The
geographic confusion of Kipp's travel fantasy reveals the hollow-
ness of his posturing, and mirrors the way in which the two
brothers move through the East German countryside. The relentlessly subjective cinematography ensures that we see with the
unseeing eyes of Kipp and Most: we are offered no legible road
signs and virtually no establishing shots; the camera keeps us
(nearly) as ignorant as they are. Early in the film, we see them

drive past an abandoned watch tower. A few moments later, Kipp looks around vaguely and asks: "Are we already in the East?" Most, unresponsive, simply keeps on driving. Unable to read a map—and, by extension, unable to decipher social codes—they are veritably fated to be taken advantage of. After struggling through their first long day of driving blind, they stop at a modern, fluorescently glowing gas station—a pool of light in the middle of a vast darkness. As the site of their first encounter not with the East, but rather with the West as Other, this "oasis" offers the first indication of the real difficulties that lie ahead. The station clerk, an opportunistic *Wessi*, senses their cluelessness and sells each of the brothers things they do not need: Most buys an entire set of wrenches when he needs just one size, and Kipp is talked into equipping the truck with an expensive first aid kit.

Like many similar scenes in the film, this one reveals two things: first, the East is no longer the "East," but rather is in the process of (quickly) becoming the West. Second, Kipp and Most are, put simply, more "Eastern" than the East itself (as is evidenced by the disdain with which the clerk exploits them); they possess only marginal awareness of the value of things in a market economy. Like the Struuz family, they have lived at some remove from this system of exchange; but whereas Jacqueline's facility in pop culture gains her access to representation and meaning, Kipp and Most have no sense of how to negotiate capitalism. While Most negotiates with the station clerk inside, Kipp sits in the truck, listening to a plaintive song that is piped through the station's speakers, about a caged bird whose flight puts it in danger ("Little bird, don't fly too far / It's snowing, it's snowing . . ."). While the scene in the gas station clearly expresses a warning about the pitfalls of capitalism, the folkloric quality of the song moves the critique into a mythic dimension: the traveling brothers resemble childlike figures from a fairy tale, and the voice is that of the storyteller, warning of dangerous weather ahead. Like the songs in *Go Trabi Go*, "Little Bird" provides commentary on the action, but with a notable difference: in contrast to the earlier film, the voice of this song does not echo the characters' sentiments, but rather identifies (with) the position of a distanced commentator.

Throughout *No More Mr. Nice Guy*, this authorial voice speaks in a register distinct from that of the characters, communicating an undercurrent of anxiety about the abiding difference of the East. This fear of an unknown terrain, which permeates the filmic vision, is most clearly expressed in the insertion of generic conventions and motifs associated with the Western. In stark contrast to the travelogue scenery of *Go Trabi Go*, here the screen fills up with images of lonely desolation: in one scene the lighting of a huge haystack casts such shadows that it evokes a rocky outcropping in the desert more than the German countryside. The particular regional setting plays a significant role here as well, for if the Saxon has become the prototypical East German, as suggested by *Go Trabi Go*, Mecklenburg epitomizes the landscape of the East. This region was already within the East German imagination considered to be remote, uncivilized, unpopulated—insignificant except as a possible tourist destination (the Baltic Sea). The convergence of the brothers' uncertainties in navigating the terrain of capitalism and the estranged "Western" scenery of the East suggests the frontier mentality of a new order that is not yet orderly: capitalism is pure chaos, not yet reigned in by the law, and the gas station clerk is a latter-day snake oil salesman.

The underlying thematic of the trip as an encounter with the foreign is concretized in the figure of Viktor, a likeable young Red Army deserter—and thus the film's first "outlaw"—toting a Kalashnikov, who forces Kipp and Most to help him on his way home to Russia. Although he is as monolingual as the brothers, Viktor possesses enough cultural understanding of the East to ensure their safe passage on the basis of his brute strength or his boyish sex appeal, depending on the particular situation.[15] More critical, perhaps, is his role in the narrative as the embodiment of the film's deeper desire, providing a corrective to Kipp's and Most's dream of going to grandmother's house (where grandmother is dead and gone), and replacing it with his mother's house (where, as the closing scene of the film shows us, there is even a literal, living mother). From this perspective, the road trip adventure merely masks the ultimate fantasy of escape from the symbolic order, figured as the return to an imagined home. Focusing on the provincial elements of Buck's film, Cosima Reif speaks of a "renaissance of the *Heimatfilm*, which . . . speaks volumes about the current need for myths in our culture" (28). If it functions as a *Heimatfilm* at all, it does so in its refashioning of the foreign as a projection site for that (specifically West German?) fantasy of home.

While he never really wants anything except to go home, Viktor operates on the seam between two sides of the narrative: with his gun (and his looks and his brain), he is also the perfect hero of the Western/road movie that persists in unfolding.[16] After a showdown with some highway thugs who seem to be lifted straight out of George Miller's apocalyptic thriller *Mad Max*,[17] he and the brothers become unwitting outlaws and the rest of the film is, unbeknownst to them, in large part a police chase. As the law tries to haul them in, it becomes clear that the gang of three has left the symbolic order of the West for good. If the Western is used to signify the residual otherness of the East—its outlaw nature (yet) beyond the grasp of the long arm of the law—the law, in turn, is represented with another imported genre entirely, namely, the detective film. The cultural clash of the two is summed up by the elegantly suited inspector in charge of the case, reminiscent of a figure from a West German TV detective show, who remarks, upon surveying the scene: "Amazing situation; it's like the Wild West."

One could argue that this film, while set in the East, marginalizes East Germans, for it reveals little of their perspectives or experiences, but this is perhaps precisely the point. The cluelessness of the two brothers itself functions as a stinging commentary on Western ignorance of the East, while simultaneously recuperating the possibility for their redemption by means of assimilation *with* the East. Kipp and Most are, after all, ill-suited for their role as colonizers from the outset, and their status as *Wessis* comes increasingly under question. Kipp's vain attempts to play the conquering hero—based on stereotyped (and outdated) notions of what it means to be an inheritor of capital—fail, for he doesn't even understand what money is: when purchasing a boat, he puts a 100 GDR-mark bill (bearing the image of Karl Marx) on the pile of cash. As their capitalist dreams evaporate, cultural and geographic boundaries become increasingly fluid, and colonizing fantasies gradually give way to the desire to escape into a new field of utopian projection, for which the boat serves as a compact cipher: its purchase leaves them penniless, but with a new mobility beyond German horizons. Following this pivotal scene, Viktor is suddenly in the driver's seat, and revealed to be the vehicle for the next phase of the brothers' cultural transformation—and the film's next generic shift. As he begins humming, then singing, a popular Soviet march, a different representational realm emerges, and the countryside is suddenly illuminated by the stirring heroism of the Soviet agricultural musical.[18] The desertlike desolation of earlier scenes gives way to a friendlier, more distinctly rural setting, as the camera tracks the old truck's path across vast tilled fields. *Heimat*, yes—but German, no.

If any doubt remained, their arrival at the brothers' destination—the manor house of Wendelohe—reveals once and for all that their goal is none. When an arrogant, aristocratic West German woman dressed in full riding gear sails in and coldly informs them that they are not, in fact, inheritors of the big house, but rather of a ramshackle cottage down the road, Kipp and Most are finally and inexorably transformed into *Ossis*. Their integration is complete, but integration into what? As the brothers finally realize that they are the inheritors of—and hence "belong" to— nothing more than a ruin, the film opens their eyes and ours to the misery of this reality: it is in the village of Wendelohe that we come closest to a ground-level view of the sorry side-effects of unification on the East German landscape. The town is deeply troubled by unemployment and discontent (evidenced, among other things, by some skinheads who sit around drinking heavily). One last time, the Western asserts itself as the three travelers approach the bar as if it were a saloon, through swinging doors; but now Viktor enters as the obvious hero, flanked by Kipp and Most.

The heroization of Viktor and simultaneous marginalization of Kipp and Most seals the film's departure from the representational grid of the West, a shift that is concretized in the abrupt blossoming of an Eastern love story. As the men enter the saloon, a shot/countershot close-up sequence establishes the mutual attraction between Viktor and the attractive barmaid Nadine. Their relationship emerges as the single point of real cross-cultural understanding in the film, for Nadine is the first person who can understand Viktor's Russian. This coupling marks a breakdown in the homosocial camaraderie of the road movie and, interestingly, sparks a conflict between the two brothers when Kipp questions Most's sexual orientation. The transference of Kipp's dashed hopes of land ownership onto Most's threatened masculinity brings us back, in a peculiar twist, to the uncertain status of Udo Struuz in *Go Trabi Go*. Where that film worked constantly toward the recuperation of the East German's virility, *No More Mr. Nice Guy* concludes with the opposite gesture. Here, the fulfilled (hetero)sexuality of Viktor and Nadine offers the viewer a point of identification beyond the brothers' social and cultural impotence.

When the three men, watching a news bulletin on the television in the bar, realize they are outlaws and murderers, road movie and detective film merge, and the question of destinations shifts altogether with the exigency of escape: escape from law and order, from capitalism and its discontents, from Germany. Not surprisingly, Nadine, originally their hostage, quickly becomes a willing partner in this venture, for this new Germany is no *Heimat* for her, either. Mythically distant lands are evoked in a scene on the beach: while Kipp and Most struggle with the unlikely boat that will carry them all away from their pursuers, Viktor stands gazing out at the Baltic Sea with Nadine. To her query: "Where are you all headed? To Vladivostock? Or China?" he replies simply, with a little grin, "Naw. Africa." In a redemptive fairy-tale twist, they all find their way "home," not to Africa but to Mother Russia, resurrecting a displaced, archaic vision of *Heimat* beyond history and conflict. With its subversion of the "real-life" plot of Western colonization of the East, *No More Mr. Nice Guy* clearly performs an act of critique; yet the escape executed in its denouement also offers a unified German film audience a way out of its own limitations, as the characters on the screen step first out of their received Western role as conquering heroes, and finally out of the status of demoralized *Ossis*, by moving into the mythical dimension of a Russia startlingly replete with clichés. In the end, Kipp and Most are, for all practical purposes, no longer Germans, but rather rural, timeless creatures tapping beer (Most) and holding forth on pig breeding and catalog shopping (Kipp) for an audience that cannot understand but is endlessly amused.

In the final scene of *No More Mr. Nice Guy*, an ancient, toothless Russian woman is shown in a close-up shot, grinning broadly at the antics of Kipp and Most. Buck's construction of utopian otherness relies heavily on an orientalizing imagery that I find just as disturbing as Rita's beautification at the close of *Go Trabi Go*. In both cases, the imbalance and anxiety that was unleashed in the course of the characters' wanderings through an estranged Germany is restored with recourse to the domestic harmonization of heterosexuality, and the idealization of a utopian other place. Yet do the troublesome conclusions of *No More Mr. Nice Guy* and *Go Trabi Go*, which certainly demonstrate the nearness of escapist fantasy and productive utopian impulse, signify critical failure?

I have argued that with the appropriation of diverse movie genres—from road movie to *Ferienfilm*, from slapstick physical comedy to Western—Peter Timm and Detlev Buck tapped into a rich cinematic language in order to articulate the contradictory experience of unification. The flip side of the coin is—and perhaps always will be, in popular cinema—their participation in deeply embedded fantasies of the resolution of both ideological and narrative conflict. However, I would assert that the residue from the tribulations that the Struuz family and the illiterate brothers in turn experience along the way is not erased by escapist endings. On the contrary, all of them fail precisely in their efforts toward resolution, that is, integration into capitalist culture—at least as long as they remain on German soil. Directly confronting the inequalities obtaining in East-West relations, and responding to the anxiety of loss and disorientation, both films imply that there are no answers inside of "Germany," as it is currently configured, to unification and its representational dilemmas. That they do so while making their audiences laugh is perhaps a sign of the utopian desire to unite, rather than polarize, their East-West German audiences.

NOTES

1. All translations from the German are mine.

2. *Go Trabi Go* and *No More Mr. Nice Guy* were both domestic box office hits, achieving significant popularity in both Eastern and Western Germany. *Go Trabi Go* was nominated for the German Film Prize in 1991 and, according to the *Süddeutsche Zeitung* (14 February 1992), sold 1.4 million tickets. Two years later, *No More Mr. Nice Guy*, with some half a million tickets sold, was also nominated for the German Film Prize. It was awarded the Film Strip in Silver for Shaping of a Feature Film, and several members of the cast and crew received awards (Film Strip in Gold): Detlev Buck and Ernst Kahl for their screenplay; Joachim Król and Horst Krause for acting; Detlef Petersen for music. The film also received the Readers' Award *(Leserpreis)* of the *Berliner Morgenpost* and garnered Jury Special Mention at the Berlinale in 1993.

3. Andreas Kilb cites the bottom line of profit margins: comedies are cheap, action films are expensive. See Kilb, "Ein allerletzter Versuch." See also Thomas Elsaesser's discussion of shifts in domestic cultural policies after 1983, as well as the changing global media landscape, in Elsaesser 309–23.

4. David Coury views the emerging new generation of directors as pursuing an autonomous vision in rebellion against the New German Cinema and the *Autorenfilm* (Coury 362–64). On the impact of Fassbinder's death, see Elsaesser 310–12. For a broad discussion of developments into the early 1990s, see Rentschler 285–322.

5. In addition to the films discussed here, see, for example, *The German Chainsaw Massacre [Das deutsche Kettensägen Massaker]* (Christoph Schlingensief, 1990), *All Lies [Alles Lüge]* (Heiko Schier, 1992), and *Good Day, Comrade [Grüß Gott, Genosse]* (Manfred Stelzer, 1993).

6. See, for example, Horton; Karpf, Kiesel, and Visarius; Matthews; and Neale and Krutnik.

7. For a rich collection of explorations of the road movie genre, see Cohan and Hark; see also Atkinson and Laderman.

8. Wim Wenders is, of course, the most prominent German fan of the American road movie; Ina Rae Hark has gone so far as to claim that Wenders "is to road movies what John Ford (or maybe Anthony Mann) is to Westerns" (210). On the particular appeal of the road movie for European directors, see Eyerman and Löfgren.

9. Timm's earlier comedy, *Meier* (1986, shortly after Timm's move to the West), also played with the topos of travel within East German consciousness. In that film, a young East German man inherits a large sum of money, with which he acquires a fake West German passport, enabling him to take an illegal trip around the world. He then uses his double identity to move freely back and forth between West and East Berlin until he is found out.

10. Within the specific context of the *Ferienfilm*, the car is a central motif, and indeed is often connected to the father's identity. In Franz Antel's 1958 vacation film, *Oh These Holidays! [Oh . . . diese Ferien!]*, the wife remarks to her husband at one point, "When you talk like that, it sounds like you're not married to me, but to this car." In its humorous anthropomorphization, the Trabant also bears a certain resemblance to Herbie of Robert Stevenson's *The Love Bug* (1969) and its sequels. The Disney films appear to have spawned a series of German takeoffs known as the "Dudu" films—written and directed by, and starring, Rudolf Zehetgruber—in which a VW Beetle also functions as a heroic central character.

11. At the same time, the film also exposes the Struuzes own implication in acts of "othering." In a hotel in Rome, Jacqueline and Rita ogle the room service, assuming that he doesn't understand them. When Jacqueline asks her mother, "Shall we have him for desert?" the Italian turns around and addresses them in perfect German, putting the lie to their own chauvinistic behavior. Similarly, Udo hurls a series of ridiculous epithets at two helpful Italian men on the highway (who push the little Trabi up a mountain pass with the nose of their own car): "Slick apes [*Lackaffen*], Mafioso, Pappap-parazzi."

12. "The material thing is what people want, are looking for / What they have a taste for is more and more and more . . ." The song, titled "Keep On Running," is performed by The Real Voices of Milli Vanilli (!). Here ostensibly played as diegetic dance music, it is the same song that Jacqueline tries to play on her boom box in the car, only to have Udo yell at her (as he does repeatedly) to turn it off. Its appearance early on in the film points to Jacqueline's alignment not only with Western pop culture, but also with the values contained in the song's lyrics.

13. This aspect may have contributed to the positive identification with this heroic family among East German audiences. Another, more immediate reason for the film's popularity in the East, however, was likely its casting. East Germans played all three lead roles: Wolfgang Stumph (Udo), Marie Gruber (Rita), and Claudia Schmutzler (Jacqueline). Stumph was particularly familiar to East German audiences from his work in television and cabaret. Casting of the Western roles is equally significant: from cabarettists Dieter Hildebrandt and Diether Krebs to *Liedermacher* Konstantin Wecker and 1960s soft porn film star Barbara Valentin (whose career Fassbinder revived by casting her in several of his films [Elsaesser 289]). The pointed inclusion of familiar actors from both parts of Germany may be another symptom of the unified, utopian vision of this film.

14. Their utter lack of awareness, combined with their physical appearance (Kipp is small and slight, Most tall and rotund), has led several reviewers to note their affinity to Laurel and Hardy. See, for example, Lux 28; Holloway 13.

15. The simple fact of his unsubtitled Russian creates two distinctly different audiences for the film. The hypothetically unified German audience that goes to see this film experiences its difference anew when East Germans (who all learned at least some Russian in school) understand Viktor and thus actually see a different film than do Westerners.

16. In the American cinema, the Western and the road movie are intricately connected genres sharing a "frontier symbolism [. . .] propelled by masculinity and a particular conception of American national identity that revolves around individualism and aggression" (Roberts 45). Viktor presents a disarming inversion of these values that allows for the elaboration of an alternative masculinity. He is always just as aggressive as the situation—and genre—within which he finds himself demands, and is otherwise completely passive.

17. One reviewer has noted a similarity of aura between this scene and the opening of Sergio Leone's *Once Upon a Time in the West*. See Sennhauser 40.

18. The song he sings, "V Put," which literally means "on the road," is not, as the closing credits assert, a Russian folk song, but rather a very popular Soviet army march. After the demise of the Soviet Union, this music experienced a certain popularity in the West as a kind of post-Red chic. The cinematic tradition evoked in this scene—with the visually expansive countryside and chorus swelling in the background—is that of the so-called kolkhoz musicals that glorified the collective farm. Most famous among these is Ivan Pyriev's *The Tractor Drivers* (1939). See Taylor 210–11 and Zorkaya 159–60, 163–64, as well as the 1997 documentary *East Side Story*, directed by Dana Ranga.

WORKS CITED

Arnold, Frank. "Wir können auch anders." Review. *epd film* 10, no. 4 (1993): 40.

Atkinson, Michael. "Crossing the Frontiers." *Sight and Sound* 4, no. 1 (1994): 14–18.

Cohan, Steven, and Ina Rae Hark, eds. *The Road Movie Book*. London and New York: Routledge, 1997.

Coury, David N. "From Aesthetics to Commercialism: Narration and the New German Comedy." *Seminar* 33, no. 4 (1997): 356–73.

Davidson, John. *Deterritorializing the New German Cinema*. Minneapolis: University of Minnesota Press, 1999.

Elsaesser, Thomas. *New German Cinema: A History*. New Brunswick, N.J.: Rutgers University Press, 1989.

Eyerman, Ron, and Orvar Löfgren. "Romancing the Road: Road Movies and Images of Mobility." *Theory, Culture & Society* 12 (1995): 53–79.

Grant, Barry Keith, ed. *Film Genre Reader*. Austin: University of Texas Press, 1986.

Hark, Ina Rae. "Fear of Flying: Yuppie Critique and the Buddy Road-Movie in the 1980s." In *The Road Movie Book*, edited by Steven Cohan and Ina Rae Hark, 204–29. London and New York: Routledge, 1997.

Herzog, Werner. "Spuren heftigster Art." Interview. *Der Spiegel* 21 (24 May 1999): 196–98.

Holloway, Dorothea. "Wir können auch anders: No More Mr. Nice Guy." Review. *Kino (German Film)* 50 (June 1993): 13–14.

Horton, Andrew, ed. *Comedy / Cinema / Theory*. Berkeley: University of California Press, 1991.

Karpf, Ernst, Doron Kiesel, and Karsten Visarius, eds. *"Ins Kino gegangen, gelacht": Filmische Konditionen eines populären Affekts*. Marburg: Schüren Verlag, 1997.

Kilb, Andreas. "Ein allerletzter Versuch, die neue deutsche Filmkomödie zu verstehen" *Die Zeit online* 16 (26 April 1996). Http://www.archiv.-zeit.de/zeit-archiv/daten/pages/komodie.txt.19960426.html

Laderman, David. "What a Trip: The Road Film and American Culture." *Journal of Film and Video* 48, no. 1–2 (1996): 41–57.

Lux, Stefan. "Wir können auch anders." Review. *Filmdienst* 46, no. 6 (16 March 1993): 28.

Matthews, Nicole. *Comic Politics: Gender in Hollywood Comedy after the New Right*. Manchester: Manchester University Press, 2000.

Neale, Steve, and Frank Krutnik. *Popular Film and Television Comedy*. New York: Routledge, 1990.

Reif, Cosima. "Die Provinz schlägt zurück: Über die Tugenden des Ländlers und Detlev Bucks neuen Heimatfilm 'Wir können auch anders.'" *Film und Fernsehen* 21, no. 2 (1993): 28–29.

Rentschler, Eric. "Film der achtziger Jahre: Endzeitspiele und Zeitgeistszenerien." In *Geschichte des deutschen Films*, edited by Wolfgang Paulsen, Anton Kaes Jacobsen, and Hans Helmut Prinzler, 285–322. Stuttgart: Metzler, 1993.

Roberts, Shari. "Western Meets Eastwood: Genre and Gender on the Road." In *The Road Movie Book*, edited by Steven Cohan and Ina Rae Hark, 45–69. London and New York: Routledge, 1997.

Schneider, Tassilo. *Genre and Ideology in the Popular German Cinema 1950–1972*. Ph.D. diss., University of Southern California, 1994.

Seeßlen, Georg. "Durch die Heimat und so weiter: Heimatfilme, Schlagerfilme und Ferienfilme der fünfziger Jahre." In *Zwischen Gestern und Morgen: Westdeutscher Nachkriegsfilm 1946–1962*, edited by Hilmar Hoffmann and Walter Schobert, 136–61. Frankfurt/M.: Deutsches Filmmuseum, 1989.

Sennhauser, Michael. "Eigensinnige Grandeur." *Filmbulletin* 35, no. 1 (1993): 37–40.

Taylor, Richard. "Ideology as Mass Entertainment: Boris Shumyatsky and Soviet Cinema in the 1930s." In *Inside the Film Factory: New Approaches to Russian and Soviet Cinema*, edited by Richard Taylor and Ian Christie, 193–216, 243–47. New York and London: Routledge, 1991.

Wood, Robin. "Ideology, Genre, Auteur." In *Film Genre Reader*, edited by Barry Keith Grant, 59–73. Austin: University of Texas Press, 1986.

Zorkaya, Neya. *The Illustrated History of the Soviet Cinema*. New York: Hippocrene Books, 1989.

FILMOGRAPHY

Go Trabi Go (Peter Timm, 1991)—not in U.S. distribution; available in PAL format, no subtitles, through German outlets (e.g., amazon.de, kaysers.de).

No More Mr. Nice Guy [Wir können auch anders] (Detlev Buck, 1993)— available for rent or purchase with subtitles through Inter Nationes.

CHAPTER 17

"Honor Your German Masters"

History, Memory, and National Identity in Joseph Vilsmaier's *Comedian Harmonists* (1997)

Lutz Koepnick

Postunification confrontations with the problem of German national identity have become sites of what historian Charles Maier understands as a "surfeit of memory" (Maier).[1] Whether they recall German history as trauma or remember the past nostalgically, recent public memorials and monuments have played a focal role in reshaping the postwall imagination, in stimulating public controversies about the meaning of national history and about Germany's future role in Europe and the world. Germany after unification has become host to a virtual memory boom, a fascination with material configurations that help evoke or even reenact history in sensuous and seemingly direct ways. As they explore possible meanings of national history from "below," postwall memory sites are designed to offer new tissues in order to connect individual lives to the narrative of the nation. They provide new zones of cultural coherence and remake the modalities of collective belonging. Memorials are often seen today as unlocking doors to what has been blocked out by professional historians across the entire spectrum. Public memory sites, according to this understanding, return subjectivity and sentience to the process of historical recollection. They privilege ethical concerns over scholarly questions and thus encourage the individual to draw relevant lessons from German history. More skeptical voices, on the other hand, question whether this sudden fixation on material memory sites might not be part of a cunning strategy of forgetting, because Germans now let monuments do the memory work for them or in fact fetishistically displace what is supposed to be remembered for the sake of memorizing itself.[2]

Current arguments about the meaning of the Nazi past and the future of German-Jewish relations often conceive of memory and history as locked into a binary opposition. Critics either discard professional history as a positivistic exercise only to valorize memory as the authentic muse of remembrance, or they demonize memory as uncritical, subjective, and mythical while hailing history as the principal conduit to critical knowledge and insight. However, as Dominick LaCapra has argued persuasively, both positions entertain equivalent blind spots and mystifications. Though memory is clearly not identical with history, we ought not consider them as radical opposites. Instead, memory and history should be understood in terms of a dialectical or supplementary relationship, one improving the work of the other without aiming at closure or totalization:

> Memory is both more and less than history, and vice-versa. History may never capture certain elements of memory: the feel of an experience, the intensity of joy or suffering, the quality of an occurrence. Yet history also includes elements that are not exhausted by memory, such as demographic, ecological, and economical factors. More important, perhaps, it tests memory and ideally leads to the emergence of both a more accurate memory and a clearer appraisal of what is or is not factual in remembrance. (LaCapra 20)

History can probe and sharpen memory; it can draw our attention to how the exigencies of representation might complicate what is usually assumed to be the genuine scripts of subjective experience. Memory, by way of contrast, may infuse history with a critical sense of what in our encounter with the past is of greater and what of lesser importance. It brings into focus what kinds of historical traditions might be preserved and what should be avoided in the future. History and memory, according to LaCapra, cannot do without the other. In fact, it is precisely by recognizing their dialectical interaction and supplementary character that victims and perpetrators alike may best work through the irrevocable traumas, ruptures, and displacements of German twentieth-century history.

LaCapra's comments about the supplementariness of memory and history are surely helpful and to the point. However, what they do not seem to take into full consideration is the enormous power of contemporary media apparatuses, in particular popular cinema, to invent and proliferate public memories that spectators can experience sensually with their own bodies, as if they had actually been there. Alison Landsberg has suggested the notion of "prosthetic memory" as a way to understand how recent technologies of memorization can induce the individual to live through imagined pasts in material ways, and how postmodern popular cinema, in so doing, profoundly alters "the individual's relationship to both their own memories and to the archive of collective cultural memories" (Landsberg 1). Moreover, while mass cultural technologies today on the one hand incessantly rerun the past as film, fiction, or fashion (Kaes 193–98), they on the other hand also exhort us to remember not historical events themselves but how they were handed down to us through mass-mediated representations.[3] Whereas LaCapra is mostly concerned about the radical splitting off of history from memory, the mass cultural production of virtual memories today results in a dramatic conflation of remembrance and history, of private and public narratives. Prosthetic experience often dons the historical in the disguise of personal memory, explores the symbolic warehouse of the past so as to fuel "nostalgia for the present" (Jameson 279–96), and thereby erases the very diacritics of synchronicity and diachronicity according to which we can define any meaningful distinction between history and memory in the first place. Remaking past realities into objects of tangible sensation, prosthetic memory therefore far from overcomes the myopic effects LaCapra associates with the dissociation of history and memory. On the contrary, as it undermines any critical exchange between public history and individual remembrance, as it often entertains the individual with the belief in unmediated access to lived experiences of the past, prosthetic memory, too, may paper over, rather than work out, lasting historical traumas, deep-seated repressions, and irretrievable losses.

This chapter examines the recent prominence of prosthetic memories not only in reimagining German-Jewish relations but, at the same time, in revising the historical narratives of German national and popular cinema. In the second half of the 1990s German cinema has witnessed a surge of historical melodramas in which the quest for popular appeal coincides with the attempt to convert German history, in particular that of the Nazi period, into flamboyant spectacles of sight and sound. Domestic feature productions such as Joseph Vilsmaier's *Comedian Harmonists* (*The Harmonists,* 1997), Max Färberböck's *Aimée & Jaguar* (1999), Rolf Schübel's *Ein Lied von Liebe und Tod—Gloomy Sunday* (1999), and Xavier Koller's *Gripsholm* (2000) thrive on panoramic views of German-Jewish history. They resort to Hollywood conventions and special effects so as to recover blocked national alternatives. What is remarkable about German cinema's renewed interest in the German-Jewish past is that films such as *The Harmonists,* on the one hand, recall German national history as one of contested, pluralistic identities, as a matrix of different histories embedded in the larger narrative of the nation. Contrary to dominant postwar models, the subject position of Jews in pre-Nazi and Nazi Germany is no longer simply seen as that of oppressed outsiders—"Jews in Germany"—but rather as that of a particular ethnic group within a (historically suppressed) multicultural society.[4] On the other hand, however, in its very process of melodramatic memorization, the new historical melodrama nonetheless tries to align its differential account of German national history with nineteenth-century notions of German cultural identity, of a unified German *Kulturnation.* What nineteenth-century ideologues were eager to naturalize as the most German of all arts, music and song (see Dennis; Potter), in the new melodrama sutures Jews and Germans into an imagined community, one that allegedly opposed the disruptive violence of public history.

In nineteenth-century discourse, the sound of music had been a crucial component in envisioning an end to internal divisions and shaping German national identity: "The idea of a German nation-state had to overcome a long history of political fragmentation and regional differences, but music represented a mode of artistic expression in which all Germans could share" (Potter ix). Recent melodramas relocate this idea—the notion of music as a panacea for the wounds of a divided society—to the terrains of the present. Playing out the seemingly authentic textures of melos and popular music against the disintegrating force of the political, popular cinema's prosthetic memory here reorders the nation's narrative, reimagines a German-Jewish past that never existed as such, and in so doing provides present audiences with a new image of ethnic consensus detached from any historical trauma. With a clear gesture of postmodern hubris, these new epic melodramas thus aspire nothing less than to redeem the past and recuperate a sense of national normalcy.

Yet, as this chapter shall argue, German cinema's renewed interest in the various narratives that have fed into the nation's story does not only serve the purpose of quieting historical disquiet. Rather, as I will show in my following reading of *The Harmonists*, this new populist focus on German-Jewish relations—films such as Dani Levy's *Meschugge* (1999) and Didi Danquart's *Viehjud Levi* (1999) come to mind as well—also plays an important function in postunification efforts to redefine the contours of German national cinema and hence revise the history of German filmmaking itself. Postwall German cinema takes recourse to the memory of Jewish-German life in Germany prior to or during the Nazi era to inaugurate a new chapter of self-confident popular filmmaking in Germany. While no longer willing to mobilize former distinctions between European art cinema and American commercial filmmaking, it produces the figure of the German Jew as an authentic mouthpiece of a better Germany in which German popular culture rebuffed industrial mass entertainment à la Hollywood. In order to do so, this new German cinema, while memorializing certain aspects of the nation's past, creates critical amnesia about others, in particular the bifurcation of German popular cinema during and after the 1930s into the paths of Nazi fantasy production and Hollywood exile. At once reinventing and repressing history, Vilsmaier's film folds prosthetic memory, the German-Jewish past, and the quest for a new German popular cinema into one coherent, albeit deeply ideological, fantasy. Triumphant images of German-Jewish collaboration naturalize what is prosthetic about the new fixation on the nation's past so as to entertain the viewer with normalizing visions of German cinema as a unified national and popular cinema.

One of the first scripts written for *The Harmonists* proposed to tell the film's story with the help of a suggestive framing device. In this frame, a young Berlin musician visits the last remaining member of the Comedian Harmonists, Roman Cycowski, in the early 1990s in order to gather information about the legendary sextet. Interested in the biographies of artists who contributed unique sounds to the history of music, this young musician inspires the nonagenarian to recall the history of the famous a cappella group. One of its three Jewish members, Cycowski then narrates the group's foundation in 1927, its rise to tremendous stardom between 1930 and 1934, and its ill-fated partition in 1935 due to Nazi persecution. The muse of personal memory, in this initial treatment, was to authenticate the film's subsequent images and sounds. It led the viewer back to a forgotten world in which popular song and music helped express great emotions and unbridled joy, a universe of melodramatic intensity whose genuine pleasures and passions, according to scriptwriter Klaus Richter, fell victim to "a fanatical ideology that stepped over dead bodies for its ideas; an entertainment industry that makes a killing the more it dulls its children with phony emotions" (Vilsmaier 8).

As if in working on this material the legend already had become fact, Vilsmaier's final version no longer includes Richter's framing device. Instead, the film's first sequence confronts the viewer directly with that curious air of nonsense and serenity, of popular appeal and high cultural travesty, of wit and sorrow, of vocal lightness and rigorous synchronization, that served as the Comedian Harmonists' trademark around 1930. Yet, the film's final cut is, of course, no less driven by a desire for past historical temporalities, for the authentic and the uninhibited, than Richter's original script. While Richter's treatment initially employed the (imagined) voice of personal memory as a kind of narrative crutch, Vilsmaier makes highly professional use of special effects, sweeping camera moves, elaborate set designs, and digitally remastered sound arrangements in order to engineer the past as a tangible site of memorization. Taking advantage of the full spectrum of current technological possibilities, Vilsmaier's film remakes memory as history so as to imagine a past in which German musicians, with a neo-Wagnerian gesture, displaced foreign models and created something of their own; in which popular diversion escaped the homogenizing protocols of political ideology and the twentieth-century culture industry alike; and in which German-Jewish alliances bridged the peculiarly modern divide between high and low culture and precisely thereby offered populist alternatives to the brutal excesses of German political history.

In 1878 Richard Wagner had declared that the essence of German national identity could be found in music. Yet, at the same time, he expressed his frustration over the impossibility exactly to define what made German music German: Bach's work had relied on French and Italian models; Handel had achieved his fame in London as a composer of Italian operas; the Austrians Haydn and Mozart had been heavily influenced by Italian music of the time. Facing the dilemma of the internationalism of German musical traditions, Wagner ended up explaining the Germanness of German music by pointing at the power of domestic composers to rework foreign sources and articulate the true

meaning of other aesthetic traditions: "[H]is is no mere idle gap-
ing at the Foreign, as such, as purely foreign; he wills to understand it 'Germanly' . . . [H]e strips the Foreign of its accidental,
its externals, of all that to him is unintelligible, and makes good
the loss by adding just so much of his own externals and acciden-
tals as it needs to set the foreign object plain and undefaced before
him" (Wagner, *Prose Works* 4:160).

Vilsmaier's film relocates Wagner's definition of what
makes German art German to the terrains of twentieth-century
culture. Reckoning with the prominent role of sound and music
in the history of both German culture and German narrative cinema, *The Harmonists* presents Harry Frommermann's foundation of the sextet in 1927 as a conscious effort to rework the
foreign and beat different cultures at their own game. Asked by
Harry (Ulrich Noethen) during the initial recruiting session about
his familiarity with the American a cappella quintet "The Revelers," Robert Biberti (Ben Becker) expresses Harry's innermost fantasies: "Hey, that's it! . . . To sing like The Revelers. Only in
German! Different. Unique." Subsequently, the act of translating
foreign inspirations into German expression, for Vilsmaier's
Frommermann, becomes an act of perfecting the other, of setting
the foreign straight and replacing it with homemade objects of
greater authenticity. It therefore should come as no surprise that
"The Revelers" enter the film's diegesis only through the mediation of shellac records and gramophone players, whereas Vilsmaier places great emphasis on picturing concerts by the
Comedian Harmonists as scenes of direct interaction between audiences and on-stage performers. Cutting back and forth between
enthralled listeners and triumphant singers, Vilsmaier's many
concert sequences, rather than picturing audiences as passive
consumers, consecrate German song as a form of unmediated
communion, as an auratic presence whose here and now escapes
the homogenizing force of modern industrial culture. Understanding the American model "Germanly," Vilsmaier's German-
Jewish sextet does not simply translate the songs of "The Revelers" into the German language. It in fact unlocks the true possibilities of the other by emancipating what is popular from
technological mediation and postauratic mass culture. What
makes this music German, in other words, is not simply the singers' predominant use of the German language, but their alleged
ability to sustain preindustrial notions of popular culture in spite
of the ever-increasing Americanization, standardization, and
deauraticization of German cultural exchange.

According to screenwriter Klaus Richter, *The Harmonists*
extols early successes of multicultural cooperation in German
history; the film recuperates forgotten links between different
ethnic groups that were disrupted by the rise of Nazi power (Vilsmaier 18). It is not difficult to see that Richter's and the film's
vision of Weimar multiculturalism is based on a deeply preserva-
tionist notion of cultural difference and particularity, one in
which different cultural entities may neatly exist side by side
without really challenging calcified concepts of cultural fixity or
encountering the other in the medium of critique and self-
critique. Multiculturalist experiments such as the Comedian
Harmonists may temporarily collapse what separates Jews and
non-Jews, but in doing so they—according to the film—raise our
awareness for and appreciation of the other's fundamental alterity, for the differential history of particular ethnic identities in
Germany. What is more interesting to discuss in our context here
is how this reifying view of cultural alterity and intercultural collaboration interacts with the film's vision of modern cultural production at large and of what Andreas Huyssen, informed by the
seminal work of Theodor W. Adorno and Max Horkheimer, has
called the great divide between mass culture and modernism
(Huyssen, *After the Great Divide*). Similar to the way in which
Frommermann's a cappella group briefly succeeds in fusing the
dissimilar itineraries of Germans and Jews, so the Comedian Harmonists mend the split of modern culture into incompatible
arenas of taste and self-expression. Combining Eichendorff and
American jazz, German folk songs and Italian opera, Vilsmaier's
Comedian Harmonists provide something for everyone and thus
restore notions of culture as unified and homogenous. Vilsmaier's
Hitler, by way of contrast, at once displaces the auratic with mechanical reproduction and the authentically popular with ideological politics. Prioritizing the radio over live performance and
disciplining the individual's desire from above, Nazi Germany
employs the most advanced means of modern industrial culture
in order to drive German society apart; it develops a Hollywood
of its own so as to discredit the consensus-building power of populist experiences. Vilsmaier's Nazis orchestrate phony scenes of
cultural accord while they at the same time remap cultural differences in terms of hierarchical segregation. Auschwitz *and*
Goebbels's "ministry of illusion" (Rentschler, *The Ministry of Illusion*), Nazi eliminationism *and* mass distraction, according to
the film's account of modern German culture, serve one and the

same purpose: they obliterate the putative power of German popular culture to fuse what is different and incompatible.

In simultaneously setting the popular against industrial mass culture, and German-Jewish multiculturalism against Nazi totalitarianism, Vilsmaier's *The Harmonists* gives a curious spin to what during the entire postwar era has offered many German intellectuals a paradigm to confront the national past and challenge their respective presents: the identification of Hitler and Hollywood, of fascist manipulation and Fordist mass culture. In Hans Jürgen Syberberg's 1977 *Hitler, ein Film aus Deutschland* (*Our Hitler*), this trope has found its no doubt most striking formulation.[5] Syberberg's six-hour opus rested on the high-cultural proposition that twentieth-century show business and fascism were virtually identical. According to Syberberg, both Hitler and Hollywood not only eliminated the autonomy of art and functionalized aesthetic experience for the purpose of mass manipulation; in doing so they also compromised the utopian power embedded in myth, in Richard Wagner's music, and in preindustrial forms of popular culture. Both Hollywood and Hitler, in Syberberg's perspective, degraded the mythic by transforming politics and culture into spellbinding movie sets; both exemplified a cynical triumph of instrumental reason over the irrational substratum of what Syberberg understands as authentic culture. Syberberg's art cinema, by way of contrast, wanted to recuperate what could make German culture authentic and an object of positive identification again. His Wagnerian exercise pitted Wagner's longings for redemption against their own legacy in Hollywood and Nazi Germany. It intended to emancipate the irrational from the grasp of instrumental reason and help Germans overcome the fact that after Hitler they had lived "in a country without homeland [Heimat]" (Syberberg 15).

At first one might contend that Vilsmaier's multicultural populism has little, if nothing, in common with Syberberg's celebration of art cinema and his denigration of industrial filmmaking. However, closer inspection reveals curious correspondences between the two positions. Not only do both Vilsmaier and Syberberg believe that in addressing the legacy of fascism German cinema may succeed in establishing a strong, nationally independent alternative to contemporary Hollywood filmmaking. Both *The Harmonists* and *Our Hitler* also base their equation of Hitler and Hollywood on Manichean understandings of modern culture as a face-off between incompatible codes of aesthetic authenticity and commodified diversion. Rather than to show, as Adorno and

Horkheimer have suggested, that the valorization of aesthetic authenticity in twentieth-century culture was born as a reaction to
the gradual commodification of cultural material during the second half of the nineteenth century (Horkheimer and Adorno 120–
67), rather than to maintain that authentic expressiveness in
modern culture in some sense at once presupposed and reinscri-
bed the existence of the culture industry, both Vilsmaier and
Syberberg present Fordist mass culture and what they understand
as authentic art as radical alterities. As a result, both Vilsmaier
and Syberberg glorify the popular dimension as a mythic site of
the irrational, of emotional excess and utopian redemption, of romantic longing and sentimental kitsch. While they disparage industrial mass culture, they at the same time deify the popular as
a critical antidote to the politicization of culture à la fascism and
the commodification of art à la Hollywood. Whereas Hitler and
Hollywood enlisted modern technologies of distraction in the service of all-inclusive deception, both *The Harmonists* and *Our
Hitler* hope to take recourse to the mythic substratum of the popular, to the suturing power of music and song, to the legacy of
Richard Wagner, in order to recuperate what it may mean to be
German after Hitler.

It has become a commonplace among Wagner scholars to
argue that compositional technique in *Die Meistersinger von
Nürnberg* denied technique and engineered the paradoxical illusion of self-contained being. Wagner's *Die Meistersinger* relied on
modern compositional practices in order to conjure the impression of older musical idioms. Following Wagner's own aesthetic
beliefs to the letter, his 1867 music drama disguised reflection
and technique as nature and spontaneity. "Nowhere, not even in
Parsifal, is Wagner's music so artificial as in the appearance of
simplicity with which it clothes itself in *Die Meistersinger*"
(Dahlhaus 75). Similarly, in his hope to reconstruct feelings of
national belonging via the emotive sounds of German music and
the German language, Wagner in *Die Meistersinger* amalgamated
various modern visions of sixteenth-century Nuremberg so as to
recuperate a mythical past in which art knew no separation from
the everyday. *Die Meistersinger* cloaked historicist reconstruction in the spellbinding guise of unmediated presence and prophetic anticipation. Wagner's Nuremberg was a dreamt one, a
populist chimera of the nineteenth-century imagination. While
Wagner was at pains to give history the appearance of historical
inevitability (Goehr 48–87), his view of Nuremberg as a site of
authentic popular culture derived "its meaning precisely from the

confrontation between past and present, between medieval community and modern industrial society" (Hohendahl 57).

In his seminal *In Search of Wagner,* Theodor W. Adorno employed the concept of "phantasmagoria" in order to describe this puzzling fusion of old and new in Wagner's *Die Meistersinger.* Phantasmagorias, in Adorno's understanding, indicate the

> occultation of production by means of the outward appearance of the product. . . . In the absence of any glimpse of the underlying forces or conditions of its production, this outer appearance can lay claim to the status of being. Its perfection is at the same time the perfection of the illusion that the work of art is a reality *sui generis* that constitutes itself in the realm of the absolute without having to renounce its claim to image the world. (Adorno 85)

Replaying the old with the help of the new and passing cultural products as self-sustaining attractions, this mystifying power of phantasmagoria is also at the core of the political and cultural program of *The Harmonists.* Like Wagner's mastersingers, Vilsmaier's vocalists rely on modern and eminently rationalized technique, on mediation and technology, in order to elicit populist perceptions of immediacy and spontaneity. Hans Sachs's interpretation of Walther's prize song—"It sounded so old—and yet it was so new" (Wagner, *Die Meistersinger von Nürnberg* 103)—not only explains the historical success of the Comedian Harmonists around 1930, it also elucidates why this success became such a concern for German filmmakers and popular audiences in the late 1990s.

"Often copied, never matched"—though themselves a remake of an American model, the historical Comedian Harmonists already in their earliest publicity campaigns and marketing slogans capitalized on the aura of originality German audiences and music distributors were eager to attribute to the acrobatic aspects of a cappella song. At the same time as the German film industry, with the critical support of the emerging record industry, ventured into the era of the talkie, the Comedian Harmonists relied heavily on phonographic records and radio broadcasts in order to spread their fame and penetrate the German music market. Lucrative deals, first with the Odeon and later with the Electrola label ("His Master's Voice"), laid the foundation for the group's enormous success. Between 1928 and 1935, the Comedian Harmonists, in fact, released no less then 150 titles on record, while live performances, such as the one in the Leipziger

Schauspielhaus in January 1930, would often reference the group's celebrity on record to enhance stage effects. Moreover, as Peter Czada has argued, the possibility of sound recording was essential to improve the style and quality of the group's performance (Czada and Große 44). From the very beginning, the record studio provided an important site for monitoring the degree of vocal harmony and coordination. Contrary to Walter Benjamin's hopes that mechanical reproducibility would eliminate the auratic elements of bourgeois art (Benjamin 217–52), then, the Comedian Harmonists—in likeness to classical cinema and its cult of stardom—aspired to reinscribe auratic values, the halo of aesthetic genius and originality, with the means of mechanical reproduction itself. Though deeply rooted in industrial culture, the group intended to provide impressions of organic integrity, of athletic uniqueness unmediated by modern machines and musical instruments. Furthermore, similar to the way in which during the early years of sound film almost all important innovations in cinema technology resulted from "the desire to produce a persuasive illusion of real people speaking real words" (Altman 7), the aura of the Comedian Harmonists originated from their extraordinary ability to bond bodies and voices—image and sound—into spectacles of synchronization. Yet what in live performances gave the outward impression of rhythmic lightness and individual spontaneity in actual fact was the product of calculated effort and formal rationalization. A cappella song around 1930 relied on a quasi-Taylorist division of vocal labor, a factory-like separation and reassembly of different musical assignments. Reminiscent of the famous Tiller Girls in Siegfried Kracauer's analysis (Kracauer 75–86), the Comedian Harmonists employed human voices as functional building blocks. They disciplined the individual's vocal organs so as to reintegrate discrete performative tasks within the orchestrated unity of a sounding human ornament. While the aura of the final product was meant to remind audiences of preindustrial modalities of musical performance, it was deeply affected by the logic of industrial culture. Elaborate technique and present-day technology generated a dreamlike semblance of the past.

It is, to speak with Adorno, this phantasmagoric aspect of a cappella song that figures central in Vilsmaier's nostalgic treatment of the historical Comedian Harmonists: the film dedicates no less than twenty minutes of screen time to picturing the group's protracted efforts to sound effortless and mystify the very process of musical production. Starving geniuses who solely follow their calling, Vilsmaier's musicians traverse various spaces—an unheated loft, a bordello, a bourgeois home, a bar—before they finally attain that unique sound necessary to reach stardom. In one of the early practice sessions, Frommermann and Biberti define their Taylorist rigor as such:

> Frommermann: None of us should try to stick out. I mean, everybody has to hold back, do his part.
> Biberti: That means the group counts, not the individual.

Nowhere is the music of Vilsmaier's Comedian Harmonists more artificial than when they finally, almost one quarter of the way through the film, reach that perfectly synchronized sound of simplicity that serves as their trademark. Interestingly enough, however, what triggers the sextet's final breakthrough into the phantasmagoric is not rigorous exertion but a loosening of functionalist discipline and rationality. Getting drunk after a failed audition, the singers join one by one into Duke Ellington's "Creole Love Song," only then to hit upon that mysterious synthesis they have been after all along. *The Harmonists*, in this crucial sequence, grafts nineteenth-century notions of music as a nonrepresentational language of the soul onto the sounds of twentieth-century culture. Emotional excess and the elimination of internal censorship, unrestrained intoxication and self-transcendence, seemingly overcome industrial rationality and offer a royal road to multicultural friendship as much as to aesthetic success. Like Wagner's aristocrat Walther, who in act 3 of *Die Meistersinger* wins the bourgeois Eva because he unconsciously understands how to reconcile rules and romantic excess, Vilsmaier's new German mastersingers learn how to generate discipline out of passion. In having booze rather than unyielding practice prompt the final breakthrough, Vilsmaier ironically retracts the film's entire first twenty minutes. As if learning from its object, the narrative itself incorporates what appears to be the singers' performative mystery: occultation of production. Not once in the remainder of the film do we witness any further practice sessions. Henceforth, both the singers' performances and the narrative itself lay claim to self-contained being. Not only has technique allegedly become nature, but nature is shown to procreate techniques that sound so old yet are so new.

It is in Vilsmaier's Wagnerian embrace of the phantasmagoric that some of the film's political and cultural agendas become the clearest. On the one hand, by glorifying German-Jewish collaborations prior to Hitler as enigmas triggered through the ineffable sounds of popular music, *The Harmonists* imagines the German nation not as composed of those who subscribe to the nation's political creeds and constitutional principles but rather as a site of religious communion, as an awe-inspiring and mythical blessing. *The Harmonists* may surely question narrow notions of German national identity that emphasize exclusive ethnic attributes, yet the film is far from reconstructing a polycentric German community based on constitutional entitlements and postnationalist principles of citizenship. Vilsmaier's *The Harmonists*, in other words, clearly does not invite the viewer to envisage the German nation "as a community of equal, right-bearing citizens, united in patriotic attachment to a shared set of political practices and values" (Ignatieff 5). According to the film's revisionist account, not the cold rule of shared rights but the numinous ability of popular culture to downplay ethnic characteristics and genealogical features allows Germans as well as Jews to access German national identity. What, in the film's perspective, makes non-Jews or Jews German is the phantasmagoric power of the popular to collapse difference and synthesize particularity rather than any political framework linking nonidentical particulars through deliberate choices and civic commitments.

Vilsmaier's grasp for the phantasmagoric, his valorization of mythical over civic forms of nationalism, on the other hand, also plays a critical role in what I understand as the film's revisionist map of German film culture and film history. As the film revisits a precarious moment in the history of German cinema at which the coming of synchronized sound sustained high-flying hopes for a nationally independent film industry, Vilsmaier's *The Harmonists* recalls the sextet's history in order to redeem those hopes and transfer them to the present. Like early sound film, Vilsmaier's Comedian Harmonists are dedicated to synthesizing heterogeneous articulations into seemingly natural harmony. Their formula of success, like that of the talkie, is to bond voice and body into collective fantasies of plenitude and presence. Although *The Harmonists* itself pays no attention to the group's actual performances in early German sound features such as *Die Drei von der Tankstelle* (1930, dir. Wilhelm Thiele) and *Bomben auf Monte Carlo* (1931, dir. Hanns Schwarz), the mystique of German song and sound buffers German popular culture and cinema against Hollywood hegemony. Nostalgically lifting a glorious past to the present, *The Harmonists* thus features the sextet's phantasmagoric sounds to resuscitate the possibilities of popular filmmaking in postunification Germany.

Even though Hollywood continued to dominate the German film market throughout the 1990s in almost all respects,[6] postwall German cinema has clearly broken away from the Americanist dilemmas of earlier *Autorenfilmer* (Rentschler, "How American Is It?"; Elsaesser, "German Postwar Cinema and Hollywood"). Unlike many representatives of the New German Cinema, younger comedy directors such as Doris Dörrie, Katja von Garnier, and Sönke Wortmann are clearly guided by Hollywood paradigms of industrial filmmaking. As Gerd Gemünden observes:

> More credit is now given to high professional standards in filming and editing, and particularly to scriptwriting, a specialization virtually nonexistent among *Autorenfilmer*. With their fast editing, stylized interiors, witty dialogues, well-paced plot development, and a strong emphasis on entertainment rather than consciousness raising, these German comedies do indeed come very close to the Hollywood cinema they seek to emulate. (212–13)

Vilsmaier's work of the 1990s has extended this new concern with proficient modes of popular filmmaking to the genre of the historical melodrama. Films such as *Stalingrad* (1992), *Brother of Sleep* (1995), *The Harmonists*, and *Marlene* (2000) recall the past through elaborate special effects and carefully constructed set designs. In the complex last shot of *The Harmonists*, this grasp for the historical has found its perhaps most emblematic expression. Initially positioned on a train track, the camera pictures an approaching steam engine from a frontal, low-angle perspective. Just in time, the camera moves suddenly to the right and—facilitated by a crane—dramatically turns around the original frame's vertical and horizontal axis. It climbs to a stunning bird's-eye point of view, which allows the viewer to see the train rushing away toward the horizon. Hollywood standards of technical expertise here provide a captivating sensation of bygone temporalities. Vilsmaier's final crane shot remembers the past by means of a cinematic aesthetics of attraction which privileges exhibitionism over voyeurism, startling display and special effect over narrative integration and the illusion of a coherent story world (Gunning, "The Cinema of Attraction[s]"; idem, "An Aesthetic of Astonishment").[7] Professional standards of filmmaking in this shot picture German history as a site of sensuous experience and consumption, a figure that excites the viewer's curiosity and sense perception in spite of all its negativity. Participating in the "mnemonic convulsions" (Huyssen, *Twilight Memory* 7) of contemporary cyber-culture, *The Harmonists* reconfigures historical memory as a (literal and metaphorical) ride through space and time, as a source of corporeal thrills engineered by the extraordinary power of present-day film technology.

"In a world of change," writes Richard Terdiman, "memory becomes complicated. Any revolution, any rapid alteration of the givens of the present places a society's connection with its history under pressure" (Terdiman 3). In Vilsmaier's *The Harmonists*, state-of-the art digitization takes over important functions to remake German cinema's connection to the past and articulate a response to the historical ruptures of the present. Yet digital technology, under Vilsmaier's direction, is not simply meant to transport the original charisma of the Comedian Harmonists to the present; its ultimate purpose is to reinvent synthetic aura with the means of most advanced information technologies itself. Revitalizing the historical penchant of German popular cinema for the music film genre (Bock, Jacobsen, and Schöning), *The Harmonists* frequently suspends the flow of narrative progress so as to provide special moments of sonic spectacle, performative interludes in which the viewer can enjoy digitally remastered versions of the original songs. "For the first time 100 percent noise-free," proclaimed the ad that promoted the release of the film's musical soundtrack on compact disk, celebrating the extent to which prosthetic memory today can correct the flaws of earlier modes of mechanical reproduction. Yet, what for the CD listener becomes a tool to render selected aspects of the past entirely present in the film itself allows Vilsmaier to build trouble-free bridges between story and spectacle, between the diegetic and the non-diegetic, between history and memory. It is precisely this digitally produced absence of noise that helps transport the viewer easily into and across the individual music numbers, that effectively coaxes us to suspend our desire for narrative development, and that in doing so lets the audience consume the past as if they experienced it with their own bodies. Similarly, the film repeatedly employs digital imaging technology in order to cater the past more palpably to the viewer's senses. A total of forty shots were digitally enhanced to recreate, among others, the Manhattan skyline circa 1930, a wintry Jewish cemetery in Berlin, and the bow of the *Europa* in the harbor of Bremerhaven (Vilsmaier 90–107). As it conjures a past in which cinematic technology itself underwent dramatic alterations, *The Harmonists* enlists film technologies that unsettle the privileged role of the photographic image in modern culture and its putative claims to veracity and objectivity (Mitchell 3–57). In order to make the past part of the present archive of personal experience, the film employs what undoes any traditional sense of authenticity and experience in the first place.

In an international perspective, Vilsmaier's professional use of digitized sounds and images, to be sure, is hardly remarkable. Digital enhancement today has become a staple of mainstream commercial filmmaking. When seen in the particular German context, however, Vilsmaier's digitization of German history strikes some more problematic cords, not because special effects here may blur the lines between the real and the imagined but because sophisticated technologies of representation shroud sites of traumatic rupture and displacement in fantasies of wholeness and historical mastery. Though the film intends to narrate the historical blockage of German popular culture due to the rise of German fascism, that is, the splitting of the popular into Nazi mass culture and Jewish exile, digital memory in *The Harmonists* ends up denying any anxiety that memory of this traumatic past may incite. It subjects trauma to the pleasure principle rather than to working through and mourning the lasting traces of suffering in German twentieth-century history.

There is surely no conceptual reason why digital representation and prosthetic memory today could not capture historical experiences of trauma and question totalizing notions of history as reconciled. Traumatic events, we should recall, rupture the fabrics of narrative, memory, and historical experience. As they destroy any sense of continuity or tradition, historical traumas erase what may enable us in the future to narrate our present as a meaningful past. Trauma, then, means to live through extreme experiences without really experiencing them. Because the traumatic challenges the very texture of memory and narrativity, any recollection of traumatic histories must negotiate the aporia of narrating what, ultimately, cannot be narrated. This challenge of representing trauma, however, does not automatically relegate the filmic treatment of traumatic histories to the realm of self-reflexive art cinema. On the contrary, to the extent to which postmodern cinema has incorporated the once hostile legacies of modernism and Fordist mass culture, popular cinema today is quite familiar with modernist techniques that may withstand the drive for closure and disrupt facile lines of narrative progression, and can thus formally acknowledge irrevocable deformations of historical experience. To critique the role of digitized memories in *The Harmonists*, therefore, does not automatically imply a favoring—nostalgically, as it were—auteur film art over popular cinema. It simply means to point out that, in this film, advanced technology is used to (re)master a traumatic past that cannot be mastered. To the extent to which special effects invoke self-contained replicas of the past for the purpose of present-day consumption, *The Harmonists* offers what Eric Santner calls a "strategy of undoing, in fantasy, the need for mourning by simulating a condition of intactness, typically by situating the site and origin of loss elsewhere" ("History beyond the Pleasure Principle" 146). Instead of using representational techniques that may defetishize both the traumatic event and the work of fantasy (for example, blockage of narrative, splitting of narrative functions, deformations and interruptions) (White 31–36), Vilsmaier's grasp of professional modes of popular filmmaking, of digitized visual and sonic spectacle, entertains fantasies about the German past in which the very power of representation can clear away any lasting trauma and historical debt. The film thus not only accommodates, as Robert Burgoyne has written in a different context, "a nation desperate to remake itself in the image of its remembered popular culture" (108). As importantly, *The Harmonists* actively promotes postwall visions of a German national cinema that disavow the traumatic course of German film history itself, the historical processes of division, doubling, and displacement during the 1930s that cannot simply be reintegrated into some kind of unified national narrative.

Miramax Films marketed the American release of *The Harmonists* in March 1999 with the catch phrase, "A true story that proves the voice is mightier than the sword." The film indeed, as much as it aspires to rewrite the German past, revels in the romantic tradition of defining linguistic and musical properties as the central components of German national identity. As I have argued previously, in the film's most intriguing sequences we witness the singers' strenuous efforts to make most complex vocal arrangements sound natural and to integrate a multiplicity of voices into one higher unity. What is process must become product, what relies on a Taylorist division of vocal labor must give the impression of organic harmony, so that both national and popular success might ensue. Vilsmaier's film renders the texture of the German language as a trigger of overwhelming experiences of collectivity. Prosthetic memory here reclaims even sites of traumatic conflict as points of national identification. It reorders the past and constructs a new social consensus. Recapturing glorious moments of German-Jewish collaboration prior to Nazism, the film's phantasmagorias of synchronized sound intend nothing less than to fix the broken vessels of German history, to detach the sonic community of the nation from what is shown as the fragmenting violence of political history.

Vilsmaier's cinematic reinscription of the German language and sound as the principle conduit to national integration did not emerge in a vacuum. Instead, it cast the nationalist murmur of many German intellectuals after unification, their elitist and often polemically anti-American desire for self-confident expressions of national belonging, into a popular idiom.[8] In his 1991 lecture, "Talking about Germany," filmmaker Wim Wenders helped inaugurate this renewed quest for a grounding of German identity and filmmaking in the fabrics of the German language. Exasperated about the way in which Hollywood images flood the German market, Wenders returned to *Genesis* 1:1—the mythic creation of being through language—in order to overturn the intermingling of cultural codes in the present: "[O]ur balm in this land of lost souls, is our German language. It is differentiated, precise, subtle, endearing, accurate, and nurturing at the same time. It is a rich language. It is the only wealth that we have in a country that believes itself to be rich when it is not. The German language is everything that our country no longer is, what it is not yet, and what it may never be" (Wenders 59). Paradoxical though it may seem, the filmmaker Wenders vowed to abandon the world of images in order to reclaim the word as a mythic predicate of national identity. He endorsed Kafka and Goethe as panaceas against the lack of integrative myths. Cinematic images can no longer produce identity in Germany, he claimed; authentic nationhood can reemerge only from the sonic spaces of poetic language.

Whereas Wenders's cinema of the 1990s itself has increasingly abandoned the project of sonic regrounding and national normalization, Vilsmaier's *The Harmonists* converted Wenders's elitist vision of 1991 into a popular box office hit.[9] The sounds of the German language, in Vilsmaier's film, fold both Germans and Jews into the mythic community of the nation and bestow bliss to the shattered topographies of German twentieth-century culture. Furthermore, when understood in its function as a metacinematic allegory, as a film trying to recuperate a national tradition of independent popular cinema, of a German Hollywood grounded in specific uses of sound, Vilsmaier's *The Harmonists* aspires to nothing less than to reconcile the dissimilar tracks of German popular cinema since the inception of synchronized sound around 1930. The film systematically displaces what is traumatic about the course of popular filmmaking in Germany, and in so doing normalizes the decisive role of sound, music, and song in Goebbels's earlier construction of Hollywood in Berlin during the 1930s.

Contrary to Vilsmaier's fetishistic reinscription of a nationally self-confident sound cinema, it remains important to insist that the history of German popular filmmaking is filled with sudden departures and enforced demises, scathing disruptions and displaced memories. Radical political and industrial caesuras impacted the course of this cinema as much as shifting cultural orientations and transnational alliances. How to group the many ambivalent moments of German popular film history into meaningful periods remains an unresolved issue; the continued debates over adequate models of periodization reveal only the highly unsettled nature of this cinema itself.[10] Although more recent scholarship has often rightly emphasized some of the underlying continuities between Weimar, Nazi, and postwar German film culture, it is impossible to consider even seemingly coherent phases of German film history as homogenous or unequivocal. German cinema may be seen at its most classical, popular, and German when it was organized under the direction of "film minister" Goebbels (Moeller). Yet even the history of Nazi popular film does not simply entail the story of how German cinema tried to drive Hollywood out of Europe; it equally includes the disjointed narrative of Berlin in Hollywood, the emigration and assimilation of German-Jewish film practitioners to the classical Hollywood studio system. While it is correct to consider the legacy of Nazi popular cinema and its political functionalization as indivisible (Witte), it is equally important to emphasize that the history of German popular filmmaking during the Nazi period became one of irreversible ruptures and fundamental unsynchronicities. Situated between Hitler and Hollywood, German popular sound cinema after 1933 developed along incompatible spatial and temporal axes. There is no way—as Vilsmaier's phantasmagorical cinema wants us to believe—to recuperate this history of imaginary doubling and enforced displacement as simple or normal. There is no way around understanding German national cinema as a differential cinema in which incongruous meanings and practices, fantasies and recollections, institutional frameworks and ideological mandates, coexist in ways they don't in other national cinemas.

As they reinvent historical traditions, reify lost legends, and camouflage the products of industrial mass culture as preindustrial emanations of the popular, recent melodramas such as *The Harmonists* disavow the traumas and displacements that surround the very category of the popular in both German history and film history. In its attempt to build a new German Hollywood, this new German "cinema of consensus" (Rentschler, "From New German Cinema to the Post-Wall Cinema of Consensus") wants to suggest that in spite of the shadows of Goebbels and Auschwitz, the codes of the popular and the nation have reattained the kind of normalcy they may enjoy somewhere else. Films such as *The Harmonists* subject the history of Jewish-German relations to the machineries of prosthetic memorization in order to erase any critical interaction between history and memory. In the final analysis, they remember the harrowing events and divisions of German history in order to forget them. Yet, no fetishistic reordering of the German past can ever really succeed in reconciling the dissimilar histories of German mass culture and filmmaking in the twentieth century. The marks left by the traumatic bifurcation of German culture and cinema during the course of the 1930s remain indelible.

NOTES

This essay continues, refocuses, and expands a set of arguments suggested in particular at the end of my *The Dark Mirror: German Cinema between Hitler and Hollywood* (2002). I am grateful to the University of California Press for allowing me to make use here of a very few previously published paragraphs.

1. On the question of memory and postwall German identity, see also, among others, Hartman, Reichel, Bodemann, Frei, Diner, Herf, Zuckermann, and Fulbrook.

2. "At some point, it may even be the activity of remembering together that becomes the shared memory; once ritualized, remembering together becomes an event in itself that is to be shared and remembered" (Young 7).

3. "'Do you remember the day Kennedy was shot?' really means 'Do you remember the day you watched Kennedy being shot all day on television?' No longer is storytelling the culture's meaning-making response; an activity closer to therapeutic practice has taken over, with acts of retelling, remembering, and repeating all pointing in the direction of obsession, fantasy, trauma" (Elsaesser, "Subject Positions, Speaking Positions" 146).

4. For more on different postwar models of Jewish-German identity, see Brumlik.

5. For extensive discussions of Syberberg's *Our Hitler*, see Kaes 37–72 and Santner, *Stranded Objects* 103–49.

6. Domestic feature productions earned as little as 9.5 percent of all German box office returns in 1998 (*FFA Intern* 7).

7. For a critical reassessment of Gunning's model, see Bordwell 139–49.

8. See, for instance, the various contributions to the influential by Schwilk and Schacht.

9. Released on December 25, 1997, *Comedian Harmonists* attracted a total of 2.8 million viewers to German cinemas. It was the by far most successful domestic production at German box offices in 1998 (*FFA Intern* 8).

10. For an instructive overview of these debates, see Petro.

WORKS CITED

Adorno, Theodor. *In Search of Wagner*. Translated by Rodney Livingstone. London: New Left Books, 1981.

Altman, Rick. "Introduction," *Yale French Studies* 60 (1980): 3–15.

Benjamin, Walter. *Illuminations: Essays and Reflections*. Translated by Harry Zohn. Edited by Hannah Arendt. New York: Schocken, 1969.

Bock, Hans Michael, Wolfgang Jacobsen, and Jörg Schöning, eds. *MusikSpektakelFilm: Musiktheater und Tanzkultur im deutschen Film 1922–1937*. Munich: Edition Text und Kritik, 1998.

Bodemann, Y. Michal, ed. *Jews, Germans, Memory: Reconstructions of Jewish Life in Germany*. Ann Arbor: University of Michigan Press, 1996.

Bordwell, David. *On the History of Film Style*. Cambridge, Mass.: Harvard University Press, 1997.

Brumlik, Micha. "The Situation of the Jews in Today's Germany." In *Jews, Germans, Memory: Reconstructions of Jewish Life in Germany*, edited by Y. Michal Bodemann, 1–18. Ann Arbor: University of Michigan Press, 1996.

Burgoyne, Robert. *Film Nation: Hollywood Looks at U.S. History*. Minneapolis: University of Minnesota Press, 1997.

Czada, Peter, and Günter Große. *Comedian Harmonists: Ein Vokalensemble erobert die Welt*. Berlin: Edition Hentrich, 1993.

Dahlhaus, Carl. *Richard Wagner's Music Dramas*. Translated by Mary Whittall. Cambridge: Cambridge University Press, 1979.

Dennis, David B. *Beethoven in German Politics, 1870–1989*. New Haven, Conn.: Yale University Press, 1996.

Diner, Dan. "On Guilt Discourse and Other Narratives: Epistemological Observations regarding the Holocaust." *History & Memory* 9 (1997): 301–20.

Elsaesser, Thomas. "German Postwar Cinema and Hollywood." In *Hollywood in Europe: Experiences of a Cultural Hegemony*, edited by David W. Ellwood and Rob Kroes, 283–302. Amsterdam: VU University Press, 1994.

————. "Subject Positions, Speaking Positions: From *Holocaust, Our Hitler,* and *Heimat* to *Shoah* and *Schindler's List.*" In *The Persistence of History: Cinema, Television, and the Modern Event,* edited by Vivian Sobchack, 145–83. New York: Routledge, 1996.

FFA Intern. 10 February 1999.

Frei, Norbert. *Vergangenheitspolitik: Die Anfänge der Bundesrepublik und die NS-Vergangenheit.* Munich: Beck, 1996.

Fulbrook, Mary. *German National Identity after the Holocaust.* Oxford: Polity Press, 1999.

Gemünden, Gerd. *Framed Visions: Popular Culture, Americanization, and the Contemporary German and Austrian Imagination.* Ann Arbor: University of Michigan Press, 1998.

Goehr, Lydia. The *Quest for Voice: On Music, Politics, and the Limits of Philosophy.* Berkeley: University of California Press, 1998.

Gunning, Tom. "The Cinema of Attraction(s)." *Wide Angle* 8, no. 3–4 (1986): 63–70.

————. "An Aesthetic of Astonishment: Early Film and the (In)Credulous Spectator." In *Viewing Positions: Ways of Seeing Film,* edited by Linda Williams, 114–33. New Brunswick, N.J.: Rutgers University Press, 1995.

Hartman, Geoffrey, ed. *Holocaust Remembrance: The Shapes of Memory.* Cambridge: Blackwell, 1994.

Herf, Jeffrey. *Divided Memory: The Nazi Past in the Two Germanys.* Cambridge, Mass.: Harvard University Press, 1997.

Hohendahl, Peter U. "Reworking History: Wagner's German Myth of Nuremberg." In *Re-Reading Wagner,* edited by Reinhold Grimm and Jost Hermand, 39–60. Madison: University of Wisconsin Press, 1993.

Horkheimer, Max, and Theodor W. Adorno. *Dialectic of Enlightenment.* Translated by John Cumming. New York: Continuum, 1995.

Huyssen, Andreas. *After the Great Divide: Modernism, Mass Culture, Postmodernism.* Bloomington: Indiana University Press, 1986.

————. *Twilight Memory: Marking Time in a Culture of Amnesia.* New York: Routledge, 1995.

Ignatieff, Michael. *Blood and Belonging: Journeys into the New Nationalism.* New York: Farrar, Straus and Giroux, 1993.

Jameson, Fredric. *Postmodernism or, The Cultural Logic of Late Capitalism.* Durham, N.C.: Duke University Press, 1991.

Kaes, Anton. *From Hitler to Heimat: The Return of History as Film.* Cambridge, Mass.: Harvard University Press, 1989.

Koepnick, Lutz. *The Dark Mirror: German Cinema between Hitler and Hollywood.* Berkeley: University of California Press, 2002.

Kracauer, Siegfried. *The Mass Ornament: Weimar Essays.* Translated by Thomas Y. Levin. Cambridge, Mass.: Harvard University Press, 1995.

LaCapra, Dominick. *History and Memory after Auschwitz.* Ithaca, N.Y.: Cornell University Press, 1998.

Landsberg, Alison. "Prosthetic Memory: The Logics and Politics of Memory in Modern American Culture." Ph.D. diss., University of Chicago, 1996.

Maier, Charles. "A Surfeit of Memory? Reflections on History, Melancholy and Denial." *History & Memory* 5 (1993): 136–51.

Mitchell, William J. *The Reconfigured Eye: Visual Truth in the Post-Photographic Era.* Cambridge, Mass.: MIT Press, 1992.

Moeller, Felix. *Der Filmminister: Goebbels und der Film im Dritten Reich.* Berlin: Henschel, 1998.

Petro, Patrice. "Nazi Cinema at the Intersection of the Classical and the Popular." *New German Critique* 74 (spring/fall 1998): 41–56.

Potter, Pamela M. *Most German of the Arts: Musicology and Society from the Weimar Republic to the End of Hitler's Reich.* New Haven, Conn.: Yale University Press, 1998.

Reichel, Peter. *Politik mit der Erinnerung: Geächtnisorte im Streit um die nationalsozialistische Vergangenheit.* Munich: Hanser, 1995.

Rentschler, Eric. "How American Is It? The U.S. as Image and Imaginary in German Film." *Persistence of Vision* 2 (1985): 5–18.

———. *The Ministry of Illusion: Nazi Cinema and Its Afterlife.* Cambridge, Mass.: Harvard University Press, 1996.

———. "From New German Cinema to the Post-Wall Cinema of Consensus." In *Cinema and Nation,* edited by Mette Hjort and Scott MacKenzie, 260–77. London: Routledge, 2000.

Santner, Eric L. *Stranded Objects: Mourning, Memory, and Film in Postwar Germany.* Ithaca, N.Y.: Cornell University Press, 1990.

———. "History beyond the Pleasure Principle." In *Probing the Limits of Representation: Nazism and the Final Solution,* edited by Saul Friedländer, 143–54. Cambridge, Mass.: Harvard University Press, 1992.

Schwilk, Heimo, and Ulrich Schacht, eds. *Die selbstbewußte Nation: "Anschwellender Bocksgesang" und weitere Beiträge zu einer deutschen Debatte.* Berlin: Ullstein, 1995.

Syberberg, Hans Jürgen. *Hitler, ein Film aus Deutschland.* Reinbek: Rowohlt, 1978.

Terdiman, Richard. *Present Past: Modernity and the Memory Crisis.* Ithaca. N.Y.: Cornell University Press, 1993.

Vilsmaier, Joseph, ed. *Comedian Harmonists: Eine Legende kehrt zurück. Der Film.* Leipzig: Gustav Kiepenheuer Verlag, 1997.

Wagner, Richard. *Prose Works.* Translated by William Ashton Ellis. New York: Broude Brothers, 1895.

———. *Die Meistersinger von Nürnberg: Opera in Three Acts.* Translated by Susan Webb. New York: Metropolitan Opera Guild, 1992.

Wenders, Wim. "Talking about Germany." In *The Cinema of Wim Wenders: Image, Narrative, and the Postmodern Condition,* edited by Roger F. Cook and Gerd Gemünden, 51–59. Detroit: Wayne State University Press, 1996.

White, Hayden. "The Modernist Event." In *The Persistence of History: Cinema, Television, and the Modern Event,* edited by Vivian Sobchack, 17–38. New York: Routledge, 1996.

Witte, Karsten. "The Indivisible Legacy of Nazi Cinema." *New German Critique* 74 (spring/summer 1998): 23–30.

Young, James. *The Texture of Memory: Holocaust Memorials and Meaning.* New Haven, Conn.: Yale University Press, 1993.

Zuckermann, Moshe. *Zweierlei Holocaust: Der Holocaust in den politischen Kulturen Israels und Deutschlands.* Göttingen: Wallstein, 1998.

FILMOGRAPHY

Comedian Harmonists (1997)
Director: Joseph Vilsmaier
Screenplay: Jürgen Büscher, Klaus Richter
Cast: Ben Becker, Heino Ferch, Ulrich Noethen, Heinrich Schafmeister, Max Tidorf, Kai Wiesinger, Meret Becker, Katja Riemann
Producers: Hanno Huth, Reinhard Klooss, Danny Krausz, Peter Sterr, Joseph Vilsmaier
Original Music: Walter Jurmann
Cinematography: Joseph Vilsmaier
Editor: Peter R. Adam
Production Companies: Bavaria Atelier GmbH, Der Film Produktionsgesellschaft GmbH, Iduna Film Produktiongesellschaft , Senator Film Produktion GmbH, Televersal
Distributors: Cipa (France), Miramax Films (USA), Senator Film
U.S. Title: The Harmonists
Run Time: 126 min.

Meschugge (1998)
Director: Dani Levy
Screenplay: Dani Levy, Maria Schrader
Cast: Maria Schrader, Dani Levy, David Strathairn, Nicole Heesters, Jeffrey Wright
Producers: Stefan Arndt, Margot Bridger, Milanka Comfort, Peter-Christian Fueter, Gebhard Henke, Dani Levy, Andreas Schreitmüller, Tom Spiess, Susann Wach-Rösza
Original Music: Niki Reiser
Cinematography: Carl-Friedrich Koschnick
Editor: Ueli Christen, Sabine Hoffmann, Dani Levy
Production Design: Teresa Mastropiero, Volker Schäfer
Production Companies: Arte, Condor Films, Extrafilm, Westdeutscher Rundfunk (WDR), X-Filme Creative Pool
Distributors: Bavaria Film International (2000, USA), German Independent (2000, USA), Jugendfilm-Verleih GmbH, Video Search of Miami (video)
U.S. Title: The Giraffe
Run Time: 103 min.

Aimée & Jaguar (1999)
Director: Max Färberböck
Screenplay: Erica Fischer (novel), Max Färberböck
Cast: Maria Schrader, Juliane Köhler, Johanna Wokalek, Heike Makatsch, Elisabeth Degen, Detlev Buck,
Producers: Hanno Huth, Feliks Pastusiak, Günter Rohrbach, Lew Rywin, Stefan Schieder, Gerhard von Halem
Original Music: Jan A. P. Kaczmarek
Cinematography: Tony Imi
Editor: Barbara Hennings
Production Design: Albrecht Konrad
Art Direction: Uli Hanisch

Production Companies: Senator Film Produktion GmbH
Distributors: Senator Film (Germany), Zeitgeist Films (2000, USA, subtitled)
Run Time: 125 min.

Viehjud Levi (1999)
Director: Didi Danquart
Screenplay: Didi Danquart, Martina Döcker
Cast: Bruno Cathomas, Caroline Ebner, Eva Mattes, Georg Olschewski,Martina Gedeck, Ulrich Noethen
Producers: Isabelle Birambaux, Martin Hagemann, Gabriele Röthemeyer, Gerhard Schedl, Andreas Schreitmüller, Susan Schulte, Susann Wach-Rösza, Christoph Weher, Marc Wehrlin
Original Music: Cornelius Schwehr
Cinematography: Johann Feindt
Editor: Katja Dringenberg
Production Design: Susanne Hopf
Production Companies: Arte, Dschoint Ventschr Filmproduktion, Lotus Film, Schweizer Fernsehen DRS, Südwestdeutscher Rundfunk (SWR), Zero Film
U.S. Title: *Jew-Boy Levi*
Run Time: 95 min.

Ein Lied von Liebe und Tod—Gloomy Sunday (1999)
Director: Rolf Schübel
Screenplay: Nick Barkow (novel), Rolf Schübel
Cast: Erika Marozsán, Joachim Król, Ben Becker, Stefano Dionisi
Producers: Michael André, Kerstin Ramcke, Martin Rohrbeck, Andreas Schreitmüller, Richard Schöps, Aron Sipos, Martin Wiebel, Winka Wulff
Original Music: Nico Fintzen
Cinematography: Edward Klosinski
Editor: Ursula Höf
Production Design: Volker Schäfer, Csaba Stork
Production Companies: Studio Hamburg Filmproduktion, Dom Film, Focus Film, PolyGram Filmproduktion, Westdeutscher Rundfunk (WDR), Arte, Premiere
Distributors: Arrow Releasing, Inc. (USA), PolyGram (Germany)
Run Time: 112 min.

Gripsholm (2000)
Director: Xavier Koller
Screenplay: Stefan Kolditz
Cast: Ulrich Noethen, Heike Makatsch, Jasmin Tabatabai, Marcus Thomas
Producers: Danny Krausz, Rainer Kölmel,Ulrich Limmer, Alfi Sinniger, Kurt Stocker, Thomas Wilkening
Original Music: David Klein, Kol Simcha, Olivier Truan
Cinematography: Pio Corradi
Editor: Patricia Rommel
Art Direction: Aïda Kalnins, Peter Manhardt
Production Companies: Catpics AG, Dor Film Produktionsgesellschaft GmbH, Kinowelt Filmproduktion, Schweizer Fernsehen DRS,

Studio Babelsberg Independents, Teleclub AG, Thomas Wilkening Filmgesellschaft, Zweites Deutsches Fernsehen (ZDF), Österreichischer Rundfunk (ORF)
Distributors: Kinowelt Filmverleih
Run Time: 100 min.

CHAPTER 18

Angst Takes a Holiday in Doris Dörrie's *Am I Beautiful?* (1998)

Margaret McCarthy

The opening shot in Doris Dörrie's *Am I Beautiful? [Bin ich schön?]* (1998) hovers above a plain, then gradually descends onto a highway as vacant as a landing strip, jetting the spectator into a mostly bare mise-en-scène. A musical version of Federico Garcia Lorca's poem *Verde que te quiero verde* offers at first only acoustic bearings; further along, Spain finds its one visual signifier in a billboard-size bull standing by the road.[1] The two-dimensional quality of space throws the German tourists who dot the landscape into high relief, while Spain's own populace is hardly seen at all. Moreover, a terrain emptied of all but the most cliched guidepost to Spanish culture connotes superficial relations between Germans and one of their longtime favorite vacation destinations.[2] Oblivious to the rousing soundtrack, they mostly remain enclosed in cars, like the family seen in the following segment listening to a cassette recording of a German children's book. Itself stripped of narrative adornment, the story imparts the childlike wish: "We're doing well . . . because we have everything the heart desires, and we don't need to be afraid of anything, because we are, of course, still strong." As embedded in a children's book, self-help for German angst also codes Spain as "the country of our dreams."[3] Even an interchangeable foreign backdrop, it seems, can sooth the German psyche.

As framed in these opening shots—visually pared down to the point of being nondescript, but psychically overinvested—Spain soon becomes a playground for German infantile fantasies: Werner (Gustav-Peter Wöhler), a fertilizer salesman, gets his bottom whipped by Linda (Franka Potente) in a hotel room, then plays air guitar to Janis Joplin's *Cry, Baby, Cry;* a flashback shows Klaus and Franzi (Steffan Wink and Anica Dobra) play-acting a bullfight in another hotel room. Specific markers of Germanness are less evident in what seems a quirky take on a standard, Merchant-Ivory formula: "tourist goes to sunny, southern country and his or her blood boils." The children's story also conjures a parallel fantasy of paring down to the carefree, unformed nature of a child susceptible to psychic (re)programming. In fact, an early shot shows Linda throwing her purse to the winds, struggling to become as unencumbered by angst as the cloud she appears to cup in one shot. The overarching and repeated visual reference to Spain, that proplike bull, either inspires sadomasochistic fantasies or becomes a cutout form in a fairytale landscape of childish yearnings. Each fantasy more accurately refers back to a German psyche stripped of adult control and repression.

Despite threadbare or comically over-the-top visual clues, these opening scenes do, in fact, provide an important map for understanding the film's subsequent trajectory. *Am I Beautiful?,* however, charts a slightly different course than the standard road movie or vacation film, with its search for happiness and exoticism or flight from dislocation. What's significantly different is the fact that Spain does emerge as a tangible presence by the film's end and effectively transforms many of the film's characters. In this manner, their tunnel vision finally registers difference, while we as spectators glimpse the contours of a new Europe united and interconnected in surprising ways. In the film's final scenes, our tourists lose themselves in crowds of Spaniards celebrating the Semana Santa, as Spain in all its cultural specificity now subsumes those previously content to frolic by the flattened bull.[4] Our German tourists finally register cultural difference in a manner that paradoxically yields, in turn, a sense of self elsewhere missing in the film. When Linda pays tribute to the Madonna in a ritual of recognition, atonement, and respect, she returns to the self cast to the winds with her purse, albeit a self in much improved form. Unlike that bull, the Madonna looks back, and we enter a world in which identity emerges in the give and take across cultural and sometimes gendered and familial differences. Whether reminiscent of Merchant Ivory or Hollywood, Dörrie's use of popular cinematic forms and strategies also looks back at and offers an ironic and, at times, utopian take on German selfhood in the larger, global context of the twenty-first century. Whether impertinently or respectfully appropriated, a whole range of borrowed cultural forms, of course, define this self. What's different, though, in Dörrie's road movie/ vacation film is not only an altered, transnational landscape of cultural forms perpetually in transit but also an altered path toward happiness, if not self-knowledge, in the ability to perceive and embrace difference in a meaningful, respectful way.

The extent to which Dörrie rewrites conventional, formulaic film genres, the ostensible task of the new German filmmakers of the 1990s, with their Hollywood-inspired comedies, generally goes unnoticed. Rather, she's more often simply "the mother of contemporary German relationship comedies," a designation that one would hardly associate with innovation. Dörrie has, in fact, been making films since the early 1980s, many featuring a jumbled mix of gendered, familial, and multicultural relations. Seen by five million spectators in Germany alone, *Men* (1985) grossed $52 million in Europe and landed Dörrie on the cover of the German magazine *Der Spiegel*.[5] International success also brought a brief but disappointing stint in Hollywood, which ended when Dörrie returned to Germany to have more control over her work.[6] If critical reception of Dörrie's subsequent films has been mixed, her films generally make money and sometimes win film prizes.[7] Attention to German film critics' less kind responses to her work, however, sheds light on Dörrie's relationship to popular film, as well as German critics' often fraught feelings toward Hollywood.

Klaus Phillips has written about the venomous attacks that German film critics have aimed at Dörrie's films, her persona, even her perfume. He writes that such negativity is predictable, given that "Dörrie seems to encourage critics' perception of her as a nonconformist outsider who . . . has little in common with the generation represented by Wim Wenders. . . . Moreover, her work abounds with sly, nagging reminders that Germans excel at making themselves and each other miserable instead of enjoying life, and that they continue to have difficulty accepting and adapting to Germany's multiculturalism" (175). Phillips's observations highlight two significant factors in the reception of Dörrie's films: her problematic status as auteur and the unpalatable political implications of her films, which, as I will demonstrate, are often lost in old-fashioned quibbling about her work's aesthetic merits. Dörrie has cited the influence on her work of American film directors like Martin Scorsese, John Cassavetes, and Bob Rafelson, not of the German *Autorenkino* that preceded her, thus aligning herself with what many critics consider a golden age of good Hollywood film.[8] This stance may also account for Anglo-American film scholars' lack of interest and respect, given their tendency to measure German film against the aims of New German Cinema. Chronologically, Dörrie emerged after Rainer Werner Fassbinder's death and the rise of the CDU/CSU/FDP coalition in 1983 when interior minister Friedrich Zimmermann began subsidizing only entertaining films. German film history currently views this trend as a downhill process, a movement away from New German Cinema's attempts to thematize the past in the present and offer something more than mindless escapism and pure commercial cinema. Given Anglo-American scholars' ongoing obsession with German identity vis-à-vis its turbulent twentieth-century history, it's unsurprising that Dörrie's films have received little attention. Such scholars will have to modify their criteria and disciplinary boundaries to follow the transformations of German culture and identity in an increasingly global economy.

The extent to which German film critics find Dörrie deficient according to Hollyword values emerged in the film reviews of *Am I Beautiful?* Again, the film's political implications generally disappeared in laments about the film's ostensibly second-rate status as compared to a superior Hollywood product. Many critics gleefully underscored the film's failings when compared to Robert Altman's *Short Cuts* (1993), since both films are based on short stories (Dörrie's own and Raymond Carver's), share a chainlike episodic structure, and feature an all-star cast of actors. Dörrie's contention that she had the idea before Altman but considered such a film unrealizable prompted a response from critics that was far from kind.[9] Hans-Günther Dicks of the newspaper *Neues Deutschland* wrote: "Dörrie as director is as little Altman as Dörrie the story-teller is Carver." (September 17, 1998, 2) Sven Gächter of the Austrian magazine *Profil* wrote: "Dörrie tries to germanize Altman, which doesn't work because of her chronic dependence on cliché" (September 14, 1998, 38). Spotting obvious parallels, German film critics were content to vent their often schizophrenic attitude toward Hollywood, normally the site of the deficient artistic merit which they here ascribe to Dörrie. (Paradoxically, criticisms of the German film industry's purported lack of popular appeal hardly apply to Dörrie, whose affinities with more obvious Hollywood values generally go unrecognized.[10]) A recent article in Munich's newspaper, *Süddeutsche Zeitung*, wonderfully and knowingly captures the German film industry's ambivalence toward Hollywood. In "Ambrosia and Dishwater: Between Two Stools, or Is There an Intelligent German Comedy?" Rolf Silber imagines a scenario where a German scriptwriter appears before a German producer to pitch the idea behind the Hollywood film *Groundhog Day*, only to receive the name of a good psychiatrist. Despite the industry's fervent desire for innovative and intelligent entertaining films, a wide chasm nonetheless persists in critics' minds between "Kunst und Dreck," or art and garbage, making the existence of something in between, like the unexpected appearance of that groundhog, hard to imagine. Because Dörrie both departs from the art house *Autorenkino* which preceded her in Germany and presumably lacks the talents of an innovative Hollywood director like Altman, she, too, receives the same dismissive incredulity as that *GroundHog* script.

As much as both Hollywood and the auteurs of New German Cinema may be insufficient reference points for a body of work with very hybrid, transatlantic influences, two key players—Altman and, perhaps more surprisingly, Fassbinder—serve as useful markers for positioning Dörrie on that tricky terrain between art and garbage. All three directors have experimented with diverse genres, even as they have employed a favored stable of actors; all have been subject to a wildly fluctuating critical response to their films and offscreen personas; and their films tend to feature over-the-top (or, to some, cliché-ridden) representations of either ugly Americans or Germans indulging in extreme behaviors. The filmic genres with which each has experimented include detective films and film noir, melodrama, literary adaptation, police/action film, and comedy; in addition, all three have worked in television intermittently during their careers.[11] Yet all of them couple Hollywood forms and conventions with a rigorous critique of the status quo, achieved via various distantiation techniques.[12] For all three the status quo bears through and through the marks of their own cultural context; indeed, for Dörrie and Fassbinder, a persistent obsession with things German may account for the fact that, despite an international reach, each remained, in his or her own way, a homebody of sorts.[13] I would also argue that Dörrie not only shares what Gerd Gemünden has called Fassbinder's self-lacerating introspection, but also that her films, too, are often "hybrid and . . . messy constructions that provoke different and contradictory responses from the audience" ("Re-fusing Brecht" 75). Most importantly, what Gemünden points to as a neglected treasure trove of contemporary themes in Fassbinder's films are also evident throughout Dörrie's, namely, "questions of identity and nationality, marginality, foreigners . . . all issues which are setting the political agenda of the 1990s for a unified Germany" (Gemünden, "Introduction" 9).

In commenting on what appealed to him in Raymond Carver's short stories, Altman points up common ground with Dörrie's films, particularly *Am I Beautiful?*, namely attention to "the wonderful idiosyncrasies of human behavior, the idiosyncrasies that exist amid the randomness of life's experiences" (quoted in Nayman 85). Bizarre and freakish behavior, as I will soon demonstrate, is much in evidence throughout *Am I Beautiful?*. "Chance and serendipity" (Scofield 390) also seem to define the geographical space traversed in both Dorrie's film and *Short Cuts*, as seemingly random characters inhabiting a sprawling horizontal space nonetheless appear to cross paths and bump up against each other as if bound together by some larger, invisible web. More generally, and perhaps most irksome to critics, such spaces seem populated by stereotypical figures, like frustrated housewives, philandering husbands, callous and uptight professionals, and perennial drifters. Both Dörrie and Atman up the ante by coupling stereotype with obvious irony, which may lead already irritated audiences to inwardly groan: Altman has a tendency to wave the American flag in precisely those moments when his characters act in their most egregious (and predictable) ways; Dörrie's perpetually down Germans are forever in search of existentially meaningful lives, yet remain doggedly attached to consumer objects as substitutes for human contact. When in both films a cast of very famous, bankable actors inhabit the stereotypes and deliver rather blunt ironies, what might otherwise be very pleasurable audience identification tips over into something more uncomfortable. As I will argue, Dörrie, in particular, is quite uninhibited about exposing her actors flagrantly mired in often unattractive, private acts.

Poised somewhere between Fassbinder and Altman, Dörrie's films create their own crossbred characteristics. Adding to the influences from the German-speaking world in *Am I Beautiful?*, as a few critics observed, is the Austrian playwright Arthur Schnitzler, whose *Reigen*, or "round-dance," examined sexual relations in fin-de-siècle Vienna. With Schnitzler in the cultural mix, an Altmanesque cast and chain of episodes becomes part of a ritualistic dance around German identity. Given precisely this unusual amalgam, it is not enough to simply label Dörrie a seondrate Altman if this means ignoring what an Altmanesque film might say about German identity. If the difficulty of Dörrie is that she stands both within and apart from German culture, the beauty of Dörrie is her ability to frame this identity via non-German cultural reference points.

Am I Beautiful? begins with credits in which names appear in pairs, as actors from various moments in German film history "partner" each other. Dörrie's film brings together a former Fassbinder player (Gottfried John), a star of the 1980s blockbuster hit *Men* (Uwe Ochsenknecht), and a new superstar of the 1990s (Franka Potente, star of *Run, Lola, Run*). Also featured are Senta Berger, whose long film career includes work in American, Italian, and German film, particularly with Berger's husband, director Michael Verhoeven; Iris Berben, perhaps best known for her role as a TV detective but also an actress with a long, distinguished film career; and Dietmar Schönherr, whose film career spans the last fifty years and includes stints on television as talk and quiz show host. First and foremost, such an ensemble challenges the traditional periodization of German film, as several generations come together in a manner that speaks to continuity, not division. Not merely a rip-off of a standard Altman cast, Dörrie's actors instead underscore the viability of German popular films of the 1990s. Moreover, pairing two actors' names in the opening credits suggests not just continuity but parity. If the extreme verticality of the opening aerial shot gives way to the horizontal plain, Dörrie's film creates a level playing field for actors otherwise subject to traditional hierarchies that privilege art house over popular films.

Yet celebrity is muted as Dörrie's actors lend themselves to sometimes graphic manifestations of the film's overarching themes: shot through not just with infantile desires, but very adult anxieties, *Am I Beautiful?* shows many of its characters coming to terms with that ultimate other: death, and its lesser forms, abandonment, neglect, and physical decline.[14] A buoyant fantasy world of clouds, bubbles, and wedding gowns, which Elke (Maria Schrader) compares to whipped cream, continually confronts decaying matter and the gravitational pull of the grave. Real life is consistently messier than fantasy, often graphically so. When Jessica (Elisabeth Romano) meets her callous married lover Herbert (Gottfried John) for a trist, she slits her wrists and performs a spectacular bloodletting all over his pristine white sheets, carpets, and walls. Werner's spanking shows us his paunchy, middle-aged body, and a sex scene between the caterers Rita (Iris Berben) and Fred (Oliver Nägele) features more undulating fat rolls, not to mention oral sex and intercourse in slow motion.[15] Over and over the film emphasizes how human bodies share affinities with the potato heads that Fred carves, shown moldering in time-lapse photography. Moreover, spent, undesirable bodies are often treated like so much garbage: an old woman (Christine Osterlein) in a wheelchair, crippled by a stroke, is abandoned by her daughter in a parking garage. Dörrie's film shows famous German actors not only literally exposing themselves, but also some of the more brutal realities of German culture, as Dörrie sees it, namely, that human bodies treated as the equivalent of consumer commodities will inevitably be discarded once desirability departs and dysfunction sets in.[16]

Given the many characters' strong attachment to the cell phones and answering machines that appear in so many scenes, material commodities often appear to supplant material bodies. The color red as thematic thread runs through Am I Beautiful?, displacing what should be the realm of emotion or blood onto lifeless consumer items like Gummi Bears, shoes, and clothing.[17] Franzi, for instance, determines her feelings for her former bull-fight partner, Klaus, by blindly reaching into a bag of Gummi Bears, hoping that a red one will signal a love still alive. Passion finds its diminution here in a shrunken candy inside a plastic bag. When consumer objects become the locus of identity, they also take on the existential qualities one would normally associate with humans: on her wedding day, Franzi almost dumps Holger (Michael Klemm), Klaus's successor, because he is the shoes that she can't stand. Similarly, consumer objects satisfy in ways that otherwise necessitate human contact: another scene shows a girl letting herself be groped by a man in order to get his trendy Bitex sunglasses, her face registering a bargain-hunter's bliss, rather than sexual ecstasy. Most often, human contact is again filtered through the tenuous connections of modern electronic equipment, which procures both psychic and geographic distance toward the many figures in the film who grow fat, go bald, or fall prey to disease.

None of the preceding sounds specifically German until one pays attention to the use of foreign language in the film. In the Dörrien universe of uptight Germans, strong emotions can be articulated only in foreign tongues. When Juan (Dietmar Schönherr) tells an awkward and speechless Klaus that his wife has just died, Klaus lets himself be schooled in the appropriate response: just say I'm sorry (lo siento), Juan tells him in Spanish. When Bodo (Uwe Ochsenknecht) reveals to Linda how he came to terms with his sister's death, he quotes an old Indian in English who told him that life has "no beginning, no end," that matter merely transforms itself. At Franzi's wedding, a duo of African-American women (the *Weather Girls*, actually) sing a song in English whose title, "Happy," names a state, according to Dörrie, unfamiliar to Germans."[18] All of this suggests that those empty spaces in the film's opening shots may symbolize emotional gaps in the German psyche fillable only by foreign forms. In other words, Spain is not merely a playground for Germans intent on cutting loose. If one considers how much language forms the very basis of identity, then Spain has the potential to mold its German tourists in profound ways, just as Juan teaches Klaus how to grow up and deal with dying, and later what it means to truly love someone.

While implicit hierarchies between German and Hollywood cinema guided many of the film's reviewers, German/Spanish relations received little analysis. In what I'll call an elaborate "dance of difference," *Am I Beautiful?* does, however, offer many perspectives—at times romantic, ironic, or utopian—on such relations. Several recent, popular culture artifacts suggest that Spain's satellite island, Majorca, is the land of many German dreams. The prime-time soap opera, *Majorca: The Search for Paradise*, offered by the German television station ProSieben, was reportedly Germany's most expensive television show to that point in time.[19] *Ballermann 6* (1997) tells the story of two working-class Germans drinking beer and sangria by the bucket on a three-day, prepackaged trip to Majorca.[20] Germans of all classes fill up the beaches in Spain and its satellite islands, while the rich and famous, like Claudia Schiffer, busily buy up much of the available real estate. Self-centered Germans in the film may, in fact, parody a takeover tourist mentality already much in evidence. Hierarchical relations that privilege Germans are, however, inverted in *Am I Beautiful?* by romantic binaries that traditionally attract tourists: if Germany is green, cold, and rainy, Spain is dry, sunny, and desertlike, the perfect antidote to crummy German weather, even if Spain's climate varies widely. If Germans are often seen enclosed in cars, if not stuck in traffic, Spain seems to consist of mostly wide open spaces. Finally, of course, if Germans are whiners, Spaniards are merely wise. At times, though, Dörrie satirizes Germans' use of exotic sources as the antidote to anomie. One frustrated German husband, Robert (Joachim Król), fetishizes hip-swinging Trinidadian woman. Later, at Franzi's wedding, he writhes and sweats to the strains of "Happy," the voluptuous, hip-swinging African-American women right behind him. In his own way, he looks as awkward as Klaus learning to be a *Mensch* in Spanish. In a more serious vein, Linda's anxieties about mortality sharply contrast the elderly couples she watches perform the flamenco, with great grace and dignity, in a hotel lobby. Childish Germans versus mature Spaniards may seem a naively romantic variation on multicultural relations, but since Germans are just as likely to get a good dose of rhythm as humanity in this dance of difference, Dörrie offsets idealism with satire.

What this dance requires, first off, is a good pair of shoes. Seen repeatedly in close-up, shoes are probably the film's favored commodity object. "I recognized you as German because of your shoes," Werner tells Linda early in the film when he picks her up by the highway. Foot apparel, of course, provides a highly unstable marker of identity, since Germans often favor Italian footwear. When Holger ditches his ugly shoes at Franzi's behest, a close-up shows him dancing in what look like Chuck Taylor hightops. In an era of loosening cultural boundaries, German identity, of course, finds its share of support from non-German commodities. As the Euro subsumes national currencies, commodities travel across borders so quickly that they sometimes lose clear markers of their original cultural context, like Turkish fladen bread next to German bread on bakery shelves.[21] Sometimes recipes do change somewhat in translation, like when German cable TV offers its own version of *The Price is Right*, much as *Majorca* may have been the German answer to *Baywatch*. In this manner, traveling cultural artifacts become a hybrid mix both of and not of the borrowing culture. Further, something formulaic then articulates a new range of cultural concerns. Dörrie's love of non-German music in her films provides another striking example, even if lyrics in a particular language seemed so closely tied to their national origins. Joplin's *Cry, Baby, Cry* becomes an anthem of repressed Germans in need of a good spanking for emotional release; Sinead O'Conner's *Nothing Compares 2U*, as I will discuss later, becomes the antidote to a throw away culture that Dörrie sees everywhere in German human relations. More important, traveling, mutating commodities challenge the presumably discreet and stable components that structure otherwise hierarchical relations among various countries. Whatever cultural superiority a German might feel toward a Turk living in Germany, for instance, is complicated by the presence of Turkish fladen bread in German bakeries.

Given a landscape of commodities in transit, it is important to note how *Am I Beautiful?* departs from the traditional backdrops informing road and vacation films. Wim Wenders's road movies of the 1970s, like *Alice in the Cities [Alice in den Städten]* (1974), *Wrong Move [Falsche Bewegung]* (1974), or *Kings of the Road [Im Laufe der Zeit]* (1976), all share a profound psychic and geographic dislocation. The empty opening scenes in *Am I Beautiful?* may pay lip service to the notion of an uncharted frontier, but in reality, Klaus can not only whip out his cell phone and chat with Franzi in Munich, he is also educated enough to be able to converse with Juan in basic Spanish. (In a pinch, many get by with a bit of English, too.) Juan is equally capable of hopping a plane to Germany and navigating (not to mention fetishizing!) a landscape of traffic snarls and lush, green forests. If Wenders's perpetual wanderers never seemed to actually arrive anywhere and remained at a psychic remove from their surroundings, Dörrie's post-European Union characters seem to move as easily as commodities not subject to trade disputes, which can be either good or bad, depending on their ability to engage their surroundings as something more than a consumer fantasy or ware up for grabs.

When cultural artifacts move with such ease, however, laments about a downward spiral to the lowest common denominator are common, much as Dörrie's appropriation of another director's cinematic vocabulary marked her as a second-rate Altman in the eyes of German film critics. In such a situation, their use remains suspect, presumably reflecting a fetishism whereby expensive Italian shoes merely shore up faltering German selves otherwise incapable of a healthy respect for Italian design. Indeed, everywhere in the film, characters attempt to fill an existential *Loch,* or hole, not only with food or sex but with cashmere sweaters and cell phones, if not extended vacations in Spain. Yet, *Am I Beautiful?* sometimes belies such unreflexive egotism, particularly when the object appropriated happens to be a subject who inspires, if not demands, respect. In its more utopian moments, *Am I Beautiful?* shows us its dance of difference as one of mutual respect and parity. Juan's long marriage to a German woman provides the film's most striking example.

Blurry cultural boundaries find positive resonance in their relationship: as Juan puts it, "I was her, she was me," in a dynamic that displaces, if not de-essentializes German and Spanish identities. Their lives offer several instances of a doubling that both challenges hierarchical relations and eclipses, at times, the marks of an originary identity. Old super eight footage of the wife dancing shows a dark-haired woman in traditional Spanish garb, no obvious signs of Germanness apparent. When he places the urn carrying his wife's ashes into German soil, Juan dances as if internally possessed of that super eight footage. Despite such doubling, acknowledgment of and respect for difference remains a fundamental piece of their marriage. In lovingly describing his wife's various personas, Juan pays tribute to her as a complicated, full-blown subject, not merely object of desire. Significantly, her German identity remains integral to him: as she lays dying, Juan listens raptly while she describes all the various types of rain in Germany. By sharing this memory with Klaus, Juan celebrates her Germanness, even as she seems to slip so easily into a Spanish identity in that super eight footage.[22]

Respect for difference carries over, at times, to familial and gendered relations. When that old woman in the wheelchair is abandoned by her daughter in a parking garage, Vera (Heike Makatsch) rescues her, then sings loudly to the strains of *Nothing Compares 2U* emanating from the car radio, in a tribute as heartfelt as one directed toward a love object. Contrary to the brutal abandonment enacted on the old woman by her own daughter, Sinead O'Connor's lyrics suggest that in some relationships, there is no possibility of a trade-in. Respect for difference across gender finds its most striking example in the caterers, Rita and Fred. First shown in a rather unattractive sex scene, Rita and Fred seem, each in their own way, to be hung up on consumer objects or food, not each other. During sex Rita thinks of the cashmere sweater waiting for her at a nearby store and all the calories she's consumed that day. Her voice-over also reveals that Fred's fat is a product of frustrations, like when she denies him sex. In a striking turnaround, though, Fred later tries to talk Rita out of her disordered body image by insisting "You are *my* Rita," and that he will love her no matter how much her *Hülle*, or exterior, deteriorates, like his withering potato heads. From Fred's perspective, nothing compares to Rita, in yet another relationship marked by respect and love for another. For some, there is only one object to fill the void, recognized despite the effects of aging or disease to retain the status of subject. The question posed by the film's title can be answered only by the presence of another looking back at and speaking to us. More important, in the give and take between two full-fledged subjects, definitions of beauty can vary widely. When difference becomes a source of respect, Germans and Spaniards can be as happily married as a conventionally attractive woman and overweight man, a utopian message that throws a different light on Fred's jiggling flesh and rotting potato heads.

The final scenes of *Am I Beautiful?* suggest that a similar dynamic is possible even if one half of the equation happens to be a ritualistic icon. Unlike tourists, who use Spain for sun, warmth, and kitschy romantic or existential fantasies, penitents in the Semana Santa require a Spain, here the Madonna, that actually looks back at them. What a German like Linda gets in paying tribute to the Madonna is not so much a pardon for the offenses of marauding tourists and real-estate hounds. Rather, she receives a fundamentally missing piece of self, much as Juan gave his wife her German self back by listening to her talk about German rain, or Fred gave Rita a sense of an inner self beneath the facade of the thin woman in the cashmere sweater.[23] Her encounter begins with a point-of-view shot that frames the Madonna, after which a second point-of-view shot from the Madonna's perspective captures Linda's appeal for courage. The acoustic component of this visual exchange is particularly striking, since Linda sings her appeal in German. Unlike her compatriots in the film, she has learned how to connect strong emotions to a German vocabulary. Happily paired off with Klaus in the film's final scenes, Linda also rediscovers her purse by the bull, and together she and Klaus leaf through its contents. Again, what emerges in the respectful exchange across difference, whether cultural or gendered, is not so much a new self but a return to a self now validated, if not completed, by the gaze of another, a dynamic that seems to provide a firmer base for identity than chic, Italian shoes. Klaus revels in the quirky contents of Linda's purse—the bubbles, the hairspray, and so on—and in her reading from a book the story we heard at the film's beginning.

Unna's (Senta Berger) desire not just for atonement but also to locate a missing piece of self prompts her to search out the lover, David (Otto Sander), with whom she lived in Spain many years before, the same man she rejected when he appeared at her doorstep years later in Munich. Having suffered a stroke and substantial memory loss, David no longer recognizes Unna when she appears at his apartment. At first glance, he seems to represent the exigencies of aging, if not the sad culmination of Linda's fantasy to reinvent herself in a foreign land. As his roommate Paco (Pierre Sanoussi-Bliss) tells Unna, David pushed the "big erase button," which, as David observes, left a big hole inside of him.[24] Although Unna remains a stranger to him, what finally fills that void is a retrieved memory of the pumpernickel bread that she used to make for him. If food is an expensive or exotic commodity or an object of guilt to our German characters, here it provides a rather different type of sustenance. A subsequent shot shows Unna and David lying together and holding hands on his bed, as

Unna repeatedly lists all the bread's ingredients at David's behest. Significantly, what they recall is a recipe from an American cookbook for German bread made from Spanish ingredients. By ticking off the bread's ingredients, Unna also conjures a self of mixed-up cultural components no longer moored to their original context in the inevitable blurring when various cultures meet. The symbolic love scene enacted on the bed not only recasts food as a sensual, as opposed to a consumer object, it also suggests again that sustenance, if not satisfaction, comes from the presence of another who restores and completes one's own identity. Unna herself finds that younger, irrational self we glimpse only occasionally in super eight footage of her turning cartwheels in the living room. David also seems to offer her the respect missing in her relationship with the philandering Herbert.

Two happy, heterosexual couplings once again beg questions about Dörrie's relations with Hollywood and its own standard happy endings. The final scene shows Linda and Klaus romping and blowing bubbles by the bull, while reading from that children's story heard in voice-over at the beginning, as the film's framing devices close in on them. Spain recedes into two-dimensionality again when Linda reads: "In Panama everything is much nicer, you know. Because in Panama everything smells like bananas. Panama is the land of our dreams. We should go there tomorrow. Because there we don't need to be afraid of anything. . . ."[25] Back to square one, it seems, where a hazy foreign backdrop is the best balm for German angst. Here *Am I Beautiful?*, for better or for worse, resembles a dynamic that Eric Rentschler has identified in German-American cinematic relations, namely that foreign terrain (America in Rentschler's analysis) functions "as a mirror that reflects and intensifies the preoccupations and imported conflicts of its visitors . . . becom[ing] a catalyst, a foreign terrain one treads while exploring oneself . . ." (280).[26] The extent to which this dynamic remains wholly self-serving is a rather tricky, vexing question; perhaps, in the case of *Am I Beautiful?*, one can be more forgiving if the outcome is new, improved Germans more adept at doing the fancy footwork required of partners in the European Union. What gets lost, however, are the funkier contours of Spain evident, for instance, in Pedro Almodóvar films, which perform a "radical sex change on Spain's national stereotype," as parodic melodramas mock and displace the traditions of Franco's Spain (Kinder 3).[27] Yet, by invoking one more auteur firmly linked to his own national context, I would also like to suggest that one's horizon of expectations should only extend so far: as much as one would critique myopic vision, it's hard to imagine Woody Allen trading his standard crew of neurotic, upper-middle-class professionals for Spike Lee's down and out African Americans.

If in Spain/Panama everything is much nicer for our self-satisfied German tourists, even if Dörrie's final shots frame them in a somewhat distanced, ironic way, one wonders again about popular German cinema's relations with Hollywood imperatives that prescribe happy endings. The notion that in Hollywood, that land of collective, cinematic dreams, "everything is much nicer," explains not only Hollywood's tendency to sanitize real life, but also the trajectory of countless contributors to the German film industry who made the trek to Hollywood. From the Weimar Republic to the present moment, the list is a very long one, indeed, and includes directors from Fritz Lang to Wolfgang Petersen, actors from Peter Lorre to Til Schweiger, and cameramen from Karl Freund to Michael Ballhaus. Yet, this trajectory is a more complicated one than that of geographical displacement followed by assimilation to Hollywood's cinematic vocabulary, big budgets, and mass appeal. If such blatant "selling out" has placed directors like Petersen beyond the pale of critical attention, other German film directors who have negotiated other kinds of relations with Hollywood also seem perennially neglected. Here I mean not just Dörrie, but someone like Monika Treut, who often films and has a faithful following among both filmgoers and film scholars in America, while their disgusted German counterparts have been known to walk out of her films. Likewise, Wim Wenders's take on America is interesting to film critics only if filtered through a New German Cinema plot about an alienated wanderer with a colonized unconscious. Wenders's films, like *The End of Violence* (1997) and *The Million Dollar Hotel* (2000), both filmed in Los Angeles with some very bankable Hollywood film stars, however, demand critical attention to the ways a German film director can turn Hollywood toward his own vision and obsessions. What critics stuck on that "art versus garbage" dichotomy seem unwilling or unable to recognize are the myriad ways that German and Hollywood films overlap, which are no longer conveniently assimilable to dichotomous rubrics. Much as Dörrie seems to aim Hollywood's cinematic mirror back across the Atlantic with lip service to conventional genres and her use of well-known German actors, her films continually refract sometimes unflattering, sometimes very funny things missing from Germans' own self-image, providing a sustained reflection on Germany identity over the last twenty years. Where her aims and methods overlap with other more critically acclaimed outsider-artistes like Altman and Fassbinder, it becomes possible to begin closing that problematic gap between art and the popular.

NOTES

1. Originally advertising for a particular kind of Spanish sherry, this bull and the many others that once existed recall Franco's Spain, or a world without regional tensions or autonomous groups, one that the world could easily associate with the cliches of bullfights, flamenco, and Carmen. Although most of the billboards were taken down, there are currently efforts to have them placed under historical preservation.

2. Spain's satellite island, Majorca, is particularly popular with Germans. Every year 6.5 million tourists vacation there, a number ten times the size of the island's population. Forty percent of these tourists, or approximately 2,800,000 people, are German, another 40 percent English, and the rest a mix of various nationalities, including Dutch and Scandinavian.

3. The story is actually about Panama; Oh, How Beautiful Is Panama (1979) is the first story written by the German author and painter Janosch. It concerns the adventures of Tiger and Little Bear, who set out to find Panama and discover what a fine place they already live in. The most widely read children's author in Germany, Janosch happens to live on the Spanish island Teneriffa. A central question in much of Dörrie's work is why Germans can be so anxiety-ridden in the face of so much material plenty, and here it seems fundamental enough to have even concerned a children's author.

4. Spain's culture, of course, is highly diverse and consists of four languages and many dialects. The Semana Santa, during which brotherhoods from various churches parade through the streets carrying a Madonna figure, is only a small but very famous part of Spanish culture.

5. In fact, she was the only woman featured on the cover of Der Spiegel in 1986. Men also beat out such Hollywood fare as Out of Africa and Rocky IV at the German box office (Phillips 173). Worldwide, six million people saw Men.

6. Dörrie's one and only Hollywood film, produced by Bernd Eichinger, was Me and Him (1987), starring Griffin Dunne. The story of a man and his talking penis, it received mixed reviews.

7. Three of Dörrie's films—Straight through the Heart (1983), Men, and Nobody Loves Me (1994) have won a variety of German film awards.

8. Dörrie actually lived in California during this Golden Age, attending the University of the Pacific in Stockton from 1973 to 1975.

9. In an interview with Klaus Phillips, Dörrie cited Altman's Short Cuts and The Player as two recent favorite movies (Phillips 177).

10. In an interview with Alice Swensen, Dörrie stated: "Many German films, and they are only 2 percent of the German market, are so strange and complicated that people don't want to see them. They say that the films are boring and unintelligible. That's why even in Germany people watch

American films which take up about 95 percent of the market. This is not to say, of course, that there are not talented German directors." (Swenson 97)

11. Loosely taken, *Men* resembles Hollywood comedy fare, just as *In the Belly of the Whale* (1985) seems a road movie and *Happy Birthday, Türke* (1992) contains elements of police action films and a touch of film noir. Closer inspection of all these films reveals uniquely German concerns about protofascist behavior and violence visited on foreigners.

12. Fassbinder has stated: "The best thing I can think of would be to create a union between something as beautiful and powerful and wonderful as Hollywood films and a critique of the status quo" (quoted in Gemünden, "Re-Fusing Brecht" 55). Gerd Gemünden has analyzed Fassbinder's various strategies for creating a "German Hollywood" by fusing Brechtian and avant-garde techniques with Hollywood formulas, the former either parodying or invoking nostalgia for the latter. In doing so, he "forces German audiences to reconsider stereotypical perceptions of Hollywood film as apolitical and serving the status quo" (Gemünden, "Re-Fusing Brecht" 75). The extent to which Germany's Hollywood-style comedies of the 1990s challenge the status quo, however, is debatable. See Halle 1–39.

13. Of Fassbinder, Thomas Elsaesser has written: "He may have had apartments in Paris, visited brothels in North Africa, and gone to the leather-bars of New York, but his home was obstinately and unambiguously West Germany. . . . In the end . . . only Munich seemed to matter; even the Berlin of *Despair* and *Berlin Alexanderplatz* was ultimately "made in Bavaria (Atelier)" (14). Bernd Eichinger has observed of Dörrie: "For [her] it's enough to be known in Schwabing" (a suburb of Munich), which he contrasted with his own desire for international renown (quoted in Rentschler 296).

14. Here an autobiographical subtext adds another layer of emotional substance: diagnosed with cancer during the filming of Dörrie's previous film, *Nobody Loves Me,* Dörrie's husband and cameraman, Helge Weindler, died during the initial filming of *Am I Beautiful?* The project would never have been finished, had producer Bernd Eichinger not intervened to revive it. Eichinger himself is quite a transatlantic phenomenon, having produced not only Dörrie's work and other German films like the blockbuster *The Never-Ending Story* (1984) but also the German production *The Name of the Rose* (1986), which featured many Hollywood stars.

15. Here a significant difference emerges between Dörrie's and Altman's films: one can hardly imagine a Hollywood actor submitting him or herself to the demands of realism in a manner that requires such personal exposure. Of the various nude scenes in *Short Cuts*, all feature, predictably, women, and conventionally attractive ones at that.

16. *Nobody Loves Me* (1994), Dörrie's previous film, also thematizes the dangers of being thrown away in an increasingly consumerist, commodified culture in a dynamic that extends from objects to people. See McCarthy 176–201.

17. Thank you Tonya Werner for calling my attention to the continued appearance of red in the film. Thanks are also in order to the entire group of seniors who participated in my seminar on the German short story and novella and brought wonderful, sharp insights to Dörrie's short story and film version of *Am I Beautiful?* Christoph Ruland also deserves very special thanks in this context.

18. Several Dörrie films offer pleasurable, acoustic suturing with foreign music. *Men* ends with "I want to Take You on My Banana Boat," and Edith Piaf's "No, je ne regrette rien" is heard four times during *Nobody Loves Me*. Asked about how she selects music for her films, Dörrie simply talked about using music in the right way: "It should reinforce what is happening, not overpower it. If you notice the music, you lose the emotion." (Phillips 181).

19. *Majorca* cost DM7,000 per minute. Relatively short-lived, it was cancelled in January 2000 due to low ratings.

20. The Internet Movie database lists *Ballermann 6* under the following keywords: bad-taste, machismo, and proles. Interestingly, it was also produced by Bernd Eichinger.

21. The Internet, of course, places products from many different cultures side by side on its own virtual shelves. Posters, bikes, toys, and wallpaper designs by Janosch, the children's author cited at the beginning of the film, can not only be found at German sources on the Web, but also together with American wares offered by Amazon.com, Ebay, and Barnes and Noble.

22. The fact that Juan is played by Austrian actor Dietmar Schönherr may also enhance the border-crossing aspects of the film. (Thank you Christian Rogowski for suggesting this reading.) It may also tick off those already offended by the fact that the Turkish lead character in Dörrie's *Happy Birthday, Türke* was also played by a German actor.

23. *Nobody Loves Me* also finds its most concentrated metaphor for the human relations it depicts in the ritual that appears in its final scenes—the *Nubbelverbrennung*, or burning in effigy of a dummy at the end of *Karneval*. The importance of rituals provides another means of understanding *Am I Beautiful?*, which shows or suggests some of Spain's more well known, if not cliched, rituals, from bullfights to flamenco to the Semana Santa, as a collective voice for ur-emotions surrounding love and death. Germans are mostly seen as wandering individuals in search of such collective rituals. Thanks, Pascal Belling, for suggesting this reading of the film

24. If the presence of the Weather Girls as exotic spice to a very white wedding seems too self-conscious to merit critique, Pierre Sanoussi-Bliss seems a rather problematic choice for the role of cultural other here, because he is, in fact, an Afro-German. Whereas *Nobody Loves Me*, in which he starred, smartly plays up the manner in which Afro-Germans are made into cultural others, here the same process seems entirely unself-reflexive.

25. Bananas are a wonderfully resonant image for a global, twenty-first century economy, since they're more often an object of trade disputes than a signifier of exoticism. West Germans demonstrated their material well-being and ostensible generosity by bringing bananas to East Germans when the wall came down in November 1989.

26. This function of foreign territory as narcissistic imaginary cuts both ways, according to Rentschler's analysis. The popularity of New German Cinema among Anglo-American scholars, he argues, was a product of American obsessions during the 1970s with our own culpability for the Vietnam War, our own preoccupations with doom and gloom in an era where global destruction no longer seemed a remote possibility. New German Cinema's ever-present angst and disaffection seemed an important counterpoint and alternative to Hollywood as "blatantly cynical dream factory" (291).

27. Here an obvious parallel emerges with Dörrie, Altman, and Fassbinder—Almodóvar's desire to revamp Hollywood paradigms, in this case to comment on Spain's own political status quo.

WORKS CITED

Dicks, Hans-Günther, "Zu hoch gezielt." *Neues Deutschland.* September 17, 1998, 2.
Dörrie, Doris. *Bin ich schön?* Zürich: Diogenes, 1994.
Elsaesser, Thomas. "Historicizing the Subject: A Body of Work?" *New German Critique* 63 (1994): 11–33.
Gächter, Sven. "Die Dinge des Lebens." *Profil,* September 14, 1998, 38.
Gemünden, Gerd. "Introduction: Remembering Fassbinder in a Year of Thirteen Moons." *New German Critique* 63 (1994): 3–9
———. "Re-fusing Brecht: The Cultural Politics of Fassbinder's German Hollywood." *New German Critique* 63 (1994): 55–75.
Halle, Randall. "Happy Ends to Crises of Heterosexual Desire: Toward a Social Psychology of Recent German Comedies." *Camera Obscura* 44 (2000): 1–39.
Janosch. *Oh, wie schön ist Panama.* Basel: Beltz Verlag, 1978.
Kinder, Marsha, ed. *Refiguring Spain: Cinema/Media/Representation.* Durham, N.C.: Duke University Press, 1997.
McCarthy, Margaret. "Teutonic Water: Effervescent Otherness in Doris Dörrie's *Nobody Loves Me.*" *Camera Obscura* 44 (2000): 179–201.
Nayman, Ira. "The Adaptable Altman." *Creative Screenwriting* 4, no. 3 (1997): 84–96.
Phillips, Klaus. "Interview with Doris Dörrie: Filmmaker, Writer, Teacher." In *Triangulated Visions. Women in Recent German Cinema,* edited by Ingeborg Majer O'Sickey and Ingeborg van Zadow, 173–84. Albany: State University of New York Press, 1998.
Rentschler, Eric. "How American Is It: The U.S. as Image and Imaginary in German Film." Reprinted in *Perspectives on German Cinema,* edited by Terri Ginsberg and Kirsten Moana Thompson, 277–94. New York: G. K. Hall & Co., 1996.
Scofield, Martin. "Closer to Home: Carver versus Altman." *Studies in Short Fiction* 33, no. 3 (1996): 387–99.
Silber, Rolf. "Ambrosia und Spülwasser. Zwischen zwei Stühlen, oder: Gibt es den intelligenten deutschen Unterhaltungsfilm?" *Süddeutsche Zeitung,* March 30, 2000, 20.
Swensen, Alice. "An Interview with Doris Dörrie." *Short Story* 2, no. 2 (1994): 96–99.

FILMOGRAPHY

Doris Dörrie:
Am I Beautiful [Bin ich schön?] (1998) DVD and video available through www.amazon.de
Nobody Loves Me [Keiner liebt mich] (1994) DVD and video available through www.amazon.de
Happy Birthday, Türke (1992) video available through www.amazon.de
Men [Männer] (1985) video available through FACETS, www.amazon.de
In the Belly of the Whale [Im Innern des Wals] (1985)
Straight through the Heart [Mitten ins Herz] (1983)

Robert Altman:
Short Cuts (1993) laserdisc available through Criterion.

CHAPTER 19

You Can Run, but You Can't Hide

Transcultural Filmmaking in
Run Lola Run (1998)

Christine Haase

Alles rennet, rettet, flüchtet
(Everyone's running, escaping, fleeing)
Friedrich Schiller, *The Song of the Bell*

Wo laufen sie denn?
(Where are they running?)
Heinz Erhardt

Run Lola Run [Lola rennt] (Tykwer, 1998) begins with a striking contrast: A quote by T. S. Eliot is juxtaposed with a quote by West Germany's beloved and highly idiosyncratic former national soccer team coach Sepp Herberger:

We shall not cease from exploration
And the end of all our exploring
Will be to arrive where we started
And know the place for the first time.
T. S.ELIOT

After the game
is before the game.
SEPP HERBERGER

Profundity and truism take each other on until they become indistinguishable. The contrast continues: seconds later, we zoom
in on an archaic and tribal-looking version of a cuckoo clock, in
which the not-so-harmless bird has been fittingly replaced by a
menacing gargoyle ferociously opening its mouth, devouring the
viewers whole. To the pulsating sounds of techno music and the
beat of time ticking away, the audience is sucked down a dark
passageway to emerge seconds later in the midst of a buzzing,
hectic crowd running around without apparent purpose. The use
of fast motion heightens the chaotic atmosphere of the scene.
Then we hear a deep, quiet, soothing voice that conjures up
nights in front of fireplaces, listening to an old storyteller, and
memories of childhood fantasies. The voice belongs to Hans Paetsch and is one of the most recognizable and recognized voices in
the Federal Republic of Germany. Not only did Paetsch have a
long, successful career as a theater actor and director, he has also
narrated many children's records, and does voice-overs for documentaries as well as literary readings. In addition, he lends his
distinguished bass to TV commercials, and can be heard on CDs
by popular German bands like *Die Ärzte* and *Die toten Hosen.*
Thus, while he generally performs in the arena of "high" culture,
Paetsch cannot be confined to this end of the cultural spectrum.
Nevertheless, his first sentences in *Run Lola Run* live up to the
expectations his sophisticated voice initially raises: "Human beings: very likely the most mysterious species on our planet. A
mystery of open questions!" A perfect introduction to any high-
brow documentary. A few minutes later, however, Paetsch's perfect diction, thoughtful articulation, and philosophical musings
give way to the comment of a rather unrefined-looking guy in a
watchman uniform that ends the introductory sequence. Amidst
the crowd the camera zooms in on him as he—talking straight
into the lens—announces in colloquial vernacular and again borrowing from Herberger: "Ball is round. Game lasts 90 minutes.
That much is for sure. Everything else is theory." The man then
picks up a soccer ball from the ground and kicks it up into the
sky, yelling: "And off you go!" And off the film takes, with a cartoon version of Lola frantically running away from the camera
down psychedelic-looking halls and tunnels as the opening credits roll.

These first minutes of *Run Lola Run* introduce in a highly
concentrated and allusive manner a number of important and recurring visual as well as content-related themes and motifs: the
use of a wide array of cinematographic techniques;[1] notions of

destiny versus volition and the idea that life is circular in shape; the nature of the action genre; and the relationship between high and low art, that is, serious and popular culture, as well as the interplay between German and American (film) culture. The last two shall be the focus of the following pages, even though all of the above will come into play during this analysis of *Run Lola Run* within the context of popular German culture.

Run Lola Run was one of the biggest commercial and critical cinematic successes from Germany in the 1990s, catapulting Tom Tykwer, the writer-director, Franka Potente, the female lead, and the male protagonist Moritz Bleibtreu into instant stardom.[2] The film received critical and popular acclaim for its visual style, quirky story, and fast-paced action. Not just the national but also the international success of *Run Lola Run* demonstrates the film's resonance with the moviegoing public. An American critic pronounced the film to be a "festival circuit smash hit from Germany that's already become a pop culture phenomenon in Europe."[3] This resonance is based on more than MTV-style aesthetics, a rushing soundtrack, and two protagonists that are hip, tattooed, and deeply romantic. It is based on the successful fusion of German and American filmmaking in a movie that allows for Hollywood pleasure without giving up its *Heimat* identity. Thus, *Run Lola Run* is an apt expression of the *zeitgeist* at the turn of the millennium: the film typifies a growing global tendency for transcultural appropriation and hybridization.

To develop the argument about Tykwer and his film, the concept of "popular appropriation," as advanced by Roger Chartier, will prove helpful. Chartier places "the notion of appropriation at the center of a cultural historical approach" to analyze "the ways in which common cultural sets are appropriated differently."[4] Chartier proposes

> a reformulation of the concept of appropriation that accentuates plural uses and diverse understandings and diverges from the meaning Michel Foucault gives appropriation when he holds "the social appropriation of discourse" to be one of the primary procedures for gaining control of discourses and putting them beyond the reach of those who were denied access to them.[5] It also parts company with the meaning hermeneutics gives to appropriation, which is identified with the process of (postulated as universal) interpretation.[6]

In Chartier's view, "appropriation involves a social history of the various uses ... of discourses and models,'"[7] whose understanding and analysis helps to break up the myth of unequivocal, stable, and one-way power relations in terms of cultural influence and control. Rather, appropriation attempts to understand popular culture in terms of the "relationships between, on one hand, the mechanisms of symbolic domination that aim to make the dominated themselves accept the very representations that qualify (or, rather, disqualify) their culture as 'popular,' and, on the other hand, the specific logic at work in the customs, practices, and ways of making one's own that which is imposed."[8]

Chartier's concept of popular appropriation—which he aims at the investigation of intranational (rather than international) relationships between elite and mass cultures—is useful for examining the ties between a prevailing popular culture and its transatlantic counterpart. Tykwer exemplifies this popular cultural appropriation with *Run Lola Run* as an instance of "practices and ways of making one's own that which is imposed."

Today, authors like Tykwer—as opposed to the more conflicted Wim Wenders, Alexander Kluge, and Margarethe von Trotta, or, to a different extent, Rainer Werner Fassbinder, for example—seem to feel more at ease "appropriating" (be it wittingly or not), that is, seem able to interact with U.S. entertainment culture in a less burdened, less inhibited, and more playful manner, than most of their German predecessors before the 1990s. Undoubtedly, the reasons for these developments are diverse: they can be found in a greater historical and personal distance to the Third Reich and the postwar period, and in the political events of the late 1980s and 1990s, but also in generally shifting attitudes toward economic considerations in regard to production, distribution, and consumption. Tykwer, and others like him, does not have to fight off Hollywood constantly, either for political-philosophical reasons or in an attempt to gain creative distance, a distance that is instrumental in the construction of space needed to define oneself.[9] Rather, in Chartier's sense, Tykwer's work recognizes the multitude and diversity of influences that have come to bear on it. In true postmodern fashion, Tykwer unabashedly, joyfully, and with a sense of irony digs into the high and the low, the German and the American funds with both hands. At the same time, he recognizes and acknowledges the importance of economic considerations in general and, thus, in regard to popular, hence traditionally nonsubsidized, cultural production. Tykwer "belongs to the new generation of German film-makers who have managed that rare feat: to make domestic productions that have mass appeal."[10]

"The Yanks have colonized our subconscious."

Kings of the Road, Wim Wenders

"To a rationalized, expansionist and at the same time centralized, clamorous, and spectacular production corresponds *another* production, called "consumption." The latter is devious, it is dispersed, but it insinuates itself everywhere, silently and almost invisibly, because it does not manifest itself through its own products, but rather through its *ways of using* the products imposed by a dominant economic order."

Michel de Certeau, *The Practice of Everyday Life*

To grow up in postwar (West) Germany meant to live in a society with a distinct structure: a cultural legacy of *Dichter und Denker* (poets and thinkers), that is, high art in the form of literature, philosophy, and classical music, and a society of *Richter und Henker (judges and executioners)*, that is, a past burdened by the atrocities of the National Socialist regime. It also meant liberation, escape, and restructuring with the help of the Allies, namely the United States of America. Enter: U.S. record companies, radio stations, TV-fare, and Hollywood. After World War II, whether it was Marilyn or Marlboro, Jeans or *Jaws*, Americans could hardly fail on the German market. The proliferation of American consumer products in German society is visible and well documented. The reasons for this presence are complex, legion, and equally well researched, and the phenomenon manifests itself most perceptibly by way of fast food, youth fashion, and in the realms of musical and visual entertainment.[11]

The generation of young filmmakers associated with the Young and New German Cinema of the 1960s and 1970s was the first after 1945 radically to challenge their parents' society as well as the classical narrative (Hollywood) paradigm dominating the film industry.[12] These writer/directors had grown up in an "Americanized," economically prosperous Germany, but in a nation that was unable and unwilling to confront its most recent past. Cultural and film theorists like Thomas Elsaesser have argued that this constellation disrupted and uprooted Germany's sense of cultural identity by obstructing access to its immediate past, declaring "the question of cultural or national identity obsolete, preferring to rephrase it either in terms of the new Europe (on the right) or by advocating internationalist political solidarity (on the left)."[13] This resulted, among other things, in the emergence of monotonous and atrophied (popular) cultural spaces that were quickly revitalized by mostly American imports. However, this explanation for the American mass-cultural success remains partial. Another pivotal aspect of the problematic status of popular culture in the Federal Republic is a particular intellectual and critical bias toward high culture. Clearly, certain intellectual and social elites have "long scorned a popular culture identified with commodified culture,"[14] as Chartier points out, the mere term "popular culture" already being "a category of the learned. . . . An intellectual category aiming to encompass and describe artefacts and behaviors situated outside learned culture. . . . On one side, then . . . popular culture is completely defined by its distance from a cultural legitimacy of which it is deprived."[15] This attitude toward mass culture in combination with certain sociohistorical perspectives forms the basis for a widely accepted explanatory model:

> Through its lucrative postwar alliance with the US, West Germany has traded off large chunks of its cultural identity. . . . This . . . has produced in the postwar generation an acute sense of alienation and anomie. . . . Robbed of their past by the infamy of Nazism and of their future by American cultural imperialism, the filmmakers of *das neue Kino* express the sense of psychological and cultural dislocation described by the film critic Michael Covino as "a worldwide homesickness."[16]

Yet, so the argument continues, the New German Cinema also was "for the seventies (and eighties), what the *nouvelle vague* was for the sixties: a questioning of received values, an intoxicating burst of energy, a love affair with the cinema, and a love-hate relationship with Hollywood."[17] This analysis of the situation, put forward here by film historian Robin Cook, is as illuminating as it is problematic, because it represents the aforementioned explanatory model primarily based on considerations of high culture. This model reflects an assessment of the history of German film production that is strongly informed by the author's critical relationship to popular culture and, thus, demonstrates in and of itself an aspect of the problematic state of filmmaking in postwar Germany.

The "love-hate relationship with Hollywood" mentioned previously can be traced to highly conflicted attitudes toward questions of national identity and toward popular and entertainment culture, an attitude evidenced and perpetuated by Cook's analysis. In order to confront and compliment this explanatory model, and better to understand (trans-)cultural production, consumption, and interpretation, German mass culture and its products need to be reexamined, especially in their increasingly globalized context. As Elsaesser states:

> What tended to be passed over entirely was a more detailed assessment of German popular culture, both before and after the war, and thus any very differentiated view of what the cinema could contribute as a popular art to the nation's life, beyond being a mere tool for reactionary values or bidding for respectability. One might call it a historical double bind: a commercial cinema that was popular with audiences found itself despised by the critics, even though arguably doing the impossible/impermissible "mourning work" for that part of the nation's identity and sense of belonging that had been formed as much by mass entertainment as by nationalist propaganda. Genre-bound and with a star-system, its lack of realism could only be perceived as reactionary, by an avantgarde for whom the popular was necessarily nationalist, because during the Nazi period, they seemed two sides of the same coin.[18]

For decades, the long-standing biases against popular culture combined with the experiences of the Nazi propaganda machine made for a problematic mixture in regard to the creation of German mass entertainment products. Looking at a director like Tom Tykwer, however, indicates that changes are afoot. The current, postwall generation of German filmmakers has, to a certain extent, overcome—or is in the process of overcoming—the discourse of "alienation and anomie," of "psychological and cultural dislocation" that has often been used to describe postwar German film.[19] Dovetailing with this development, these directors also seem to oppose and prevail over "a quasi-universal disapproval of popular culture in general" that is looming large in their nation.[20] In *Run Lola Run*, Tykwer attempts to synthesize those two notions long perceived and articulated as oxymoronic by many in Germany: Culture and the popular.

> "I think this is going to be an experimental film for a mass audience."
>
> Tom Tykwer

The story line for *Run Lola Run* can be quickly summarized: Lola and her boyfriend, Manni, a small-time underworld operator, are somewhat punkish twenty-somethings living in Berlin. One day, Lola receives a frantic phone call from Manni, who has just lost the DM 100,000 he is supposed to deliver to his brutal and unforgiving crime boss. If he can't come up with the money by noon—which is in twenty minutes, film time—he'll most likely end up as fish food at the bottom of the Spree. So Lola starts running, trying to come up with the cash. This scenario is repeated three times, offering three different versions of the plot with three different endings, much in the fashion of "what if" films like Krzysztof Kieslowski's *Blind Chance* (*Przypadek*, 1981), or *Sliding Doors* by Peter Howitt (1998). If the plot itself does not seem entirely remarkable, the way in which it is realized and performed certainly is.

The ironic fusion of German/American, that is, serious/popular culture dichotomies as well as the equally ironic representations of the economic influences underlying and connecting these issues can be found everywhere in *Run Lola Run*. Yet there is also a general mingling of homegrown and imported cultures throughout the film. In this sense, *Run Lola Run* consistently points to a growing global trend of transnational movements in terms of culture and capital, and to the vital importance of financial considerations overall: from the Japanese domino spectacle on Lola's TV at the beginning of the film to the border-crossing criminal activities of Manni, who seems to be trafficking in stolen cars with Poland; from the bag containing the money sporting a Cyrillic caviar ad that Manni forgets in the subway to the variety of international bills that—blown up and framed—decorate the office of Lola's father, a high-ranking banker, and to the multicultural audience populating the casino of Lola's final triumph: the presence and interlacing of different cultures in one location, and the pivotal part that economy and capital play in connecting them, manifests itself in the film's story line as well as in its mise-en-scène. After all, the character that sets off the film's entire narrative is called *Manni*.

In regard to the intermingling of diverse yet nonspecific cultures, Lola's visit to the casino is a good example. The problem of "one of these things is not like the others" in the scene is obvious: Lola has neither the appropriate funding nor the attire for such an establishment, a fact the receptionist points out in her warning, "You can't get in here like this!" Both of these shortcomings, however, seem to be of little consequence in the face of at least minimal monetary resources that Lola can present, since seconds later she is permitted and ready to gamble away her and

Manni's future at a roulette table. Once again, money proves, here as later, to be the lowest common denominator and the ultimate Shibboleth of capitalist consumer societies. Under the eyes of a very distinguished and international-looking crowd of people who are as well mannered as they are dressed, Lola screams at the top of her lungs, flaunts her tattoos and her carrot-colored hair, and finally carries off her booty of DM 100.000 in a plastic trash bag, demonstrating that you don't have to be like them to participate in what they are doing. The flipside, though, is that this also demonstrates the undeniable hegemonic and conformist powers of capital and economy across cultures and countries.

The one specific national cultural connection that is most palpable and apparent in *Run Lola Run* refers to the United States. The film acknowledges these ties in terms of the action genre, certain visual aesthetics and detailing of the filmscape, as well as the soundtrack, while at the same time reasserting its German roots and cultural background. The dominant MTV-style music video aesthetic, as well as the interspersed cartoon sequences are nods to American forms of popular entertainment. The sports allegory as the opening narrative springboard of the film quotes a widely used Hollywood trope while giving it a German spin by using *Kaiser Fussball* (emperor soccer) as its reference point. In this way, *Run Lola Run* consistently points to the "interconnectedness of all things," in terms of the growing hybridity of German and American (and, indeed, most national) cultures, and also—in a way by extension—of high and low art. These aspects are exemplified by various elements in the film. The side-by-side quotations of one of the United States's most eminent poets, who was himself already a cultural mix as an American-born poet living in Britain, and one of Germany's most eminent sports figures can serve as one example, the eclectic music mix that characterizes the soundtrack as another. Dynamic, pulsating techno music (a branch of twentieth-century popular music that is recognized as one of the few and originally European contributions to this field, with Germany playing a pace-setting part in it) is interrupted by the Dinah Washington hit *What a Difference a Day Makes* and the classical Charles Ives piece *The Unanswered Question*. Already within these epigraphic and musical choices, Tykwer shifts preconceived cultural notions: Germany, the supposed home of poets and philosophers, is represented by a popular soccer coach, whereas the United States, home of Michael Jordan, the genre of the sports movie, and self-help bestsellers, is introduced by a demanding poet par excellence. Likewise, the musical choice linked up with the Federal Republic, stereotypically known as Bach and Beethoven country, is an example of pure twentieth-century entertainment culture, consumed and designed mostly by and for an age group in the wake of Generation X. On the other hand, the lyrical, vulnerable, and elegiac music of a classical American composer represents the United States, land of Rock 'n Roll, the invention of supermarket music, and MTV. Here, general stereotypes of the respective cultures of both nations are clearly turned on their heads.

Echoing this challenging of expectations and the compartmentalizing of cultural products in *Run Lola Run* is the way in which low and high art are brought together. Obviously, the music as well as the opening quotations already entail a juxtaposition not only of German and American culture but also of the realms of the popular and the serious. The flippant comment of an admired coach is locking arms with the poetic insights of an admired writer, classical music takes turns with techno. Yet, from the beginning to the end of the movie there is fusion between these binarily constructed cultural camps. The introductory sequence mentioned earlier is a prime example. The film begins by posing fundamental questions of human existence: "Who are we? Where do we come from? Where do we go? How do we know what we believe to know? Why do we believe anything at all?" These questions may not be answered, but are certainly addressed by the folksy words of the watchman: "Ball is round. Game lasts 90 minutes. That much is for sure. Everything else is theory." Following the ball that the watchman kicks into the sky, the camera pulls up to assume a bird's-eye view. Then, out of the chaos of aimlessly running people, the spectators look down onto the words *"Run Lola Run"* as the bodies form them in the field. Chaos turns into structure and, presumably, just as easily into chaos again. Just as profundity can easily turn into banality, "high" culture quickly into "low" culture and back.

Another example of such apparently contradictory cultures—which nonetheless contain, or so the film seems to suggest, various simultaneous potentials for the situation at hand—can be observed in the changing life scenarios of the people Lola runs into during her race against time. In these scenes, the action proper is suspended for a few seconds after Lola crosses paths with three different people during her run. The film stops, so to speak, and the viewers are presented with a lightning round of still photographs that resemble a slide show, illustrating different

versions of what became of the person after the chance encounter
with the heroine. There are seven of these "destiny in a nutshell"
sequences depicting and summarizing future lives in a matter of
seconds before the "regular" film resumes and the viewers rejoin
Lola on her quest.

At the start of her run, Lola encounters a woman with a
baby carriage, who in the first version of the story loses her child
to state care because of alcoholism. Desperate and confused, she
steals a baby in a park. This rather grim scenario undergoes a dramatic change in the story's second round with the woman now
winning a fortune in the lottery and posing with her family in a
luxury convertible in front of their mansion on the cover page of
the *Bild-Zeitung*, a notorious German tabloid. Finally, in a third
reversal of fortune she finds God and becomes a Jehovah's Witness, standing at a street corner with *The Watchtower* in hand.

A little later in the film, a young guy is trying to sell his
obviously stolen bicycle to the breathlessly running Lola. In his
first "slide show," he marries a nurse whom he meets in a hospital after he is beaten up by a bunch of thugs. He thus turns into a
respectable and useful citizen. In his second sequence, on the
other hand, he ends up homeless and dies of drug abuse in a public
restroom.

The last person Lola encounters is a woman who works
at her father's bank. In the first plot line, she becomes quadri-
plegic after a car wreck and ultimately commits suicide. In the
second version, she finds fulfillment and happiness in an S&M
relationship with a coworker.

These "nutshell" scenes are digressions and superfluous
in terms of plot economy. They therefore challenge the classical
narrative commandment of efficiency in storytelling. Conceptu-
ally and philosophically, the developments represent extremes on
a continuum and not mutually exclusive elements. Thus, they
can be viewed as miniature reflections of some of the film's larger
issues of economic determinism and fate, or contingency versus
volition. These questions are raised by the three plot versions as
well as by the fate of the bum who takes off with the DM 100,000
and, for twenty minutes, faces a very bright future. These are
complex issues, on which *Run Lola Run* does not offer simple,
definitive opinions but rather plays the potential of their indeter-
minacy for all its worth.

After investigating more general issues concerning the
question of high versus popular culture, a more specific analysis

of American versus German filmmaking in *Run Lola Run* is necessary. In this analysis, the former will be equated with the classical narrative paradigm and the latter with an alternative or diverging one.[21]

Even though the film was generally billed as a "breathless ride," a "hyperkinetic pop culture fire cracker," and "a film of nonstop motion," it is more than an action adventure.[22] It is also in part a dystopian family drama and an exercise in social critique. Whenever the running stops, and it does so regularly and conspicuously, other genres and styles take over, in terms of content as well as cinematography. For example, the quiet and intimate scenes between Lola's father and his mistress—captured on grainy video—and the dialogues between Lola and Manni in bed counterbalance and rupture the action sequences. Fundamentally, though, *Run Lola Run* is the epitome of an action film, a genre that is in turn for many the epitome of mass entertainment and Hollywood culture. Yet, *Run Lola Run* is not so much a story conceived of and told in terms of an action movie as it is a study of what an action movie really is. *Run Lola Run* investigates this genre with such radicality that the result is an almost contentless enactment of the genre's defining traits. In other words, the film presents all the formal elements of the action genre, but refuses to fill them with more than the barest narrative content. Paradoxically, it thus turns itself into the entertaining narrative production of a theoretical generic paradigm. *Run Lola Run* in a way does for the action genre what Michael Snow's *Wavelength* did for the zoom.

The defining feature of the traditional action thriller is a race against time in a battle between good and evil. Additionally, the story usually hinges upon a hero who overcomes obstacles and odds and triumphs in the end. Or, as David Bordwell puts it, the conventions of classical Hollywood cinema—of which the traditional action film is a part—call for "psychologically defined individuals who struggle to solve a clear-cut problem or to attain specific goals. In the course of this struggle, the characters enter into conflict with others or with external circumstances. The story ends with a decisive victory or defeat, a resolution of the problem and a clear achievement or non-achievement of the goals. The principal causal agency is thus the character."[23] Formally, the script approximates a classical three-act structure, with an initial exposition, a dramatic climax, that is, peripetia, and the ensuing resolution of the threatening situation: "[T]he classical film respects the canonic pattern of establishing an initial state of affairs which gets violated and which must then be set right. . . . [T]he plot consists of an undisturbed stage, the disturbance, the struggle, and the elimination of the disturbance."[24] More often than not, everything culminates in a happy ending and the formation of a heterosexual couple, because usually, the film offers a "double causal structure, two plot lines: one involving heterosexual romance . . . , the other line involving another sphere—work, war, a mission or quest, other personal relationships. . . . In most cases, the romance sphere and the other sphere of action are distinct but interdependent. The plot may close off one line before the other, but often the two lines coincide at the climax."[25] Lastly, according to Bordwell, the time factor mentioned previously does not only play a crucial part in action films. Rather, he emphasizes the "deadline" as a "device highly characteristic of classical narration. A deadline can be measured by calendars . . . , by clocks . . . , or simply by cues that time is running out (the last-minute rescue). That the climax of a film is often a deadline shows the structural power of defining dramatic duration as the time it takes to achieve or fail to achieve a goal."[26]

What deserves attention in an analysis of *Run Lola Run* is how it uses, quotes, and diverges from this familiar paradigm. The film thematizes all of the preceding elements, distilling their main features from an entire crop of classical (action) movies. The title heralds the bottom line: there is a protagonist and she will run. That, and the giant, menacing-looking clock ticking away in the first scene, devouring the viewers, already sets up the things to come in an ostentatious and rather ironic way: the audience will witness a scary race against time. The extremely tight deadline propels the film forward, and the cutting to clocks and watches happens with such frequency that it is difficult not to see it as an ironic quote of the traditional "measuring of a deadline" in action films with the countdown of digital bomb displays, ticking away of train station and airport clocks, wristwatches, and church towers striking "High Noon."[27] There is the clock from the opening credits, one across from Manni's phone booth, another one in Lola's room, two more in the bank and the casino, and strangers are asked what time it is. Equally if not more blatant is the use of running itself: a little over half of the screen time is occupied by Lola pounding the pavement, without any other relevant information being conveyed. In terms of limited informational content as well as aesthetic style, these sequences are striking quotations of music videos. Accompanied by the hypnotic sounds of techno, Lola's run leads her through an urban cityscape connected only by editing, since no human being could traverse the vast distances between the depicted (East and West) Berlin locations in twenty minutes. These scenes portray pure adrenalin-pumping motion stripped of almost all pretenses but the unrelenting communication of urgency and the protagonist's determination. It is almost racing for racing's sake as a celebration of thrill and excitement, the pointlessness of it emphasized by the fact that Lola's efforts turn out to be in vain every single time. The first time, she is too late and ends up dying. The second time, she arrives just on the dot but Manni gets run over by an ambulance. In the third version, she arrives in time only to find out that Manni has already solved the problem himself, making her whole marathon redundant in a life-saving sense. The film thus divests Lola's running of narrative meaning and undermines the classical assumption of "principal causal agency" as resting with the character, because the causal relations between Lola's actions and the outcome of the episodes are tenuous and unverifiable at best. At the same time, on a visual level the film stoutly reaffirms and magnifies the importance of the eponymous heroine and her actions by granting her run most of the screen time. Again, *Run Lola Run* displays the action film elements as spelled out by traditional genre etiquette, but gives them a twist of its own.

Just as it overdoes the clock motive, it overemphasizes dramatic structure while simultaneously subverting it: there is the initial exposition in the phone call between Manni and Lola, where the "disturbance" is introduced, and the final "elimination of the disturbance," but there is no clear-cut "undisturbed stage" at the outset of the film; instead, that stage is represented intermittently throughout the film in flashbacks and the two bed scenes.

The script follows the overall three-act structure and resolves the conflict with a "decisive victory or defeat," but it remains hazy in terms of "clear achievement or nonachievement of the goals"—finding DM 100,000 and saving Manni—until the very end. Twice the couple produces the money but one of them dies, thus partially achieving the goal but tearing apart the heterosexual unit the movie is expected to produce, until finally the film resolves into a happy ending, reaffirming the couple and its love in unambiguous Hollywood fashion. The first two versions hence play like ironic reminders of stereotypical views on German (art) cinema: that it is bleak, depressing, and usually won't end on a happy note. It apparently takes several rounds until the film catches on to the proper mass entertainment tradition, until it—tongue in cheek—finally gets it right.

One last element of the action genre, particularly of the last decade, is the common and often excessive use of violence, a feature that is almost entirely absent from *Run Lola Run*.[28] The movie clearly bucks the violence trend of the 1990s epitomized by works like James Cameron's *Terminator II—Judgement Day* (1990) or *True Lies* (1995), John Woo's *Face/Off* (1997), or the British *Lock, Stock, and Two Smoking Barrels* (1998), whose initial premise is almost identical to Tykwer's film. There are a number of verbal threats in *Lola*, but ultimately, the only two people who get hurt in the film are Lola and Manni. There is exactly one shot fired, which kills Lola, and one fatal car accident that costs Manni his life. Both scenes show the clearly shocked and horrified perpetrator after the act, that is, the policeman and the ambulance driver. These shots add to the viewer's strong sense of dread after witnessing the violent deaths of the film's heroes. Here, brutality and death are not just pecadillos for entertainment's sake. They are not employed as trivialized and trivializing means of enhancing a thrill ride or turning the hero into a hyper-cool *Übermensch*. Quite the contrary: for Tykwer, every bullet counts and comes with a price tag attached. The violence is intricately linked to its potential outcome in a manner that takes itself for what it is: dead serious.[29]

The film goes even further in playing with generic trends and habits. As mentioned before, embedded within the action movie are scenes from other genres and of different styles. These scenes are set apart from their surroundings visually as well as in terms of content, in a striking manner. The focus in the following will be on the scenes involving Lola's father and his mistress, even though the interludes of Lola and Manni lying in bed, engulfed in deep red light, could serve as examples, as could the "destinies in a nutshell" series of vignettes discussed earlier.

The three versions of the intimate conversation between Lola's father, who is a high-ranking banker (pointing, once again, to the pivotal role of the world of finance) and his mistress, a colleague of his, could belong to a different film. They are shot on grainy video and partly filmed with a handheld camera, which gives them a super 8 home movie quality. A quiet mood is created by the close-framed, fairly static composition of the scenes and their washed out colors, intimate close-ups, and halting shots, which appear twice as slow in comparison to the hyperkinetic environment from which these scenarios emerged. The quiet atmosphere is further amplified by the slow-paced editing and by the substitution of the fast-driving underlying music with faint and serene spheric sounds in these scenes. In addition, the topic of the conversation, and the manner in which it is conducted, intensify the menacing air of an unfolding family drama. The scenes seem like nods to directors like Fassbinder or von Trotta, or any other New German specialist on the dissection and breakdown of traditional family values and scenarios, in fact, to the stereotypical "European art school" on the whole, from Bergman to *Dogma 95*.[30] The homemade dystopia that takes shape in front of the viewers is really not part of the action movie being watched. It is the intrusion of another genre and, with it, another intellectual level and reality.

The dialogue between Lola's father and his girlfriend, Frau Hansen, is about the couple's future, and it is not an entirely happy one. Frau Hansen reveals to her lover her fears and anxieties of time wasted, opportunities missed, and more than anything else loneliness, pushing him to either break off the relationship with her or leave his alcoholic wife and family. So far, this is nothing special. The cruel black humor of their talk lies in the differing lengths it takes up in the three different versions, and, thus, the amount and nature of the information that is exchanged. Frau Hansen is pregnant and in all variants of the plot manages to tell her lover that she is expecting a baby. After she reveals this to him, she goes on to ask: "Say, do you want to have a baby with me?" to which he, clearly moved, responds: "Yes!" In the first version, this is where Lola interrupts them by bursting into her father's office, turning the spotlight away from their affair and onto the father-daughter relationship. This relationship, which hardly deserves to be called that, bears all the hallmarks of an alienated, estranged, highly conflicted, and rather hateful family constellation. Lola's father reacts with incredulity and annoyance to her request for money, displaying no sympathy for her ordeal or the fact that he is jeopardizing someone's life by his banker-by-the-book coldness. This someone is, after all, his daughter's boyfriend, whom he fails to remember, even though, as Lola points out to him, they have been together for more than a year and Lola does still live at home. The father has his daughter thrown out of the bank, demonstrating beyond any doubt that her personal life and feelings are of no consequence or interest to him. Then he adds for good measure that he will leave his wife and family, marry another woman, and that Lola is not his biological child anyway, as if this would rid him of all responsibility toward her and could justify his behavior: "All I'll say is cuckoo's egg! The guy who fathered you didn't even stick around long enough for your birth." This horrifying news, thrown at her with indifference to the presence of the watchman, who looks on in disbelief, breaks Lola and, metaphorically and literally, kills her: the first plot version ends with Lola's empty-handed death.

In the second take, Lola arrives at the office a little later, giving the couple inside a chance to get further along in their conversation: after the initial announcement of the pregnancy, Frau Hansen reveals to her lover that he is actually not the biological father of her baby. He does not take kindly to the news, which puts a very ironic spin on his earlier happiness about it and on his nasty spat with Lola, another nonbiological child of his. This time, Lola interrupts the couple's fight and does not have to listen to her father's cruel revelations about her own birth. Instead, she takes action, throws a total fit, and, interestingly enough, of all the different currencies at her disposal decorating the office walls, she rips off the enlarged and framed dollar bills and smashes them on the ground. This time, she does not leave the bank empty-handed. However, the fight between the lovers seems to have foreshadowed the end of the protagonistic couple, since now it is Manni's turn to die, just as the first fight with the father had represented Lola's death and that of their family. Thus she arrives at the meeting point with DM 100,000 just in time to witness Manni being run over by an ambulance.

Moving on to the third scenario, Hollywood takes over to a large extent. Lola's father has to leave the office earlier, because someone is picking him up who had been delayed involuntarily by Lola herself in the first two versions. Out of time, the father cuts off the conversation with his mistress before she can tell him about the baby not being his, leaving the situation, and the relationship, on a friendly, harmonious note: "That is the most beautiful present you can give me. . . . We'll see each other later, okay!" Then he takes off and is gone by the time Lola arrives at the bank. None of the conflicts from before come to light in this last version: neither the family problematic (which, as mentioned before, also includes references to the alcoholism of the wife, Lola's mother) nor the crisis in the extramarital relationship. Promptly, with all conflicts safely circumvented and silenced, Fortuna smiles on Lola, letting her win all the money she needs at the roulette table. Yet Manni gets lucky, too, retrieving his DM 100.000 from the bum who had stolen them earlier, thus granting the loving couple an extra DM 100.000 as a foundation for their everlasting happiness. As Lola always said: "Love can do anything!"

If compared, these three scenarios seem like ironic commentaries on stereotypical notions about German filmmaking of the serious culture variety—a non-glossy or glamorous, faux documentary style combined with *Problembewußtsein*, critical consciousness and analyses, an examination of psychological and emotional crises, and a questioning of societal norms and values—and, on the other hand, on conventional Hollywood entertainment movies, with their colorful, vivacious style, fast cutting, mood-enhancing music, happy endings, triumphant heroes, and, if they appear at all, divorcing of individual and societal problems and conflicts from any systemic causes, thereby reaffirming the established order.

So, whereas the first two versions entail family and social drama as well as individual suffering and tragedy, culminating in the death of a main protagonist, the last version ends with the suppression of all former conflicts and the resolution of the primary problems. The couple is not only saved but they have become wealthy, too; Lola's illusions about her birth are not shattered, nor are her father's about his girlfriend; Lola, in a metaphysical labor of love that defies rational explanations, rescues the watchman from an almost fatal heart attack; and the only destiny vignette in the Hollywood version shows the woman with the baby carriage being religiously awakened, joining the Jehovah's Witness. In this version, fate's salvation lies in God. Summarizing the Hollywood American way of life, the underlying message here seems to be that supported by a love strong enough, initiative, some luck, and firm belief and faith, everything will work out in the end. Or, as Manni wraps it up in the film: "Don't worry. Everything's fine!"

In the spirit of reworking and innovation, Tykwer even turns the final moments of *Run Lola Run* on their conventional head in a subtle but surprising way: the credits roll down from the top to the bottom of the screen instead of vice versa, which is the customary way of doing it. Watching this for the first time, the viewers just perceive difference without immediately being able to put a finger on its source. Upon realizing the cause, however, it becomes apparent that it is entirely possible to create an unprecedented and characteristic structure using old and conventional building blocs.

Run Lola Run in many ways exemplifies an inventive and

creative instance of "practices and ways of making one's own that which is imposed," and of how to fuse and synthesize the imposed reference with that which *is* one's own. The irreverent mix of high and popular culture and of Hollywood and German filmmaking clearly struck a chord with Tykwer's contemporaries. The smart, assertive, and ironic way in which he quotes and uses genres and styles resonated with a transnational cultural *zeitgeist.* Tykwer appropriates by way of innovation and reinterpretation, bringing together the old and the new, the serious and the entertaining, the transatlantic and the continental, offering a fresh perspective on sights that have become all too common, habitual, and accepted. By the same token, his work opens up questions about the "nationality" of Hollywood and popular culture in general, and whether it is still adequate to conceive as "American" the mass entertainment paradigms and phenomena in question as they exist and emerge globally today. Or, to put it differently: Is a pizza topped with caviar, prepared by an Austrian chef, and sold in Tokyo to a Finnish tourist still Italian?

NOTES

1. The film offers almost every trick in the bag in terms of visuals: Tykwer makes use of animated sequences, still photography, and black-and-white footage; he intersperses his 35mm film with grainy video shots, slow and fast motion, and split screens; and he mixes together a barrage of diverse camera angles and cuts, all of which are edited dramatically for tempo and "jolt value."

2. Tom Tykwer, born in 1965 in Wuppertal, directed only two feature films before *Lola: Die tödliche Maria [The Deadly Maria]* (1994) and *Winterschläfer [Winter Sleepers]* (1997). Franka Potente, born in 1974, made her first appearance in the 1996 comedy *Nach 5 im Urwald [After 5 in the Jungle]* by Hans-Christian Schmid, and acted in Doris Dörrie's *Bin ich schön? [Am I Beautiful?]* as well as in the successful TV adaptation of Joseph Haslinger's novel *Opernball [Opera Ball]*, both from 1998. Moritz Bleibtreu, born in 1971 and already well established as an actor when *Lola* was made, has appeared in more than twenty TV and movie productions, starting as a child in 1980.

3. Rob Blackwelder, review of *Run Lola Run, SPLICED Online,* 1999. *Http://www.splicedonline.com/99reviews/runlolarun.html*

4. Roger Chartier, *Forms and Meanings: Texts, Performances, and Audiences from Codex to Computer.* (Philadelphia: University of Pennsylvania Press, 1995), 89.

5. Michel Foucault, "The Discourse on Language," in *The Archeology of Knowledge* (New York: Pantheon, 1972), 229. Originally published as *L'ordre du discours* (Paris: Gallimard, 1971), 54. Quoted in Chartier, *Forms and Meanings,* 111.

6. Chartier, 89.

7. Ibid.

8. Ibid., 90.

9. Writer/directors like Katja von Garnier, Detlef Buck, Wolfgang Becker II., Sönke Wortmann and Leander Haußmann can serve as examples here, as can Joseph Vilsmaier or Doris Dörrie, though of an older generation.

10. David Stratton, review of *Run Lola Run*, *The Australian*, 23 October 1999, R 20. Online edition at: *Http://entertainment.news.com.au/film/archive/91023a.htm*

11. The German involvement with American consumer goods and popular culture reaches further back, and significant scholarship has been devoted to these aspects of pre-World War II Germany. See, for example, Thomas Saunder's study *Hollywood in Berlin: American Cinema and Weimar Germany* (Berkeley/Los Angeles/London: University of California Press, 1994) or the collection of texts in Frank Trommler and Joseph McVeigh, eds., *America and the Germans* (Philadelphia: University of Pennsylvania Press, 1985).

12. For a condensed discussion of the concept of "classical narrative paradigm," see David Bordwell's "Classical Hollywood Cinema: Narrational Principles and Procedures," in *Narrative, Apparatus, Ideology: A Film Theory Reader*, ed. Philip Rosen (New York: Columbia University Press, 1986), 17–34. For a thorough account of the same see David Bordwell, Janet Staiger, and Kristin Thompson, *The Classical Hollywood Cinema: Film Style and Mode of Production to 1960* (New York: Columbia University Press, 1985). A more general background for this context is also provided in David Bordwell and Kristin Thompson, *Film Art: An Introduction*. (Reading, Mass.: Addison-Wesley, 1979).

13. Thomas Elsaesser, *Fassbinder's Germany: History, Identity, Subject*. (Amsterdam: Amsterdam University Press, 1996), 15.

14. Chartier, 88.

15. Ibid., 83.

16. Robin Cook, *A History of Narrative Film*. (New York and London: W. W. Norton & Company, 1981), 854.

17. Ibid., 874

18. Elsaesser, 15.

19. Cook, 854.

20. Elsaesser, 17.

21. This does not mean to imply that there are not plenty of examples of classical narrative filmmaking in Germany and of an alternative cinema in the United States. The positing of these national conceptual affiliations is primarily heuristic here, aimed at facilitating the analysis of the go-between: a film that investigates the spaces and exchanges between the two paradigms.

22. Jonathan Foreman, "A Dash of Brilliance," review of *Run Lola Run*, *New York Post*, 18 June 1999, p. 56. Online edition at: http://www.nypost.com/movies/9472.htm. Kenneth Turan, "'Run Lola' Keeps Playful Tale Moving," *Los Angeles Times*, 18 June 1999. Online edition at: *http://www.calendarlive.com:8081/s . . . 7admimg%2F&Theme = &Company = LA + Times*. Roger Ebert, review of *Run Lola Run*, *Chicago Sun-Times*, 1999. Online edition at: *http://www.suntimes.com/ebert/ebert_reviews/1999/07/070203.html*

23. Bordwell, "Classical Hollywood Cinema," 18.
24. Ibid., 19.
25. Ibid.
26. Ibid.
27. "High Noon" (1952), incidentally also a film by a German speaking director, Fred Zinnemann, has obviously been an influence on Tykwer, because not only is midday the hour of judgment for both the protagonists, Manni (Moritz Bleibtreu) and Will Kane (Gary Cooper), but both films also purport to take place in real time, *High Noon* in ninety minutes, *Run Lola Run* in three times twenty, plus set up, intermezzi, and resolution, coming out to about eighty minutes (which also happens to be roughly the length of a regular soccer game).
28. Another element that is often a crucial part of Hollywood action films, and one that is largely absent in *Run Lola Run*, is special effects.
29. There are two other scenes that involve physically violent behavior. Both mark very serious occasions in nonfrivolous ways, thereby distinguishing themselves from common generic ways of using violence in action movies. The first is the brief flashback in which Manni is beaten up by his brutal boss. This scene forcefully drives home to the viewers and to Lola what kind of danger Manni is in: the danger of losing his life. The other scene is Lola's second encounter with her father in his office, where he slaps her in the face, denoting the brutal demolition of his family and their relationship. Thus, every instance of violence in the film contains either a glimpse or a full frontal look at its ultimate consequence: destruction.
30. Obviously, the breakdown of the traditional family and family values does appear in Hollywood productions as well (*Independence Day* by Roland Emmerich [1996] can serve as an example here, as well as *Die Hard* by John Mc Tiernan [1988] or *Fatal Attraction* by Adrian Lyne [1987]). The difference generally lies in the way the conflict is positioned and finally reconciled in the film: in Hollywood action films such conflicts usually appear for dramatic arching and ultimately are resolved happily, without leaving loose ends or really questioning social institutions like marriage or parenthood.

CONTRIBUTORS

ANTJE ASCHEID is assistant professor of film studies at the University of Georgia at Athens, where she teaches film history, theory, and production. She is the author of several articles on film in translation and on Nazi Cinema. Her first book, *Hitler's Heroines! Stardom, Womanhood and the Popular in Nazi Cinema*, is forthcoming with Temple University Press.

HESTER BAER is assistant professor of German and film and video studies at the University of Oklahoma. She received her Ph.D. in German, with a concentration in women's studies, from Washington University in St. Louis. She is currently completing a book, based on her dissertation, about gender, spectatorship, and visual culture in West Germany in the early postwar period. Her new research focuses on discourses of the popular in postunification German literature and film.

TIM BERGFELDER is a lecturer in film studies at the University of Southampton/UK. His research interests include popular European cinema and its genres, international co-productions, and the relationship between film and tourism. Forthcoming books include *The German Cinema Book* (BFI, co-edited with Erica Carter and Deniz Göktürk) and a monograph on popular German cinema of the 1960s.

JOHN E. DAVIDSON is an associate professor in Germanic languages and literatures at Ohio State University. In addition to teaching film, literature, and cultural theory, he currently serves as director of graduate studies in German. His scholarship includes articles on representations of the radical Right, Nazi cinema, and ecological issues in film. He is presently following up his *Deterritorializing the New German Cinema* (University of Minnesota Press, 1999) with a study of postwall cinema.

417

GERD GEMÜNDEN is professor of German and comparative literature at Dartmouth College. He is the author of *Framed Visions: Popular Culture, Americanization, and the Contemporary German and Austrian Imagination* (1998), and he is co-editor of *Wim Wenders: Einstellungen* (1993), *The Cinema of Wim Wenders* (1997), and *Germans and Indians: Fantasies, Encounters, Projections* (2002). He is currently working on a study of exiles and émigrés in Hollywood.

ALISON GUENTHER-PAL is a doctoral student in German studies at the University of Minnesota, Twin Cities, where she also received her M.A. The essay in this volume is an abridged chapter of her dissertation, which focuses on homosexuality in 1950s West Germany. She is also editing a volume with Richard W. McCormick on German film criticism.

CHRISTINE HAASE is assistant professor of German at the University of Georgia in Athens. Her research interests include twentieth-century popular culture, film, and cultural studies. The essay in this volume is part of a book project on connections and dialogues between German and American filmmaking over the last thirty years, especially in regard to appropriations of Hollywood paradigms by German directors working in both countries.

RANDALL HALLE is assistant professor of German and film studies in the Department of Modern Languages and Cultures at the University of Rochester. He co-edited with Sharon Willis the special issue of *Camera Obscura* on marginality and alterity in contemporary European cinema and is currently researching and presenting his work for *Frames of Belonging: German Film from National to Transnational Productions*.

ALASDAIR KING is senior lecturer in German studies at the University of Portsmouth. He has published on the popular cinema industry during National Socialism and on Hans Magnus Enzensberger. He is currently working on the films of Doris Dörrie and co-editing a book on women in recent European cinema.

LUTZ KOEPNICK is associate professor of German, film and media studies at Washington University in St. Louis. He is the author of *Walter Benjamin and the Aesthetics of Power*, for which he received the MLA's Aldo and Jeanne Scaglione Prize for Studies in Germanic Languages and Literatures in 2000; and of

Nothungs Modernität: Wagners Ring und die Poesie der Politik im neunzehnten Jahrhundert. His latest book, *The Dark Mirror: German Cinema between Hitler and Hollywood,* is forthcoming.

JANET MCCABE is a lecturer in film studies at Trinity College, Dublin. She has just completed her doctoral thesis on feminist theory and the writing of film history, entitled *Addicted to Distractions: Imagined Female Spectator-Participants and the Early German Popular as Discourse, 1910–1919.*

MARGARET MCCARTHY is associate professor of German at Davidson College, where she teaches twentieth-century German literature and film. She has published essays on Ingeborg Bachmann, Jutta Brückner, Luc Besson, G. W. Pabst, and Wim Wenders. She is presently at work on a monograph on Doris Dörrie.

RICK (RICHARD W.) MCCORMICK is an associate professor of German at the University of Minnesota, where he teaches German film, literature, and culture. He is the author of *Gender and Sexuality in Weimar Modernity: Film, Literature, and "New Objectivity"* (Palgrave/St. Martin's, 2002) and *Politics of the Self: Feminism and the Postmodern in West German Literature in Film* (Princeton University Press, 1991); he is a co-editor of the anthology *Gender and German Cinema: Feminist Interventions* (Berg, 1993); and he has written a number of articles on Weimar and postwar German cinema.

ELIZABETH MITTMAN is associate professor of German at Michigan State University, where she teaches German literature, cultural studies, and film. Her publications include numerous articles on East German literature, postunification literature, and curricular issues in German studies. She is co-editor of two volumes, *The Politics of the Essay: Feminist Perspectives* (Indiana University Press) and *Theory as Practice: A Critical Anthology of Early German Romantic Writings* (University of Minnesota Press), and is currently at work on a book on gender and national identity in the former GDR.

NANCY P. NENNO is assistant professor in the German program at the College of Charleston, where she teaches German language and literature, culture, and film.

BRAD PRAGER is an assistant professor in the Department of German and Russian at the University of Missouri, Columbia. He teaches both film and literature, and he has written articles for *New German Critique, Seminar, Literature/ Film Quarterly* and *Art History*, among others. He is currently completing his book manuscript on German romanticism.

ROBERT C. REIMER is professor of German and director of the minor in film studies at the University of North Carolina Charlotte. He has published essays and papers on post-1945 German film and is coauthor with Carol Reimer of *Nazi-Retro Film: How German Narrative Cinema Remembers the Past* (Twayne Publishers,1992) and editor of *Cultural History through a National Socialist Lens: Essays on the Cinema of the Third Reich* (Camden House, 2000).

CHRISTIAN ROGOWSKI is professor of German at Amherst College. He is author of two books on Robert Musil and has published articles on, among others, Ingeborg Bachmann, Heiner Müller, Wim Wenders, Thomas Brasch, the Medea myth, and German studies in the United States. His current research interests include the use of multimedia in cultural studies, German film history, the legacy of German colonialism, and the popular culture of the Weimar Republic.

STEFAN SOLDOVIERI teaches in the German Department at Northwestern University. He is the author of several articles on East German cinema and is currently pursuing projects on genre film efforts in the GDR and German-German film relations.

INDEX

INDEX OF FILMS

For an updated listing of books in this series, please visit our Web site at http://wsupress.wayne.edu